COMMUNICATION IN THE LEGAL PROCESS

COMMUNICATION IN THE LEGAL PROCESS

RONALD J. MATLON
TOWSON STATE UNIVERSITY

HOLT, RINEHART AND WINSTON, INC.

NEW YORK   CHICAGO   SAN FRANCISCO
PHILADELPHIA   MONTREAL   TORONTO   LONDON   SYDNEY   TOKYO

Library of Congress Cataloging-in-Publication Data

Matlon, Ronald J., 1938–
  Communication in the legal process.

  Bibliography: p.
  Includes index.
  1. Trial practice—United States.   2. Forensic
oratory.   3. Persuasion (Psychology)   I. Title.
KF8915.M375   1988   347.73′7   87-16852
                            347.3077

0-03-062771-0

Requests for permission to make copies of any part of the work should be mailed
to:
Permissions
Holt, Rinehart and Winston, Inc.
111 Fifth Avenue
New York, NY 10003
Printed in the United States of America

8 9 0 1   016   9 8 7 6 5 4 3 2

Holt, Rinehart and Winston, Inc.
The Dryden Press
Saunders College Publishing

PREFACE

This book focuses on communication questions and communication skills which lawyers, judges, litigants, and jurors face in criminal and civil justice. Particular attention is given to a survey of research related to the verbal and nonverbal aspects of communication for the expressed purpose of noting the application of these to the legal concerns of interview, negotiation and pretrial maneuvers, and litigation. This research review is supplemented by applicable rhetorical and communication theory, as well as anecdotal documentation by experienced trial lawyers and legal educators.

Often referred to as counseling, the legal concern of *interview* involves a consideration of fact-gathering and advising. In studying the legal interview, readers will become aware of the verbal and nonverbal factors which play a role in the success or failure of the interaction. They will be exposed to the philosophy that the interview situation is a get-and-give situation; the lawyer's primary goal is to secure facts, interpretations, and opinions related to a case—both favorable and unfavorable. While doing so, however, lawyers—willfully or otherwise—are inevitably giving clients advice as well as various messages regarding their interpersonal relationship, professional competence, and integrity.

Since most cases never evolve into a courtroom experience (an estimated 90 percent are settled out of court), it is important that those trying to better understand communication in the legal process achieve some measure of understanding of the process of *negotiation and pretrial strategy*. With this in mind, readers will be exposed to the verbal and nonverbal aspects of conflict resolution, information management, and issue analysis. Attention is given to the nature and type of communication activity which contributes to the mosaic entitled negotiation. In addition, various pretrial strategies, such as investigation, pleadings, discovery, issue and theme development, motions practice, and pretrial conferences, are closely tied to the effectiveness of negotiation and trial preparation.

Without doubt the strongest beacon which interests people in the legal profession is their concept of *litigation*. It is, in the eyes of most people, the *sine qua non* of lawyering. Yet, even for many practicing lawyers, it remains an enigma, largely because they have failed to explore the various phases of litigation with an eye toward determining the precise role of communication in each phase. What dominates the process (and/or its separate phases) is the dialogue: attorney-judge; attorney-attorney; attorney-client-witnesses; attorney-jury; jury-jury; judge-jury. In each instance, verbal and nonverbal factors interact to produce the final trial experience. Readers will be asked to attend to communication principles and strategies applied during the phases of jury selection, opening statements, examination of witnesses, summations, the judge's charges, and jury decision making.

The book is intended primarily for undergraduate upper-division students, although throughout this work I had in mind four categories of potential readers: communication majors who wish to know more about legal processes, pre-law students who wish to know more about communication studies, law and other graduate students, and practicing lawyers. The ideal reader is one who has had some prior knowledge of the fundamentals of communication and/or law.

In sum, the approach used in this book is to apply several subdisciplines of communication to the study, practice, and understanding of the legal process. The principal subdivisions that are adapted to the legal situation are argumentation, persuasion, dyadic communication, small group communication, and public speaking. This is not a book which will emphasize the law, although some understanding of the legal system is necessary to make the book meaningful to the reader. Rather, this book is designed for the purpose of better understanding how verbal and nonverbal communication skills and strategies of persuasion are used in a variety of legal settings.

Of particular help were the comments and suggestions of the following individuals: William L. Benoit, Bowling Green State University; Don Boileau, Director of Educational Services, Speech Communication Association; Wayne Callaway, University of Wyoming; Craig Dudczak, Syracuse University; Michael Fahs, California Polytechnic State University; Joan B. Kessler, California State University—Northridge; Bruce Landis, Kent State University; Nancy G. McDermid, San Francisco State University; Ruth McGaffey, University of Wisconsin at Milwaukee; Gerald Miller, Michigan State University; Scott Nobles, Macalester College; Richard D. Rieke, University of Utah; Rita James Simon, American University; David Smith, University of Southern Florida; Charles Stewart, Purdue University; Ralph Towne, Temple University; Ruth Walden, University of Utah; George Ziegelmueller, Wayne State University; and Gordon Zimmerman, University of Nevada at Reno. I would also like to express my appreciation to the fine staff at Holt, Rinehart and Winston.

R.J.M.

CONTENTS

CONTENTS

CHAPTER 10

CLOSING ARGUMENTS   268

CHAPTER 11

TRIAL JUDGE COMMUNICATION   288

CHAPTER 12

JURY DECISION MAKING   300

CONTENTS

APPENDICES

COMMUNICATION
IN THE
LEGAL PROCESS

INTRODUCTION

COMMUNICATION
THEORY AND LAW

THE LAW, THE LEGAL PROFESSION, AND THE AMERICAN JUDICIAL SYSTEM
Becoming a Lawyer / The Legal System in America

THE RELATIONSHIP OF LAW TO COMMUNICATION AND RHETORIC

This book analyzes communication designed to inform and persuade. Communication that informs enlightens the understanding; communication that persuades influences the beliefs, attitudes, and actions of a listener. The specific environment in which communication will be analyzed here is the legal setting—communication between and among lawyers, clients, witnesses, judges, and juries. The book is aimed at students of communication as well as students and practitioners of law who want to better understand how communication functions in the legal process. This is *not* a book about the law. However, since some knowledge of legal process is necessary in order to get the best possible understanding of communication strategies throughout the practice of law, we need to begin our analysis with an overview of the American legal system.

THE LAW, THE LEGAL PROFESSION, AND THE AMERICAN JUDICIAL SYSTEM

The United States has an extremely large legal system. On a per capita basis, our system is about three times as large as that found in Great Britain. In 1950, there were approximately 220,000 lawyers in America. That number grew to over 300,000 by the mid-1960s, and stood at nearly 650,000 in 1985.[1] That meant that there were 2.7 lawyers for every 1,000 persons in the United States. By 1995, the number of lawyers in the United States is expected to double, making law one of the fastest-growing professions.[2]

The number of students interested in law is on the rise as well. In the past decade, the number of individuals taking the Law School Aptitude Test (LSAT) has increased nearly three times, to roughly 100,000 per year. The 174 approved law schools in the United States receive about 65,000 applications annually but accept only 30,000 of the applicants. Nearly 130,000 students are currently enrolled in American law schools, and that

figure is double the number of a decade ago.[3] Each year, approximately 35,000 persons graduate from law schools,[4] but only about two-thirds of them find jobs in law after they graduate.

Yet the growth continues. Why? One turning point came several years ago when the Supreme Court said that every citizen is entitled to an attorney. Since then, more and more Americans have gained easy access to legal counsel. Now, with advertising, legal clinics, and prepaid legal plans, millions of people each year consult attorneys. In addition, more and more disputes of all kinds that might have been settled within a family or community are becoming matters of legal concern. Going to court is a great indoor sport!

The legal profession is attractive to many. Although starting attorney salaries average only $25,000 a year,[5] senior partners in law firms earn incomes well into six figures. Being an attorney is also attractive because many see lawyering as the road to power. For instance, being a lawyer is an excellent springboard to political office. What often attracts prelaw students most is the thrill of someday being able to go to trial, probably the most exciting element of lawyering.

Becoming a Lawyer

After receiving an undergraduate degree, students spend three full years in law school to earn the J.D. (doctor of jurisprudence) degree. Certain common courses on the law and legal research are taken by all students, regardless of the law schools they attend. Required courses include civil procedure, criminal law and process, torts, contracts, property, and evidence. Some lawyering skills and communication techniques courses in trial advocacy, interviewing, and negotiation are offered at the upper level, but they are considered nontraditional and are almost always elective in nature.

The teaching method used in law schools

is Socratic, designed to get students "to think like lawyers." The Socratic method is an inductive approach to education in which the students have masses of raw data from court cases dumped in their laps. From these data, students are asked question after question about judicial opinions to lead them to an understanding of the legal principles involved, to a recognition of the complexity and ambiguity of the law, and eventually to an ability to think on their feet and defend their ideas.

Upon graduation from law school, an individual seeks admission to a state bar. Each state has its own bar examination, and one usually cannot get a license to practice law in a state without passing the examination. The bar examination is said to be more difficult than any examination a student takes while enrolled in law school, and the national pass rate is roughly 67 percent.[6]

Once the bar examination is passed, the new lawyer may try to join an established firm. One out of every three does so.[7] As a beginning associate in the firm, the lawyer performs much legal research and has little direct contact with clients. Rather, most of the communication in this job is with lawyers and staff in the firm. Middle-range and upper-range associates achieve increased responsibilities in consulting with clients, negotiating contracts, and so forth. A senior associate or junior (or middle) partner in a law firm is the one who is contacted directly by clients, assigns research to others, offers legal advice, and maybe does some trial work. Several years down the line, after setting an outstanding track record, a lawyer can become a senior partner in the firm. Senior partners are broad-based advisors and office managers. They counsel younger attorneys. They are called upon by bar associations to perform certain professional functions. And they serve as advocates in major trials.

Of course, not all graduates from law school follow these same career steps. One out of three sets up his or her own practice; one out of ten is employed by private indus-try; one out of ten becomes a district attorney or public defender; and others assist judges, teach, or work in law-related occupations.[8]

Whatever career paths lawyers choose, there are certain specific tasks common to all. Lawyers *read* a great deal. Much of this reading is legal research necessary to draft documents, advise clients, and try cases. Lawyers *negotiate* a great deal. They try to get people with other interests to accommodate their own views, and they attempt to manage conflict. Lawyers *write* a great deal, and they must deal with considerable detail carefully and clearly. Finally, lawyers *talk* a great deal. They spend considerable time informing and persuading clients, witnesses, experts in many fields, other lawyers, judges, and jurors. Reading, negotiating, writing, and speaking skills are essential to an attorney.

Lawyers specialize in criminal or civil law. In *criminal law,* the government (national, state, or local) brings charges against an individual or group for breaking a law. Representatives of the state in criminal law are the *prosecutors* or *district attorneys.* Sometimes they are elected to their positions; other times they are appointed. Prosecutors are full-time employees in most jurisdictions, although there are still some part-time district attorneys in rural areas. If a prosecutor is only part-time, he or she may also have a private practice but may not handle criminal cases for the defense. Many *defense attorneys* in criminal cases also work for the state. They are called *public defenders;* they represent individuals who cannot afford to hire their own attorneys. Of course, there are criminal defense attorneys in private practice too.

In *civil law,* where most attorneys practice, citizens file complaints against other citizens or groups for recovery of damages or property, or to compel certain conduct such as honoring a contract.[9] Attorneys who file complaints in civil litigation are called *plaintiff's lawyers.* Their opposition is once again called the defense counsel. Attorneys in civil law frequently specialize (e.g., contracts, wills and trusts, medical negligence cases, tax law, patent law). In 1981, more than 13 million civil suits were filed in our courts. In contrast, Japan—a nation with a population one-half that of the United States—had only 282,000 such suits.[10]

The Legal System in America

Our system of justice is very much like that found in Great Britain. The rights, duties, liberties, and privileges of individual citizens are similar in both countries. Yet, our systems are also quite different. State autonomy has played an important part in United States history, so we have no national criminal law, no uniform law of torts and property, no nationwide divorce law, and so on. Furthermore, courts in one state are not bound by decisions of courts in other states.

In America, we have over 3,500 state courts of general jurisdiction. They are called circuit, district, or superior courts, depending on where you live. These state trial courts are empowered to hear and decide a large variety of civil and criminal cases. Also, there are several thousand courts of limited jurisdiction. These are courts that deal with particular matters, such as petty crime, probate (wills), small claims, domestic relations (divorces and child custody), and juvenile problems. Municipal courts and justice-of-the-peace courts are known as courts of limited jurisdiction. They have jurisdiction in matters arising out of city and town ordinances (e.g., traffic violations). In each state, there is a supreme tribunal to hear appeals from the decisions of courts inferior to them. Some larger states have intermediate appellate courts to better manage the case load and prevent every matter on appeal from going to the supreme courts.

Alongside these fifty state court systems there is another system at the federal level. Ninety-four district courts exist in the federal system. These courts deal with violations of federal and interstate crimes, such as narcotics violations, smuggling, income tax evasion, and treason and espionage. Many organized crime cases go through the federal district courts since they involve alleged violations in interstate commerce. Eleven federal appellate courts also exist. These courts cannot hear state court appeals, but only appeals from federal district courts. Decisions in one federal appellate court are not binding in other federal appellate courts. Finally, the United State Supreme Court is the highest and most powerful court in the country. The nine justices of the Supreme Court can review lower court decisions that involve questions of federal and constitutional law, but they choose which cases to review.

Next, let us examine the procedure that eventually leads to a trial. In *criminal law,* the typical situation is to have a suspected offender arrested and booked by the police. The suspect is advised of certain rights. The case is brought before a prosecutor who decides whether or not to *charge* the suspect with committing a crime and, if so, for which criminal offense. The act of charging involves the filing of a complaint (called an information) by the state. The charge is read to the suspect by a magistrate (judge). If the crime is especially serious,[11] the court takes steps to guarantee that the suspect will be present for a possible trial. Hence, the accused is detained in jail unless the necessary bail can be paid. Bail is a sum of money which must be paid by the accused to get out of jail. That money is returned to the suspect only if he or she is present throughout the course of trial. If the charge is not serious, the accused may be released with instructions not to leave the jurisdiction during the processing of the case.

Shortly after the arrest, the filing of the charge, and the setting of bail, a preliminary hearing is held to determine whether there is probable cause (sufficient reason) to believe the suspect might be guilty of the charge. If probable cause exists, the defendant is bound over to a proper court of trial jurisdiction.

Otherwise, the suspect is released. To establish probable cause, a prosecutor files a formal accusation called the *indictment*. Sometimes a defendant is bound over by a single judge; other times, a group of approximately 16 to 23 citizens issues indictments. This citizens' group is called the grand jury.[12] An indictment can be issued by a simple majority vote from the grand jurors. At the preliminary hearing to decide whether to indict, the defendant typically presents no evidence. The only evidence heard is that which comes from the prosecuting attorney.

After the indicted defendant is bound over to a proper court of trial jurisdiction, an *arraignment* is held. The purpose of the arraignment is to get a plea on the indictment. The charge is read aloud, and then counsel for the defense files a plea. The plea can be "guilty," in which case the judge sets a time for sentencing. The plea can be *"nolo contendere"* (no contest), which has the same effect as a guilty plea in the matter at hand but cannot be used as an admission for subsequent criminal or civil litigation. The plea can also be "not guilty"—or "not guilty by reason of insanity," a rarely used plea. If a not guilty plea is filed, a trial date is set. Between the arraignment and the trial, delicate negotiating takes place to see if an agreement can be reached between the prosecutor and the defense counsel to prevent the case from going to trial. This is called *plea bargaining*. Should no settlement be reached, a trial is held before a single judge or a petit jury. At trial, the prosecutor must prove guilt beyond a reasonable doubt. This requirement is known as the *burden of proof*. If the defendant is found not guilty (is acquitted) at trial, he or she walks away free. If the defendant is found guilty (is convicted), the presiding judge imposes an appropriate sentence.

Civil cases follow similar procedures. A civil case begins with a cause of action, an alleged wrongful act for which a lawsuit is brought. For instance, if you sign an agreement to buy a house and the seller refuses to go through with the deal, you have a cause of action: a breach of contract. So, working with a lawyer, you lay out the facts behind this cause of action in a document called the *complaint*, which is filed in court. The court, in turn, issues a summons to the defendant to answer the complaint. Negotiating between both sides follows, and should no settlement be reached, a trial occurs. At trial, the plaintiff must prove a case by the preponderance of the evidence. If the jury finds for the plaintiff, money damages will usually be awarded.

THE RELATIONSHIP OF LAW TO COMMUNICATION AND RHETORIC

All lawyers must be masters of communication. They must have interpersonal communication skills for interviewing, negotiation skills for bargaining, and public speaking skills for appearing in court. Several sources attest to the importance of communication in the practice of lawyering. Hunsaker writes, "Since law . . . is a communicative system, chiefly rhetorical in nature, . . . the lawyer [becomes] an agent of rhetorical change. . . . Through his skill in using linguistic tools, he shapes, alters, and restructures social reality."[13] Goodpaster claims that to be an effective lawyer requires "very high level abilities not only to communicate, but also to perceive the full range of what is being communicated by the parties; and . . . a good knowledge, intuitive or acquired, of the psychology of communication and persuasion and . . . a repertoire of specific communication and persuasion techniques which can be used in or adjusted to various situations."[14] Similar opinions are found in the following quotations:

Ability to make use of the spoken word may be one of the lawyer's principal assets. Just a glance at some of the activities of today's attorney show that his effectiveness may be limited by his ability as a speaker. . . . An ability to communicate and to "handle" clients with persuasive speech is very helpful.[15]

I realize how much of a lawyer's work is involved in dealing with people—listening to clients, developing rapport with them, handling them, . . . persuading judges or opponents, and so on. . . . The skills of the successful lawyer lay in mastery of the human interaction— . . . how to listen, how to persuade, how to meet emotional and psychological needs of clients, opponents, judges, indeed everyone they dealt with professionally.[16]

Effective communication between the judge, lawyers, witnesses, and jury is critical to the proper functioning of the system. It is self-evident that if the communication process is not effective—if jurors are unsure about the evidence, unclear on the meaning of the law, confused by legal jargon, bewildered by trial procedure, uncertain of the role they are to play—the jury cannot be expected to perform its function intelligently. . . . Such a condition of pervasive confusion . . . is largely a result of poor communication.[17]

Fundamental to the broad spectrum of the lawyer's work is the art of communication— communication both sending and receiving, communication in the relatively informal setting of . . . interviewing . . . clients, witnesses, or associates, communication in the relative formality of the courtroom, communication in the negotiation process, communication (perhaps to an unidentified audience) through the written word. . . . Nor, as we have recently been made aware, can the subtleties of non-verbal communication be ignored.[18]

In its *Prelaw Handbook,* the Association of American Law Schools assents to these opinions by advising undergraduates that "as long as you receive a quality education and learn critical analysis, logical reasoning, and written and oral expression, the range of acceptable college majors is very broad."[19] The Association also declares that the highest skills in expression can be mastered by studying speech and debate.[20]

The close relationship in western civiliza-tion between communication and law has been around a long time, although the road traveled has been a rocky one. The study of the art of persuasion, called *rhetoric,* began in the fifth century B.C. in Greece. This period was filled with turmoil and conflict. A series of revolts and invasions by tyrants led to com-plex disputes over land titles and citizenship rights. There were no lawyers to assist the cit-izens. Hence, the populace was eager to learn about rhetoric and law as a matter of social preservation. The ancient Greeks had a court system, and the need to present cases in those courts led to the development of clas-sical rhetoric.

A Sicilian, Corax, was one of the earliest teachers of rhetoric; he wrote the first system-atic approach to the study of persuasion in the court system. Aristotle refined Corax's work with his treatise *Rhetoric.*[21] Aristotle dis-cussed the use of logical, emotional, and per-sonal proofs and lines of argument to influ-ence Greek juries. He urged persuaders to examine each setting to determine the most appropriate techniques of rhetoric to use. Ar-istotle's writing, in which he maintained that justice can be reached through rational deci-sion making, became a cornerstone of legal and rhetorical theory.[22]

Lawyers flourished in ancient Rome. Among the best was Cicero, also an outstand-ing orator and statesman. Cicero wrote a text-book discussing everything from the stock is-sues in a criminal case (particulars of the crime, reason for the accused to commit the crime, and personal circumstances of the ac-cused) to specific techniques for persuading in the courtroom.[23] Quintilian, also a famous pleader in the courts and a teacher, empha-sized in his *Institutes of Oratory* that an effec-tive litigator is "a good man speaking well."[24] Rhetoric was indeed a central factor in Roman legal education. The techniques and strate-gies of persuasion became vehicles for teach-ing legal concepts to students of law.

During the medieval and Renaissance periods, both rhetoric and law declined. The early church fathers distrusted the pagan rhetorics of Greece and Rome, even though they borrowed the tenets of classical rhetoric when they wrote about homiletics, or preaching (e.g., St. Augustine's *On Christian Doctrine*).[25] Feudalism meant that there were no orderly governments, no senates, no political discussions, and, of course, no courts. Legal education was unnecessary. So, advancements in the theory of law came to a halt, and rhetoric became a tool of the sermon maker.

Peter Ramus, a sixteenth-century French monk who attempted to categorize all human knowledge, was extremely influential in Europe in the development of educational disciplines and curricula. Ramus believed that the study of the discovery of ideas *(invention)* and the arrangement of ideas *(disposition)* belonged to the discipline of logic, or *dialetic*. Rhetoric was to be treated merely as the study of delivery *(elocution)* and figures of speech *(style)*.[26] In antiquity, invention, disposition, elocution, style, and memory had been the canons of rhetoric to be studied by legal advocates. In the sixteenth century, rhetoric traveled a path separate from the analytical dimension of forensic, or legal, speaking. Later, great legal thinkers and philosophers, such as Locke, Hobbes, Coke, and Blackstone (who were educated in England), were attracted to dialectic but not to rhetoric. Legal and rhetorical theory took separate paths, with rhetoric focusing on the art of amplifying and beautifying one's thoughts in speech. As law developed in England, neither the solicitors (those who do legal research) nor the barristers (those who engage in trial appearances) knew much rhetoric.

American legal education was patterned after the case method developed by Christopher Columbus Langdell at Harvard Law School. This method was designed to systematically teach logical thinking and reasoning. Langdell was a legal positivist who maintained that juridic decisions were reached by examining rules, laws, and logic. Thus, justice was a means of arriving at an absolute and universal truth. Langdell believed that rhetoric only confused and distorted the search for truth.[27] Law students at Harvard (and elsewhere, since Harvard served as a model) got no training in the techniques of persuasion.[28] They studied law in the library, learned relevant rules, and decided how to apply the rules to facts to determine what was "correct and true." Meanwhile, rhetorical theory was being advanced for use by politicians and the clergy. Some of this theory was limited to language and presentation, and some focused on invention,[29] but all of it was largely ignored in legal education.

The legal realists of the late nineteenth and twentieth centuries vigorously attacked Langdell and the positivists. They were led initially by Oliver Wendell Holmes, who in 1898 penned the classic line "The life of the law has not been logic, it has been experience."[30] Holmes admitted that legal decisions have logical form, but he said that judges and juries have personal experiences and values that must be considered as well. Benjamin Cardozo, an appellate court judge and an influential legal realist who later became a Supreme Court justice, agreed with Holmes that courts do not locate the truth. Instead, they establish situational standards of right conduct as a reflection of societal values.[31]

In his fascinating work *Courts on Trial,* Jerome Frank viciously criticized the syllogistic certainty of judicial thinking as he explored the study of attitudes and values.[32] Frank said that legal training ought to include extralegal considerations such as audience analysis and adaptation in the process of courtroom persuasion. After all, neither case facts nor final decisions constitute "truth."

To illustrate his point, Frank asks us to consider *United States v. Shipp.*[33] A man named Johnson had been convicted in Tennessee on a rape charge. Johnson's attorney appealed the case, and while the appeal was pending,

Johnson was kept in custody by a sheriff named Shipp. While in custody, Johnson was seized by a mob and lynched. Sheriff Shipp was charged with aiding, abetting, and conspiring with the lynch mob. The Supreme Court appointed a commissioner to gather testimony about the incident. The information was presented to the Court without recommendation. After hearing oral arguments from both sides, the Supreme Court split in a 5–3 vote against the sheriff. Writing for the majority, Chief Justice Fuller said that the facts showed that Shipp made the work of the mob easy and that a conspiracy had indeed taken place. Writing for the minority, Justice Peckham said that there was not one particle of evidence regarding the conspiracy claim. Frank points out that both sides had the same information.

Which side was right? Which one was wrong? How can anyone say that there is an objective means for testing the correctness of any finding? The law is written and interpreted by human beings who are capable of error. There is no absolute method of determining which witnesses are most worthy of belief. There is no standard for determining what evidence is sufficient to induce a certain belief. There is no fixed meaning to language. All the courts can do is determine what is probable, and they do that subjectively. In other words, *United States v. Shipp* clearly shows that there is no such thing as truth; there is only the probability of truth.

While Frank was addressing the legal profession, rhetoricians were developing their own theory of persuasion, based also on uncertainty and probability. In other words, rhetoricians began focusing on how speakers could establish enough probability in their messages to convince audiences that what they were saying should be accepted as worthy of belief. In the process, rhetoricians got increasingly interested in courtroom argument.

Today, not only the rhetorician, but also the lawyer, is interested in learning more about human communication and persuasion. Rhetoric and law are coming together again in new and exciting ventures.[34] While law school curricula are only beginning to demonstrate this interest through pragmatic courses in interviewing, negotiating, and trial advocacy skills,[35] practicing lawyers are enrolling in increasing numbers in continuing legal education courses that emphasize communication and persuasion skills,[36] and prelaw students are discovering courses in their communication departments that focus on communication in the legal process.[37] This book attempts to further tighten the law-and-communication relationship by pulling together remarks made by experienced trial attorneys with applicable behavioral research conducted by communicologists and other social scientists.

Notes

[1]American Bar Association Membership Report (1985), unpaged.

[2]*Prelaw Handbook* (Washington, D.C.: Association of American Law Schools and the Law School Admission Council, 1978), 9.

[3]*Prelaw Handbook* (Washington, D.C.: Association of American Law Schools and the Law School Admission Council, 1985), 13; *Prelaw Quarterly* (Washington, D.C.: Law School Admission Council, 1985), 9.

[4]Mark W. Cannon, "Contentious and Burdensome Litigation: A Need for Alternatives," *National Forum* 63 (Fall 1983), 10.

[5]"Questioning the Bar Exams," *Time* (February 25, 1980), 44.

[6]Ibid.

[7]*Prelaw Handbook* (1978), 9.

[8]Ibid., 9–10.

[9]Henry J. Abraham, *The Judicial Process: An Introductory Analysis of the Courts of the United States, England, and France* (New York: Oxford University Press, 1968), 22–23.

[10]Cannon, op. cit., 10.

[11]Serious crimes are called felonies. Other crimes are called misdemeanors.

[12]Today 31 states allow charges to be brought without an indictment by a grand jury; a single judge decides the issue. "Behind Closed Doors," *Time* (April 8, 1985), 33.

[13]David M. Hunsaker, "Law, Humanism, and Communication: Suggestions for Limited Curricular Reform," *Journal of Legal Education* 30 (1980), 423.

[14]Gary S. Goodpaster, "The Human Arts of Lawyering: Interviewing and Counseling," *Journal of Legal Education* 27 (1975), 22.

[15]Ronald C. Dahl and Robert Davis, *Effective Speaking for Lawyers* (Buffalo: William S. Hein, 1969), 3.

[16]Goodpaster, op. cit., 3.

[17]Robert F. Forston, "Sense and Non-Sense: Jury Trial Communication," *Brigham Young University Law Review* (1975), 605–606.

[18]Richard W. Nanstoll, "Regulating Professional Qualification," in Geoffrey C. Hazard, Jr., ed., *Law in a Changing America* (New York: American Assembly, 1968), 129.

[19]*Prelaw Handbook* (1985), 16.

[20]*Prelaw Handbook* (1978), 18.

[21]Lane Cooper, trans., *The Rhetoric of Aristotle* (New York: Appleton-Century-Crofts, 1960).

[22]Robert F. Hanley, "Brush Up Your Aristotle," *Litigation* (Winter 1986), 39–42.

[23]G. L. Hendrickson, Trans., *Cicero's Brutus* (Cambridge: Harvard University Press, Loeb Classical Library, 1952); H. M. Hubbell, trans., *Cicero's Orator* (Cambridge: Harvard University Press, Loeb Classical Library, 1952).

[24]H. E. Butler, trans., *The Institutio Oratoria of Quintilian,* 4 vols. (Cambridge: Harvard University Press, Loeb Classical Library, 1920–1922).

[25]D. W. Robertson, trans., *Augustine's On Christian Doctrine* (New York: Bobbs-Merrill Library of Liberal Arts, 1958).

[26]Carole Newlands and James J. Murphy, trans., *Peter Ramus' Arguments in Rhetoric Against Quintilian* (DeKalb: Northern Illinois University Press, 1983).

[27]"The lawyer-client relation, the numerous non-rational factors involved in persuasion . . . at trial, the face-to-face appeals to the emotions of juries, the elements that go to make up what is loosely known as the 'atmosphere' of a case . . . [were] virtually unknown (and therefore meaningless) to Langdell." Jerome Frank, "Why Not a Clinical Lawyer School?" *University of Pennsylvania Law Review* 81 (1933), 907–908.

[28]Yale was the rare exception to Harvard. "A different philosophy . . . existed between Harvard and Yale toward legal education. Yale attempted to teach a more practical course. . . . In this philosophy, it was concerned with developing a rhetorical theory of legal practice. . . . Representative of this theory is William C. Robinson's *Forensic Oratory: A Manual for Advocates.* Robinson, a professor of law at Yale University writing in 1893, expresses the underlying philosophy of his book in the Preface, 'Nothing is more desirable than that young advocates should be well trained in the principles and practice of this art (forensic oratory).' . . . Robinson's *Forensic Oratory* . . . stands as an example of an effort to relate formal legal education and rhetorical theory in a way that had not been done for centuries. It is of interest that this sort of an effort was made during the formative years of American law schools, and one can speculate what changes might have taken place had Yale become one of the leading and most influential of the law schools. However, it was . . . Harvard that . . . set the example for other law schools." Richard D. Rieke, "Rhetorical Theory in Legal Practice," Ph.D diss. (Columbus: Ohio State University, 1964), 76–77, 81.

[29]Winifred Bryan Horner, "The Eighteenth Century," in Winifred Bryan Horner, ed., *The Present State of Scholarship in Historical and Contemporary Rhetoric* (Columbia: University of Missouri Press, 1983), 101–133.

[30]Oliver Wendell Holmes, *The Common Law* (Boston: Little, Brown, 1898), 1.

[31]Benjamin N. Cardozo, *The Nature of the Judicial Process* (New Haven: Yale University Press, 1921).

[32]Jerome Frank, *Courts on Trial: Myth and Reality in American Justice* (Princeton, N.J.: Princeton University Press, 1949).

[33]*United States v. Shipp,* 214 U.S. 386 (1908).

[34]For a detailed discussion of this phenomenon,

see Ronald J. Matlon, "Bridging the Gap Between Communication Education and Legal Education," *Communication Education* 31 (1982), 39–53.

[35]The case method remains the modus operandi in legal education. However, as the drive to make the curriculum more practical and communication-oriented continues, "law schools . . . remain torn between the influence of Dean Langdell and the Realists. . . . The resulting tension has been diagnosed . . . as a deep 'schizophrenia' in legal education." George S. Grossman, "Clinical Legal Education: History and Diagnosis," *Journal of Legal Education* 26 (1974), 167.

[36]Matlon, op. cit.

[37]Ronald J. Matlon, "Communication in the Legal Process: A Pre-Law Course at the University of Arizona," *Journal of Legal Education* 31 (1982), 589–603; Ronald J. Matlon, "Teaching Communication in the Legal Process," *Communication Education* 30 (1981), 399–409.

PART ONE

COMMUNICATION THEORY AND PRACTICE IN THE PRETRIAL PROCESS

CHAPTER

INTERVIEWING

THE NATURE OF DYADIC COMMUNICATION AND OF INTERVIEWING

DYADIC COMMUNICATION IN THE LEGAL INTERVIEW

INTERVIEWING BARRIERS AND DISTORTING INFLUENCES
Mood Influences / Background Influences /
Nonverbal Influences / Language Influences / Role
Influences / Environmental Influences

STAGES OF A SUCCESSFUL INITIAL LAWYER-CLIENT INTERVIEW
The First Stage: Developing Rapport / The Second
Stage: Gathering Information / The Third Stage:
Counseling

While preparing for and settling cases, an attorney will spend many hours in legal interviewing. Whether interviewing a client, a potential witness, or other attorneys, the savvy lawyer will want to develop a communication strategy for asking meaningful questions and for understanding the responses. This chapter can help the student of legal interviewing gain a better understanding of the nature of dyadic communication, specifically applied to the lawyer-client relationship in a legal interview. Because overcoming communication barriers and distorting influences is vital to the success of an initial interview, six important influences are analyzed. Finally, an examination of the three stages of an interview will complete the chapter.

THE NATURE OF DYADIC COMMUNICATION AND OF INTERVIEWING

Communication is a process in which a source sends a message through a channel to a receiver, who then provides a response. It is people sharing thoughts and feelings in a sort of "joint venture, with both participants adjusting continually to what happens from moment to moment."[1] The most basic unit of communication is a one-to-one situation, such as your talking with a friend. A pair of persons is called a *dyad*. Hence, two-party communication is referred to as *dyadic communication*. The model is quite simple, as is seen in Figure 1.1. In this model, person 1 says something to person 2; person 2 responds, and person 1 picks up the message.

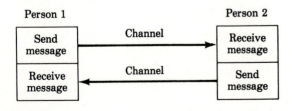

Person 1 | | Person 2

Send message → Channel → Receive message

Receive message ← Channel ← Send message

FIGURE 1.1 MODEL OF DYADIC COMMUNICATION

Both members of this dyad are supplying *feedback* to each other. Feedback is response to a message. Persons engaged in two-way communication control the interaction that ensues.

In dyadic communication, certain unique qualities exist. For instance, in a direct visual contact dyad, the communicators are physically quite close to each other. This closeness, or *proximity,* allows the most innocuous of movements to call attention to itself. The message sender looks at the clock, and the message receiver thinks the conversation should be coming to a close. The message sender yawns, and the message receiver thinks the sender is uninterested. Because of proximity, communication behaviors are often magnified out of proportion.

Another quality of dyadic communication is usually *informality*. Messages are not as carefully prepared in advance as they are for a public speech to a large audience. Although people in dyads sometimes have certain goals in mind, their communication is usually more random and intimate than in more formal settings.

Finally, *simultaneous and mutual message exchange* is a key factor. In fact, in good dyadic communication, it is often difficult to distinguish message senders from message receivers, since both parties constantly move in and out of both roles. Poor dyadic communication occurs when there is relatively little relevant feedback from one or both dyadic partners.

An interview is one form of dyadic communication. As in other forms, the pair is in close proximity, acts rather informally, and engages in simultaneous and mutual message exchanges. However, an interview has one characteristic that distinguishes it from other dyadic communications. An interview is not just random conversation. Although a good interview may appear to be highly conversational, it actually is initiated for a specific purpose. An interview has "a predetermined and

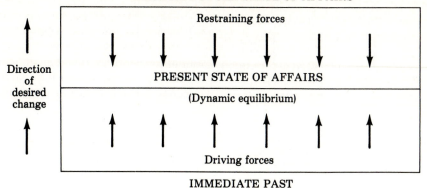

FIGURE 1.2 FORCE FIELD THEORY

serious purpose designed to interchange behavior and involve the asking and answering of questions."[2] It has been defined as "a specialized form of oral, face-to-face communication between people in an interpersonal relationship that is entered into for a specific task-related purpose associated with a particular subject matter."[3] In other words, an interview is a particular form of dyadic communication in which people have purposes, things they want to accomplish. "It is this task-related purpose that differentiates an interview from mere conversation."[4]

In a legal interview with a client, an attorney has the specific purpose of helping the client, and the client has the specific purpose of securing help with a problem. From the lawyer's point of view, a legal interview is *a process of human interaction in which the attorney's primary purposes are procurement of information, diagnosis, and advice.* Let us now look more closely at the interviewer-interviewee relationship and at the nature of effective dyadic communication in the legal interview setting.

DYADIC COMMUNICATION IN THE LEGAL INTERVIEW

A good way to begin consideration of dyadic communication in the legal interview is to apply *force-field theory.* A force field is a volume of space occupied by certain kinds of energy. Field theory has been widely applied in social psychology, although it originated in physics. Individuals, groups, and institutions can be studied by viewing the forces operating interdependently between them. Any action or behavior in a field is a result of those psychological forces operating on a person. If forces are in a state of equilibrium, the field is in equilibrium. Equilibrium means that the person's behavior is not changing. However, if tension enters the system through a change in forces, the field as a whole is changed, and a change in behavior ensues. "Action is thus the result of forces operating in the present field."[5]

Although it is somewhat an overgeneralization to do so, the interview between attorney and client can be explained by considering it as an illustration of force-field theory. In Figure 1.2, the arrows represent the psychological forces making up the force field. The direction of each arrow indicates that force's tendency to change; the length of the arrow indicates the strength of the force. The center lines (called "present state of affairs") is equilibrium, or the present arrangement of the forces.

In a legal interview, the attorney-interviewer is the agent of change; the attorney is

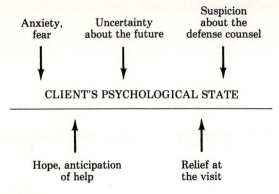

FIGURE 1.3 LAWYER-CLIENT INTERVIEW: PHASE ONE

interested in moving toward a desired future state of affairs with a client. The attorney must, from the client's present unsettling state of affairs, limit or remove the number and intensity of restraining psychological forces and strengthen in number and intensity the positive, driving forces. Naturally, each new person interviewed presents a new and different situation for a lawyer.

Let us consider an example. Suppose a male lawyer has been assigned to defend in a criminal case a 23-year-old male client who has just been arrested along with a codefendant. When they were stopped in a car, heroin was discovered hidden in the trunk. The codefendant has a history of drug abuse; the

client has no prior record of any kind. The charges against the client are conspiracy to sell and possession of drugs. During the arrest, the client told the police that the codefendant was not involved at all. What the police do not know is that the client was lying because he was afraid of what the codefendant might do to him.

The initial interview between attorney and client is about to take place. What is the psychological force field of the client? Figure 1.3 shows that he is experiencing anxiety, fear, and uncertainty because he does not want an arrest record. The client is also uncertain and somewhat suspicious about the defense counsel, because the counsel is a public defender, and the client does not understand why the government is trying to prosecute him on one hand and defend him on the other. On the positive side, the client is at least relieved that he now has an attorney to talk to. He hopes the attorney will be able to "get him off."

In the first few moments of the interview, the attorney identifies himself and explains the role of a public defender. This explanation reduces the client's suspicion and increases his positive feelings toward the attorney (see Figure 1.4). To some extent, anxiety and uncertainty are also mitigated. The client now begins to cooperate.

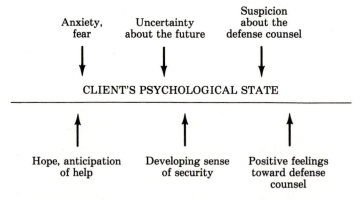

FIGURE 1.4 LAWYER-CLIENT INTERVIEW: PHASE TWO

After some discussion, the attorney begins to suspect a cover-up of the involvement of the codefendant. He asks the client if he is telling the truth. Figure 1.5 shows what happens to the force field. It dramatically changes. An unfavorable array of forces increases. Motivation of the client to cooperate declines. The client may even repeat the lie he told the police or choose not to talk to his attorney anymore.

Force-field theory demonstrates the extraordinary sensitivity an attorney must have during a legal interview. After all, the relative weights of the elements in the model vary constantly. Contingencies and variables in the client's psychological field can change from moment to moment. Lawyers must depend upon a "sophisticated awareness of how humans are likely to act or react in any given situation; upon very high-level abilities not only to communicate, but also to perceive the full range of what is being communicated by the parties; and finally, upon a good knowledge, intuitive or acquired, of the psychology of communication and persuasion techniques which can be used in or adjusted to various situations."[6] Recognizing emotions and drawing reasonable inferences about them are essential to an effective legal interview.

I do not want to leave you with the impression that the client is "an irrational bundle of needs to be gratified and fears to be purged" while the rational lawyer has "all of the best qualities of the professional thinker and therapist" to "discover what deep-seated drives or repressed desires are controlling the client's behavior."[7] This view of the personas involved is incorrect. Lawyers have irrational impulses and serious frustrations too. Yet, as professionals, they are expected to control those impulses and act as understanding counselors with the ability to maintain "a metatheoretical position on the process of interaction as a whole"[8] and to control the force field of the client. That is a tall order indeed.

INTERVIEWING BARRIERS AND DISTORTING INFLUENCES

There are six potential barriers or distorting influences that attorneys need to recognize before and during any legal interview. What follows is an analysis of these barriers along with suggestions for overcoming them.

Mood Influences

A trip to a lawyer's office is potentially a dreadful experience for many clients. In the waiting room, clients may experience considerable apprehension about an upcoming interview because each believes he or she has a serious need or life problem, be it a divorce, a contract dispute, a criminal charge, or the

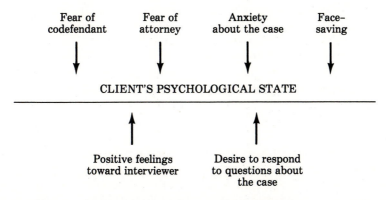

FIGURE 1.5 LAWYER-CLIENT INTERVIEW: PHASE THREE

drafting of a will. They are apprehensive because they have no idea how "the case" will turn out. They are probably not knowledgeable about the law. They may have heard that lawyers cannot be trusted or that they always charge far too much money.

The lawyer must anticipate this apprehensive mood of clients. In the interview, the lawyer has to dispel the mood and give the client as much of a sense of security as possible. Since most legal problems require a number of interviews before they can be resolved, the client will probably still have a problem when he or she leaves the lawyer's office the first time, but at least the client will feel somewhat better if the initial interview has been properly conducted.

The lawyer, too, has a certain mood or emotional set that affects the interview. Before the interview begins, the attorney may feel tired or downhearted. Perhaps an upsetting conversation with a disliked client has just ended. Or perhaps a case has just been settled, earning a good fee and causing the lawyer to feel especially upbeat. No matter what the situation, the lawyer should make a concerted effort to be aware of the mood he or she is in before the interview begins and to deal with it in a way that will not interfere with what must be accomplished in the upcoming interview. As seen in the force-field example earlier, certain social-psychological components inhibit the flow of information in a legal interview, and the moods of both attorney and client before the interview begins affect the way in which the interview proceeds.

Occasionally, emotional disturbances can affect the mood and influence the outcome of a legal interview. Interviewees sometimes express feelings of embarrassment, guilt, or pain. Some cry. Some get hysterical. What should the interviewer do? Move away? Change the subject? Certainly not. Lawyer-interviewers should be empathetic. Empathy is feeling with, not sympathy for, someone else. As lawyers demonstrate this empathetic understanding, they should nevertheless remain calm. An emotional disturbance by an interviewee may actually create a positive mood in the interview. Catharsis—a release of tension—can be an appropriate response to an anxious situation. The lawyer should just let it happen and, when it shows signs of subsiding, offer comfort and understanding, not to the point of agreeing about the cause of the disturbance, but to the point of offering to do whatever is possible and necessary to help the person in distress.[9]

Background Influences

Our personal backgrounds have a tremendous influence over our personalities, our attitudes, and our value systems. Certainly no one completely abandons his or her background when entering an interview situation. Backgrounds, called by sociologists cultural factors, create major expectations in the interviewee (client) and the interviewer (attorney) before and during their exchange.

One background influence is social class. If the interviewer and the interviewee come from different socioeconomic backgrounds (i.e., life-styles that are different because of differences in wealth), the difference in backgrounds could create a communication barrier in an interview. Young lawyers working in poverty law frequently find their clients "laying trips" on them because of perceived differences in wealth. The client's negative preconceptions about wealthy people create a problem for the interviewer.

Not only might the client have preconceptions based on social class, but the lawyer too should be conscious of any preconceptions he or she might hold about the client. There is a natural tendency to categorize people. For example, let us assume that the client is a young woman who dyes her hair odd colors and wears black, metal-studded leather clothes. The 60-year-old male lawyer has a perceptual set that categorizes the client. To the lawyer, the category "punk" means the client does not wash, has no money, uses drugs, and is untrustworthy. Of course, none of these characteristics necessarily apply to the client, who could be a wealthy, hardworking accountant who just happens to prefer oddly colored hair and black, metal-studded leather clothes. The lawyer's predisposition is inaccurate and will interfere with his ability to communicate with the client.

Two techniques can relieve the tendency of perceived differences in social class to interfere with the interview. One technique is for the lawyer to be aware of and check this tendency to categorize. When lawyers meet clients, they should silently ask themselves if a client's appearance may be causing them to categorize the client in any particular way. The other technique is for the lawyer to minimize the barrier by focusing on the issues that brought attorney and client together. The attorney should work toward that objective and not toward bridging the socioeconomic gap. The issues provide a common objective for attorney and client. A socioeconomic gap, real or imagined, may persist throughout the attorney-client contact, but no attempt should be made to alter it in any way.

Another background influence is *education and experience*. Tensions on the part of the less educated often restrict their flow of communication with more highly educated people. Unfortunately, less educated people frequently believe difference in schooling experiences makes communication with more highly educated individuals impossible. How many of us have experienced this in our daily lives, particularly in the feeling that there is a problem communicating with a relative who has had no college education? Or, how often have you felt uncomfortable talking with a college dean or professor?

A similar barrier to effective communication can occur among equally educated and equally experienced persons. A study has shown that there can be considerable tension between "educated" sections of a community.[10] For example, in a legal interview, a lawyer may find a doctor hard to pin down because of the physician's reluctance to put his or her career on the line. The physician may divulge information very cautiously because she or he knows she or he is talking to an equally educated person from another profession.

In the situations just noted, the net result is that the interviewee behaves in a reticent manner. Sensitive lawyers can overcome this education and experience barrier by creating an atmosphere in which people feel comfortable talking with them regardless of differences. Lawyers create such an atmosphere by learning how to listen and respond to people in different "languages."[11] Later in this chapter, some attention will be given to establishing rapport between attorney and client. That advice can be used to overcome any education and experience barrier to effective communication.

Sex and age are potential barriers too. At times, there may be problems in dyadic communication just because the dyad is male-male, female-female, female-male, or young-old. Let us consider some examples. If a male client has for years been dominated by a harsh and critical mother, he may have difficulty listening to and accepting the advice of a female attorney. If a female client strongly believes that men are always sources of poor treatment, she may view a male attorney as an enemy. And we have long heard about the generation gap. Youth have trouble understanding the elderly, and vice versa. These problems occasionally lie outside the immediate awareness of the interviewee. Yet the problems are formidable ones and should be addressed frankly once they are perceived by the interviewing lawyer. Sometimes the problems are so serious that a change of attorney is necessary.

To adjust to all these potential barriers (social class, education and experience, sex, and age), attorneys must be good listeners and must feel their way into interviewees' backgrounds. Feeling is, after all, what empathy is. Keeping these background influences in mind will go a long way toward maximizing the effectiveness of the interview.

Nonverbal Influences

Communication in the dyad takes place through a number of channels, all of which are important if the interview is to proceed smoothly. What we are concerned with here are the channels that are not verbal. Specifically, how do physical and vocal delivery affect feedback between interviewer and interviewee?

Eye contact is very important as people talk to each other. For instance, people tend to look at each other with longer gazes when listening intently. They tend to look away when they dislike the other person or when they are embarrassed or lying. A lawyer can greatly enhance the willingness of a client to communicate freely by looking directly at the client during the interview. The lawyer should remove, insofar as possible, all temptations to look elsewhere. Of course, "it is possible to carry eye contact too far, although the vast majority of interviewers are on the side of too little rather than too much contact. Once in a while, though, an interviewer who is a very intense person will establish too much eye contact, so that he or she seems to be staring"[12] at the interviewee. That can make a client uncomfortable. If a client appears uncomfortable, it is a good idea for the lawyer to use a little more or a little less eye contact. The best eye contact occurs when the lawyer looks directly at the client, with a thoughtful or pleasant facial expression, "so that the overall picture is of someone who is listening with real interest and understanding."[13]

Body movements and gestures also affect the messages we are trying to communicate. Regardless of the mental attitude you may have in a given situation, your gestures and body movements communicate certain attitudes by themselves. For example, a clenched fist might communicate anger. Sitting stiffly might communicate formality. Frowning can be discouraging. Picking at your fingernails might communicate nervousness or boredom. A "dead fish" handshake does not inspire confidence or interest. Hence, lawyers need to be aware of using inappropriate physical movement. That is no easy task because most body movements and gestures are made subconsciously. Others, however, can be more readily and consciously controlled. For instance, if an attorney gets in the habit of leaning back in his or her chair, that position can be interpreted by a client as a willingness to listen. If an attorney offers a client a cigarette, the offer can be interpreted as an invitation to relax (although it may be an annoying gesture to a nonsmoking interviewee). Nodding the head can be interpreted as agreement or understanding. Certain actions should *not* be used, such as playing with a pen or pencil, chewing gum, constantly shuffling papers, drumming the fingers on a desk or table, constantly fiddling around with a pipe, or doing anything else that could be distracting, annoying, or rude or that could be interpreted as showing lack of interest in the client.

Vocal delivery is as important to effective communication as is physical delivery. Speech that is too fast, too loud, too soft, slurred, or high-pitched will distract from the message the interviewer is trying to get across. A lawyer should be careful to speak slow enough to be understood, but not so slow as to bore the client. As a rule, a lawyer should neither shout at a client nor speak so softly as not to be heard. If the lawyer's speech is as conversational as possible, the client will not be distracted by a speaking voice inappropriate to the interview.

As well as understanding how their own nonverbal communication affects the interview, astute lawyers will also learn from the nonverbal cues of clients. Clients communicate much without putting all messages into words. Uncomfortable and anxious clients may perspire, have halting speech, lack eye contact, speak in a high pitch, drum their fingers, and so forth. These are signs that clients are unable to communicate freely because of their feelings of anxiety. If the signs change and become more positive during an interview, it is an indication that the client is relaxing. However, the signs can surface again at any time if the exchange of thoughts becomes threatening to the client. The interviewer may have to "back off" when these signs appear. To do so can open up communication channels once again.

A note of caution: Nonverbal signs are not always accurate signs; that is, they are not easy to interpret correctly. "Many respondents have learned to hide certain nonverbal clues to their feelings and attitudes. This control is usually exercised by maintaining a neutral or noncommittal expression or by pretending an opposite feeling."[14] It is, however, extremely difficult to control all of one's nonverbal responses at one time. Therefore, the interviewer needs to develop the habit of observing the total of body and vocal responses rather than concentrating only on the other person's eyes, hands, or vocal pitch. There might be a calm facial expression and a casual tone of voice, but the same person could also be constantly tapping on the tabletop. In later interviews with the same client, it becomes easier to accurately evaluate contradictions in nonverbal cues and to make more reliable judgments about a person's emotional state. In sum, nonverbal cues that are inconsistent with verbal messages, or sudden changes in the interviewee's nonverbal activity, are signs that there are problems in the interview that need to be addressed by the interviewer.

Language Influences

Word choice and sentence structure can either impose constraints on communication or go far in making communication more ef-fective. One precaution is obvious. The lawyer must use legal terminology sparingly. Legal jargon is unlikely to be familiar to a non-lawyer. If technical words must be used, the lawyer should be careful to explain these terms so that the client understands them. Also, a lawyer should frequently ask questions to discover if the client understands what has been said (e.g., "Do you know what a class action suit entails?"). Finding the appropriate language and being clearly understood are crucial.

Role Influences

Both the interviewer and the interviewee have certain expectations of the other party, such as empathy, good listening, good advice, and cooperation. To build a trusting relationship based on fulfillment of those expectations, both persons should recognize and accommodate their respective roles in the interview.

What are some of the things a lawyer can do to meet the role expectations of the client? First, as noted earlier, attorneys should show empathy toward clients; clients need someone who can share and understand their innermost feelings. Attorneys must project a genuine, warm interest in clients in order to produce confidence and candor. Even words of praise by the attorney for efforts to answer questions can be quite rewarding to the client. Clients expect and deserve empathy.

Second, lawyers should be good and objective listeners throughout interviews. Listening is a very important behavior. Yet many attorneys seems more concerned with what they will say during an interview than with what they will hear. A good indication of faulty listening is the failure to follow up on some of the key clues a client gives in response to the attorney's questions. How many times have you, when asking questions, concentrated so greatly on asking your next question that you missed the last answer? Lawyers must not tune out clients as though they were commercial breaks in a television program. Too much can be missed. Clients expect and deserve attentive lawyers.

Third, lawyers are expected to counsel, not just to listen to problems. Of course, early in an interview, lawyers must discipline themselves against giving advice until adequate data have been provided. However, what might appear to the client as a detached attitude will soon begin to disturb the advice-seeking interviewee, and at some point in the interview, the lawyer should attempt to put the client at ease by offering some advice just to relieve the client's anxieties.

Lawyers also have role expectations. The ideal interviewee is one who cooperates. The attorney may have to give a short speech pointing out to the client that a legal interview is an information-gathering setting. The attorney might also tell what has to be done by both parties to achieve this information-gathering objective. If the interviewee is reluctant to talk because he or she perceives an insurmountable superior-subordinate role barrier, the lawyer may have to discuss the problem with the client. Guarded comments are often an indication of such a perception. How many times have you been hesitant to talk to a professor openly about a particular problem? Was it because you perceived your audience (the professor) to be in a superior role to you? When this hesitancy occurs in a legal interview, it is difficult for the attorney to get all the facts that are needed. The lawyer must break down the barrier as soon as possible.

Some interviewees believe that their role is to give only the facts that they think will help their case and then to rely on the attorney to "get them off the hook." Of course, this attitude inhibits effective communication also. Once again, clients must be instructed to provide all information, no matter how unpleasant the information is or how desirable it is to conceal it. The attorney may also have to explain to a client that a lawyer is not in a position to "figure a way out" of problems without regard for what is right and reasonable. That misconception oversimplifies an attorney's role. Because clients are usually unprepared for legal complexities and because they usually want their problems settled quickly, they frequently become annoyed and impatient. So they need advice about the respective roles of attorney and client.

Environmental Influences

The physical surroundings of a legal interview can be quite important whether the interview is in a lawyer's office, a jail, someone's home, or a work place. "The cardinal point to remember is that wherever the interview takes place, the setting will stimulate reactions and their consequences should be scrutinized closely."[15] Rooms that are too hot, too cold, too plush, too unkempt, and so forth, should be avoided. The ideal physical surrounding is one in which the interviewee feels comfortable—a businesslike location, but one that creates a feeling of quiet ease.

Since most interviews are conducted in a lawyer's office, what can the lawyer do to make that office a businesslike place that creates a comfortable feeling for the interviewee? Here is a checklist of recommendations:

1. Clients should not be kept in the waiting room. Long delays can create irritation and build apprehension, causing the interview to get started on the wrong foot.

2. Keep interruptions to a minimum. They stop the flow of ideas. For instance, avoid a ringing telephone. Be sure the phone is disconnected.

3. Privacy must be ensured so that lawyer and client can talk more easily. Do not allow the tapping of typewriters or other such noise outside the office to enter the interviewing room.

4. Consider carefully the placement of

furniture. Desks between the two parties can serve as a barrier. Such an office arrangement only enhances the authority image of the attorney. The solution is to place a chair beside the desk or to have the attorney and interviewee sit in comfortable, but not too soft, chairs approximately three to eight feet apart.[16]

5. Be certain the interviewee is not facing glaring lights or sun. The client should not feel as though he or she is being "grilled."[17]

6. The attorney should be careful not to be too conspicuous about taking notes, particularly during an initial interview. If possible, notes should not be taken at all, or only a few cryptic references should be recorded. The physical movements of writing may distract the interviewee. Eye contact is easily broken. The attorney may get too involved in the mechanical task of writing. Also, interviewees may be overcautious if they see that their words are being recorded in writing. What, then, about the possibility of using a stenographer? That is not a good idea because it is inhibiting too. The client may be ill at ease about disclosing all the information, especially confidential facts, if another person is present. What can be done by a lawyer is to personally transcribe a detailed statement about the interview immediately after it is over. This allows for the retention of information without the distractions of note taking in the interview itself. This rule of thumb about not taking notes is not, however, absolute. After the initial telling of the story by the client, the interviewer can explain the need for recording detail, and then only when the client is willing and is comfortable with the taking of notes should a lawyer proceed to do so.

7. Making an electronic tape of an interview avoids many of the problems involved with note taking and gives an attorney a permanent record of the interview, but new problems are introduced.

Interviewees become reluctant to talk because of the threat of preserving their exact words. They may also have doubts about why recording is really necessary. Under any circumstances, if a recording device is used, "the interviewee should be told about the machine . . . and that a tape will be made of the conversation."[18] Even then, it may be best not to start recording "until after some rapport and some trust have been established."[19]

8. If more than one lawyer is interviewing a client, the responsibilities should be divided before the interview begins. If there are two lawyers, perhaps one could take responsibility for talking; the other could observe, remember, and later counsel. The lawyers should not seat the client between them; it is uncomfortable for the client to continually turn back and forth to see both lawyers.

STAGES OF A SUCCESSFUL INITIAL LAWYER-CLIENT INTERVIEW

For some reason a man or a woman comes to a lawyer's office seeking help. Why does the person want help? Why does the person need to see a lawyer? Why has this particular lawyer been chosen? Why is the person coming at this time? What does this person hope to accomplish? These are the kinds of questions a lawyer will need to get answers for in an initial legal interview. Cases do not walk into lawyers' offices; people with problems do. The person may only need moral support, friendship, or a rock to cling to. In any case, the potential client comes to the lawyer hoping to find an understanding listener. How the lawyer and the client build a trusting relationship depends on the unique personality requirements of both individuals involved.

In a civil matter, a potential plaintiff appears in the lawyer's office with what he or she perceives to be a legitimate claim. The client's natural inclination is to tell the lawyer only the most favorable side of the story. Lawyers need to be cautious about getting too enthusiastic about what a potential plaintiff has to say. Rather, they should be reserved in their evaluations and conservative regarding prophecies on the success of any litigation for a plaintiff.[20]

In a civil or criminal matter, a defendant, who is usually confused and under considerable stress, contacts a lawyer for help. The lawyer must be a good listener and counselor. The story must be obtained from the defendant, but the person must also be kept as calm as possible. It is generally unwise to ask a client whether he or she is guilty or innocent of the charge or liable for the complaint. "Many people believe they are guilty of a crime when in fact they are not, while others believe they are innocent when in fact they may be guilty."[21] The defense attorney is an advocate; he or she is neither judge nor jury. The defense counsel's function is to support the client to the utmost of his or her ability.

If the initial lawyer-client interview goes poorly, any future relationship between that client and the lawyer could be one without mutual trust and confidence. This is not what a lawyer desires, of course. In order for the initial interview to go well, a lawyer must establish three key objectives: (1) develop rapport with the client, (2) gather information from the client, and (3) advise and counsel the client satisfactorily. These objectives can be translated into three stages of a legal interview.

The First Stage: Developing Rapport

When a lawyer and a client first meet, they consciously and subconsciously receive initial impressions of each other. This initial mutual evaluation is made quickly by both parties. The first impression is often a lasting impression. Hence, it is extremely important that the

lawyer try to make the client as comfortable as possible. As the client becomes comfortable, rapport (effective communication) can be established between the parties involved.

Unfortunately, many interviews begin on the wrong foot. For instance, some interviews start with such questions as "What is your name?" "What is your address?" "How old are you?" "Are you married?" "Where do you work and what do you do?" These personal data can be obtained in writing by a legal secretary before the interview begins. To gather them at the beginning of a lawyer-client interview is impersonal and cold. By the same token, a lawyer who begins an interview by saying that there is probably a great deal of information to obtain, that there is not much time to get that information, that all he or she wants is "the story" in a nutshell, and that he or she wants the client to be accurate and truthful will no doubt put inappropriate pressure on the client. If the initial interview begins in ways like those described, rapport is unlikely to be established, and the relationship between the two parties is unlikely to be a particularly good one.

In his "valuable research"[22] on lawyer-client relationships, Goldsmith found that the most common complaint of clients is that lawyers seem not to empathize with them.[23] A survey of Missouri clients showed that their dissatisfaction with lawyers was usually based, not on losing a case, but on the indifferent manner and attitude of lawyers.[24] Apparently, lawyers make clients feel as though there is little interest in their problems, and many seem "aloof, unconcerned, . . . bored, . . . [and] uncommunicative."[25] Since interviews with lawyers can be unnerving experiences for clients anyway, it is essential that a lawyer build a supportive climate for a client as early in an interview as possible. How can this be done? How can a client be made to feel important and yet be put at ease?

Initially, the interview should begin with a few pleasantries. A friendly and informal, but professional, introduction is appropriate. The attorney should stand up and greet the client pleasantly by name (e.g., "Good afternoon, Ms. Johnson. May I call you Pat?") These few first moments, if appropriately handled by counsel, can create a low-threat environment for the client. Small talk helps break the ice too. However, this small talk should not put clients on the spot by making them feel pressure to talk about themselves. Nor should the small talk last too long, because clients generally want to get down to business.[26]

After introductions and small talk, the lawyer should invite the client to talk about his or her problem as much as possible. Discussion should start in an area chosen by the client. Letting clients choose where to begin will allow them to relax, and it may bolster their self-esteem to let them talk in the areas where they initially feel most comfortable.[27] They ought to be allowed to talk without interruption. Clarification of details should be saved for stage 2. Interrupting with questions may lessen the client's candor, make the client defensive, and possibly shift the interview in an inappropriate direction. A catharsis should occur if necessary. Clients are often worried and want to talk. They may have talked to no one else about their problem until the time they first see a lawyer. They are often eager to tell their stories. Attorneys should let them. In this way, rapport can be enhanced. So, after the initial pleasantries and introductions, the lawyer's best question is "What can I do to help you today?"

From this point, the lawyer should settle back and be an attentive listener. Unfortunately, "poor listening . . . is the most serious problem in attorney-client relations."[28] Why is this so? "Partly, . . . it has to do with a basic insecurity with the professional role. Professionals are 'supposed to be' in command. One sure way to be in command is to ask questions."[29] But interrupting with questions does not allow clients to narrate their own problems, and this narration is essential.

Flashy, insightful questions must therefore be repressed by attorneys in the early stages of an interview.

It may seen a bit abnormal to a lawyer at first just sitting there listening to what a client is saying rather than concentrating on what to ask next. Nevertheless, concentration must be on what the client says. This kind of active listening quickly builds empathetic identification and rapport. It is astounding to the client to actually be listened to. It encourages the client to get to the level of true feelings. For instance, it is useful in a child custody case to hear the statement "I've been stupid for years in the way I've ignored my children." But a statement like that can come only from emotions built up by a person freely narrating his or her own story to an empathetic listener.

Listening is a difficult skill. Essentially, it is the talent of learning something through attentive, receptive silence. We are able to listen to about five hundred words per minute. "How we fill in the hiatus determines whether or not we are doing a good job of listening."[30] If we listen not only to what is said, but also to what is not said, then we are using our listening time well.

What about silence? Is it awkward? Not necessarily so. Silence in an interview can be quite meaningful. Research indicates that there is a positive correlation between interviewer silence and respondent spontaneity.[31] Silence serves to punctuate a thoughtful mood. "If the silence is accompanied by a facial or postural expression of interest and thoughtfulness, it gives the respondent the impression that the interviewer is vitally interested in the story."[32] Silence is not awkward when the silence is allowing the client to think about such things as a relationship between elements in the story or about whether or not to reveal additional facts.

Too much silence is possible, too. Excessive silence can build up client anxiety. Silence becomes excessive when a client has stopped talking because he or she has nothing more to say. In that situation, the lawyer is wrong being silent. Lawyers need to be sensitive so that silence does not embarrass a client. Pacing this part of the interview is something that is learned through extensive interviewing practice.

On rare occasions, clients will not open up and talk.[33] The client frankly assumes he or she is to sit there and only answer questions. When this occurs, the attorney may have to inject brief words of encouragement (e.g., "Fine. You're doing just fine. Go on."). Maybe there still is no narration, possibly because the client feels awkward telling the story. If so, the attorney might interject something like this: "Many people feel uncomfortable talking about the kind of problem you seem to have. I understand that. But it really is important that I get a full account of what took place. So won't you please continue?" With such urging, the client may begin to talk.

Finally, the lawyer needs to remember that stage 1 is not the time when crucial information is gathered; this is rapport-building time only. All interviews have two important dimensions: content and relationship.[34] Content (getting and giving information) is not the primary focus in the first stage of the interview; relationship is. Relationship may well determine whether or not information is adequately exchanged. For revelations to be made, a high degree of interpersonal trust must be established early.

When clients ramble on and on, they are building a trusting relationship with a lawyer. Lawyers must be very careful not to get impatient with what they think is the reporting of extraneous or trivial matters. Clients must be allowed to talk freely, and lawyers must not halt that kind of talk.

The first stage of a legal interview is therefore one in which an attorney should be courteous and should show interest in a client's story. To build good rapport, the lawyer does what is necessary to bring about an open, trusting, caring relationship within the dyad.

Unconstrained talk on the part of the client should be encouraged, and the attorney should not hurry this talk along. However, once the client begins to "wind down," the lawyer can then ease into the next part of the interview by orienting the client to what the lawyer wants to accomplish, namely, the gathering of information, which will serve as the foundation for giving advice.

The Second Stage: Gathering Information

Information helps the attorney discover issues in a case. Since information is extremely important to a lawyer, the importance of this stage of a legal interview can hardly be overstated. It should be said at the outset, however, that this second stage of the interview does *not* involve counseling or problem solving. There is always the temptation to slip into giving advice before the second stage is completed. Advice should not be given until as much relevant information as possible has been gathered by the interviewer. Pressure will be placed on the attorney to offer advice early, but the attorney must resist until the data base is established. Occasionally during the second stage, the interviewing lawyer may have to say, "Of course, I'll give you some advice today. But try to be patient a few more moments while I get more information from you. After all, I want to give you the best advice possible, and I really can't until I have all the relevant information from you. So let me ask you a few more questions."

Two main overall interviewing approaches can be used to gather data. The *direct approach* begins by asking relatively specific questions (e.g., "Where were you Tuesday, November 5, between 6:00 and 8:00 P.M.?"). The advantage of being direct is that information is gathered efficiently and is structured around what the attorney sees as important. "If specific facts and opinions are needed rather than more complex structural relationships, a more specific question will be efficient. For example, if we wish to know a person's age, religion, and marital status, and if such information is not ego threatening under the circumstances, then it would be ridiculous to attempt to obtain the information by asking, 'Would you please tell me about yourself?'"[35] The disadvantage of being so direct is that, since the original story is undoubtedly incomplete, the attorney could leave out something critical during the questioning. In addition, the client might see this approach as too mechanical and interrogatory in nature and might therefore become defensive, losing some of the initial rapport that was established.

The *indirect approach* begins by asking rather general or broad questions. There is not a great deal of interviewer control here. This approach encourages lengthier responses from the interviewee. The broad question allows information to be elicited without the potential for distortion that exists when a more specific question is posed. In other words, broad questions help the attorney because they "prevent early questions from conditioning or biasing the responses to those which come later."[36] "Tell me about" might begin several of the lawyer's questions using the indirect approach.

Research on the two approaches shows that it is best for the lawyer to begin the information-gathering stage with the indirect approach. Goldsmith found that clients were "happier" when this approach was used.[37] Jones also discovered that information gathering is improved when the interviewer moves in a sequence from the indirect to the more direct. He calls this a *funnel sequence*.[38]

In a funnel sequence, each successive question has a narrower scope than the previous question, although it is included in or related to the previous question. For example:

"What do you think are some of the most important social problems of the day?"

"Of all those you mentioned, which one do you think is the most urgent to solve?"

"Since you think the abortion issue is the most urgent, what is your opinion on that subject?"

"Where do you get most of your information on abortion?"

"You mention *Time*. Are you a regular reader of that magazine?"

Notice the path of association between these questions. Notice also that the questions are worded so that each reflects the interviewee's frame of reference in the preceding answer. The interviewer is not only gathering information, but also continuing to build rapport by using the interviewee's answers as the foundation for questions asked. The interviewee knows that the interviewer is listening.

Even though the client may go off on a tangent from time to time, the lawyer can maintain considerable topic control by using the funnel whenever the interview reaches a crucial place and it seems necessary to become more specific and direct. The entire interview does not proceed from general to specific. Rather, at vital points in the information-gathering process, the lawyer makes use of more specific, closed-ended questioning. Once the bottom of a particular funnel has been reached and there is no more crucial information related to that subject to be discovered, the lawyer shifts to more indirect and open-ended questioning once again. Examples of closed-ended and open-ended questions are seen in Figure 1.6.

Note the implication of what has been said. If diagrammed, the fact-gathering stage of an interview is essentially a series of funnels. Each line of questioning or each funnel can be thought of as a mini-interview. Within each mini-interview, the attorney moves from a fairly general and open-ended question and response to increasingly more specific and closed-ended questions and responses that allow him or her to dig out details. So the funnel takes its shape from the type of questions posed. By setting up a series of funnels, the

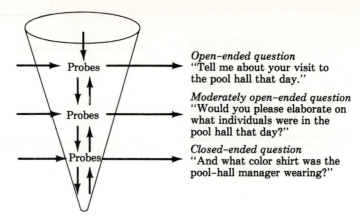

Open-ended question
"Tell me about your visit to the pool hall that day."

Moderately open-ended question
"Would you please elaborate on what individuals were in the pool hall that day?"

Closed-ended question
"And what color shirt was the pool-hall manager wearing?"

FIGURE 1.6   INTERVIEWING FUNNEL

attorney can program into the interview the topics he or she needs to cover to meet essential information-gathering objectives. No attempt will be made here to list topics for the funnels; each client's situation is unique, and each inquiry should be unique as well.

In Figure 1.6, the top of the funnel begins with the open-ended question, "Tell me about your visit to the pool hall that day." This question opens up the topic of the pool hall event with something other than a yes-or-no response. It suggests that the lawyer wants the client to answer with something more than a brief phrase or sentence. The question does not inform the client what specific kinds of information about the pool hall event the lawyer wants. Nor does it suggest what aspects of the pool hall event the attorney considers important. There is no "right answer" implied. The client can say anything he or she wishes to say about the particular pool hall event.

The middle of the funnel in Figure 1.6 contains a moderately open-ended question ("Would you please elaborate on what individuals were in the pool hall that day?"). The funnel has narrowed, but it is not yet tight. This question is narrower than the one at the top of the funnel, but it is not yet a closed-ended question, that is, one that can be an-

swered by a yes, no, or a very terse reply. The moderately open-ended question depends on and pertains to part of the answer to the open-ended question. In our example, it is clear from the response to the open-ended question that there were other people in the pool hall when the interviewee arrived.

The bottom of the funnel in Figure 1.6 uses a closed-ended question ("And what color shirt was the pool-hall manager wearing?"). This kind of question can be answered briefly—for example, "Red" or "Green and white stripes." Some closed-ended questions can even be answered by a simple yes or no. These kinds of questions get bits and pieces of information that were not elicited by open-ended quesitons. These questions near or at the bottom of a funnel may also occasionally threaten a client because they may be especially sensitive kinds of questions. It is possible for a client to feel "pinned down" to giving uncomfortable specific facts; those facts which were underemphasized or omitted are often facts the client believes are not in his or her favor. Since closed-ended questions can be awkward for clients, lawyers must pose them with tact.

Once the attorney is satisfied that all the pertinent information available on a particular topic has been gathered, he or she eases the client on to the next funnel. Moving from one funnel (topic) to the next must be apparent to the client. An attorney might say, "Carl, I think I have a rather good understanding of what you did in the pool hall that day. Now, I wonder if we might talk a while about where you went immediately after you left the pool hall. Please tell me about that." The attorney has thus closed the funnel and provided a transition to the top of another funnel with an open-ended question. The client should clearly know when the topic has been changed.

Sometimes the client will change the topic without prompting from the lawyer. This is satisfactory if the client is an orderly thinker and the topic just discussed has been covered adequately. However, a client sometimes changes the topic because (a) what was being discussed is too painful or too difficult to continue or (b) the topic seems irrelevant or of little personal interest. If a topic appears too painful for the client to discuss, an attorney might postpone it until a later interview. If a topic the lawyer thinks important is not significant to the client, and the client jumps to something that seems to him or her more pressing, the lawyer should either pick up the old topic immediately or return to it later.

Often clients do not realize they have changed topics. When this happens, the phenomenon of free association is occurring. For instance, a woman who is talking about problems in getting along with her landlord suddenly shifts to a discussion about an uncle she disliked as a child. The landlord and uncle may be unconsciously connected in her mind. A lawyer should watch for such relationships by letting a client continue an apparent topic shift for a while.

Throughout the funnel sequence, it is essential to employ the *probe*. A probe is a question or sign indicating to an interviewee that he or she should add something to the last reply. Probes are especially efficient at getting information, and they help interview-

ees remember some information they might have otherwise forgotten. A probe can be used at any point in an interview as illustrated in Figure 1.6. After all, incomplete interviewee replies can occur anywhere inside one of the funnels. However, attorneys must be very careful that the verbal probe not become a leading question, or the information gathered may be inaccurate. A leading question suggests an answer by the form of the question. It may even be designed to guide the interviewee to give a particular response. For instance, a lawyer asks, "Isn't it true that Jack liked to go to Las Vegas as often as possible?" The lawyer is obviously looking for an affirmative answer. To ask questions in this way is to bias fact-gathering, which is not a good idea. This question above should be framed, "How did Jack feel about going to Las Vegas?"

Many probes will take the form of *mirror questions;* that is, an attorney will go after additional information reflecting a client's previous response. "Mirror questions . . . are designed to sustain talk. They force a respondent to expand upon or clarify statements."[39] For instance, the lawyer asks, "Where were you when the car broke down?" The client says, "Well, I was actually driving the car at the time, and I remember Mary turning to me and saying. . . . " Now, this is the first time the attorney has heard about someone named Mary. Therefore, the attorney uses a mirror question, which is built on the client's response, and says, "Mary. Mary who?" When used properly, mirror questions are an excellent way for an interviewer to maintain topic control when gathering information. After all, a probe is an attempt to get a more relevant, more complete, or clearer answer to a previous question or questions.

Let us look more closely at four types of probes, moving from the somewhat indirect kinds to the most direct ones. Naturally, the more direct the lawyer's question, the more topic control the lawyer has. One type of indirect and nonverbal probe is simple *silence*. Here the attorney says nothing at all following a client's comment but instead waits for the client to continue. The silent probe indicates to the client that he or she should go on with the story.

Another indirect, but verbal, approach is a brief word of *encouragement* for what is being said. This includes such abbreviated acceptances as "Uh-huh," "I see," "Go on," and "Is that so?" These responses indicate to the client that the lawyer accepts what has been said and that the client should continue speaking, although it is not clear what he or she should be talking about. Silent probes and brief words of encouragement are indirect probes, which are beneficial for maintaining some degree of topic control at or near the top of a funnel.

If the attorney wants more topic control, he or she can use questions of *elaboration*. These are probes designed to get clients to complete their stories or thoughts (e.g., "Then what happened immediately after that incident?"). They are still not highly specific questions, but they are a little more direct than silence or encouragement. The elaboration probes really say, "Tell me more about some aspect of your story." Elaboration probes are an especially valuable way to follow up on broad questions. They encourage the client to continue without making specific suggestions as to what to say. Questions of elaboration may be asked immediately (at the moment the attorney hears something he or she wants elaborated) or retrospectively (to elaborate something said earlier). The advantage of an immediate elaboration is that the lawyer gets the information while it is fresh in his or her mind; the advantage of a retrospective elaboration is that it does not interrupt the client's speaking.

The most direct probe an attorney can use is a question of immediate or retrospective *clarification*. Probes of clarification focus on some particular aspect of previous response.

Examples include: "At what time did it happen?" "Was the sun shining or was it cloudy?" "What did you say to your father when you looked out the window?" These are all questions asking for specific kinds of additional information. Hence, they are useful when elaboration probes are no longer producing much pertinent information.

Several aspects of probing deserve attention. First, probes are not used to drive clients immediately, directly, and continuously to the bottom of a funnel. Rather, they are used to keep the discussion moving within a funnel until the attorney has all the information he or she desires about a particular topic. As the arrows in Figure 1.6 indicate, interview probes (unlike liquids being poured through a funnel) can go up, down, or around the funnel. They go up as the questioning gets more general; they go down as the questions become more specific; they go around as the questions remain at one level for a while.

Second, the most direct probes may or may not be beneficial for effective information gathering. Sometimes the continuous use of direct probes lowers a client's motivation to talk. The client tends to play a more passive role in the interview when lots of direct probes are used by the attorney. On the other hand, direct probes are quite useful when a client is not presenting much information. Direct probes are also helpful when a client rambles on and on with irrelevant information.

Third, an attorney should not interrupt too frequently when probing. A client should be allowed to finish a sentence or thought.

Fourth, the client's own words should be used as often as possible when phrasing a probe. Referring exactly to something that was said in a previous answer shows careful listening. For instance, suppose the client says, "I get along fine with my brother. Oh, we have a little scuffle now and then, but basically I think we like each other very much." A good clarification probe should be "I see.

[Pause.] Tell me more about those scuffles you have now and then. What are they all about?" A poor clarification probe would be "Who lost the fights?" Both probes want additional information about the sibling conflict. Yet the first probe shows attorney interest, understanding, and careful listening, as seen in the "I see" remark and in the use of the client's own words ("scuffles . . . now and then"). The second probe assumes someone "lost" the scuffles. It also assumes, rightly or wrongly, that scuffles were actual fights.

Fifth, when probing, a lawyer must be as careful as possible to avoid confrontation with a client, especially in the initial interview. For instance, clients often contradict themselves. It is clearly wrong for an attorney to say, "Earlier you stated this. I distinctly heard you. Now you say the opposite. Come on now. Make up your mind!" This abrasive approach goes a long way toward reversing any rapport that has been established. It sets up an unnecessary power struggle. Attorneys must be tactful. When the problem of a contradiction arises, the attorney might probe with something like "I believe you said such and such earlier, and then you said this. Now, this confuses me somewhat. Perhaps you can help me out." Notice that this response shifts the problem or the contradiction to the mental processes of the lawyer, away from the client. Tact is extremely important here.

Next, let us consider what must be done with clients who distort information in interviews. Sometimes, a lawyer must be quite firm, particularly when a client is not resolving a contradiction in the story, is obviously lying, or is doing something else that results in misinformation. Without getting angry, the lawyer should discuss these client behaviors if they persist. An appropriate and firm response by an attorney is, "I'm sorry, but unless this behavior changes, nothing can really be accomplished because I can't get what I need from this interview." The client must "be encouraged to speak frankly and to with-

hold nothing. He should be advised that no attorney can represent him adequately unless all the facts are at the attorney's disposal."[40] This bit of instruction and warning may change the information the client is giving the attorney without sacrificing any loss of rapport between the two. Admittedly, this change is difficult. Once a client "has taken the false position, he will feel honor bound to defend it even though he may regret his falsification."[41] That is why it is so essential that an attorney be straightforward with clients who work themselves into such positions.

Not all distorted information in a legal interview comes from continuing contradiction or from lies. Some of it occurs because a client is honestly forgetful. In such cases, the lawyer can review some of the already-elicited salient facts that have emotional impact for the client, hoping these facts will foster remembering. Often distorted information can be the result of chronological confusion. If the questioning attorney has some idea of the correct order of events, he or she must help the client unscramble the sequence. Both forgetfulness and chronological confusion can be reduced by reviewing what took place. Here is an illustration:

We have so far been able to establish the order of some events that you remember from the day of the accident here in Smithville. First, there was the fire in the building at the corner of Main and Elm streets. Then you said you heard a hissing noise coming from the area where you saw the fire. Then you saw someone run out of the burning building and down Main Street. Now, exactly where were you standing when you made these observations?

Reviewing known facts may help the person recall forgotten information (the person's precise location while watching the fire) as well as subsequent, additional observations and actions. In both cases, accidental misinformation or omission of information should not be treated in the same manner as conscious misleading.

At the end of stage 2 and prior to stage 3 of a legal interview, a lawyer should take time to recapitulate. Briefly reviewing the story told by the client has many advantages. Reviewing provides chronological order to the story that was told. It is a cross-check that demonstrates to both attorney and client that the attorney understands the story. Reviewing is one last attempt by the attorney to get the client to add any pertinent new detail before they get to the advice-giving stage. In fact, after the recapitulation, the attorney should ask, "Is there anything else I should know?" Finally, reviewing serves as a bridge between the end of the information-gathering stage and the beginning of counseling.

The Third Stage: Counseling

This stage requires the application of information obtained during the second stage of the interview. The lawyer shifts from being a somewhat passive listener to being an active and directive advisor. This final stage of the interview should produce closure, or results.

Counseling actually begins in the mind of the lawyer while the information-gathering stage of the interview is progressing. The lawyer needs to be constantly evaluating more than just the adequacy of the information. He or she also needs to be constantly and critically analyzing the client's problem and, in particular, considering whether any part of that problem is soluble through the legal system. The following questions may be asked by a lawyer in making a critical analysis:[42]

☐ What are the operative situational facts?
☐ Is this a problem that the legal system can resolve?
☐ If so, what area of law controls, or is there more than one?

☐ What are the applicable legal principles, whether case law or statutory?
☐ In view of the facts and legal principles, does the client have a provable case?
☐ If the client has a legally provable case, in terms of results compared with chances of success, is it worth pursuing?

Once the problem has been analyzed, the lawyer should then present possible courses of action the client can take. They may include nonlegal counseling,[43] additional information gathering, informal bargaining with "the opposition," the beginning of preparation for litigation, and a host of other possibilities. The lawyer may even point out to the client the manner in which the client is contributing to the problem. This is a delicate undertaking, but sometimes very necessary. With each policy alternative, the lawyer should indicate the risks involved. For instance, if litigation is a possibility, the client should know the hard realities (i.e., what laws might be relevant, what the strong and weak points of the case seem to be, what the attorney can and cannot do for the client, that success in court cannot be guaranteed, that the wheels of justice move slowly, and that there undoubtedly would be some cost to the client).

Costs for services should be clearly delineated in the first interview when the potential client is relaxed. This should be done in a mellow tone of voice and with precision so that nothing comes as a surprise to the client later. The nature of the fee agreement will vary according to the nature and complexity of the case. Many lawyers work on contingency; that is, the lawyer receives a percentage (usually 25 to 35 percent) of any amount received in settlement or by judgment, with the percentage increasing if a retrial is required or if the case must be appealed. This type of fee structure enables a lawyer to render services to those unable to guarantee payment. It is also quite common for attorneys to operate on fixed fees, hourly rates, or some combination of these two methods of cost determination. During or shortly after the interview, the client should sign a retainer agreement or should agree in some fashion to pay the fee.

After the courses of action are laid out, the lawyer should ask which the client prefers to follow. Note that this is the client's selection; the essence of good counseling is allowing the client to have freedom of choice. The lawyer can guide the decision and suggest (not insist) which action might be preferable, but the client should ultimately decide which path to follow. Naturally, the lawyer is a legal advisor only and should be competent in the area of advice given. If not, the client should be sent to another professional (e.g., another lawyer, a psychiatrist, a physician, an accountant, a social worker).

Occasionally, a client will resist choosing a course of action. In a criminal case, for example, there may have to be a decision about whether or not to plead guilty prior to trial. The accused may seek to place the burden for this decision on the lawyer's shoulders, saying, "I'll do whatever you say. You're the lawyer." The lawyer should respond by saying he or she is only a technical advisor. The lawyer can develop insights into alternatives and thereby assist decision making, but cannot actually make major decisions about another person's life.

Near the end of the interview, it is essential that the lawyer explain to the client how they will continue to communicate with each other and how often. A common client complaint is that retained lawyers do not maintain enough contact and do not keep them advised of what is happening. The attorney should tell the client exactly what he or she intends to do with the case. Some lawyers send copies of all subsequent written communications to the client. Although sending everything in writing to clients might consti-

tute information overload, an attorney should at least periodically send letters to a client about the case.[44]

At the very end of the interview, the attorney should promise the client no more than can be delivered. The final words should not be in the form of a confident gladiator's guarantee, such as, "Well, we'll certainly win this one for you." On the other hand, the attorney should not end the interview in a fashion that is too low-key (e.g., "We'll be in touch"). While the parties are warmly shaking hands in the last moments of the initial interview, realistic words of encouragement should come from the attorney's mouth, such as, "I will certainly do my best to help you." Now, we hope, a sense of trust exists between attorney and client, and the work can proceed from there. "That trust will not be based on blind faith, but rather will be the product of a jointly experienced, goal-directed, problem-solving involvement. The longer this relationship endures and the more involved it becomes, the deeper will be the developed trust."[45]

How long should this initial interview last? Like fifth graders spelling the word "banana," lawyers sometimes do not know when to stop. So, "they conduct a full-blown interview, asking detailed questions and inviting a lengthy narration of past events in every instance."[46] This is not a good idea, particularly if the lawyer winds up declining representation of that client. Time is wasted for all parties involved. Even if it looks as though the case is going to be accepted, extending an initial interview past two hours might be counterproductive. Usually an interview will last from 30 to 60 minutes. A series of interviews affords better pacing and is less tedious for everyone involved than one long inerview. One final thought: the time scheduled for the initial interview should be long enough that the attorney can comfortably get through the three essential stages. It is unwise to rush the client through the latter part of any consultation. However, the complexity of the issue and the emotional state of the client will also affect the amount of interview time needed.[47]

This chapter has dealt with client-lawyer relationships in the process of interviewing and counseling. Two experienced California attorneys summarize what we have said here with the following checklist of objectives to make the lawyer-client interview team function well.[48]

1. To succeed, the lawyer must ease the anxiety the client naturally feels. He or she must inspire a sense of confidence, rapport, and trust if the relationship is to develop.

2. The lawyer must obtain and sort out the legally relevant facts.

3. The lawyer must make an initial determination about the legal merit of his or her client's position.

4. The lawyer must analyze the risk and potential cost to decide whether the matter is worth pursuing in a legal context.

5. The lawyer must make a tentative recommendation of approaches or procedures available for addressing the client's situation.

6. The lawyer and client must agree on the terms and conditions of the ongoing relationship.

At the end of the initial interview, the lawyer must leave the client with a sense of satisfaction and with confidence that the case rests in professional hands. "Properly performed, the initial interview is the cornerstone of the trust relationship between the client and the attorney."[49]

Notes

[1]William S. Howell, *The Empathic Communicator* (Belmont, Calif.: Wadsworth, 1982), 25.

[2]Charles Stewart and William B. Cash, *Interviewing* (Dubuque, Iowa: William C. Brown, 1978), 5.

[3]Cal W. Downs, G. Paul Smeyak, and Ernest Martin, *Professional Interviewing* (New York: Harper & Row, 1980), 5.

[4]Ibid., 6.

[5]Gary S. Goodpaster, "The Human Arts of Lawyering: Interviewing and Counseling," *Journal of Legal Education* 27 (1975), 24.

[6]Ibid., 22.

[7]David B. Hingstman, "Legal Interviewing and Counseling: Communication as Process," in Ronald J. Matlon and Richard J. Crawford, eds., *Communication Strategies in the Practice of Lawyering* (Annandale, Va.: Speech Communication Association, 1983), 56.

[8]Ibid., 57.

[9]Mark K. Schoenfield and Barbara Pearlman Schoenfield, *Interviewing and Counseling* (Philadelphia: American Law Institute, 1981), 15–16.

[10]Erwin O. Smigel, "Interviewing a Legal Elite: The Wall Street Lawyer," *American Journal of Sociology* 64 (1958), 159–164.

[11]Andrew S. Watson, *The Lawyer in the Interviewing and Counseling Process* (Indianapolis: Bobbs-Merrill, 1976), 34.

[12]Thomas L. Moffatt, *Selection Interviewing for Managers* (New York: Harper & Row, 1979), 13.

[13]Ibid., 27.

[14]Raymond L. Gorden, *Interviewing: Strategy, Techniques, and Tactics* (Homewood, Ill.: Dorsey Press, 1969), 66.

[15]Watson, op. cit., 5–6.

[16]Mark K. Schoenfield and Barbara Pearlman Schoenfield, "The Art of Interviewing and Counseling, Part I," *The Practical Lawyer* (January 15, 1978), 69.

[17]Ibid.

[18]Robert McFigg, Ralph C. McCullough II, and James L. Underwood, *Civil Trial Manual* (Los Angeles: Joint Committee in Legal Education of the American Law Institute and the American Bar Association, 1974), 49.

[19]Harrop A. Freeman and Henry Weihofen, *Clinical Law Training: Interviewing and Counseling* (St. Paul, Minn.: West Publishing, 1972), 22.

[20]McFigg, McCullough, and Underwood, op. cit., 45.

[21]Frederick D. Fahrenz and Monty L. Preiser, "The Initial Client Interview: A Critical Prelude to Every Criminal Case," *Trial* (October 1980), 45.

[22]Jesse G. Delia, "'The Initial Attorney/Client Counsultation': A Comment," *Southern Speech Communication Journal* 45 (1980), 408–410.

[23]John Daniel Goldsmith, "The Initial Attorney/Client Relationship: A Case History," *Southern Speech Communication Journal* 45 (1980), 394–407.

[24]William S. Bailey, "The Attorney/Client Relationship: The Hidden Dimension of Advocacy," *Trial Diplomacy Journal* (Fall 1985), 17.

[25]Allen Smith and Patrick Nester, "Lawyers, Clients, and Communication Skills," *Brigham Young University Law Review* (1977), 275.

[26]Joseph H. Savitz, "How to Handle a New Client—The Initial Interview with a Business Client," *Practical Lawyer* (December 1975), 17.

[27]Schoenfield and Schoenfield, "The Art of Interviewing," 74.

[28]Wayne N. Thompson and S. John Insalata, "Communication from Attorney to Client," *Journal of Communication* 14 (1964), 31.

[29]Kenney F. Hegland, *Trial and Practice Skills in a Nutshell* (St. Paul, Minn.: West Publishing, 1978), 197.

[30]Freeman and Weihofen, op. cit., 16.

[31]Gorden, op. cit., 187–188.

[32]Ibid., 187.

[33]For a fuller discussion of the reluctant client, see David A. Binder and Susan C. Price, *Legal Interviewing and Counseling: A Client-Centered Approach* (St. Paul, Minn.: West Publishing, 1977), chap. 6.

[34]Downs, Smeyak, and Martin, op. cit., 13–14.

[35]Gorden, op. cit., 208.

[36]Robert L. Kahn and Charles F. Cannell, *The Dynamics of Interviewing* (New York: John Wiley and Sons, 1957), 158.

[37]Goldsmith, op. cit.

[38]Stanley E. Jones, "Directivity vs. Non-Directivity: Implications of the Examination of Witnesses in Law for the Fact-Finding Interview," *Journal of Communication* 19 (1969), 64–75.

[39]T. Richard Cheatham and Keith V. Erickson, *The Police Officer's Guide to Better Communication* (Glenview, Ill.: Scott, Foresman, 1984), 47.

[40]Laurence V. Hastings, "Interviewing the Client," in *American Jurisprudence: Trials,* Vol. I (Rochester, N.Y.: The Lawyers Co-operative Publishing Co., 1964), 15.

[41]Gorden, op. cit., 197.

[42]Mark K. Schoenfield and Barbara Pearlman Schoenfield, "The Art of Interviewing and Counseling, Part II," *Practical Lawyer* (March 1, 1978), 8–49.

[43]Some client problems are nonlegal in nature. The student who wants to sue a university for not giving him a degree may not have a legal case if, in fact, he has not completed all his course work and the university is giving him the opportunity to do so. The client just does not want to return to school and is trying to make a legal claim out of the situation. In this case, the attorney should advise the person to seek counseling at the university.

[44]Watson, op. cit., 145.

[45]Ibid., 146.

[46]Robert L. Simmons, *Winning Before Trial* (Englewood Cliffs, N.J.: Executive Reports Corporation, 1974), 106.

[47]William A. Haskins, "Interviewing Clients in a Legal Setting: A Dialogic Approach," *Trial Diplomacy Journal* (Summer 1985), 28.

[48]Don Howarth and Thrace Hetrick, "How to Interview the Client," *Litigation* (Summer 1983), 25–26.

[49]Lawrence J. Smith and Loretta A. Malandro, *Courtroom Communication Strategies* (New York: Kluwer, 1985), 453.

2
CHAPTER

NEGOTIATING

The goal of negotiating is settlement. Settlements can occur before a case is brought to trial, at any point during a trial, or even after a trial, as when there is a hung jury and another trial is imminent, or when a verdict is in and a long series of appeals is about to begin.

Most of America's legal problems are negotiated. Approximately 90 percent of all criminal and civil litigation is settled at some point before going to court.[1] Eighty percent of all processed criminal felonies and misdemeanors are disposed of through negotiations before trial.[2] Well over 95 percent of personal injury suits are settled prior to trial.[3] Clearly, trial lawyers are occupied much more with negotiating than they are with courtroom advocacy. Former Chief Justice Warren E. Burger concludes, ''Of all the skills needed for the practicing lawyer, skill in negotiation must rank very high.''[4] Unfortunately, negotiation training is not widespread in American legal education.[5]

THE NATURE OF NEGOTIATION

Although some writers have attempted to distinguish between negotiation and bargaining, the distinction is often unclear and is, for our purposes, unimportant. Here the terms shall be used interchangeably. All legal negotiations involve the striking of bargains.

Just what is negotiation? Essentially it is a process through which competing parties try to cooperate in order to adjust their differences. Differences are resolved when each side makes concessions. In other words, an agreement lies somewhere between the original positions of both sides and, presumably, is in each participant's best interest.[6] Bargaining, then, is a mixed-motive game: advocates are cooperating, and they are also competing. ''The parties must both trust each other enough to exchange information vital to reaching agreement, and distrust each other enough so that they withhold information that the other side could use to dominate the bargain.''[7] This is unlike a trial, which is essentially an all-or-nothing, pure-competition game.

As bargaining occurs, five conditions are essential.[8] First, at least two parties must be involved. In legal negotiations, you must bring together the attorneys from both sides as a minimal requirement, although others (e.g., judges and outside mediators) may enter the negotiations as well. Second, the parties involved must have a conflict with respect to one or more difficult issues. The issues in a legal negotiation arise out of the plaintiff's complaint or the prosecution's charge against the defendant. Third, the parties must be joined together in a special kind of voluntary relationship. The use of the word *voluntary* is crucial. Both sides entering legal negotiations are there by choice, not by compulsion. Both sides choose to enter the relationship, and both sides choose whether or not to remain in the relationship. Each side chooses the demands it will make, the concessions it will give, and the agreements it will accept or reject. Fourth, activity in the relationship must concern the division or exchange of one or more specific resources or the resolution of one or more issues among the parties. In negotiation, there is an outcome for each party. The attorney for one side is dependent on the attorney for the other side for the quality of the outcome. Fifth, negotiating must involve the presentation of demands or proposals by one party, evaluation of those by the other party, and then concessions and counterproposals. Bargaining activity is thus sequential rather than simultaneous. This exchange of preferences constitutes an exchange of information and arguments. All five of these conditions must exist for bargaining to occur.

Once these five conditions are in place, the pattern of negotiation consists of three stages.[9] In the first stage, negotiators search for the issues. They attempt to discover the range of the negotiations. Extreme demands are established and exchanged. Both sides give the illusion of being fixed in their positions. In the second stage, both sides begin offering alternative solutions, which fall between the extreme demands. They shift from talking about their own positions, and each begins obtaining information about the other side's true position and objectives.[10] In doing so, they find clues to where concessions might take place.[11] In the third and final stage, a crisis is reached in which the parties must ascertain the last offer of the other side and then decide whether to accept it. Agreement is reached or there is a breakdown in the negotiations.

TYPES OF LEGAL NEGOTIATION

Bargaining takes place in both civil and criminal cases. In civil matters, it often takes the form of a *settlement negotiation*. The assumption underlying a settlement negotiation is that a range of values exists from zero to a very high quantity of benefits, money, land, or some other object of negotiation. Both sides in a settlement negotiation generally have points of resistance, that is, the lowest the plaintiff and the highest the defense are willing to go. When negotiating, each side tries to discover the other's point of resistance. This point is critical, often-hidden information in the negotiations. If there is overlap in the ranges of the two parties, settlement is possible. The final product is either a lump sum payment to the plaintiff or a structured settlement, one in which the defendant agrees to pay the plaintiff a certain amount on a regular basis over a period of time.[12]

Settlement negotiations are conducted directly by lawyers for both sides. Other settlement programs, civil as well as criminal, take the form of *mediation* or *alternative dispute resolution*. Here an impartial third person attempts to get aggrieved parties to settle their differences and reach agreement on the issues in dispute. "The mediator has no authority to make decisions for the parties, how-

ever."[13] Many see mediation as a partial remedy to the enormous, costly increase in case loads confronting our judicial system. Throughout the country mediators are being trained to referee disputes. Some programs are private; others are created by the courts. Some states (e.g., New York and Pennsylvania) have now adopted compulsory third-party arbitration for all claims up to a few thousand dollars. Florida and California have established neighborhood justice courts.[14] There are over one hundred community mediation programs in the country today,[15] and they are rapidly becoming good alternatives to lawsuits, particularly for minor disputes. For instance, in 1984, of 132 civil claims against insurance companies mediated by members of the American Arbitration Association, only 4 failed to settle, and most discussions took less than a day.[16]

An illustration of mediation is a situation in which a trained mediator meets some evening in an unoccupied courtroom with the parties in conflict for the purpose of negotiating a solution to their problem. Meeting in the courthouse gives the litigants a feeling that justice can be served. The mediator (usually a volunteer lawyer, social scientist, arbitrator, or trained local citizen) is, in actuality, a communication consultant who combines storytelling, subtle forms of argumentation, and conflict resolution practices in solving problems for people who have ongoing faulty relationships. In a study of 30 trained mediators, it was found that most of them use a process of communication that allows the litigants to explore solutions rather than having the mediator pressure, intervene, and persuade in order to modify attitudes and behavior.[17] The effectiveness of the trained mediator in tracking the reasoning of the disputants is associated with the outcome of the hearings.[18] Most disputants rely heavily on their own authority when arguing. For instance, one party claims that a neighbor's children threw rocks through their windows. The other party says they should not have to put up with lots of noise late at night from the first party's howling dog. The mediator hears both stories. This is technically not a legal proceeding. Nor is the mediator necessarily after the truth. After the stories have been told and the anger and frustration have been vented, the mediator assists the disputing parties in seeking a compromise solution before seeking legal redress. Once both sides are given an opportunity to air their grievances, they begin looking for solutions.[19] If a solution is negotiated, the mediator may have the parties affix their signatures to a handwritten negotiated settlement (e.g., one promises to pay for half the cost of repairing the broken windows; the other promises to keep the dog inside at night).

Negotiating in criminal cases occurs through *plea bargaining,* "a process by which the defendant in a criminal case relinquishes his right to go to trial in exchange for a reduction in charge and/or sentence."[20] Here is how it typically works. After the accused is indicted, the prosecutor, the defense attorney, and perhaps a judge participate in negotiation. There is considerable jockeying, which often goes on for weeks and months, with offers and counteroffers. This can be done up to the date of the trial. The defendant is usually not present at any of these negotiating sessions. The objective of plea bargaining for the state is to get the defendant to admit guilt of a lesser crime, such as obtaining money under false pretenses when the original and more serious charge was forgery. The objective of plea bargaining for the defense is to get the prosecutor to reduce, dismiss, or combine some of the charges, or recommend leniency in sentencing by the judge. Once an agreement has been reached by both sides, a judge is asked to review the agreement and then issue an appropriate sentence to the accused.[21] Additional discussion of the judge's role in all forms of negotiation can be found in Chapter 11.

Either counsel may initiate plea bargaining action. Some believe the first move should be made by the defense before the prosecutor has invested too much in the case. Others say that it "should be one of the last questions a defense attorney addresses on a client's behalf. Copping a plea, after all, is never the preferred treatment."[22] In any case, the bargaining is usually quite informal—in the hallways of the courthouse, over coffee, and so on.

Although it has become the dominant method of resolving criminal cases, plea bargaining carries with it certain negative connotations. A plea bargain is often called a "cop-out" or a "deal."[23] Resentment of plea bargaining in Alaska led to its ban in 1975.[24] Alaska's action is atypical, but it does reflect uncomfortableness with the practice. Meanwhile, those who favor plea bargaining (and negotiated settlements as well) see certain advantages to be claimed by both sides.

ADVANTAGES OF LEGAL NEGOTIATION

Why is out-of-court settlement so widely used? There are a number of reasons. For prosecutors, it gives them astronomical conviction rates. In some cases, prosecutors know that the defendants are guilty, but they also know that a judge or jury will not likely find the defendants guilty should the cases go to trial. With a plea bargain, at least they get some sort of conviction. Another advantage for prosecutors is that their case loads are reduced. Prosecuting attorneys everywhere are overwhelmed with cases, and of necessity the less important or potentially less successful ones must be plea bargained on a cost-benefit basis to allow those prosecutors to do well in the cases that do go to trial.

For plaintiffs, settlement ensures that they will recover some damages at less cost, with less pain, and with more certainty than if they went to trial, because of the reduction in the time it takes to resolve a matter; "the economics of law practice today are such that an average lawyer cannot afford to bury himself in unnecessary trial procedures when good settlement procedures are available."[25]

For the defense, the advantage of bargaining is that the judgment in a civil case or the maximum sentence in a criminal case is lessened. This means that the client pays a potentially lower claim or fine, is incarcerated for a reduced time, or is placed in a somewhat more desirable imprisonment situation, such as a minimum security detention center instead of a maximum security prison. Another advantage to the defendant is, once again, that the cost, time, delay, uncertainty, and pain of a trial experience are avoided.

For the court, negotiation reduces the number of cases going to trial, and it is common knowledge that the court backlog for trials is a national disgrace.

Finally, negotiation is a commendable process. Irrespective of the results, it allows the attorneys an informal discovery of information and of the potential strengths and weaknesses of their cases. This informality also benefits clients. For instance, people with legal problems do not necessarily want lawsuits and trials in which one wins and the other loses. What people often prefer is a satisfactory compromise. Negotiation is their answer.

THE NATURE OF CONFLICT

The remainder of this chapter will lay out the skills and strategies needed to be an effective legal negotiator. An appropriate starting point is to explain initially the notion of conflict, since the goal of all bargaining is to reduce conflict. *Conflict* is a state that exists whenever incompatible activities occur. It is a struggle for dominance between individuals or groups with differing preferences or goals, which are perceived to be mutually exclusive. One individual or group tries to influence another, the other resists, and you have conflict. It is natural and inevitable among humans. Conflict occurs either when people fail to understand each other or when they fully understand each other but disagree. When kept under control, conflict can help stimulate communication, but when conflict gets out of control, it needs to be harnessed.

Given this explanation, "negotiation can be described as a form of social conflict, since it involves the defense of opposing positions. It also can be described as a form of conflict resolution, since the roots of conflict are often examined and rectified during negotiation."[26] In other words, negotiation grows out of conflict, and negotiation resolves conflict.

Starr identifies three bases for conflict from which negotiation flows.[27] First, *conflicts may occur over ends or means*. When there are different goals (I want X and you want Y) or when there is only one goal, which cannot be shared (I want X and so do you, but only one of us can have it), then we have a conflict of ends. When we agree on a goal, but disagree on the method to achieve it, then we have a conflict of means. Conflicts over ends are generally more difficult to negotiate than conflicts over means.

Second, *conflicts may be personal or impersonal*. If someone steals my money, I am more personally involved in the conflict than if someone steals an unknown person's money. An attorney who "really cares" about a case approaches conflict personally. An attorney who is involved only to the extent of fulfilling an obligation to a client is approaching conflict impersonally. Personal approaches to conflict are generally more emotional and therefore more difficult to negotiate.

Third, *conflicts may be disagreements over interests or values*. A conflict of interests stems from a situation of scarcity. Both parties want the same thing, but there is not enough of it to be had. For instance, in real estate, a seller wants more money than the buyer is willing to pay. This type of conflict, one of differing interests, is particularly prone to compromise.[28] This is so because both the seller and the purchaser of the house can bargain without sacrificing basic deep-seated values or principles. Moreover, the gain of one party is not wholly a loss to the other party. On the other hand, conflicts of values are conflicts over fundamental normative principles. When there is a conflict over values, negotiation is possible, but extremely difficult. Even settlements in the form of laws or treaties are apt to break down. This type of conflict has characterized religious and ideological wars for centuries. In conflicts of this type, communication between the conflicting parties is very strained and sometimes ceases entirely. This type of conflict can lead to uncontrolled and uncontrollable behaviors, such as have been exhibited for many years in the Middle East. Attorneys are more often than not involved in conflicts of interests, not conflicts of values. This is so because conflicts of interests work to draw antagonists together, whereas conflicts of values work to disassociate antagonists.

To summarize, negotiation is more likely to be successful when the conflict that caused bargaining is over means, not ends; is impersonal, not personal; and is over interests, not values. In the discussion that follows, an analysis will be made of ways of reducing conflict stemming from these different bases.

THE RESOLUTION OF CONFLICT IN LEGAL SETTINGS

Conflict resolution is the termination of a manifest conflict. Resolution is accomplished either by making the opposition powerless or by compromising. The former method sometimes makes the conflict worse; the latter method can reduce aggravation for both sides. Thus, in law, negotiation toward compromise over conflicts is utilized. Parties are temporarily joined in a voluntary relationship. Each knows what can be gained; each knows what can be lost. Each tries to gain from the relationship, but knows that something will be lost in the process. A wise agreement can be defined as one that meets at least some of the legitimate interests of each side.[29]

Legal negotiators must aim for nonzero-sum solutions. Nonzero-sum solutions stem from compromise, in which the gain of one party is not equal to the loss of the other, because the parties associate different satisfactions with the same outcomes. By contrast, zero-sum solutions are those in which the gain of one party is always identical to the loss of another. A zero-sum solution is not conflict resolution based on compromise. For example, instead of a tenant's saying, "Sue the bastard!" (zero sum), in a case in which a landlord allows a leaky roof to ruin some furniture, the focus in negotiations is on sharing the cost of cleanup and on repairing the roof in the future (nonzero sum). This form of conflict resolution creates the appearance of winning for *both* the landlord and the tenant. The landlord does not have to pay for all the damage, and the tenant can rest assured that the roof will not leak again. Both parties gain in satisfaction by the single outcome.

There are several ways to explore the process of nonzero-sum conflict resolution in legal settings. One is to consider ways parties can resolve problems by exploring and adapting to the bases for each conflict. Another is to think of bargaining as a game and examine the various developmental stages in the game. Yet another way to analyze nonzero-sum conflict resolution is to understand the communication dynamics that occur when conflicts are being resolved. Each perspective on conflict resolution offers further insight into the process.

Adaptation to the Bases for Conflict

Here, we return to the three bases for conflict and see how nonzero-sum resolutions fit each occasion. As noted earlier, it is easier to resolve conflicts of means than conflicts of ends. Some theorists suggest, then, that a way to reduce any conflict's severity "is to redefine the situation so that ends are seen as ultimately common, with the conflict centered on means."[30] For example, an injured plaintiff files a lawsuit for $1 million, but really wants only fair compensation for his injuries. If the defense is initially willing to pay $100,000, then the $900,000 difference is viewed as a conflict of ends. However, if the defense attorney enters negotiations with the end of determining adequate compensation for injuries, then the conflict is over means; the negotiating mood becomes more mellow, and settlement is more likely.

It is also easier to resolve impersonal conflicts than personal ones. Persons entering legal negotiations, if they genuinely desire settlement, should carefully assess the extent of personal or emotional involvement in an issue or a case. Compromise is much more likely when emotions can be kept under control. This is one reason lawyers make better negotiators than the parties themselves. Even then, if negotiation becomes a heated ego trip for one attorney, the other attorney must keep a cool head and depersonalize the discussion as soon as possible.

Finally, conflicts of interests are more negotiable than conflicts of values. When a lawyer says, "But it's the principle that matters," the conflict has shifted to one of values. When such a shift occurs, the conflict becomes difficult to resolve, because compromise on "the principle" is apt to look like a sellout. Converting a conflict of values into one of interests opens up the possibility of settlement. The conversion is accomplished by returning to a discussion of the facts. "When a problem is converted to one of fact, . . . it is 'objectivized.'"[31] For example, in a divorce case, rather than attempting to decide whether a particular behavior that led to a marriage dissolution was "moral," it is more appropriate to focus on such matters as the monetary value of the joint estate. Showing

that concessions can be made without violating certain principles allows rationalization of those concessions and facilitates cooperation in negotiation.

Adaptation to the Stages of Conflict Resolution

In the first part of this chapter, the three stages of bargaining were noted. An attorney sincerely interested in settlement should recognize that those three stages of conflict resolution constitute a game, and as in so many games, knowledge of the mind set needed at each stage along the way is essential for the competent negotiator. What follows on page 43 is a review of those three stages, in the left column, and an appropriate mind set or set of expectations for the attorney playing this conflict-resolution game, in the right column.[32] The lawyer who understands these mind sets or expectations during the various stages of an interview will be in a position to satisfactorily compete with his adversary.

Communication Dynamics and Conflict Resolution

Obviously, communication is a primary ingredient in the negotiation process. "'Talking it out' is functional rather than dysfunctional"[34] in resolving conflict. In fact, there are times counsel may want to get together just to talk over the case with the opposition without moving into formal negotiations. A word of caution is in order. There is an adage that goes as follows: "If you can only get them to communicate with each other, their conflicts can be resolved." As ideal as this maxim sounds, it is a naive observation. "The mere availability of communication channels provides no guarantee that they will be used or used effectively. To the contrary, it appears that a variety of conditions, such as the intensity of

Stage of Conflict Resolution

1. A working relationship is established. Initial negotiating demands are presented. Issues are explored.

Mind Set (Expectations)

Tension can be expected, particularly if one attorney assumes a dominant position. Some demands may be realistic; others will be unrealistic. Neither side is providing all the information needed for resolving the conflict, although each party is trying to find out the opponent's real preferences. In the process, issues become more clearly defined, and the strengths and weaknesses of the case become more obvious to both sides. Both sides begin to learn what additional research into the factual and legal elements of the case is necessary. Both sides learn whether the other side is flexible or inflexible regarding their demands. Signs of flexibility are that the demands are over means and interests and that the demands are impersonally presented.

2. Demands are evaluated, more information is shared, and concessions are offered. Some compromises occur. Alternative solutions are explored.

Debate can be expected to intensify. Arguments are developed for both sides. Rationalizations are given to legitimize one's own proposals. Information and persuasion are a two-way exchange. Decisions must be made along the way as to whether bargaining should be pursued. If so, concessions should be weighed. Tensions can be expected to continue, although there can be a graduated defusing of hostility if one side announces "unilateral and noncontingent rewards . . . to the adversary with a request of some form of reciprocation."[33] Compromise puts the two sides closer.

3. The last offer is made and evaluated. A crisis stage is at hand. Either deadlock or agreement is reached. If an agreement is reached, a negotiation wrap-up is necessary.

This may follow several rounds of negotiation. The bargaining issues are narrowed. A point is now reached, at which it is decided if there is a realistic settlement zone for both sides. Threats are commonplace. A deadline for settling increases the psychological pressure and, in turn, the bargaining activity. The question for bargainers is ultimately how much they are willing to relinquish to their adversaries. Whatever the result, battle fatigue sets in.

conflict, the relationship between the bargainers, and the importance of the issues at stake, are likely to be just as important in determining the quality and quantity of communication as the mere fact that opportunities for it exist."[35] Bargaining effectiveness can be enhanced by communication, but communication effectiveness cannot be the sole determinant of good bargaining.

Nevertheless, attorneys can improve their capacity to negotiate by better understanding and applying certain communication principles essential for effective bargaining. Most of the principles discussed here emphasize the importance of cooperation in the negotiation setting. A list of seven of them follows.

First, postpone difficult confrontation as long as possible when negotiating. In many negotiations, communication is blocked because serious confrontation comes too early. "Negotiation becomes much easier when the desire to settle is tempered with positive atmospheres instead of hostile negative approaches."[36] A positive atmosphere can be established in the first stage of a bargaining session by being a brainstorming communicator as opposed to one who is eager to evaluate offers from the other side. When brainstorming, an attorney tries to suggest as many options for discussion as possible. Consider this example:[37]

Q: As I understand it, it is your position that our company should merely agree to be acquired by you with no safeguards for our management group other than whatever you see fit to grant after acquisition, is that correct?
A: No, we are willing to place in our offering material, a provision that it is our current intention to retain present management.
Q: As I understand it, this would be solely

an intention which you would be able to change at any time.
A: That is true, but we would be willing to give present management an employment contract with the parent company for ten years.
Q: What would happen if the parent company itself were to change form?
A: I believe that there would be successor liability under a number of circumstances.
Q: Would you be willing to put that in writing?

Notice that the tone of the questioner is to get feedback for understanding. Notice, too, how the parties avoid direct confrontation, allowing themselves to communicate openly. This in no way means that confrontation should never be accelerated. Quite the contrary: there is a time at which this communicative behavior is recommended. Initially, however, serious confrontation should be delayed.

Second, pay attention. In order for rapport to be established between the negotiating parties, they must listen carefully to each other. Listening involves more than the hearing of words; it is the alert reception and correct interpretation of those words. Preoccupation, rapid thought, a desire to talk, and faulty preconceptions of what will be said are sure signs of inattentiveness when listening.[38] Negotiators should avoid these pitfalls and listen intently to everything their opponents say. Listening fosters understanding, and understanding fosters accommodation. Listening is no easy task. In fact, it is rare to find outstanding listeners. So bargaining attorneys must work on their listening skills.

Third, use meaningful language. Meaningful language is language that is clearly understood. It may mean, for example, a reduction in complex vocabulary and jargon. If an attorney is negotiating a settlement for a client who fell down some "old, unrepaired stairs" in a department store, why not talk about the stairs in those terms rather than as a ''curable functional obsolescence''? When speaking, lawyers should always ask if their listeners understand. And an attorney who hears something he or she does not understand should always ask for clarification.

Fourth, keep anxieties restrained. Highly anxious negotiators are likely to be too cautious, too conservative, and too competitive. They expect the worst from the negotiations. In attempting to minimize their anticipated losses, they let their anxieties show through their competitive behavior.[39] Anxious negotiators begin attacking each other as a way to vent their frustrations, and, in turn, reducing their chances of reaching settlements. Negotiators should be aware of transmitting and communicating cues of anxiety. If they are doing so, they should try to restrain themselves or call an intermission in the bargaining until they can pull themselves together. Patience is a powerful weapon in the negotiator's arsenal.

Fifth, display trust. Highly suspicious persons disrupt communication. They are selfish, hostile, and excitable. Because they expect the worst, they try to beat others at the game. If you are negotiating with a suspicious person, you should attempt to convince that person that your motives are worthy ones. Only then can constructive decision making take place.[40]

Sixth, observe and evaluate nonverbal cues. Vital information can be given to and obtained from the person with whom you are bargaining. Inadvertent disclosures are made by sudden changes in nonverbal form.[41] The face can suddenly show pleasure or anxiety. Wringing hands can be a sign of frustration. Open, uplifted hands can express sincerity. Crossed arms or legs can be a combative or defensive posture. Not looking a person in the eye may just be a bad habit, or it may be a sign of anxiety or insincerity. To make an adversary feel more uncomfortable when ne-gotiating, counsel might invade the other's personal space by moving closer to that person. Signs of discomfort in return might be looking away, leaning away, giving a hostile glance, or blocking with hands and arms.

Careful observation of nonverbal communication is also a way to assess deception and bluffing by an adversary. Inevitably, some deception and bluffing are built into any negotiation model.[42] How is deception perceived nonverbally? Research shows that deceivers show physical signs of nervousness and reticence.[43] They speak for shorter periods of time[44] and at an unusually high pitch.[45] They pause frequently[46] and increase object manipulations with their hands.[47] If an attorney detects deception, the best response is honesty. Honesty converts deceivers into cooperative partners; honesty deters threateners from sending threats.[48]

Although bargaining attorneys cannot completely rely on the accuracy of all nonverbal cues, such cues are signs of what might be going on in the mind of the other side. It is advisable for any negotiator to acquire a keen ability to assimilate and analyze these cues. Note taking should be limited during bargaining so that visual attention can be fixed on the opponent. This also means that negotiating by telephone or by correspondence is disadvantageous because of counsel's inability to see and judge the nonverbal cues of an adversary. Face-to-face negotiating is best.[49]

Seventh, understand and apply communication (social interaction) principles. All the elements noted in the previous chapter on interviewing and counseling must be present in negotiation too. Among them are a strong interpersonal relationship, maximum information flow, empathy, careful observing and listening, knowing and being yourself, knowing and respecting your opponent, knowing when to be assertive, and recognizing the needs and prejudices of all concerned. In a survey of more than one hundred lawyers, O'Rourke and Sparrow found that the most important communication variables for negotiating are, in rank order, abilities to be perceived as honest, to listen, to persuade, to generate alternative solutions, to state one's position, to compromise, to be perceived as cooperative, to keep negotiation focused, to question, to answer, and to perceive deceptions and bluffs.[50] Pulling these elements together is an art form that, for polished negotiators, becomes smooth, relaxed, spontaneous, and efficient in moving toward the desired objective.

The bottom line on communication in legal negotiation is that attorneys must learn what works best for them, namely, whether they ought to be conciliatory types; competitive, aggressive, litigative types; or versatile negotiators. "Negotiation is a skill requiring knowledge of a good deal more than how to build a power base, stand firm, and pound on the table. A good negotiator should know the various tactics for moving toward accommodation without serious position or image loss."[51] After interviewing and observing over six hundred negotiating attorneys in Denver and Phoenix during a two-and-a-half-year period, a team of scholars was able to categorize virtually all practicing lawyers into one of two basic negotiating patterns—cooperative and aggressive. About 60 percent of the lawyers fell into the cooperative pattern, and 40 percent into the aggressive pattern.[52] Effective cooperative negotiators are fair, courteous, personable, tactful, honest, astute, prepared, reasonable, and realistic. Effective aggressive negotiators are dominating, forceful, ambitious, clever, honest, prepared, perceptive, analytical, and convincing. Cooperatives who become too sociable, friendly, gentle, adaptable, and forgiving are ineffective negotiators. Aggressives who become too irritating, secretive, bluffing, argumentative, unreasonable, demanding, headstrong, intolerant, arrogant, and hostile are ineffective negotiators. Neither pattern has a monopoly on effectiveness. Rather, there are effective and ineffective communication behaviors in both patterns.

In order for attorneys to become proficient in negotiating, they should be familiar with Williams's explanation of the communication dynamics of cooperative and aggressive negotiating patterns.[53] The aggressive style is to use language that emphasizes the differences between the advocates who are negotiating. The aggressive lawyer intimidates, threatens, accuses, and ridicules in order to put pressure on an opponent to make concessions. The aggressive lawyer is always right and superior; the opponent is always wrong and inferior. Aggressive negotiators believe that if they do not behave this way, the opponent will get the upper hand and win. They believe all opponents are going to be combative, and when they confront cooperative types, they perceive them to be weak, naive, and deserving of exploitation. Even when they compromise, aggressives do so grudgingly and continue to appear inflexible.

The advantage of being aggressive is that rarely is too much given away in negotiations. Also, aggressives are particularly effective in gaining concessions from ineffective cooperatives. The disadvantage of being aggressive is that greater tension and mistrust are generated between the negotiators. Tension and mistrust cause increases in misunderstanding, hardened attitudes, deadlocks over issues, magnification of trivial issues, frustration (which can lead to retaliation), and longer negotiations.

The cooperative style moves toward the opposition; attempts are made to establish common ground, and to demonstrate shared interests, attitudes, and values. Cooperatives find aggressives to be manipulative, exploitive, overbearing, selfish, and undignified. Cooperatives want to negotiate in a low-key, open, and trusting atmosphere. They believe that communication is enhanced when threats are avoided, rational persuasion is emphasized, fairness is the objective, and unilateral concessions are made in good faith. They admit weaknesses and problems in their own cases. The reason for cooperation is to encourage the other side to reciprocate in order to get an outcome that is fair to both parties.

The advantage of being cooperative is that mutual understanding is promoted and agreement is more likely than it is when one or both of the negotiators are aggressive. The disadvantage of being cooperative is vulnerability to exploitation by skillful aggressive types. "The risk for cooperatives is that they will make concession upon concession in a vain attempt to impose a moral obligation on the opponent to reciprocate."[54]

Is the aggressive approach or the cooperative approach better as a negotiating pattern? "The best answer is neither of the above. The most effective strategy is a selective combination of the cooperative and aggressive strategies. The challenge for the skillful negotiator is to put the best of both strategies together in an artful and persuasive manner."[55] Above all, lawyers should use the pattern they do best.

STRATEGIES FOR RESOLVING CONFLICT

Bargaining is a two-edged sword. On one hand, cooperation is the name of the game. On the other hand, competition and winning are essential elements of the game, too. The remainder of this chapter presents several strategies legal negotiators can employ to help them win as much as they can from the bargaining game. The 19 suggested strategies that follow are designed to give an attorney leverage in bargaining or to enhance his or her credibility as an effective bargainer or to do both.

Strategy 1: Determine the objectives to be sought through bargaining. After assessing his or her own case, an attorney should establish an aspiration level for the negotiations. Attorneys who start with high aspirations usually do better than those who do not. Counsel should, therefore, seek a principled and high, yet seemingly reasonable, position to present to the opponent and a plan as to how best to

present that position. Attorneys going into bargaining who have no clear or specific idea of what they want and how to get it can get into trouble. The notion that "I will get as much as I can" is too vague. The limits for settlements should be specifically established and rationalized.

Limits are set by (1) assessing the likely result of litigation and (2) considering factors collateral to the litigation that affect the settlement worth of the case.[56] In assessing the likely result of litigation, an attorney asks about the probability of victory and the judgment that could be expected on the merits of the case. An attorney looks at his or her case from the viewpoint of judge or jury and, essentially, whistles in the dark when predicting. In addition, certain collateral factors must be considered, such as attorneys' fees for litigation, a client's fear of appearance at or desire for trial, the desire to encourage or avoid publicity, and the competence of the attorney for the other side. Once the objectives of negotiation have been determined, they must be communicated to the client.

Ask for his authorization to settle on this basis, promising to work for better terms, but stating that in your opinion the goal represents the best bargain you are likely to get. Explain how the goal terms contrast with the consequences to him of an adverse trial result. If, after explaining your goal, the client refuses consent or gives it only with extreme reluctance, do not proceed with negotiations with this as your aim. Ask him what settlement terms, if any, will satisfy him; then do your best to procure them. If he refuses to authorize a . . . bargain, . . . make no settlement proposal and prepare for trial.[57]

Strategy 2: Know the facts of the case thoroughly. Information is one of the keys to success in negotiation. Unprepared lawyers are clearly at a disadvantage. In fact, Williams found that a negotiator who is not adequately prepared, and who uses aggressiveness to compensate for the lack of preparation, will be ineffective.[58] "Uncertainty creates insecurity during settlement negotiations and prevents . . . a proper evaluation and successful settlement"[59] of a client's claim. Unprepared lawyers may also concede points too easily, because compromising is better than revealing and apologizing for their ignorance. Winning adversaries live by the maxim, "Knowledge is power."

Strategy 3: Obtain as much information from the other side as possible. In addition to knowing the facts before entering negotiations, an attorney should develop skills for obtaining information from the other side when bargaining. "The more extensive your knowledge base, the better position you will be in to deal effectively with the opposition."[60] All social encounters yield an exchange of information. The question is how to get more reliable information than one must provide to the opposition. Here are some tips.

A negotiator is more of an information seeker than an information provider when he or she poses timely questions to discover additional facts and reasons from an opponent. When one attorney says, "We must have $50,000," the other attorney should ask, "Why?" Questioning the reason for something can give the information seeker a basis for rejecting the $50,000 demand. In other words, the asking of questions controls the agenda for the negotiations.

General questions are useful for probing and are best during the early stage of negotiation. As matters unfold, however, it is usually better to refrain from asking them in order not . . . to unfavorably reflect upon the negotiator's thoroughness of preparation or grasp of the subject matter. . . . Specific questions are much safer to venture out with, since they call for fairly confined answers. They're useful in any phase of the negotiation, but more so in the latter stages when the negotiator is more apt to know precisely what he is after when asking. . . . Leading questions are excellent for maintaining control of the negotiation.[61]

Questions on facts and reasons can pay rich dividends for negotiators.

Another tip for getting information is to reduce the pressure when a critical disclosure from the other side is about to be made. Reducing pressure keeps the other side from knowing just how critical the information is to the attorney seeking it. To accomplish pressure reduction, simply change the subject by saying, for example, "Oh, by the way, did you know that . . . ?" instead of using the probe "Tell me more about what you just said." This ploy can make the other side momentarily forget the game that is being played and, as a result, offer the important information.

Strategy 4: Know the opponent well. Attorneys should assume at the outset that their opponents are at least as capable in negotiating as they are. Whenever it is possible to learn something about the bargaining skills and strategies of the opposition, it is essential to do so. Is the opposition an aggressive or a cooperative type? Is the other attorney experienced in negotiating? An able negotiator? Does he or she settle many cases or very few? Make concessions easily or reluctantly? Wait until the day before the trial to negotiate in earnest? Is the other attorney honest and fair? Does he or she exaggerate? Lots of advice can be obtained by talking with fellow lawyers in the community. It is especially useful to learn something about an opponent's motives for the positions that he or she takes. Knowing why people do things aids in predicting what they will do in the future.

Once an attorney knows something about an opponent, adaptation can follow. For instance, an attorney who likes to move fast and often interrupts discussion is one who might make decisions quickly, perhaps too quickly in facing a more thoughtful and slow-moving opponent. An attorney who likes to think things over is more easily moved to a decision if an opponent fully substantiates his or her positions. An attorney should not allow the hostility and quarrelsomeness of an aggressive type to bully or cajole him or her into a concession. Enormous self-control is the best adaptation to an opposing negotiator. Of course, not using the same negotiation strategies and tactics every time makes it difficult for others to analyze a lawyer's bargaining approach. Such variation is an effective counterstrategy to strategy 4.

Are there any significant differences when negotiating with a member of the opposite sex? Little empirical research exists on this question. However, what we do know is that women lawyers are treated differently from men by aggressive male negotiators. Female lawyers experience derogatory gender-related remarks from their male opponents (e.g., "Honey, you just don't understand how things work in the corporate world"). The word "honey" is patronizing, and the "corporate world" is assumed to be a man's business. It is yet another form of intimidation by the aggressive style of attorney. If a female attorney knows she is going to face an aggressive male, she should exercise self-control and not let the intimidation attempt show any effect. Other than in this one phenomenon, male negotiators do not generally change their behavior or strategies to respond to a member of the opposite sex.[62]

Strategy 5: Time the negotiations to your own advantage. When anyone feels hurried in bargaining, that person loses too much. Therefore, attorneys should agree to negotiate when they have lots of time and particularly when an adversary is short on time. To avoid a further loss of time, that adversary may make hasty concessions. Some public interest lawyers claim that they frequently schedule negotiations with government lawyers late in the day, at night, or on weekends because civil service lawyers usually end their workdays at 5:00 P.M. Monday through Friday and, hence, bargain quickly and carelessly on their own time.[63] It is surely not a sign of weakness to be the first one to suggest talking, and an advantage of broaching the sub-

ject first is the opportunity to suggest a meeting time most suitable to one's own personal makeup. The wrong time to negotiate is when you need rest, have just eaten too much food, or have a headache or some other ailment.[64] "The lawyer should consider his biological rhythm and attempt to negotiate at a time when he functions best."[65] Good timing is as important for an attorney who is negotiating as it is for a baseball player swinging at a ball.

Strategy 6: Negotiate on your own turf if possible. People generally feel more comfortable on their own home field than in the arena of an adversary. "When Party A is invited into Party B's office to discuss a problem, A is less secure than B, and A's problem-solving capabilities may be diminished as a result of anxiety."[66] It feels good to have opposing counsel come to you. It constrains opposing counsel from leaving and gives the host more power in terminating discussions. And a psychological disadvantage falls over the visitor if he or she has to tackle conflict in alien surroundings.[67] In selecting the place to bargain, go to your own turf first, neutral territory second, and the opposition's ball park last.

In the movie classic *The Great Dictator,* Charles Chaplin plays a role reminiscent of Adolf Hitler. In one scene, "Hitler" invites someone like a Mussolini to talk with him on his own ground. Hitler arranges the meeting in a room Mussolini will enter far from the führer's desk and chair. Then, so that he will feel small, Mussolini will have to walk a great distance across the room to an elevated area, on which Hitler is seated. Mussolini is then to sit in a low chair below that of Hitler's. Surprise overcomes Chaplin's Hitler when Mussolini enters a back door and proceeds to sit on top of Hitler's desk, looking down at the führer. The two then adjourn to a nearby barber shop to continue their negotiations.

All well-laid plans do not necessarily go the way Chaplin's plans did. For instance, many neighborhood poverty lawyers successfully negotiate with banking and real estate attorneys in ghetto surroundings. Seeing the shocking housing conditions reduces the bargaining effectiveness of the landlord lawyers. One final note of reality: To a large extent, most negotiations regularly scheduled by lawyers do not occur in offices at all, but rather by telephone, in hallways, or over coffee or lunch in some neutral territory.[68]

Strategy 7: Plan to balance or outnumber the other side. This is accomplished by having at least the same number or possibly a larger number of attorneys than the other side brings to the negotiations. The side with fewer representatives tends to tire more quickly. They also have less control over the flow of the discussion. One should not go overboard with this strategy, however, because it may cause the adversary to feel insecure and not to want to bargain at all. If additional persons are in attendance, their presence should be justified. For example, perhaps they are new members of the law firm; perhaps they are technical experts. There is strength in numbers.[69]

Strategy 8: Make the meeting of a demand a precondition of negotiation. If the other side wants to initiate talk, an appropriate response for a lawyer is to say that one of his or her demands is to name the time and place to meet. If the other side agrees, the attorney who set the precondition is already at some psychological advantage as bargaining begins.

Strategy 9: Get the other side to tender the first substantive offer. A substantive offer is a concrete proposal (e.g., "I am willing to give your client $500 for his broken toe"). Although no firm rule exists in legal negotiations as to who should make the initial offer, it is generally believed that it is better to have an opponent do it. To use this strategy well, an attorney should just sit in silence for a while. The opposition may feel compelled to break the ice. Another approach might be for the defense lawyer to say, "Why don't you give us an idea of your position? How much do

you want for that broken toe?" In response, the negotiating plaintiff might say, "Well, how much are you willing to pay? What does your client want to do?" There is a real advantage to being the receiver rather than the giver of the first offer. Here again, information is power. The risk in this strategy should also be noted: it lets the party making the first offer advantageously set the agenda for the negotiations.

Strategy 10: Make the first demand high. Most lawyers expect initial demands to be negotiable; that is, the initial position stated should offer room for some bargaining. This practice in the legal setting is unlike an alternative strategy, sometimes used in labor-management disputes, called "Boulwareism,"[70] which involves stating a demand, sticking with it, and not haggling over it. The first demand in that setting is nearly identical with the least favorable terms that the negotiator making the demand is willing to accept. This take-it-or-leave-it approach is seldom used by attorneys.[71]

The first demand by an attorney should lie outside the acceptable settlement limits (beyond the other party's resistance point).[72] This procedure should be followed even though both parties generally know this strategy is being used. It is a commonly accepted way of instituting bargaining without having to set the level at the outset. By making initially high demands, a bargainer avoids the pitfall of seeming to be too generous, gives him- or herself more time to get information about the other side's preferences, and makes subsequent demands look more attractive to the other side. The end result is that bargainers attain higher and more satisfactory outcomes when they begin their interaction with high demands.[73] One word of caution is appropriate, however. If the first demand is too outrageous, it may look as though the person making it is not seriously interested in the negotiations, and the discussion may break apart in a hurry.[74]

Strategy 11: Make concessions slowly, and occasionally raise new demands. In bargaining, both sides are trying to make the size of their average concession "equal or less than that offered by the opponent."[75] The successful negotiator also raises demands as concessions are carefully measured and slowly made.[76] Raising new demands means doing some backtracking in the negotiations. Some topics that were set aside should be reopened for discussion. Maybe one demand should be raised and justified for every two concessions made. New concessions from the other side should be obtained for each concession made. To illustrate, a defense counsel commits the defendant to pay a certain sum of money to the plaintiff. Now that attorney should start to acquire concessions, such as more time to pay. The result is a reduction in the aggregate number of concessions for the side of the lawyer using this strategy. This strategy can have the effect of tiring the opposition and forcing him or her into ending the negotiations more quickly, making some mistakes along the way. No one should want to end bargaining in haste.

Strategy 12: Place major demands at the beginning of the agenda. Often there is a honeymoon period as bargaining begins, in which negotiators compromise freely. As negotiations proceed, progress toward a settlement tends to tighten, and the major demands may not be met. Also, it is rather offensive for one side to suddenly discover that the other side's major demand is made near the end of bargaining. In the past, delaying major demands has caused negotiations to fail.

Strategy 13: Use multiple negotiators in tough roles and mellow roles. One is a hardliner; the other is not.[77] "The 'good guys–bad guys' technique is where one person on the lawyer's team is the 'good guy' who is reasonable and willing to go along with what the other side requests, and another person on the lawyer's team is the 'bad guy' who refuses to accept the other side's request."[78] Occa-sionally, the two may argue with each other. To the other side, the person making small concessions (the "good guy" lawyer) seems reasonable. Behind this ploy, it is the mellow attorney's positions that are really desired by the negotiating team.

Strategy 14: Invoke the law. Because of their training, lawyers are impressed by authority citations. So demands should be tied to case or statute references, particularly when the other side is unfamiliar with the citations being used.[79] In addition, lengthy analytical discussion of law is a good way to kill time without disclosing information about particular case facts.

Strategy 15: Know when to settle. Settlement cannot be premature, and it cannot be too late. A premature settlement can be disadvantageous. One study of bargaining behavior suggests that the longer one party is able to maintain a position outside the range in which the other side will settle, the more likely he or she is to obtain a disproportionately favorable agreement.[80] Some attorneys wait until just moments before a trial begins, or even until sometime during the trial, to settle. What is important for a lawyer to perceive is when to accept a "final offer" as the other side's last offer. The final offer should be better than the probable results of a trial.

Each case is unique, but generally the comparison that should be made is between the offer facing the negotiator and the best possible outcome of a courtroom trial. Is the cost of a trial justified? "Small or medium cases should be, and usually can be, settled directly with the insurance company without the necessity of suit or litigation."[81] Also, if a personal injury plaintiff is hostile and has a hard demeanor, the claim on paper may look better than the claim in court, and the plaintiff's attorney should settle.

Making this decision has become quite an art for lawyers. There are no magic formulas for knowing precisely when to settle, although some have tried to create them.[82] Like a physician, an attorney "has a set of facts and must arrive at a diagnosis mainly through his skill and experience at evaluation."[83]

Strategy 16: Bargain in good faith. Giving up too much and going too far in relation to the adversary's demands and concessions is one problem; it means a bad deal for clients. But an equally serious problem is really wanting to go to trial, but going through the motions of bargaining anyway. This is usually done to gain time or to obtain information from the adversary. This bargaining practice is fraudulent because it actually subverts negotiation. Good-faith bargaining means that negotiators "must want to reach an agreement."[84] Attorneys expect honesty, fairness, sincerity, and cooperation from their opposition.[85] Trust is essential. If it is violated, the chances of settlement are greatly reduced.

Strategy 17: Clear a bargained agreement with a client before making it final. Consulting with the client is crucial. It is, in fact, an attorney's ethical obligation to do so. This contact with the client often involves explanation and persuasion. For example, suppose a defense attorney has just struck a plea bargain with a prosecutor. When communicating this to the defendant, it is essential for counsel to prepare the defendant for the consequences of voluntarily admitting criminal conduct in open court. For example, a felony conviction entails the loss of certain rights, such as carrying a firearm or voting. Also, the defendant's employment opportunities may be reduced, and ostracism by one's family is possible. In other words, an attorney must inform a client of both the negative and positive aspects of the bargained agreement. In a personal injury case in which a client has a high settlement figure in mind, it is sometimes necessary to explain that no jury is going to understand and appreciate the full extent of the damages to the extent the plaintiff does. The jury never felt the pain of the plaintiff. So persuasion toward accepting the defense offer is needed. However, ultimately, the client is the one

who grants permission to finalize any agreement.

Strategy 18: If a written agreement is to be used, volunteer to draft the document. Perhaps there are slightly differing interpretations of one or more points in the agreement, and when it is drafted by one party, it will contain the language that that party chooses to use. That language reflects the drafter's own interpretation of the terms of the settlement. Also, certain omissions can be filled and ambiguities can be resolved by the draftsperson. An attorney who is not the drafter of a written agreement should certainly be a careful editor at a later time. One word in passing: most legal disputes are not resolved by binding written agreements, but there is nothing that precludes any attorney from suggesting an agreement be put in writing.

Strategy 19: At the end of the negotiations, an attorney should make the adversary feel good. It is not profitable to gloat over a settlement. In fact, such behavior could cause an opponent to renounce the agreement and reopen neogitations, or it could affect a future negotiation with that individual.[86] When ending a negotiation, a lawyer should congratulate the other side for driving a hard bargain and doing such a good job. This builds rapport which serves as a worthwhile foundation for future negotiations. An attorney's reputation is established, in part, by his or her behavior with other attorneys in adversarial situations.

These nineteen strategies, or tactics, in negotiating are catalogued here in the spirit of giving an attorney an extra edge when bargaining. Not every strategy is appropriate for every negotiation; the use of the strategies depends on the particular case and opponent. Furthermore, the propriety of each of them should be closely examined by an attorney before it is put into use. Some of the sneakier ones may even be ethically dubious tactics.[87] Unfortunately, there is nothing in the American Bar Association Code of Professional Responsibility that relates specifically to the ethical constraints upon the lawyer as a negotiator.[88] The code generally forbids dishonesty, fraud, deceit, or misrepresentation, including such ploys as hiding facts from an opponent or bluffing. The code also calls for maintenance of the integrity and competence of the legal profession (Canon 1) and zealous representation within the bounds of the law (Canon 7). Certainly these requirements have a bearing on the lawyer's role as a negotiator. Balancing what may appear to be manipulative strategies with ethical behavior is a complex task, to be sure.[89]

Although legal negotiations are designed to resolve disputes, attorneys always face the prospect of taking cases to trial should bargaining fail. Trial provides an important recourse for the lawyer who, for one reason or another, cannot successfully bargain with the other side. While, on one hand, the prospect of trial inevitably provides a strong impetus toward fair, tough bargaining, preparation for trial must always be kept in mind by a negotiating attorney.

Notes

[1]Michael J. Saks and Reid Hastie, *Social Psychology in Court* (New York: Van Nostrand Reinhold, 1978), 100.

[2]Robert L. Simmons, *Winning Before Trial* (Englewood Cliffs, N.J.: Executive Reports Corporation, 1974), 904.

[3]Bill Wagner and Alan F. Wagner, "The Settlement Process," *Trial* (August 1984), 62.

[4]Warren E. Burger, "Conflict Resolution: Isn't There a Better Way?" *National Forum* (Fall 1983), 3.

[5]Ibid.; E. Gordon Gee and Donald W. Jackson, "Current Studies of Legal Education: Findings and Recommendations," *Journal of Legal Education* 32 (1982), 481; Bernard M. Ortwein, "Teaching Negotiation: A Valuable Experience," *Journal of Legal Education* 31 (1981), 108–127.

[6]Morton Deutsch and Robert M. Krauss, "Studies of Interpersonal Bargaining," *Journal of Conflict Resolution* 6 (1962), 53.

[7]Saks and Hastie, op. cit., 121.

[8]Jeffrey Z. Rubin and Bert R. Brown, *The Social Psychology of Bargaining and Negotiation* (New York: Academic Press, 1975), 6–18.

[9]Ann Douglas, *Industrial Peacemaking* (New York: Columbia University Press, 1962), 13–99.

[10]When applying this stage to legal negotiations, Craver suggests the following: "(A) Seek as much information from the opponent as possible, but be careful not to disclose inadvertently counsel's own side's confidential information. (B) Observe carefully and probe the opponent to ascertain his/her perception of the situation, because it may be more favorable to your side than you had anticipated." Charles B. Craver, *The Art of Legal Negotiating* (Berkeley: California Continuing Education of the Bar, 1980), 5–6.

[11]Hegland offers the following advice about getting concessions: The worth of the case is not an objective fact. It exists solely in your mind and in that of your opponent. In other words, we are dealing in hokum. Your objective in negotiation is to create uncertainty in your opponent as to his assessment of the case. First, he foolishly miscalculated his chances of victory at trial; second, he totally blew his assessment of the damages; finally, he grossly underestimates his collateral costs of litigation while overestimating yours. . . . Create uncertainty. Tell your opponent why he should be uncertain. If his theory is weak, let him know it. If you have a strong witness, tell him. Kenney F. Hegland, *Trial and Practice Skills in a Nutshell* (St. Paul, Minn.: West Publishing, 1978), 290–291.

[12]For a discussion of the pros and cons of structured settlements, see Neil Shayne, "Structured Settlements," *Trial Diplomacy Journal* (Summer 1983), 15–17.

[13]Robert Coulson, "Alternative Dispute Resolution: Threat or Invitation?" *Trial* (October 1985), 22.

[14]For a full explanation of one such program, see Luis Salas and Ronald Schneider, "Evaluating the Dade County Citizen Dispute Settlement Program," *Judicature* 63 (1979), 174–183.

[15]Richard D. Rieke and Renee G. Zundel, "Alternative Means of Dispute Resolution," Paper

presented at the Speech Communication Association convention (Chicago, 1984).

[16]Coulson, op. cit., 22.

[17]Maureen M. Desjardins and Deanna F. Womack, "An Empirical Investigation of the Use of Communication and Mediator Styles in Small Claims Court," Paper presented at the Speech Communication Association convention (Denver, 1985).

[18]Rieke and Zundel, op. cit. In addition, a description of the Citizen Complaint Center in Tulsa, Okla., is found in Michele Cruncleton, "Beyond Dispute," *American Way* (November 26, 1985), 49–55.

[19]Ibid.

[20]Milton Heumann, *Plea Bargaining* (Chicago: University of Chicago Press, 1978), 1.

[21]In a new development in Arizona, some crime victims and law enforcement officers have a chance to tell a judge whether they condone the plea agreements reached in their cases, before the judge accepts the plea. See *Arizona Daily Star*, Tucson, Arizona, February 25, 1982.

[22]George Beall, "Negotiating the Disposition of Criminal Charges," *Trial* (October 1980), 48.

[23]Albert W. Alschuler, "Plea Bargaining and Its History," *Law and Society Review* 13 (1979), 211–215.

[24]Michael L. Rubenstein and Teresa J. White, "Alaska's Ban on Plea Bargaining," in William F. McDonald and James A. Cramer, eds., *Plea Bargaining* (Lexington, Mass.: Lexington Books, 1980), 25–56.

[25]Robert McFigg, Ralph C. McCullough II, and James L. Underwood, *Civil Trial Manual* (Los Angeles: Joint Committee on Legal Education of the American Law Institute and the American Bar Association, 1974), 319.

[26]Dean G. Pruitt, *Negotiation Behavior* (New York: Academic Press, 1981), 6.

[27]V. Hale Starr, "Communication, Conflict and Negotiation," in Mary Frances Edwards, ed., *Settlement of Plea Bargaining* (Washington, D.C.: Association of Trial Lawyers of America, 1981), 82–97.

[28]Lawrence M. Friedman and Stewart Macaulay, *Law and the Behavioral Sciences* (Indianapolis: Bobbs-Merrill, 1969), 176.

[29]Roger Fisher and William Ury, *Getting to Yes: Negotiating Agreement Without Giving In* (Boston: Houghton Mifflin, 1981), 4.

[30]Thomas Steinfatt and Gerald R. Miller, *Perspectives in Communication in Social Conflict* (Englewood Cliffs, N.J.: Prentice-Hall, 1974), 15.

[31]Friedman and Macaulay op. cit., 92.

[32]Numerous models exist of the process of negotiation. For instance, see Ottomar J. Bartos, *Process and Outcome of Negotiations* (New York: Columbia University Press, 1974); P. H. Gulliver, *Disputes and Negotiations: A Cross Cultural Perspective* (New York: Academic Press, 1979); Linda L. Putnam and Tricia S. Jones, "The Role of Communication in Bargaining," *Human Communication* 8 (1982), 262–280; Howard Raiffa, *The Act and Science of Negotiation* (Cambridge: Harvard University Press, 1982).

[33]James T. Tedeschi and Paul Rosenfield, "Communication in Bargaining and Negotiation," in Michael E. Roloff and Gerald R. Miller, eds., *Persuasion: New Directions in Theory and Research* (Beverly Hills, Calif.: Sage, 1980), 239.

[34]David H. Smith, "Communication and Negotiation Outcome," *Journal of Communication* 19 (1969), 254.

[35]Rubin and Brown, op. cit., 92.

[36]Neil Hurowitz, *Support Practice Handbook* (New York: Kluwer, 1985), 292.

[37]Richard A. Givens, *Advocacy: The Art of Pleading a Cause* (Colorado Springs: Shepard's/McGraw-Hill, 1980), 246–247.

[38]Ronald B. Adler and George Rodman, *Understanding Human Communication* (New York: Holt, Rinehart and Winston, 1982), 99–100.

[39]Margaret G. Hermann and Nathan Kogan, "Effects of Negotiators' Personalities on Negotiating Behavior," in Daniel Druckman, ed., *Negotiations: Social Psychological Perspectives* (Beverly Hills, Calif.: Sage, 1977), 247–274; William Anthony Donohue, "An Empirical Framework for Examining Negotiating Processes and Outcomes," *Communication Monographs* 45 (1978), 247–257.

[40]Hermann and Kogan, op. cit.; Barbara D. Slack and John Oliver Cook, "Authoritarian Behavior in a Conflict Situation," *Journal of Personality and Social Psychology* 25 (1973), 130–136.

[41]Edward T. Hall, *The Silent Language* (Garden City, N.Y.: Doubleday, 1959); Mark L. Knapp, *Nonverbal Communication in Human Interaction* (New York: Holt, Rinehart and Winston, 1978); Miles L. Patterson, "An Arousal Model of Interpersonal Intimacy," *Psychological Review* 83 (1976), 235–245; Nancy F. Russo, "Connotations of Seating Arrangements," *Cornell Journal of Social Relations* 2 (1967), 37–44; Robert Sommer, *Personal Space: The Behavioral Basis of Design* (Englewood Cliffs, N.J.: Prentice-Hall, 1969).

[42]Putnam and Jones, op. cit., 269.

[43]Mark L. Knapp, Roderick P. Hart, and Harry S. Dennis, "An Exploration of Deception as a Communication Construct," *Human Communication Research* 1 (1975), 15–29.

[44]Ibid.; Robert E. Kraut, "Verbal and Nonverbal Cues in the Perception of Lying," *Journal of Personality and Social Psychology* 36 (1978), 380–391.

[45]Paul Ekman, Wallace V. Friesan, and Klaus R. Scherer, "Body Movement and Voice Pitch in Deceptive Interaction," *Semiotica* 16 (1976), 23–27; Lynn A. Streeter et al., "Pitch Changes During Attempted Deception," *Journal of Personality and Social Psychology* 35 (1977), 345–350.

[46]Glen D. Baskett and Roy O. Freddie, "Aspects of Language Pragmatics and the Social Perception of Lying," *Journal of Psycholinguistic Research* 3 (1974), 117–131; Kraut, op. cit.

[47]Knapp, Hart, and Dennis, op. cit.

[48]Frank J. Monteverde, Richard Paschke, and James T. Tedeschi, "The Effectiveness of Honesty and Deceit in Influence Tactics," *Sociometry* 37 (1974), 583–591.

[49]Harry T. Edwards and James J. White, *Problems, Readings and Materials on the Lawyer as a Negotiator* (St. Paul, Minn.: West Publishing, 1977), 152–164.

[50]Sean Patrick O'Rourke and Janet Sparrow, "From the Communication Profession: Communication Strategies and Research Needs in Legal Negotiating and Bargaining," in Ronald J. Matlon and Richard J. Crawford, eds., *Communication Strategies in the Practice of Lawyering* (Annandale, Va.: Speech Communication Association, 1983), 149–175.

[51]Dean G. Pruitt, "Indirect Communication and the Search for Agreement in Negotiation," *Journal of Applied Social Psychology* 1 (1971), 205–239.

[52]Gerald R. Williams, J. Lynn England, Larry Farmer, and Murray Blumenthal, "Effectiveness in Legal Negotiation," in Harry T. Edwards and James J. White, eds., *The Lawyer as a Negotiator* (St. Paul, Minn.: West Publishing, 1977), 8–28.

[53]Gerald R. Williams, *Effective Negotiation and Settlement* (Provo, Utah: Gerald R. Williams for the National Practice Institute, 1981), 21–26.

[54]Ibid., 25.

[55]Ibid., 56.

[56]Hegland, op. cit., 280.

[57]Simmons, op. cit., 919.

[58]Williams, op. cit., 23.

[59]Wagner and Wagner, op. cit., 62.

[60]Xavier M. Frascogna, Jr., and H. Lee Heatherington, *Negotiation Strategy for Lawyers* (Englewood Cliffs, N.J.: Prentice-Hall, 1984), 67.

[61]John Ilich, *The Art and Skill of Successful Negotiation* (Englewood Cliffs, N.J.: Prentice-Hall, 1973), 49.

[62]Williams, op. cit., 29–30.

[63]Michael Meltsner and Philip G. Schrag, "Negotiating Tactics for Legal Services Lawyers," *Clearinghouse Review* 7 (1973), 259–263.

[64]Ilich, op. cit., 21–22.

[65]Norbert S. Jacker, "From the Legal Profession: Legal Strategies and Research Needs in Negotiating and Bargaining," in Ronald J. Matlon and Richard J. Crawford, eds., *Communication Strategies in the Practice of Lawyering* (Annandale, Va.: Speech Communication Association, 1983), 130.

[66]Alan C. Filley, *Interpersonal Conflict Resolution* (Palo Alto, Calif.: Scott, Foresman, 1975), 82.

[67]In one study, subjects were paired in 30 separate dyads and were asked to bargain over a single issue, namely, the penalty to be given a guilty defendant in a fictional legal case. Subjects played the roles of prosecutors and defense attorneys. Territorial dominance was varied by manipulating the location in which the negotiations took place. Fifteen pairs met in the living quarters of the prosecutor. Proceedings were tape-recorded and analyzed by computer. Subjects negotiating in their home territory

dominated the negotiations and would win more points than their visitors. Penalties were significantly shorter when defense lawyers negotiated on their own turf. D. A. Martindale, "Territorial Dominance Behavior in Dyadic Verbal Interactions," *Proceedings of the 79th Annual Conference of the American Psychological Association* 6 (1971), 305–306.

[68]Gary Bellow and Bea Moulton, *The Lawyering Process: Materials for Clinical Instruction in Advocacy* (Mineola, N.Y.: Foundation Press, 1978), 562.

[69]See Meltsner and Schrag, op. cit.

[70]This technique is named after its chief proponent, Lemuel Boulware of the General Electric Company.

[71]Bellow and Moulton, op. cit., 101.

[72]Nancy A. Coleman, "Teaching the Theory and Practice of Bargaining to Lawyers and Students," *Journal of Legal Education* 30 (1980), 473.

[73]Jerome M. Chertkoff and Melinda Conley, "Opening Offer and Frequency of Concession as Bargaining Strategies," *Journal of Personality and Social Psychology* 7 (1967), 181–185; Bernard L. Hinton, W. Clay Hamner, and Michael F. Pohlen, "The Influence of Reward Magnitude, Opening Bid, and Concession Rate on Profit Earned in a Managerial Negotiation Game," *Behavioral Science* 19 (1974), 197–203.

[74]"It is our experience that most lawyers, whatever the type of case, expect the initial demand to be negotiable. That is, it is generally assumed that, no matter how firmly stated, the initial position of every party offers some room for bargaining." Bellow and Moulton, op. cit., 530.

[75]S. S. Komorita and Arline R. Brenner, "Bargaining and Concession Making Under Bilateral Monopoly," *Journal of Personality and Social Psychology* 9 (1968), 15–20.

[76]W. Clay Hamner and Gary A. Yuhl, "The Effects of Different Offer Strategies in Bargaining," in Druckman, op. cit., 139.

[77]Police use this Mutt-and-Jeff technique. One is a friendly interrogator; the other is nasty. They claim it is easier to extract statements from reluctant interviewees this way. Edwards and White, op. cit., 137.

[78]Jacker, op. cit., 133.

[79]Wagner and Wagner, op. cit., 62.

[80]Hinton, Hamner, and Pohlen, op. cit.

[81]Tom H. Davis, "Settlement Negotiations: Strategy and Tactics," *Trial* 19 (July 1983), 83.

[82]Sixteen important considerations are listed for plea-bargaining offers in criminal cases in Simmons, op. cit., 910–913.

[83]McFigg, McCullough, and Underwood, op. cit., 322.

[84]H. L. Ross, *Settled out of Court* (Chicago: Aldine, 1970), 148.

[85]Harold Baer and Aaron J. Broder, *How to Prepare and Negotiate Cases for Settlement* (New York: Law-Arts, 1973), 97–98; Philip J. Hermann, *Better Settlements Through Leverage* (New York: Aqueduct, 1965), 139–144; Gerard I. Nierenberg, *Fundamentals of Negotiating* (New York: Hawthorn, 1973), 22–24; Gerald R. Williams, J. Lynn England, Larry C. Farmer, and Murray Blumenthal, "Effectiveness in Legal Negotiation," in Gordon Bermant, Charlan Nemeth, and Neil Vidmar, eds., *Psychology and the Law* (Lexington, Mass.: Lexington Books, 1976), 124–128.

[86]Williams, op. cit., 40.

[87]For additional information on negotiating ethics, see Alvin Rubin, "A Causerie for Lawyer's Ethics in Negotiation," *Louisiana Law Review* 35 (1975), 577–583; and Thomas L. Shaffer, "Negotiation Ethics: A Report to Cartaphila," *Litigation* (Winter 1981), 37–40, 55–56.

[88]The Code of Professional Responsibility, which consists of canons, ethical considerations, and disciplinary rules, was adopted by the American Bar Association in 1969. Most states have adopted the ABA code in one form or another as the body of rules that regulate attorneys in that state.

[89]Gary Bellow and Bea Moulton, *The Lawyering Process: Negotiation* (Mineola, N.Y.: Foundation Press, 1981), 13–14.

CHAPTER

PRETRIAL PREPARATION

INVESTIGATION
Real Evidence / Oral Testimony / Memory and
Perception / Expert Witnesses / Organizing the Case

PLEADINGS

DISCOVERY
Depositions / Interrogatories / Production of
Documents / Requests for Physical or Mental
Examinations / Requests for Admission / Pros and
Cons of Discovery

ISSUE ANALYSIS
Rhetorical Invention and the Location of Issues /
Building Case Arguments and Developing a Case Theme

MOTIONS PRACTICE

PRETRIAL CONFERENCES

Preparation for trial should begin early and be continued diligently. This chapter will explore several preparation strategies used by attorneys during various pretrial stages, namely, investigation, pleadings, discovery, issue analysis, motions practice, and pretrial conferences. The focus will be on how information, logic, and communication strategies can be used by an attorney to get better trial advantage during this preparation stage.

INVESTIGATION

In preparation for trial, a lawyer constantly gathers and organizes information about a case. This work is called investigation into the facts and the law. The investigation should be an objective, step-by-step compilation of information designed to help a lawyer preserve evidence and calculate key issues. "Each fact discovered as a result of the investigation amounts to a component part of the whole, and if any necessary component part remains undiscovered, the lawsuit can be in jeopardy."[1] Good lawyers, then, probe for every shred of information they can find.

Investigation into the facts is basically an art. "Mastery cannot be acquired from the pages of a book. The difficult techniques . . . must be learned through a long apprenticeship of practice and self-analysis."[2] These techniques involve the power of reasoning, tested knowledge, effective communication, and a lawyer's much-needed ingenuity. There are basically two kinds of fact investigation. One is an in-house investigation of the client and supporters of the client's position. The other is to get facts, admissions, and other kinds of material from the opposite side, a process called *discovery*, which will be discussed later in the chapter.

In addition to investigating case facts, an attorney must also identify relevant law. What substantive rules govern the case? What competing rules apply? Although an attorney's

need for a detailed investigation of law with respect to each case decreases as his or her litigation experience increases, it is always best to conduct some legal investigation or at least be sure there are no unanswered questions of law as a detailed fact investigation is undertaken. Eventually the facts and the law must fit together. The scope of each investigation is influenced by the results of the other.

During fact investigation, two forms of evidence are gathered. One is real evidence; the other is oral testimony. To assist attorneys in their investigative work, independent private investigators are frequently contracted to gather both kinds of evidence. Usually these "private eyes" are hired (if a client can afford it) to perform some special assignment, not to do all the investigative work for an attorney.[3] Naturally, close communication between a private investigator and an attorney is needed to determine the areas an investigation should cover in order to build a prima facie case.

Real Evidence

Real, or demonstrative, evidence comes in the form of exhibits, for example, pictures. When there has been an automobile accident and damage has been done to the vehicles, it is helpful to secure a photograph of the damaged cars. Photographs are frequently taken by police or free-lance photographers at the scene of an accident. If a photograph is to be used as real evidence, promptness is essential in getting it taken. Accident scenes can and do change. Shadows and lighting can alter scenes. A fallen tree could be removed, or a broken sidewalk could be repaired. If a lawyer waits to obtain a picture of the accident scene after the removal or repair, the picture may be inadmissible at trial because the scene that the jury or judge would view in the photo is not the actual postaccident scene. Occasionally at trial, you will find that an attorney has enlarged a photograph for the entire jury to study. Such an enlargement can be very dramatic and persuasive, especially if the photograph taken is clear and in color.[4]

In addition to photographs, diagrams are particularly good for witnesses when they are describing something such as the scene of an accident. The best diagrams or drawings are those prepared in advance rather than on-the-spot chalk drawings. An easily understood diagram of a traffic accident is found in Figure 3.1. Important physical details of the accident are all included. These include the directions and positions of the automobiles, the location of traffic controls, the positions of witnesses, details about the intersection, such as street names and nearby buildings, and a compass indicating direction. A diagram like this is "worth a thousand words"!

Another type of exhibit is an actual physical object itself. A weapon such as a gun or a knife falls into this category. So do fingerprints, jewelry, false teeth, hair, bloodstained items of apparel, and many other objects. A car fender from the automobile accident shown in Figure 3.1 is an example of an actual object that can be brought into court.

Finally, documents are a form of real evidence. Wills, hospital records, deeds, police reports, fire reports, coroner's inquests, tax returns, and contracts constitute examples of documentary proof. They are all potentially valuable because "jurors sometimes attribute unmerited importance to the printed word."[5] In order for a document to be admissible as evidence, it must be authenticated by pretrial stipulation or by proof or stipulation during the trial itself. For instance, if an income tax return is to be admitted, it must be shown to be an original copy from the party in question. It can in no way be "sanitized"; that is, information on the return can be neither added nor deleted. Because the complete return must be presented as evidence, a lawyer may decide not to use the document. For instance, if a tax return coincidentally shows some questionable and potentially damaging charitable contributions by a client, the attorney may well want to find another way to get the needed information into the trial rather than using that return.

The possibilities for real evidence are almost unlimited. Maps, charts, and models are effective. Slides, X rays, and motion pictures are used. Skeletons are brought to trial in cases involving bone or organ injuries. In one negligence case, an attorney demonstrated a waxing machine and the wax that had been used on a floor. In another case, a plaintiff suing a bottling company had her lawyer conduct an actual experiment in which a bottle exploded from excessive internal pressure under certain temperatures. Real evidence communicates a lot. It has the ability to exercise a strong and continuing influence over

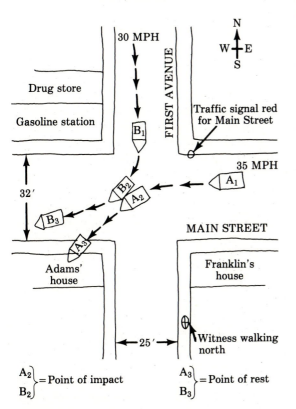

FIGURE 3.1   DIAGRAM OF A TRAFFIC ACCIDENT

judge and jury alike. Psychologists long ago estimated that 85 percent of what we learn is conveyed to our mind through what we see![6] Attorneys who know and use this statistic make extensive use of real evidence to awaken and quicken the judge's or juror's interest and to get their own points across.

One final word of caution about demonstrative evidence: It must not be overused. The use of unnecessarily elaborate visual aids to illustrate insignificant points can turn a trial into a three-ring circus. As a result, attorneys should use demonstrative evidence only to graphically illustrate key aspects of their cases.

Oral Testimony

The second and much more common form of evidence in a trial is oral testimony. Oral testimony is given when witnesses are brought to court in person to present information. As attorneys investigate their cases, potential witnesses should be evaluated carefully for what they can contribute from the witness stand. Potential witnesses should also be viewed as leads to additional sources of information. Here are some recommendations attorneys should follow in locating potential witnesses and leads.

First, an attorney should visit the scene of an occurrence before interviewing many potential witnesses. Familiarity with the scene makes it easier to determine the accuracy of a witness's testimony. It also allows the lawyer to help a witness remember some of the details of the scene and the event.

Second, potential witnesses should be interviewed as soon after an occurrence as possible. Speed is essential. Why? People usually are eager to talk immediately after an event. Their memories are sharper then. And they tend to remain more loyal to the first party who interviews them. More will be said about eyewitnesses in Chapter 9.

Third, attorneys should almost never pay lay witnesses.[7] Not only is payment a serious ethical question, but also it looks bad in a trial

for a witness to admit he or she was paid for testimony in court. The exception pertains to expert witnesses, and more will be said about them later.

Fourth, potential witnesses should be interviewed in comfortable surroundings. As noted in earlier chapters, the physical environment is important in information-gathering interviews. The potential witness must feel at ease in order for a free and open discussion to take place. Other persons should not be present. There should be no distractions or interruptions. Some believe that a likely place is the potential witness's own home, although there are those who maintain that the home should be the location of last resort because privacy is hard to guarantee there.

Fifth, the investigator should display a positive and engaging personality. If a potential witness does not like the attorney, he or she surely will not like the attorney's cause. Investigative interviews are not to be conducted like cross-examination sessions. The interviewer should be friendly and tactful, but candid and firm. He or she should be patient and even-tempered and a good listener. There should be no pressuring or intimidation. Entering the inverview, the investigator should have no prejudices or preconceived ideas. Positive interviewing traits yield enormous benefits, particularly if the interviewee is to be a witness for that side at trial.

Sixth, investigative interviews should be conducted in simple, easy-to-understand language. Legal jargon should be kept to a minimum or avoided. On occasion, witnesses later repudiate what they have said in investigative interviews, and they say they do so because they did not fully understand everything that was being asked earlier.

Seventh, a potential witness should be sized up during the investigative interview. Will this person impress the jury? Is he or she alert, sincere, pleasant, articulate, and thoughtful or pompous, evasive, inarticulate, and careless?

Let us examine articulateness in greater

depth. Witnesses must be able to convert images into words that effectively communicate those images to others. People fill in gaps with inferences, not facts. For instance, if someone says, "It was a *cold day,* and I was *wearing my winter gloves,*" it is unclear whether these are both facts or one statement is a fact while the other statement is an inferred piece of information from the statement of fact. If one of the statements is inferred, we have an example of how witnesses fill in informational gaps. There is a tendency on the part of all of us to fill in gaps with what sounds like factual information. More will be said about this subject later, in a discussion of memory and perception. Suffice it to say for now that the ability to "tell it like it was" factually is a sign of an articulate witness.

When sizing up a possible witness, counsel must recognize that "the credibility of a witness varies inversely to the closeness of the relationship between client and witness, and to the degree of benefit his testimony confers upon the client."[8] Any testimony that benefits one side is less persuasive the closer the witness is to the client on that side. Ranked by relationship from the least credible to the most credible, a witness may be (1) a close relative, (2) a close friend, (3) a professional colleague whose income is related to the client's job, (4) a distant relative, (5) a frequent social acquaintance, (6) a fellow employee and frequent contact, (7) an acquaintance with irregular contacts, or (8) a stranger. Strangers are initially more credible than close relatives. But, regardless of the relationship, potential witnesses, especially less credible ones, must always be urged to be accurate and fair with their information.

Along with these recommendations for conducting an investigative interview, much of what was said in Chapter 1 concerning interviewing applies here. For instance, the interview should be kept relatively casual; very few, if any, notes should be taken; and the funnel sequence should be employed.

During an investigation, a lawyer will build up a collection of potential witnesses who feel they owe an allegiance to that attorney's cause. These cooperative individuals can be called *friendly witnesses.* Their services should be exploited with vigor. Simmons suggests five objectives to be kept in mind as an attorney communicates with a friendly witness.[9]

☐ *Enlist his active and partisan support for your case.* He comes to you almost as a volunteer for duty. Explain his importance to the case and the client's chance of winning it. . . .
☐ *Obtain and preserve all favorable facts.* . . . Establish all that you can through friendly witnesses. . . .
☐ *Obtain and subordinate unfavorable facts.* Knowledge of "bad" facts is as important as knowledge of "good" facts, for in a legal setting knowledge is indeed power. . . . You must orient the witness in his partisan role by emphasizing his facts that help your case and by subordinating (not suppressing) those that hurt it. . . .
☐ *Obtain leads to other facts, evidence, and witnesses.* . . . The treasure a lawyer seeks . . . often can only be found by pursuing leads friends supply. . . .
☐ *Obtain sufficient personal data about the witness so you can locate him whenever necessary later.* A good witness who cannot be produced when needed is as much use as a million dollars that cannot be spent. . . .

Some potential witnesses are not quite friendly, but are merely lukewarm. In order to get these people as supporters, an attorney must show them how they can profit from enlisting in the cause. The merits of a particular case should be discussed early in the interview. The importance of winning should be emphasized. The potential witness should be told that he or she is vital to the victory. In other words, a lawyer must build up a positive self-image in each potential witness. Words like these can be very motivating: "Mr. Bryson, you're a key person in this case. I need your help. As an eyewitness to the accident on the corner of First and Main, you were in a unique and excellent position to see what happened. And since you're not a party in this case, your words will carry a great deal of weight. I think there is a chance of winning this case for my client, but only if I can have your help." The potential witness may now have a stake in what is to follow.

During an investigation, it is always possible that counsel will come across potential witnesses who cause problems. Skillful interviewing and investigating techniques are needed when adapting to these problems. Let us note just a few to illustrate what is meant here.

Sometimes an unfriendly witness displays hostility. The hostility may stem from that person's relationship with one of the parties on the other side; it may be dislike for the investigator; it may just be a defense mechanism for overcoming shyness; or the hostility may exist because the person simply does not want to get involved in the case. Attorneys need to determine the basis for any hostility. This determination can be made through the use of probing questions, such as those that follow:

Q: May I ask you a few questions about the scuffle you saw the other day?
A: No. I really don't want to talk about it.
Q: Well, do you have any reason for not wanting to talk to me about it?
A: I just don't want to get involved in anybody's lawsuit.
Q: But aren't you already involved, since you were apparently the only one who saw what took place? You know, you could get a subpoena to testify in court.[10] But if you give me some information now, I might be able to get this thing settled out of court, and then you really wouldn't be quite so involved.
A: I still don't want to get involved. Sorry.

The investigator now knows why this potential witness does not want to talk. Notice next how the attorney adapts to the situation and changes the potential witness's mind about cooperating:

Q: Let me just ask you if you knew either of the two people involved in the fight.
A: Yes, one of them was my neighbor.
Q: Your neightbor? A friend of yours?
A: I guess so.
Q: Well, I'm sure you want your neighbor and friend to have his day in court, don't you?
A: Uh . . .
Q: Wouldn't you even want the other person to have his day in court, too?
A: Sure, I suppose so.
Q: Did you know that both men are in the hospital now?
A: I heard that.
Q: They may be there for up to two months. That's pretty hard on their families, wouldn't you say so?
A: I suppose it is.
Q: Well then, don't you think it's only fair to get all the facts of this case out so the matter can be settled quickly and equitably for both of them?
A: Oh, you're probably right.

This kind of appeal to sympathy and fairness may overcome the interviewee's hostility. Generally, people being interviewed by lawyers will hold back until their sympathetic interest has been aroused enough that they want to be helpful.[11]

Another problem witness is one who does not tell the truth. Of course, lying must be distinguished from exaggeration. The latter is quite common, particularly in someone talking about an emotional incident. It may seem to a potential witness that a car involved in an accident was traveling 90 miles per hour, when in reality it was going only 70 miles per hour. It may seem that a pickpocket was "one of the tallest men I've ever seen," when in reality the person was six feet one inch tall. These are typical responses from an exaggerating witness. To find out if a person is a lying witness, other questions ought to be asked, about unemotional information not related to the event in question. When it is as easy to lead a witness as in the admittedly exaggerated example that follows, the person may be a compulsive liar.

Q: Do you know Mr. Smith?
A: Sure, he's my best friend.
Q: How long have you known him?
A: About five years.
Q: Maybe even ten?
A: Sure, maybe it was ten.
Q: And you say he was a drinker?
A: Yeh, he would occasionally have a drink or two with me.
Q: Maybe even more?
A: Sometimes.
Q: Did you ever see him drunk?
A: Sure, lots of times.
Q: Drunk to the point that he couldn't even stand up?
A: Staggering all around and falling down.
Q: How often? Once a week?
A: Every week.
Q: Every day?
A: At least.

In this case, it is very difficult to know when the interviewee is telling the truth and when he is deliberately falsifying or concealing. Having entangled himself in deceit already, the person must be dealt with firmly, and counsel should point out possible falsehoods to the witness.

After getting a potential witness's story, the investigating lawyer should attempt to summarize it (e.g., "Now, as I understand the situation as you have told it to me, . . ."). The interviewee's own words should be echoed,

and attorney coloring of the information should be avoided. Feedback from the potential witness should be requested to be sure the story has been accurately understood by the lawyer.

This leads us to getting a written account of the information obtained. Written summaries of what potential witnesses have said are designed to preserve any information obtained as possible evidence. A written statement is also useful for avoiding misunderstandings between a lawyer and a potential witness. After an interview, the investigator carefully reduces to writing all the relevant information the person provided, organizes it chronologically, and has it signed by the source of the information. The statement should be comprehensive and specific, the language should be conversational and simple, sentences should be short, and a first-person narrative should be used.[12] The potential witness gets a copy of the statement after it is prepared. A well-written statement becomes part of a diary for a lawyer building a case.

Memory and Perception

Because witnesses easily forget or distort events, attorneys should understand the intricacies of memory and perception. Jerome Frank, in *Courts on Trial,* made the pessimistic claim that witnesses are probably correct only 50 percent of the time.[13] So throughout the investigative interviews, counsel must discreetly test each witness's memory and perception.

Memory is a fallible thing. We commonly see and hear much more than we can remember and report. However, we remember best experiences that occur frequently, or with great intensity, or recently, or that leave us with a feeling of considerable pleasure or pain. First, we tend to remember what we observe or recall with *frequency.* Advertisers for Coke and Kleenex have gotten consumers to ask for soft drinks and facial tissues by those two brand names rather than by the generic words for the products. They have done this through frequent repetition of their advertising messages. Unfortunately, witnesses to an event probably see it only once, not frequently. Second, we tend to remember events of considerable *intensity*. When something occurs that is vivid, striking, or impressive, it sticks in our memory more clearly than do rather humdrum events. We focus our attention most strongly on the extraordinary or the novel. Third, we tend to remember events of greatest *recency*. The more recent the experience, the easier it is for us to remember it. You may remember what you wore to classes yesterday, but do you remember what you wore the second day of the semester? Clearly, "we quickly forget the bulk of what we perceive, our retention decreasing as the time interval increases."[14] Fourth, we tend to remember experiences of *pleasure or pain*. We remember best what we like most, next what we dislike most, and lastly those things about which we are relatively indifferent. Children talk about their most favorite and least favorite foods, but not about all foods in general.

Memory, then, is sharpened by events that happen often and are intense, recent, and pleasurable or painful. Memory is also helped when observed events are studied for a while, but, alas, witnesses do not always have opportunities for study and reflection. Therefore, potential witnesses need coaching to jog their memories. Coaching involves going over the same story again and again; it means trying to identify a witness's emotional attachment to an incident; it also means trying to understand feelings of pleasure or pain that the witness experienced at the time the event took place. By keeping these aspects of memory jogging in mind, an investigating attorney can gain more from potential witnesses and can tell which of them is most likely to possess the best memory at trial.

Some potential witnesses appear to have poor memories; they claim they do not know or remember certain information. Such claims initially should not be taken at face value. What the respondent may really want is more time to think. The best communication strategy for an attorney to use in that situation is to give the person time—say nothing and wait. If silence produces nothing, a lawyer should then say something like, "I realize that it may be difficult answering that question without having some time to think about it. So go right ahead and think for a while."

If still no answer comes, an attorney should avoid pressing further at that moment. Perhaps a more relaxed relationship and some suggestions on recollection sometime in the future can yield more positive results. On occasion, hypnosis has been used to refresh a person's memory.[15] However, a word of caution is in order. Refreshing a potential witness's memory through leading questions has the detrimental effect of reducing the accuracy of the information. Spontaneous testimony is generally more accurate than refreshed testimony, especially for people who are personality oriented, that is, people who are getting and accepting cues from authority figures.[16] Coaching must be done with extreme care!

Perception is another important dimension of witness believability. The more perceptive a witness, the more credible is his or her testimony. Generally, a believable witness is one who *was in a position* to witness the event, *had a reason* to observe the event carefully, and *took overt action* during the event.

Suppose an investigator is working on a case dealing with a hit-and-run accident involving a little girl. The accident took place in a parking lot next to a high-rise apartment building. The investigator is questioning residents, trying to discover eyewitnesses to the accident. Sure enough, the investigator finds an elderly man who saw what happened. But, is he a potentially good witness? *Was he in a position to really see the event?* There are balconies extending over the parking lot from each apartment. He happened to be standing on his third-floor balcony at the time of the accident. *Did he have a reason to observe the event carefully?* The old man said that he saw the little girl playing in the parking lot and he was watching her closely because she reminded him of his granddaughter, whom he had not seen in nearly two years. *Did he take any overt action at the time of the accident?* Yes, when he saw the car approaching, he shouted, "Watch out!" He immediately went downstairs to the scene of the accident after it took place. The potential for keen perception by this witness is excellent because he meets these three essential elements for effective eyewitness testimony.

However, there are other, overlapping elements affecting the perception of witnesses, which apply to our sample witness too. Potential witnesses are more perceptive when they have good vision, hearing, feeling, and judgment.

Vision is an essential element in perception. All of us do not see with the same accuracy. If a person is farsighted or nearsighted, it may be important to know if the person was wearing eyeglasses at the time of a particular incident. In New England at one time, the traffic lights at some intersections showed the green light on the top and the red light on the bottom. A red-green colorblind person might have given incorrect testimony about these traffic signals if asked, "Are you sure the red light was on in the north-south direction?" The answer might incorrectly have been "yes" if the colorblind person believed the top light actually was the red one. Another element in vision is that acuity is reduced with decreased illumination; for instance, it is difficult to notice minute details at dusk or dawn. Still another visual factor is overestimating or underestimating the size of some of the things we see. If a dagger is placed on a table with several pocketknives, the dagger will appear larger than it really is. If a five-foot, one-inch woman is standing with several men, all over six feet in height, she seems much smaller than she really is. Our eyes play tricks on us and affect our perception.

Hearing is an aspect of perception too. Only 50 percent of those from ages seven to eighteen can hear an ordinary conversation from 50 feet away.[17] Younger people are generally better at hearing greater distances than older people. These facts certainly have implications for people who claim to have overheard one person say something to another. Also, estimates of speed based on sound can be unreliable. For instance, motorcycles seem to be going faster than automobiles when we rely on sound as our basis for judgment. Louder noises are equated with faster speeds.

Feeling is a third element of perception. Cold, smooth surfaces can actually feel wet, thereby playing tricks on our perceptive abilities. Tastes vary depending on where in the mouth the taste buds are at work. This fact can be important when investigating something like a poisoning case.

Finally, it is possible for details of an event to be distorted because of poor *judgment*. For instance, sometimes a potential witness has a poor sense of direction. Another may tend to exaggerate length of time, particularly during periods of emotional stress. Our judgment, or inference-making ability, is greatly affected by the mental state we are in at the time events occur. Sometimes we tend to see what we expect to see. If we fear being robbed, innocent bystanders begin to look like thieves. Hence, we report what we guess had taken place, not what actually did take place; we "distort" reality.

What has been said here about perception is not intended to make the reader think that there is such a thing as a true perception. When two automobiles collide, observers seeing the accident do not see the identical collision. Perception is our awareness of a happening, but it is conditioned by varying experiences from the past. Even in the simplest observation, "the mind takes over and adjusts what the senses report to the past perceptual experience in order to maintain that stability of environment on which the human organism flourishes."[18] This mental phenomenon has been demonstrated repeatedly in psychology experiments using a wide range of perception stimuli. What it means is that even though the perceptiveness of witnesses is important for attorneys to evaluate, the trial process is in no way geared to produce in a person the perfect capacity to perceive.

Memory and perception are fragile items. Nevertheless, they are items that investigators need to evaluate when locating evidence from potential witnesses.

Expert Witnesses

During the course of an investigation, attorneys may want to use expert witnesses. "An expert is someone in any field of endeavor who has achieved a high level of education, a great deal of experience, and a high degree of skill enabling him to render an opinion on matters that fall within his expertise."[19] Because expert witnesses can clarify or interpret certain case facts and offer a jury the benefit of their greater knowledge on specific topics, they are called upon to state opinions on relevant matters for which they have special qualifications. For instance, an attorney may want to make use of a firearms identification expert, a handwriting analyst, a clinical psychologist, or a heart surgeon. The opportunities for use of skilled experts are limited only by a trial lawyer's ingenuity.[20]

How does an attorney find the most appropriate expert? A starting point is to contact professional organizations. For instance, who does the local chapter of the American Medical Association recommend as a good physician to testify about contusions and lacerations?[21] Many of the recommended experts will be old pros, that is, persons who basically earn their living by testifying in court. The disadvantages of using experts of that kind is that jurors might be suspicious of their willingness to testify over and over again "for a price." The advantage of using the pros is that they have learned to adapt to trial combat and can express themselves persuasively before juries.

There are three criteria that should be employed in selecting expert witnesses. They are competency in the field, availability and cost, and personal traits.

First, an expert must be *competent in the field*. Competence does not necessarily mean holding several academic degrees. Rather, competence means lots of experience in the area of testimony. The experience should be recent enough to demonstrate that the person is up-to-date in a certain area of claimed specialization. Competency and specialty are closely related. For instance, all physicians cannot testify competently about drug overdoses. Only those physicians who can demonstrate that it is their specialty should be used as experts on that subject matter. Even after deciding that a particular individual is competent, attorneys should check in two further directions. They should corroborate that person's opinions with other recognized experts in the field. They should also examine any and all books or articles written by the potential expert witness to be sure there are no inconsistencies with the person's proposed testimony at the future trial.[22]

Second, an expert should be *readily available at a just cost*. These two factors often go hand in hand. There may not be enough at stake in a case to justify hiring a very expensive expert. After all, many experts are paid several hundred dollars an hour. "It is inadvisable, . . . from the tactical point of view as well as that of economy, . . . to expend sums for expert testimony that are sizable in comparison with the amount of the claim."[23] Also, the more expensive experts may have so many other commitments that when it actually comes time for them to testify, they may not be available to appear in court.

Third, an expert must have *positive personal traits*. This includes a satisfactory appearance, demeanor, personality, and speaking ability. The expert should be neither too old nor too young. The person should display honesty and obvious intelligence. After all, often it is personality, not the details of the testimony, that impresses a jury. After reviewing the literature on the effectiveness of expert witnesses, one author concludes:

Most practical guides to the use of experts stress that the credibility of an expert witness is the crucial element in determining success. Credibility is sometimes referred to as ethos or even prestige. It is a term which describes the listener's image of the speaker. In the courtroom, the juror's opinion of a witness appears to be the most important element in the decision to believe that witness instead of another.[24]

In one study of the specific factors of credibility for expert witnesses, likability appeared to be the most important dimension.[25] Experts who are snide, arrogant, patronizing, unclear, or defensive lack credibility and should be replaced by those with more positive and likable personal characteristics. Furthermore, experts should be willing to defend their opinions under cross-examination. Cross-examination of expert witnesses frequently focuses on having them qualify their opinions. Chosen experts cannot be passive and compromising at this point in a trial. They must be willing to stand on their own opinions without hesitation.

After experts are chosen, close communication should be maintained with those persons by the attorney as trial preparation continues. Experts should be informed about the lawsuit in detail. The attorney should discover how they feel about the case. (Naturally, experts should believe in it, or else they could cave in under cross-examination.) Practice in direct-examination questioning with experts is always in order, and particular attention should be given to helping experts use lay language in their answers. The lawyer, too, must become knowledgeable in the area in which the expert witnesses will testify. In this sense, an expert becomes a kind of superparalegal to an attorney. Experts can educate a lawyer by explaining technical information, suggesting literature to be read, analyzing and evaluating certain case facts, framing technical interrogatories, interpreting documents produced during discovery, and evaluating complex settlement proposals. This means that clear and close communication networks must be established between attorneys and their experts. As new and relevant information surfaces, both the expert and the lawyer should be aware of it. In other words, expert witnesses and attorneys serve as advisors to each other during pretrial preparation.

Organizing the Case

As investigation continues, a system for processing the case must be established. Getting a case together is like driving cattle into a pen. It begins with a client or case file, which contains pertinent information (e.g., court papers, records of evidence, attorney notes and correspondence, and a checklist of tasks to perform). In time, the paperwork may grow to the point of requiring a more systematic and orderly filing system. The day of the stereotypical lawyer groping through his or her legal pad and briefcase for essential information is long gone, or should be.

Eventually, a trial notebook containing easily accessible case records is prepared. It becomes a blueprint for presentation—a basic organizing and indexing tool for trying a legal case. It is usually in a three-ring binder with separator tabs to categorize the material efficiently and meaningfully for the attorney. Some attorneys have started to use computer programs to assemble these notebooks. A sample trial notebook can be found in Appendix A. This is not a magic model notebook; it is but one logical way to organize and retrieve information. Each notebook should be custom-made to fit particular needs.

A well-polished trial notebook is called the *trial brief.* This polished final product can be an excellent confidence builder for the neophyte lawyer or for one who does not try cases very often. It gives the attorney a feeling of being fully prepared when he or she walks into court.[26] "Used properly, the notebook should be one of the few things in front of the lawyer in the courtroom."[27] A notebook reduces clutter and causes an attorney to communicate a certain degree of professionalism to the judge and the jury.

PLEADINGS

Pleadings are a vehicle by which parties in civil litigation attempt to isolate the precise and real questions in dispute before trial. They are an attempt to exclude irrelevancies which have no bearing on what is dividing the conflicting parties. There are three basic parts to the pleadings. They are the *complaint* filed by the plaintiff, an *answer* filed by the defendant, and a *reply,* filed also by the plaintiff. This exchange of information, when handled orally in court, is done by a judge questioning the two sides. Pleadings can also be an exchange of written statements in advance of a hearing with a judge. At trial, only those issues outlined in the pleadings are permitted to surface. For example, a plaintiff pleads property damage to his car and presents supporting facts. At trial, the same plaintiff cannot bring up the matter of his broken ankle, since that was not an issue in the pleadings. However, if both issues (the broken ankle and property damage) are entered in the pleadings, both of

them (or just one of them) may be introduced at trial.

Let us analyze each of the three parts of the pleadings in greater depth. The written complaint, once filed with the court, initiates a lawsuit. Shortly thereafter, a court clerk issues a summons to the defendant, which requires that person to answer the complaint within a specified period of time. The complaint must be crisp and to the point. "In a field like litigation where imponderables abound, a good first impression is invaluable. . . . 'Bull's-eye' pleading lets the court instantly grasp" an attorney's position.[28] The complaint should, furthermore, be arranged in logical order. As an illustration, take the following automobile accident case. In the first paragraph, the complaint says that Defendant X rear-ended Plaintiff Y about three weeks ago at Mason Street and Dixon Avenue at 3:13 P.M. In the second paragraph is an allegation of negligence, noting the errant behavior of Defendant X. It accuses him of excessive speed and of negligent failure to avoid the accident. In paragraph 3 is a list of injuries of Plaintiff Y, which include fractured bones, torn muscles, a dislocated shoulder, a sprained ankle, and numerous abrasions and lacerations. Anguish of mind is also mentioned. The claimed result is lost earnings and substantial medical expenses in the past and in the future. The final paragraph is a request for a remedy—$80,000.[29]

The answer is the defendant's response to the plaintiff. An answer may contain either a denial of each allegation, and possibly a statement of counterclaim,[30] or an admission of what happened with a denial that the plaintiff is entitled to a remedy, perhaps because defense facts are asserted. The first answer is an issue of fact (e.g., what happened); the second answer is an issue of law (e.g., what ought to be done). If no answer is provided, a court can declare judgment by default and demand that the plaintiff be guaranteed relief.

The reply is required when the court upholds a defendant's motion for such a response from the plaintiff. Tactically, it is wise for a defendant to make such a request. It can give a defendant added information about the plaintiff's strategy. In a reply, the plaintiff responds to the denial, counterclaim, or refutation of remedy from the defendant. This ends the pleadings unless they need subsequent amending in some way by either side.

Generally speaking, pleadings should be filed by a plaintiff after (1) several potential witnesses have been investigated and statements from them have been obtained, (2) substantive law questions have been researched so that a reasonable theory for the case has been formed, and (3) some attempt has been made to settle the claim.[31] Once these steps have been completed and the pleadings have been filed, the pleadings have the advantage of allowing each side to know more about their opposition. Learning more about the other side then allows an attorney to maneuver for position. It may also facilitate negotiation.

The weaknesses of pleadings unfortunately seem to be greater than their strengths. If a plaintiff is certain of his or her proof, the complaint can be very specific. However, in most cases, the complaint lacks specificity. Little information is revealed. Plaintiffs, in order to be sure of securing something from their cases, file complaints as broad as possible. This broadness makes the "real complaint" obscure. Largely because of this deficiency, the importance of formal pleadings has substantially decreased over the years. Pleadings have not fulfilled their main goal, which was to clarify and narrow the issues in a case.

In the middle and late 1800s, an attempt was made to strengthen pleadings. The complaint, the answer, and the reply were accompanied by specific questions and requests for documents to be answered by the other side. These questions and requests were called *in-terrogatories*. The answers and documents were subpoenaed by the court under what was called a *bill of discovery*. Although this procedure encouraged greater information sharing, it was very time-consuming, mainly because attorneys had to prove to the court in each instance that certain information from the other side was vital to their case. Gradually, the process of "discovering" information from the other side became less restricted and formal. This is when the pleadings were supplemented by discovery.

DISCOVERY

Because pleadings had become impotent, the first legislative action to promote discovery was in Texas in 1907. Shortly thereafter, it rapidly expanded to other states. In response to pressure from bar associations across the United States, the process of discovery was developed through a revision of the Federal Rules of Civil Procedure in 1938 and is now common in virtually all court jurisdictions.

Discovery is a procedure that has been designed to enable both sides to obtain information from each other during a pretrial investigation. It is supposed to reduce the sporting theory of justice by promoting full disclosure rather than surprise or trial by ambush. If it were to operate perfectly, both parties would have the same opportunities and capacities for investigation and equal facilities for producing all necessary discoverable material.

What is open to discovery? The answer, according to Federal Rule 26 is, essentially, any information that is not privileged and that is "relevant to the subject matter involved in the pending action."[32] "Relevant" does not mean "admissible as evidence." Even inadmissible matter may be obtained if it might lead to the possible discovery of admissible evidence.[33] The information sought does not have to be relevant to the issues, but rather "to the subject matter." After all, the issues defined by the pleadings might later be amended. It can easily be seen, then, that the scope of discovery is quite broad. If an attorney is refused information from the other side, he or she can ask the court to rule whether or not it is discoverable. In such cases, the burden of persuasion rests on the party trying to limit discovery.

Today, no lawyer, unless the case is quite minor, would think of preparing for trial without making use of discovery. It would be like a physician beginning major bone surgery without looking at X rays first. But proper timing of discovery is important. What time is best? "Most lawyers act instinctively. They want to beat their opponents to the draw. . . . Their desire arises in part from wishing to show clients their alertness and aggressiveness."[34] However, this may not be a good idea. Counsel should wait to be sure they are really ready to inquire about the other side's case before starting discovery.

There are five specific and formal discovery techniques: depositions, interrogatories, requests for the production of documents, requests for physical or mental examinations, and requests for admission. "As a painter uses a mix of colors in proper proportion for a desired effect, an attorney should use a mix of discovery methods as well, in a sequence, at a time, and to whatever permitted extent profits a case."[35] Counsel should use all five discovery methods in every civil suit unless (a) the suit is one of the few specialized actions for which the methods are not authorized (i.e., admiralty, bankruptcy, and copyright), or (b) it is obvious that no possible benefit can come from the use of one or more of the particular techniques.

Depositions

Discovery depositions, covered by Federal Rule 30, are used more frequently than any other discovery device.[36] They should be taken early in the discovery process, preferably as soon as possible after a case is filed.[37] The purpose of a discovery deposition "is to determine from the witness all the facts which he may have in his possession which may assist the trial lawyer in the preparation and settlement or trial of his lawsuit."[38] Specifically, the advantages of depositions are that they (1) assist a lawyer in the investigation and preparation of the case for trial, (2) assist a lawyer in evaluating the case for settlement negotiations, (3) are used to gain information as substantive proof, for admissions, or for impeachment during a trial, and (4) are a remarkably flexible discovery technique.

The first advantage of depositions is that they greatly assist a lawyer when investigating and preparing a case for trial. The information obtained eliminates or greatly reduces the chance for surprise at trial. Information discovered is also often used for additional investigation. For example, if a plaintiff-deponent says that she was confined to home and unable to drive her car for three months after an accident, the questioning attorney may want to find witnesses who can testify to the contrary.

A second advantage of depositions is that they help settlement negotiations. Depositions allow both sides to measure their own and their opponent's strengths and weaknesses. Sometimes, counsel knows of certain weaknesses in the testimony of one of his or her witnesses and will, as a result, seek to negotiate before the deposition of that witness is taken. Such opportunities for evaluation often lead to more intensified bargaining. "Indeed, many pretrial settlements are a direct result of the deposition discovery procedure."[39]

Third, should a case go to trial, the deposition helps counsel prepare strategies for cross-examining the other side's witnesses. Part or all of the deposition can be admitted as evidence at the time of the trial. When a witness's testimony on the stand conflicts with testimony during a deposition, "the pertinent portion of his deposition can be read to him on cross-examination for the purpose of discrediting and impeaching him because of the discrepancy."[40] Another way the taking of an oral deposition can help lawyers is that it gives them an opportunity to see and appraise a particular witness in a close approximation of a cross-examination session. Will this witness be evasive or get angry? Does this witness have "jury appeal"? Answering these kinds of questions helps an attorney prepare a certain strategy for each witness who deposes.

The fourth advantage of depositions is the flexibility they offer as a discovery technique. Questions can be rephrased on the spot. Deponents have trouble getting by with incomplete or evasive replies. Answers to questions open up new areas of inquiry, which can be pursued immediately. In other words, a lawyer can alter a line of questioning quickly according to the information he or she is getting at the time.

Of course, discovery depositions are not always such a useful technique. There are times when they should not be taken. When it is obvious that an opponent is preparing for negotiation rather than trial, depositions from the other side's witnesses may prove unnecessary. When a deponent lives far away, the cost might be too great compared with the need for the information that person possesses. If an attorney requests a deposition from a witness who is elderly or gravely ill and the deposition is audiotaped or videotaped, sympathy for the deponent can actually work for the other side if this deposition is heard or seen in court. If a deponent would become better educated by having what is essentially a practice session in cross-examination, it might be best to waive the deposition, although examining attorneys can always choose to confine their questioning to those aspects which will not educate the opponent. Finally, depositions are not always the best

strategy for the less-than-fluent lawyer, inasmuch as every sound uttered is recorded by the court reporter. Unnecessary and frequent "ah" or "uh" sounds reflect negatively on attorneys when their depositions are read in open court at a later time.

Generally, however, depositions are a splended discovery technique, and their advantages outweigh their disadvantages. The broad scope and relatively informal atmosphere of a deposition provide lawyers with an opportunity to probe a deponent's knowledge of the facts and circumstances of the litigation in great detail and depth. Given this nearly ideal opportunity for communication and information exchange, let us look at depositions more closely by posing seven inquiries about them.

How should a deposition start? The atmosphere should be casual and relaxed. In such an atmosphere, the deponent is likely to be less guarded. Depositions are frequently taken at an attorney's office or in a room in the courthouse. Some believe that "the atmosphere of the courtroom . . . is conducive to less bickering between counsel than a room in a law office."[41] Both counsel are present, and the examining lawyer who is seeking information from the other side's witness begins with the question "The usual stipulations, Counsel?" These usually agreed-upon stipulations are that the opposing attorney may advise a witness not to answer certain questions, that objections to certain questions may be raised, that the statement is to be transcribed in writing by a certified reporter, and that even if the witness, hereafter called the deponent, does not sign the deposition, it may still be used later with the same force and effect as if it had been signed.[42] A brief opening statement and some questions to put the deponent at ease provide a good start. Here is an example:

Lawyer: Good morning, Mr. Phillips. My name is Perry Mason, I am with the law firm representing Ms. Kraft. Has Mr. Bond, attorney for your insurance company, explained what a deposition is all about?

Deponent: Yes.

Lawyer: Good. I just have a few preliminary matters to discuss with you before I ask some questions. First, I'd like you to feel comfortable and be relaxed. I expect we'll be here for several hours, and if at any time you would like to take a break, please let me know. OK?

Deponent: Sure.

Lawyer: As Mr. Bond has probably advised you, I am going to ask you some questions about the lawsuit Ms. Kraft has filed against the insurance company. If any of my questions are unclear to you, please tell me and I will ask them again. All right?

Deponent: Yes.

Lawyer: Ms. Turner, the court reporter, will take down both the questions I ask and the answers you give, as well as any discussion I might have with Mr. Bond. Later this will all be transcribed into a booklet, which you will have a chance to read and correct. Do you understand?

Deponent: Yes.

Lawyer: Now, is there anything that prevents you from answering my questions accurately and completely today?

Deponent: I don't think so.

Lawyer: Good, then let's begin.

How should counsel prepare for a deposition? It is, of course, obvious that a lawyer taking a deposition needs to prepare certain lines of inquiry in advance. The checklist should be based on the goals of that particular deposition. Initially at the deposition background data on the deponent are requested. After this initial information is obtained, counsel should follow an outline of the general topics and key points to be covered.[43] The most important questions should be written out in advance, particularly those an attorney may want to have read aloud during a trial.[44] The

outline will prevent the proceeding from becoming disjointed and, hence, less useful. It will also allow the questioner to remain alert and perceptive because, while listening to one answer, he or she will not have to be devising the next question. Although the ideal outline covers all relevant topics in a certain sequence, it must be structurally flexible to allow a lawyer to explore unexpected areas that will inevitably surface during the course of the examination.

In addition to following a general agenda for the deposition, counsel should review the following questioning techniques and strategies in order to get maximum results. First, broad, open questions should be used extensively. They permit storytelling, which may in turn uncover testimony harmful to the opposition. Second, deponents who give rambling answers should not be cut off. Volunteered information could be quite beneficial. Loquacious deponents may say things to their own side's discredit.[45] If counsel pauses frequently, some deponents cannot stand silence and will fill the void with an expansion on an answer. Third, specific follow-up questions should be asked to pin down a deponent to a particular position and to obtain admissions. This should be done only after a witness has more or less finished with a topic. At that time, counsel should summarize the topic and then ask a question that calls for a yes or no answer, such as, "Do you agree?" Fourth, follow-up questions should be avoided after favorable responses have been provided. Further questioning on a point gives a deponent an opportunity to realize what he or she has said and then to cloud the earlier answer or alter it in some way. This dilutes the reply the attorney originally wanted and got.[46] Fifth, when a deponent gives an evasive answer, the question should be repeated persistently until a responsive reply is given.[47] Sixth, each topic should be exhausted before questioning moves on to the next. Successful depositions unfold logically, not erratically. The only reason it might be necessary to intentionally disorganize an examination is to throw off balance a deponent who is evasive or distorting the facts.[48] Seventh, wrap-up questions should be asked. As each topic area is exhausted, an attorney should ask, "Is that all?" A deponent should not be left with additional testimony that might come up only at the trial.

What is an appropriate demeanor for the attorney? Although there is no single right manner for conducting a deposition, a lawyer must generally employ certain behaviors that have proven profitable to others.

☐ *Sit in a strategic location.* Depositions are preferably taken around a table. To psychologically create an impression of dominance, the deposing counsel should sit at the head of the table opposite the deponent. Associates or paralegals who provide counsel with assistance during the deposition should sit on either side of the deponent to further intimidate the witness.[49]

☐ *Watch for nonverbal cues from the deponent.* For instance, if the deponent is worried about what he is saying, there may be a sudden shift of eyes, change in voice, shift in seating position, or nervous gesture, such as putting a hand to the face. Humans find it very difficult to conceal tension.[50]

☐ *Listen carefully.* Counsel often become preoccupied with their own questions instead of with the deponent's answers. This is not a good idea. Each answer must be understood fully by the examiner. An attorney cannot really know whether a deponent has answered a question until the content of that answer has been assimilated.

☐ *Generally adopt an easygoing and courteous manner.* At the beginning and perhaps throughout a deposition, everyone should be treated with respect. This induces the deponent to open up and talk freely, and it is the purpose of a discovery deposition to get the deponent to say as much as possible.

The exception is when the deponent remains uncooperative and evasive. When that occurs, counsel may want to begin leading the deponent at a rapid pace, demanding answers rather than just asking for them.

☐ *Be aware of physical appearance.* Making a good impression on the opposition is important. Counsel should appear at a deposition dressed as he or she would expect to dress when going to trial. At the same time, an attorney wants to keep the atmosphere as relaxed and informal as possible because "a relaxed witness is more likely to volunteer information and is less likely to be on guard."[51] Suggesting that people take off their jackets and offering them coffee or a cola creates an appropriate environment for the questioner.

How should the deponent prepare for a deposition? Although it is strongly advisable, unfortunately it is not common to find attorneys preparing their own witnesses for depositions.[52] Prior to deposition, lawyers should properly instruct their witnesses just as though they are getting ready to testify in court. (A discussion of witness preparation for court is found in Chapter 9.) Each major point of the anticipated deposition should be reviewed. Also, because the deponent must make a favorable impression, he or she should dress as if in court, think through all answers carefully, always tell the truth, never exaggerate, remain polite, avoid anger, not be afraid, give concise replies, never volunteer information unless it is specifically asked for, admit honest deficiencies in knowledge, and ask for explanation of questions that are not understood. Counsel must coach a deponent in all of these areas. Perhaps a mock deposition can be conducted in which the attorney asks potentially harmful questions and then directs the deponent toward favorable responses.[53] By doing so, the attorney will also have an opportunity to see how that deponent might stand up under cross-examination in a trial. Appendix B consists of a checklist of items a lawyer may wish to go over as he or she prepares someone for a deposition.[54]

How can cross-examination and objections be used effectively during a deposition? Cross-examination is conducted by the lawyer whose own witness is serving as the deponent.[55] The purpose of cross-examination is to correct any errors in the testimony of a deponent who has testified mistakenly. In other words, this is an attorney's opportunity to clear up errors in his or her deponent's answers. Cross-examination is also an opportunity to "clarify some part of the witness' testimony because it is misleading in the incomplete form,"[56] particularly when that deponent is expected to testify in the forthcoming trial. However, rarely will it be to a lawyer's advantage to ask too many questions of his or her own witness when a deposition is being taken by an adversary.[57]

Objections may be made by either side during a deposition. The examining attorney may want to object to leading questions during cross-examination. For example, assume that a deponent has been examined by the opposing lawyer and is now being questioned by counsel representing the side for which the deponent is testifying. This question is asked: "Did you make any attempt to kick Mr. Jones in the shins?" This is a blatant leading question, and an objection should be voiced. Conversely, when the deponent's attorney finds the form of a certain question improper, the examining counsel "should withdraw the question and substitute a question in a form which is not objectionable"[58] if he or she thinks the objection is valid. If the questioning attorney thinks the objection is invalid, he or she should request that the deponent be allowed to answer and that the objecting attorney later ask the court to rule. If the request is denied and the deponent is advised not to answer the question,[59] the examiner can go to court for a ruling. This is done after the com-

pletion of the entire examination.[60] In addition to form, objections can also be made to requests for privileged (e.g., "That's what your husband told you, wasn't it?") or irrelevant (e.g., "Do you generally win or lose at the racetrack?") information. Attorneys hearing objections from opposing counsel should ask them to state the grounds for the objections unless they are obvious. Such an explanation either helps the attorney correct the deficient question, thereby eliminating the objection, or reveals that the objection lacks merit.[61]

When should attorneys allow their deponents to answer objectionable questions, and when should they instruct deponents to remain silent? Generally, answers should be allowed. Too many refusals may appear to be obstructionistic. After all, an objection to having the answer read to a jury can always be raised at trial. The only time it may be wise not to allow a deponent to answer a question is when a case "will be materially damaged by the mere disclosure of a fact"[62] that is irrelevant or privileged.

How often should objections be raised? In case of the slightest doubt about the question, a lawyer should voice an objection. Once on the record, the objection is visible. So an attorney should be reasonably liberal about raising objections during a discovery deposition.

How should a deposition be ended? Near the end of a deposition, the questioning lawyer should ask the deponent if he or she understood all the questions. If the answer is no, some questions should be rephrased or asked again. The lawyer should then ask if there are any answers the deponent would like to modify. Normally, the weary deponent will not be able to think of any corrections and will therefore answer in the negative.[63] After the deposition is typed, the deponent is then asked to sign a transcribed copy of the questions and answers. This transcript may later be read into the record of a trial.

Should the signature be waived? Probably not, although "the parties by stipulation frequently waive the formalities of authenticating . . . depositions,"[64] especially when they feel comfortable with the particular court reporter who was present at the time. Without a waiver, the transcript can always be read and corrected by a deponent with the advice of his or her counsel. Furthermore, whether it is signed or not, "it may be used with the same force and effect as though it had been read, corrected, and signed."[65] So it is usually good advice for a deponent to check a transcript with care and sign it.

Should depositions be taped? Depositions can be audiotaped or videotaped. Rule 30(b)(4) provides that an application may be made to the court for recording a deposition by nonstenographic means. Since taped depositions are become more and more common, considerable attention will be given here to their use. Generally, they are used when (a) a deponent is unable to attend a trial in person, (b) counsel wants to study the demeanor of a deponent (e.g., watch for subtle signs of uncertainty or lying), or (c) it is easier for a lawyer to impeach a witness by showing a jury his or her demeanor during the deposition.[66]

Videotaping usually is conducted in a studio or an office. Lawyers for both sides are present, along with the witness to be questioned and a film crew.[67] As the witness testifies, a time-date digital clock electronically superimposed on the picture shows the year, month, day, hour, minute, and second. Whenever an attorney makes an objection, the television technician logs the time. A judge who later reviews the tape can use those times to find the objections and rule on them.[68] Lawyers proceed with the deposition without knowing which way a judge will rule. If the objection is based on the relevance of a question, then the attorney must first assume that the judge sustained the objection, and then later assume that the judge over-

ruled the objection and again proceed. The judge can later delete from the tape any questions and answers based on sustained objections so that the jury will never see or hear the question, answer, or objection. However, if an objection is overruled, the jury sees the question and answer, but the objection is deleted.[69] In case of an appeal, the original tape is kept intact and stored.

Videotaped depositions have not only been used for discovery purposes, but also for putting together complete trials. The ground-breaking article on the videotape trial was written with remarkable prescience in 1970 by Alan E. Morrill. He said, "One day very soon now, a courtroom somewhere in this illustrious land will introduce a sweeping change in the present system of trial by jury. . . . A jury will have decided the issues of a lawsuit by merely viewing and hearing the entire proceedings of a trial on a television screen."[70] He was right. The first known instance of a prerecorded videotape trial from depositions (PRVTT) took place in the civil case of *McCall v. Clemons* before the Honorable James L. McCrystal in Sandusky (Erie County), Ohio, on November 18, 1971.[71] In July of the following year, the Ohio legislature approved Civil Rule 40, which granted official sanction to the use of PRVTT throughout the state. Other states were soon to follow.[72] While the majority of PRVTT cases have been civil, some states have actually granted authority for this use of television in criminal cases as well.[73] Today, few trials are conducted entirely by use of videotaped testimony, as they are in Judge McCrystal's court. However, thousands upon thousands of videotaped depositions are in use nationwide.[74]

Since the PRVTT was first used, there has been steady opposition to it. Kosky offers this warning: "With the PRVTT, the legal profession finds itself faced with a total elimination of the traditional Anglo-Saxon trial and its replacement by essentially a series of edited tapes of depositions played to a jury. This is a fundamental change of the first order which brings with it many ramifications."[75] Five objections to having a jury view all or part of a trial on videotape are noted. First, there is the matter of cost. Costs of videotaping testimony vary considerably but can run to several thousand dollars an hour, giving the party with greater financial ability an unfair advantage.[76] Second, there are certain technical problems when videotaped depositions are presented in court. Acoustical conditions during taping may make the voice on tape difficult to hear or understand at times. Likewise, poor acoustics in the courtroom may also make the televised message difficult to comprehend. A siren, a person's coughing, and other extraneous noise can interfere with the taping.

Third, there are potential psychological concerns regarding PRVTT. For instance, perceived witness credibility (trustworthiness and sociability) is somewhat higher with televised depositions than with live presentations.[77] As a result, if some testimony is videotaped and some testimony is not videotaped, the status of the videotaped sources may be markedly enhanced by their having appeared on the television screen. As Miller and Fontes note, "The fact that the testimony has been committed to tape may confer it a disproportionate persuasive advantage, particularly if jurors interpret the deviation as arising from the added importance of the witness."[78] Is this fair to a live witness?

Other psychological concerns that may arise are as follows: "How much and how well can they [the jurors] remember and sift through what is presented to them, and how does this compare with their memories and analytic capabilities when the same facts are presented to them in a live trial format? . . . How does the presentation of legal material on videotape affect the level and quality of emotional arousal, particularly when compared with the effects of presenting the same material during a live trial? . . . Do the com-

bined cognitive-emotional changes (if any) associated with the presentation of videotape material lead to changes in the validity of the jurors' judgment?"[79] To partially answer these questions, one study discovered that jurors viewing the same testimony retain slightly more of the information communicated to them when they view witnesses on black-and-white television sets than when they view witnesses on color sets.[80] Why? Perhaps color television evokes a richer visual stimulus field and is associated with entertainment rather than education. Perhaps, also, a greater cognitive effort is required to watch black-and-white television than to watch color television. After all, "color videotape is more realistic [and] . . . perhaps this greater realism places fewer cognitive demands on jurors, culminating in a state of reduced stimulation that could explain the lower amount of information retention."[81] Even though jurors are more attentive to black-and-white images than they are to color images, witnesses appear more credible when they appear on color screens than when they appear on black-and-white screens. No matter whether the witness is highly credible or low in credibility, the credibility level overall increases on color television over the same image on black-and-white television,[82] although there is no discernible difference in verdicts or in damages awarded between black-and-white and color PRVTT.[83] Finally, expert witnesses on color television are more credible (i.e., have higher status) than expert witnesses giving their testimony live.[84]

Fourth, there are alleged problems regarding the impact television sets have on the dignified atmosphere of the courtroom. Lay jurors are used to watching television for entertainment. They bring to court their media experiences—watching soap operas, westerns, and gangster movies. Will they view the PRVTT in the same manner, or will they view the television screen with the same seriousness of mind with which they view the live witness in the stand? Can the jury fully separate watching television as entertainment from watching television as reality? We do not know "what unconscious forces might be at work affecting our judgment when we see a . . . trial in the form of a television program or movie."[85]

Fifth, there may be constitutional problems with a PRVTT, none of which have been tested yet. Most of these problems deal with PRVTTs in criminal cases rather than in civil cases. The Sixth Amendment gives defendants the right to confront witnesses against themselves in a court of law in order to observe and insure the cross-examination of those witnesses. However, when videotaped depositions are taken, the accused is not present.[86] Must a direct confrontation take place live and in front of a jury? So far, the courts have answered negatively.[87] Yet, Doret states, "The right to be present is perhaps the most serious constitutional obstacle to the application, to criminal proceedings, of video recording."[88] Furthermore, the jury views an edited tape with all disputes and procedural questions resolved. This puts considerable power in the hands of the judiciary. Armstrong writes, "By concealing court rulings and acts from the public, videotape . . . may contribute to public skepticism of judicial processes."[89]

In addition, the Fourteenth Amendment ensures the right to a fair trial. However, if evidence is distorted as the camera lens becomes the jurors' eyes, a fair trial might be jeopardized. In moving from one medium to another, editorializing always occurs.[90] In a PRVTT, the jury's view is restricted to what the camera has recorded. Because the jury can no longer look freely at the entire setting, either some nonverbal information may not be communicated at all and subtle nuances may be missed, or nonverbal cues that are on the screen may be magnified out of propor-

tion. The television camera is, after all, a highly selective instrument. Kaminski and Miller discovered that strong witnesses (fluent, assertive, and attentive) appeared most qualified to testify (authoritative) when seen in a close-up shot, whereas weak witnesses (uncertain, hesitant, fumbling, and inattentive) got their lowest ratings with the close-up shot, although long shots are bad, too, if they reveal a lack of composure.[91] For those who appear on the screen from the shoulders up, their nonverbal (particularly facial) cues are magnified greatly over the same cues in a live trial. Meanwhile, many nonverbal cues are, in fact, missing from the video deposition because they are outside the camera's field of view.[92] So the message is altered insofar as there is increased focus on nonverbal communication when television is the medium. So far, however, the courts have rejected such claims based on the Fourteenth Amendment.[93]

All is not so bleak with the PRVTT; it has its good points too. First, witnesses can testify at their own convenience inasmuch as the videotaping can be scheduled around definite appointments. Witnesses called to court to offer live testimony often have to waste hours, days, or weeks waiting to be called to the stand. The unpredictable schedule of the courtroom frequently draws cases out longer than expected. So lawyers cannot tell witnesses with any precision what time or even what day they will be testifying in court. For someone like a physician who is to testify, time is too precious to waste. Both witnesses and lawyers going to trial have previous professional commitments, vacations, relocations, or illnesses. A witness "will certainly be more cooperative when he can appear before the camera at a time that does not interfere with his personal activities, rather than being unexpectedly dragged from his job at a most inconvenient time by threat of subpoena."[94] A PRVTT solves scheduling problems and may even prevent the loss of some witnesses that might be unable to attend a courtroom trial.

Second, an impromptu slip of the tongue that could prejudice a live trial can be corrected in a videotaped deposition. The lawyer or witness who contaminates the trial by saying something inappropriate can create grounds for a new trial. Retrials are time-consuming and expensive. Millions of dollars have been lost due to the immaterial, irrelevant, or incompetent remark that plagues trials. Even though a trial judge can admonish a jury to disregard contaminating remarks, the admonishment does not always reduce the damage done. Editing such inadvertent remarks for a PRVTT enables a purer presentation of evidence to the jury.[95]

Third, witnesses are sharper in a PRVTT than they are in a live trial. Several jurisdictions have considerable court backlogs; witnesses have been known to wait for five or six years after an event to testify.[96] Naturally, a witness's memory and perception diminishes over time. For a PRVTT the lawyers can take a deposition from a witness shortly after an event occurs. The videotape sitting on a shelf somewhere will retain a lot more information from that witness than if the same person is asked to have the power of recall about an event several years later. In addition, research has shown that witnesses do not appear more nervous or experience greater stress with a television camera in front of them than they do in a live setting.[97] There are no noticeable differences in their responsiveness or decisiveness in either setting.[98] One study even found that witnesses remembered more specific details and fewer wrong details in the televised condition than in the nontelevised condition.[99]

Fourth, court time is saved. For example, in Judge McCrystal's Erie County court, a dual docket is used. The judge conducts a live trial while he has a jury in another room viewing a completely videotaped trial. The judge can al-ways be working on two trials at once. Roughly 30 percent of Erie County's trials are now PRVTTs.[100] The PRVTT jury hears a videotaped trial, which is much shorter than a live trial inasmuch as counsel objections, bench conferences, and recesses are eliminated. McCrystal says that a trial can be conducted in one-half or one-third less time.[101] From 1974 to 1977, when the dual-docket system was fully implemented in McCrystal's court, with filings remaining constant, the backlog of civil cases was reduced 22 percent.[102] Waiting time for pending cases was reduced to 13 months from 23 months.[103] A recent survey of 630 district and circuit court judges and 800 trial attorneys showed that the PRVTT results in important time savings to parties, judges, jurors, witnesses, and attorneys alike.[104] In addition, if a jury is unable to come to a decision in a case, another jury can view the same tape without rescheduling and reassembling all the trial participants.[105]

These, then, are the advantages of the PRVTT. In one study, 96 percent of the jurors who watched videotaped testimonies said they were satisfied with the process.[106] In another study, "numerous jurors . . . expressed enthusiasm for the potential of videotape . . . and indicated that in litigation of their own, they would prefer a videotaped to a live trial."[107] A National Bureau of Standards survey questioned 178 jurors who served in both kinds of civil trials, and 61 percent of them said they preferred a videotaped trial.[108] Likewise, jurors in Ohio who have served in both PRVTTs and live trials found the PRVTT less confusing, less emotionally involving, and legally more sound with respect to inadmissible evidence.[109] Yet, arguments continue to be waged as to whether these advantages outweigh the disadvantages noted earlier. The debate over videotaped depositions will probably continue for a long time to come, but there is no doubt that televised testimony will be an increasingly common courtroom phenomenon.[110]

Much has been said here about depositions, because they are the most widely used discovery device. But they are not the only way for an attorney to learn about the other side. Let us go on to consider the remaining discovery techniques that are available.

Interrogatories

Rule 33 authorizes sending adverse parties written interrogatories at any time as long as they are within the bounds of reasonableness.[111] A written interrogatory consists of a question about facts and contentions related to a particular suit (e.g., "Please state by brand name each drug prescribed by Dr. Howell for Carolyn Maxwell during the period from June 1, 1987, to October 30, 1987"). The questions should be pertinent, clear, and precise, not sweeping (e.g., "Tell me all you know about a particular incident"). In fact, courts will not allow extensive and burdensome interrogatories to be used.[112]

Answers are returned to the lawyer seeking information, and they are offered in writing under oath. If the answers are incomplete and evasive, the questioning attorney can get a court order for a better reply. Just as depositions, they may later be used as trial evidence.[113] Unless it is stipulated otherwise, answers should be returned to the other side in roughly two to six weeks. Of course, specific objections to certain questions or requests for extensions in providing answers can always be filed with the court.

Written interrogatories are used to supplement depositions. It is a good idea to combine these two discovery techniques. Interrogatories can follow up on certain answers obtained during depositions. For instance, certain additional information, such as the identity of people who know relevant facts, information about an expert's credentials, or detailed financial information such as income and sales, may not have been available at the time of the deposition and can be obtained

later through the use of interrogatories. In this way, interrogatories enhance precision in the discovery process. Furthermore, an interrogatory is a much less expensive form of discovery than engaging in another oral deposition to get the same information. After all, there are no transportation or court reporter costs with an interrogatory.

Some attorneys also use interrogatories before depositions because they feel that the written answers to the interrogatories help them better prepare deposition questions. "Many trial specialists feel that interrogatories should be routinely filed, as soon as permitted by the rules, in order to ascertain the identity and location of individuals who should be subsequently deposed. . . ."[114] Appendix C offers sample written interrogatories used for that purpose.

Generally, however, oral depositions are better than written interrogatories in discovery, because a lawyer is able to immediately and spontaneously follow up on unclear or incomplete answers. A lawyer can also watch a deponent's demeanor and nonverbal cues, which obviously are not a part of the interrogatory method. Furthermore, since the answers to interrogatories usually are drafted by an opposing attorney, it is far more difficult to obtain damaging statements from an adverse party. " . . . questions that call for . . . long narrative answers which are probably . . . prepared by counsel are far better suited for depositions."[115]

Production of Documents

Rule 34 allows a party to inspect documents and other physical objects in the possession of an adversary.[116] However, this rule does not permit free invasion of an opponent's files. If necessary, a court-orderd subpoena is issued for a desired document, and an adversary has 30 days to respond to the subpoena. Actually, most inspections and copying of documents are done simply by informal agreements between the opposing attorneys. Many of these agreements occur after a witness has referred to a particular document during an oral deposition, at which time "the interrogating lawyer may simply make an oral request on the record that the document be produced."[117]

Requests for Physical or Mental Examinations

Rule 35 allows a court to order a physical or mental examination if a person's physical or mental condition is in question. "Good cause" must be demonstrated to get this information from the other side, although most examinations are done by informal agreement between the attorneys and never go through court. For instance, it is common for a defendant in a personal injury case to require a medical examination of the plaintiff. This is generally agreed to by the plaintiff because, after all, he or she should have nothing to hide. The examining physician may be court ordered—selected by neither the plaintiff nor the defendant—or the attorney requesting an examination can use one of his or her own doctors. If the attorney chooses the physician, it is best to avoid a biased doctor, because that person's bias can easily be exposed at trial; an objective and highly qualified specialist is best. In all cases, the examined party has the right to receive a copy of the physician's report.

Requests for Admission

Rule 36 allows a request of the other party to admit that certain case facts (not opinions) are genuine and not in dispute. For example, in a slip-and-fall (on some stairs) case, a plaintiff's attorney may ask the defense attorney to admit that no repairs had been made to the stairs since they were originally built. If there is no adverse reply or request for an extension of time within 30 days, it is assumed that the information is "admitted," that is, agreed to

by both sides. Admissions may be presented at trial as evidence. Although an admission is not really discovery of any new facts, but only a stipulation to existing facts, it is a way for both parties in litigation to save the time and expense of investigating and proving certain facts. Requests for admission narrow the issues that have to be proven and should be used early in any litigation in order to avoid unnecessary trial preparation.

If requests for admission are denied by one side, "the court may award the adversary the costs of proving the matters at trial."[118] Even though a fact or circumstance may be undisputed, some attorneys actually prefer to prove it through witnesses as part of the persuasive development of their cases. Generally, however, it is to a lawyer's "advantage to obtain as many admissions as possible in advance of trial so as to reduce the expense, time, and inconvenience of proving matters not actually in dispute."[119]

Pros and Cons of Discovery

Since the development of these five discovery techniques, having a surprise witness suddenly appear in court is very rare. Both sides today generally know what the other side is going to do at trial. As a result, discovery has accomplished what pleadings originally set out to do. Discovery has several clear advantages. It offers an attorney access to evidence that an opponent possesses. It makes it easier to size up a case for possible settlement. It allows the person conducting the discovery to judge the strengths and weaknesses of the opposition's witnesses. It is little wonder, then, that discovery procedures are well received by the legal profession. This is clearly confirmed in a survey of nearly one thousand plaintiff and defense lawyers in 37 districts throughout the country. "Seventy-eight percent said discovery helped, 21 percent reported it made no difference, and only eight . . . thought discovery was a hindrance."[120]

While discovery has its many fans, it has some opposition as well. "As in any adversarial situation, the proponents and critics of discovery have offered persuasive but contradictory arguments, with divergent images of the facts. If the opponents' conception of the facts is correct, discovery seriously hampers litigation and needs fundamental changes in scope and procedure."[121]

There are four major drawbacks that may make a lawyer pause before embarking on discovery. First, discovery costs too much. Because discovery is expensive, "litigants with plenty of resources can harass opponents who are less fortunate."[122] Second, the fruits of discovery are available to both sides. An opponent can learn a lot at the discoverer's expense. Third, discovery causes extensive delay. Attorneys have been accused of engaging in unnecessary discovery when a case needs prompt disposition through an early settlement. Lundquist claims that unnecessary discovery produces useless warehouses of documents, interrogatories, and depositions, each of which has been "word processed with alacrity if not intelligence [and] . . . comes at a high price in terms of increased delay."[123] Indeed, with all this added discovery, "both sides become so well prepared they tend to fight longer and harder."[124] Fourth, discovery has jeopardized trial skills. Attorneys miss the crucial information by going for the majority of information in a dispute. Lundquist continues, "Having discovered everything, they [litigators] now want to prove everything. Litigators often fail to recognize the difference between discovery for trial purpose and discovery for discovery-oriented litigation."[125]

In conclusion, the critics of discovery believe that lawyers overemphasize its importance. Lundquist expresses himself well with this analogy:

Discovery has replaced the trial as the mechanism for resolving disputes. Litigators march forth from law firms flanked by junior partners, associates and paralegals much as fifteenth-century Italian armies ventured from warring city-states. These armies left home and lived well off the land as they proceeded to confront the enemy. They avoided direct combat at all costs. The process leading to it was too rewarding, while battle itself was too risky. Thus does litigation proceed today.[126]

Undoubtedly, discovery abuses are possible and do occur. Some critics call for limiting discovery further; others want greater judicial involvement. However, it is doubtful that major changes will be made, because most attorneys believe that the skillful employment of discovery techniques is a valuable asset. It is important, then, that all counsel be intimately familiar with the potential and the dynamics of each discovery device in order to choose intelligently among them.

ISSUE ANALYSIS

Two kinds of analytical procedures are involved when a lawyer prepares a case for trial: substantive analysis and audience analysis. Audience analysis is considered at various points in the chapters on trial advocacy. Substantive analysis, which is the primary concern of this chapter, is the process of finding the issues, or possible points of conflict, in the forthcoming litigation. Failure to do this can result in making a weak case, in defending one's own case poorly, and in attacking the opponent's case ineptly. Substantive pretrial case analysis is discussed in terms of rhetorical invention and the location of issues, as well as building case arguments and developing case themes.

Rhetorical Invention and the Location of Issues

A critical stage in pretrial strategy involves delineating the issues in a case. Issue analysis has been theorized and written about for nearly 25 centuries in a field of study known as rhetoric. In ancient Greek and Roman rhetoric, invention was that division (or canon) which dealt with the gathering and analysis of material for persuasive communication. When we discuss substantive analysis, we refer to the phase of invention that involves sizing up a controversial situation for the purpose of determining its general nature and finding the potential arguments.

The subtopic of ancient invention theory from which our contemporary version of substantive analysis evolved was called *stasis* by the Greeks and *status* by the Romans. As Cicero and Quintilian explained it in relation to forensic rhetoric, or speaking in court, *status* was the determination of the main character of the case and the locating of the main issues. It was done by asking certain formulary questions. As Cicero explained it, after concluding a client interview, the lawyer would pose these questions, some of which he said were involved in *all* disputes: What has been done, is being done, or will be done? Of what nature is it? How should it be designated?[127] Quintilian wrote of three similar possible issues: of fact, of definition, and of general considerations.[128] For instance, in Greek mythology, Orestes admittedly killed Clytemnestra and Aegisthus (fact), a situation clearly classifiable as murder (definition), but the killing was defended as justifiable homicide on the grounds of sacred duty to avenge the murder of his father (general considerations). The issue therefore concerned the rightness of a son's killing his mother because she had murdered his father.

Today, the starting point in substantive analysis is roughly the same as it was in antiquity—the finding of potential issues. Before completing the investigative procedure, a lawyer typically lists the possible points of conflict in the litigation. These are potential issues, otherwise known as questions that may become issues when the other side is heard from. After the potential issues are stated, the process of narrowing begins. Some potential issues may be waived because they

are irrelevant, and others may be admitted through discovery and the pleadings because it seems unwise to contest them. The clashes that remain after waivers and admissions are the actual issues. An issue is "a single, certain, and material point, deduced by the pleadings of the parties, which is affirmed on one side and denied on the other."[129]

How does a lawyer who is looking for potential issues find them? Experience with similar cases in the past may serve as a guide. Or one may invite associates to brainstorm and offer suggestions, which may survive as issues. Role reversal is another invention procedure. In it a lawyer behaves as if he or she were the opponent, looking at issues from that viewpoint.

Much as in the *status* of old, two general categories of issues need to be determined: issues of fact and issues of law. Issues of fact flow from the processes of investigation and discovery noted earlier in this chapter. Some possible issues of fact are (1) Had her apartment been broken into and entered? (2) Was the accused present at the scene? (3) What prompted the accused to commit the act? Issues of fact are resolved in a trial by the trier or triers of fact, namely, the judge or the jury. They decide which side's version of the facts is to be affirmed. In other words, they answer the question: "How did something happen?" This question encompasses the traditional journalism inquiries for reporting stories: who, what, when, where, and why.[130]

Issues of law are discovered in law libraries. Possible issues of law are (1) Was it proper to use a wiretap in gathering the evidence? (2) How do you define contributory negligence? Issues of law are usually resolved by motions in advance of trial. Motions are discussed in greater detail later in this chapter. Generally, there are four types of issues of law that an attorney is able to raise: of language, of legal intent, of precedent, and of policy. An issue of language arose from the Roth pornography ruling by the Supreme Court.[131] It was held that pornographic materials were "utterly without redeeming social importance." Many defense lawyers in pornography cases thereafter argued that this language was ambiguous and that pornography was indefinable. Legal intent has also been an issue in pornography cases. For instance, one prosecutor argued that the framers of the Constitution never intended to allow the right of free speech to extend to pornography. Arguments from precedent claim that the present case is analogous to an earlier one that was decided in a certain way and that this one should be decided similarly. The doctrine that rules announced in earlier decisions should be applied to the current case is known as *stare decisis,* meaning "to stand by decided cases." Finally, a question of policy concerns fairness in applying laws. If an attorney argues that the death penalty is only selectively applied and generally opposed by the populace, he or she is debating the merits of a policy in claiming that the penalty should not be used in this particular instance. These four types of legal issues represent possible focal points in any given case.

Issues, then, are questions that are appropriate for sizing up any controversial situation. They provide the overall structure for analysis and are the first step in locating case arguments.

Building Case Arguments and Developing a Case Theme

Suppose you have an argument with your roommate over who should pay a certain portion of the telephone bill that just arrived. In this sense, an argument could be the same as a fight, a controversy, a dispute, a quarrel, or a contention. It could be an endless argument, or it could be a one-sentence argument. In legal communication, we limit the term *argument* to the end product in issue development.

In rhetoric, we have a word for argument. It is called the *enthymeme.* In its simplest form, an argument (enthymeme) is a conclusion with a supporting reason, and these two elements may appear in either order. Thus, one might say, "Because the teller at the credit union has been living beyond her means, I think she should be investigated as a possible embezzler." Or the clauses could be inverted: "I think the teller at the credit union should be investigated as a possible embezzler because she has been living beyond her means." A conclusion and at least one reason constitute the basic unit in argumentative discourse. Conclusions are typically introduced by such words as *therefore, so, proves that,* and *consequently.* Supporting reasons are usually introduced by *because, since, for, as indicated by,* and so on. Of course, the two brief arguments above are devoid of evidence.

Philosopher Stephen Toulmin gives us an appropriate model of a legal argument, which allows us to examine relationships among evidence, reasons, and conclusions.[132] He diagrams for us what may be involved when a lawyer uses facts to support a conclusion or claim. In Toulmin's layout (Figure 3.2), (C) is

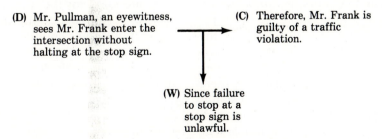

(D) Mr. Pullman, an eyewitness, sees Mr. Frank enter the intersection without halting at the stop sign.

(C) Therefore, Mr. Frank is guilty of a traffic violation.

(W) Since failure to stop at a stop sign is unlawful.

FIGURE 3.2   BASIC TOULMIN LEGAL ARGUMENT MODEL

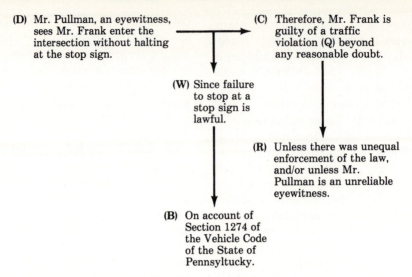

(D) Mr. Pullman, an eyewitness, sees Mr. Frank enter the intersection without halting at the stop sign.

(C) Therefore, Mr. Frank is guilty of a traffic violation (Q) beyond any reasonable doubt.

(W) Since failure to stop at a stop sign is lawful.

(R) Unless there was unequal enforcement of the law, and/or unless Mr. Pullman is an unreliable eyewitness.

(B) On account of Section 1274 of the Vehicle Code of the State of Pennsyltucky.

FIGURE 3.3   COMPLETE TOULMIN LEGAL ARGUMENT MODEL

the claim or conclusion to be supported; it is a stand or position the lawyer wants to discuss. The letter (D) represents data or facts cited as the basis of the claim; it is the grounds or information that is required if the claim is to be accepted as reasonable. The letter (W) stands for warrant, bridge, or inference. The warrant answers the question "How did you justify getting from data to claim?" Some appropriate warrant is needed if the step from data to claim is to be seen as a trustworthy one. Notice that (D) would be evidence heard in court (an issue of fact), whereas (W) would be an issue of law. The warrant, (W), is the reason that Mr. Frank's action constitutes a crime. The claim, (C), is the ultimate issue the jury must resolve.

If the data and the warrant do not show the conclusion to be true, but only probable, we must add a qualifier, (Q), before the claim. Familiar legal qualifiers are "according to the preponderance of the evidence" and "beyond any reasonable doubt." Further, there may be reservations to the conclusion; there may be instances in which the conclusion is invalid. If so, Toulmin provides (R), for rebuttal or reservations, with the typical linking

word being *unless*. The sixth and last part of the model is backing, (B), which provides authority or support for the warrant. In the diagram just shown, it would be a citation of a specific law. The six-part model now looks like Figure 3.3. This argument would be used by a prosecutor except that (R) may generate argument for the defense.

Arguments, such as the one diagrammed above, always begin with data (D). Facts serve as the foundation for argument and case construction. What this means, then, is that lawyers build cases inductively; that is, they reason from particular to general or from particular to particular. The five types of inductive reasoning are generalization, cause, sign, analogy, and argument from authority.

In an argument from generalization, several cases are cited for the purpose of making a general conclusion about the group as a whole. If plaintiff's counsel provides data (D) that his client's telephone was bugged four times, the four particular instances allow that attorney to generalize in the claim (C) that there has been an invasion of privacy. Hard data serve as support for an induction to a generalization.

Causal argument attempts to show that a conclusion or event of one sort is the cause (or effect) of a condition or event of another sort. If, in a tort case concerning negligence, it is argued that the failure to repair the furnace (D) was a cause producing the effect of a sudden fire and explosion (C), an attorney is arguing here from cause.

Sign argument consists of inferring close relationships between variables. The relationship is so close that the presence or absence of one is an indication of the presence or absence of the other. For example, a history of prior instances of exaggerating or lying (D) may be used to make the sign inference that the person is doing the same thing in court today (C).

Analogy, or argument from comparison, occurs frequently in legal cases; in fact, that is what *stare decisis* is about. When an attorney cites cases comparable to the one in litigation (D), and argues that the present case should be decided according to those precedents (C), he or she is using analogy.

Finally, in argument for authority, the conclusion (C) is accepted because it is drawn from the testimony of an expert (D). This has been called the *prestige argument* because it uses the acts or opinions of an authority in support of a claim.[133] When attorneys rely on testimony from psychiatrists, physicians, and other experts as data (D), they are arguing from authority.

Being aware of these types of inductive arguments and of ways in which they can be tested is useful to an attorney in building, refuting, and defending case positions. Several textbooks in argumentation and debate elaborate on these tests,[134] but here, in summary form, are some of the ways to evaluate and select arguments:

☐ *Argument from generalization.* Do the sample cases cover a relevant time period? Is the sample typical of the class? How many instances can be verified? Are there exceptions?

☐ *Causal argument.* Is the cause inevitable, sufficient, and necessary? Could there have been other effects? Could something have intervened to alter the causal relationship?

☐ *Sign argument.* Could the sign be only coincidence? Are there any disrupting signs?

☐ *Argument from analogy.* In how many respects are the cases similar? Are these similarities critical to the comparison? Are there dissimilarities? Are these dissimilarities critical to the comparison?

☐ *Argument from authority.* Has the person had access to the data on which the judgment rests? Does the person have the education, training, and experience to be considered an expert? Do other specialists acknowledge this person as an expert in the area in which he or she is expressing a judgment? Is this the best available expert?

As arguments are tested and selected, a lawyer must also be thinking of a case theme. The theme must be cohesive, logical, and persuasive. Five steps should be followed in developing a case theme.[135] First, each of the elements that originally caused the action to be brought should be reviewed. This information should be found in the trial notebook. Second, the evidence that can be presented through witnesses and exhibits should be evaluated. Where is it strong and where is it weak? Third, the evidence that can be presented through an adversary's witnesses and exhibits should be evaluated. Where is it strong and where is it weak? Fourth, a thorough analysis should be made of the predicted admissibility of evidence on both sides of the case. Fifth, given what evidence the lawyer thinks will be admissible, an analysis must be made of the strengths and weaknesses of both sides of the case. If an attorney finds his or her case weak in certain areas, and these areas are central to the proposed theme, either those areas have to be strengthened, or the theme has to be altered to adjust to the strongest arguments in the case.

Once these steps have been followed, a singular and unique case theme must be developed. Unique or novel themes help to make a lawyer's case unforgettable and influential.[136] "Counsel should be able to state a case theme in one sentence of no more than ten words. The retention value is higher and the theme can be easily repeated. A theme statement that is too long or cumbersome will not stick in the jurors' minds."[137] For example, in a medical negligence case in which I assisted a plaintiff's attorney, four novel words were chosen during a brainstorming session as a simple case theme. The complaint was against an industrial physician who failed to take an X ray of an employee's infected foot but kept writing in his records, "The patient's better," after which he sent the patient back to his job in the plant. The employee eventually had to have his foot amputated. The theme for the case focused on the doctor's repeated insensitivity. It was as though he had a rubber stamp that he mechanically used after each patient visit. That stamp read, "Better. Back to work." Hence, the catchy theme of the case, said over and over again, became "Better. Back to work."

What we have said here is that thorough trial preparation involves an analysis of issues as a prelude to a selection of arguments and a novel case theme. The job of each advocate is to locate those issues, arguments, and themes which can convince a judge or jury.

MOTIONS PRACTICE

A motion is a request addressed to the court, an application for an order. It is made either to obtain relief from the court or to preserve a denial of relief on record for appeal.[138] In a trial, an attorney raising an objection is actually making a motion. But motions occur before trial also, and they are an important part of pretrial communication strategy. "Parties will be joined or dismissed, peripheral or untenable legal theories will be discarded or dismissed and in some cases the issues will be decided by the court as a result of the use of appropriate motions."[139] Even the most ordinary lawyer can obtain advantages from astute motions practice, advantages that a far more gifted opponent cannot overcome.

Pretrial motions inevitably involve risk. They can be used by lawyers to gain significant advantages, but they can be unfortunate moves as well. Like a backgammon player relating every move to ultimately winning the game, an attorney must carefully study the consequences of each motion made.

Most motions are written. They can be filed with the court on a notice-of-motion form at any time prior to trial. Written notice of the motion and of a time for a hearing is then given to the adverse party. The written motion consists of a statement of facts, the grounds for granting a request, and a request to the court for relief.[140] Courts must rule on all motions filed. They do so after reading and perhaps hearing the information. The ruling becomes a permanent part of the court file.

When a motion is filed, a lawyer can request to argue it before a judge. If there is oral argument, it should be kept rather short. The oral argument should be a brief picture of what a case is about followed by an understandable argument and a motion showing the proper benefits to be gained from court relief. The emphasis should be only on what is essential; "the key to oral argument is . . . selectivity."[141] During oral argument, an attorney need not rail vehemently. This is not the place to try to win first prize in an oratory contest. Reading verbatim also detracts from the presentation and must be avoided. The attorney should be calm, sincere, serious, vivid, clear, and—once again—brief. After a few minutes of argument, counsel should not be interrupted by an embarrassing question from the judge: "Counsel, just what is this motion all about?"

If an attorney knows which judge will hear his or her motion, that judge (the audience) ought to be studied thoroughly. Some judges read the briefs in advance of the argument, and others do not. This should affect the amount of detail an attorney adds to the discussion. If a lawyer is uncertain about the judge's familiarity with the motion, he or she can state simply, "I assume that your honor has read the motion, and if there is anything about it you would like me to discuss, I will gladly do so." Some judges favor one type of relief over another. Some judges want juries to hear certain things and other judges do not. If judges pride themselves on being innovative and intellectual, they may be receptive to new and unusual procedures. If a judge frequently uses the word "fairness," an attorney should couch his motion in terms of its fundamental fairness. Most judges are sympathetic to motions that will save judicial time—either by avoiding the trial or by shortening it. Probably all judges get annoyed when counsel presents arguments on the law that are so basic that first-year law school students could make "correct" rulings; such argumentation insults a judge's intelligence. In sum, the judge should be analyzed with care. Background information on judges' personalities and their rulings on motions can be studied by consulting the court's law journal. The success of motions practice often lies in the way the motion is presented, a matter of rhetorical form.

What are some of the motions that can be filed? Here are just a few common motions, which are, of necessity, underdescribed. Many motions are omitted from this discussion.

One motion is for a *change of venue*. Under most circumstances, the trial of a criminal defendant will be held in the county or district where an alleged wrongdoing was committed. Change of venue is a motion in which an attorney says that there is reason to believe the defendant could not get a fair trial in the place is which the case was filed, because the community is so infected with prejudice. Therefore, the case should be moved elsewhere. For instance, the media may have saturated the community with publicity adverse to the defendant's cause. Verdicts should not be the result of preconceived ideas jurors gain from extrajudicial sources. So the court can either continue the trial to a time when public discussion of the case has simmered down, order the jurors to be sequestered, or honor the change-of-venue request. If the court takes the last course of action, the decision is usually based on evidence from public opinion surveys showing greater bias in one community than in another community.[142]

Another motion is to *dismiss* the charge or complaint. This is a motion used by the defense when he or she feels the other side lacks adequate information to pursue the case any further. In a criminal case, for example, there might be insufficient facts alleged to constitute the crime charged, a charge levied against the defendant might be unknown in criminal law, or a charge might be countered with a new fact and a point of law. As an example of the last situation, assume that Carolyn Manning was ticketed by Highway Patrol Officer Harley Higgins for following too close on the freeway. Ms. Manning does not contest the fact that she tailgated, but she argues that the case should be dismissed over a question of law, namely, that she was the victim of wrongful discrimination and unequal enforcement of the law inasmuch as the investigation revealed that Officer Higgins had earlier stopped a fellow officer for drunken driving but had not cited him! The defense argues that laws should be enforced equally or not at all and that the officer's failure to ticket a fellow officer was unequal enforcement. The judge is asked to grant a dismissal. In the end, most motions to dismiss are overruled.[143]

Nevertheless, the filing of such a motion allows additional case preparation time.

Trials can be delayed through another motion, the request for a *continuance*. In this motion, one of the attorneys asks for additional time before the start of the trial. The question of additional time is usually balanced by the ruling judge against inconvenience, increased cost, and the interest of justice in avoiding delay. Frequently, this motion is made by attorneys who have certain witnesses unavailable at the scheduled time of the trial.

Another relatively popular motion is to *suppress*. Here, the court is asked to abort the presentation of some evidence from the other side. The exclusionary rule forbids the introduction of evidence obtained in violation of the Constitution or certain statutes. However, the rule is not self-executing. Hence, the defendant may move to suppress any evidence that he or she wishes to have excluded from consideration by the jury. Obvious examples are motions to suppress certain information gathered through illegal searches and seizures, wiretaps, or confessions.

The *summary judgment* motion is designed to get partial[144] or complete judicial disposition of an issue or claim. A complete disposition has the effect of depriving a party of his or her day in court. If an attorney recognizes that he or she has obtained a significantly stronger set of facts than the opposition, a summary judgment motion might be filed to get an early decision on the merits of a case from a judge, although courts are increasingly hesitant to provide such radical relief. Even if unsuccessful, the motion can serve as an instrument of discovery, since it requires arguments and disclosure of facts relevant to the merits of the action from the other side.

Finally, there is the *motion in limine*. A flaw in our jury system is the tendency of jurors to be swayed by evidence that is not material to the issues of the lawsuit. The motion *in limine* is designed to prevent immaterial and potentially prejudicial facts from creeping into the case. For instance, one evening a married male plaintiff was spending the night in bed with a woman other than his wife. The couple was in a bed in that woman's home. The plaintiff had been drinking heavily and was in the act of sexual intercourse when suddenly a defect in a nearby water heater caused an explosion. A piece of metal from the heater struck the plaintiff, and he is now seeking a just award. Liability is very clear, but might not the jury be influenced by what the plaintiff was doing? A motion *in limine* can be presented not to allow the defense attorney or any defense witness to mention or suggest the possible impropriety. Should the plaintiff's motion be approved by the court, mention of where he was and what he was doing would be prohibited on the grounds that its inflammatory effect far outweighs its probative value.[145] Should the motion be denied, however, moving counsel must then determine whether to proceed to make objection during trial when the evidence is proffered, or to allow it to be heard and to demonstrate reversible error in the ruling through a subsequent appeal.[146]

These are but a few of the possible motions that can be filed prior to trial. The number of pretrial motions in our court system is limited only by the ingenuity and imagination of counsel. New motions are always being improvised for better trial position.

PRETRIAL CONFERENCES

At a meeting called the pretrial conference, attorneys meet with a judge at the courthouse. This meeting can significantly affect the course of litigation. Several matters are considered, such as simplification of the issues,[147] the witnesses to be used and a brief summary of what each will say, objections to evidence the other side wants to have presented, identification of documents and certification of their genuineness, stipulation of certain facts (the result of requests for admission),[148] determination of how visual aids might be used in court, limitations on the number of experts used, and the setting of a trial date. All of these and other matters are considered to "increase the speed and orderliness of the trial by eliminating unnecessary disputes and error-producing surprise."[149] After the conference, a pretrial order containing all agreements and decisions is issued by the judge. This order governs the procedure at trial and is difficult to amend. The order virtually freezes the case.

Generally speaking, a pretrial conference is designed to avoid communication breakdowns at trial, particularly on procedural matters. Because of its importance, very careful preparation should be made. "It is good practice for counsel, in preparation for the conference, to make an outline of the matters which he desires to bring up for consideration at the conference."[150] It is also essential for an attorney to appear at the conference in person and not to turn this responsibility over to someone else.

Procedures for pretrial conferences have been adopted in all states. In some places, the conference is uniformly ignored; in other places, it is uniformly employed. Sometimes the conference is a perfunctory social get-together; other times it is virtually a minitrial. The timing of the conferences also varies. Ideally, these conferences are held two to three weeks before trial.[151] In reality, they take place anywhere from the day before to three years before the trial begins. Some are automatic; others are called by the judge; still others must come upon request of counsel.

Pretrial conferences were first used extensively in Scotland, beginning in 1868. A pretrial conference was then called the "adjustment of issues." The conference would be held to adjust the pleadings after they were filed. The English made pretrial conferences mandatory beginning in 1893. The British model for adjusting issues before trial was first used in the United States in New Jersey in 1912, but the attempt was highly unsuccessful. The conference was discretionary with the lawyers, and few of them used it, because they did not want to reveal any of the secrets of their cases. In 1929, Judge Ira Jayne in the Circuit Court of Wayne County, Michigan, systematically and routinely used the pretrial conference to find ways to either bring about conciliation or simplify the coming trial. Then, in 1938, when Rule 16 of the Federal Rules of Civil Procedure was approved, pretrial conferences were adopted as an alternative to filing the pleadings. Similar rules were soon promulgated in the state courts.

Pretrial conferences fail when there is inertia on the bench; the judge is the pivotal person in making conferences work. The bench must provide the impetus although the judge is not empowered "to decide issues of fact or law, but only to seek agreement of the parties."[152] The judge must take an active administrative and educational role by keeping the conference well focused. This is a critical communication burden on any judge. Yet there are conflicting thoughts about what a judge is supposed to accomplish at a pretrial conference. Some say the goal of a conference is to bring the opposing attorneys together and *prepare for* trial. Others say that the goal of a pretrial conference is to *avoid* trial by encouraging a negotiated settlement.[153] Some jurisdictions even have two pretrial conferences, one to discuss settlement and the other to narrow issues and simplify proof.

If a pretrial conference is related to settlement outside of court,[154] a judge focuses on the attempts that have been made to negotiate in the past and the reasons no agreement has been reached. A judge with settlement in mind urges the attorneys to engage in additional bargaining in the remaining time before trial. Those who say this is an inappropriate role for the judge to play argue that litigants are entitled to their day in court and judges should not try to prevent this opportunity.

Nevertheless, settlement offers can always be refused. Nothing can be imposed on either side by a judge. It seems to me that settlement matters are perfectly appropriate areas for discussion in pretrial conferences. In fact, in cases in which lawyers are reluctant to initiate negotiation because they see it as a sign of weakness, judges can be the ones to break the impasse by acting as friendly, official, impartial, mediating catalysts.

Here is a classic example of a pretrial conference that succeeded in promotiong successful negotiation: A student body president from a small Midwestern college was arrested and charged with selling marijuana to other students. Lots of publicity surfaced in the small town where this event happened. The student was the son of a prominent businessman. He was academically outstanding, handsome, clean-cut, and popular. Now he was facing a serious felony charge with the prospect of receiving a long prison term. The prosecution evidence was strong; the student had sold a substantial quantity of the weed to a police informant. Since the defense counsel was preparing a case based on entrapment, however, the prosecutor was tempted to reduce the charge to possession, a misdemeanor. But he never made the offer, fearing public anger. At the pretrial conference, defense counsel confidently brought his client to the judge and argued, through full disclosure of evidence and law, that his case could be won on appeal if not at trial. The judge quickly urged acceptance of the lesser charge proposal, indicating that it was warranted in this case. The prosecutor assented. Justice had been done. The judge informed the public that he suggested this disposition of the case. Public criticism was nonexistent. The defendant received court supervision under probation. He graduated with his class and with academic honors.[155]

In the example just given, a trial was avoided. Often the pretrial conference does not reach that objective. When it does not result in settlement, does the pretrial conference then have an impact on the trial itself? An empirical study in New Jersey comparing trials following conferences to those which did not use conferences found that the pretrial conference improved the clarity and quality of attorney presentations while reducing surprise, gaps in evidence, and repetition of evidence.[156] Pretrial conferences appear to have a positive effect on communication in the courtroom.

This chapter has explored several steps lawyers must follow in preparation for trial. Through investigation, pleadings, discovery, issue analysis, motions practice, and pretrial conferences, lawyers are actively engaged in information processing, critical and strategic thinking, and communication in an attempt to secure the best possible trial advantage for their clients. Pretrial work is an art. Each trial brings with it a new pretrial experience, and skilled trial lawyers must adapt their perspectives and techniques to fit the needs of each case. Indeed, this is a most challenging mission.

Notes

[1]Alan E. Morrill, *Trial Diplomacy* (Chicago: Court Practice Institute, 1972), 168.

[2]William W. Turner, "Investigating the Criminal Case: General Principles," in *American Jurisprudence: Trials* (San Francisco: Bancroft-Whitney, 1964), vol. I, 485.

[3]In fact, an attorney who does his or her own investigation will likely be better versed in the case details.

[4]Robert Keeton, *Trial Tactics and Methods* (Boston: Little, Brown, 1973), 317–319.

[5]Robert McFigg, Ralph C. McCullough II, and James L. Underwood, *Civil Trial Manual* (Los Angeles: Joint Committee on Legal Education of the American Law Institute and the American Bar Association, 1974), 285.

[6]Lewis Lake, *How to Win Lawsuits Before Juries* (New York: Prentice-Hall, 1954), 83.

[7]When a witness incurs an expense, such as losing pay, in order to accommodate an investigator, then reimbursement might be in order.

[8]Robert L. Simmons, *Winning Before Trial* (Englewood Cliffs, N.J.: Executive Reports Corporation, 1974), 220.

[9]Ibid., 205–206.

[10]Subpoenas are available to compel unwilling witnesses to appear and testify. As a matter of tactics, subpoenas should rarely be used, since unwilling witnesses can do more harm than good.

[11]Keeton, op. cit., 311.

[12]"A rambling, long-winded statement wastes the time of those reviewing the file and destroys attention of the jurors." P. Magarick, "Investigating the Civil Case," in *American Jurisprudence: Trials,* op. cit., 413.

[13]Jerome Frank, *Courts on Trial* (Princeton, N.J.: Princeton University Press, 1973).

[14]Dillard S. Gardner, "The Perception and Memory of Witnesses," *Cornell Law Quarterly* 18 (1933), 393.

[15]Ephraim Margolin and Sandra Coliver, "Forensic Uses of Hypnosis: An Update," *Trial* (October 1983), 45–50; Thomas Sannito and Paul Mueller, "The Use of Hypnosis in a Double Manslaughter Defense," *Trial Diplomacy Journal* (Fall 1980), 30–35.

[16]James Marshall, *Law and Psychology in Conflict* (Indianapolis: Bobbs-Merrill, 1966), 29.

[17]Harrop Arthur Freeman and Henry Weihofen, *Clinical Law Training: Interviewing and Counseling* (St. Paul, Minn.: West Publishing, 1972), 40.

[18]Marshall, op. cit., 11.

[19]Neil Hurowitz, *Support Practice Handbook* (New York: Kluwer, 1985), 222.

[20]Under the Federal Rules of Evidence (F.R.E. Rule 702), the criterion is whether the expert witness's knowledge, training, or experience will assist the trier of fact in understanding the evidence or determining a fact at issue.

[21]Professional associations are not the only reference point for securing physicians. When searching for an appropriate doctor, lawyers might also ask teaching hospitals for advice. Or they could review medical literature through MEDLINE, a computer source, or the *Directory of Medical Specialists* published by Marquis Who's Who, Inc., in Chicago, Ill.

[22]Morgan P. Ames, "Preparation of the Expert Witness," *Trial* (August 1977), 22.

[23]Keeton, op. cit., 322.

[24]Ruth McGaffey, "The Expert Witness and Source Credibility—The Communication Perspective," *American Journal of Trial Advocacy* 2 (1978), 58.

[25]Subjects viewed videotaped testimony of a malpractice trial in which the experts were physicians. In addition to likability, dynamism and expertise were found to be additional dimensions of credibility. R. Rickun, *Credibility in the Courtoom,* M.A. thesis (Milwaukee: University of Wisconsin, 1977).

[26]Joseph P. Zammit, "The Trial Brief and the Trial Memorandum," *Practical Lawyer* (March 1, 1978), 74.

[27]John J. McCann, "Order out of Chaos: Using a Trial Notebook," *Trial* (January 1986), 34.

[28]George Vetter, *Successful Civil Litigation* (Englewood Cliffs, N.J.: Prentice-Hall, 1977), 37.

[29]Remedies could be in the form of damages, as in this illustration, or they could be recovery of property, injunctions (court orders directing defendants to do or to refrain from doing something), or statements of declaratory relief regarding rights and duties of the parties involved.

[30]A counterclaim against a plaintiff creates, in effect, another lawsuit, which may form the basis of an entirely separate litigation. If a counterclaim is drafted, it must be accompanied by supporting facts.

[31]Hubert Hickman and Thomas M. Scanlon, *Preparation for Trial* (Philadelphia: ALI and ABA Joint Committee on Continuing Legal Education, 1963), 42–43.

[32]Federal Rule of Civil Procedure 26(b)(1). "The rules of evidence in each state specify situations where there is a privilege to withhold information because of a presumed greater social interest in keeping the information confidential than in

disclosing it to help decide a lawsuit correctly. In all jurisdictions an attorney-client privilege is recognized, protecting communications between a lawyer and his client. . . . Other privileges exist—doctor-patient, priest-penitent, and the like—varying greatly from one state to another." Delmar Karlen, *Procedure Before Trial in a Nutshell* (St. Paul, Minn.: West Publishing, 1972), 190.

[33]See *Uttis v. General Motors Corp.*, 58 F.R.D. 450, 452–453 (E.D. Pa., 1972).

[34]Walter Barthold, *Attorney's Guide to Effective Discovery Techniques* (Englewood Cliffs, N.J.: Prentice-Hall, 1975), 51.

[35]Simmons, op. cit., 1306.

[36]William A. Glaser, *Pretrial Discovery and the Adversary System* (New York: Russell Sage Foundation, 1968), 52.

[37]Keeton, op. cit., 395.

[38]Al J. Cone and Verne Lawyer, *The Act of Persuasion in Litigation* (Des Moines: Dean-Hicks, 1966), 112.

[39]Jay S. Blumenkopf, "Deposition Strategy and Tactics," *American Journal of Trial Advocacy* 5 (1981), 231.

[40]Hickman and Scanlon, op. cit., 108. See Federal Rule of Civil Procedure 32(a).

[41]Hickman and Scanlon, op. cit., 111.

[42]Guy O. Kornblum, "The Oral Civil Deposition: Preparation and Examination of Witnesses," *Practical Lawyer* (May 1971), 15.

[43]Blumenkopf, op. cit., 234.

[44]Barthold, op. cit., 75.

[45]McFigg, McCullough, and Underwood, op. cit., 202.

[46]Vetter, op. cit., 135.

[47]Kornblum, op. cit., 19–20.

[48]Morrill, op. cit., 183.

[49]Lawrence J. Smith and Loretta A. Malandro, *Courtroom Communication Strategies* (New York: Kluwer, 1985), 504–509.

[50]Mark L. Knapp, Roderick P. Hart, and Harry S. Dennis, "An Exploration of Deception as a Communication Construct," *Human Communication Research* 1 (1974), 15–29; Glenn E. Littlepage and Martin A. Pineault, "Detection of

Deceptive Factual Statements from the Body and the Face," *Personality and Social Psychology Bulletin* 5 (1979), 325–328.

[51]Jacob A. Stein, "Going Through the Motions," *Litigation* (Winter 1985), 22.

[52]Hickman and Scanlon, op. cit., 120–121.

[53]Wayne Brazil, "The Adversary Character of Civil Disobedience: A Critique and Proposal for Change," *Vanderbilt University Law Review* 31 (1978), 1331.

[54]An additional list can be found in Phillip J. Kolczynski, "Depositions as Evidence," *Litigation* (Winter 1983), 25–29.

[55]The term *cross-examine* is a misnomer in this context. A lawyer does not really cross-examine his own deponent after an adversary's questioning. Cross-examination in the context of a deposition only means questioning a deponent after the instigator of the deposition has finished.

[56]Keeton, op. cit., 409.

[57]Ibid., 410.

[58]Harry Bodin, *Civil Litigation and Trial Techniques* (New York: Practicing Law Institute, 1976), 166.

[59]Problems arise when deponents are too eager and answer questions before counsel has an opportunity to object. To prevent this, an attorney should sit next to his or her deponent and lightly touch the deponent's arm as soon as an objectionable question is asked. This should be a prearranged communication signal to the deponent to refrain from answering a question. Kornblum, op. cit., 26.

[60]"If the question is so critical that the deposition cannot continue without an answer, the lawyer seeking the information must apply for an immediate court ruling whether the deponent must answer the question. In the event that an immediate court ruling cannot be obtained, the deposition can be continued to a specified date or continued generally." Morrill, op. cit., 182.

[61]Barthold, op. cit., 98.

[62]Ibid., 126.

[63]Cone and Lawyer, op. cit., 120.

[64]Karlen, op. cit., 194.

[65]Kornblum, op. cit., 15.

[66]McFigg, McCullough, and Underwood, op. cit.,

200; Thomas J. Murray, Jr., "Videotaped Depositions: The Ohio Experience," *Judicature* 61 (1978), 259.

[67]James L. McCrystal, "Videotaped Trials: A Primer," *Judicature* 61 (1978), 251.

[68]Ernest H. Short and Associates, "A Report to the Judicial Council on Videotape Recording in the California Criminal Justice System," (Sacramento: Judicial Council of California, 1976), 58–79.

[69]McCrystal, "Videotaped Trials: A Primer," op. cit., 252.

[70]Alan E. Morrill, "Enter the Video Tape Trial," *John Marshall Journal of Practice and Procedure* 3 (1970), 237.

[71]James L. McCrystal, "Videotaped Trials: Relief for Our Congested Courts," *Denver Law Journal* 49 (1973), 463–467.

[72]Barbara Lane Hart, "Effects of Videotaped Testimony on Juror Behavior," Ph.D. diss. (Columbus: Ohio State University, 1979), 43: Elizabeth M. Robertson, *Juror Response to Prerecorded Videotaped Trials* (Washington: National Bureau of Standards, 1979), 1.

[73]Short and Associates, op. cit., 4.

[74]Federal Rule of Civil Procedure 39(b)(4) and Federal Rule of Criminal Procedure 15; Thomas J. Murray, Jr., "Videotape Depositions: A New Frontier of Advocacy," in Melvin M. Belli, Sr., *Modern Trials,* vol. 5 (St. Paul, Minn.: West Publishing, 1982), 380.

[75]Irving Kosky, "Videotape in Ohio: Take Two," *Judicature* 59 (1975), 238.

[76]H. Allen Benowitz, "Legal Applications of Videotape," *Florida Bar Journal* 48 (1974), 87–91.

[77]F. Joseph Boster, Gerald R. Miller, and Norman E. Fontes, "Videotape in the Courtroom: Effects in Live Trials," *Trial* (June 1978), 49–51.

[78]Gerald R. Miller and Norman E. Fontes, *Videotape on Trial: A View from the Jury Box* (Beverly Hills, Calif.: Sage, 1979), 26.

[79]Gordon Bermant, "Critique—Data in Search of Theory in Search of Policy: Behavioral Responses to Videotape in the Courtroom," *Brigham Young University Law Review* (1975), 470.

[80]Miller and Fontes, op. cit., 87–100; Gerald R. Miller et al., "The Effects of Videotaped Testimony in Jury Trials: Studies on Juror Decision Making, Information Retention, and Emotional Arousal," *Brigham Young University Law Review* (1975), 362–363.

[81]Miller, et al., op. cit., 364.

[82]Ibid., 363–364; Gerald R. Miller and Fred Siebert, "Effects of Videotaped Testimony on Information Processing and Decision-Making in Jury Trials: Final Report," Unpublished monograph, Department of Communication, Michigan State University (1975), NSF-RANN #GI-38398.

[83]Hart, op. cit., 98: Gerald R. Williams, et al., "Juror Perceptions of Trial Testimony as a Function of the Method of Presentation: A Comparison of Live, Color Video, Black-and-White Video, Audio, and Transcript Presentations," *Brigham Young University Law Review* (1975), 401–402.

[84]Larry C. Farmer, et al., "The Effect of the Method of Presenting Trial Testimony on Juror Decisional Processes," in Bruce Dennis Sales, ed., *Psychology in the Legal Process* (New York: Spectrum, 1977), 66.

[85]Marshall J. Hartman, "Second Thoughts on Videotaped Trials," *Judicature* 61 (1978), 257.

[86]"Obvious difficulties arise in transporting the incarcerated defendant to many different locations, or even to a fixed location at many different times. When the accused is charged with a felony and has a known record of violent behavior, this problem is compounded." Francis J. Taillefer, Ernest H. Short, J. Michael Greenwood, and R. Grant Brady for the National Center for State Courts, "Video Support in the Criminal Courts,"*Journal of Communication* 24 (1974), 119.

[87]*People v. Moran,* 39 Cal.App.3d 398, 114 Cal.Rptr. 413 (1974). A chief prosecution witness was dying of cancer. He was not expected to live to testify at trial and in fact died shortly after the trial began. His eight-hour testimony had been videotaped and was admitted into evidence at trial over the defendant's objection. The California Court of Appeal found no merit to the defendant's contention that the videotape had deprived him of his Sixth Amendment right to confront witnesses. After all, defense counsel had

conducted an extensive cross-examination on the videotape.

[88]David M. Doret, "Trial by Videotape—Can Justice Be Seen to Be Done?" *Temple Law Quarterly* 47 (1974), 228–268.

[89]James J. Armstrong, "The Criminal Videotape Trial: Serious Constitutional Questions," *Oregon Law Review* 55 (1976), 573.

[90]Gordon Bermant and Daniel Jacoubovitch, "Fish out of Water: A Brief Overview of Social and Psychological Concerns about Videotaped Trials," *Hastings Law Journal* 26 (1975), 999–1011.

[91]Edmund P. Kaminski and Gerald R. Miller, "How Jurors Respond to Videotaped Witnesses," *Journal of Communication* 34 (1984), 88–102.

[92]Gerald R. Miller and Michale J. Sunnafrank, "Theoretical Dimensions of Applied Communication," *Quarterly Journal of Speech* 70 (1984), 258.

[93]*State v. Moffitt,* 133 Vt. 366, 340 A.2d 39 (1975). In a driving-while-intoxicated case, the court held that the defendant was not damaged by his separation in time and space from jurors. Information communicated by the videotape process was not significantly or meaningfully distorted.

[94]Allan E. Morrill, "Enter the Videotaped Trial," *Insurance Law Journal* (July 1970), 408.

[95]John A. Shutkin, "Videotape Trials: Legal and Practical Implications," *Columbia Journal of Law and Social Problems* 9 (1973), 363–393; Raymond Watts, "Comments on a Videotape Trial from Counsel for the Defense (McCall v. Clemens)," *Ohio Bar Journal* 45 (1972), 51–56.

[96]Morrill, "Enter the Videotaped Trial," 412.

[97]Robert T. Cunningham, Jr., "Videotape Evidence: Technological Innovation in the Trial Process," *The Alabama Lawyer* 36 (1975), 241; Short and Associates, op. cit., 28.

[98]Ernest H. Short, B. Thomas Florence, and Mary Alice Marsh, "An Assessment of Videotape in the Criminal Court," *Brigham Young University Law Review* (1975), 423–465.

[99]James L. Hoyt, "Courtroom Coverage: The Effects of Being Televised," *Journal of Broadcasting* 21 (1977), 489–495.

[100]James L. McCrystal and Ann B. Maschari, "PRVTT: A Lifeline for the Jury System, *Trial* (March 1983), 72.

[101]McCrystal, "Videotaped Trials: A Primer," op. cit., 253.

[102]Ibid., 254.

[103]McCrystal and Maschari, op. cit., 72.

[104]Comment, "Opening Pandora's Box: Asking Judges and Attorneys to React to the Videotape Trial," *Brigham Young University Law Review* (1975), 489–490.

[105]J. K. Lieberman, "Will Courts Meet the Challenge of Technology?" *Judicature* 60 (1976), 84–91.

[106]Robertson, op. cit., 4.

[107]Miller and Fontes, op. cit., 73.

[108]"How Jurors Feel About Videotaped Trials," *Criminal Justice Newsletter* 11 (May 26, 1980), 7.

[109]Gordon Bermant, et al., "Juror Responses to Prerecorded Videotape Trial Presentations in California and Ohio," *Hastings Law Journal* 26 (1975), 991.

[110]David M. Balabanian, "Medium v. Tedium: Video Depositions Come of Age," *Litigation* (Fall 1980), 26–27.

[111]Although no clear rule defines "reasonableness," it generally means that the discovering party should not shift the burden of preparing his or her own case to the responding party through the use of interrogatories. "Reasonableness" is usually ascertained by balancing the need for the information against the time and effort the responding party must expend to get the information.

[112]James L. Underwood, *Supplement to a Guide to Federal Discovery Rules* (Philadelphia: American Law Institute, 1983), 99.

[113]They are often used as admissions by a party against his or her interest. Counsel may also use them for impeachment purposes. See Chapter 8.

[114]Cone and Lawyer, op. cit., 107.

[115]Timothy C. Klenk, "Using and Abusing Interrogatories," *Litigation* (Winter 1985), 27.

[116]Rule 43(a) explicitly includes "writing, drawings, graphs, charts, photographs, phono-records, and other data compilations."

[117]Michael J. Fox, "Planning and Conducting a Discovery Program," *Litigation* (Summer 1981), 16.

[118]Glaser, op. cit., 34 (Note: A refusal to admit does not constitute a denial.)

[119]Keeton, op. cit., 418.

[120]Glaser, op. cit., 112.

[121]Ibid., 36.

[122]Karlen, op. cit., 215.

[123]Weyman I. Lundquist, "Trial Lawyer or Litigator," *Litigation* (Summer 1981), 3.

[124]Karlen, op. cit., 214–215.

[125]Lundquist, op. cit., 4.

[126]Ibid.

[127]Cicero, *De Oratore,* E. W. Sutton and H. Rackham, trans. (London: Loeb Classical Library, 1967), bk. 2, chap. 24.

[128]H.E. Butler, trans., *The Institutio Oratoria of Quintilian,* 4 vols. (Cambridge: Harvard University Press, Loeb Classical Library, 1920–1922), bk.3, chap. 6.

[129]*Black's Law Dictionary* (St. Paul, Minn.: West Publishing, 1951), 964–965.

[130]These stock issues for criminal cases have also been called subject, definition, locus, means, and purpose. Subject is who committed the act. Definition (what) refers to whether or not a certain act (crime) was committed. Locus refers to the time and place of the act (when). Means asks how the act was committed. Purpose refers to the motives of the accused in committing the act (why). See Craig R. Smith and David M. Hunsaker, *The Bases of Argument* (Indianapolis: Bobbs-Merrill, 1972), 28.

[131]*Roth v. United States,* 354 U.S. 476 (1957).

[132]Stephen Toulmin, *The Uses of Argument* (Cambridge: Cambridge University Press, 1958), chap. 3; Stephen Toulmin, Richard Rieke, and Allan Janik, *An Introduction to Reasoning* (New York: Macmillan, 1984).

[133]Chaim Perelman and L. Olbrechts-Tyteca, *The New Rhetoric: A Treatise on Argumentation* (Notre Dame, Indiana: University of Notre Dame Press, 1969), 305–310.

[134]For example, see George W. Ziegelmueller and Charles A. Dause, *Argumentation: Inquiry and Advocacy* (Englewood Cliffs, N.J.: Prentice-Hall, 1975), chap. 8.

[135]Thomas A. Mauet, *Fundamentals of Trial Technique* (Boston: Little, Brown, 1980), 8.

[136]David O. Sears and Jonathan L. Freedman, "Effects of Expected Familiarity with Arguments Upon Opinion Change and Selective Exposure," *Journal of Personality and Social Psychology* 2 (1965), 420–426.

[137]Smith and Malandro, op. cit., 316.

[138]Morrill, *Trial Diplomacy,* 217.

[139]Jeffrey H. Hartje, "Pre-Trial Motions," *American Journal of Trial Advocacy* (Summer 1981), 16.

[140]"Unless the motion is routine, it should be accompanied by a memorandum of law citing cases or statutory authority in support of the relief sought." Morrill, *Trial Diplomacy,* 218.

[141]Hartje, op. cit., 31.

[142]Michael T. Nietzel and Ronald C. Dillehay, "Psychologists as Consultants for Changes of Venue: The Use of Public Opinion Surveys," *Law and Human Behavior* 7 (1983), 309–335.

[143]Joseph Kelner and Francis E. McGovern, *Successful Litigation Techniques* (New York: Matthew Bender, 1981), 9-3.

[144]For example, judgment could be made by the court on liability, but a trial is deemed necessary on damages. Or a judgment could be made for one of the defendants, but not all of them.

[145]Tom Davis, "Motions *in Limine:* Tools for a Fair Trial," *Trial* (November 1982), 90.

[146]Jerome Lerner, "The Motion *in Limine:* A Useful Trial Tool," *Trial Diplomacy Journal* (Spring 1981), 17.

[147]This is a process by which the issues in a controversy are defined and framed so that extraneous disputes can be discarded.

[148]Here the facts to be proven are separated from those to be stipulated. This process avoids the unnecessary presentation of indisputable proofs at trial. However, there is a great danger in stipulations. They may be tantamount to asking an attorney to forsake the crucial consideration of the effect of testimony. After all, "nothing . . . can have less of an impact than a stipulation read to a jury." Vetter, op. cit., 278. Also, "there is another

danger, piecemeal stipulations. Evidence must be presented with a theme. A block of evidence must be internally related. A number of blocks of evidence often must be related to each other. To stipulate a bit of evidence here and a bit there could make a hodge-podge of your presentation. You may get facts admitted but find that the jury does not understand what is going on." Ibid.

[149]McFigg, McCullough, and Underwood, op. cit., 305.

[150]Hickman and Scanlon, op. cit., 205.

[151]"Pretrial Conference Procedures," *South Carolina Law Review* 26 (1980), 501.

[152]Karlen, op. cit., 219–220.

[153]"Pretrial Conference Procedures," op. cit., 485–486.

[154]Rule 16 contains no specific authorization for settlement discussion. So settlement is viewed as a natural by-product of the pretrial conference and not explicitly as a goal.

[155]Simmons, op. cit., 930–931.

[156]Maurice Rosenberg, *The Pretrial Conference and Effective Justice: A Controlled Test in Personal Injury Litigation* (New York: Columbia University Press, 1964).

PART TWO

COMMUNICATION THEORY AND PRACTICE IN THE TRIAL PROCESS

CHAPTER

TRIALS

This chapter presents an overview of the trial, "a formal event prescribed by law, as an official, socially sanctioned manner of determining facts, applying law to the facts, and pronouncing an official conclusion, called a verdict. In the simplest and most common situation, the verdict as an output terminates the dispute for all official purposes."[1] Fontes and Bundens further identify a trial as "a dynamic, rule-governed, persuasive proceeding in which information is the primary commodity processed."[2]

The key participants in most trials are a judge, two or more attorneys, one or more plaintiffs (civil cases only), one or more defendants, witnesses, and jurors. The trial generally begins with the selection of jurors, a process which is called *voir dire*. After a jury is chosen, the judge gives the jurors preliminary instructions, after which the attorneys may make opening statements. Following opening statements, the prosecution (criminal law) or plaintiff (civil law) begins its presentation of the evidence. Witnesses are examined and then are cross-examined by the defense. When the prosecution or plaintiff has finished presenting its case, the defense presents its position through witness testimony. After both sides have rested their cases, closing arguments are offered by the opposing attorneys. The judge reads the charge or complaint to the jury, which then goes off to deliberate before reaching a verdict. In a nutshell, this is what happens during a trial.

OVERVIEW OF THE TRIAL PROCESS

A trial is based on an adversarial model; that is, both sides represent their respective positions to the best of their ability. Attorneys choose evidence and claims they believe will win cases for them. As both lawyers openly and actively argue for their sides, we trust that justice will emerge as a balance between these opposing forces. A judge or jury is expected to determine where that balance lies.[3] The bulk of research on the consequences of the adversarial model shows that trial participants believe the process to be overwhelmingly fair and satisfying regardless of their success in court.[4]

Our American jury system is British in origin. It grew out of Norman inquisitions in which the king autonomously gathered information on his subjects and their behaviors. The king compelled a group of twelve to take an oath and report to him on matters concerning his subjects. Each report was based on the group's investigation, not on witness testimony in court. This procedure was used mostly to settle disputes involving land titles. The party who obtained twelve oaths for his side was declared the winner of the dispute. Gradually, the king's judges adopted a practice of hearing directly from the defendant, and at a later time, the defendant was given the right to be judged by his own neighbors. When this occurred, a group of twelve was again used, acting no longer on its own information, but on testimony it heard from others.

When the colonists came to the New World, they made jury trials a part of their system.[5] Later the Bill of Rights and the written constitutions of the states guaranteed a right to trial by jury. The Bill of Rights provides for grand juries (Fifth Amendment), criminal trial juries (Sixth Amendment), and civil trial juries (Seventh Amendment).[6] All state constitutions (except Louisiana) contain broad provisions respecting the right to trial by jury. The most universally accepted motive for the existence of juries is to have them find the facts and, in turn, "the truth," even though they never actually experience the events they hear about in the course of a trial. Rather, they receive representations or interpretations of those events, after which they must find the facts and base their decisions on those representations. So a verdict "is not a statement of truth, it is a statement of fact."[7]

Whereas juries generally resolve issues of fact, it is commonly believed that it is the judge's function to decide issues of law. The judge determines what the law is and its applicability to each and every case, but in the final analysis, juries are also judges of the law. After the attorneys have rested their cases and after the judge has instructed the jury as to the law, the jury proceeds to deliberate on applying the law to the facts. In doing so, the jury selects the principles of law that apply and decides what the law means. For instance, is a game of bingo for money in the church hall gambling, or is it not? Or if a physician shuts off the life support machine on a hospital patient, is that act murder or not? In resolving such questions, juries become *interpreters of law* as well as *finders of fact*.

Throughout the trial process, we protect a jury's fact-finding and law-interpreting mission zealously. Decisions cannot be questioned or impeached as to the reasons for them. Rarely is a verdict set aside. Inquests cannot be conducted into what went on in the jury room during the deliberations. The sanctity of the jury room is closely guarded by the judiciary, and it is the mystery about what takes place there that helps inspire public confidence in the jury as finders of fact and interpreters of law.

JURY TRIALS VERSUS JUDGE TRIALS

Not all trials go to a jury; sometimes a jury is waived, and the case is heard by a judge. Such a trial is called a *bench trial*. Lawyers frequently face this important queston: "When is a bench trial, as opposed to a jury trial, most likely to result in a verdict favorable to our side?" One of the first research efforts focusing on this question was conducted by Kalven and Zeisel in their landmark work, *The American Jury*.[8] They sent numerous questionnaires to trial judges, asking them how much in agreement they were with juries in cases they observed together. They found that judges agreed with juries in 78 percent of the 3576 criminal cases heard.[9] When judges and juries disagreed in the remaining 22 percent of the cases, juries were more lenient than judges in 19 percent of those cases; and judges were more lenient then juries in 3 percent of those cases. They concluded, then, that with juries, "the defendant fares better 19 percent of the time than he or she would have in a bench trial."[10] Of course, this is a relatively small sample and pertains only to criminal cases. One ought not to conclude from the data that the odds are always better for the defendant in a jury trial over a bench trial. For instance, there may be unique mitigating circumstances, significant variables, or strategic reasons that the defense may find a certain judge more lenient.

It is up to the defendant to personally waive the right to a jury trial. He or she may do this either in writing or in open court. Defendants may not withdraw waivers once a trial begins. However, judges occasionally allow the withdrawal of waivers just prior to the commencement of a trial.

Should a jury be waived or not? There are three arguments for jury trials. The first argument is a philosophical one. Many citizens believe they should take full advantage of their constitutional right to have a trial by a jury of their peers. The right to a jury trial is well established. Article III, Section 2, of our federal Constitution specifies that "the trial of all crimes, except in cases of impeachment, shall be by jury." The Seventh Amendment extends the jury trial to federal civil cases in which the amount at stake is above a minimal figure. The United States Supreme Court has further held that the due process clause of the Fourteenth Amendment imposes on the states the requirements of Article III, Section 2, and of the Sixth Amendment.[11] As a result, state constitutions routinely provide the right to a jury trial. Historically, then, the right to a trial is inviolate when the alleged offenses are not petty. This right is a creature of the common law and, although it is not absolute and does not guarantee a jury trial in all cases, "it cannot be denied by the legislature or by judicial decree."[12]

The second argument is also philosophical. Juries are a more democratic way of making decisions than are judges. The jury is an epxression of public opinion; the court expresses the power of the state.[13] Juries constitute unique opportunities for nongovernmental people to play an important role in our judicial process. It is not that we lack faith in our judges to evaluate human conduct, but we have even greater faith in turning to the collective decision of average citizens in each legal case.

The third argument is a practical one. "A jury trial is best for the defendant if the outcome of the case is a gamble."[14] This argument is simply an application of the findings noted earlier in Kalven and Zeisel, that juries tend to be more lenient on defendants than are the judges.

There are two arguments against jury trials, but both of these systemic arguments are easily refuted. First, jury trials take longer than bench trials and thereby cause docket congestion. Extra time must be used to select a jury, explain the charge to them, and then allow them to deliberate. The refutation is that, in spite of this claim, there is little evidence to suggest that there is a significant time difference between jury and nonjury trials. Court backlog seems to be prevalent in both jury and bench dispositions. Second, jury trials are more expensive than bench trials. It is true that jurors are paid nominally for their services. However, the cost differential between jury trials and judge trials is not an enormous one.

If we were to stop the comparison between jury and bench trials here, a conclusion could be reached that jury trials are preferable. Generally, this is true, and my bias is admittedly showing. However, there are tactical considerations that ought to further govern this decision for the defendant. These factors are the experience of counsel, the type of case, the appeal of the parties in the case, the judge involved, and the potential jurors.

The attorney is a critical factor in the decision to opt for a judge or a jury trial. Perhaps counsel is popular in the community, but unpopular with a judge, or vice versa. Perhaps he or she is a particularly effective or ineffective advocate before juries, and his or her attractiveness has the potential of swaying juries. Perhaps he or she is an unseasoned trial lawyer, and litigation would be less complex to handle if it were held before a single judge. Perhaps he or she simply enjoys appearing before juries and will feel more comfortable under those circumstances. Attorneys need to diagnose themselves in choosing a bench trial over a jury trial.

The type of case should further influence the decision of going before the bench or a jury. Although there is no evidence that judges are better than juries in complex cases or in cases that are strong on the facts but weak on the law,[15] there are some case considerations that make a difference. If a case looks close, and the defendant can be made attractive, a jury is preferable to a judge because "the credibility of the defendant was a stronger variable with the jury than with the judge when the evidence was close."[16] If a client has a prior record and it will be brought out in court, a jury might be irreparably prejudiced, and the case might be better tried before a judge.[17] Finally, if the case deals with a matter for which there is little chance of reparation (e.g., sex crimes against children), juries are generally more strict than judges. The case makes a difference.

So does the personal appeal of the parties in a case. For instance, almost all professional groups, with the exception of engineers, recover in civil cases tried to juries far less often than the population of plaintiffs as a whole. The recovery rate for the total population is

61.3 percent. For professors and teachers, it is 50 percent; for accountants and auditors, it is 38 percent; for attorneys, it is 27 percent; for doctors and dentists, it is 22 percent. Moreover, the higher-paid the profession, the lower the damages awarded to the plaintiff.[18] These low recovery rates for professionals may be due to the fact that most juries are composed of nonprofessional and low-socio-economic-status people, who have little identification with the already-wealthy plaintiff. In criminal cases, if any sympathy can be generated for the defendant, a jury is better than a judge. In 22 percent of cases in which judge and jury disagreed, the judges reported to Kalven and Zeisel that sentimentality by a jury for the defendant was an important determinant.[19] A jury may have such feelings for a person that is crippled, a widow, elderly, a member of the clergy, pregnant, repentant, or sad. On the other hand, notoriety, looking horrible, being arrogant, having an undignified occupation, or being divorced several times can lead to greater strictness from a jury than a judge.

The judge is a factor too. Some judges are known to favor the prosecutor or plaintiff and others are known as defendant's judges. Leanings of judges who have been on the bench for some time can be read like an open book. Decisions should be based on whether or not a judge is apt to lean strongly toward one side or the other. Furthermore, the relationship between the judge and the attorney and the attitudes of the judge toward the type of case, the persons involved, their life-styles, the kinds of evidence, and any extenuating circumstances are critical. For example, judges differ in their treatment of drug, traffic, or liquor law violators. Some hesitate to ruin the career of a professional, such as a physician or another lawyer. Some judges are strict with prostitutes, but not with their customers. Some judges might sentence a defendant to a hefty fine and imprisonment for price fixing in an antitrust case; others might ask guilty business executives to present monthly public speeches about their criminal activity to business organizations for one year. Attorneys need criteria for judging judges, just as effective public speakers need criteria for analyzing audiences. Having a judge biased against a case probably calls for a jury trial.

The jury pool is the final factor to be considered in making a judge or jury decision. It is crucial that attorneys analyze potential jurors and their anticipated attitudes toward the case. Once again, persuading a jury basically entails analysis of and adaptation to the audience.

The attorneys, the type of case, the appeal of the parties in the case, the judge, and the jurors are all factors that must be considered by counsel in deciding whether to have a jury trial or a bench trial. After a considerable amount of information has been weighed, the safe procedure, if in doubt, is to demand a jury. If circumstances later indicate that this was the wrong decision, the request can be withdrawn.

PERSUASABILITY

Persuasability refers to susceptibility to persuasion, irrespective of source, subject, or message.[20] Some persons are easier to influence than others, irrespective of the topics and appeals used.[21] In an adversarial situation, it is important to know which persons are particularly susceptible, not only for aiming one's own arguments, but also to consider blunting the effectiveness of the opponent's arguments too.

Prior beliefs, attitudes, and values are major factors in our understanding of persuasability. Beliefs are the ideas that people accept as true or false about something.[22] Lawyers should consistently search for and use beliefs that the jury holds as the means for leading them to the conclusion that is the lawyer's objective. Attitudes are judgments about whether beliefs are good or bad,[23] and lawyers should search for and use attitudes that are congruent with jury attitudes regarding what is dangerous, evil, praiseworthy, moral, and so on. When expressed openly, attitudes are called opinions. Values are organized sets of related attitudes. They are usually the starting points for evaluating persuasive statements, and it is therefore imperative that a lawyer understand the values a jury cherishes so that the themes in the persuasive message can be connected to such values as security, peace, equality, freedom, respect for others, salvation, and wisdom.

Beliefs, attitudes, and values affect human behavior and, in turn, explain the process of persuasion. For example, you might *believe* God exists. You might have the *attitude* that worshiping God will produce favorable results in your life. You also *value* salvation. Therefore, you behave in ways that reflect what you believe is God's will (e.g., going to church each Sunday).

The intensity of our beliefs, attitudes, and values at times causes us to resist persuasion from our opposition. For instance, we may have fundamentalist religious attitudes, our attitudes may be emotionally involved, or we may sense too much difference between our attitudes, beliefs, and values and those an opposing advocate (e.g., an atheist) offers. Conversely, one can expect more success in persuading persons that have moderate beliefs and attitudes, little emotional involvement with their attitudes, no public commitment to a belief, no obligation to be loyal to the views of a group they belong to or look to for guidance, and less perceived dissonance or disagreement between their views and those an advocate offers.[24]

An important step in trial preparation for attorneys is to understand the beliefs, attitudes, and values of the audience. A significant portion of the remainder of this book will attend to the lawyer's task of bringing about change. After all, in a trial, the attitude of the judge or jury must be brought from a position of neutrality to a position of supportiveness. To accomplish that change, the advocate-persuader must follow two essential steps in the process of persuasion: analyze the audience and adapt to that audience. Noted advocate James Jeans wrote that the effective advocate-persuader does not confine his efforts to the sterile adduction of facts.

Every action, every word, every gesture of the attorney, his client, his witnesses will filter through the mind of each juror, assume the flavor of his experience and background, blend with the distillates from his fellow "fact finders" and generate a feeling for the case. This then will be the concern of the advocate—to create the proper "feeling," cultivate the response mood, generate a DESIRE to reach the "right" conclusion. In doing so, you will incidentally, but only incidentally, produce the facts that will support that desire.[25]

In other words, audience motivation is the key to success in persuasion. Juries must believe in an attorney's information, they must form favorable attitudes toward that information, and those attitudes should reinforce already-held basic values.

THE TRIAL AS A PERSUASION MODEL

Because our "formal justice procedures . . . must engage some parallel form of social judgment that anchors legal questions in everyday understandings,"[26] storytelling becomes the "everyday form of communication that enables a diverse cast of courtroom characters to follow the development of a case and reason about the issues in it."[27] The story is the underlying judgment scheme by which vastly different people communicate with each other about issues and evidence in legal cases. Through storytelling techniques, lawyers present their issues and evidence in a way that adapts to the particular audience. Then, in order to understand and take part in trials and to reconcile reality with justice, the jury transforms the issues and evidence into stories. "Stories are systematic means of storing, bringing up to date, rearranging, comparing, testing, and interpreting available information about social behavior."[28] Attorneys must help juries symbolically construct events and actions through storytelling, a particularly effective means by which attorneys can analyze and adapt to their audiences. Stories allow juries to coherently structure an event or action in much the same way they unravel a mystery novel, a movie, a news story, or a television situation comedy.

Unfortunately, many trial lawyers fail to recognize the psychological and storytelling dimensions of a trial. The conviction that "trial outcomes should be decided on the grounds of the facts, evidence, and reasoned arguments presented by the contesting parties is one of the most consensually shared values of members of our legal system."[29] This vision of the trial portrays it as a rational, rule-governed, collective search for the truth. Juries and judges are to determine what really existed or happened. Even though this may be what a trial should be, it does "not accurately mirror the psychological and sociological realities of what a trial *actually is.*"[30]

If trials are not viewed solely as rational, rule-governed events, then they must be seen as places where judges and juries weigh heavily the veracity of informational sources to piece together stories that make sense to them. The way in which evidence is presented and the qualifications and trustworthiness of witnesses and attorneys are quite relevant to decision making in the courtroom. More will be said about this aspect of the trial in Chapter 9.

In order for an attorney to cause a judge-jury attitude shift from neutral to supportive, he or she must involve them "in the process of planning and installing the [attitude] change."[31] As noted in the previous section, this involvement means emotionally stimulating their motives and needs to the point where attitudes become favorable to counsel's cause. Although there are numerous courses an advocate can pursue to create change, let us follow one approach to illustrate once more the persuasive nature of a trial.

Nearly all trials contain conflicting evidence for the jury to resolve. One way they can resolve the conflict and restore balance is to cease thinking about the evidence, that is, to deny that the conflicting evidence exists. An attorney who wants a jury to disregard evidence of this nature might play on this dissonance in the jury by ignoring or belittling the evidence so that it appears unimportant. Or, better yet, an attorney can attempt to reduce dissonance over the conflicting evidence by bringing added social support to reinforce acceptance of the desired change. This is done by getting the jury to like his sources of evidence better than the opponent's sources of evidence. After all, we tend to accept ideas more readily from people we admire, and we reject ideas with ease from people we dislike. The persons liked may be counsel or witnesses or both, and it is their words that can reduce dissonance and cause attitude change. Social acceptance correlates positively with reasonability, balance, and consonance. The attorney-advocate who is knowledgeable in such techniques of persuasion can gain an edge in the drama of the courtroom.

Every part of the trial must be an integrated effort by opposing counsel to sell their cases and secure attitude change. There is no recess from persuasion during a trial. It exists in jury selection, opening statements, examination of witnesses, closing arguments, the judge's instructions to the jury, and jury deliberations. To better understand how the trial serves as a model for persuasion, it is beneficial to recognize the interrelationships among communication process, persuasibility, and the trial itself.

The process of communication can be broken down into five elements. They are *the source* (attorneys and witnesses), *the message* (facts, opinions, and arguments), *the channel* (voices and visual aids), *the audience* (jury and judge), and *feedback*. There are naturally an infinite number of variables linking these five elements of the communication process together, and what we know about these variables has resulted in large part from research on the art of persuasion.

Source

Persuasion research consistently shows that the higher the credibility of the source, the more persuasive the message from that source is for the audience.[32] Because of media coverage of the highly sensational cases he has defended, noted attorney Gerry Spence is going to have a credibility advantage over a lesser-known attorney in most courtroom proceedings. Likewise, witnesses who appear dynamic, knowledgeable, and trustworthy possess greater believability in a trial. Dynamism includes such characteristics as being emphatic, bold, active, and energetic rather than hesitant, timid, passive, and tired.[33] Lawyers and witnesses are knowledgeable when they appear to be intelligent, authoritative, experienced, skilled, informed, competent, and professional.[34] For instance, lawyers should know what they are talking about and their witnesses should be able to deal with the weaknesses and negative aspects of their testimony.[35] Trustworthiness is the extent to which people appear honest, open-minded, fair, friendly, warm, well mannered, and reliable.[36] Thus, the credibility of the source of the message is an element of communication serving an important role in persuasion.

Message

The word is the attorney's paramount tool. Yet there are no meanings in words themselves; meanings exist in our heads. Communication depends on our perceptions of the words we hear and read. This is a phenomenon no attorney should ignore. In order for words to communicate and persuade, they must be clear, powerful, and of interest to the audience. Some of the words we use have greater impact than other words. Since we cannot retain all of the words we receive, we select and retain only certain of them. For example, our tendency is to select and retain congenial words (those which support our beliefs, attitudes, and values) over uncongenial words. Uncongenial information, if it is to be retained at all, is often assimilated, rationalized, or distorted to fit our preconceptions. So, if juries and judges see what they want to see, hear what they want to hear, and remember what they want to remember, attorneys should adapt and select language and messages that best fit the audience's own language, beliefs, and attitudes.

Channel

Most messages during a trial are delivered by the spoken voice. In order for effective communication and persuasion to occur, each voice must be loud enough, clear enough, varied enough in tone, and paced appropriately to keep the audience alert and interested in the message.

Audience

The closer that audiences are mentally to a message and its source, the more likely they can be persuaded by that source. Audiences are not all alike; they differ in many ways. Even judges differ from each other. By way of an illustration, consider this defense against a speeding ticket by a theoretical physicist from the Oak Ridge Scientific Laboratory in Tennessee. He argued that the ionized air that precedes a thunderstorm affects police radar units and that such a storm occurred soon after he was stopped for going 33 in a 25 miles-per-hour zone. The judge who found the accused not guilty was likewise a theoretical physicist! Only in a place like Oak Ridge and with a judge like the one described could a defendant use a principle of advanced physics in his defense and have the judge understand what he was saying. Of course, a juror with a comparable background could have done as well. Audience analysis is intricately related to the message or issue analysis (see Chapter 4). This relationship is important, and it is folly to ignore either kind of analysis. One who ignores issue analysis may lose by default for want of a convincing case, and one who ignores audience analysis is likely to fail to persuade.

Feedback

This is an essential element of effective communication in any setting. Attorneys must be certain their messages are getting across. The final feedback in a trial comes in the form of the verdict. However, during the trial, lawyers should watch the judge and the jury as much as possible, for feedback can often tell lawyers if they should be clarifying the message or emphasizing or deemphasizing certain arguments and evidence.

The five basic elements in a communication model (source, message, channel, audience, and feedback) are the basic elements in a model of persuasion. These elements exist in all persuasion settings, and certainly the courtroom is no exception.

ETHICS AND PERSUASION

Even though a trial is a dramatic event in which persuasion is the goal, attitude change is not to be attempted without keeping in mind certain constraints. The paramount constraint that ought to face lawyers is ethics. An attorney needs to be constantly aware of right and wrong behavior before and during a trial. What are some of those kinds of behavior?

When an attorney sets the judical machinery in motion in behalf of another, he or she needs to do so carefully and cautiously. That is, if going to court will do a client no good, then it should not be attempted. And, if litigation is attempted, "a lawyer should represent a client zealously within the bounds of the law."[37] Such representation means urging a client's strong points and minimizing the weak points through every reasonable and lawful avenue and not through fraud, chicanery, deception, or disrespect. Furthermore, attorneys should never attempt to handle alone something for which they know they are incompetent.

A lawyer should also "preserve the confidences and secrets of a client."[38] Information given by clients to attorneys is privileged. Clients need to understand that in order to feel free to discuss whatever they wish with attorneys. Attorneys ought never to reveal client confidence or secrets to the advantage of another party unless that client consents. This duty not to divulge outlasts even the life of the client.

It is also unethical for lawyers to let their personal interests or those of other clients or third parties impair their loyalty to clients. If tempted, an attorney should withdraw from a case. Such situations include a conflict of interest stemming from multiple clients or a prospect of gaining anything from the outcome other than a reasonable fee. Additionally, gifts from clients should be avoided, including publication rights to a client's story. Other rules of professional conduct pertaining to lawyer-client relations are as follows: a lawyer must never take advantage of a client's fragile state of mind; a lawyer must never hold out false hope and promises to a client; a lawyer must never let an intimate relationship develop with a client; a lawyer should never downgrade a client before others. To behave unprofessionally can seriously jeopardize the general credibility of a trial attorney.[39]

During a trial, a lawyer serves as an officer

of the court. He or she must assist in making the legal process work and must simultaneously represent the client as effectively as possible. Lawyers who try to win cases at all costs have violated their ethical duties both as officers of the court and as attorneys. This balancing of duties is delicate and challenging. For example, as a court officer, an attorney must avoid absurd, frivolous, malicious, and specious arguments, but as an advocate, he or she must make every arguable point and procedural move necessary to aid a client's cause.

Some conduct in court is clearly unethical behavior on the part of any attorney. Facts and laws must never be intentionally fabricated, misstated, or misquoted. Courtesy and respect to the court should be exercised continuously. Undignified exchanges with a judge are verboten. Punctuality must always be attempted. Dilatory tactics, such as unreasonably delaying a trial, should be avoided. No attorney should engage in attacking an opposing lawyer's ability or personality. A lawyer must never attempt to bribe another court official, a juror, or a witness. A lawyer may not communicate improperly with a juror in the case. The list goes on and on. The point to be made here is that ethical considerations must pervade lawyers' minds throughout their professional careers. Admittedly, minor attention has been given here to the subject of ethics. The brevity of this treatment is in no way a commentary on the relative importance of ethics in the legal process. Volumes have been written about ethics, both in human communication and legal communication, all of which should be consulted as companions to this book.[40]

Now that you have been introduced to the trial, let us proceed step by step through it as a paradigm of persuasion. However, before we do, one final observation is in order. Much of the information in the following chapters has been gleaned from observations by legal professionals and research by social scientists.

Only in recent years has an intellectual courtship between the two groups begun, and some still believe that lawyers and social scientists are incompatible partners. "The testable hypotheses, statistical paraphernalia, and ostensibly value-free milieu of the social scientist have been viewed as a world apart from the rule-governed, rhetorical (in the best sense of that term), and value-laden environment of the legal professional."[41] Nevertheless, slowly but surely, this viewpoint is diminishing, and the two groups of professionals are discovering congruence with each other.

Since the middle of the twentieth century, rhetoricians, communicologists, and psychologists have become increasingly fascinated with courtroom behavior. The courtroom is certainly an alluring object of inquiry for testing theories about decision making, information processing, memory, motivation, credibility, and a host of assumptions about communication and attitude formation. The purpose of the remaining chapters is to review the attempts that have been made thus far to study communication in the courtroom.

Notes

[1] Jay A. Sigler, *An Introduction to the Legal System* (Homewood, Ill.: Dorsey, 1968), 119.

[2] Norman E. Fontes and Robert W. Bundens, "Persuasion During the Trial Process," in Michael E. Roloff and Gerald R. Miller, eds., *Persuasion: New Directions in Theory and Research* (Beverly Hills, Calif.: Sage, 1980), 252.

[3] This is in stark contrast to the model used in French courts, where the presiding judge conducts most of the questioning of witnesses. Although attorneys are present, French trials are more firmly in the hands of a judge. Having adopted a nonadversarial and inquisitorial model, the French have an impartial court representative investigate the dispute and present a dossier to the judge before the trial.

[4] John W. Thibaut and Laurens Walker, *Procedural Justice: A Psychological Analysis* (New York:

Erlbaum/Halstead, 1975); E. Allan Lind et al., "Procedure and Outcome Effects on Reactions to Adjudicated Resolution of Conflicts of Interest," *Journal of Personality and Social Psychology* 39 (1980), 643–653.

5Trial by jury was mandated in the colony of Virginia in 1606.

6The distinction between grand and petit juries is noted in Chapter 1.

7John Gossett, "Stock Issues in Legal Argumentation: The Role of 'Fact,' " Paper presented at the Speech Communication Association convention (New York, November 1980), 7.

8Harry Kalven, Jr., and Hans Zeisel, *The American Jury* (Boston: Little, Brown, 1966).

9The judges in the Kalven and Zeisel survey were asked to speculate as to the reasons for their disagreements with juries. Most often, they believed that evidence was the key factor. When evidence was close or ambiguous, jurors were thought to have more doubt about evidence from both sides than did the judges. When facts were unclear, jurors were also thought to rely more on their own values and sentiments. Also, the credibility of the defendant was thought to be a stronger variable with juries than with judges.

10Kalven and Zeisel, op. cit., 59.

11The vitality of the jury process has been discussed and upheld in court decisions such as *Singer v. United States,* 380 U.S. 24 (1965); *Similer v. Conner,* 372 U.S. 221 (1963); *Beacon Theaters, Inc. v. Westover,* 359 U.S. 500 (1959); *Patton v. United States,* 281 U.S. 276 (1930) and *Dyke v. Taylor Implement Mfg. Co.,* 391 U.S. 216 (1968).

12Walter E. Jordan, *Jury Selection* (Colorado Springs: Shepard's/McGraw-Hill, 1980), 10.

13James Marshall, *Law and Psychology in Conflict* (Indianapolis: Bobbs-Merrill, 1966), 87.

14James P. Nunnelly, "When a Trial by Jury," in Glenn R. Winters, ed., *Selected Readings: The Jury* (Chicago: American Judicature Society, 1971), 26.

15Thomas A. Demetrio, "Should Juries Decide Complex Cases?" *Trial* (August 1985), 44–49.

16This is a comment on the Kalven and Zeisel findings from Amiram Elwork, Bruce Dennis Sales, and Davis Suggs, "The Trial: A Research Review," in Bruce Dennis Sales, ed., *Perspectives in Law*

and *Psychology: The Trial Process* (New York: Plenum, 1981), 10.

17Orville Richardson, "Jury or Bench Trial? Considerations," *Trial* (September 1983), 61.

18Jury Verdict Research, *Injury Valuation Volumes* (Solon, Ohio: Jury Verdict Research, 1974).

19Kalven and Zeisel, op. cit., chaps. 15 and 30.

20Irving L. Janis et al., *Personality and Persuasibility* (New Haven: Yale University Press, 1959), 13–14.

21Paul F. Secord and Carl W. Backman, *Social Psychology* (New York: McGraw-Hill, 1964), 168–169.

22Richard E. Petty and John T. Cacioppo, *Attitudes and Persuasion: Classic and Contemporary Approaches* (Dubuque, Iowa: William C. Brown, 1981), 7.

23Martin Fishbein and Icek Ajzen, *Belief, Attitude, Intention, and Behavior* (Boston: Addison-Wesley, 1975), 5.

24Leon Festinger, *A Theory of Cognitive Dissonance* (New York: Harper & Row, 1957); Fritz Heider, "Attitudes and Cognitive Organization," *Journal of Psychology* 21 (1946), 107–112.

25James Jeans, *Trial Advocacy* (St. Paul, Minn.: West Publishing, 1975), 144.

26W. Lance Bennett and Martha S. Feldman, *Reconstructing Reality in the Courtroom: Justice and Judgment in American Culture* (New Brunswick, N.J.: Rutgers University Press, 1981), 3.

27Ibid.

28Ibid., 4.

29Gerald R. Miller and F. Joseph Boster, "Three Images of the Trial: Their Implications for Psychological Research," in Bruce Dennis Sales, ed., *Psychology in the Legal Process* (New York: Spectrum, 1977), 23.

30Ibid., 24.

31Marshall, op. cit., 84.

32Jesse G. Delia, "A Constructivist Analysis of the Concept of Credibility," *Quarterly Journal of Speech* 62 (1976), 361–375.

33David K. Berlo, James B. Lemert, and Robert J. Mertz, "Dimensions for Evaluating the Acceptability of Message Sources," *Public Opinion Quarterly* 33 (1969–70), 563–576.

34James C. McCroskey and Thomas J. Young,

"Ethos and Credibility: The Construct and Its Measurement After Three Decades, *Central States Speech Journal* 32 (1981), 25–34; Don Schweitzer and Gerald P. Ginsberg, "Factors of Communicator Credibility," in Carl W. Backman and Paul F. Secord, eds., *Problems in Social Psychology: Selected Readings* (New York: McGraw-Hill, 1966), 94–102.

[35]Robert V. Wells, "Lawyer Credibility: How the Jury Perceives It," *Trial* (July 1985), 69–72.

[36]Berlo, Lemert, and Mertz, op. cit., 574–575; Carl I. Hovland, Irving L. Janis, and Harold H. Kelley, *Communication and Persuasion* (New Haven: Yale University Press, 1953), 23–24; Schweitzer and Ginsberg, op. cit., 98.

[37]Canon 7, American Bar Association Code of Professional Responsibility.

[38]Canon 4, American Bar Association Code of Professional Responsibility.

[39]Neil Hurowitz, *Support Practice Handbook* (New York: Kluwer, 1985), chap. 14.

[40]Richard L. Johannesen, *Ethics in Human Communication* (Columbus, Ohio: Charles E. Merrill, 1975); Charles U. Larson, *Persuasion: Perception and Responsibility* (Belmont, Calif.: Wadsworth, 1973), chap. 9; Wayne C. Minnick, *The Art of Persuasion* (Boston: Houghton Mifflin, 1968), chap. 11; Thomas R. Nilsen, *Ethics of Speech Communication* (Indianapolis: Bobbs-Merrill, 1974); Robert T. Oliver, *The Psychology of Persuasive Speech* (New York: David McKay, 1968), chap. 2.

[41]Miller and Boster, op. cit., 19.

CHAPTER

JURY SELECTION PROCEDURES

several theories and considerable speculation surround the subject of jury selection. Some lawyers believe that any audience will be impartial, and they take the selection process lightly; others believe that jury selection is what really wins or loses cases. It is my own belief that jury selection is the engine that propels the vehicle of persuasion. Hence, lawyers must be encouraged to strip away their local myths and stereotypes and to replace (or perhaps substantiate) them with an increasing body of knowledge regarding jury behavior.

THE ISSUE OF IMPARTIALITY IN JURY SELECTION

The maximum practical benefit of a jury trial "hinges on the capability of the system to generate a jury pool from which unbiased, impartial jurors are selected to determine a particular factual controversy."[1] The federal government first addressed the matter of procedures by which jury pools are generated with the passage of the Judiciary Act of 1789. It permitted each state the opportunity to establish whatever it wished concerning qualifications for prospective jurors. As might be expected, considerable variations in jury selection procedures existed then and throughout most of the nineteenth century.

In 1879, the Supreme Court set aside a state statute on jury selection that excluded black people from jury service.[2] The Court said this violated the equal protection clause of the Fourteenth Amendment to the Constitution. This was the first time the federal government became involved in the jury selection process within the states. The second time was in 1940, when the Court required that source lists for jury pools be representative of a cross-section of the community.[3] In 1946, the Court further declared that impartial juries are not those which represent narrow class interests or are the instrument of the socially and economically privileged.[4] With the passage of the Civil Rights Act of 1957 (Section 1861), uniform juror qualifications were put into place for all federal courts. The qualifications specified who could be excluded from jury duty, but did not identify who was to be included or what constituted a "fair cross-representation" of a community.

In 1961, the United States Commission on Civil Rights reported that underrepresentation of blacks, Hispanics, the poor, and the young in jury service was commonplace.[5] This finding spurred Congress to pass the Federal Jury Selection and Service Act of 1968 and the 1970 Uniform Jury Selection and Service Act of 1970. This legislation was the first attempt to deal with jury selection systematically and thoroughly. Prior to these acts, Congress had never addressed the issues of sources of names for prospective jurors, selection of those names, or the bases for eliminating certain persons. Federal courts had been choosing jurors through a key-man system, under which court clerks consulted with civic or political leaders for suggestions regarding prospective jurors. These leaders traditionally proposed jurors who were esteemed in their community as persons "of good character, approved integrity, sound judgment, and fair education."[6] The federal courts had, in fact, boasted about the quality of these "blue ribbon" juries, in spite of the fact that they were far from representative of the community and consisted mostly of middle-aged, middle-to-upper-class white males.[7]

The new legislation was based on the premise that local jury selection customs were not always suitable for arriving at justice. Many people had been denied the right to serve jury duty, and the laws were designed to ensure "that jury service will be spread among our citizens more evenly—and more equitably."[8] Three general principles were set forth in the legislation. First, jurors must be selected from voter lists by some random method. This principle was designed to reduce discrimination in jury selection, since voter lists were considered to be broad-based. Second, in order to do away with blue ribbon juries, only objective criteria can be used to determine if a prospective juror is qualified or should be excused from service. Prior to the laws, some courts had used such criteria as verbal intelligence for eligibility for jury duty. Objective criteria are such factors as age, citizenship, residence, or absence of criminal record. Third, greater uniformity in jury selection between the federal and state systems and among the states was desired.[9] Although these laws better ensure that we have impartial juries, critics say much more needs to be accomplished.

COMPILING JURY LISTS

The goal of the first stage of jury selection is the compilation of a list of citizens in each community who are potentially qualified for service. While the list must represent a cross-section of the community, it need not contain the name of every citizen in that community. It must only be a "reasonable" cross-section. As noted above, voter registration lists are the principal source of information, but when a community believes that voter lists are inappropriate or unrepresentative, supplemental lists may be used to correct the perceived imbalance.[10] Sources commonly used include lists of paying utility customers, welfare rolls, telephone directories, city directories, taxpayer lists, and driver's license lists.

There remains some opposition to voter lists, even though they are the most widely employed method of securing names.[11] An argument against them is that not everyone registers to vote. For instance, 73 percent of whites and only 44 percent of Hispanics are registered. Over 80 percent of individuals over the age of 55 are registered to vote, but only 58 percent of those in the 18-to-20-year-old group register. Over 84 percent of college-educated people register, compared with less than 62 percent of those with an eighth-grade education or less.[12] It is easy to

see, then, that whites over the age of 55 in the upper-educated segment of our society could disproportionately be chosen for jury duty, the result being that poor minorities are systematically underrepresented.[13] In defense of the voter lists, however, registering is simply a matter of individual choice, and no one is barred from voting on the basis of race, age, or education.[14]

In each jurisdiction, a local citizen jury commission, as required by the 1970 federal law, compiles the names of potential jurors by the use of voter lists and perhaps supplemental lists as well. Once the commission has prepared a list of potential jurors, a screening process begins. This often takes the form of a random public drawing for the purpose of creating a master list of jury panels. For example, from a voter list of ten thousand persons, an interval number of twenty is used to get a jury pool of five hundred people. The interval number is based on the percentage of persons the commission anticipates it will need for jury duty in a particular term. Names are taken at the chosen interval from the list. Only in a few locations is the old system of drawing names from a drum in the jury commissioner's office being used; computerized data processing systems are becoming more commonplace. The names drawn become the jury pool. Each of those persons is sent a questionnaire so that the jury commission can next examine the competence, qualifications, eligibility, and liability of each person to serve.

When the jury pool questionnaire is returned, the commission may remove the names of certain people who happen to fall into occupational groups that are excluded from jury duty. These predetermined occupational groups are generally positions that are so important to the public that absence from the job cannot be tolerated. Among the most common ones are police, firefighters, physicians, nurses, clergy, military personnel, pilots, teachers, and elected public officials. Certain special occupations, such as embalmers, morticians, ferryboat operators, and chiropractors in Louisiana, millers in Mississippi, law students in Wisconsin, and lighthouse keepers in Massachusetts, are also included in the lists of exempted occupations. In New York State, the list of occupational exemptions was so long that it prompted Judge John C. Knox to say, ''Millions of persons, possessing the best and most intelligent brains in all the land, are relieved, by law, of the necessity of lending aid to the courts in their search for justice.''[15] In recent years, many states have reduced the number of occupational exemptions.[16]

In addition to occupation, some people might be excluded from jury duty because of home or family problems, such as a serious illness or incapacity, small children to care for, or—if they live a long distance from the courthouse—a lack of easily obtainable transportation. Economic sacrifice is generally not considered a reason for being excused; jurors are paid from five to thirty dollars a day, and some employers continue paying their employees while they serve.

The names that have not been removed are placed in a qualified-jury wheel. It is from those remaining names that jury panels are chosen. At any given time, there may be several hundred to several thousand names in the jury pool, and it is from those names that potential jurors are drawn for a particular term of court. After the qualified jury pool has been created, potential jurors whose names are drawn are then summoned for jury duty. Within a specified amount of time, excuses can be sent to the court by potential jurors who want to be dismissed from jury responsibility. About sixty percent of all people summoned ask to be excused.[17] The court issues rulings on each of these submitted excuses, and the standards used vary widely across jurisdictions. Many of the standards leave wide room for discretion by the court's clerical officials.

After receiving a summons to appear on a certain date, a prospective juror shows up at the courthouse, is assigned a number, is given some orientation about jury duty, and is asked to wait in a large hall with others who have been called. As cases come forth for trial, numbers are drawn at random. A set number of names is drawn, and these people are escorted to a courtroom and seated in the jury box, the gallery, or in seats especially for jury selection. This group is called the *venire*. The venire may contain two or three times the number of persons necessary for a trial. By questioning them in a process called voir dire, attorneys will try to determine which ones are inappropriate for a particular case. Only a portion of them will be selected as jurors for a given trial. If possible, the jury will be chosen from the initial venire, but if that is exhausted, others will be called in from the jury pool until a full jury plus alternates has been chosen.

GOALS AND SCOPE OF THE VOIR DIRE EXAMINATION

The process of selecting members of the venire to serve as a jury is called *voir dire,* a French term meaning ''to speak the truth'' or ''truly to say.'' Voir dire is the judicial name for the oral face-to-face questioning of prospective jurors by judges and lawyers for the purpose of determining the jurors' competence to serve.

Intangibles such as local, county, or district practices or the idiosyncrasies of an individual judge are factors that cause voir dire to vary from jurisdiction to jurisdiction or from case to case.[18] What follows is a discussion of just one of those variations, albeit a rather typical one. A number of venirepersons are brought into the courtroom at the same time and seated by the bailiff. An oath is administered to them by the presiding judge, after which the judge greets the panel and offers opening remarks, briefly explaining in general terms what the case is about. The judge may also note some basic principles of justice, in words that might be similar to these: "Trial by jury is a basic right guaranteed to all of us. Those who come before you are entitled to a fair hearing, as free from outside prejudices as possible. Under our legal system, we must ensure that all parties will have cases decided by the facts as presented, rather than by experiences that you, the jurors, have had elsewhere. It is therefore necessary for us to ask you questions to identify your experiences and beliefs in order to ensure an impartial hearing for both the plaintiff (or prosecutor) and the defendant. This part of the trial is called the voir dire."

The judge will proceed by identifying the opposing attorneys and the parties involved in the case and then asking if anyone in the jury pool is acquainted with anyone in the case. Near the end of the judge's remarks, he or she will ask the jurors if there is any reason they believe they might not be fair and impartial in this trial. If a potential juror raises his or her hand, the judge may question that person further and, if necessary, send the person back to the jury pool to await further instructions.

Voir dire is now ready to proceed. From the constitutional perspective, the goal of voir dire is to secure, in theory at least, the most impartial jury possible.[19] A leading court decision ensuring the right to voir dire involved a bearded black civil rights worker who was a defendant in South Carolina.[20] The defense attorney asked the judge to put certain questions to the jury. Two of the questions dealt with racial prejudice. Another was about beards. The Supreme Court ruled that the beard question had no constitutional significance. However, the racial prejudice voir dire questions were guaranteed as part of due process.

Even though the court views impartiality as the goal of voir dire, this view is not shared by the competing attorneys. For them, three goals of voir dire exist: (1) to gather information about the venire, upon which to select the best possible jury, (2) to sell himself or herself as counsel, thereby building rapport and facilitating communication, and (3) to familiarize the jury with certain legal and factual concepts while, at the same time, selling the client's case. The first goal allows attorneys to select the best jurors available from the standpoint of each particular case; the other goals ensure that the jurors who are selected enter the trial in the best possible frame of mind.[21]

The first goal of voir dire for attorneys is to obtain information in order to secure a jury attitudinally biased toward their side and away from the other side. (It is assumed that if both sides work hard toward accomplishing this goal, the net result will be impartiality; in other words, fairness emerges from the confrontation of well-matched opponents.) Voir dire has the potential to discover information about the beliefs, attitudes, and values of the venire. For instance, a lawyer for the defense in a criminal trial would probably ask prospective jurors about their relationships with law enforcement personnel, their experiences with crime, their acquaintance with any witness for the prosecution, their exposure to news media, and any prior experience with criminal trials. In the 1975 Los Angeles trial of members of the Symbionese Liberation Army for the alleged attempted murder of a policeman during a shoot-out, the defense asked prospective jurors about their views of revolutionary politics: "Do you mind that the defendants are called revolutionaries?" "Can you keep the overall cloud of the SLA out of your mind?" The goal of the defense was to cull out those persons unfavorably disposed toward SLA activities. Their main interest was to "obtain a jury favorable to their clients."[22]

The second goal for an attorney conducting voir dire is to establish credibility and rapport with the jury. Some attorneys believe this is the "most useful function"[23] of voir dire. It helps counsel immensely to attain a relationship of trust, respect, and understanding from the very beginning of the trial. Jurors do not reach decisions solely because one lawyer is more credible than the other, but an attorney does appear to have an edge if he or she seems honest, sincere, persuasive, and likable. Attorneys who do their homework concerning the potential jurors in the audience can do much to build bridges between their side of the case and the audience's appreciation for that side.

The third goal for attorneys in voir dire is to educate the jurors about the case. Although this is technically not to be done until the opening statement, it is quite permissible and certainly informative and persuasive to instruct jurors about case facts, theories, and the law prior to asking them questions about any of these matters. "The voir dire examination should flow easily into the opening statement, so that there is continuity in the story being told to the jury."[24] To illustrate, a basic purpose of the story in a personal injury suit might be to have the jury understand the nature and extent of the compensation sought by a client. "Accordingly, it is permissible to condition the jury as to the jurors' ability to award a large sum of money, specific in amount."[25] Questions as to each juror's willingness to compensate an injured plaintiff consistent with thousands and millions of dollars are deemed appropriate by the courts.[26]

One study found that lawyers do, in fact, attempt to fulfill the latter two goals (the social influence goals) as well as the former one. In that study, more than 40 percent of the lawyers' communications to the jury in voir dire were concerned with creating a good impression and laying the foundation for the case. The authors emphasize the importance of this socializing influence of voir dire, calling it "a rite of passage."[27] In another study, it was discovered that 80 percent of voir dire time is spent on the socializing influence, and only 20 percent of the time is used by attorneys in

an attempt to elicit information by which favorable and unfavorable jurors can be distinguished.[28]

What can be covered during the voir dire examination? In the early English jury, questions could pertain only to a specific bias, such as blood, marriage, or economic relationship to a litigant. A nonspecific bias, such as ill feeling toward a litigant's case, could not be probed. This limited voir dire was used in the American colonies. However, once controversial political trials began, the revolutionaries demanded and got the right to query potential jurors about their prejudices. Patrick Henry said he would prefer that a judge hear the case if he did not have the right to question the venire about their attitudes. This position was implicitly included in the Constitution's references to "impartial juries."

An expansive voir dire was officially sanctioned by Chief Justice John Marshall in 1807 in the treason trial of Aaron Burr.[29] Burr had been vice-president under Thomas Jefferson although they were longtime political enemies. In 1804, Burr killed Alexander Hamilton in a gun duel. Burr fled to Kentucky and assembled a small army, causing Jefferson to bring treason charges against him. The print media publicized the case widely, and both sides became increasingly concerned about obtaining an impartial jury. Justice Marshall, no friend of Jefferson's, made a number of rulings calling for the disqualification of jurors who had preconceived ideas about the dispute. He permitted voir dire questions based on juror attitudes toward the evidence. Marshall's decision was so persuasive that it was subsequently adopted by nearly all the state courts. Since that time, potential jurors have been subject to questions in areas of nonspecific bias.[30]

Today, venirepersons are questioned on a wide range of matters, encompassing anything "relevant to the issues on trial which would disclose bias or prejudice against any person or on any issue."[31] Typical exclusions from voir dire are the mention of the existence of liability insurance in a civil case, questions about verdicts in past cases heard by the prospective jurors, highly personal questions about habits of the jurors, and information about prior convictions of the defendant in a criminal trial.[32]

Questioning generally is related to one of four possible areas. First, questions are asked regarding the law.[33] Such a question might be, "Are you in sympathy with and could you follow the rule of law which states that . . . ?" Or, "Do you have any bias against a defense based on insanity?" Second, questions are asked concerning expected testimony. Such a question might be, "Would you give more weight to testimony from a policeman solely because he is a policeman?" Third, questions are asked concerning the potential juror's own background. Although attorneys get some personal information on a juror report form, they may want additional information from some or all of the panel. This information includes such matters as any relationship or acquaintance the potential juror might have with persons participating in the trial, knowledge or hearsay information concerning any matters relevant to the trial, and bias that may affect the final judgment. Fourth, questions are asked concerning sentencing. For instance, "Are you predisposed for or against capital punishment?" A sample voir dire covering these areas is found in Appendix D. Jurors are sworn to answer all voir dire questions truthfully.

Before we go further in our discussion of voir dire, it should be noted that there is disagreement among legal practitioners concerning its value. Some counsel say that it is only random guessing and that it is impossible to identify biased jurors by questioning them. Those practitioners are willing to accept any venirepersons as impartial and fair. Judge Alan E. Morrill claims that these lawyers are either "lacking an aptitude for jury trial work" or have "little or no trial experience" and that voir dire should have "first priority in importance."[34] I tend to agree with Morrill and believe that, considering the many possibilities of juror prejudice that exist, lawyers should not lightly waive the right to conduct a voir dire. The authors of one study, after comparing juries impaneled through the voir dire process with those selected merely at random, found that the voir dire jury was (1) much better in considering mitigating circumstances, (2) much less influenced by prejudicial publicity, (3) much better at following the applicable law, and (4) less shifting in its opinion during deliberations.[35]

JUDGE-CONDUCTED VERSUS COUNSEL-CONDUCTED VOIR DIRE

With the passage of Rule 47 of the 1938 Federal Rules of Civil Procedure, judges were permitted to either conduct the voir dire themselves or permit counsel to do it. Today, in practically all federal courts, judges conduct most, if not all, of the voir dire. Attorneys conduct the voir dire in 44 percent of state courts, judges in 30 percent, and both attorneys and judges in the remaining 26 percent.[36] Generally, the steady trend today is toward curtailing counsel's opportunity in favor of the judge. With this shift in voir dire responsibility, there is considerable debate in the legal community over who, ideally, should conduct the questioning.

There are two main advantages to having a judge-conducted voir dire. First, some say the judge-conducted voir dire saves time.[37] The New York State Commission on the Administration of Justice found that the average attorney-conducted voir dire took 12.7 hours, whereas a judge-conducted voir dire took an average of 2.5 hours.[38] A judge usually tells the jury panel something about the lawsuit and then asks general questions as to their knowledge of the case or acquaintance with parties in the case. Attorneys left alone to accomplish the same purpose tend to be "long, dull, and repetitious,"[39] whereas a judge, in the interest of time, can end the same voir dire more quickly. One should note, however, that not all of the studies have found that judge-conducted voir dire is faster.[40]

Second, judge-conducted voir dire can halt abusive practices by counsel. When counsel questions potential jurors, the judge does not have the opportunity to screen the questions in advance. Occasionally, improper questions are asked (e.g., embarrassing questions and questions assuming certain facts still to be proved).[41] These questions are deemed unfair. In addition, some claim that lawyers should not have the opportunity to use voir dire for the purpose of ingratiating themselves with the jury; they say ingratiation is an improper goal to set.[42]

The three advantages of counsel-conducted voir dire focus on the premise that it is good to have direct two-way communication between counsel and juror. Voir dire is the only phase of the trial in which this can be accomplished. First, since it is the attorneys who ultimately decide which jurors will and will not serve, they ought to be the source of rooting out any hidden background experiences or attitudes affecting the prospective juror's judgment. It is the attorneys, not the court, who are more familiar with the case at hand and are therefore better equipped to ask more deeply probing questions.[43] Furthermore, when attorneys are permitted to question, they can assess directly the nonverbal communication cues from the panel, since these cues are directed toward the questioner.[44] This valuable information is lost when counsel cannot question.

Second, counsel-conducted voir dire allows the lawyers to introduce themselves, let the jury get used to their style, and establish rapport. This was the second goal of voir dire

as previously noted. If one accepts that as a proper goal, "it seems apparent that [it is] . . . lost if the judge conducts the voir dire examination."[45]

Third, venirepersons respond to the court's questions with less candid self-disclosure than if the questions are posed by counsel. A survey of jurors found that they look upon the judge as an important authority figure and are therefore reluctant to displease him.[46] Seeking approval from a judge, venirepersons portray themselves in the best possible or most socially desirable light, not wanting to admit they might be biased.[47] They are determined to appear honest and open-minded because that is what they believe the judge wants from them.[48] Attorneys, with apparently less status in the courtroom, "are more likely to elicit candid answers from jurors. . . . When the social distance between the questioner and the respondent is decreased the respondent is more likely to be forthright in answering questions."[49] Also, lawyers are in a better position than the judges to be more open, informal, and personal with the jurors, thereby influencing the potential juror's liking, warmth, and capability for self-disclosure.[50] One study found that jurors are much more consistently honest with their answers when questioned by an attorney than when questioned by a judge, regardless of the interpersonal style of the questioner.[51]

There is little empirical research validating or invalidating any of the above claims. However, a recent study shows that the traditional role of judges constrains them from eliciting juror self-disclosure while the low image of attorneys prevents them from securing maximum self-disclosure as well. In addition, judges and lawyers are so dissimilar from most jurors that open and free talk with either of them is impeded. The authors of this study boldly suggest that the courts appoint citizens who are especially skilled in obtaining self-disclosure and who are more similar to the jurors in their way of life to conduct the preliminary voir dire, with follow-up questions from judges and attorneys.[52]

STRATEGY AND CONDUCT OF THE EXAMINERS

Certain special strategic and behavioral opportunities for trial lawyers arise when they are permitted to question the venire personally. These opportunities are related to the information-gathering, source-credibility, rapport-building and case education objectives of voir dire. As Crawford notes, "there is a direct correlation between the *degree* of credibility attributed to a speaker and the *quantity* of attitude change he can produce."[53] Let us look at twelve strategies and attorney behaviors that make voir dire effective for trial lawyers.

First, *file strategic pretrial motions related to voir dire*. For instance, prior to jury selection, the filing of a motion *in limine* can prohibit opposing counsel from communicating to the jury any irrelevant or prejudicial facts. If a party's divorce, wealth, drunkenness, or tax evasion comes out in voir dire, no admonitions from the bench will erase this information from the venirepersons' minds, even though the information has nothing to do with the case. The damage is done. So attorneys must anticipate ways in which their imaginative adversaries may try to directly or indirectly communicate prejudicial facts to the panel and must try to get a protective order from the court by filing an *in limine* motion.

In addition, counsel might also consider filing motions concerning the conduct of the voir dire, the number of challenges, and the impaneling procedure. All motions should be well documented. For example, defense attorneys who are trying to convince judges that there is a general community bias against their clients should ask for an expanded voir dire. Documentation for this request can come from such surveys as the nationwide study that showed that 37 percent of Americans believe that a defendant should prove innocence.[54] It can be argued that an expanded voir dire is needed by defense attorneys to know which venirepersons make up that 37 percent.

One creative pretrial motion is to request that the client participate in the voir dire. This participation can be a masterful stroke from a communication standpoint. A brief introductory statement from a client can evoke many responses from the venirepersons. Some may smile at the client; others may frown. Some may maintain eye contact; others may pull their legs and arms close to their bodies and look away. These are valuable clues for the questioning attorney. In that introductory statement, a client can state his or her name, indicate the reason for being in court, and ask the jury for full cooperation with his or her attorney during the voir dire. Some clients might even be able to ask a few questions of the panel. For instance, when American Indian Movement leader Russell Means was on trial for murder in South Dakota, he asked some of the voir dire questions himself. If clients are to participate in the voir dire, they should have the kind of personality and communication skills needed to establish a positive relationship with a jury panel. Clients who are incapable of establishing this kind of relationship through direct interaction with the venirepersons should not be asked to participate.

Second, *be clear*. Unfamiliar terms should be explained, and whenever possible, more commonly used synonyms should be employed. For example, a prosecutor or plaintiff's attorney can explain the technical legal term *negligence* as synonymous with "carelessness" or "fault." Complex language can confuse and antagonize a jury. The result may be misleading answers to an attorney's technical questions or hostility toward a display of legal brilliance. For example:

Suppose you are defending a person charged with assault and your defense is that the accused acted in self-defense. Some lawyers might phrase the question in this manner: "Do you believe that a person is justified in injuring his attacker, if, by the exercise of ordinary discretion and care, he has reasonable ground to believe that he is in imminent danger of losing his life or of incurring great bodily harm?" The accuracy of the law involved in that question is not to be doubted, but its value as a question is. The lay mind would have difficulty grasping it. The response therefore, would be worthless.

I would suggest a more simplified question, such as follows: "Do you believe that a person is justified in injuring another if he honestly believes that he is in actual danger of being harmed by his attacker?"

This question employs simple, everyday language. It also explains to the jury the law of self-defense.[55]

Third, *convey a sense of professionalism during voir dire.* There are lawyers who appear to believe they can build rapport by giving the impression they are only half competent. In reality, juries do not expect such commonness; they prefer thoroughness, knowledge, accuracy, and professionalism throughout the voir dire. Acting half-competent reduces attorney power and seriousness regarding the promotion of justice. Blunk and Sales note, "To the extent that counsel is able to develop perceived expertise in the eyes of the veniremen (specifically through a demeanor of confidence, efficiency, and moderate display of knowledge) his persuasive impact will be enhanced; however, emphasis on recondite points of law or a pedantic display of legal expertise may alienate the veniremen by a loss of perceived similarity."[56]

Professionalism is also fostered when attorneys, while asking questions in voir dire, make it clear which juror is to speak. If a question is asked of the entire group, the form of the answer should be specified (e.g., "Raise your hand if you agree with this statement"). Efficiency of this sort enhances counsel credibility. "Beginning a trial at opening statement time with a deficiency in credibility . . . is tantamount to losing a case which might have been won."[57]

Professionalism is further conveyed if the lawyer avoids boring the venirepersons. Routine questions, not the kind noted in the eighth strategy discussed below, should never be repeated over and over again. Rather, these questions can be asked of the jury as a whole or in small groups. Or a routine question can be asked of one panelist, such as, "Do you know or have you ever heard of the painter Thomas Gonzales?" After the respondent replies, the attorney may then say to the full panel, "If I were to ask the rest of you that same question, would anyone answer it differently?" This procedure keeps the voir dire moving along satisfactorily, and a jury appreciates an attorney's attempt to be efficient. Voir dire should be kept as short as possible to avoid boring the venire.

Fourth, *decide on the techniques to be used to immunize the jury. Immunization,* also called *inoculation,* is an attempt by an advocate to fight off persuasive messages from an opponent. Immunization involves *commitment* and *anchoring* techniques to induce resistance to counterpersuasive efforts.

All of us strive to be cognitively consistent with our beliefs, attitudes, and values. Irrevocable commitments that lawyers ask prospective jurors to make during voir dire are a form of immunization technique. Here are some examples. A criminal defense lawyer asks a jury to set aside prejudice against an "ex-con." A plaintiff's attorney poses this query: "Will you, as a juror in this case, promise to bring in a verdict for the plaintiff if we establish our case by a greater weight of the evidence, not proof beyond any reasonable doubt?" Or, defense counsel asks, "Will you promise to me and commit yourself to me not to let any of your natural sympathies influence your verdict?''

In each of these instances, the commitment made by the juror is most powerful if it is made verbally in front of the court rather than as a simple nodding of the head with the group. Then, after the verbal commitment is made, it should be paraphrased by the lawyer to call attention to the importance of commitment so that the juror will not forget it.[58] To illustrate, a juror says, "Even though I sat on a jury that heard a similar case, I can put bias from that case aside." The attorney should then say, "Fine, Mr. Juror. I understand that you are saying that you will not let any bias that you have from the other trial enter into this case. Thank you." The attorney's response reinforces the juror's commitment.

Commitments are further strengthened when they are put in writing.[59] People who commit themselves in written form are most dogged in maintaining their committed positions over a period of time. Of course, jurors cannot be asked to actually put their commitments in writing. However, the court reporter is "writing" the voir dire proceedings. So all counsel has to do is point out to the jury that their commitments are in written form. "When the time for summation arrives, drive home the commitment by showing the jury the transcript of their commitment on an overhead, blown up and projected onto a big screen. It will appear larger than life to them; it is the closest thing to having the jurors read it in their own handwriting."[60]

Promises and commitments can become very important to counsel when final arguments are made. The theory is that having given such a commitment, a juror is more likely to follow it, because changing the commitment is awkward or costly to a juror's self-esteem. In one discussion of commitment techniques, the authors conclude that "the evidence clearly demonstrates that forcing a person to publicly commit himself to a belief is an effective way of increasing resistance to subsequent persuasive appeals."[61] Of course, psychological reactance theory also tells us that trying to get people to promise to behave in ways that run counter to common sense and good judgment might backfire.[62] So an attorney should not try to go too far in securing juror commitments. More will be said about commitment in Chapter 10.

Anchoring techniques can also be used to induce resistance to persuasive appeals from the other side. Anchoring involves the connection of attorney beliefs to other beliefs, attitudes, or values already held by the jury panel or by individuals or groups liked by the panel.[63] Such connections produce resistance to persuasion because a change in the belief, attitude, or value would require that the panelist either change other linked beliefs, attitudes, or values correspondingly or endure the discomfort of cognitive inconsistency. Linking beliefs to accepted values makes those beliefs more resistant to change. For instance, if the defendant is a teenager accused of selling cocaine, it is assumed that older jurors are undesirable. However, if the defense attorney appeals to the widely held belief that defendants deserve a fair trial and are to be considered innocent until firmly proven guilty, that defense attorney is anchoring the case in the jurors' beliefs that all citizens, including teenagers, ought to have the same constitutional safeguards of justice and equality in our legal system. "To the extent that counsel may present specific aspects of the case to the veniremen, . . . the anchoring and the committing approaches to immunization against persuasion should serve as helpful voir dire techniques."[64]

Fifth, *decide on the means to be used to indoctrinate the jury*. Indoctrination as a tactical device means designing questions to make educational statements about the case.[65] Indoctrination further involves seeking out juror predispositions and adapting to them so that the juror is impressed with the merits of the case. One book provides us with the following example and explanation from a defense attorney's point of view. Notice how the attorney educates the jury and tries to adapt to their basic values.

"I would be naive if I didn't recognize that many persons have strong feelings regarding the use of intoxicating beverages by persons who operate motor vehicles. Many of us may belong to religious denominations which prohibit the use of intoxicants and consider such behavior as being morally wrong. In this case the evidence will be that my client, Tom Brown, drank several beers before the collision occurred. The evidence will further indicate that he was not under the influence of liquor at the time of the occurrence. Now my problem is this—that someone may be so offended by Tom's behavior in drinking the beer that they might find it difficult to sit as a juror in this case and return a verdict based solely on the law and the evidence. (Addressing a juror personally) Mrs. Green, how do you feel about this?"

The style might vary but the pattern is clear.

1. Recognize the potentially dangerous attitude.
2. Speak solicitously of those who share this attitude.
3. Acknowledge that the problem exists.
4. Confront the jurors personally.
5. Seek an expression of opinion, not a monosyllabic affirmation.
6. Get a commitment.[66]

If Mrs. Green thinks all drunken drivers ought to be thrown in jail, she ought to be excused. If she thinks she wants to hear the evidence about how Brown's drinking affected his driving, she has been indoctrinated and is now ready to make a commitment. Obviously, indoctrination and immunization are closely related phenomena. Indoctrination involves educating the jury about the case and then reinforcing predispositions; immunization involves building a resistance to an opponent's persuasive appeals.

Indoctrination is accomplished when attorneys develop a perception of relevant similarities between themselves and the potential jurors. If the jury shares with an advocate a belief that the American system of jurisprudence is effective, persuasibility is enhanced for that advocate. Attraction to shared beliefs, attitudes, and values is a major determinant in message acceptance.[67] This includes attraction as a function of attitudinal similarity of personality, similarity of need, and similarity of economic background.[68] "When the receiver of the persuasive communication perceives a similarity with the sender of the message, the receiver assumes that they share common goals and values. The receiver then may change his or her attitudes to match those desired by the sender in order to bring the attitudes in line with what is perceived to be appropriate for someone having those goals and values."[69]

Furthermore, similarity between lawyer and juror is enhanced linguistically when the lawyer uses a technique called *pacing*.[70] This technique must be applied to each juror individually as he or she is being questioned. What a lawyer does when pacing is listen to each juror's key words and phrases, then mirror that language in follow-up remarks. If a juror says, "Well, I would look for . . . ," the attorney next says, "I understand that you would look for . . . " Such language pacing builds a perception in the jurors' minds that the lawyer is similar to themselves.

So attorneys can indoctrinate prospective jurors by developing and encouraging a perception of shared similarities, and this can be done through carefully selected and matched voir dire questions. However, if attorneys are too blatant in their attempts to indoctrinate a jury, an objection can be raised by opposing counsel, and a judge can restrict or prohibit the use of such questions. For instance, it would be inappropriate to ask a potential juror's verdict in a hypothetical, but quite analogous, case. It also is inappropriate to ask a juror what an appropriate settlement sum might be in a case such as the one to be tried.[71] It looks bad for an attorney to ask a question such as this and then have an opposing counsel's objection sustained by the judge. Good sense in voir dire questioning must be practiced, if for no other reason than to establish and maintain credibility with the jury.

Sixth, *decide on what is possible and necessary to ingratiate yourself with the jury.* Ingratiation is the building of attorney esteem.[72] It is grounded in the notion that juries base some of their decisions on their likes or dislikes for the lawyers in the trial; jurors will give more favors and respond more favorably to lawyers they like.[73] Unfortunately, some lawyers try to ingratiate themselves with too many grandstand plays. For instance, some attorneys loudly announce they choose to waive voir dire since they have so much faith in the integrity and fairness of the particular panels at hand.[74] This boast could have a boomerang effect because it is an obvious attempt at a persuasive ploy or because it appears that the lawyers are being too careless in their work.

An effective way to begin voir dire is with some self-disclosure by counsel. For instance, a lawyer might tell the audience how nervous he is at the beginning of every trial and say that he assumes the jurors are nervous too. This ingratiation technique not only gets the jurors to empathize with and like the lawyer, but encourages self-disclosure from the jurors as well. Some of the other ingratiation methods include flattery of the panel, demonstrated concern for the health of older panel members, joking with the venirepersons, or identification of activities in common, such as playing tennis.[75] Used sparingly, such tactics can ingratiate, although no empirical research "has been performed to determine the frequency or efficacy of such ingratiatory tactics in the voir dire."[76] Used blatantly, these techniques can backfire. Detroit lawyer

Charles Bair claims, "Juries spot phonies and don't like them."[77] For instance, the attorney who intentionally plants a homey and corny tale runs the risk of appearing insincere. What would you think of a lawyer who said, "The case is sort of like what the old farmer said about his bread: 'No matter how thin I slice it, there is always two sides' "? Ingratiation works best when natural opportunities and not pre-planned ones come along. Constant gushing over a jury in an exaggerated way appears phony, but the radiation of friendship, good will, and subtle charm can go a long way.

What the attorney wants in voir dire is a warm relationship with the jury. Such a relationship can be developed at the beginning of voir dire as the lawyer makes a self-introduction and introduces the client as well. If counsel touches the client physically when making the introduction, jurors will respect the warm and personal bond between the two persons. The lawyer's client should be referred to in a natural, matter-of-fact way as "Mary Jones," not "Ms. Jones" or "plaintiff" or "defendant." Of course, while counsel uses a client's first name, a contrast should be made by using the opponent's last name or "plaintiff" or "defendant." The former usage is personalized, informal, and endearing; the latter is depersonalized, formal, and cold.

Another way for lawyers to achieve a warm relationship with a jury is to be aware of their own nonverbal communication during voir dire. Nonverbal cues are constantly being sent to and interpreted unconsciously by jurors. For instance, standing sets up a power relationship, particularly if the lawyer is behind a lectern. Sitting on the edge of a table has a softer and more personal look and makes eye contact between the lawyer and the sitting jury easier to accomplish. Several lawyers conduct voir dire 20–30 feet from the prospective jurors. This is a rather large and formal interaction distance. This may be satisfactory when questioning the entire group, but in questioning individuals, a closer distance (3–6 feet), rather than a public distance, is more appropriate. Getting too close—less than 2 feet away—is too intimate and runs the risk of making the juror feel uncomfortable.[78] Of course, exact distances vary with the setting, the lawyer, and the panel. For example, most women and small men can move in closer to the jury; tall and large people should move back. Generally, a casual and informal approach to voir dire goes a long way toward building rapport, whereas excessive formality hinders self-disclosure and builds walls between venirepersons and counsel.

Counsel can further ingratiate themselves with juries by being polite and fair. Being considerate of other people does not mean making saccharine moves. But tact and kindness throughout the questioning period are generally more successful than "investigating" the jurors with regard to their personal biases. Voir dire is not the equivalent of cross-examination. Jurors should not be made to feel as though they are on trial. The questioning attorney must indicate not only by statement but also by attitude and manner that he or she has no personal feeling toward the examinee but is only doing what is necessary for his or her own side's cause.

A lawyer should never interrupt in the middle of an answer; it cuts off comunication. An attorney's voice should never be raised in anger, and the questions should never be asked in an accusing or judgmental tone. Even though venireperson answers are not always clear and may not be the desired ones, an attorney should remain calm, unruffled, and nonargumentative throughout the questioning process. Getting into an argument with a potential juror creates a very poor impression of the attorney. Also, sarcasm, including puns and wisecracks at a juror's expense, should be avoided at all costs. Finally, it never hurts to sprinkle the questioning with an occasional "please" and "thank you." "This is not only a good display of common courtesy and politeness, but will leave a much better general impression with the jury panel than if the lawyer has never uttered these common words."[79] In sum, "voir dire must be used by the lawyer to 'sell' himself to the jury."[80] That is what ingratiation entails—being interested in and nice to people.

Seventh, *deal with each potential juror as an individual.* Panel members may be interrogated as a whole, in small groups, individually, or both as a group and individually. This is a matter of court and lawyer discretion. One problem in questioning the entire panel as a group at once is that it is extremely difficult to monitor all the answers. Another problem is the phenomenon of peer group pressure. Individuals often do not like to deviate from the attitudes of others in their group. The hesitant juror may pause a moment to see how the rest of the group is going to respond, and then, not wanting to seem different, respond in like manner. It is much easier to gauge some of the more subtle aspects of a potential juror's attitudes and reactions to the case by having that person open up and talk awhile. Such talk is difficult to achieve in collective questioning. Probably the only advantage of collective questioning in which the group responds vocally or by a show of hands is that it avoids repetition and saves time.

Although potential jurors think of themselves as members of a group, they also like to be recognized on their own individual merits as well. They like to think of themselves as important people. Therefore, it is best for an attorney to show an interest in each juror's occupation, hobbies, and other interests. It is also good for an attorney to single out individuals and offer them positive reinforcement for certain answers they provide.[81] Words of approval (e.g., "Good," "Excellent," "Correct") single out a respondent and promote identification between that respondent and the approving lawyer. Expressions of approval to individuals should be sprinkled throughout the examination in order to dampen the negative effects of judgmental inquiries.[82]

During questioning, the lawyer should look at individual panelists, not at his or her feet, the ceiling, or other people. Eye contact elicits greater self-disclosure and verbalization from venirepersons, as long as it is intermittent and frequent rather than a constant staring.[83] In addition, "counsel should talk with jurors not at them."[84] Talking casually with jurors makes them feel at ease and not threatened by counsel.

Finally, jurors can be thought of as individuals if they are addressed by name (e.g., "Mr. Smith," "Ms. Jones"). A chart of names can be prepared by the questioner to help him or her remember the individual names of the panelists. Addressing them from memory is even better than reading from the chart; it is quite impressive. Jurors will appreciate this courtesy, especially if their names are pronounced correctly! If necessary, the name should be written down by the attorney phonetically. People are usually sensitive about the pronunciation of their names.

Eighth, *get the jurors talking*. To get the most and best information from the venire, it is important to get all of them to unlatch their thinking on critical, not routine, questions. Question phrasing is crucial in that regard. A very poor question is, "In spite of the fact my client was intoxicated, you would make every effort to be fair and impartial, wouldn't you?" This leading question is weak because it does not allow any description of the prospective juror's experiences, impressions, and opinions; it yields little information because no one likes to think he or she would intentionally be unfair to someone just because that person was intoxicated. If anything, this type of question demeans the questioner. The "will you be fair" leading question should generally be avoided, unless it is designed to immunize or indoctrinate the panel. As noted earlier, immunization and indoctrination rely on a pattern of leading questions. Here, we are considering only the goal of obtaining information about each juror.

In order to impose at least some burden of candor on the venireperson, a question can be posed this way: "Have you ever had any personal experience with intoxication in your life that you think might influence your vote even slightly in favor of one side if you serve on this jury? You understand we have to rely on your sincerity and honesty because we have no way of knowing what might influence your judgment as a juror." To go further, the attorney might reassure the venireperson that prejudice is a normal phenomenon by conceding to his or her own prejudices, for example, "Even I sometimes prejudge people because of their appearance or conduct. Such feelings are normal, and we certainly don't need to be ashamed of them." An open-ended question, such as the one about a juror's personal experiences, requires narration rather than a yes or no response. Questions like these start with words such as "how," "why," and "what" rather than "do you agree" or "do you believe." A good question would be, "What is your attitude toward intoxication?" The yes or no reply does not accurately gauge prejudice or intellect; the narrative response produces more and better information for the attorney. "If the juror can be drawn out to engage in 'conversation' on the issue under discussion, a truer reflection of the juror's real thoughts will be revealed."[85]

One word of warning, however: open discussion can produce an occasional unexpected answer that may have a negative impact on other jurors.[86] For example, a juror might say to a defense attorney, "I think being drunk is the worst form of human irresponsibility," and then proceed to give countless horror stories about intoxicated individuals. So the least risky form of open-ended question is one that asks the jurors to talk about their jobs, their families, and their interests as windows to their attitudes and personalities.

Ninth, *disclose weaknesses*. It is generally a good idea to disclose the unattractive features in one's case as soon and as gracefully as possible. Assume that a defense counsel has a client who was drunk at the time of an accident, which is the focal point of a trial. This information can be explosive and damaging. It is softened considerably if the defense counsel brings this information out in his or her own voir dire questioning. The lawyer can ask this question: "Mr. Jones, what do you think of the fact that my client, Dorothy Jessup, was inebriated at the time of the accident?" The jury will learn of this information anyway, and they might as well hear it from the source. It then looks like a confession of sins. Think of the conditions in which you are most likely to forgive another person for something that person did wrong. Are you not more tempted to forgive people when they inform you of their wrongdoing than when they remain silent or get defensive about it? Juries, too, appreciate sincerity and candor of this sort. It helps to build both the questioning attorney's and, in this case, Dorothy Jessup's credibility.

Tenth, *if necessary, ask for a private voir dire.* If an attorney wishes to ask one or more potential jurors some highly personal questions, it is appropriate to request that each of these jurors be questioned out of the presence of the others in the group. Venirepersons should never be embarrassed in public, for they may become hostile to the attorney asking the questions. If a sensitive matter, such as having been the victim of a physical attack, needs to be probed in a rape trial, the questioning attorney should ask for a sequestered voir dire. In this way, the personal privacy of the respondent is protected, and freer disclosure is possible.[87] Also, potentially harsh questioning of one panelist, which may antagonize others in open court, may call for a private voir dire session, which is usually conducted in the judge's conference room with only the venireperson, the judge, both attorneys, the defendant, the plaintiff, a court reporter, and court staff present.

Eleventh, *explain why awkward questions must be posed to the respondents.* Jurors do not like the nosy, intimate question, but they must not be allowed to take out their resentment on the lawyer who needs to ask such a question. So the lawyer might precede a highly personal question with a comment such as, "Please forgive me for asking prying questions at this time. I will try not to get too personal. However, I am sure you understand that I am not trying to satisfy my own curiosity. Rather, in order to get a fair and impartial consideration of the facts in this trial, it is necessary for me to learn about your background and about personal experiences in your life that might affect your fairness and impartiality to both sides." Notice the appeal to the American ideal of fair play. It is not a matter of prying into the private lives of the venirepersons. Rather, it is a lawyer's *duty* to ensure an impartial jury for his or her client.

Twelfth, *explain the significance of being excused.* Excuse of a potential juror may offend that juror and others as well. So it should be explained carefully why some people might not be selected for jury duty in this trial. An attorney can say to the entire panel in advance, "It is possible that there is something in your past that I might think would make it difficult for you to judge this case impartially. Therefore, if you are excused, please do not think I do so because of any general personal impression I have of you." Even excusing a person should be done with utmost courtesy. Animosity must be avoided. When a venireperson is excused, the less said, the better. The excuse should be exercised quietly and without undue emphasis.

These twelve examiner strategies and conducts produce maximally effective counsel communication in voir dire. Again, the techniques are as follows: (1) file strategic pretrial motions, (2) be clear, (3) be professional, (4) immunize the jury with commitments and anchoring, (5) indoctrinate the jury, (6) ingratiate yourself with the jury, (7) treat the jurors as individuals, (8) get the jurors talking, (9) disclose weaknesses, (10) consider a private voir dire, (11) explain the need for posing awkward questions, and (12) explain what excusing certain jurors means.

PREPARING FOR VOIR DIRE

By thinking early in the game about the probable juror mix, an attorney becomes better able to draw reliable conclusions about juror responses. Voir dire information should be placed in the jury selection section of the trial notebook. A few weeks before trial, a voir dire conference should be held in order for the lawyer and his or her assistants, possibly along with a jury consultant, to discuss the case and its relationship to the jury, with particular emphasis on which cues (based upon research) best suggest how the potential jurors will make their decisions.[88] An effective voir dire takes considerable preparation time, and attorneys should not approach it with only a vague idea of what they want to accomplish.

Some of the questions can be structured in advance. After all, it is a rare attorney who instinctively knows all the right questions while in the pressure cooker of voir dire. There are standard areas of examination common to every trial. For example, Jordan provides us with the following checklist to infer possible bias or prejudice:

Relationship by blood or marriage to a party
Relationship by blood or marriage to an attorney or an attorney's partner
Friendship for, or acquaintance with, a party, a party's business associates, or family
Friendship for, or acquaintance with, an attorney, attorney's partner, or attorney's family
Business relations with attorney or party
—employer or employee
—client
—customer or salesman
—landlord or tenant
—indebtedness
Social relations with an attorney or a party
—club, society, or association
—church
—fraternal order
—school
—politics
—participation in sports
Relationship to, friendship for, or acquaintance with any prospective witness
Interest in case
—reading about it in the newspaper
—discussing it or hearing it discussed
—participation in similar case as party, witness, or juror
—stockholder, officer, or employee of corporate party
—stockholder, officer, agent, or employee, or in any way interested in insurance company insuring against liability or injury to person or property
—direct or indirect financial benefit or detriment of any kind affected by the outcome of the case
Prejudice
—racial prejudice
—religious prejudice
Preconceived opinions
Sympathy
Prior personal experience of prior jury service
Prior knowledge of the facts[89]

Although extensive, the list is by no means complete. Specific questions must be tailored to specific cases. Unless counsel has an infallible memory, a list of questions should be outlined on a legal pad and periodically examined during the voir dire period. However, the pad should be consulted as infrequently as possible so that the notes are not a distraction for the panel and do not serve as a barrier to effective lawyer-panel eye contact.

Other specific questions can be prepared in advance by knowing the case strategy and studying jury lists and juror information forms. Jury lists contain the names of those selected for service, and these lists are open for inspection. A noted Miami lawyer finds it useful to ride past the jurors' homes, observe the neighborhoods, and—if they own businesses—look them over as well.[90] Sometimes it is helpful for a lawyer with time, money, and ingenuity to hire a jury investigation service, which may, among other things, indicate the members of the venire who served on prior juries and the outcome of those cases. The FBI makes a practice of investigating jurors in this way when the United States is a party in a court case.[91]

Juror information forms contain even more detail than jury lists. These forms are given to an attorney by the court clerk before voir dire begins. If time allows, it is possible to hire outside agents to study and interpret this material. Although the information on these forms is useful, lawyers must be aware that some of it may be incomplete or inaccurate. For instance, a juror may hold two jobs but list only one of them. Or a juror may indicate he is divorced, but actually may have married again. Nevertheless, from these data, some voir dire questions can be prepared. What a lawyer must not get in the habit of doing is using voir dire questions that are too routine. "A lawyer's greatest enemy is habit. Each trial case involves different considerations. The selection of a jury cannot be followed by rote."[92]

If jurors are called to the box for voir dire, a diagram of the jury box can be prepared with a square for each seat. Information about each person is placed in an appropriate square on the grid so that individualized voir dire questions can be posed. A sample diagram follows:

| 7 | 8 | 9 | 10 | 11 | 12 | P: Peremptory Challenges |
| 1 | 2 | 3 | 4 | 5 | 6 | D: |

As each name is called, information about that person is placed in the space corresponding to the seat he or she will occupy. During questioning, additional information is recorded on the diagram by using a meaningful shorthand system. As a potential juror is challenged and excused, that individual's name is removed from the chart and replaced with information on the new panelist. To accomplish this feat, the information on each juror is placed on cards or sheets, which are taped onto the squares of the diagram. The margin on the right side of the diagram is to keep track of the challenges used by each side.

Another aspect of voir dire preparation is directed toward the clients, who should be instructed by counsel to be attentive but relaxed, to be interested in the answers venirepersons give, and to remain pleasant and confident throughout voir dire questioning. A client should not react openly (orally or nonverbally) to jurors' answers. However, the client may want to record a simple *good* or *bad* on a pad of paper in order to advise counsel regarding the ultimate selection of panelists. Because clients have neither knowledge nor experience in jury selection, their opinions ought not to be determinative, but rather advisory in nature.

UTILIZING CHALLENGES

Early juries were handpicked by the crown. If someone unacceptable appeared, the crown could remove that person or any number of persons by a simple declaration of challenge. In 1305, the English Parliament, trying to restrict the crown, passed a statute limiting challenges to certain causes. By 1531, there were seven recognized challenges for removing a potential juror from hearing a trial. In the New World, the challenge system became much more firmly established. As one British barrister put it, "In England, the trial begins when the jury is picked; in America, the trial is over when the jury is picked." There is a point here, despite the hyperbole.

The first remedy for removing objectionable jurors is the *challenge to the array*. This is an infrequently used procedure that is basically a common law challenge to the validity of the entire pool from which the jury is drawn.[93] In other words, it is a claim that the panel is not representative of the community. Perhaps there has been a technical defect or irregularity in putting together the venire. If so, an attorney files a motion stating this challenge and asking that the panel be quashed. The motion is filed before voir dire begins. The burden of evidence falls on the party filing the motion to quash. Attorneys cannot object to individual persons in the venire or to the statutes governing the way a venire is assembled; they only can object that the statutes have not been followed. Examples of successful challenges to the array include one in which a sheriff who participated in the drawing of the jury list was also a party to the action[94] and one in which a jury commission had systematically excluded blacks from the panel.[95]

The second remedy is the *challenge for cause*. If a juror seems biased, a lawyer should try to get that person to disqualify himself or herself. The lawyer might say something like, "Mr. Parker, I realize that because of the experience you had when your own child was injured, you might have a problem being impartial in this particular trial. You understand that when you accept a responsibility to serve as a juror, you cannot let your past experience or sympathy interfere with your decision, don't you?" At this point, counsel has made it relatively easy for Mr. Parker to remove himself from the panel, although sometimes it requires a few more follow-up questions for him to recognize that he would rather not sit on this jury. Other times, panelists like Mr. Parker will admit they are sympathetic to one party but will say that the feeling will not influence them and that they will return a verdict based solely on the evidence. If Parker asks to be dismissed, other venirepersons with similar sympathies may feel that it would be extremely difficult to be fair in this particular trial, and they may ask to be disqualified too. This is especially true if a painstaking case is built for disqualification through the questions posed. The balance of the jury, rather than risk similar interrogation, might come forth with candor.[96]

Challenge for cause recognizes that a potential juror has a bias against one party or has an interest in the outcome of the litigation, but it is a challenge to be honored at the discretion of the court. The reasons for lack of fitness are generally stated in the statutes.[97] They include such matters as (a) being related to one of the parties in the case, (b) having prejudicial knowledge of the facts, (c) possibly benefiting from the decision, such as being a stockholder of a corporate party or a depositor in a bank, (d) lacking mental integrity (e.g., having an unsound mind or deficient intelligence),[98] and (e) having a definite, fixed opinion about the case or covering law. Fixed opinions about a case might include a bias against dentists on the part of a potential juror in an oral surgery malpractice case, or the belief of a panelist in a personal injury case that people injured in accidents should endure their suffering and never sue for damages.

The challenge for cause is made in court during voir dire and before the trial begins. When a venireperson first gives a clue of prejudice, counsel must probe in order to get fuller disclosure of possible bias. Nonjudgmental, open-ended questions best accomplish this goal. Questioning should continue until either the attorney realizes that the bias is not substantial, or until the juror demonstrates enough bias to either ask for removal from the panel or be challenged. The challenge should be made as soon as grounds appear for it. Since the prosecution or the plaintiff questions first, that side exercises the initial challenges for cause. Counsel should be prepared to state the statutory basis and supporting facts for the challenge, although the judge may not call upon counsel to do so.[99] Once the case has been laid for disqualifying a juror for cause, an attorney simply asks the court to dismiss that person and commends the juror in question for his or her forthrightness and honesty. Challenge for cause should be attempted by counsel whenever possible because, if successful, it does not count against the quota of challenges each attorney has for eliminating persons from the jury. In other words, the number of challenges for cause is unlimited. And because challenges for cause are unlimited, counsel must not give up too easily on them.

Sometimes jurors begin to feel uncomfortable about being brought to the point of admitting prejudice. They start backtracking and trying to prove they can be fair. To avoid this behavior, questioning counsel should shift to closed-ended questions like, "Now, Ms. Jenkins, in view of all you have told us today about your feelings toward Puerto Ricans, don't you think it would be better if you didn't serve on this particular jury?" If Ms. Jenkins says no, counsel should approach the bench, marshal all of the juror's statements showing bias, and argue for a challenge for cause.

A book on trial techniques provides us with the following example of a challenge for cause in a case in which a plaintiff is suing a truck driver for injuries arising out of a highway accident.

Plaintiff Counsel: Mr. Smith, what kind of work do you do?
Juror: I'm a truck driver.
Plaintiff Counsel: For how many years?
Juror: Eighteen years.
Plaintiff Counsel: Over those eighteen years, were you ever involved in collisions with automobiles?
Juror: Yes, three of them.
Plaintiff Counsel: Were you ever involved in lawsuits as a result of those incidents?
Juror: Well, on one of those I got sued.
Plaintiff Counsel: Mr. Smith, because you have the same occupation as the defendant, and, like him, were also the defendant in a lawsuit, do you think you

might start off in this case a little on the defendant's side?
Juror: It's possible.
Plaintiff Counsel: Looking at it from the other side, can you promise us that you have a completely fair and impartial frame of mind and can give my client a fair verdict based solely on the evidence you hear during the trial?
Juror: I'm not sure.
Plaintiff Counsel: Your honor, to be fair to both sides here, we ask that Mr. Smith be excused, for cause.
Court: Mr. Smith, you will be excused. Thank you for your candor in this matter.[100]

The success of such a challenge rests with the court. The mere fact that a juror was once involved in a similar lawsuit may not in itself be sufficient to disqualify that person for cause. But it might be sufficient if that person directly or indirectly reveals a bias that would justify his or her removal.

When challenges for cause have been completed, *peremptory challenges* begin. The peremptory challenge is derived from English common law[101] and is often based on hunch or instinct.[102] There is technically no legal barrier that prevents the juror from serving, but the challenging lawyer suspects some kind of bias that justifies removing that person from the panel.[103] No reasons for this challenge need to be disclosed, and the judge passes no judgment on the challenge. These are simply requests by an attorney, which are automatically granted by the court, not to have some person or persons serve on a particular jury. The challenging lawyer simply says, "If the court please, we thank and excuse Mr. Foster." Of course, "the overruling of the challenge of a juror for cause is the signal to exercise a peremptory challenge."[104] On the other hand, a peremptory challenge should not be used for a juror who is subject to a challenge for cause. Once a peremptory strike is made, it cannot be withdrawn. If a strike is not made before the jury is sworn, the challenge is lost.

The number of peremptory challenges an attorney gets is limited by law.[105] For instance, an attorney may get in a federal criminal court anywhere from 3 to 20 strikes for a 12-person jury. In civil cases in federal court, each party is entitled to only three peremptory challenges for a 6-person jury, although exceptions can be granted. Where alternate jurors are used, each party is entitled to additional peremptory challenges. On a joint trial of several defendants, each defendant is customarily allowed one-half the number of peremptory challenges otherwise allowed to one defendant, with no additional peremptory challenges allowed a prosecutor. Both sides tend to get the same number of peremptory challenges, although some jurisdictions give the prosecutor or plaintiff a lesser number of choices. In a federal felony trial, for example, the prosecution has 6 peremptories, and the defense has 10. This means that at least 28 potential jurors must survive any challenges for cause before peremptories can be exercised to get a 12-person jury.

Strategy is very important in dismissing jurors. It is often analogous to a game of chess. It is a battle of wits and maneuvering often more exciting than the rest of the trial. Sometimes the plaintiff or the prosecution proceeds first in open court, the defense follows, and this process continues *sequentially*. Other times, the opposing attorneys adjourn to separate rooms and *simultaneously* strike a set number from the list of venirepersons. If peremptories fail to whittle the venire down to its final size and the jury is still too large, the judge randomly excuses surplus jurors.[106]

Peremptory challenging follows the complete examination of the panel by both adversaries. However, certain strategies are unique to either the sequential or the simultaneous system. In sequential striking, it is extremely important to be aware of the com-position of the full panel. If the panel looks good, it is important to ''pass'' and quit striking jurors. After all, a worse panel could probably be brought in. In simultaneous striking, there is more time to ponder. The strategy there ought to be a thorough comparison of all potential jurors. Jurors should be ranked from best to worst.

As peremptory challenges are being exercised, it is important for attorneys to keep their eyes on the reserves ready to fill the vacant chairs. Morrill offers this illustration:

Assume for one reason or another that both you and your opponent know that older men would be preferable as jurors for your side of the case. Assume further that . . . you see that the last panel in the jury box answers your needs because there are four elderly men. At the same time, you see that the reserve jurors in the back of the room are practically all young women except for two or three older men. . . . At this point you should take a hard look at the . . . panel with a view toward keeping them unless they are clearly undesirable. . . . You could clearly find yourself in a most uncomfortable position of having two or three dangerous jurors move into the box and being helpless to do anything about it. If, on the other hand, the reserve forces should appear to be what you want because they are practically all older men, you may want to use up your challenges . . . by getting rid of questionable jurors.[107]

Jurors are randomly chosen from the reserve group to reconstitute the panel. Since attorneys have almost no control over who these jurors are, it is wise to save at least one peremptory challenge. If any challenges are left, new jurors may be challenged. ''The cases are legion in which one lawyer used all his challenges before the complete jury was picked only to discover that the last juror seated was disastrous for him.''[108] In sum, then, peremptory challenges are limited in number, made without inquiry by the court, and an extremely important tool. Noted attorney Louis

Nizer calls the peremptory challenge a "precious opportunity [that] should be used with all the resourcefulness at [an attorney's] command."[109]

Once a panel is acceptable to counsel, he or she simply informs the court and, if appropriate, tenders it to the other side (e.g., "Your Honor, defense accepts the panel and tenders it to the prosecution"). Once the acceptance is made, lawyers should feel as though they have a jury partial to their side at best and an impartial jury at worst.

But do these challenges really make a difference? Almost no empirical data exist to answer this question except for one study.[110] The authors arranged for the peremptorily challenged venirepersons in twelve criminal trials to serve as shadow jurors—to remain in court throughout the trial and to reach a verdict. After interviewing the real jury, the authors were able to reconstruct what the vote of the jury would have been without any peremptory challenges. In 7 of the 12 trials studied, the effect of the lawyer's challenges was minimal; the verdicts of the two groups would have been identical. In the remaining 5 cases, the differences would have been substantial on the first ballot, and in 2 or 3 instances, the final verdict would have been different.[111] In spite of some methodological shortcomings in the study,[112] it shows that "there are cases in which the jury verdict is seriously affected, if not determined by the voir dire."[113]

In closing this discussion, it should be noted that there is some concern in certain circles that challenges can result in "the radical reduction or total elimination of a particular segment of the population"[114] in some trials. For instance, the prosecution in the 1975 murder trial of Joan Little used 8 of its 9 peremptory challenges to completely eliminate blacks from the jury. Through the use of peremptories, the prosecution eliminated all but one black from the jury in the 1968 murder trial of Black Panther Huey P. Newton. The defense in the 1974 John Mitchell–Mau-rice Stans perjury, conspiracy, and obstruction of justice trial used 20 peremptories to eliminate all college-educated persons from the jury.[115] Maneuvering to alter the representative qualities of the jury through challenges, and possibly altering the verdict, is commonplace. After all, trial lawyers have no duty to select panels that are objective. Indeed, they should select panels that they think are the most favorable to their side.[116] But, in doing so, they can use challenges to turn representative juries into unrepresentative ones, and some argue that the number of peremptories should be significantly reduced, particularly for the prosecution or plaintiff.

Notes

[1]Robert J. Feldhake, "From the Legal Profession: Legal Strategies and Research Needs in the Selection of Juries," in Ronald J. Matlon and Richard J. Crawford, eds., *Communication Strategies in the Practice of Lawyering* (Annandale, Va.: Speech Communication Association, 1983), 227.

[2]*Strauder v. West Virginia,* 100 U.S. 303 (1879).

[3]*Smith v. Texas,* 311 U.S. 128 (1940). Mr. Justice Murphy, speaking for the Court, declared, "The American tradition of trial by jury, considered in connection with either criminal or civil proceedings, necessarily contemplates an impartial jury drawn from a cross-section of the community. This means that prospective jurors shall be selected without systematic and intentional exclusion of economic, racial, political and geographic groups."

[4]*Thiel v. Southern Pacific Co.,* 328 U.S. 217 (1946).

[5]Rita J. Simon, *The Jury: Its Role in American Society* (Lexington, Mass.: Lexington Books, 1980), 30.

[6]Letter from the Clerk of the U.S. District Court, Western District of Texas, printed in Subcommittee on Improvements in Judiciary Machinery of the Senate Judiciary Committee, *Hearings: Federal Jury Service,* 90th Cong., 1st sess., March 21–July 20, 1967, pp. 415–416.

[7]Blue ribbon juries made their first appearance in

England in 1730. Court officials would choose forty-eight men to serve the crown's bench. These juries were not statutorily abolished in Great Britain until 1971.

[8]Irving R. Kaufman, "The Judges and Jurors," in Glenn R. Winters, ed., *Selected Readings: The Jury* (Chicago: American Judicature Society, 1971), 45.

[9]V. Hale Starr and Mark McCormick, *Jury Selection* (Boston: Little, Brown, 1985), 34.

[10]Benjamin S. Mackoff, "Jury Selection for the Seventies," *Judicature* 55 (1971), 101.

[11]David Kairys, Joseph B. Kadane, and John P. Lehoczky, "Jury Representativeness: A Mandate for Multiple Source Lists," *California Law Review* 65 (1977), 776–827.

[12]Bureau of the Census, "Voting and Registration in the Election of November 1972," *Current Population Reports,* series P-20, no. 253 (Washington: Government Printing Office, 1973).

[13]Gordon Bermant and John Shapard, *The Voir Dire Examination, Juror Challenges, and Adversary Advocacy* (Washington: Federal Judicial Center, 1978), 5–8. A similar, earlier finding appears in Fred A. Summer, "Voter Registration Lists: Do They Yield a Jury Representative of the Community?" *University of Michigan Journal of Law Reform* 5 (1972), 385–407.

[14]Hayward R. Alker et al., "Jury Selection as a Biased Social Process: The Case of Eastern Massachusetts," *Law and Society Review* 11 (1976), 9–41.

[15]John C. Knox, "Jury Selection," *New York University Law Quarterly Review* 22 (1947), 437.

[16]George B. Merry, "Jury Duty on Trial," *Christian Science Monitor,* February 9, 1979, B12.

[17]Jon M. Van Dyke, *Jury Selection Procedures* (Cambridge, Mass.: Ballinger, 1977), 111.

[18]Daniel J. Ryan and Peter J. Neeson, "Voir Dire: A Trial Technique in Transition," *American Journal of Trial Advocacy* 4 (1980–81), 526.

[19]*Swain v. Alabama,* 380 U.S. 202, 219 (1964).

[20]*Harn v. South Carolina,* 409 U.S. 524 (1973).

[21]Max R. Israelson, "Selecting the Jury—Plaintiff's View," in *Am Jur Trials,* vol. 5 (San Francisco: Bancroft-Whitney, 1966), 152.

[22]Robert G. Begam, "Voir Dire: The Attorney's Job," *Trial* (March 1977), 3.

[23]Edward Burke Arnolds and Thomas Sannito, "Jury Study Results Part II: Making Use of the Findings," *Trial Diplomacy Journal* (Summer 1982), 13.

[24]Leonard M. Ring, "Voir Dire: Some Thoughtful Notes on the Selection Process," *Trial* (July 1983), 75.

[25]James Krueger, "Jury Selection and Jury Instructions," *Trial* (August 1981), 22.

[26]*Bunda v. Harwick,* 138 N.W.2d 305 (Mich. 1975); *Murphy v. Lindahl,* 155 N.E.2d 340 (Ill.App. 1960).

[27]Robert W. Balch et al., "The Socialization of Jurors: The Voir Dire as a *Rite* of Passage," *Journal of Criminal Justice* 4 (1976), 271.

[28]Dale W. Broeder, "Voir Dire Examinations: An Empirical Study," *Southern California Law Review* 38 (1965), 503–528.

[29]*United States v. Burr,* 25 F.Cas. 49 (No. 14, 692g) (D. Va. 1807).

[30]S. Mac Gutman, "The Attorney-Conducted Voir Dire of Jurors: A Constitutional Right," *Brooklyn Law Review* 39 (1972), 307–308.

[31]Walter E. Jordan, *Jury Selection* (Colorado Springs: Shepard's/McGraw-Hill, 1980), 32.

[32]Margaret Covington, "Jury Selection: Innovative Approaches to Both Civil and Criminal Litigation," *St. Mary's Law Journal* 16 (1984–85), 584–585.

[33]"The latitude allowed in discussing the 'law' with jurors varies from state to state. This critical area of inquiry is being fenced off by our courts more and more." Herald P. Fahringer, "In the Valley of the Blind: A Primer on Jury Selection in a Criminal Case," *Law and Contemporary Problems* 43 (1980), 120.

[34]Alan E. Morrill, *Trial Diplomacy* (Chicago: Court Practice Institute, 1979), 1.

[35]Alice M. Pawader-Singer, Andrew Singer, and Rickie Singer, "Voir Dire by Two Lawyers: An Essential Safeguard," *Judicature* 57 (1974), 386–391.

[36]Sonya Hamlin, *What Makes Juries Listen* (New York: Harcourt Brace Jovanovich, 1985), 32.

[37]The average voir dire time by judges is 64 minutes, versus 111 minutes spent by counsel. William H. Levit et al., "Expediting Voir Dire: An Empirical Study," *Southern California Law Review*

44 (1971), 916. Also, see E. Maurice Braswell, "Voir Dire: Use and Abuse," *Wake Forest Law Review* 7 (1970), 49–65; Anne Rankin Mahoney, "American Jury Voir Dire and the Ideal of Equal Justice," *Journal of Applied Behavioral Science* 18 (1982), 481–494; David F. Rolewick, "Voir Dire Examination of Jurors," *DePaul Law Review* 25 (1975), 50–63.

[38]Maureen A. Tighe, "The Need for Attorney-Conducted Voir Dire in New Jersey Capital Cases," *Rutgers Law Review* 36 (1983–84), 915–946.

[39]Jordan, op. cit., 23.

[40]Philip H. Corboy, "Opening Statement," *Litigation* (Fall 1980), 1; Jon M. Van Dyke, "Voir Dire: How Should It Be Conducted to Ensure That Our Juries Are Representative and Impartial?" *Hastings Constitutional Law Quarterly* 3 (1976), 65–97.

[41]David Suggs and Bruce Dennis Sales, "Juror Self-Disclosure During Voir Dire," *Indiana Law Journal* 56 (1981), 245–271.

[42]William H. Fortune, "Voir Dire in Kentucky: An Empirical Study of Voir Dire in Kentucky Circuit Courts," *Kentucky Law Journal* 69 (1980–81), 293.

[43]Van Dyke, "Voir Dire," op. cit.

[44]Walter E. Jordan, "Voir Dire Examination," *Trial Diplomacy Journal* (Summer 1981), 18–21, 40–41; Suggs and Sales, op. cit.

[45]C. Clyde Atkins, "Jury Voir Dire by Counsel—Let's Preserve It," *Insurance Counsel Journal* 31 (1964), 689.

[46]See affidavits of Alice M. Padawer-Singer *In re Antitrust Actions,* No. 4-71 Civ. 435 (C.D. Minn., filed June 7, 1971).

[47]Affidavit of Richard Christie, *In re Coordinated Pretrial Proceedings in Antibiotic Antitrust Action* (D. Minn., 1974), 410 F.Supp. 659; "Judges' Nonverbal Behavior in Jury Trials: A Threat to Judicial Impartiality," *Virginia Law Review* 61 (1975), 1266–1298; Milton J. Rosenberg, "When Dissonance Fails: On Eliminating Evaluation Apprehension from Attitude Measurement," *Journal of Personality and Social Psychology* 1 (1965), 28–42.

[48]Affidavit of Charles Haney *In Support of Defendant's Motion Regarding Voir Dire Procedures in re Maryland v. Sailes* (Circuit Court, Prince Georges County, Maryland, No. 82-352, 1982).

[49]Elissa Krauss and Neal Bush, "Improving Voir Dire Conditions," in Beth Bonora and Elissa Krauss, eds., *Jurywork: Systematic Techniques* (Oakland, Calif.: National Jury Project, 1979), 37–38.

[50]Barbara Allen Babcock, "Voir Dire: Preserving Its Wonderful Power," *Stanford Law Review* 27 (1975), 545–565; Robert G. Begam, "Who Should Conduct the Voir Dire? The Attorneys," *Judicature* 61 (1977), 76–78; Neal Bush, "The Case for an Expansive Voir Dire," *Law and Psychology Review* 2 (1976), 9–30; Padawer-Singer, Singer, and Singer, op. cit.; Suggs and Sales, op. cit.

[51]Susan E. Jones, "Judge Versus Attorney Conducted Voir Dire: An Empirical Investigation of Juror Candor," Ph.D. diss. (University: University of Alabama, 1985).

[52]Ronald J. Matlon and Peter C. Facciola, "Voir Dire by Judges and Attorneys: A Study of the Role Expectations of Potential Jurors," Paper presented at the Speech Communication Association convention (Chicago, November 1986).

[53]Richard J. Crawford, "Defense Voir Dire: Communication Strategy," *Criminal Defense* (May–June 1979), 6.

[54]Daniel Yankelovich, *The Public Image of the Courts: A National Survey of the General Public, Judges, Lawyers, and Community Leaders* (National Center for State Courts, March 1978).

[55]Henry B. Rothblatt, *Successful Techniques in the Trial of Criminal Cases* (Englewood Cliffs, N.J.: Prentice-Hall, 1961), 20.

[56]Richard Ahern Blunk and Bruce Dennis Sales, "Persuasion During the Voir Dire," in Bruce Dennis Sales, ed., *Psychology in the Legal Process* (New York: Halstead, 1977), 48.

[57]Crawford, op. cit., 6.

[58]Lawrence J. Smith and Loretta A. Malandro, *Courtroom Communication Strategies* (New York: Kluwer, 1985), 175–176.

[59]Martin Deutsch and Harold Gerard, "A Study of Normative and Informational Social Influence Upon Judgment," *Journal of Abnormal and Social Psychology* 51 (1955), 629–636.

[60]Smith and Malandro, op. cit., 571.

[61]Gerald R. Miller and Michael Burgoon, *New*

Techniques of Persuasion (New York: Harper & Row, 1973), 28.

[62]Jack W. Brehm, *A Theory of Psychological Reactance* (New York: Academic Press, 1966); Robert A. Wickland, *Freedom and Reactance* (Hillsdale, N.J.: Lawrence Erlbaum, 1973).

[63]For a comprehensive discussion of anchoring, see Edith Becker Bennett, "Discussion, Decision, Commitment and Consensus in Group Decisions," *Human Relations* 8 (1955), 251–273; William J. McGuire, "The Nature of Attitudes and Attitude Change," in Gardner Lindzey and Elliot Aronson, eds., *The Handbook of Social Psychology,* vol. 3 (Reading, Mass.: Addison-Wesley, 1968), chap. 21.

[64]Blunk and Sales, op. cit., 51.

[65]Ronald M. Holdway, "Voir Dire: A Neglected Tool of the Art of Advocacy," *Military Law Review* 40 (1968), 2; Robert A. Wenke, *The Art of Selecting a Jury* (Los Angeles: Parker and Son, 1979), 35.

[66]James W. Jeans, *Trial Advocacy* (St. Paul, Minn.: West Publishing, 1975), 192.

[67]Ellen Berscheid, "Opinion Change and Communicator-Communicatee Similarity and Dissimilarity," *Journal of Personality and Social Psychology* 4 (1966), 670–680; Timothy C. Brock, "Communicator-Recipient Similarity and Decision Change," *Journal of Personality and Social Psychology* 1 (1965), 650–654; Herbert C. Kelman, "Process of Opinion Change," *Public Opinion Quarterly* 25 (1961), 57–58.

[68]Donn Byrne, "Interpersonal Attraction and Attitude Similarity," *Journal of Abnormal and Social Psychology* 62 (1961), 713–715; Stephen W. King and Kenneth K. Sereno, "Attitude Change as a Function of Degree and Type of Interpersonal Similarity and Message Type," *Western Speech* 37 (1973), 218–232; Henry E. McGuckin, Jr., "The Persuasive Force of Similarity in Cognitive Style Between Advocate and Audience," *Speech Monographs* 34 (1967), 145–151; Anthony J. Smith, "Similarity of Values and Its Relation to Acceptance and the Projection of Similarity," *Journal of Psychology* 43 (April 1957), 251–260; Charles F. Vick and Roy V. Wood, "Similarity of Past Experience and the Communication of Meaning," *Speech Monographs* 36 (1969), 159–162.

[69]David Suggs and Bruce Dennis Sales, "The Art and Science of Conducting the Voir Dire," *Professional Psychology* 9 (1978), 372.

[70]Smith and Malandro, op. cit., 550–551.

[71]Max E. Wildman, "Selecting the Jury-Defense View," *Am Jur Trials,* vol. 5 (San Francisco: Bancroft-Whitney, 1966), 256.

[72]For a comprehensive discussion of how ingratiation persuades, see Edward Ellsworth Jones, *Ingratiation: A Social Psychological Process* (New York: Appleton-Century-Crofts, 1964); and Edward Ellsworth Jones and Camille B. Wortman, *Ingratiation: An Attributional Approach* (Morristown, N.J.: General Learning Press, 1973).

[73]Smith and Malandro, op. cit., 178; Gerry Spence, "Address," Paper presented at the Association of Trial Lawyers of America convention (Reno, Nev., June 1980).

[74]Lyman Field, "Voir Dire Examination—A Neglected Art," *University of Missouri at Kansas City Law Review* 33 (1965), 171–187.

[75]Suggs and Sales, "Conducting the Voir Dire," 371.

[76]Ibid.

[77] Ann Fagan Ginger, *Jury Selection in Civil and Criminal Trials* (Tiburon, Calif.: Lawpress, 1984), 830.

[78]Hamlin, op. cit., 53.

[79]Jordan, *Jury Selection,* 38.

[80]David L. Herbert and Roger K. Barrett, *Attorney's Master Guide to Courtroom Psychology* (Englewood Cliffs, N. J.: Executive Reports Corporation, 1980), 405.

[81]Suggs and Sales, "Juror Self-Disclosure," 254–255.

[82]Henry R. Rothblatt, "How to Profile a Jury," *Trial Diplomacy Journal* (Spring 1984), 19.

[83]Albert Mehrabian, "A Semantic Space for Nonverbal Behavior," *Journal of Consulting and Clinical Psychology* 35 (1970), 248; Michael M. Reece and Robert N. Whitman, "Expressive Movements, Warmth and Verbal Reinforcement," *Journal of Abnormal and Social Psychology* 64 (1962), 234.

[84]David Cromwell Johnson, "Voir Dire in the Criminal Case: A Primer," *Trial* (October 1983), 63.

[85]Krueger, op. cit., 23.

[86]"Many lawyers fear the loss of control that comes with allowing a juror to speak openly in the courtroom; however, it is better to lose control . . . during voir dire than it is to lose control of the jury after it has adjourned to the jury room for deliberations." Starr and McCormick, op. cit., 278.

[87]Michael L. Fahs, "Voir Dire and Our Knowledge of Human Communication: Indictments of the Relationship," Paper presented at the Western Speech Communication Association convention (Denver, Colo., February 1982).

[88]R. William Wood, "Preparation for Voir Dire," *Trial Diplomacy Journal* (Spring 1985), 17–19.

[89]Jordan, *Jury Selection*, 67–68.

[90]Murray Sams, Jr., "Persuasion in the Voir Dire: The Plaintiff's Approach," in Grace W. Holmes, ed., *Persuasion: The Key to Damages* (Ann Arbor, Mich.: The Institute of Continuing Legal Education, 1969), 6.

[91]Joshua Okun, "Investigation of Jurors by Counsel: Its Impact on the Decision Process," *Georgetown Law Journal* 56 (1968), 852.

[92]Fahringer, op. cit., 127.

[93]*United States v. Gordon,* 253 F.2d 177 (7th Cir. 1958).

[94]*Jones v. Woodworth,* 24 S.D. 583, 124 N.W. 844 (1910).

[95]*Allen v. State,* 110 Ga. App. 56, 137 S.E.2d 711 (1965).

[96]Arne Werchick, "Method, Not Madness: Selecting Today's Jury," *Trial* (December 1982), 68.

[97]Even if they are not stated in the statutes, grounds for challenge for cause existing at common law may be asserted. *Lewis v. State,* 260 Ala. 368, 70 So.2d 790 (1954); *Johnson v. Missouri-K-T RR,* 374 S.W.2d 1 (Mo. 1963); *State v. Gates,* 131 Mont. 78, 307 P.2d 248 (1957); *Moss v. Fidelity + Cas Co.,* 439 S.W.2d 734 (Tex. Civ. App. 1969); *Nolan v. Venus Motors, Inc.,* 64 Wis.2d 215, 218 N.W.2d 507 (1974).

[98]This has included such matters as not knowing the English language, being feebleminded, not understanding instructions, and having psychiatric disabilities.

[99]In one case, the New York Court of Appeals said that it is better for a court to err by excusing jurors than by letting them sit in a trial where some risk is apparent. *People v. Culhane,* 33 N.Y.2d 390, 350 N.Y.S.2d 381, 305 N.E.2d 469 (1973).

[100]Thomas A. Mauet, *Fundamentals of Trial Techniques* (Boston: Little, Brown, 1980), 30.

[101]Under English common law, peremptory challenges were initially allowed only in capital felony cases. Later, they were extended to all common law felony trials. In the United States in 1790, Congress codified the criminal defendant's right of peremptory challenge in felony cases. The right was extended to the prosecution in 1865. In 1872, the right to peremptory challenges was further extended, to both sides in misdemeanors and civil cases. This development at the federal level was paralleled in the states as well. Although the right to peremptorily challenge does not arise from the Constitution, it is recognized by the courts as one of the most important rights for both litigants. See *Pointer v. United States,* 151 U.S. 396, 408 (1894); *Hayes v. Missouri,* 120 U.S. 68, 70 (1887); *Swain v. Alabama,* 380 U.S. 202, 217 & n. 20 (1965).

[102]Denver lawyer Joseph Jaudon (of Long and Jaudon) has both the client and himself prepare strike sheets. The information recorded is purely a gut reaction to the potential juror. A plus (+) is recorded for jurors that are liked; a minus (−) is recorded for jurors that are not liked; a zero (0) is recorded for jurors that leave no strong impression on the recorder. Jaudon and his client then compare sheets at the end of the voir dire and strike the worst jurors (those with the most minuses) first. The recorded marks are based strictly on the recorder's feelings about the venireperson and whether or not it appeared as though the venireperson liked the recorder. Joseph C. Jaudon, "Jury Selection: Communicating Information and Challenges," Audiotape JS-4, Jury Selection Series (St. Paul, Minn.: National Institute for Trial Advocacy, Legal Education Center).

[103]In essence, then, the court allows counsel to stereotype people. Steven Penrod and Daniel Linz, "Voir Dire: Uses and Abuses," in Martin F. Kaplan, ed., *The Impact of Social Psychology on Procedural Justice* (Springfield, Ill.: Charles C. Thomas, 1986), 137.

[104]Ward Wagner, Jr., *Art of Advocacy: Jury Selection* (New York: Matthew Bender, 1981), 2–13.

[105]In the sensational 1966 trial of Richard Speck, who was convicted of the murder of eight Chicago nurses, Judge Herbert C. Paschen permitted an unprecedented total of 320 peremptory challenges! Each side was permitted twenty for each of the eight murder charges. A grand total of 2500 jurors were questioned.

[106]There are many variations on this system. In the 1972 Harrisburg Seven trial, 46 qualified jurors remained after challenging for cause. The defense had 28 strikes; the prosecution had 6. They reduced the jury in alternating patterns until they had 12 members. In Virginia civil cases, both sides are given a list of 13 names and asked to cross off 3 of them. In Alabama, if a 6-person jury is used, each side has 6 peremptory challenges from a panel of 18. If more than 6 remain after the voir dire is completed, the first 6 called become the jury, and the seventh person is the alternate. The rest are released.

[107]Morrill, op. cit., 6–7.

[108]Mauet, op. cit., 28.

[109]Louis A. Nizer, "The Art of the Jury Trial," *Cornell Law Quarterly* 32 (1946), 59, 62.

[110]Hans Zeisel and Shari Seidman Diamond, "The Effect of Peremptory Challenges on Jury and Verdict: An Experiment in a Federal District Court," *Stanford Law Review* 30 (1978), 491–531.

[111]The real jury was less likely to convict the accused than the reconstructed jury in all instances.

[112]Bermant and Shapard, op. cit., 37–49.

[113]John Monahan and Laurens Walker, *Social Science in Law: Cases and Materials* (Mineola, N.Y.: Foundation Press, 1985), 496.

[114]Van Dyke, *Jury Selection Procedures,* 154.

[115]Judge Lee P. Gagliardi granted 20 peremptories to the defense and only 8 to the prosecution because of "acute pre-trial publicity."

[116]Melvin M. Belli, Sr., *Modern Trials,* vol. 3 (St. Paul, Minn.: West Publishing, 1982), 428.

6

CHAPTER

JURY

ANALYSIS

HOW JURY BIAS IS RECOGNIZED
*Attitudinal Analysis / Personality Analysis /
Nonverbal Analysis / Demographic Analysis*

SOCIAL SCIENCE RESEARCH APPLIED TO JURY SELECTION

Now that the mechanics of jury selection have been covered in Chapter 5, it is time to consider the psychological makeup of the jury for purposes of eliminating those individuals who could harm the advocate's cause.

HOW JURY BIAS IS RECOGNIZED

All humans are prejudiced to some degree, and complete objectivity is impossible. What lawyers must really consider for their peremptory challenges is the extent to which jurors are unable to set aside their beliefs, attitudes, and values when rendering a decision. How biased will they be?

It must be recognized at the outset that prospective jurors are rarely going to say in voir dire, "I am too prejudiced to render a fair verdict in this case." If they do, it is often because they believe that "other obligations are more important than their duty to serve on a jury."[1] But when they are hesitant to admit to bias, the hesitance may be due to the unfamiliar environment,[2] a fear of being rejected for jury duty,[3] an inability to recognize their own prejudice,[4] a desire to say what is socially acceptable,[5] an opportunity to avoid answering voir dire questions about prejudice directly,[6] or intentional deception.[7] A survey done by the National Jury Project during a New Jersey murder prosecution found that 71 percent of eligible jurors thought a certain defendant was guilty. Yet only 15 percent of the persons drawn for jury duty admitted this predisposition during voir dire. A later investigation of the chosen jury showed that many of them really had different predispositions about the case than they had indicated in voir dire.[8] One wonders if the situation would improve if the judge said prior to voir dire, "You know, folks, one of the serious problems in American courts today is that jurors won't readily admit bias when they have it."

Whatever the jurors' reasons for not telling the truth, lawyers must do their best to surmise the degree of prejudice by reading and understanding the results of voir dire and by making educated guesses about each juror. This is why it is essential, as noted earlier, for an attorney to get prospective jurors to communicate as much as possible about themselves, even though complete self-disclosure cannot be expected.

In recent years, "many attorneys, . . . not really satisfied with their own dependence on whims and hunches"[9] in picking juries, have become more scientific in their attempts to weed out prejudice through a careful attitudinal, personality, nonverbal, and demographic analysis of each panelist. It must be understood as we go through each of these scientific methods of evaluating jurors that (1) no one method is more assured of success over any other method, (2) no two people are identical—we all have highly individualized perceptual systems that provide meaning to sensation—and (3) judgments about potential jurors must be made not only about them as individuals, but also about their possible social interaction with other individuals functioning as a group. At best, each of these methods can only give an attorney some degree of extra insight into the way a potential juror might perceive communication in the courtroom.

Attitudinal Analysis

Any evaluation of prospective jurors should, of course, be based on what they say in response to counsel questions. After all, attitudes (general feelings of favorableness or unfavorableness) and behavior are reciprocally interrelated.[10] For instance, if someone is an economic conservative in daily life, he or she is not likely to give away large sums of money at trial. And in a hunting accident case, the plaintiff wants jurors with pro-gun-control attitudes, and the defense wants the opposite.

There are some standard areas of questioning that may reveal biased feelings about a particular case. As noted in Chapter 5, the first and most obvious is whether or not the potential juror has any close relationship with any party, witness, or attorney in the case. Such relationships include family relationships, business associations, and social connections. The extent of these relationships must be pursued in voir dire. Certainly, such relationships could affect a juror's vote. The relationship may not even be a personal one. For example, the defense lawyer in a product liability case ought to be skeptical about persons who identify with consumers rather than manufacturers.

Some of our attitudes are formed from past law-related activity. It is important to know which panelists or family members or close friends of panelists have ever been engaged in a lawsuit, what kind it was, what their role was, what the result was, and what attitudes they have toward the suit. It might also be a good idea to find out which panelists have attended law school or have had law-related careers. If a person with a legal background remains on the jury, he or she could be quite influential, meaning that his or her attitudes toward the case should be pursued in depth.

General prejudices, such as racial intolerance, should be probed as well. Most individuals will profess tolerance. Yet, if racial prejudice is relevant, jurors must be brought to the point of having the courage to admit race could be a factor in their decisions. What is important is that the lawyer uncover the degree of a prospective juror's prejudice. This can be accomplished by asking questions about the venireperson's personal experiences with people of other races. Here are some possible questions:

☐ What does the term *racism* mean to you?
☐ Have you or an immediate member of your family had any direct experience with discrimination? If so, please describe it.
☐ Have you ever felt racial tension on the street, in a store, in a bar, in a barracks, in your neighborhood, or anywhere else? If so, please describe it.
☐ Do you think blacks are treated unfairly in courts, in employment, or in schools?
☐ Why do you think that, on a per capita basis, more blacks are convicted of violent crimes than whites?
☐ Do blacks live in your neighborhood? Do you have contact with them?
☐ Do you work with black people? What is your relationship with them?
☐ Do your children attend school with black pupils? If so, do you have any contact with their parents?
☐ How do you feel about interracial dating and marriages?

Questions such as these should be asked beginning with the most nonthreatening and moving to the more threatening ones in order to coax honesty from the juror. The same is true for religious prejudice, economic prejudice, regional prejudice, occupational prejudice, and so forth.

In criminal cases, attitudes toward crime and criminal justice should be explored. Here are some questions that might be posed:

☐ What is your attitude toward capital punishment?
☐ How serious a problem do you think crime is in our city?
☐ Do you think the courts are too soft on crime?
☐ The judge has told you that a defendant is presumed innocent until proven guilty beyond a reasonable doubt. What does "presumption of innocence" mean to you?

Answers to questions such as these often yield considerable information regarding pro-prosecution and prodefense jurors. Several studies have found that persons who favor capital punishment are more inclined to render a guilty verdict regardless of the amount of evidence presented than are those who oppose the death penalty.[11]

It is also important to know if the potential jurors could be affected by the outcome of the case. When a personal stake is involved, impartiality is reduced. To illustrate, the case might involve stock divestiture, and the juror might own stock in the company. Or a venireperson's business rival might be one of the litigants in the case, and the venireperson would thus benefit from a financial loss suffered by that party. None of this happens very often, but a trial lawyer should be alert to this factor and include the information in excusing jurors.

Prior information about the case may be important too.[12] Has the juror received any newspaper, radio, television, or personal accounts of the case? If so, to what extent has he or she received information, and might the publicity bias the decision? Case publicity can have an impact on juror attitudes. For example, when potential jurors in the Joan Little case in North Carolina were asked what they had heard or read about Ms. Little, descriptions "varied from 'She's a black woman charged with the murder of a prison guard who was attempting to rape her' to 'She's that colored girl who stabbed the jailer to death, 18 times with an ice pick.'"[13] The words, along with the tone of voice used, certainly reveal how pretrial publicity affects attitudes. Granted, situations like the Joan Little case, the John Hinckley case over the attempted assassination of President Reagan, or the Patty Hearst case in California, are rare, but pretrial publicity is still a reality in some instances.

Personality Analysis

Another method of evaluating juror responses is to examine personalities. Some inferences can be made by linking personality types to certain cases. In a manslaughter case, the issue is whether the death was an accident or the result of the defendant's irresponsibility. Hence, the defense wants careless personalities, and the prosecutor wants careful people who will feel vindicated by punishing inattention. Table 6.1 lists some other possibilities for personality analysis associated with certain offenses.[14] Each of these personalities is identified with or opposed to the psychological makeup of the type of personality we expect of people accused of committing a certain act. For example, we assume that insecure people will sympathize with a victim of burglary while bold and daring people will "find a thief an attractive rogue"[15] or that, in a medical malpractice case, a person who is dependent on doctors (or others) will be ill at ease

TABLE 6.1

PERSONALITY TYPES AND CASE TYPES

Type of Case	Proprosecution or Proplaintiff Personality	Prodefense Personality
Bad checks	Frugal	Reckless
Medical malpractice	Independent	Dependent
Burglary	Insecure	Bold, daring
Product liability	Accountable	Unaccountable, easygoing
Embezzlement	Austere	Hedonistic
Wrongful death against a railroad	Impatient	Patient
Forgery	Forthright	Devious
False arrest	Recalcitrant	Deferential to authority

TABLE 6.2

EGO STATES AND ATTITUDES

Parent

A. *Critical Parent*

  1. Characteristics
    a. Blaming
    b. Critical
    c. Strong
    d. Faultfinding
    e. Righteous
    f. Assertive
    g. Forceful
    h. Bossy
    i. Demanding
    j. Supercilious
    k. Hostile
    l. Dogmatic
  2. Attitudes as a juror
    a. If he's on trial, he must be guilty.
    b. That attorney has beady eyes, and you can't trust him.
    c. Young people have no respect for anyone.
    d. People don't need big handouts to survive.
    e. That scar on the plaintiff's face won't hurt anything.
    f. Proprosecution

B. *Nurturing Parent*

  1. Characteristics
    a. Soothing
    b. Comforting
    c. Kind
    d. Sympathetic
    e. Indulgent
    f. Soft-hearted
    g. Affectionate
  2. Attitudes as a juror
    a. Those dear children will have a hard time if we don't help the mother.
    b. Let's compromise.
    c. That poor man will have to spend a long

Child

A. *Adapted Child*

  1. Characteristics
    a. Compliant
    b. Withdrawn
    c. Whiny
    d. Despondent
    e. Forgetful
    f. Stubborn
    g. Pleasant
    h. Sulky
    i. Depressed
    j. Courteous
    k. Rebellious
    l. Vindictive
  2. Attitudes as a juror
    a. I'll never be able to make that decision.
    b. I'm not sure about that point. I just don't know.
    c. That scar is awful. I'd die if it happened to me.

B. *Natural Child*

  1. Characteristics
    a. Self-indulgent
    b. Fun-loving
    c. Spontaneous
    d. Charming
  2. Attitudes as a juror
    a. I think we should award as much money as possible.
    b. If that scar were Z-shaped, she could say Zorro got her!
    c. Proplaintiff
    d. Prodefense in criminal cases.

Adult

  1. Characteristics
    a. Rational
    b. Factual
    c. Unemotional
    d. Open-minded
    e. Objective
  2. Attitudes as a juror
    a. Let's look carefully at the evidence and see what it indicates.
    b. I would like to read that deposition myself.
    c. I think $50,000 is a fair amount for an injury like that.
    d. I don't know what impact that will have on her. I'll wait to hear the testimony.
    e. Fair and unbiased for both sides.

TABLE 6.2 (*Continued*)

Parent

B. *Nurturing Parent*

        time in jail if we con-
        vict him.

   d. That person is an
      underdog and really
      needs help.

   e. Just look at that terri-
      ble scar on the plain-
      tiff's face.

   f. Proplaintiff in personal
      injury cases.

criticizing them. Voir dire questions can be prepared for each personality dimension. For reckless–frugal, it could be "Are you in favor of nuclear power or solar energy?" For powerful–weak, it could be "How do you react to people who disagree with you?" For careless–careful, it could be "Do you like to plan your vacations or take them on the spur of the moment?" Matching personalities is an important procedure to be used in jury selection.

One approach to studying personalities received its impetus from Eric Berne's 1964 book on social transactions,[16] which has been amplified in hundreds of other places. Berne developed his transactional analysis (TA) theory of human behavior as an alternative approach to psychotherapy. "He viewed TA as a model, couched in simple language, from which people could gain personal awareness and effect behavior change."[17]

To best get a basic understanding of this approach, it is necessary to comprehend the meaning of *ego states*, behaviors that exist in each of us from birth. Ego states are parts of each individual's personality. Berne classifies these parts of the personality according to three types: *parent*, *child*, and *adult*. The parent ego state contains behaviors, feelings, and attitudes that are learned from people who serve as our parent figures. Some of those

parent behaviors are nurturing types (caring, showing consideration or concern, being protective, being sympathetic, giving positive strokes, loving, listening, helping); others are critical types of parent behavior (evaluating, hurting, punishing, being prejudiced or condescending, being dictatorial, rigid, closed-minded, or nasty, ridiculing others). The child ego state contains behaviors from our youth. Some of those behaviors are natural (uninhibited, carefree, and spontaneous); others are adapted or socialized by parent messages and behavior, such as various forms of obedience. The adult ego state contains behavior that is objective and unemotional. The adult is an information processor, functioning much the same way as a computer does in gathering data, storing it in memory banks, processing it, and then arriving at decisions. Table 6.2 illustrates more specifically the relationship between each ego state and certain attitudes.[18]

Using this approach, an attorney figures out the predominant ego state each potential juror communicates. For instance, the plaintiff in a case in which a woman received a scar on the forehead would want a jury made up of nurturing parents, natural children, and adapted children; the defense would want a jury made up of critical parents, adults, and adapted children. If the defense did the better

TABLE 6.3

WORDS AND PERSONALITY TYPES

Critical Parent	Nurturing Parent	Adapted Child	Natural Child	Adult
1. Should	1. There now	1. Want	1. Love	1. How
2. Must	2. Honey	2. Hope	2. Play	2. When
3. Ought to	3. Poor thing	3. Wish	3. Yes	3. Where
4. Have to	4. Good	4. Won't	4. Wow	4. Why
5. Don't	5. Cute	5. If you want to	5. Delightful	5. What
6. Always	6. Doesn't hurt to try	6. I don't know	6. Happy	6. Who
7. If I were you	7. Try this	7. So	7. Excited	7. Tell me more
8. I said so	8. Feel better	8. Did I do it	8. Curious	8. Think
9. Ridiculous	9. Don't worry	right?		9. Alternatives
10. Stupid				10. It's possible
11. Bad				11. Could it be
12. Disgusting				12. It says here
13. Absurd				13. My understanding is
14. Shocking				
15. Lazy				
16. Horrible				
17. You can't				
18. Now what				
19. When I was a kid				
20. You'd better				
21. I knew it all along				

job of jury selection, it would presumably wind up with a group of people strongly committed to rules, authority, power, and absolute truth. If the plaintiff did the better job of jury selection, the group would believe in friendship and harmony, want to help the underdog, and be suggestible. To make the best use of Berne's system, an attorney or trained professional helping an attorney should have a good background in social psychology or communication in order to make such discriminating judgments from verbal and nonverbal responses.

Language cues help to identify personality types. Language cues consist of spoken words and their syntactical arrangement. Table 6.3 offers a list of words frequently used by each of the personality types identified.[19] Language cues also help to identify the anxious personality. (The real value of seeking such information during voir dire will be discussed in the following section, on nonverbal analysis.) One way to study anxiety is through the concept of immediacy. Immediacy is the verbal or nonverbal distance between people when they interact.[20] If jurors refer to "that" and "those" rather than any direct object, they are engaging in nonimmediate language and displaying anxiety. If they use mostly future or past tense rather than present tense, they are displaying anxiety. When nonimmediate language is employed, the source is usually feeling negative about the topic being discussed. Consider these two answers from prospective jurors being asked if they are prejudiced against Jehovah's Witnesses:

Panelist A: "No, I don't think I'm biased
against Jehovah's Witnesses."
Panelist B: "No, I don't think I'm biased
against those people."

Panelist B exhibits more nonimmediacy and is therefore displaying greater anxiety toward Jehovah's Witnesses.

Finally, there is the authoritarian personality. Authoritarianism has been a widely studied personality construct ever since the atrocities of World War II. This research allows authoritarianism to be one of the strongest among all the personality predictors of juror behavior.[21] An authoritarian person is one who is striving for power and elitism and who uses conformity to gain favor from those who are in power; it is a person who will be obsequious and deferential to those above him or her and severe to those below.[22] Political and economic conservatives fit an authoritarian image.[23]

What has the research concluded about authoritarians? The author of one study used personality questionnaires to divide simulated jurors into the categories authoritarian, antiauthoritarian, and egalitarian. She had jurors observe a mock trial involving a charge of manslaughter. The findings were that egalitarians lack bias and are open-minded in reaching criminal trial decisions. Antiauthoritarians stand for acquittals; they want to thwart authority. Meanwhile, authoritarians side with prosecutors and favor guilty verdicts and harsh punishments.[24] This is especially true if the defendant is a member of a minority group and charged with the crime of murder. Other studies confirm that authoritarian personalities are generally antidefendant[25] and that they are more influenced by prosecution testimony than by defense testimony.[26] The exception is in sexual assault trials. There authoritarians "tend to hold negative attitudes toward the rape victim and therefore are unlikely to be conviction prone."[27]

Another study involved a student who was accused of stealing an examination prior to its administration. Simulated jurors received information about how the accused felt about college life overall. Each juror was categorized according to an authoritarian–egalitarian scale. The results were that when the accused had different values about college life from those of the authoritarian jurors, strong punishment was recommended. However, when the accused shared values with the authoritarian jurors, they were uncertain about punishment. Egalitarians were steady in their views on punishment regardless of the defendant's views on college life. This study shows that attraction significantly affects the jury decisions of authoritarians but not egalitarians. Authoritarians can be expected to be highly punitive toward dissimilar defendants.[28]

Still another study demonstrated that high authoritarians are especially punitive toward low-status defendants. Furthermore, high authoritarians are more influenced by character than they are by the evidence.[29] Looked at another way, authoritarian jurors will not always render verdicts on the basis of testimony, but will have a predisposition toward certain decisions based on the credibility of the litigants. The author of another study learned that authoritarians generally vote for the prosecution except when they feel a similarity to the defendant, in which case they vote for acquittal.[30] Authoritarian jurors who want to convict may even ignore a judge's instructions to disregard inadmissible incriminating evidence.[31]

Additional studies on authoritarian jurors present a variety of results. One found that when authoritarians serve on juries, they evidence much more anxiety and create more tension during the deliberations than do their nonauthoritarian colleagues.[32] An additional and rather curious finding of another study was that, in criminal cases, authoritarian jurors appear to be malleable in the decision-making process, that is, they try to identify with the in-group and are willing to change toward the majority position on the jury. They are willing to change their attitudes toward the larger number, even more so than egalitarians. Perhaps this change occurs because the power rests with the majority of jurors.[33]

What can we conclude from all this research on authoritarian jurors in criminal litigation? They are creators of tension. They rely heavily on extralegal information in reaching their independent judgments. "For judgments of punitiveness high authoritarians tend to be more harsh than low authoritarians, but for judgments of guilt the influence of authoritarianism remains to be clarified,"[34] particularly since their opinions can be influenced by a majority of other jury members.

How, then, can a lawyer spot an authoritarian personality? For the most part, authoritarians favor capital punishment and discipline of children; respect personal accomplishment, family security, and national security; care little for equality; and are not very loving or forgiving. The authoritarian can be expected to adhere to conventional values, submit to authority figures, adhere to stereotypes, punish violators of norms, identify with power figures, and project his or her own feelings and attitudes on others.[35] A juror's authoritarianism can be detected (a) by questions related to any of the above attitudes (e.g., "Do you believe that programs for the gifted have been neglected in favor of aid to the underprivileged?") (b) by questions related to personal experiences (e.g., "To what organizations do you belong?"); and (c) by the juror's submissive and deferential manner with the court, hanging on the judge's words and modifying personal statements in accordance with what the court seems to desire. The frequent use of the word "sir" is a further indication of the authoritarian personality, unless the person has been raised in an area of the country where such language is commonplace.

In seeking out authoritarians, counsel should distinguish between high authoritarians and soft ones. The former are more clearly prosecution-prone in criminal trials. A soft authoritarian is a person who agrees with most authoritarian positions, but not all of them. So soft types repeat authoritarian cliches, but are not themselves authoritarian leaders. Lower-status authoritarians may be acceptable to the defense, particularly if it appears that no high authoritarians will be serving on the jury.

One caution in striking authoritarians is warranted. The nature of the defendant's personality must be considered. Authoritarians are generally biased in favor of the prosecution, but "when the defendants are high-status authority figures themselves, as in the Watergate trials, low-authoritarian jurors may actually be a better choice for [the prosecution].[36] This would be true, for example, in a case in which a police officer is a defendant who says that he or she was acting under orders[37] or in a military case in which an enlisted person was ordered to kill a civilian (e.g., Lieutenant Calley's trial for the My Lai Massacre in Vietnam). In these instances, authoritarian jurors are less likely to convict than nonauthoritarian jurors because they can associate with a defendant who obeys orders.[38]

Closely related to this matter of authoritarianism is susceptibility to conformity pressure. The assumption is that the prosecution should strive for interjuror conformity whereas the defense should strive for individual dissent within the jury. Prosecutors want jurors who can mesh. The reason for this is that a hung, or undecided, jury is much more damaging for the prosecution than it is for the defense. Conformity relates to authoritarianism because of the covariation between the two elements; high conformists tend to side with authority.[39] When sources are respected authorities, the authoritarian message receiver becomes highly suggestible; that is, he or she yields with ease to the persuasive message of the source. Hence, prosecutors should seek out true conformists who are predisposed toward suggestibility, while defense lawyers should choose jurors with opposite predispositions.

Nonverbal Analysis

"A great deal of nonverbal communication takes place . . . in the confined setting of the jury box."[40] Observing this mode of communication "is a potentially rich source of information about internal emotive states [and] . . . the status of interpersonal relationships."[41] So, as voir dire questioning gets under way, it is meaningful for lawyers to watch and interpret nonverbal signals. But a word of caution is warranted. To understand the meaning of a word, you usually have to read the entire sentence in which that word is used. The same is true in the study of nonverbal cues. By themselves, gestures, movement, and vocal cues have no specific, accurate, or universal meanings. Instead, nonverbal behavior is idiosyncratic. Meanings vary from person to person. Thus, vocal and body codes must be observed in repeated clusters because an isolated clue can easily be confused or contradicted by a previous or subsequent one. However, if sequential patterns endorse one another and fall into congruent clusters, nonverbal cues can reflect juror bias.

To begin this method of analysis, an attorney must first determine baseline nonverbal behavior for each person and then look for changes in that behavior. Baseline behavior is what a person usually does. Nervous fidgeting does not tell an attorney much if a person always fidgets. However, if a person starts fidgeting at a certain point during voir dire, this may be a good predictor of anxiety, and one particularly useful method of eliminating jurors is to understand personal anxiety. "Initial observations or baselines provide general information about the juror's nonverbal style which enable [an attorney] to recognize shifts or changes later on."[42] It is critical, then, to

keep a constant eye on the panel when they come into the courtroom and throughout voir dire.

Nonverbal behavior has two dimensions to it: paralinguistic and kinesic. The *paralinguistic* dimension consists of vocal cues, such as pauses, pitch, volume, rate, tone, and breathing. The *kinesic* dimension consists of physical cues, such as gestures, body movement, eye contact, and facial expressions. Paralinguistic and kinesic cues are used to express emotion and maintain interpersonal relations appropriate to the sender of the cues.[43]

There are several paralinguistic manifestations of anxiety. Research has shown that, paralinguistically, anxious people tend to (a) speak in unfinished sentences, break in with new thoughts, repeat phrases, and stutter; (b) sigh or take deep breaths and say "I don't know" in disgust; (c) laugh inappropriately; (d) make sudden voice changes;[44] (e) switch from an informal style to a more pompous and stilted manner;[45] or (f) talk noticeably faster than usual.[46] In addition, a sudden change in vocal pitch (high and low of the speaking voice) is a dependable indicator of anxiety and possible deception by a potential juror.[47] There are a number of kinesic manifestations as well. Anxious people (a) make frequent lateral eye movements;[48] (b) reduce visual interactions with others;[49] (c) sustain rigid body postures;[50] (d) increase their frequency of body movements;[51] or (e) wring their hands, tap their fingers, or touch their faces or other parts of their bodies with some frequency.[52]

What, now, is the value of identifying these nonverbal manifestations of anxiety during voir dire? Suggs and Sales tell us that anxiety has four possible causes: (a) the person is anxious because he or she is speaking in public; (b) the person is anxious because he or she has a negative personal feeling about the lawyer conducting the voir dire; (c) the person is anxious because of the strong emotional attachment to the subject matter being discussed; or (d) the person is anxious because he or she is being deceptive and does not want to be discovered.[53] If deception is a possibility, paralinguistic cues are better predictors than kinesic cues.[54] The source of the anxiety can be isolated by observing and recording baseline nonverbal behavior during the initial background information questions and later studying the same behaviors when sensitive attitudinal questions are posed. Observers can compare a person's nonverbal responses with each series of questions.

Here is an example. During the baseline phase of voir dire, a prospective juror has a relaxed posture and direct eye contact with a lawyer. The lawyer asks that juror to look at the defendant and indicate whether he or she has any opinion about that person's guilt or innocence. After a rapid glance at the defendant, the prospective juror says, "No," and suddenly breaks eye contact with the lawyer and builds up a tense body posture. The discrepancy between the baseline behavior and later nonverbal behavior indicates that there is indeed a feeling about the defendant's guilt or innocence. Further attorney questioning regarding the direction of that feeling is warranted.

It may seem as though there is an overwhelming amount of data that need to be evaluated systematically in making this aspect of nonverbal analysis work during voir dire. "The technique requires the use of observers who can rate a potential juror's nonverbal behavior . . . on several scales"[55] measuring anxiety. Suggs and Sales have given us an experimental rating scale that adds to the utility of the system.[56] A version of their rating grid for baseline information, as I have revised it, is found in Table 6.4. The evaluation of our hypothetical juror in Table 6.4 indicates that this might be a person the defense attorney wishes to challenge. Some signs of anxiety (lateral eye movements and increased body movements) occurred only during the de-

fense attorney's questioning. Also, the body posture became somewhat more rigid than when being questioned by the judge or the prosecutor.

Changes from baseline nonverbal behavior can guide the attorney in jury selection. Here are several examples of such cues. If a person starts to swallow hard, the questions might be getting difficult to answer. If a person suddenly folds his or her arms, he or she might not be accepting what is being said and may be getting antagonistic. If a person starts talking through his or her teeth, he or she might be getting hostile. If a person's shoulders become more rounded and the chest increasingly caves in, he or she might be feeling unsure of an answer and defeated. On the contrary, if someone shifts to a more square-shouldered, relaxed-back position, he or she

TABLE 6.4

NONVERBAL RATING SCALE

NAME	J	P	D
Unfinished sentences, stuttering	0	0	0
Sighing, deep breathing	0	0	0
Inappropriate laughter	0	0	0
Sudden voice changes	0	0	0
Switch to stilted manner	0	+	+
Increased speaking speed	0	+	0
Frequent lateral eye movements	0	+	−
Reduced eye contact	+	+	+
Rigid body posture	+	+	0
Increased body movements	0	0	−
Increased gestures	+	+	+

Column J = Juror's responses to baseline phase of questioning by the judge.
Column P = Juror's responses to baseline phase of questioning by the prosecutor or plaintiff.
Column D = Juror's responses to baseline phase of questioning by the defense.
+ = Positive nonverbal responses.
0 = Neutral or unclear nonverbal responses.
− = Negative nonverbal responses (anxiety).

is feeling more comfortable and confident. If a person's legs become twisted in a knot, that person could be nervous. If a respondent quickly pushes back and leans away, he or she could be experiencing a negative reaction even if the response is outwardly agreeable. On the other hand, if a person leans forward, the reaction shows friendliness and favor.

Trying to make too many judgments from nonverbal cues is a risky business. For instance, does a person's clothing offer the attorney any information? Not really; it is easy to be fooled here. For some, jury duty is a golden opportunity to put on good clothes or not to get dressed up as one might for work in a professional career. Maybe the person who is immaculate, with everything matching, is more sensitive to cognitive detail and less sensitive to emotionalism than the person who is sloppily attired—and maybe not. Maybe a juror who wears an American flag or a lodge pin in a lapel is conservative and good for the prosecution in criminal cases—and maybe not. Maybe the wearing of punk clothing indicates a hostility to the establishment—and maybe not. Maybe jurors who smile at counsel and nod their heads affirmatively when being asked questions are reacting favorably to that side—or maybe they are being cagey and trying to ingratiate themselves with the lawyer so that they will not be challenged.[57] Smiles can be favorable responses, or they can be the kiss of death.

About thirty to forty years ago, there was much research on the relationship of body shapes to attitudes. Some of Sheldon's body-type findings are unfortunately still part of the folklore in selecting juries.[58] For instance, in civil cases, ectomorphs (tall, skinny people) are supposed to be good for the defense because they are stingy with money in awarding damages. They are considered good for the prosecutor in criminal cases because of their anxious, introverted natures. Endomorphs (obese people) are supposed to be more likely to award large sums in damages be-

cause of their friendly, relaxed natures. They are also considered good for the defense in criminal cases because of their slow and complacent natures. It should be noted, however, that "Sheldon's somatotype theory has fallen out of favor . . . and that there are no empirical data by which to assess the efficacy of evaluating jurors by this method."[59]

There are some, like Houston criminal defense attorney Percy Foreman,[60] who swear by nonverbal techniques as a tool in jury selection. There are others who maintain that attempts to measure attitudes through nonverbal analysis are faulty because "people can and do conceal their attitudes nonverbally as readily as they do verbally."[61] Nonverbal analysis should neither be relied on with fervor nor be completely dismissed as unsophisticated and unscientific: the jury is still out on its effectiveness, because "the casual application of general nonverbal research to specific trial predictions is in its embryonic stage."[62]

Demographic Analysis

Ever since Clarence Darrow's classic remarks on juror stereotypes,[63] generalities have attained the status of maxims of legal lore. Darrow made claims such as that an Irishman is emotional, kindly, and sympathetic; a German is not so keen about individual rights; a Presbyterian is cold as the grave and seldom finds anything right; Baptists are even more hopeless than Presbyterians for the defense; Scandinavians are almost sure to convict; Christian Scientists are too serious; wealthy men convict unless the defendant is accused of violating an antitrust; and women serving on a jury ought to make any lawyer feel uncomfortable! Some of these generalities are irrational and not supported by any behavioral research; other demographic generalities have proven more reliable. What are reported here are, I hope, the more reliable findings regarding jury selection based on a juror's *sex*, age, ethnic and racial characteristics, social and occupational status, and prior jury experience. Religion is not included, because it appears to be a declining source of personal bias in jury decisions. The research findings are presented here in order to show how they might be considered during voir dire. The premise underlying the demographic approach is that a person's background denotes a certain kind of socializing history for that person. Different histories causes people to react differently and to hold different beliefs, attitudes, and values.

Several studies reveal positive correlations between demographic factors of jurors and the personal characteristics of the trial participants that jurors find influential in making their decisions.[64] In other words, likenesses attract. "Jurors tend to prefer their own kind. The greater the perceived similarity between a party and a juror, the more likely it will be that the juror will vote in that party's favor."[65] One study found that a juror's identification or familiarity with the occupation of the defendant results more often in acquittals than if there is a lack of identification with that occupation.[66] Another study shows that the likelihood of conviction increases when there is a greater discrepancy between the socioeconomic and occupational level of the defendant and that of the juror.[67] A group of studies confirms the notion that jurors are more lenient with defendants whose attitudes or appearance is similar to their own.[68] The advice for attorneys to generally follow, then, is to demographically match the jury with their client or key witnesses.

Occasionally, gender makes a difference in jury trials, although it is not one of the best predictors of behavior.[69] The earliest demographic studies of juries came on the heels of women being allowed to serve on juries after the turn of century.[70] Psychologists were curious to find out if females made a difference in jury deliberations. In the 1950s, ongoing re-

search showed that men were assertive in initiating rhetorical acts in jury deliberations, while women only reacted.[71] One group of researchers discovered that men, particularly those in high status occupations, were the jury leaders and participated in jury deliberations more actively than women.[72] Furthermore, females' comments were more emotional in nature, whereas males were more task-oriented, focusing on the issues at hand.[73]

Times have changed dramatically since the 1950s, when "men performed as breadwinners and as task-oriented leaders and . . . women performed as sources of nurturance, love and stability."[74] Later research cannot confirm the earlier results. Although some studies still find that males participate more than females,[75] other studies deny this finding. For instance, one study found that women are quite active in jury discussions.[76] Another researcher found that women participate as actively and task-orientedly as men in criminal juries.[77] She also found that women are more active mediators on juries than are their male counterparts. Women do a better job of breaking tension and helping the group come to an agreement.[78] Generally, however, juror participation differences today cannot be ascribed to gender per se.

What about certain jury verdicts, using gender as a variable? Women appear to find more often for minority plaintiffs than men do, although women favor lower awards than men.[79] On liability, we know that a woman is somewhat more desirable for the defendant if the defendant or the defense lawyer is a young, handsome male. Meanwhile, men are desirable if the defendant (but not the attorney) is a young, attractive female.[80] However, the research does not allow us to offer the sweeping claim that jurors have a general tendency to be less forgiving of their own sex and more forgiving of the opposite sex.[81] On damages, two studies confirm that male jurors give higher awards than female jurors do, especially to a male plaintiff in a personal injury case.[82] However, if the plaintiff is female, female jurors favor higher awards than male jurors.[83]

In criminal cases, guilt-prone men are family-oriented, conventionally socialized, authoritarian, and honest (fearful of lying in court). Meanwhile, guilt-prone women believe in a natural correlation between virtue and reward, are authoritarian on legal issues, believe in their responsibility in the administration of justice, and believe in a just world.[84] Generally, although women are more likely to prejudge defendant guilt than males,[85] there are no significant differences in verdicts based on juror gender.[86] The one exception was for rape cases, in which women jurors appear to be more tense[87] and conviction-prone than their male counterparts.[88] Only one known experimental study shows that women make good defense jurors in rape trials, whereas men are better for the state.[89]

One final observation should be made about gender. Women are more affected by the channel of nonverbal communication than men.[90] Whether nonverbal sensitivity is a condition of motherhood or is learned as a way to advance or survive in the world, we have no adequate explanation for this phenomenon. But it exists. Therefore, if a lawyer or client emits particularly positive or negative nonverbal cues, those cues could carry more weight for a female juror, and this factor should be considered during peremptory challenges.

Another demographic variable is age. In civil cases, some believe that older jurors tend to be more plaintiff-prone, perhaps because they have experienced aches and pains and can, as a result, more closely identify with the injured party.[91] On the other hand, older people may discount subjective complaints on the causes of pain insofar as they have developed similar pains for other reasons.

Whatever position one believes, there is little doubt that older people usually tend to favor settlements on the low side. In additon, older people are good for the defense in antitrust cases.[92] And in criminal cases, older persons may be more suspicious than younger folks. One study found that 84 percent of the jurors over age 60 and only 12 percent of the jurors in the 18-to-30 age group agree that a witness who takes the Fifth Amendment is hiding guilt.[93] Another study showed that jurors' guilty verdicts generally increase with age, particularly for rape cases, but less so in murder cases.[94]

Younger jurors (under age 30) are consistently more forgiving (unless it is in favor of wealthy parties) and tend to be more lenient toward the defense in both criminal and civil law.[95] Young people are more likely to accept scientifically discovered evidence (e.g., the results of a psychiatric test), and they are generally less fixed in their ideas than are the elderly.[96]

Some other conclusions about age should be noted in passing. First, in terms of their contributions to deliberations, the oldest and youngest jurors tend to participate slightly less than jurors in intermediate age groups (34–56).[97] Young people in particular are not very influential on jury panels.[98] In addition, actual comprehension of the case facts and judge's instructions bear an inverse relationship to age. Older jurors exhibit particularly low recall of specific components of the trial testimony and judge instructions. Although these studies on age point in certain directions, firm judgments about the effects of age on jury decisions are inconclusive until further research is conducted.[99]

Ethnic and racial characteristics can make a difference also. This assumes that attitudes and values flow from one's ethnic background. This assumption was more reliable several years ago, when there were many first-generation immigrants on jury panels. It was widely believed by lawyers that northern Europeans demanded more evidence and relied less on emotions than did southern Europeans. It was also claimed that blacks, Chicanos, Irish, Italians, and Jews sympathized with the plaintiffs in civil suits and the defendants in criminal actions, whereas the reverse was true for the British, Germans, and Scandinavians. There is very little scientific confirmation for these beliefs today, because of the dispersion and assimilation of ethnic groups. One study found that 74 percent of the Irish and 50 percent of the Italians voted guilty and that 62 percent of the British and only 46 percent of the Germans voted guilty.[100]

Using national origin stereotyping is clearly wrong. However, depending on racial stereotyping as a prediction of juror behavior may have some validity. Whites are more likely than blacks to convict blacks[101] and will stick with their first-ballot decisions to find black defendants guilty.[102] Meanwhile, black jurors support underdog defendants in litigation,[103] regardless of the race of the perceived underdog.[104] If a "not guilty by reason of insanity" plea is filed, . . . blacks . . . are suitable defense jurors.[105] In civil cases, blacks favor larger-than-average personal injury awards for plaintiffs.[106] Finally, jurors who favor those of the same ethnic or racial derivation as themselves should be sought by an attorney whose client is of that derivation, unless the client is regarded as a discredit to that national origin or race.[107]

Social status and occupational status are much more telling than ethnic or racial background.[108] Social status includes such matters as juror income and education. Low-income people, particularly racial minorities, are defense-oriented in criminal cases and plaintiff-oriented in civil cases. However, this is true only if the defendant and plaintiff have like socioeconomic backgrounds to the juror. Jurors whose occupations make it appear as though they have wealth are less likely to find for the plaintiff, but when they do, they are

generous in the amount of damages they award.[109]

Closely related to income is the matter of education. Jurors that are well educated cope well with the concept of a large verdict. Surveys show they are favorable to the plaintiff in antitrust cases.[110] They are also desirable in cases where a lawyer "intends to conduct a vigorous cross-examination and/or introduce strong impeaching evidence. They tend to be less biased in favor of their own ethnic or racial groups than those less well endowed. They also tend to be good prosecution jurors in criminal cases, unless the People's case depends on weak circumstantial evidence."[111] In addition, those jurors who have high levels of educational attainment feel a greater responsibility for changing other juror's minds. Compared to their less well-educated counterparts, they talk more in deliberations.[112]

Research with ten mock criminal juries showed that more poorly educated jurors put more emphasis on their own personal life experiences than do better-educated jurors, while the better-educated put more emphasis on the judge's instructions, case detail, and jury room procedures than do the less well-educated jurors. Understanding of the court's instructions increases with the educational attainment level of the juror. College-educated jurors also make more attempts at facilitating group discussion than do jurors with less education,[113] and educated jurors generally are the most persuasive members of a panel during deliberations.[114] However, there is no clear pattern in the research between guilty verdicts and any particular educational level.[115] One study found that better-educated jurors more frequently voted for conviction;[116] but another study found no such correlation.[117] The only exception is that the more educated the jurors, the smaller the chance of a verdict of not guilty by reason of insanity.[118]

Occupation may well be the most important variable in jury deliberation. In a study linking occupation to criminal cases, it was discovered that managers and secretaries convict in rape trials "with alarming frequency."[119] No such pattern exists in rape cases for any other occupational group. Other high criminal conviction rates are found among engineers, computer programmers, machinists, bankers, accountants, and bookkeepers.[120] Generally, the higher the occupational status of a juror, the more likely he or she is to vote guilty.[121] One study found, to no one's surprise, that teachers and housewives strongly favor conviction in negligence cases involving an injury to a child.[122] Finally, farmers are more likely to vote guilty than people with jobs in urban areas.[123]

Studying the decisions of 6,266 jurors nationwide, Jury Verdict Research found several clear relationships between occupations and decisions in civil cases.[124] In the civil cases they studied, they classified several occupational types by the extent of their deviation from the national average vote for the plaintiff. Table 6.5 shows the results for overall liability in seven different types of civil cases and for overall damages.

Across the board, clerical workers, professionals, and skilled tradesmen are the best jurors for the plaintiff, although the amount of damages awarded by the last group is substantially below the national average. Some additional findings of the Jury Verdict Research group regarding proplaintiff jurors are as follows:

☐   Blue-collar and clerical workers show the most prejudice against corporate defendants, both in liability and damages.
☐   Skilled tradesmen, professional people, and executives show the least prejudice against plaintiffs who are minors.
☐   Salespersons, professional people, and clerical workers show the least prejudice against plaintiffs who are unemployed.
☐   Although skilled tradesmen are generally good plaintiff jurors, they show prejudice against plaintiffs who are salespersons or among the unemployed.
☐   Although professional people are generally good plaintiff jurors, they show prejudice against plaintiffs who are executives.

Table 6.6 further delineates jurors by occupation, comparing their decisions with the national recovery rate (61 percent) and the average award in all types of civil cases and with the recovery rate in vehicle collision cases.[125] The most proplaintiff jurors on liability are butchers, printers, tool and die makers, accounting clerks, painters, bookkeepers, musicians, artists, and typists, although only printers, among this group, are strong on damages. Liability in vehicle collision cases is found most often among butchers, statisticians, tool and die makers, plumbers, draftsmen, accounting clerks, and food service workers, although none of them are particularly strong on damages. So who should a plaintiff's attorney put on a jury to argue for high damages? The best groups would be accountants and auditors, office machine operators, sales clerks, general clerks, realtors, and printers.

Table 6.5 shows that strong prodefense jurors are business executives (except in occupier and product liability cases), housewives in some cases (and especially on damages), and salespersons, even though attorney folklore claims that salespeople will be for the plaintiff because they think in big-money terms and do not pay attention to detail.[126] Some additional findings of the Jury Verdict Research group regarding prodefendant jurors in civil cases are as follows:

☐   Professional people and skilled tradesmen show the least prejudice against corporate defendants, both in liability and damages.

TABLE 6.5

OCCUPATION AND JURY VOTING BEHAVIOR I

Types of Cases and Damages	Blue-Collar Workers[1] (N = 948)	Clerical Workers[2] (N = 2031)	Executives[3] (N = 589)	Housewives (N = 863)	Professionals[4] (N = 584)	Retired People (N = 489)	Salespersons[5] (N = 228)	Self-Employed[6] (N = 114)	Skilled Tradesmen[7] (N = 420)
All Cases									
Deviation from average vote for plaintiff (61%)	0	+4	−2	−4	+9	−7	−7	0	+16
Intentional Injury Cases									
Deviation from Average vote for plaintiff (66%)	−24	+11	−17	+17	+2	+11	0	0	0
Malpractice Cases									
Deviation from average vote for plaintiff (33%)	+12	+48	−58	+15	+67	+33	−24	−24	+52
Occupier Liability Cases									
Deviation from average vote for plaintiff (46%)	+24	+28	+26	+17	+26	0	−2	0	+52
Pedestrian–Vehicle Cases									
Deviation from average vote for plaintiff (53%)	−9	+4	+4	−4	+15	−4	−6	−6	+15

Types of Cases and Damages	Blue-Collar Workers[1] (N = 948)	Clerical Workers[2] (N = 2031)	Executives[3] (N = 589)	Housewives (N = 863)	Professionals[4] (N = 584)	Retired People (N = 489)	Salespersons[5] (N = 228)	Self-Employed[6] (N = 114)	Skilled Tradesmen[7] (N = 420)
Product Liability Cases									
Deviation from average vote for plaintiff (49%)	+27	+12	+69	+41	+69	+76	0	0	+31
Vehicle Collision Cases									
Deviation from average vote for plaintiff (62%)	+6	+10	-2	+2	+13	0	+8	0	+34
Work Accident Cases									
Deviation from average vote for plaintiff (76%)	-3	-5	0	-7	+11	-11	-34	0	-3
Size of Awards									
Above or below national average	0	+5	0	-8	+6	+4	+5	+4	-7

[1]Includes food service workers, foremen, inspectors, maintenance and service persons, metalworkers, mechanics, machinists, production workers, transportation workers, civil servants, utility workers, vehicle drivers, and warehousemen.

[2]Includes accounting clerks, bank tellers, bookkeepers, general clerks, office machine operators, postal clerks, secretaries, and typists.

[3]Includes public relations and personnel executives, editors, writers, bank executives, corporation executives, purchasers, buyers, managers, and supervisors.

[4]Includes accountants, auditors, artists, interior decorators, engineers, mathematicians, statisticians, scientists, nurses, teachers, surveyors, social workers, designers, appraisers, and architects.

[5]Includes sales clerks, real estate salespersons, and sales representatives.

[6]Includes musicians, artists, realtors, brokers, and owners of small businesses.

[7]Includes draftsmen, electricians, printers, carpenters, radiomen, mechanics, butchers, technicians, plumbers, programmers, beauticians, masons, photographers, lithographers, pressmen, printers, upholsterers, seamstresses, cabinetmakers, tool and die makers, watchmakers, blacksmiths, and metal craftsmen.

TABLE 6.6

OCCUPATION AND JURY VOTING BEHAVIOR II

Type of Occupation	DEVIATION FROM AVERAGE VOTE FOR PLAINTIFF (%)		
	On Liability	On Damages	On Liability in Vehicle Collision Cases
Accountants and auditors	+4	+21	+15
Accounting clerks	+31	−5	+31
Artists and interior decorators	−4	+21	−32
Bank executives	+4	−6	+3
Bank tellers	+14	−8	+16
Beauty operators	+3	0	+8
Blue-collar workers, retired	−17	−9	−10
Blue-collar workers, spouses of	+1	−21	+8
Bookkeepers	+24	−6	+26
Butchers	+44	−10	+40
Carpenters	+1	−5	+3
Civil servants	−5	+4	+5
Clerical workers, retired	0	+3	+10
Corporate executives	−30	0	−29
Draftsmen	+9	−15	+5
Editors and writers	+16	−13	+34
Electricians	+16	−20	+23
Engineers	+19	0	+18
Executives, retired	−54	−11	−47
Executives, spouses of	−2	−12	+8
Food service workers	−2	−1	+27
Foremen and inspectors	+3	+1	+15
General clerks	+3	+15	+6
Managers of businesses	+4	−5	0
Maintenance and servicemen	+3	−1	+19
Mathematicians and statisticians	+17	+3	+39
Mechanics, machinists, and metalworkers	0	−2	−2
Musicians and artists	+22	−17	+15
Nurses	−9	−5	+13
Office machine operators	−4	+20	+13
Owners of small business	−5	+2	0
Painters	+29	0	−11
Plumbers	+17	0	+34
Postal clerks	+1	0	+6
Printers	+39	+8	+15
Production workers	−2	+3	−3
Professional people, retired	+4	+17	−19
Professional people, spouses of	−5	−12	+8
Public relations and personnel executives	−36	+1	−37
Purchasers and buyers	−9	+4	+5
Real estate salespersons	−48	+2	−19

TABLE 6.6 (*Continued*)

OCCUPATION AND JURY VOTING BEHAVIOR II

Type of Occupation	DEVIATION FROM AVERAGE VOTE FOR PLAINTIFF (%)		
	On Liability	On Damages	On Liability in Vehicle Collision Cases
Realtors and brokers	+4	+36	−19
Retired workers, spouses of	−20	−3	−5
Sales clerks	+1	+15	+18
Sales personnel, retired	−18	−21	−5
Sales personnel, spouses of	−22	−5	−35
Scientists	+16	+1	+11
Secretaries	−4	+2	+2
Self-employed people, retired	−30	+9	−50
Self-employed people, spouses of	+11	+7	+19
Skilled tradesmen, retired	+1	+14	−5
Skilled tradesmen, spouses of	−10	+11	−16
Supervisors	+3	+4	+2
Teachers	−9	−5	+13
Technicians	−2	+20	−3
Tool and die makers	+39	−7	+34
Transportation workers	+8	+2	+26
Typists	+21	−14	+26
Unemployed, spouses of	−46	−12	−47
Utility workers	−5	+4	−2
Vehicle drivers	−12	0	+10
Warehousemen	+9	−1	+8
Widows	−2	+1	+5

☐ Self-employed people, salespersons, and housewives show the most prejudice against plaintiffs who are minors.

☐ Housewives, executives, and blue-collar workers show the most prejudice against plaintiffs who are unemployed.

☐ Although salespersons are generally good defense jurors, they show prejudice in favor of plaintiffs who are clerical workers and the unemployed.

Other studies show that defense-oriented jurors in civil cases include retired professional military personnel, insurance company employees, and farmers.[127]

Table 6.6 shows that the most prodefendant jurors on liability are retired executives, real estate salespersons, spouses of unemployed persons, public relations and personnel executives, retired self-employed persons, and spouses of sales personnel and retired folks. Liability in vehicle collision cases is difficult for the plaintiff to prove to retired self-employed persons, spouses of unemployed persons, retired executives, public relations and personnel executives, spouses of sales personnel, interior decorators, and corporate executives. Jurors arguing for the lowest damages possible in all cases are spouses of blue-collar workers, retired sales personnel, electricians, musicians and artists, draftsmen, and typists.[128]

The University of Chicago Jury Project also demonstrated how jurors' occupational backgrounds correlate with their judgments. In a civil case, proprietor white-collar jurors sided with the defendant (a railroad) and laboring blue-collar jurors sided with the plaintiff (a railroad worker). The conclusion reached by this study was that "occupational bias was the central characteristic of the . . . deliberations and of the thinking of the . . . jurors with regard to the case."[129]

Professional and skilled persons have the highest participation rates in jury discussions[130] and are more influential on jury panels than members of unskilled occupational groups and housewives.[131] High-status jurors make more procedural remarks and are more helpful in reaching decisions than are low-status jurors.[132] Finally, the greater the disparity in social status between a juror and a party in litigation, the more difficult it is for identification and empathy to occur between the two parties. For example, successful people tend to be biased against the unemployed. "High discrepancy between defendant and jurors is more likely to lead to a conviction than a trial situation in which low status discrepancy occurs."[133] Finally, "a juror belonging to an occupation or profession traditionally antagonistic to the occupation or profession of the client or witness is more likely to return an unfavorable verdict."[134]

Although all of this information points in certain directions, caution about its use is warranted. At best, the profile serves only as a starting point in using occupational information in jury selection. After all, the profiles do not show what influenced the juror's decision. Was it an outstanding trial performance, a lopsided case, or a persuasive fellow juror? Not knowing the answer to this ques-

tion puts limitations on all demographic information.

Does prior juror experience influence juror judgment on subsequent assignments? Lawyers seem to think so. And, they are right. An anecdotal survey of more than two hundred jurors in federal court showed that jurors use past experiences as a basis for premature conclusions.[135] Evidence of a previous case becomes the model against which a new case is judged,[136] although no direct references in deliberation are made by jurors to prior jury duty.[137] So, in civil cases, a plaintiff's attorney should probably excuse jurors who sat on prior cases that involved more serious injuries, because the injury in this case may look miniscule by comparison. In criminal cases, prospective jurors who sat on earlier juries that returned guilty verdicts will be good defense jurors this time around if the prosecution's case in the immediate trial is not as strong as the prosecution cases in earlier trials.[138] Unfortunately, many jurisdictions will not allow lawyers to discover the outcome of prior trials during voir dire.

There is a mixed voting pattern among jurors in criminal cases who sat on previous criminal trial panels. Some studies have found no relationship between experience and verdicts.[139] Yet, studies in Louisiana,[140] Utah,[141] and Kentucky[142] did find that panels with large proportions of experienced jurors tended to convict more often. However, no correlation between prior jury service and the amount or kind of contributions made to the deliberations has been found,[143] although the credibility of jurors with previous experiences is enhanced among the rest of a panel.[144] One difference that has been discovered is that prior experience appears to increase jurors' overall satisfaction with their roles as jurors,[145] as well as "their confidence in their current verdict."[146]

Attorneys may find demographic data useful,[147] but blind adherence to these generalizations is risky. In separate studies, researchers found that demographic variables of jurors account for 3 to 16 percent of the variance in juror votes.[148] Crawford says, "Matters of age, size of family, years lived in a county, etc., do not tell you whether you have found a good or bad juror. Rather, the predisposition to respond favorably to a certain . . . pitch rests on personality variables, including values, attitudes, and belief systems."[149] Although he does not discount demographic information entirely, and generally accepts occupational information as useful, he shares my belief that demographic heuristics cannot be generalized too far as predictors.

Furthermore, although each of these individual difference variables in group composition determines behavior to some extent, "an analysis of single predictors does not tell you how they combine to influence jurors' verdicts."[150] Gender, age, occupation, prior jury service, and so on are not in and of themselves strongly reliable predictors of a juror's vote. However, "when their combined effect is studied, we may learn that one combination convicts significantly more than another and is, therefore, a good predictor of verdict."[151]

Finally, the dynamics of the group as a whole must be considered in jury selection. The whole is not greater than the sum of its parts. The combination of different personalities and demographic types that are brought into interaction and the social forces that suddenly appear affect the decision-making process. How will a conservative, authoritarian male banker interrelate with a nurturing young housewife? And how will each of them relate to the remaining jurors? A consideration of group dynamics is especially helpful in avoiding or hoping for a hung jury. For instance, defense attorneys may want some rugged individualists on the panel who will not easily conform to group pressure. Bright, well-educated, high-status, relaxed people fit the pattern.[152] Or having two strong people with predicted opposing views on a jury may destroy the possibility of unanimity. The de-

mographic and personality mix must be considered.

Here is a brief summary of much of the research on individual difference variables as they relate to jury decision making. The importance of these findings will vary from trial to trial; that is, because of the case, some demographic variables ought to be weighed heavier (given greater value) than other demographic variables as predictors of salient juror attitudes and behaviors.

Gender

☐ Sex is not a highly reliable predictor of jury leadership roles.

☐ Women favor lower damage awards than men, unless the plaintiff is female.

☐ Gender is not a reliable predictor of decisions in criminal cases, except in rape trials. Women are more conviction-prone than men in rape cases.

☐ Women favor young, handsome male lawyers and parties in litigation; men favor young, attractive defendants.

☐ Women evaluate nonverbal signals more carefully than men.

Age

☐ Older and younger jurors generally do not assume leadership roles.

☐ Older jurors recall less information in the deliberations than do younger jurors.

☐ Older jurors favor lower damages than do younger people on jury duty.

☐ Younger jurors are more lenient in civil and criminal cases than older jurors.

Ethnicity

☐ Black jurors favor perceived underdogs in litigation. They favor large awards for underdog plaintiffs and acquittal for underdog criminal defendants, regardless of the race of the underdog.

☐ Whites are more likely to convict blacks than are blacks.

☐ National origin of a juror is not a reliable predictor of decisions.

Social and Occupational Status

☐ Low-income people are defense-oriented in criminal cases and plaintiff-oriented in civil cases, particularly when the plaintiff is socioeconomically similar to them.

☐ Persons with high levels of educational attainment will most likely be jury leaders.

☐ The best-educated jurors base their decisions on case detail and jury instructions. The worst-educated jurors rely more on their own personal life experiences.

☐ Professional and skilled persons are more likely to be jury leaders than unskilled persons and housewives.

☐ Engineers, computer programmers, machinists, bankers, accountants, bookkeepers, and farmers are proprosecution jurors.

☐ Managers and secretaries are conviction-prone in rape trials.

☐ Teachers and housewives are conviction-prone and are plaintiff-prone in negligence cases involving injuries to children.

☐ Proplaintiff jurors include butchers, printers, tool and die makers, accounting clerks, painters, bookkeepers, entertainers, artists, musicians, auditors, office machine operators, sales clerks, general clerks, realtors, brokers, and secretaries.

☐ Prodefendant jurors in civil suits include retired military personnel, insurance company employees, farmers, executives and other professionals, retired executives, salespersons, retired persons, electricians, draftsmen, and housewives.

☐ Jurors identify with parties in litigation whose occupations are similar to their own.

Prior Jury Experience

☐ Prior jury service sets standards for jurors performing later jury service, although the prior experience is rarely discussed in subsequent case deliberations.

☐ Prior jury experience is a fairly good predictor of jury leadership.

SOCIAL SCIENCE RESEARCH APPLIED TO JURY SELECTION

As previously noted, attorneys have for centuries relied on intuition, folklore, and personal experience in picking the "right" jurors. However, in recent years, psychologists, sociologists, communicologists, and other social scientists have contended that the process of jury selection should go beyond intuition and folklore to a more sophisticated plane, enabling selection decisions to be made with the benefit of knowledge acquired through the use of systematic empirical techniques. They maintain that broadly defined stereotypes cannot predict how an individual will vote, especially when each geographic region and case has its own special characteristics.

Empirical techniques are far from new; it is the application of the techniques to the problem of jury selection that is new. The union of law and behavioral science "has been a slow and considered process."[153] The necessary mathematical and probability formulas were developed before the 20th century; the attitude-change measurement and scaling techniques were developed by the late 1920s; development of standardized attitude and personality scales, and awareness of the relationships among them and demographic characteristics to better understand human nature, were under way by 1950; and when electronic technology came into common use by the social scientists, around 1960, "the capability for selecting juries scientifically might have been described more as easy than as feasible."[154] No one knows exactly how widely scientific jury research is currently being used. It has yet to be planted permanently in the legal landscape. Certainly, we are many years away from the time when, if ever, the problem of choosing the right juror will be alleviated as all pertinent data are fed into a hand-held computer that will give its recommendation right in the courtroom.

The first major effort to use social science knowledge was made on behalf of Philip Berrigan and the other members of the Harrisburg Seven in their conspiracy trial in the winter of 1971–72. Berrigan and the others were antiwar activists accused of conspiracy to destroy draft board records, kidnap Secretary of State Henry Kissinger, and blow up heating tunnels in Washington, D.C.[155] Sociologist Jay Schulman left his teaching job at City College of New York to become active in the anti–Vietnam War movement. He became deeply concerned about the outcome of the Harrisburg Seven trial. Harrisburg was a relatively conservative community and seemed to be prejudiced against antiwar activity. Schulman recalls how jury research was born:

I kept thinking . . . there must be something I, as a social scientist, can do to help my friends. But what? The answer—I could use my skills to get a fair jury. I went to Richard Christie, . . . a social psychologist at Columbia, and talked it over with him. . . . We . . . designed a major survey . . . and got volunteers to do . . . interviews; . . . then we wangled computer time to process our data. The defense lawyers—Ramsey Clark, Paul O'Dwyer, . . . among others—weren't interested at first, but we had some useful surprises for them. For instance, we discovered that Catholics would be O.K. on the issue of social protest. . . . Also, contrary to what our lawyers expected, college-educated people were not likely to be liberal in Harrisburg. . . . With access to such findings, the lawyers were able to ask probing questions and . . . got dozens of jurors excused for cause.[156]

Based on a telephone poll of 840 people, followed by in-depth interviews of 252 people who were representative of potential jurors, Schulman advised the defense that the ideal juror was a semiskilled female Democrat with no religious preference. When the trial was over, the hung-jury decision was 10–2 for acquittal.

Jury analysis techniques were subsequently used in other highly publicized trials, including the trial and acquittal in Camden, New Jersey, of 28 radical Catholics in connection with a draft board raid; the trial in Gainesville, Florida, of some militant members of Vietnam Veterans Against the War, in which a jury that included some men of draft age voted for acquittal; the trial of Daniel Ellsberg and Anthony Russo, in which, although the case was dismissed partway through, follow-up study showed that the jury was likely to have voted for acquittal; and the trial and acquittal of John Mitchell and Maurice Stans, in which Long Island consultant Martin Herbst helped the defense lawyers select an appropriate jury.[157]

Schulman and his associates were involved in the trial and acquittal of the black militant Angela Davis.[158] Prior to the trial, Davis was on the FBI's most-wanted list. She was an admitted member of the Communist Party. In 1972, her name was more widely recognized than that of presidential candidate George McGovern, although she certainly was not a figure that aroused sympathy. In their preliminary door-to-door research, the scientific jury advisors determined that only low-income blacks and Mexican-Americans would be able to give Angela Davis a fair trial. They knew it was highly unlikely that they could get a jury made up entirely of these groups, so they continued their research into the case by analyzing other dimensions of group dynamics and personality traits. They discovered that Davis might be able to get a fair trial, regardless of the ethnic and racial makeup of the jury, if they could get people who basically had not heard of Angela Davis, who were uninformed about current events, and who were not socially conscious. On the day of voir dire, only one black was present, and the prosecutor used his peremptory strike against her. No Mexican-Americans were present. Nevertheless, based on this preliminary research as well as in-court observations by five psychologists, a jury was chosen that found Angela Davis not guilty of murder, kidnapping, and conspiracy. This verdict was due, in part, to the fact that the jury was eventually made up of people with no strong biases or convictions of any kind.

The National Jury Project was founded in 1975 by Schulman and a group of social scientists, legal workers, and lawyers who had been involved in political trials in the early 1970s. In those cases, defendants were on trial because of the political struggles they had participated in and represented—anti–Vietnam War activities; the Attica Prison rebellion, after which more than one thousand counts were charged against the inmates; and the Wounded Knee Occupation, the Indian takeover of Wounded Knee, South Dakota, from which a series of trials arose, including the trial of Dennis Banks and Russell Means, leaders of the American Indian Movement. Defense committees and progressive social scientists were part of the defense teams, and they joined with lawyers and legal workers to focus exclusively on the problems of jury selection.[159] The primary work of the NJP continues to be the defense of members of progressive movements—American Indians, labor, gay rights, women's rights, antinuclear power, tenants' rights, war resistors' rights, and so on. NJP is a self-funding organization with offices in Berkeley, Minneapolis, Atlanta, and Boston.

Another such company is Litigation Sciences, a Palos Verdes, California, firm experienced in product liability, antitrust, breach of contract, corporate criminal defense, and major tax dispute litigation. The scientists there are not lawyers but, as their brochure states, "experts in human behavior."[160] The staff consists of specialists in communication, social psychology, sociology, consumer behavior, research psychology, econometrics, and marketing science. The concept of Litigation Sciences was born in 1977, when Donald E. Vinson, then a University of Southern California marketing professor, was hired by IBM for advice in a major antitrust case. Since the company was founded, it has worked almost exclusively for law firms representing large American corporations.

Social scientists of all kinds are involved in jury selection today for all sorts of cases, big and small. They tend to view trials quite differently from most attorneys. This difference is largely due to the fact that the two groups of professionals have quite different histories of academic specialization, as Christie explains:

Graduate training in the social sciences places a heavy emphasis on research methodology. Questions are viewed as best answered by the application of statistically based techniques. Thus, the selection of a fair and unbiased jury is viewed as analogous to a research problem. Legal training, on the other hand, is characterized by the study of previous cases and the whole intricate system of legal precedent that may apply to a particular case. The practice of . . . law demands the effective implementation of these principles through argument in a specific arena—the courtroom. Here, skills in advocacy . . . are paramount.

The basic point in making this distinction is that social scientists and lawyers tend, by virtue of differential training and professional experiences, to have different conceptual approaches to the problem of jury selection. This is neither good nor bad; it simply is.[161]

Has the marriage between social science and law been effective? Apparently so. Those lawyers who have used social scientists to help them pick juries are usually complimentary about the services rendered. The authors of one book claim that scientific jury selection "can be a worthwhile investment when it is limited to a specific court district and focuses on general attitudes that are related to the juror's role."[162]

Before we examine the techniques used by these social scientists, it should be mentioned that some of their research is used, not to select juries alone, but to test the venue generally in order to assist attorneys who want to file pretrial change-of-venue motions (see Chapter 3). A venue survey is designed to ascertain whether people have formed opinions about a case or are so biased against some party that the ability to obtain a fair jury in that community is endangered. Results of venue surveys are presented in court to show that a certain party cannot receive a fair trial. For instance, in *North Carolina v. Joan Little,* a survey was conducted on a random sample of registered voters (the source of jurors) in the county where the crime took place and in several adjacent counties. The case involved the killing of a white male guard in the women's section of a jail. Ms. Little was a 20-year-old black inmate in the jail. The key questions were (1) measurement of how much the person had heard about the case, (2) preconception of guilt, and (3) racism (e.g., "Do you believe that black women have lower morals than white women?"). The results showed a much higher degree of case knowledge, preconception of guilt, and racism among potential jurors in the county of the crime than in the adjacent and more urban counties. The defense team, armed with these data, argued for a change of venue. The judge, convinced that racism would hamper a fair trial, ordered the trial moved from Beaufort County to the more urban Wake County. Many observers were later convinced that the granting of a change of venue was the main reason for the ultimate acquittal of Joan Little.[163] Some regard community polls of this type "as the most persuasive evidence for obtaining a change of venue."[164]

Two models of scientific jury selection predominate. Jay Schulman has called these the *demographic model* and the *clinical model.*[165] The former emphasizes the link between attitudes and demographic characteristics, as in the Harrisburg trial; the latter emphasizes psychological and communication constructs, as in the Angela Davis trial.[166] Of course, the two models can be coupled.

The demographic model of scientific jury selection relies heavily on telephone surveys and in-depth, person-to-person interviews of a random and representative sample (usually 300–500 persons) from the area where a trial is to occur.[167] The best sample is drawn from those people who have been called for jury service in the past.[168] The interviewers seek information about potential jurors' attitudes toward such matters as economic prejudice, youth, capital punishment, amount of damages in a civil case, law enforcement officers, rape victims, or other elements of the particular case being tried. For example, in a consumer electronics case in Florida, respondents were read a brief scenario of the case and were then probed as to their attitudes toward the specific product, after which certain demographic data were collected.[169] Prospective jurors themselves are not questioned, although interviewers in some surveys do question jurors' neighbors or make inquiries about their employment.[170] Community surveys are based on two assumptions: (1) that people's attitudes are stable and will be linked to their voting behavior on a jury, and (2) that people with different attitudes possess different background characteristics.[171]

Attitudinal data are fed into a computer and paired with demographic factors to arrive at a prediction equation. This equation tells the social scientist which background variables in that particular community are most important in predicting a potential juror's attitude and biases toward issues central to the case.[172] "The advantage of having demographic predictors is that as soon as a prospective juror states his age, occupation, income, and so on, the attorney has some idea of how most people who have this particular set of characteristics feel about the case. The advantage of having indirect predictors [attitudes] is that the lawyer has a set of questions to ask during the voir dire, the answers to which will increase his knowledge of the juror's predisposition without the juror being aware (and thus being able to manipulate his responses) and without increasing the opposing attorney's knowledge of the juror."[173]

So, in voir dire, an attorney asks the prospective juror questions that will elicit a self-description of the demographic variables found to be significant in the original sample survey. The responses of the juror are then put into a multiple regression analysis formula that assigns a weighted numerical value to each of the various demographic characteristics; the sum of the values which indicates whether the person is likely to be a favorable or, at least, an unbiased juror.[174] For example, a survey of the jurors in Wake County was used to develop a mathematical model of the ideal defense juror in the Joan Little trial. The $35,000 poll matched pertinent case attitudes with demographic characteristics of the respondents in the sample. The result was a prediction equation for each type of juror as to the likelihood such jurors would find Joan Little guilty. Among the streams of information, it was discovered that health food waitresses and record store employees were found to be fairer to Ms. Little than IBM engineers, both in the survey and in the actual trial, since these occupational types surfaced when she went into court.[175]

The 1976 Pinto reckless-homicide case was the occasion for one of the most famous of these demographic surveys. Ford was accused of ignoring safety defects that contributed to the death of three teenage girls in a crash. Hans Zeisel, a University of Chicago Law School professor, was hired by the automobile company, and his work basically involved asking people whether they thought indicting Ford for homicide was a good thing. Compiling demographic profiles, he discovered that young women were the most likely to convict, hardly surprising since young women were the victims. The best jurors for Ford were men. Then Zeisel found something interesting. If a young woman drove a truck, she effectively became, as far as the verdict went, a man![176]

Other demographic surveys have yielded useful and sometimes surprising information

as well. The defense team in the Watergate-era criminal trial of former Attorney General John Mitchell and Maurice Stans found the worst possible juror to be a liberal, Jewish Democrat who read the *New York Times* or the *Washington Post,* listened to Walter Cronkite, and was well informed about Watergate and public affairs in general.[177] In the case involving the Berrigan brothers in the middle district of Pennsylvania, attorneys knew that many of the citizens of the community read the *New York Times.* Hence they assumed that these people were liberals and would be defense-oriented jurors. But a survey showed that those who read the *Times* were actually quite conservative, the explanation being that the major newspapers published in the middle district of Pennsylvania were afternoon papers. Most of the people who got the morning *Times* did so to get the closing stock prices and to read the business news. They were almost all conservative business people.[178]

Is the demographic survey method successful? The major drawback of demographic surveys is that they cannot determine whether the particular prospective juror being examined holds the same opinions and attitudes as his or her demographic group. Pollsters can deal only in probabilities and not in certainties. It may be that the particular prospective juror holds views contrary to those commonly held by members of his or her demographic group, or will not hold the same opinions on the particular subject at hand. These possibilities are likely to occur in situations in which the juror belongs to a demographic subgroup with differing tendencies from the main group. For example, survey data may indicate that urban Jews are favorably disposed and rural Republicans are negatively biased toward a particular defendant. The prospective juror that is both an urban Jew and a conservative Republican presents a problem in analysis. Does the juror identify more with urban Judaism or with rural, conservative Republicanism? And even if the question can be answered, how do we factor in such matters as the strength of the evidence in a case? The numerous variables are far too complex to be summarized in a pollster's statistics. Nevertheless, in a number of cases, practitioners of the method have conducted posttrial interviews with both actual jurors and prospective jurors that had been dismissed. They have concluded that "the demographic survey is accurate about 70% of the time in predicting individual jurors' attitudes and dispositions."[179] One author is more positive. He compares human intuition in jury selection to a demographic model:

When the same information is available to a human decisionmaker and a mathematical model, almost without exception the mathematical model makes more reliable and accurate predictions [of attitudes]. After 60 studies comparing clinical versus statistical prediction, the humans beat the computer only once. . . . These findings . . . were as much of a shock . . . to the people who discovered them as to you who read about them. The original intention was to aid human decisionmakers by providing a floor of statistical accuracy below which they could not fall. But the floor turned out to be a ceiling. We are indeed fallible creatures. In the Harrisburg trial, one of the two jurors who held out for conviction had been vetoed by the computer. That advice, however, was overruled by Ramsey Clark, who felt certain the juror was a good choice.[180]

Even if the findings of a demographic study are not used to predict attitudes, they at least allow a trial team to know what voir dire questions should be prepared for each potential juror to get at relevant predispositions.

The clinical model relies on in-court observation of prospective jurors. It has been described by some as an "intuitive approach to jury selection"[181] where the emphasis is placed on the answers, actions, personalities, and mannerisms revealed in court by the in-

formants. Two steps are involved: (1) defining the types of jurors desired and not desired in a case and (2) identifying those jurors in a courtroom situation. Prior to voir dire, profiles of ideal jurors and risky jurors are designed. These profiles are based on previous social science studies of large numbers of people over long periods of time. Many of those studies have been reported in this chapter. The reliability of each profile increases as more and more data are used in constructing it. Even then, each judicial district "has its own unique social and cultural patterning which must be understood and taken into account in jury selection."[182] Jurors in Bar Harbor, Maine, differ from jurors in Miami, Florida. Ideally, then, the clinical model should be supplemented by the demographic model in jury selection. However, "when time and/ or resources prevent research on a specific case, the jury selector should apply only the previous research that has been shown to be generalizable to the specific case at hand."[183] That information is used to prepare a juror profile. Then, during voir dire, each individual respondent is compared with the profile and rated, and the overall pool is ranked according to the traits the prospective jurors reveal. At the end of voir dire, recommendations for deselection are discussed by the consultant and the attorneys. As each prospective juror's name comes up, an assessment of that person is made. "Those jurors whom everyone agrees are very good or very bad for one side are quickly identified, and the remainder of the meeting is spent discussing the pros and cons of the veniremen who are rated in the middle or about whom there is disagreement."[184]

In the Joan Little trial, a team of consultants performed a personality analysis and a nonverbal analysis of the panel. The personality analysis was designed to get at authoritarianism. The defense did not want authoritarians on the jury, thinking that they would be rigid, racist, politically conservative, and highly punitive. Each panelist was rated on an authoritarianism scale from 1 to 30, based on in-court observation. Jurors with a score higher than 20 were rejected. (The final panel had an average rating of 12.95.) Subsequent interviews showed that these "in-court ratings of authoritarianism were indeed related to post-trial measures of authoritarianism."[185] Additionally, paralinguistic and kinesic analysis helped to assess levels of juror anxiety on a scale from 1 to 5, a high score indicating low anxiety. Near the end of voir dire, members of the consulting team and the lawyers huddled to decide whether to accept, reject, or obtain more information from the jurors. After a five-week trial and 78 minutes of jury deliberation, Ms. Little was found not guilty on all charges.[186]

In addition to the demographic and clinical models of scientific jury selection, two other methods have been employed in recent years too. First, the *mock jury*, or *focus group, approach* "is a nonstatistical method of eliciting direct feelings and attitudes toward the issues"[187] before an actual trial begins.[188] In this method, old jury lists are used to assemble from the community a group of eight to ten people that will match the real jury as closely as possible. These "jurors" are placed in a simulated trial setting with a mock judge. Opposing counsel is impersonated by another attorney in the same law firm who is familiar with the facts of the case and who can fairly represent the interests of the other side. Either the real witnesses or actors pretending to be the witnesses present an abbreviated version of the trial. An alternative to the minitrial is to have a group leader, the trial consultant, present unbiased information from both sides of the case to the focus group and then leave the room.

No matter which approach is used, the group is next asked to deliberate as a jury, and these proceedings are videotaped, or the jurors are observed through a one-way mirror, or both. Once deliberations are completed, the social scientists conduct individual de-

briefings with the jurors to determine the basis for their decisions and the factors that may have confused them. By doing this, the social scientists identify potential strengths and trouble spots with the case. To avoid the possibility of obtaining a jury with unusual idiosyncrasies, at least 3 focus groups should deliberate after they have all heard the minitrial.[189] In a well-known case in which SCM Corporation filed an antitrust action against Xerox, 20 focus group sessions were used by SCM, although such a large number of groups is atypical.[190]

This technique is "principally beneficial in (1) developing a cohesive and comprehensive trial strategy, (2) formulating a preferential rating system of juror profiles, and (3) organizing a list of voir dire questions which will explore juror attitudes and opinions and allow counsel the opportunity to know and rate the jurors."[191] Here is a report on one case in which the mock jury approach was used in 1980, prior to a real jury award of $1.8 billion to the plaintiff:

In an antitrust suit brought by MCI Communications Corporation against the American Telephone and Telegraph Company, . . . Jenner and Block had hired Leo J. Shapiro and Associates, a sizable Chicago market-research firm, . . . to conduct a survey in the Chicago area from which prospective jurors would be drawn. Through both telephone and face-to-face interviews, the researchers learned which predictor variables correlated with a tendency to side with a slant toward AT&T. Shapiro's team then recruited three mock juries of eight, each group being a measured mix of persons likely to favor one litigant or the other. The pseudojuries met . . . to hear a Jenner and Block lawyer present a 45-minute version of MCI's case. Next, another Jenner and Block lawyer offered AT&T's side, making as strong a case as he could. Then the jurors . . . deliberated while the lawyers and Shapiro's staffers observed them . . . through a one-way mirror.[192]

The *shadow jury approach* uses a surrogate jury, matched demographically to an actual panel. They sit in the courtroom while an actual trial is in progress day after day and are available each evening for detailed interviews. The techniques used in the shadow jury are a modified form of participant observation research, in which "the researcher takes the role of a participant in a given situation and then reflects on what it is like to be the person who is actually in the role under study. Surrogate jurors ... become participants, observing everything the actual jurors observe, hearing everything the jurors hear, and suffering the same admonitions."[193] The shadow jurors do not, however, deliberate among themselves.

Members of a shadow jury are recruited as full-time paid members of a research team. They cannot ask, nor are they told, the source of funding for the project. Each night of a trial, they report to the project leader (the hired consultant) by telephone. They answer questions to elicit their feelings about the court proceedings, the lawyers, the witnesses, the exhibits, and their general reactions to the case. Advice on juror response is then passed on to the attorneys who hired the consultant in the case. Comments are used to make testimony more understandable and to shape the final arguments.

In 1976, IBM's general counsel Nicholas B. Katzenbach and David Boies, conceived the idea of engaging Donald E. Vinson of the University of Southern California to recruit a jury that would mirror the demographic and psychological traits of the actual jurors in a multimillion-dollar antitrust suit brought against IBM by California Computer Products of Anaheim. "'They were very concerned about what the jury would be thinking during the trial,' Vinson recalled. 'None of the jurors had any experience or expertise in computer technology. And they were to be presented with very complex and sophisticated evidence.'"[194] Through the use of this jury, IBM's attorneys hoped to be able to evaluate the extent to which jurors with no previous understanding of the technical matters at issue

could understand what was being discussed in the trial. Once the actual jury in the trial was impaneled, Vinson quickly developed a jury profile and recruited six people whose traits matched those of the real jurors. Daily monitoring of the surrogate jury and their reactions to the attorneys and witnesses yielded a substantial amount of information to IBM's counsel. "One of the most valuable returns from the shadow jury research was insight into why jurors either understand or fail to understand evidence. One of the principal reasons jurors fail to understand complex technical information is that lawyers themselves, through long study of the case, become experts in the subject under litigation and tend to forget that they are presenting their case to lay people, often quite unsophisticated. Attorneys frequently are not effective communicators."[195]

To some, the clinical model, mock trials, and shadow juries remain nostrums rather than truly scientific methods of jury selection. The clinical model is only as good as the in-court methodology that is used to evaluate jurors. Mock and shadow jury decisions come from people who know their verdicts will not count and, as a result, perceive things differently and may reach different decisions from real juries. These methods offer "no uniform set of predictor variables that can be applied universally."[196] In addition, how do you blend conflicting results from a variety of methods, or how do you resolve a difference of opinion between "scientific" test results and lawyer intuition? How should priorities be placed on the various sources of information? How should their interrelationships be evaluated? The only advice that can be offered is to use both intuition and some methods of scientific jury selection together. To the extent hunch and "science" agree, the deselection of certain jurors can be deemed wise.

Should an attorney desire to hire a social scientist for jury selection, he or she should provide the consultant with a detailed summary of the facts of the case, a list of the legal issues involved, descriptions of important witnesses expected to testify for both sides along with their anticipated testimony, and a list of demonstrative evidence. The expert consultant can then make an evaluation of counsel, client, and ideal jury.[197] After the social scientist makes recommendations to an inquiring lawyer, "the attorney would do well to listen to his consultant, and then integrate his recommendations into the approach and intuitive style with which the attorney feels most comfortable. If the verdict comes out against the client, it is the attorney who bears the responsibility—not the consultant."[198] Lists of recommended consultants may be obtained from the American Society of Trial Consultants.[199]

This brings us to the end of our consideration of jury selection. As can be seen, there is a lot involved in the jury-picking process. A great deal of the process is guesswork and speculation; yet attorneys must still master certain specially developed techniques to help achieve their objective of getting the best possible audiences for their presentations. They must consider jury selection with utmost care, and only after the final oath is administered to the last juror can they relax and try to put the jury selection process out of mind until the next trial. Jury selection is indeed a challenging and exciting part of trial work.

Notes

[1] V. Hale Starr and Mark McCormick, *Jury Selection* (Boston: Little, Brown, 1985), 238.

[2] "This group of strangers is brought into the courtroom, where they have probably never been before, and are seated by a uniformed court officer in some kind of order. Then they are stared at for a considerable length of time by strange looking lawyers, litigants, and a rather austere looking fellow in a black robe seated at an elevated bench. They are eventually asked all kinds of questions about their attitudes, their experience, their personal feelings and habits, and many other personal things. It is a strange world for this jury panel." Walter E. Jordan, "A Trial Judge's Observations About Voir Dire Examination," *Defense Law Journal* 30 (1981), 225.

[3] Starr and McCormick, op. cit., 238.

[4] "Most residents of South Dakota who live near an Indian reservation 'know' that Indians are lacking in a strong work ethic and that they are prone to be drunkards—they know this because they have heard such expressed by honored members of the community from birth and, besides, they have seen examples of such behavior with their own eyes. These individuals would not view this 'knowledge' as prejudice, but merely as an indication of their ability to draw correct conclusions from observed 'evidence.' Such individuals, with all good and clear conscience, feel that there is no prejudice in their own minds against Indians. This level of prejudice is perhaps the most difficult to expose and the most difficult to discern during voir dire." V. Hale Starr, "Behavioral Science in the Courtroom," *Trial Diplomacy Journal* (Summer 1981), 9.

[5] Starr and McCormick, op. cit., 238.

[6] Here is an example. After Lester Maddox threatened to use an ax handle on blacks he believed were disrespectful, he answered questions from the press when running for governor claiming he was fair-minded and unbiased toward blacks.

[7] "Jurors often, either consciously or unconsciously, lie on voir dire." Dale W. Broeder, "Voir dire Examinations: An Empirical Study," *Southern California Law Review* 38 (1965), 528.

[8] Lori B. Andrews, "Mind Control in the Courtroom," *Psychology Today* (March 1982), 70.

[9] Nancy Gossage McDermid, "Response Paper: Jury Selection and Jury Behavior," in Ronald J. Matlon and Richard J. Crawford, eds., *Communication Strategies in the Practice of Lawyering* (Annandale, Va.: Speech Communication Association, 1983), 280.

[10] Lynn R. Kahle and John J. Berman, "Attitudes Cause Behaviors: A Cross-Lagged Panel Analysis," *Journal of Personality and Social Psychology* 37 (1979), 315–321; Herbert C. Kelman, "Attitudes Are Alive and Well and Gainfully Employed in the Sphere of Action," *American Psychologist* 29

(1974), 324; William J. McGuire, "The Concept of Attitudes and Their Relations to Behaviors," in H. Wallace Sinaiko and L. A. Broedling, eds., *Perspectives on Attitude Assessment: Surveys and Their Alternatives* (Champaign, Ill.: Pendleton, 1976); William A. Watts, "Relative Persistence of Opinion Charge Induced by Active Compared to Passive Participation," *Journal of Personality and Social Psychology* 5 (1967), 4–15.

[11] Edward J. Bronson, "On the Conviction Proneness and Representativeness of the Death-Qualified Jury: An Empirical Study of Colorado Veniremen," *University of Colorado Law Review* 42 (1970), 1–32; Edward J. Bronson, "Does the Exclusion of Scrupled Jurors in Capital Cases Make the Jury More Likely to Convict? Some Evidence from California," *Woodrow Wilson Journal of Law* 3 (1980), 11–34; Robert Fitzgerald and Phoebe C. Ellsworth, "Due Process vs. Crime Control: Death Qualification and Jury Attitudes," *Law and Human Behavior* 8 (1984), 31–51; William C. Thompson et al., "Death Penalty Attitudes and Conviction Proneness: The Translation of Attitudes Into Verdicts," *Law and Human Behavior* 8 (1984), 95–113; K. Phillip Taylor and Raymond W. Buchanan, "The Effects of Attitude Toward Capital Punishment on the Evaluation of Evidence and the Determination of Guilt," Paper presented at the Speech Communication Association Convention (Louisville, Ky., November 1982).

[12] In her review of numerous published empirical studies on pretrial publicity, Simon found that juries are able and willing to put aside extraneous information and base their decisions on the case evidence. In spite of considerable adverse publicity against Angela Davis and John Mitchell, both were acquitted, indicating that, once again, jurors might be able to withstand pretrial information. Rita James Simon, "Comments on Jury Selection and Jury Behavior Papers," in Ronald J. Matlon and Richard J. Crawford, eds., *Communication Strategies in the Practice of Lawyering* (Annandale, Va.: Speech Communication Association, 1983), 274–275.

[13] Beth Bonora and Elissa Krauss, eds., *Jurywork: Systematic Techniques* (Oakland: National Jury Project, 1979), 185.

[14] Thomas Sannito and Peter J. McGovern, *Courtroom Psychology for Trial Lawyers* (New York: John Wiley, 1985), 18–23, 35.

[15] Ibid., 20.

[16] Eric Berne, *Games People Play* (New York: Grove Press, 1964).

[17] Gerald M. Goldhaber and Marylynn B. Goldhaber, *Transactional Analysis: Principles and Applications* (Boston: Allyn and Bacon, 1976), vii.

[18] Adapted from Jay Burke, *Jury Selection: The TA System for Trial Attorneys* (Hialeah, Fla.: Burke Publications, 1980), 1–18.

[19] Ibid.

[20] Albert Mehrabian, "Immediacy: An Indicator of Attitudes in Linguistic Communication," *Journal of Personality* 34 (1966), 24–34; Albert Mehrabian, "Attitudes Inferred from Non-Immediacy of Verbal Communicators," *Journal of Verbal Learning and Verbal Behavior* 6 (1967), 294–295; Albert Mehrabian and Morton Wiener, "Non-Immediacy Between Communicator and Object of Communication in a Verbal Message: Application to the Inference of Attitudes," *Journal of Consulting Psychology* 30 (1966), 420–425.

[21] Arthur H. Patterson, "Scientific Jury Selection: The Need for a Case Specific Approach," *Social Action and the Law* 11 (1986), 105–109.

[22] Thomas Sannito, *A Psychologist's Voir Dire* (Dubuque, Iowa: Forensic Psychologists, 1979), 11.

[23] Theodore W. Adorno et al., *The Authoritarian Personality* (New York: Harper, 1950), 255.

[24] V. R. Boehm, "Mr. Prejudice, Miss Sympathy, and the Authoritarian Personality: An Application of Psychological Measuring Techniques to the Problem of Jury Bias," *Wisconsin Law Review* (1968), 734–750.

[25] Robert M. Bray and Audrey M. Noble, "Authoritarianism and Decisions of Mock Juries," *Journal of Personality and Social Psychology* 36 (1978), 1424–1430; Richard Centers, Robert W. Shomer, and Aroldo Rodrigues, "A Field Experiment in Interpersonal Persuasion Using Authoritative Influence," *Journal of Personality* 38 (1970), 392–403; Robert F. Crosson, "An Investigation Into Certain Personality Variables Among Capital Trial Jurors," Ph.D. diss. (Cleveland: Western Reserve University, 1966); Ralph Epstein, "Aggression Toward Outgroups as

a Function of Authoritarianism and Imitation of Aggressive Models," *Journal of Personality and Social Psychology* 3 (1966), 574–579; Michael Fried, Kalman J. Kaplan, and Katherine W. Klein, "Juror Selection: An Analysis of Voir Dire," in Rita James Simon, ed., *The Jury System in America: A Critical Overview* (Beverly Hills, Calif.: Sage, 1975), 51; George L. Jurow, "New Data on the Effect of a 'Death-Qualified' Jury on the Guilt Determination Process," *Harvard Law Review* 84 (1971), 567–611; Ramsey McGowen and Glen D. King, "Effects of Authoritarian, Anti-Authoritarian, and Egalitarian Legal Attitudes on Mock Juror and Jury Decisions," *Psychological Reports* 51 (1982), 1067–1074; Neil Vidmar, "Retributive and Utilitarian Motives and Other Correlatives of Canadian Attitudes Toward the Death Penalty," *Canadian Psychologist* 15 (1974), 337–356.

[26]Stanley Sue, Ronald E. Smith, and George Pedroza, "Authoritarianism, Pretrial Publicity, and Awareness of Bias in Simulated Jurors," *Psychological Reports* 37 (1975), 1299–1302.

[27]Roberta Wyper Shell, "Scientific Jury Selection: Does It Work?" *Barrister* (Summer 1980), 48.

[28]Herman E. Mitchell and Donn Byrne, "The Defendant's Dilemma: Effects of Jurors' Attitudes and Authoritarianism," *Journal of Personality and Social Psychology* 25 (1973), 123–129.

[29]Kathleen Stirrett Berg and Neil Vidmar, "Authoritarianism and Recall of Evidence About Criminal Behavior," *Journal of Research in Personality* 9 (1975), 147–157.

[30]Dee Ann Soder, "Testing a Jury Selection Scale and Theory in Court," Ph.D. diss. (Norman: University of Oklahoma, 1976).

[31]Carol M. Werner, Dorothy K. Kagehiro, and Michael J. Strube, "Conviction Proneness and the Authoritarian Juror: Inability to Disregard Information or Attitudinal Bias?" *Journal of Applied Psychology* 67 (1982), 629–636.

[32]Jacqueline Goldman, Kenneth F. Freundlich, and Victoria A. Casey, "Jury Emotional Response and Deliberation Style," *Journal of Psychiatry and Law* 11 (1983), 319–334.

[33]John Lambert, Edith Krieger, and Susanne Shay, "Juror Decision Making: A Case of Attitude Change Mediated by Authoritarianism," *Journal of Research in Personality* 16 (1982), 419–434.

[34]James H. Davis, Robert M. Bray, and Robert W. Holt, "The Empirical Study of Decision Processes in Juries," in J. L. Tapp and F. J. Levine, eds., *Law, Justice, and the Individual in Society: Psychological and Legal Issues* (New York: Holt, Rinehart and Winston, 1977), 330.

[35]Jeffrey T. Frederick, "Jury Behavior: A Psychologist Examines Jury Selection," *Ohio Northern University Law Review* 5 (1978), 575.

[36]Fried, Kaplan, and Klein, op. cit., 52.

[37]V. Lee Hamilton, "Obedience and Responsibility: A Jury Simulation," *Journal of Personality and Social Psychology* 36 (1978), 126–146.

[38]V. Lee Hamilton, "Individual Differences in Ascriptions of Responsibility, Guilt and Appropriate Punishment," in Gordon Bermant, Charlan Nemeth, and Neil Vidmar, eds., *Psychology and the Law* (Lexington, Mass.: D. C. Heath, 1976), 239–264.

[39]Robert N. Vidulich and Ivan P. Kaiman, "The Effects of Information Source Status and Dogmatism Upon Conformity Behavior," *Journal of Abnormal and Social Psychology* 63 (1961), 639–642.

[40]Terry W. Mackey, "Jury Selection: Developing the Third Edge," *Trial* (October 1980), 24.

[41]C. David Mortensen, *Communication: The Study of Human Interaction* (New York: Harper & Row, 1972), 210.

[42]Bonora and Krauss, op. cit., 210.

[43]Michael Argyle, *Social Interaction* (London: Methuen, 1969); Albert Mehrabian and Susan R. Ferris, "Inference of Attitudes from Nonverbal Communication in Two Channels," *Journal of Consulting Psychology* 31 (1967), 248–252; Albert Mehrabian and Morton Wiener, "Decoding of Inconsistent Communications," *Journal of Personality and Social Psychology* 6 (1967), 109–114.

[44]Andrew S. Dibner, "Cue-Counting: A Measure of Anxiety in Interviews," *Journal of Consulting Psychology* 20 (1956), 475–477; Stanislav V. Kasl and George F. Mahl, "The Relationship of Disturbances and Hesitations in Spontaneous Speech to Anxiety," *Journal of Personality and Social Psychology* 1 (1965), 425, 430; Benjamin Pope and Aron Wolfe Siegman, "Interviewer

Warmth and Verbal Communication in the Initial Interview," in *Proceedings of the 75th Annual Convention of the American Psychological Association* 2 (1967), 245–246.

[45]David Suggs and Bruce Dennis Sales, "Using Communication Cues to Evaluate Prospective Jurors During the Voir Dire," *Arizona Law Review* 20 (1978), 633.

[46]Frieda Goldman-Eisler, "Speech-Breathing Activity—A Measure of Tension and Affect During Interviews," *British Journal of Psychology* 46 (1955), 53, 60–62.

[47]Agnes Hankiss, "Games Con Men Play: The Semiosis of Deceptive Interaction," *Journal of Communication* 30 (1980), 108.

[48]Merle E. Day, "An Eye-Movement Indicator of Type and Level of Anxiety: Some Clinical Observations," *Journal of Clinical Psychology* 23 (1967) 438–439.

[49]Paul Ekman and Wallace V. Friesen, "Nonverbal Leakage and Clues to Deception," in Shirley Weitz, ed., *Nonverbal Communication* (New York: Oxford University Press, 1974), 269, 279; Albert Mehrabian, "Nonverbal Betrayal of Feeling," *Journal of Experimental Research in Personality* 5 (1971), 64–73. B. Anderson Mitcham, "Psychotherapy Techniques in Voir Dire Selection," *Trial* (September 1980), 52. Further, we know that increased eye contact indicates a positive feeling toward another individual. See Michael Argyle and Janet Dean, "Eye Contact, Distance and Affiliation," *Sociometry* 28 (1965), 289.

[50]Albert Mehrabian, "Orientation Behaviors and Nonverbal Attitude Communication," *Journal of Communication* 17 (1967), 324, 330–331; Albert Mehrabian and John T. Friar, "Encoding of Attitude by a Seated Communicator via Posture and Position Cues," *Journal of Consulting and Clinical Psychology* 33 (1969), 330, 335–336.

[51]Albert E. Scheflen, "The Significance of Posture in Communication Systems" *Psychiatry* 27 (1964), 316, 319–321.

[52]Norbert Freedman and Stanley P. Hoffman, "Kinetic Behavior in Altered Clinical States: Approach to Objective Analysis of Motor Behavior During Clinical Interviews," *Perceptual and Motor Skills* 24 (1967), 532–533, 537–538;

Paul Ekman and Wallace V. Friesen, "Hand Movements," *Journal of Communication* 22 (1972), 353, 359–363.

[53]Suggs and Sales, "Using Communication Cues," 638. If lying is suspected, it should be noted that "people lie better from the neck up than they do from the neck down." K. Phillip Taylor, Raymond W. Buchanan, and David U. Strawn, *Communication Strategies for Trial Attorneys* (Glenview, Ill.: Scott, Foresman, 1984), 59.

[54]Judee K. Burgoon, "Nonverbal Cues in Jury Selection," Paper presented at the Western Speech Association Convention (Tucson, Ariz., February 1986).

[55]Jeffrey T. Frederick, op. cit., 584.

[56]Suggs and Sales, "Using Communication Cues," 638–639.

[57]Lawrence J. Smith and Loretta A. Malandro, *Courtroom Communication Strategies* (New York: Kluwer, 1985), 554–555.

[58]Henry B. Rothblatt, "Techniques for Jury Selection," *Criminal Law Bulletin* 2 (1966), 14–29.

[59]David Suggs and Bruce Dennis Sales, "The Art and Science of Conducting the Voir Dire," *Professional Psychology* 9 (1978), 378.

[60]"In voir dire I don't pay attention to what a juror or jury tells me in answer to a question. It is the way he tells me. . . . The way anybody answers [a] question will tell you more than whatever they say. . . . The shape of the mouth, the slight delay in the answer . . . tells you a whole lot more." Percy Foreman, "Keynote Address," in Ronald J. Matlon and Richard J. Crawford, eds., *Communication Strategies in the Practice of Lawyering* (Annandale, Va.: Speech Communication Association, 1983), 9.

[61]Michael J. Saks and Reid Hastie, *Social Psychology in Court* (New York: Van Nostrand Reinhold, 1978), 61.

[62]John C. Reinard, "Nonverbal Communication Research in Legal Settings: Consideration of Limits and Effects," Paper presented at the Western Speech Communication Association Convention (Tucson, Ariz., February 1986), 3.

[63]Clarence Darrow, "Attorney for the Defense," *Esquire* (May 1936), 36; "Clarence Darrow: Ace Jury Picker," *Literary Digest* (May 16, 1936), 35.

[64]Thomas E. Salisbury, "Forensic Sociology and Psychology: New Tools for the Criminal Defense Attorney," *Tulsa Law Journal* 12 (1976), 278–279; Linda Muncher Welsh, "Factors Which Influence the Decision-Making of Jurors," Ed.D. diss. (Philadelphia: Temple University, 1978).

[65]Lawrence J. Leigh, "A Theory of Jury Trial Advocacy," *Utah Law Review* 1984 (1984), 783.

[66]Dale W. Broeder, "Occupational Expertise and Bias as Affecting Juror Behavior: A Preliminary Look," *New York University Law Review* 20 (1965), 1079, 1099.

[67]Freda Adler, "Socio-economic Factors Influencing Jury Verdicts," *New York University Review of Law and Social Change* 3 (1973), 1, 6–10.

[68]Michael G. Efran, "The Effect of Physical Appearance on the Judgment of Guilt, Interpersonal Attraction, and Severity of Recommended Punishment in a Simulated Jury Task," *Journal of Research in Personality* 8 (1974), 45–54; William Griffitt and Thomas Jackson, "Simulated Jury Decisions: The Influence of Jury-Defendant Attitude Similarity-Dissimilarity," *Social Behavior and Personality* 1 (1973), 1–7; Richard R. Izzett and Walter Leginski, "Group Discussion and the Influence of Defendant Characteristics in a Simulated Jury Setting," *Journal of Social Psychology* 93 (1974), 271–279.

[69]Saks and Hastie, op. cit., 63.

[70]William M. Marston, "Studies in Testimony," *Journal of the American Institute of Criminal Law and Criminology* 15 (1924), 5–31; Hugo Munsterberg, *On the Witness Stand: Essays on Psychology and Crime* (New York: Doubleday, 1915); H. P. Weld and E. R. Danzig, "A Study of the Way in Which Verdict Is Reached by a Jury," *American Journal of Psychology* 53 (1940), 536.

[71]Fred L. Strodtbeck and Richard D. Mann, "Sex Role Differentiation in Jury Deliberations," *Sociometry* 19 (1956), 3–11.

[72]Fred L. Strodtbeck, Rita M. James, and Charles Hawkins, "Social Status in Jury Deliberations," *American Sociological Review* 22 (1957), 713–719.

[73]Strodtbeck and Mann, op. cit.

[74]Rita J. Simon, *The Jury: Its Role in American Society* (Lexington, Mass.: Lexington Books, 1980), 42.

[75]Patricia Hayes Andrews, "Performance, Self-Esteem and Perceptions of Leadership Emergence: A Comparative Study of Men and Women," *Western Journal of Speech Communication* 48 (1984), 1–2.

[76]Eloise C. Snyder, "Sex Role Differential and Juror Decisions," *Sociology and Social Research* 55 (1971), 442–448.

[77]Simon, *The Jury: Its Role,* 43.

[78]Rita James Simon, interview by Wallace M. Rudolph, "Women on Juries: Voluntary or Compulsory?" *Journal of American Judicature Society* 44 (1961), 209.

[79]Snyder, op. cit.

[80]Martin Blinder, in Ann Fagan Ginger, *Jury Selection in Civil and Criminal Trials* (Tiburon, Calif.: Lawpress, 1984), 855.

[81]Anne Rankin Mahoney, "American Jury Voir Dire and the Ideal of Equal Justice," *Journal of Applied Behavioral Science* 18 (1982), 485.

[82]Stuart S. Nagel and Lenore J. Weitzman, "Women as Litigants," *Hastings Law Journal* 23 (1971), 171–198; Cookie Stephan and Judy C. Tully, "The Influence of Physical Attractiveness of a Plaintiff on the Decisions of Simulated Jurors," *Journal of Social Psychology* 101 (1977), 149–160.

[83]Nagel and Weitzman, op. cit.

[84]Gary Moran and John Craig Comfort, "Scientific Juror Selection: Sex as a Moderator of Demographic and Personality Predictors of Impaneled Felony Jury Behavior," *Journal of Personality and Social Psychology* 41 (1982), 1052–1063.

[85]Edmond Constantini, Michael Mallery, and Diane M. Yapundich, "Gender and Juror Partiality: Are Women More Likely to Prejudge Guilt?" *Judicature* 67 (1983), 120–133.

[86]Bray and Noble, op. cit.; Susan V. Eisen and Leslie Z. McArthur, "Evaluating and Sentencing a Defendant as a Function of His Salience and the Perceiver's Set," *Personality and Social Psychology Bulletin* 5 (1979), 48–52; David B. Gray and Richard D. Ashmore, "Biasing Influence of Defendants' Characteristics on Simulated Sentencing," *Psychological Reports* 38 (1976), 727–738; Charlan Nemeth, Jeffrey Endicott, and Joel Wachtler, "From the '50's to the '70's:

Women in Jury Deliberations," *Sociometry* 39 (1976), 293–304; Steven D. Penrod, "Study of Attorney and 'Scientific' Jury Selection Models," Ph.D. diss. (Cambridge: Harvard University, 1979); A. P. Sealy and W. R. Cornish, "Jurors and Their Verdicts," *Modern Law Review* 36 (1973), 496–508; Rita James Simon, *The Jury and the Defense of Insanity* (Boston: Little, Brown, 1967); Jon M. Van Dyke, *Jury Selection Procedures,* (Cambridge, Mass.: Ballinger, 1977), 42; Glen D. White, "Sex Bias in Experimental Juries," Ph.D. diss. (College Park: University of Maryland, 1960).

[87]Goldman, Freundlich, and Casey, op. cit.

[88]Lawrence G. Calhoun, James W. Selby, and Louise J. Warring, "Social Perception of the Victim's Causal Role in Rape: An Exploratory Examination of Four Factors," *Human Relations* 29 (1976), 517–526; James H. Davis et al., "Victim Consequences, Sentence Severity, and the Decision Processes in Mock Juries," *Organizational Behavior and Human Performance* 18 (1977), 346–365; E. Hawrish and E. Tate, "Determinants of Jury Selection," *Saskatchewan Law Review* 39 (1975), 285–292; Marina Miller and Jay Hewitt, "Conviction of a Defendant as a Function of Juror-Victim Racial Similarity," *Journal of Social Psychology* 105 (1978), 159–160; Carol J. Mills and Wayne E. Bohannon, "Juror Characteristics: To What Extent Are They Related to Jury Verdicts?" *Judicature* 64 (1980), 22–31; Michael G. Rumsey and Judith M. Rumsey, "A Case of Rape: Sentencing Judgments of Males and Females," *Psychological Reports* 41 (1977), 459–465; Ronald E. Smith et al., "Role and Justice Considerations in the Attribution of Responsibility to a Rape Victim," *Journal of Research in Personality* 10 (1976), 346–357.

[89]John R. Snortum and Victor H. Ashear, "Prejudice, Punitiveness and Personality," *Journal of Personality Assessment* 36 (1972), 291–296.

[90]Michael Argyle, "The Communication of Inferior and Superior Attitudes by Verbal and Nonverbal Signals," *British Journal of Sociology and Clinical Psychology* 9 (1970), 231; Robert Rosenthal, "Body Talk and Tone of Voice: The Language Without Words," *Psychology Today* (September 1974), 64–66.

[91]Alan E. Morrill, *Trial Diplomacy* (Chicago: Court Practice Institute, 1979), 18.

[92]Ann Fagan Ginger, *Jury Selection in Civil and Criminal Trials* (Tiburon, Calif.: Lawpress, 1984), 228.

[93]Donald H. Ziegler, "Young Adults as a Cognizable Group in Jury Selection," *Michigan Law Review* 76 (1978), 1045–1110.

[94]Mills and Bohannon, op. cit.

[95]W. R. Cornish, *The Jury* (London: Allen Lane Penguin Press, 1968); Mills and Bohannon, op. cit., 27; Sealy and Cornish, op. cit.

[96]Walter E. Jordan, *Jury Selection* (Colorado Springs: Shepard's/McGraw-Hill, 1980), 302.

[97]Reid Hastie, Steven D. Penrod, and Nancy Pennington, *Inside the Jury* (Cambridge: Harvard University Press, 1983), 142.

[98]Robert A. Wenke, *The Art of Selecting a Jury* (Los Angeles: Parker and Son, 1979), 84.

[99]Stephan and Tully, op. cit.

[100]Thomas Sannito and Edward Burke Arnolds, "Jury Study Results: The Factors at Work," *Trial Diplomacy Journal* (Spring 1982), 9–10.

[101]Taylor, Buchanan, and Strawn, op. cit., 59; Denis Chimaeze E. Ugwuegbu, "Racial and Evidential Factors in Jury Attribution of Legal Responsibility," *Journal of Experimental Social Psychology* 15 (1979), 133–146.

[102]J. L. Bernard, "Interaction Between the Race of the Defendant and That of Jurors in Determining Verdicts," *Law and Psychology Review* 5 (1979), 104–111.

[103]Dale W. Broeder, "The Negro in Court," *Duke Law Journal* (Winter 1965), 29; Dale W. Broeder, "The University of Chicago Jury Project," *Nebraska Law Review* 38 (1959), 744–760; Simon, *The Jury and the Defense of Insanity,* op. cit.

[104]Bernard, op. cit.

[105]Simon, *The Jury and Insanity,* op. cit.

[106]Broeder, "The Negro in Court," op. cit.; Ibid.

[107]Ethnic dissimilarity is also a two-edged sword. One study shows that persons are more tolerant of racially dissimilar individuals who hold dissimilar attitudes than of racially similar persons holding dissimilar attitudes. It is possible to feel charitable, excusing people exactly because they are ethnically unlike ourselves. Donn Byrne and Terry J. Wong, "Racial Prejudice, Interpersonal Attraction, and Assumed Dissimilarity of

Attitudes," *Journal of Abnormal and Social Psychology* 65 (1962), 246–253.

[108]Phillip Taylor and John W. Wright, "Review of Research on Jury Selection and Jury Behavior," in Ronald J. Matlon and Richard J. Crawford, eds., *Communication Strategies in the Practice of Lawyering* (Annandale, Va.: Speech Communication Association, 1983), 209.

[109]Ruth McGaffey, "Communication Strategies and Research Needs in Selecting Juries," in Ronald J. Matlon and Richard J. Crawford, eds., *Communication Strategies in the Practice of Lawyering* (Annandale, Va.: Speech Communication Association, 1983), 261.

[110]Ginger, op. cit., 228.

[111]Wenke, op. cit., 82.

[112]Reid Hastie, Steven D. Penrod, and Nancy Pennington, "What Goes On in a Jury Deliberation," *American Bar Association Journal* 69 (1983), 1849; Mills and Bohannon, op. cit.

[113]Rita M. James, "Status and Competence of Jurors," *American Journal of Sociology* 69 (1959), 563–570.

[114]Hastie, Penrod, and Pennington, *Inside the Jury,* 145.

[115]Mills and Bohannon, op. cit.

[116]Reed, op. cit.

[117]Gray and Ashmore, op. cit.

[118]Simon, *The Jury and Insanity,* 107–108.

[119]Sannito and Arnolds, op. cit., 9.

[120]Sannito and McGovern, op. cit., 84.

[121]Reed, op. cit.

[122]Edward Green, "The Reasonable Man: Legal Fiction or Psychosocial Reality?" *Law and Society Review* 2 (1967), 241–257.

[123]Thomas L. Grisham and Stephen F. Lawless, "Jurors Judge Justice," *New Mexico Law Review* 3 (1973), 352.

[124]*Personal Injury Valuation Handbooks,* vol. 8 (Solon, Ohio: Jury Verdict Research, 1969). See summary in P. J. Hermann, "Occupations of Jurors as an Influence on Their Verdict," *The Forum* 5 (1970), 150–155.

[125]Ibid.

[126]Smith and Malandro, op. cit., 572.

[127]James C. Adkins, "Jury Selection: An Art? A Science? Or Luck?" *Trial* (December 1968– January 1969), 37–39; Louis S. Katz, "The Twelve Man Jury," *Trial* (December 1968–January 1969), 39–42.

[128]*Personal Injury Valuation Handbooks,* vol. 8.

[129]Dale W. Broeder, "Occupational Expertise and Bias as Affecting Juror Behavior," op. cit., 1090.

[130]Hastie, Penrod, and Pennington, *Inside the Jury,* 138.

[131]Simon, *The Jury and Insanity,* 117.

[132]Strodtbeck, James, and Hawkins, op. cit.

[133]Adler, op. cit., 10.

[134]F. Lee Bailey and Henry B. Rothblatt, *Successful Techniques for Criminal Trials* (New York: Lawyers Cooperative, 1971).

[135]Dale W. Broeder, "Previous Jury Trial Service Affecting Juror Behavior," *Insurance Law Journal* (March 1965), 138–143.

[136]Norbert L. Kerr, Douglas L. Harmon, and James L. Graves, "Independence of Multiple Verdicts by Jurors and Juries," *Journal of Applied Social Psychology* 12 (1982), 12–29.

[137]Saul M. Kassin and Ralph Juhnke, "Juror Experience and Decision Making," *Journal of Personality and Social Psychology* 44 (1983), 1182–1191.

[138]Norbert L. Kerr, "Effects of Prior Juror Experience on Juror Behavior," *Basic and Applied Social Psychology* 2 (1981), 175–193.

[139]Kassin and Juhnke, op. cit.; Ibid.; Dennis H. Nagao and James H. Davis, "The Effects of Prior Experience on Mock Juror Case Judgments," *Social Psychology Quarterly* 43 (1980), 190–199; Sealy and Cornish, op. cit.

[140]Over four hundred juries in East Baton Rouge Parish were surveyed. Reed, op. cit.

[141]Carol M. Werner et al., "The Impact of Case Characteristics and Prior Jury Experience on Jury Verdicts," *Journal of Applied Social Psychology* 15 (1985), 409–427.

[142]The study was of 175 criminal trials in Fayette County. When up to half of a jury's members had experience, guilty verdicts were rendered about 47 percent of the time. When more than half of the jurors had been in a jury box before, the conviction rate rose to 63 percent. If all twelve jurors had done their duty before, the guilty

verdicts jumped to 81 percent. Ronald C. Dillehay and Michael T. Nietzel, "Juror Experience and Jury Verdicts," *Law and Human Behavior* 9 (1985), 179–191.

[143]Hastie, Penrod, and Pennington, *Inside the Jury,* 144.

[144]Broeder, "Previous Jury Trial Service," op. cit.

[145]Richard M. Durand, William O. Bearden, and A. William Gustafson, "Previous Jury Service as a Moderating Influence on Jurors' Beliefs and Attitudes," *Psychological Reports* 42 (1978), 567–572; William R. Pabst, Jr., G. Thomas Munsterman, and Chester H. Mount, "The Myth of the Unwilling Juror," *Judicature* 60 (1976), 164–171.

[146]Kerr, op. cit., 182.

[147]For a detailed discussion of how demographic analysis can be useful in jury selection, see Starr and McCormick, op. cit., chap. 7.

[148]Steven Penrod, "'Scientific' Juror Selection Debunked," *American Bar Association Journal* 66 (1980), 1197; Michael J. Saks, *Jury Verdicts: The Role of Group Size and Social Decision Rule* (Lexington, Mass.: D. C. Heath, 1977), 65–66, 128–129.

[149]Richard J. Crawford, "Defense Voir Dire: Communication Strategy," *Criminal Defense* (May–June 1979), 6.

[150]Sannito and Arnolds, op. cit., 10.

[151]Ibid.

[152]Leonard Berkowitz and Richard M. Lundy, "Personality Characteristics Related to Susceptibility to Influence by Peers or Authority Figures," *Journal of Personality* 25 (1957), 306–316; Kay H. Smith and Barrie Richards, "Effects of a Rational Appeal and of Anxiety on Conformity Behavior," *Journal of Personality and Social Psychology* 5 (1967), 122–126.

[153]Starr, op. cit., 10.

[154]Saks and Hastie, op. cit., 55.

[155]The jury selection for the Harrisburg trial is reported in detail in Jay Schulman et al., "Recipe for a Jury," *Psychology Today* (May 1973), 37–44, 77–84.

[156]Morton Hunt, "Putting Juries on the Couch," *New York Times Magazine* (November 28, 1982), 78.

[157]Deborah Shapley, "Jury Selection: Social Scientists Gamble in an Already Loaded Game," *Science* 185 (1974), 1033.

[158]Wayne Sage, "Psychology and the Angela Davis Jury," *Human Behavior* (January 1973), 56–61.

[159]Bonora and Krauss, op. cit., 1.

[160]Judith Dancoff, "Hidden Persuaders of the Courtroom," *Barrister* (Winter 1982), 16.

[161]Richard Christie, "Probability v. Precedence: The Social Psychology of Jury Selection," in Gordon Bermant, Charlan Nemeth, and Neil Vidmar, eds., *Psychology and the Law* (Lexington, Mass.: Lexington Books, 1976), 265.

[162]Katherine W. Ellison and Robert Buckhout, *Psychology and Criminal Justice* (New York: Harper & Row, 1981), 190.

[163]Ibid., 184.

[164]John A. Cannito and K. L. Becker, "The Case for Limited Use of Polls in the Jury Selection Process," *Rutgers Journal of Computers and the Law* 7 (1979), 124.

[165]Jay Schulman, "A Systematic Approach to Successful Jury Selection," *Guild Notes* (November 1973), 14–19.

[166]Ann Ginger, *Jury Selection in Criminal Trials* (Tiburon, Calif.: Lawpress, 1980), 11.9–11.30.

[167]For an in-depth discussion of community attitude assessments, see Starr and McCormick, op. cit., chap. 5.

[168]Ginger, op. cit., 209.

[169]Donald E. Vinson and Philip K. Anthony, *Social Science Research Methods for Litigation* (Charlottesville, Va.: Michie, 1985), 12–13.

[170]"In *Dow v. Carnegie-Illinois Steel Corp.,* 224 F.2d 414 (3d Cir. 1955), the court approved an investigator's questioning of neighbors and friends of a potential juror. . . . If friends, neighbors, or co-workers are contacted, it is likely that the prospective juror will hear of it. This will not be a problem when individual voir dire is conducted. . . . At that time, the juror can be told about the investigation. . . . Sometimes however, the resentment and anger is so deep that the juror must be removed by either a challenge for cause or a peremptory challenge. This option may be a high price to pay for the pretrial investigation." Starr and McCormick, op. cit., 90–93.

[171]Shell, op. cit., 48.

[172]Ibid.

[173]John Berman and Bruce Dennis Sales, "A Critical Evaluation of the Systematic Approach to Jury Selection," *Criminal Justice and Behavior* 4 (1977), 221.

[174]"When a survey is being done to present in court it is always necessary to have at least one person involved in the work who can be qualified as an expert to testify to the validity of the procedures followed and the data collected." Bonora and Krauss, op. cit., 119.

[175]John B. McConahay, Courtney J. Mullin, and Jeffrey Frederick, "The Use of Social Science in Trials with Political and Racial Overtones: The Trial of Joan Little," *Law and Contemporary Problems* 41 (1977), 205–229.

[176]Ellen Hopkins, "Jury Roulette: How Lawyers Play Hunches in Picking Jurors," *New York* (December 12, 1983), 69.

[177]Hans Zeisel and Shari S. Diamond, "The Jury Selection in the Mitchell-Stans Conspiracy Trial," *American Bar Foundation Research Journal* (1976), 151.

[178]Neal Bush, "Scientific Jury Selection," in Grace W. Holmes, ed., *New Frontiers in Litigation* (Ann Arbor, Mich.: Institute of Continuing Legal Education, 1979), 5.

[179]Suggs and Sales, "Conducting the Voir Dire," 376.

[180]Michael J. Saks, "Social Scientists Can't Rig Juries," *Psychology Today* (January 1976), 49–50.

[181]Richard A. Berk, Michael Hennessy, and James Swan, "The Vagaries and Vulgarities of 'Scientific' Jury Selection," *Evaluation Quarterly* 1 (1977), 146.

[182]Ginger, op. cit., 225.

[183]Patterson, op. cit., 108.

[184]Berman and Sales, op. cit., 223.

[185]Margaret Covington, "Use of Expert Assistance in Jury Selection," *Case and Comment* (July–August 1985), 23.

[186]McConahay, Mullin, and Frederick, op. cit.

[187]Jeffrey T. Frederick, "Social Science Involvement in Voir Dire: Preliminary Data on the Effectiveness of 'Scientific Jury Selection,'" *Behavioral Sciences and the Law* 2 (1984), 391.

[188]For an in-depth discussion of trial simulations, see Starr and McCormick, op. cit., chap. 6.

[189]Saul M. Kassin, "Mock Jury Trials," *Trial Diplomacy Journal* (Summer 1984), 28.

[190]Curt Schleier, "Lawyers Court Help in Jury Selection," *Advertising Age* (November 14, 1985), 30–32.

[191]Daniel J. Ryan and Peter J. Neeson, "Voir Dire: A Trial Technique in Transition," *American Journal of Trial Advocacy* 4 (1980–81).

[192]Hunt, op. cit., 70–71.

[193]Donald E. Vinson, "The Shadow Jury," *American Bar Association Journal* 68 (1982), 1243.

[194]Edwin Chen, "Firms Seek Insights Into Jury Panels," *Los Angeles Times* (November 2, 1981).

[195]Vinson, op. cit., 1246.

[196]John R. Hepburn, "The Objective Reality of Evidence and the Utility of Systematic Jury Selection," *Law and Human Behavior* 4 (1980), 90.

[197]Ralph W. Gallagher, "The Use of a Consultant in Voir Dire," *Trial Diplomacy Journal* (Winter 1984–1985), 24–28.

[198]Martin Blinder, "Picking Juries," *Trial Diplomacy Journal* (Spring 1978), 8.

[199]ASTC, Department of Speech and Mass Communication, Towson State University, Towson, Md. 21204.

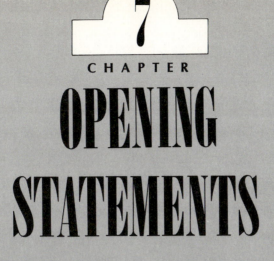

CHAPTER

OPENING STATEMENTS

The trial, from beginning to end, is a persuasive campaign. No single stage alone yields a favorable or unfavorable decision from a judge or jury; it is a collection of communication events, from voir dire through closing arguments, which forms images that ultimately persuade decision makers.

One way of thinking about the trial as a persuasive campaign is to consider it akin to a play with a very strong message from the author. The author attempts to get the audience voluntarily to change their beliefs, attitudes, or behavior in response to the play's plot line. The same is true in court, where the lawyers become the playwrights. Voir dire is the time for the audience to buy their tickets and learn something about the production. The opening statement is similar to the first scene in the play; it is designed to capture the audience's attention. The first scene in many of Shakespeare's plays is a prologue—an introductory speech that was designed specifically to capture the audience's imagination and beliefs. So it goes with the opening statement in court. After the jurors have been impaneled, attorneys for both sides are invited to present opening statements, or prologues, to their cases per se. Since the opening statement immediately follows voir dire in the persuasive campaign, it can actually be viewed as an extension of jury selection.[1] The prosecution or the plaintiff speaks first; the defense speaks next. The side that has the burden of proof generally gives the first opening statement.[2]

The opening statement is considered by some lawyers to be the most crucial part of a trial. One of them writes, "There was a time when I believed the most important part of the trial was cross-examination. . . . Later I thought summation the most important. In my present evaluation, however, opening statement is at least as important as summation."[3] The pioneer piece of research on the importance of the opening statement was done by H. P. Weld and E. R. Danzig, who questioned mock jurors and found that some of them formed strong opinions after opening statements and interpreted all of the subsequent evidence in light of those initial impressions.[4] Continued support for the belief that openings are important came as a result of the University of Chicago Jury Project, which found that only 20 percent of the jurors surveyed changed their minds about a liability decision after they heard opening statements. The remaining 80 percent of the jurors formed judgments immediately after opening statements and stayed with those judgments as they entered deliberations later. Hence, the initial impression for most was the lasting impression.[5] A later study at the University of Chicago yielded similar results, although the figures changed to 35 percent and 65 percent, respectively.[6] Of course, these data do not mean that opening statements *alone* account for 65 to 80 percent of the decisions. It is possible that what actually happens in court after opening statements is more important in terms of decision making and that it is this later communication that reinforces an impression created during the opening remarks. It is also possible that jurors who do not change their minds after opening statements are "more influenced by their life experiences and beliefs than by evidence and argument."[7] As noted in Chapter 6, these are usually lesser-educated jurors. In any case, the University of Chicago findings cannot allow us to claim the opening statement is the most important part of any trial; the research only points to the conclusion that openings are an important weapon in the arsenal of the trial attorney.

Recently, at the University of Kansas, an investigation was conducted on the effect that in-depth versus abbreviated opening statements have on jurors' verdicts. Some openings contained very brief and vague preview conditions; other openings were more detailed, interesting, and extensive. The mock criminal trial study found that jurors are heavily influenced by the first in-depth or extensive opening they hear. If the prosecution's opening is impressive, the defendant is found guilty, regardless of the extensiveness of the defense's opening statement. If the prosecution's opening is scanty and the defense makes impressive and extensive remarks, the verdict in the same case is not guilty. It appears that if one side offers an opening statement that is comparatively stronger than the other side's statement, jurors may be biased toward that side, even though the evidence in the trial is balanced.[8]

No one can quantify with much more precision how important opening statements are in litigation. We at least know they are of such importance that every attorney should attempt to prepare and present an opening statement that virtually cripples the opposition. Just as in a football game, an attorney should try to get the game out of reach through the opening statement and have the other side play catch-up for the rest of the trial. As one witty writer succinctly put it, "the opening statement is not the time for foreplay; it is the time to score!"[9]

In spite of an abundance of legal literature about the importance of the opening statement, many lawyers seem to give it short shrift. "Sadly, most opening statements are thrown together almost as an afterthought, even by lawyers who pride themselves as being good litigators."[10] Openings in court are often dull, listless, and disjointed. This chapter is written in the hope that opening statements in the courtroom will be taken more seriously by counsel in the future.

GOALS OF THE OPENING STATEMENT

Two goals should be kept in mind by counsel as they present the opening statement. The first goal is to introduce the case theme to the court and jury.[11] After opening statements, a case unfolds in bits and pieces and not necessarily in any organized manner. The open-

ing statement is thus an opportunity for counsel to put an entire story in a compact package so that the jury will be able to get a bird's-eye view and better comprehend and appreciate the issues and the evidence. The opening statement is analogous to a preview, roadmap, or synopsis of what is to follow. Its place in the trial follows the old bromide for public speakers: "Tell them what you're going to tell them (opening statement), tell them (evidence), and tell them what you told them (closing argument)."

In order to facilitate the processing of information, the opening statement must provide one or more themes that jurors can use to later integrate the witnesses' testimony. Every lawsuit has a theme, and the establishment of this theme must be sounded in the opening statement. A thematic framework has been described as "a subset of existing knowledge, based on prior experience and relevant to a limited domain, that people use as a framework to guide their observation, organization, and retrieval from memory of perceived events."[12] These frameworks help jurors make sense out of the rather disjointed array of information that comes forward in a trial. One book on trial advocacy offers the following illustration of an attorney's theme development:

Plaintiff is injured when struck by a blade which disengages from a rotary lawn mower operated by A and owned by B. A is a college student who earns money during the summer cutting grass. He has operated many lawn mowers, is an engineering student, and is familiar with their mechanics. He has worked for B on other occasions, was familiar with B's lawn mower. On a previous occasion he had noticed that the blade was wobbly and had notified B. B had owned the lawn mower for four years and had never had it repaired or overhauled. B acknowledges that A had told him that the blade was wobbly.

Assume your suit is against A alone. Your opening statement will attempt to exonerate B from any wrongdoing and lay the blame at A's feet. The theme to be developed will be as follows:

A is trained and experienced with lawn mowers. He discovered that the mower was faulty but continued to use it knowing and appreciating the risks that were involved. B, on the other hand, had reason to believe the lawn mower was in working order. It had functioned properly for four years without the need of repair. He was told by A that the blade was wobbly, but he didn't think that this was a dangerous situation. He knew that A was an engineering student, well versed in the handling of lawn mowers, and relied on him to make any necessary repairs or at least tell B that the mower was dangerous and needed repair.

If the suit was against B alone the theme would be substantially different and proceed as follows:

B had owned this lawn mower for four years and during the entire 48 months had not attended to its servicing or repair. He had been told specifically that the blade was wobbly but rather than have the blade replaced at minimal cost he elected to expose A and others to the dangers of a malfunctioning power lawn mower. A, a hard-working and conscientious college student, having told B of the defect assumed that the simple repair had been made.[13]

The facts are the same; only the slant is changed. Once the appropriate theme is determined, counsel plants it in the minds of the jury in the opening statement, emphasizes it through the questioning of witnesses, and pulls it through again in summation.

Theme development must be accompanied by a clear statement of goals for the major parties in litigation. In the illustration above, the college student's goal was to earn money, whereas the lawn mower owner's goal was to get his grass cut. Experiments show that we best understand and recall characters in stories and their desires when we identify with character goals.[14] Further experimental work illustrates that as people enhance their understanding of a character's goals, motives, and plans, that character's ac-

tions are better recalled.[15] In that experiment, subjects were given a story about a farmer who tried to put his donkey into its shed. Some of the subjects read a paragraph with this goal explicitly stated. Others read a themeless paragraph that did not mention the ultimate goal. Both paragraphs had 34 other action propositions contained therein. When the ultimate goal was omitted, subjects found the text only half as comprehensible, and they remembered 20 percent fewer action propositions than the first group. Stories with stated themes accompanied by stated character goals help audiences effectively integrate information.

Leonard Decof identified four representative themes in his comprehensive treatise on opening statements.[16] The *underdog theme* might be developed by a plaintiff suing a giant corporation. The underdog is a little person trying to fight city hall, a person with whom many jurors can empathize. Remember how Rocky, who was an underdog, got the movie audience to cheer! The *undefeated theme* focuses on the indomitable fighter who never quits, regardless of the odds. Ernest Hemingway's bullfighter, Manolete, and his old man in *The Old Man and the Sea* are classic examples of the undefeated person. The disfigured and paralyzed plaintiff who continues to function and fight may appear truly heroic to a jury. The *victim theme* deals with people who are put upon by everyone. Charlie Chaplin's characters were victims of society and progress. In *Modern Times,* he was actually sucked into the gears of a machine and spit out the other end. The plaintiff in a consumer fraud case can be portrayed as a victim of advertising, causing the jury to become outraged toward the defendant. The *contrast theme* creates startling images for the jury, such as small-big, weak-strong, human-impersonal, simple-complex, moral-immoral, or careful-careless. In a child dart-out case, think of what can be done by contrasting the 38-pound little girl with the 2-ton van that hit the girl.

Themes are powerful concepts; they require no exaggeration on the part of the attorney because they are so deeply rooted in our belief-attitude-value structure. Lawyers need to search for themes as they think about accomplishing this first objective for opening statements.

The second goal is to establish rapport with the court and jury. Voir dire offered the first opportunity to reach this goal. The second opportunity to command juror interest, to get the jury to like the attorney,[17] and also to get the jury to identify with a lawyer's cause is found in the opening statement. Generally, the attorney should come across as sincere, honest, understanding, intelligent, dependable, considerate, warm, kind, friendly, and cheerful. He or she should not be ill-mannered, unfriendly, hostile, loud-mouthed, conceited, insincere, unkind, untrustworthy, malicious, or obnoxious.[18] This advice may seem obvious, but alas, "the number of lawyers who alienate their juries by rank discourtesy is unpleasantly large."[19]

TIMING OF THE OPENING STATEMENT

What about not giving an opening statement at all? Complete waivers of the opening statement by both sides or by just one side are rare in the American judicial system. If they occur, they are much more common in bench trials, in which the judge may already have read the pleadings and the briefs. Partial waivers, or delays in presenting the opening statement, are possible, however. These occur when the defense attorney waits to present an opening statement until the plaintiff or prosecution has called all of its witnesses.

There are no advantages to waiving an opening altogether. There are some advantages, however, in having the defense attorney postpone the time for the delivery of the opening statement. One advantage is that it buys time, which in turn allows flexibility in theme development. The defense counsel may have more than one possible theme and be unable to determine which one is best until the other side has called all its witnesses and presented its case in chief.[20] To illustrate, in a murder case, a defense attorney who wants to focus on either lack of identification or self-defense may really want to hear the prosecutor's evidence on identification before deciding which approach to emphasize. Another advantage of the delayed opening is that it conceals strategies from opposing counsel until later in the trial. (The first advantage seems more valid than the second, however, since the development of pretrial conferences and discovery makes the surprise element in the opening statement highly unlikely.) A third advantage is one of continuity. The thrust and force of the defendant's case "will be enhanced if it is preceded by a forceful opening statement immediately before the adduction of [the defendant's] evidence."[21] Story continuity is tied to juror comprehension and recall of the defendant's evidence.[22] On the other hand, as a matter of strategy, the defense breaks up the prosecutor's or plaintiff's continuity by not delaying the presentation of the opening statement.[23]

Two interrelated disadvantages exist regarding postponement of the opening statement by the defense. The first is that the jury may infer that the defense case is weak when they hear no immediate opening statement. The second drawback is that the primacy advantage, which a prosecutor or plaintiff may have in speaking first, is not diminished. In other words, providing a thematic structure beforehand has stronger effects than providing it after counterinformation is presented.[24] More will be said about this primacy advantage later in the chapter. For now, this illustration explains the point:

A killing occurred a few years back in my county on a dance floor with roughly fifty people present. The single eyewitness of the shooting was named Lucy and the victim was her father-in-law (with whom she was living at the time and the two were a couple at the dance lounge that night). With some vigor and intensity, the defense gave an early opening statement focusing primarily on Lucy's character, especially the fact that she was living with her father-in-law. Although such habitation circumstances may not seem shocking to the reader, there are still people in rural Colorado who find them so. In any event, during the speech, the defense did a pretty good impeachment job on the state's single eyewitness. The drama of the trial, in one sense, came as the defense sat down from opening statement and the state called as their first witness, Lucy. As she walked through the courtroom to take her seat in the witness box, the jury gave her a long and cold small-town stare. She had been fatally contaminated by the defense. Of course, the defense could have waited and could have hurt her during cross-examination, but she would have testified for an hour under direct testimony as a pristine bereaved lady and the impact would have probably made a lasting impression on the jury. But because the defense made the proper choice of offering the opening statement early, the direct testimony of Lucy was viewed with suspicion at best. The jury, then, saw and heard a *different* state case than had the opening statement been held for later presentation. The defense had ground the glasses for the jury and had influenced what they saw.[25]

Although the preponderance of advice from practicing attorneys is that it is not a sound strategy to reserve an opening statement until the conclusion of the prosecutor's or plaintiff's case, some behavioral research in the area of one-sided presentations versus two-sided presentations may indicate otherwise. Trials, of course, are designed for two-sided communication insofar as jurors are charged to hear both sides of an issue. Delaying the opening statement allows jurors to hear initially only one side of the question. One researcher found that when people expect to hear another side of an issue, such as that presented by the defense, the initial presentation seems biased, and they will suspend judgment on one side's argument until both

sides have presented their cases.[26] Jurors will be fair to the defense and wait to hear that side's argument. In another experiment, it was found that one-sided arguments are much less effective when the jury knows there are two sides.[27] One side alone seems biased and unfair. Again, the jury will withhold judgment until that other side is presented. This research shows that the defense team will not be treated unfairly just because they have postponed the presentation of the opening statement. In sum, there is no definite answer to the question of when it is best for a defense attorney to give the opening statement.

CONTENT AND STRUCTURE OF THE OPENING STATEMENT

What we will consider here are the substance and the organizational pattern of the opening statement. As in any good speech, there is an introduction, a body, and a conclusion. The model opening statement in Appendix E contains all three elements in a well-developed fashion.

In an *introduction,* the purpose of the opening statement is explained,[28] the order of the trial is noted (if this has not already been done by the judge), and key persons are introduced. These key persons, who are asked to stand for all the jury to see, include the plaintiff in a civil case, the defendant, and critical witnesses. Of course, an attorney introduces only those parties he or she intends to call to the stand to build the case. Each introduction of one's own parties should be designed to humanize them so that the jury can relate to them as real persons. For instance, plaintiff's attorney might say: "Mary Jane Fox is an elementary school teacher. Before November 22, 1986, she was a very healthy young woman, twenty-eight years of age. She had been teaching at Pelham Elementary School for six years. Mary Jane is married and the mother of one three-year-old son, Jason. She enjoyed jogging, bicycling, and tennis. Never during the course of any of these activities did she have any trouble with her leg." If there are other people seated at counsel's table, they should be introduced too, in order to satisfy the curiosity of the jury. These standard introductory routines, combined with matters to spark the jury's attention, get the jury ready to hear the important part of the message, which comes next, in the body of the speech.

The *body* of the opening statement contains most of the information. This information should not be presented perfunctorily. If it is kept general, a jury might perceive a lawyer as uninterested, unprepared, and uncommitted to his or her position. Detail must be provided. Counsel should not just claim that his or her client was driving carefully, but should state the facts supporting that claim. Of course, an attorney can go overboard with detail and use a shotgun approach. This, too, should be avoided! Pertinent detail is essential; every single detail is poor strategy.

The body should begin with an explanation of the key issues. For instance, in a personal injury case, the opening sentence in the body of the speech should be a capsule description of the wrong complained of.[29] What did the defendant do that was wrong? What happened to the plaintiff? What are the nature and severity of the plaintiff's injuries? All of this is usually developed in the body of the speech, and it should be capsulized early in the opening statement. Here is an illustration from an automobile rear-end collision case: "Ladies and gentlemen, this lawsuit was filed because the defendant's car was following too closely behind the car of Mary Jane Fox, the plaintiff. The defendant, Mr. Hare, was not paying attention to the traffic ahead of him. As a result, Mary Jane was hit from behind by Mr. Hare. She suffered a broken and separated leg, and she will have this injury for the rest of her life." Notice how the wheat is distinguished from the chaff. Not everything that will develop in the case is here. The im-

portant has been separated from the unimportant, and in this brief remark we have the focal point of the trial from the plaintiff's vantage point. "Good trial lawyers follow the practice of narrowing the issues as much as possible. . . . All the experts agree that simplicity should be the goal of the lawyer in every case. Most jurors lose interest if the task before them appears to be a complicated one."[30]

After the case has been capsulized, the next step for a plaintiff or prosecutor is to present the story's detail. The overall structure of the story should be chronological, in contrast to a review of what each witness will say at trial. In the civil case regarding Mrs. Fox, the attorney should focus on scene, liability, injury, and—if permitted—damages. A chronological sequence of events unfolds. Audiences like stories that have beginnings, middles, and endings; the opening statement should not deviate from this simple pattern.

In many civil and criminal cases, scene is important. It must be meticulously described so that the jury can visualize where something took place and what happened. For instance, the scene of the occurrence in which Mr. Hare hit Mrs. Fox from behind was an urban traffic intersection. The details of that occurrence must be provided. They might include a description of the vehicles, the date and the time, a description of weather conditions, and a description of road conditions where the action took place.

As the story of what took place comes to an end, the question of why it took place should next be addressed. It is at this point that the attorney assigns liability to the defendant. This ought to be a motivational peak in the plaintiff's speech; counsel must show with some emotion why the defendant is to blame.

The discussion of injury should be a vivid account of the resulting harms. It is important, however, that the jury understand any medical jargon that must be used. The discussion of injury can begin by describing the anatomy of the injured area or organ, by describing the injury in both lay person's and medical terms, and by describing the treatment both in lay terms and in technical terminology: "Doctor Harris had to perform surgery on Mary Jane's leg, and you will hear him tell you about that surgery. The operation is called an open reduction of the tibia and fibula. Briefly, what Dr. Harris did was to cut open the lower part of her leg so he could see and handle the two lower leg bones which had been broken and separated in the accident. Then, with his hands, he actually moved the bones back together in their normal position. To hold these broken pieces together while the bones healed, he then drilled holes in the bones with an electric drill so that screws could be placed in Mary Jane's bones, locking them together." After this description, the prognosis, medication, and therapy for Mrs. Fox are described, and medical experts who will testify about her situation are introduced.

Many states do not allow counsel to mention the amount of compensation sought in a civil lawsuit. In other jurisdictions, recoverable damages or legal losses can be discussed in the opening statement. An attorney must be careful here not to exaggerate; more should not be claimed for the client than can be reasonably expected from the jury. Regardless of the dollar figure, counsel must explain how the evidence will demonstrate each loss category.[31] How much should be recovered for out-of-pocket expenses, loss of earnings, pain and suffering, mental anguish, inability to lead a normal life, and so on? The amount requested by the plaintiff's attorney is called the *prayer for relief*. Even where the prayer for relief can be discussed in an opening statement, an attorney should give it only cursory treatment, because a jury is not psychologically ready to probe into the matter of damages so early in a trial.

In the *conclusion* of the opening statement, the prosecutor or the plaintiff's counsel should recapitulate the highlights of the case,

the witnesses to be presented, the issues to be proven, and the theme or theory to be developed. These closing words should be upbeat and crisp. The conclusion should contain an explicit, not an implicit, appeal. The jury should not have to infer what the attorney wants; they should know specifically what they should feel, believe, and do (e.g., "I am confident that you will return a verdict for Mary Jane in the amount of $300,000"). Several studies support this conclusion about being explicit.[32] Although attorneys are prohibited from revealing their personal feelings about the case, this prohibition does not preclude them from directly stating to a jury the decision or decisions the group should reach. A good opening statement does not just set a few things in motion; it closes the psychological doors of the jury so that they are predisposed to render a decision for the side having made the most impressive presentation.

So far, we have looked only at opening statements for the plaintiff or the prosecutor. What about the other side? Opening statements for the defense essentially follow the same pattern, retelling the same story, but with different emphases or a different set of developing themes.[33] The jury should be told at the outset that there are at least two sides to every story and that they should not reach a decision in the case until they hear from the defense side. For instance, the attorney for Mr. Hare, wishing to make liability the key issue in conflict, might express regret that Mrs. Fox was injured, but indicate that the accident was her fault. The key issue then becomes liability.

During the defense lawyer's opening statement, a sense of identification should be established between the defendant and the jury. A common bond of sympathy should be found and exploited. For example, if the plaintiff says, in a negligence case, that it was the ice and snow on the sidewalk in front of the Ferris hardware store that caused the plaintiff to slip and fall, the defense attorney who recognizes that most of the jurors are property owners can show that the owner, Mr. Ferris, did everything a prudent person could have done to get the sidewalk as clean as possible. Audience adaptation is critical!

In addition, a defense lawyer should indicate which plaintiff or prosecution issues or facts are acceptable and point out that he or she does not have to assume the burden of proving innocence or freedom from liability. It is also best not to disclose damaging evidence that can catch the prosecutor or plaintiff by surprise. "This evidence will have greater impact on the jury if introduced into the case by witnesses. Commenting on such evidence in the opening statement will merely soften the blow."[34] Finally, in the conclusion of the speech, the defense lawyer should remind the jurors of their duty to keep an open mind.

Now that we have considered the content and organization of opening statements, let us look at some additional considerations all attorneys should make regarding substance. One consideration is whether or not to admit case weaknesses. There is obviously no point in volunteering this information if counsel for the other side has no intention of raising the weakness at trial. However, if the weakness is to become an issue, it is best if the attorney does not try to sweep it under the rug. The weakness should be mentioned, but diminished in importance and certainly never accompanied by an apology. If a defendant in a homicide case was smoking marijuana during the incident in question, it is best to refer to this in a matter-of-fact way as the facts are being reconstructed. This takes the sting out of the weakness right away. Openings "provide counsel with an opportunity to talk frankly with a jury, and every such manifestation of a lawyer's fairness adds to his effectiveness."[35]

Attorneys should always take notes on the content of their opposition's opening statements. This is a good way to check on the other side's promised proof. Naturally, the best advice for an attorney is not to open a case so wide with promises that it cannot be closed. Lawyers should never go further than their proof will allow. To do so can be disastrous, since jurors or opposing counsel inevitably discover the overstated representation. The failure to live up to a promise makes a case appear far weaker than it really is. One group of researchers found that opening statements that exaggerate the strength of the evidence create more lenient verdicts for prosecutors than statements that avoid overstated promises, particularly when the other side points the exaggeration out in summation.[36] If proof promised in an opening is not provided when the case evidence is presented, opposing counsel can note those unfulfilled promises to the jury. It is even possible that "the deliberate inclusion in an opening statement of matters which cannot be established by admissible evidence may constitute reversible error."[37] For instance, a mistrial can be declared if a criminal prosecutor makes a remark like "I suspect the defendant has done things far worse than we can prove. He really is a rotten guy!"

During opening, the opposition's case should be neither summarized nor refuted in great detail. If the opposition case is debated in an opening statement, the jury might presume that the case is more formidable than it really is. After all, the opposition has not yet really presented any of its evidence. This is not to say that the opposition's case should be entirely ignored. Although rebuttal is technically disallowed in openings, and attorneys cannot directly allude to evidence they expect the opposition to produce, they can subtly forewarn the jury to watch for certain attempts at counterpersuasion. Research shows that the attitudes and beliefs of message receivers are more resistant to counterinfluence when the receivers have been inoculated by prior exposure to the arguments involved.[38] This principle is analogous to being inoculated biologically against disease. But here, instead of making a jury resistant to some future attacking virus, an attorney shows jurors how to protect themselves against persuasive appeals by learning how to respond to the proposed counterargument.[39]

The following experiment is illuminating: Researchers took one group of college students and told them they would be hearing a lecture from a campus housing director advocating that all freshmen and sophomores be required to live in dormitories. Another group were asked to write out their thoughts on the subject but were not forewarned about the speaker. A third group were told nothing. All three groups then heard the lecture. Those who were forewarned about the persuasion attempt and those who were asked to think and write about the topic were more resistant to the lecturer than were those who got no instructions. Hence, forewarning apparently induces thinking and hesitation.[40] The notion of forewarning persons that they are about to hear something designed to change their minds is particularly a useful tactic for plaintiffs and prosecutors. What they should do is to briefly inform a jury about a strongly held position of the opposition, and to motivate them to build and practice defensive responses against that position.

Asking the jury to compare the persuasive strength of one's own arguments with the weaknesses in the opposition's arguments (called two-sided presentation) is also most attractive, particularly with well-educated juries, because educated people like to be cognitively active participants in the trial.[41] "In contrast, affective jurors are looking for guidance of a different sort from the attorney. . . . Affective jurors do not respond well to long, drawn-out, step-by-step accounts that . . . will be too tedious and complex for them to absorb. Rather, affective jurors are most appreciative of the attorney who provides them with . . . three or four critical points upon which [to] base their verdicts."[42]

For them, two-sided presentations might be avoided.

One final word should be said about the content of the opening statement. Following common law, it must not be perceived as argument. Argument or persuasion is *technically* to be saved until all the evidence is in and summations are offered for the jury. In other words, attorneys are prevented "from encouraging inferences or conclusions from abstracted data until the abstracted data has been actually adduced in the trial event."[43] Openings are only supposed to state "facts."[44]

Here is an example of argument in the opening statement, which could be ruled out of order. An attorney says, "The defendant, Mr. Hare, negligently drove at an excessive rate of speed." This is argument because it is up to the jury to decide if Hare was negligent. The attorney cannot draw that conclusion. Neither can Mr. Hare nor any of the witnesses. This rule does not mean that openings must be lukewarm and sterile. Quite the contrary. The attorney can still say, "The speedometer read seventy-three miles per hour, and Mr. Hare was traveling in a fifty-miles-per-hour zone." The attorney can even say, "Mr. Hare was racing down the road at seventy-three miles per hour!" All this can be said because there are witnesses who will appear on the stand to state these facts to the court. But the negligence conclusion cannot be uttered in the opening statement, because it constitutes argument.

Determining where to draw the line is not easy, and trial court "judges differ widely in their interpretation of what constitutes impermissible argument."[45] Can the jury make such a fine distinction as well? Probably not. After all, "there are many ways that one may persuade without arguing,"[46] and the distinction is a subtle one. According to one writer, the rule that attorneys can be persuasive only in closing arguments "ignore[s] clear reality. Communication theorists . . . now accept the broad concept that being persuaded relates to three behavioral outcomes: attitude formation, attitude reinforcement, and attitude change. What we call 'informative communication' serves a persuasive function in that it conditions jurors to respond in a certain way. Attitude formation begins at the point where the jurors receive their first piece of information and intensifies as more information is supplied."[47] This kind of persuasion certainly typifies the opening statement.

PRESENTATION OF THE OPENING STATEMENT

Like any effective public speech, the opening statement must make use of certain rhetorical techniques that enhance its persuasive potential. Three categories of technique will be discussed: narrative style, attention factors, and subtle persuasion.

Narrative Style

One writer found in analyzing nearly one hundred trials that good storytelling is the essence of effective narrative style.[48] "The opening statement is basically a story and the techniques to be followed are those of the traditional storyteller."[49] To make narration effective, certain word choices and sentence structures must be used to create the correct impression for both sides. An investigation of attorney language use in criminal trials resulted in some interesting observations.[50] Successful prosecutors are verbally assertive and direct; unsuccessful prosecutors are polite and hesitant. After all, they must fulfill their burden of proof. Prosecutors should avoid such words as "please," "I hope," "I think," and "maybe" in favor of such words as "very" and "certain." Successful defense lawyers are abstract and ambiguous; unsuccessful defense attorneys are clear and specific. After all, they need only create doubt. For them, too many adverbs increase specific-

ity and all "ly" words (e.g., "obviously") should be avoided.[51]

Mark Twain once said, "The difference between the right word and the almost right word is like the difference between lightning and the lightning bug."[52] Here are several other illustrations of the importance of word choice in narrative style. Prosecutors should not refer to "the state"; that is too cold and official. Rather, a federal prosecutor ought to refer to "America" to invoke patriotism, and all prosecutors should talk about "the people" as the party against the defendant. And who are "the people"? Naturally, they include the victim and the jury! Attorneys should use language that personalizes their side and depersonalizes the opposition. In our hypothetical civil case of *Fox v. Hare,* the defense lawyer should refer to "the plaintiff" and to "Ed Hare." The client's name should be used whenever possible. The attorney for the plaintiff may also describe the client as "the injured party."

Many openings lose their effectiveness because the lawyers repeatedly say, "What I or my opponent says is not evidence." The court has "already told the jury this. Lawyers should not give the jury any more reasons for tuning out their remarks."[53] In addition, words like "the evidence will show" or "we expect to prove beyond a reasonable doubt" disrupt the flow of the story and should be avoided or noted only once (e.g., "The evidence in this case will show that this is what happened"). Then, go on with the story. Instead of repeatedly using weak language such as "we believe the evidence will show," counsel should go directly to the facts, saying, "The defendant, driving east on Main Street, speeds right through the red light, never slows down, and crashes right into the back of Mary Jane Fox's car." Also, notice that this sentence is in the present tense, to make it easier for the jury to visualize the incident.

Some words in storytelling are more appropriate for one side than they are for the other side. To the plaintiff there is "wrong"; to the defendant the same thing is "unavoidable." Plaintiff's counsel can refer to a plaintiff's being "maimed" in a "collision," "crash," "wreck," or "tragedy"; defense counsel might talk about "an accident," "a mishap," "an act of God," or "one of those things." If an automobile accident involves an injured child, the plaintiff calls the youngster a "playing child," while the defendant's lawyer refers to a "darting child." In a criminal case, a prosecutor may want to emotionally charge the relatively neutral word "gun" by calling it a "deadly weapon." Or a defense attorney in a rape case may want to use the term "sexual intercourse" rather than "rape." Appropriate language needs to be selected carefully for each case and each side.

Technical, medical, and legal terms need to be explained in lay language in order to bridge the gap between the jury's vocabulary and that of the attorneys and their witnesses. Lacerations, abrasions, contusions, and closed fractures must be called cuts, scrapes, bruises, and broken bones. Legalese (dead legal phrases and terms such as "statute of limitations," "collateral," and "certiorari") should be avoided.[54] "I represent the executrix of Samuel Diamond" ought to be replaced by "In this case, I am here for the widow of Samuel Diamond." If technical language must be used, it should be defined in lay terms. After all, technical terms are mind stoppers; they communicate little.

Whenever possible, simple words should replace complex ones. In one study, only one out of 35 jurors understood what a "proximate cause" was after all were told that it is a cause that, in natural and continuous sequence, produces an injury. Without that proximate cause, the injury would not have occurred. Many people confused the word "proximate" with "approximate." The only person to understand what this complex language meant was a Ph.D.![55] "Before" is better than "prior to," and "after" is better than "subsequent to." "Crossed the highway" is better than "traversed the highway." "Asked the doctor" is better than "interrogated the physician." "Began the operation" is better than "commenced the surgery." "Total," "suggest," and "if" are simpler and clearer than "aggregate," "submit," and "in the event that." Lawyers must be clearly understood by the least educated people in the jury box, and this goal can be accomplished through the use of simple words.

The obvious follow-up advice to that offered in the preceding paragraph is that simple sentence structure should replace complex structure. This, too, enhances clarity and reduces verbosity and pomposity. It does not mean being antiseptic and uninteresting; it means being crisp and clear. Attorneys must resist showing how erudite many of them really can be. Complex structure often takes the form of redundancy and overstatement. Consider these examples: "each and every," "full and complete," "final and conclusive," "absolute and definite," and the suspicious claim, "my honest opinion."

In order to transform the ordinary into the exciting, the attorney should incorporate imagery into the opening statement. Imagery involves an appeal to the senses. The ideal situation for a lawyer would be to have a film reenacting the story shown during opening statement. But a lawyer cannot use this technique and must resort to words to bring a story to life. Words must make the image vivid, not hazy. These images can appeal to all the senses—sight, sound, touch, taste, smell, muscular or kinesthetic feeling, and internal or organic sensations. Here are some sentences using words that appeal to three senses commonly appealed to in the courtroom:

☐ The injured plaintiff is *crushed* and *impaled* in the collision. His arm is *torn off,* his face is *shredded,* and his leg is made to look like a *broomstick.* (visual imagery)

☐ That noise is the unmistakable *timpani*

of automobiles colliding and sheet metal *buckling*. (auditory imagery)

☐ As she starts running, she notices tiny *cramps* in her lower legs. Then, *shooting pains* begin to work their way upward. She feels her knees *pounding* with each step, and the muscles in her thighs are *complaining bitterly*, but she has to escape. (kinesthetic imagery)

Notice the use of the broomstick analogy in the first example. "Analogies supply an equal sign between something strange and something familiar and are a powerful participatory persuasion tool."[56] Analogies are stirring because they link case information to the experiences, knowledge, and ideas of the jurors. They are interesting and they persuade. Craig Spangenberg illustrates the power of the analogy with this explanation of a case that depends on circumstantial (inferential) evidence:

This reminds me of my father reading *Robinson Crusoe* to me when I was a little boy. Remember when Robinson was on the island for such a long time all alone? One morning he went down to the beach and there was a footprint in the sand. Knowing that someone else was on the island, he was so overcome with emotion, he fainted.

And why did he faint? Did he see a man? He woke to find Friday standing beside him, who was to be his friend on the island, but he didn't see Friday. Did he see a foot? No. He saw a footprint. That is, he saw marks in the sand, the kind of marks that are made by a human foot. He saw circumstantial evidence. But it was true, it was valid, it was compelling, as it would be to all of you. We live with it all of our lives. So let's look at the facts of this case—for those tracks that prove the truth.[57]

This analogy is designed to motivate the jury to accept the attorney as a credible and decent person, as credible and decent as any good father is to his child.

In sum, "the advocate who is insensitive to the importance of language in impression formation may increase the probability of a jury's creating unfavorable impressions"[58] about the case. Narrative language is important in storytelling. The following two sentences allow us to compare a drab and colorless sentence with an effective and lively one:

Wrong Way: This is a dram shop lawsuit and my client, a quadriplegic, seeks damages against the defendant tavern.

Right Way: This is the case of a young mother of three small children who, for the rest of her natural life, will be paralyzed from the neck down because the defendant's tavern sold too much beer to a young driver.[59]

Good trial lawyers may spend hours and days selecting the right words, as well they should. More will be said about the power of language in the courtroom in Chapter 9.

Attention Factors

Persuasiveness depends on maintaining the attention of the jury. They cannot accept that to which they do not attend.[60] People do not pay complete attention to everything. Rather, they focus selectively on certain stimuli.[61] It is the attorney's job in an opening statement to obtain and retain juror interest. How is this done? One of the best-selling public speaking textbooks suggests several techniques,[62] some of which are noted here.

If one actor on a stage is moving and another is standing still, members of the audience probably attend more closely to the moving figure. *Activity* is an attention getter. It involves not only physical movement for the lawyer, but movement of ideas, too. We have already suggested how the narrative style facilitates verbal activity in storytelling. The opening statement should march forward through the use of such style. Too much time should not be spent dwelling on any one point.

Referring to someone present in the courtroom, to some object close at hand, to the immediate litigation occasion, or to something that just happened in voir dire makes use of the attention factor called *proximity*. Referring to things juries face in their everyday lives makes use of *familiarity* as an attention factor. Describing vividly a commonly known intersection in town, an ice storm typical of those experienced often in a given community, or problems in changing a tire in a consumer product safety case can trigger an old-friend or old-nemesis image in the minds of a jury.

Another approach to building interest in the opening statement is to focus on *conflict*. The opposition of forces compels attention. This is basically why we get interested in sports events and political contests. In a medical malpractice case, the struggle against disease by both the doctor and the patient can be vividly developed. In an abuse case, the conflict between parent and child can be described. Communicating a sense of conflict is a natural attention factor in the drama of a courtroom.

An element of the art of good storytelling is to inject *mystery and suspense*. It was noted earlier that the full story should be told in capsule form at the beginning of the body of the speech. At times, a lawyer may wish to wait and offer that summary at the end of the body of the story. The story can build to a climax, keeping the jury in the dark until the end of the tale. Another very effective way to build suspense is by using the parallel actions technique. For example, the accused and the victim in a manslaughter trial could be shown starting out from two separate places at two separate times. The actions of each would be followed separately, building, of course, to the incident that brought the two of them together and in which one of them was killed.

Visual aids can be used in most courts to enhance a juror's attention and interest. They make use of an attention factor called *reality*. Charts, photographs, models, drawings, and the like give jurors a visual connection to an attorney's claims. They make a deeper impression than words alone. Most courts permit visuals during the opening statement, although a few limit counsel to blackboard drawings. In the hypothetical case of *Fox v. Hare,* a diagram of the street location where the accident took place helps the jury see the paths of the cars. Visual aids should be prepared professionally in advance of the trial. They should be accurate and simple. The detail must be easily seen, and the user must not block the view or talk to the aids. Visual aids are not evidence, but they help in gettting the story across to the jury, especially if the story is complex. Research on the intersection between message modality and message complexity confirms this thesis. An experiment was conducted in which college students were asked to read, listen to an audiotape, or watch a videotape of a persuasive speech. Sometimes the message was simple, and other times it was complex. The students were much more influenced by the simple message on audiotape or videotape, but the complex message had more of an impact when it was in written form.[63] An attorney confronted with a complex opening statement may well want to outline in summary form the major events and issues for the jury on a visual aid so that the jurors can see the case before them graphically while the attorney is speaking. Even if prepared visual aids cannot be used, an attorney can use props in the courtroom as visual aids: "While he was traveling seventy-three miles an hour, Mr. Hare was about as far from Mary Jane as it is from this window to the back of the room." Many courtrooms seem to come to life when such language is used; the visual element enhances the persuasiveness of the message.

Although attention factors should be incorporated throughout the opening statement, it is especially important to select carefully the ones to be used at the very beginning. In show business, an early attention getter is called "the hook." The hook evokes an image the attorney wants to portray. When we think of facial tissue, the image is Kleenex. When we think of a soft drink, the image is Coke. When a jury thinks about a case, those thoughts should be linked to a slogan developed at the beginning of the opening statement and carried on throughout the trial. In one case in which I served as a trial consultant, the plaintiff was claiming that a fraudulent will had been drafted by the late husband of the defendant. Not so, said the defense. The deceased had left virtually his entire estate to a child from a second marriage. Why? It seems that he wanted that child to receive a good education, and he wanted his money to be spent toward that end. You might say he had a "fervor for education." Continuous use of that "fervor" slogan throughout the trial was quite persuasive. Jurors granted a unanimous decision for the defendant. The hook ("fervor for education") in the opening statement guided their deliberations.

Subtle Persuasion

There are additional and sometimes subtle aspects of the opening statement that can further enhance its persuasiveness. How long should it be? What demeanor should the lawyer assume? Should notes be used? Should humor be used? Where should the lawyer position himself or herself when delivering the opening statement? How important is nonverbal communication? Should objections be used as a tool of persuasion? These questions will be answered here.

One element of subtle persuasion is that the opening should be as brief as possible. It should not be a cursory statement, nor should prolixity abound. Rather, it should be only long enough to make the necessary points and hold the jury's interest. Obviously, no dogmatically fixed time limit can be placed on the opening, but orating too long and boring the jury is counterproductive. Opening statements usually run from twenty minutes to an hour. Some say twenty to thirty minutes is preferable;[64] others feel the need for twenty minutes per each week the trial is expected to run.[65] Many federal courts already are asking lawyers to complete their speeches to the jury in twenty minutes or less.

Also, the opening statement should be delivered in a natural and calm manner. If nothing else, it makes the presenter *appear* confident and logical. A relaxed, friendly attitude is important. The delivery can be almost conversational, as though the story were being told to a group of friends. Opening statement is not the time for formalism, theatrics, or high-flown oratory. Excitement during opening statements may be wasted, as the jury has not yet heard anything to get excited about.

The opening statement should be delivered using no notes, or if notes are used, they should be sparse and unobtrusive. In no instance should the opening be read from manuscript.[66] It is important for an attorney to maintain good eye contact with the jury, and notes can be distracting. Furthermore, a speech delivered without notes makes the speaker look more spontaneous and sincere.

Even though many public speeches begin with a funny story, levity or humor should be avoided in the courtroom. Trials are a serious business for jurors. They do not know counsel very well during the opening statements. A planned joke for the opening statement runs counter to the jurors' belief that their task is a serious one. The joke makes an attorney seem insincere, and it may make the jury feel uncomfortable. Of course, if something humorous inadvertently occurs, a warm smile or a chuckle from attorneys humanizes them a bit. In such situations, a cautious reaction to levity is permissible.

Choosing where to position themselves in the courtroom during opening statement is another decision attorneys must make. Tall, heavy, and loud lawyers must stand somewhat farther away from the jury box than their short, thin, soft-spoken counterparts, or else they might overpower the jury. Ideally, the opening should be given four to twelve feet away from the jury. Moving in too close makes jurors feel uncomfortable; standing too far away reduces the presence of the speaker. A formal public speaking distance is twelve feet or more from the audience; a social distance (ideal for the opening statement) is four to twelve feet away; a distance of four feet or less is too personal and intimate.[67] The lawyer should stand directly in front of the jury as well; speaking from one side of the jury box gives the impression that the people at the other end are being ignored.

Despite typical overstatements about non-verbal communication in the legal literature, there is no doubt that it is of some importance to the persuasiveness of the opening statement. Of particular importance are eye contact, gestures and movement, dress, and voice. Attorneys must maintain eye contact with all members of the jury when the opening statement is delivered. It is not a good idea to concentrate only on those that look the most sympathetic. "The speaker who looks down at the floor instead of at listeners, who reads excessively from notes, . . . or who delivers a speech to the back wall has severed visual bonding. Our culture has come to expect eye-to-eye contact from speakers."[68] An attorney should watch the jurors' eyes as well. The pioneer study on pupillary reflex by Eckhard Hess gives insight into juror reactions to an opening statement. Hess found that sudden widening or narrowing of pupils can be related to attitudes and that, generally, our pupils dilate when we see something we like, contract when we see things we find distasteful, and remain unchanged when we are indifferent.[69] Anthropologist Edward Hall notes that Arabs have known about pupil response for years and "since people can't control the response of their eyes, . . . many Arabs, like Arafat, wear dark glasses, even indoors."[70] During opening statement, attorneys might be able to observe pupillary phenomena to better interpret jury reactions to what they are saying.

Gestures and movement are another dimension of nonverbal communication that must be considered. The lawyer who constantly points at the jury with his pen, twirls his Phi Beta Kappa key, scratches his nose, or jingles the change in his pocket is using mannerisms distracting to the audience. Gestures and movement that are too effusive or repetitive, unrelated to the content, uncoordinated, or indefinite also create a poor image for counsel. Standing with arms folded is an unimpressive speaking position. If one needs occasional support, it is better to occasionally lean against a table or chair than to use one's own body for support by crossing the arms across the midsection. Pacing back and forth in front of the jury is also a bad idea. So is rooting to one spot and never moving. This happens a lot when speakers plant themselves behind a lectern. If a lectern is used, counsel should move around it to the side or occasionally go to the front of it. Good movement comes when there is a break in thought (transition) or when counsel is stressing a particularly important point. If permitted, lawyers should avoid giving opening statements while standing behind lecterns. The lectern shields the speaker from the audience and makes the speaker appear cold and rigid. The best advice to overcome poor physical delivery is just to forget about it when speaking. If lawyers keep their minds on what is being said, how it is being said will be self-corrective.

Attorney dress should convey an image of professionalism and warmth combined. Neat appearance and good grooming (e.g., polished shoes, clothes free from wrinkles, and good cuticle care) enhance lawyer credibility. Table 7.1 contains a checklist for attorneys to follow.[71] If a lawyer's personality is warm, he or she should dress to strengthen the professional image. On the other hand, if a lawyer's personality shows confidence and power, he or she should dress to accomplish an image of greater warmth. Balance between the two is important.

Voice control is important as well. During the opening, the voice should be pleasant

TABLE 7.1

ATTORNEY APPEARANCE

Male: Professionalism

Traditional two-piece suit. Wool or wool-blend. Small pinstripe, subtle plaid, or solid. Gray or navy blue.

Conservative tie.

Solid long-sleeved shirt with classic collar. Cotton fabric. White or light blue.

Conservative tied shoes.

Conservative leather belt.

Very limited jewelry.

If eyeglasses, conservative frames and clear lenses.

Short, conservative hair style.

Male: Warmth

Sports jacket or two-piece suit. Tweed, small plaid, or solid. Tan, beige, or brown.

Conservative tie.

Solid or striped long-sleeved shirt with button-down collar. Cotton fabric. Pastel color.

Conservative tied shoes.

Conservative leather belt.

Very limited jewelry.

If eyeglasses, conservative frames and clear lenses.

Short, conservative hair style.

Female: Professionalism

Traditional two-piece suit. Matching skirt and jacket. Solid, small plaid, or small stripe. Wool, wool-blend, or summer fabric. Gray, off-white, beige, or navy blue.

Cotton or silk blouse. Bows or pleats. Solid white or light blue. Conservative belt.

Closed-toe heels of 2½ inches or less. Classic.

Limited jewelry.

If eyeglasses, conservative frames.

Classic, conservative fairly short hair style.

Little to moderate makeup.

Female: Warmth

Traditional two-piece suit. Contrasting skirt and jacket, or a dress with or without a jacket. Solids, small plaids, or small stripes. Wool or wool-blend. Brown, gray, blue, or rose.

Cotton or silk blouse. Bows, pleats, ruffles, or soft ties. Normal neckline. Blue, pink, light rose, or light green.

Conservative belt.

Closed-toe heels of 2½ inches or less. Classic. Limited, conservative jewelry.

If eyeglasses, conservative frames.

Soft hair style. Subtle curls or waves. Shoulder length or shorter.

Little to moderate makeup.

and moderate, but audible. Rate is crucial; the speech should be neither rushed nor plodding. A monotone or a bland pitch is dull and will not uplift the jury. Vocal variety adds interest. A voice therapist notes: "Many a juror has considered a man's argument weak because his voice and manner were against him."[72]

Objections can be another form of subtle persuasion. They should be used sparingly during opening statements. They might be used if opposing counsel makes an inference but presents it as fact, if issues of law are being analyzed, or if certain facts that were declared inadmissible on pretrial motions are alluded to in the presentation by counsel for the other side. Lawyers should raise objections only if they are reasonably certain that the judge will sustain them. After all, lawyers can create initially poor impressions if their objections are constantly being overruled while the other side is speaking. The jury may regard these interruptions during opening statement as attempts by the objecting party to confuse the opponent and break up his or her line of thought.

To avoid an objection to the content of an opening statement, objectionable material, such as noted in the preceding paragraph, should be omitted. One writer further maintains that a restrained delivery is a better deterrent to objections than is a forceful delivery.[73] Additional worthwhile advice comes from another writer:

If an objection is sustained because an opening statement is argumentative, the appropriate remark to make is something along these lines: "I apologize to the court and the jury for having been carried away by my enthusiasm for my client's cause. I will try to confine myself to outlining what we intend to prove and ask your indulgence. Returning now to the facts. . . ."

If the objection is sustained because the opening contained a reference to improper evidence, defense counsel might state: "I apologize to the court and jury for the statement

which the court held objectionable. I had no intention of making any statement which was not in accordance with my understanding of the law. Honest differences of opinion do exist, but in the trial of every case, the trial judge's ruling is final and binding. I therefore sincerely ask you to forgive me and to disregard the remark. Returning now to the facts. . . ."[74]

The bottom line on the presentation of opening statements is that, like good bedtime stories, they should be told with honesty, simplicity, and conviction. Embellishments and purple passages are to be saved for another time and another place. Most important, the trial lawyer should be his or her natural self during the opening statement, be it before judge or before jury.[75]

PREPARING THE OPENING STATEMENT

"The great loss . . . is the lawyer who stands up to speak and makes one realize that that moment is the first time he has really thought about the opening statement."[76] Advance planning for the opening is critical! After the facts are gathered, the issues decided, and the witnesses coached, a lawyer should carefully prepare a written outline for the opening statement. "Generally, the opening statement should be prepared as the last item before commencement of the trial. It should be reviewed quickly after the jury has been selected to determine whether any alterations should be made in substance, or approach, based on the jurors selected to hear the case."[77] The organizational pattern for this outline has already been discussed. Although the outline might be altered somewhat during the actual presentation, writing it up forces an attorney to take preparation of the opening seriously.

After the outline is prepared, counsel should practice giving the opening statement, first with notes and later without them, or with nothing more than a "crib card" containing a few words at most. Lots of rehearsal time will increase an attorney's proficiency in presenting an effective opening.[78] Knowing a case is not the equivalent of stating it. Practicing aloud might be done before relatives, friends, or other lay persons in order to get feedback and helpful criticism. Lawyers should carefully listen to and evaluate their own opening statements before they make them in court. Practicing with a video- or audiotape recorder can be an invaluable experience, too.

PRIMACY AND THE OPENING STATEMENT

The rule of primacy is basically that first impressions are lasting impressions. What we believe first, we believe more intensely, retain more strongly, and resist changing more forcefully. (Primacy is not to be confused with the principle of recency, which is that the last message heard is the easiest one to remember.) Primacy relates to belief and attitude formation. Whichever side of an issue is presented first will have a greater influence on beliefs and attitudes than an equally potent but later presentation by the opposite side.

Most of the primacy research to date has been derived from studies conducted under the artificial and controlled conditions of communication and psychology laboratories. In most cases, two communications of equal persuasive content on a controversial issue have been presented, reversing the order with each group of subjects (pro–con and con–pro). There have been two types of laboratory studies conducted. With experimental primacy studies, it is quite possible that audiences that receive the persuasive communications have already been exposed to information about the topic, and they may have formed attitudes about it. Sometimes, individuals with prior case information serve on juries; more often they do not. With true primacy experiments, there is not the possibility

of prior exposure to information, because the information is fictitious. True primacy studies have suggested that "the nearer one comes to achieving primacy in the sense of the first presentation of unfamiliar material, the more apt one is to obtain primacy effects."[79] *Generally, the first information received by the audience is more influential in forming impressions than the information presented in the second communication.*

Primacy research began in the 1920s with F. H. Lund, who concluded that arguments presented first in a sequence of messages are more effective in terms of belief and attitude formation than arguments on the same topic presented at a later time.[80] Primacy research was continued in the 1950s by Carl Hovland and his associates. They tended to find exceptions to the importance of primacy, but they recognized that, under certain conditions, it certainly could play a key role in belief and attitude formation.[81] The Asch and Luchins studies also illustrate the impact of first impressions on later judgments. Solomon E. Asch was an information integration theorist who gave subjects information about a hypothetical person, arranging it from favorable to unfavorable or in reverse order. Subjects rated the personality of that individual, and the results show a primacy effect. Attitudes were more favorable when favorable information appeared first on the list and more negative when unfavorable information was presented first.[82] A. S. Luchins designed two paragraphs that describe a fictitious person, Jim, as either extroverted or introverted. Four groups of students were given the paragraphs and asked to evaluate Jim as friendly or unfriendly. Those who read only the introvert description rated Jim as unfriendly. When subjects read both paragraphs, they rated Jim as friendly when they read the extrovert paragraph first, and unfriendly when they read the introvert paragraph first. The first block of information was the most influential, and thus the primacy effect was apparent. Once people form an initial impression, they give less credence to subsequent information that conflicts with that initial impression.[83]

The principle of primacy seems to apply to the order of opening statements in the courtroom as well. Two-thirds of the mock jurors in one study reached a verdict consistent with the first presented opening statement, regardless of which side delivered its speech first (half of the subjects heard the prosecution first, and half heard the defense first).[84] In fact, some attorneys believe that "the right to speak first is even more important than the right to argue last."[85]

In much of the research confirming the existence of a primacy effect, it was found to occur because the first speech was more fully attended to than the second speech,[86] the first speech had less interference for the audience than the second speech,[87] and the first speech had the advantage of structuring the context and interpretation of subsequent information for the audience.[88] Put another way, interesting subject matter, controversial topics, and highly familiar stories tend toward a primacy effect.[89] This may well mean that if a case in court is inherently dramatic, interesting, and not too technical—for example, an emotionally contested divorce, a savage murder, or a rape—it will tend toward a primacy effect, and the side to open first has a distinct advantage. Cases that are uninteresting, colorless, dull, or highly technical—for example, a condemnation proceeding, a tax claim, or a dispute over title to real property—may lack any primacy effect.[90] In these latter cases, in particular, counsel must use the rhetorical techniques discussed in this chapter to try to get primacy working for them.

Those who de-emphasize the importance of primacy in litigation do so because the courtroom conditions are quite different from the conditions in most primacy experiments. Conditions are indeed important. One study found that primacy is not "an indubitable factor in persuasion," but occurs only on certain occasions.[91] The major condition in the true primacy experiments in which a primacy effect is found is that there are opposing sides presenting conflicting and controversial messages to uninformed audiences. One writer notes, however, that the jury has information prior to the opening statements; it gets it from the period of voir dire.[92] Furthermore, the prosecution and the plaintiff also have a burden of proof, which is not a burden found in nonlegal conditions. So the verdict on the importance of primacy in the trial setting is yet to be determined.[93] More will be said about primacy when its counterpart, recency, is discussed in Chapter 11.

Notes

[1]Sometimes opening statements are given before voir dire so that the jurors can learn about the case and thereby provide better answers to the voir dire questions.

[2]Where the allegations of the complaint have been admitted, however, the defendant has the right to open. In this situation, the defendant has either pleaded affirmative defenses or set forth a counterclaim. Jerome Stern, "Opening Statements—Defense View," in *Am Jur Trials,* vol. 5 (San Francisco: Bancroft-Whitney, 1966), 320–321.

[3]Alfred S. Julien, *Opening Statements* (Wilmette, Ill.: Callaghan and Company, 1980), 2.

[4]H. P. Weld and E. R. Danzig, "A Study of the Way in Which a Verdict Is Reached by a Jury," *American Journal of Psychology* 53 (1940), 518–536.

[5]Dale E. Broeder, "The University of Chicago Jury Project," *Nebraska Law Review* 38 (1958), 744–761.

[6]John Alan Appleman, *Preparation and Trial* (Vienna, Va.: Coiner Publications, 1967), 189.

[7]G. David Hughes and Henry S. Hsiao, "Does the Opening Determine the Verdict?" *Trial* (February 1986), 70.

[8]Thomas A. Pyszczynski and Lawrence S. Wrightsman, "The Effects of Opening Statements

on Mock Jurors' Verdicts in a Simulated Criminal Trial," *Journal of Applied Social Psychology* 11 (1981), 301–313.

[9]Richard J. Crawford, "Opening Statement for the Defense—A Patch of Blue," Paper presented at the Speech Communication Association Convention (Anaheim, Calif., November 1981), 2.

[10]James W. McElhaney, *Trial Notebook* (Chicago: American Bar Association, 1981), 37.

[11]In a landmark case on opening statements, the Supreme Court noted, "The opening statement of counsel is ordinarily intended to do no more than to inform the jury in a general way of the nature of the action and defense so that they may better be prepared to understand the evidence." *Best v. District of Columbia,* 291 U.S. 411, 54 S.Ct. 487, 78 L.Ed. 882 (1934).

[12]John H. Lingle and Thomas M. Ostrom, "Principles of Memory and Cognition in Attitude Formation," in Richard E. Petty, Thomas M. Ostrom, and Timothy C. Brock, eds., *Cognitive Responses in Persuasion* (Hillsdale, N.J.: Erlbaum, 1981), 401.

[13]James W. Jeans, *Trial Advocacy* (St. Paul, Minn.: West Publishing, 1975), 200–201.

[14]Gordon H. Bower, "Cognitive Psychology: An Introduction," in W. K. Estes, ed., *Handbook of Learning and Cognitive Processes,* vol. 1 (Hillsdale, N.J.: Erlbaum, 1975), 25–80.

[15]Perry W. Thorndyke, "Cognitive Structures in Comprehension and Memory of Narrative Discourse," *Cognitive Psychology* 9 (1977), 77–110.

[16]Leonard Decof, *Art of Advocacy: Opening Statement* (New York: Matthew Bender, 1982), 1/40–1/42.

[17]Liking a person positively influences our thinking. W. Curtis Banks, "The Effects of Perceived Similarity Upon the Use of Reward and Punishment," *Journal of Experimental Social Psychology* 12 (1976), 131–138; William Griffit and Thomas Jackson, "Influence of Ability and Nonability Information on Personnel Selection Decisions," *Psychological Reports* 27 (1970), 959–962; Thomas Sannito and Edward B. Arnolds "Jury Study Results: The Factors at Work," *Trial Diplomacy Journal* (Spring 1982), 6; Ibid. (Summer, 1982), 13; Yong H. Sung, "Effects of

Attitude Similarity and Favorableness of Information on Bayesian Decision Making in a Realistic Task," *Journal of Applied Psychology* 60 (1975), 616–620.

[18]Norman H. Anderson, "Likableness Ratings of 555 Personality-Trait Words," *Journal of Personality and Social Psychology* 9 (1968), 272–279.

[19]Abraham P. Ordover, "Persuasion and the Opening Statement," *Litigation* (Winter 1986), 67.

[20]The case in chief refers to the presentation of the entire case.

[21]Jeans, op. cit., 210.

[22]Gordon H. Bower, "Experiments on Story Understanding and Recall," *Quarterly Journal of Experimental Psychology* 28 (1976), 511–534; Walter Kintsch, Theodore S. Mandel, and Ely Kozminsky, "Summarizing Scrambled Stories," *Memory and Cognition* 5 (1977), 547–552.

[23]Gary L. Wells, Lawrence S. Wrightsman, and Peter K. Miene, "The Timing of the Defense Opening Statement: Don't Wait Until the Evidence Is In," *Journal of Applied Social Psychology* 15 (1985), 758–772.

[24]John W. Howard and Myron Rothbart, "Social Categorization and Memory for Ingroup and Outgroup Behavior," *Journal of Personality and Social Psychology* 38 (1980), 301–310; Robert S. Wyer et al., "Effects of Processing Objectives on the Recall of Prose Material," *Journal of Personality and Social Psychology* 43 (1982), 674–688.

[25]Crawford, op. cit., 6.

[26]Godwin C. Chu, "Prior Familiarity, Perceived Bias, and One-Sided Versus Two-Sided Communications," *Journal of Experimental Social Psychology* 3 (1967), 243–254.

[27]Russell A. Jones and Jack W. Brehm, "Persuasiveness of One- and Two-Sided Communications as a Function of Awareness That There Are Two Sides," *Journal of Experimental Social Psychology* 6 (1970), 47–56.

[28]Here is an example: "This is my first opportunity to talk to you about this case. It is not my intention to persuade you to my point of view or to argue a specific point of the case for the purpose of selling the same to you. I would rather

like to give you at this time a fair picture of the facts, a skeleton or framework upon which you can place the testimony as it unfolds at the trial. I believe that with this framework you will better be able to grasp the issues involved." Robert C. McFigg et al., *Civil Trial Manual* (Los Angeles: Joint Committee on Legal Education of the American Law Institute and the American Bar Association, 1974), 395.

[29]George A. LaMarca, "Opening Statements—Effective Techniques," in John J. Kennelly, ed., *Trial Lawyer's Guide: 1977 Annual* (Wilmette, Ill.: Callaghan and Company, 1977), 447.

[30]Al J. Cone and Verne Lawyer, *The Act of Persuasion in Litigation* (Des Moines: Dean-Hicks, 1966), 268.

[31]"The University of Chicago studies concerning jury deliberation present an interesting conclusion. A case involving several items of damage was submitted to numerous juries in two different ways. On the one hand, a separate verdict was rendered by the jury on each item of damage, while on the other hand, a lump sum verdict was rendered. Where separate verdicts were returned on each of the items of damage, they totaled a higher amount than where a lump sum verdict was returned. This would indicate that it is the duty of the attorney, in states where the use of per diem formulas is allowed, to use them in cases where separate items of damage exist." Ibid., 269.

[32]Eunice Cooper and Helen Dinerman, "Analysis of the Film 'Don't Be a Sucker': A Study in Communication," *Public Opinion Quarterly* 15 (1951), 243–264; Bernard J. Fine, "Conclusion-Drawing, Communicator Credibility, and Anxiety as Factors in Opinion Change," *Journal of Abnormal and Social Psychology* 54 (1957), 369–374; Carl I. Hovland and Wallace Mandell, "An Experimental Comparison of Conclusion-Drawing by the Communicator and the Audience," *Journal of Abnormal and Social Psychology* 47 (1952), 581–588; Norman R. F. Maier and Richard A. Maier, "An Experimental Test of the Effects of 'Developmental' Versus 'Free' Discussion on the Quality of Group Decision," *Journal of Applied Psychology* 41 (1957), 320–323.

[33]"The idea of the opening is always the same whether I am representing the defendant or the plaintiff; it is very detailed. Why is it so detailed on the defendant's side? After all, many experienced trial lawyers have been saying for years that they like to keep things in reserve on the defense so that they can surprise the jury after the case has gone on for some time. That may have been good thinking at one time, but it isn't anymore. In these days of complete discovery, . . . through the use of pre-trial motions, there is little opportunity for complete surprise." Alfred Julien, "Opening Statement—An Interview," *Trial Diplomacy Journal* (Summer 1983), 5.

[34]William H. Mitchell, "Voir Dire and Opening Statement/The Defense Takes the Offense," *Federation of Insurance Counsel Quarterly* 26 (1976), 141.

[35]Jacob D. Fuchsberg, "Opening Statements—Plaintiff's View," in *Am Jur Trials*, vol. 5 (San Francisco: Bancroft-Whitney, 1966), 296.

[36]Thomas A. Pyszczynski et al., "Opening Statements in a Jury Trial: The Effect of Promising More Than the Evidence Can Show," *Journal of Applied Social Psychology* 11 (1981), 434–444.

[37]Francis Xavier Busch, *Trial Procedure Materials* (Indianapolis: Bobbs-Merrill, 1961), 137.

[38]William J. McGuire, "Inducing Resistance to Persuasion," in Leonard Berkowitz, ed., *Advances in Experimental Social Psychology*, vol. 1 (New York: Academic Press, 1964), 192–231.

[39]The reason forewarning results in less persuasion is that when individuals learn of a pending persuasion attempt, they immediately begin to generate counterarguments to what they anticipate hearing. William J. McGuire and Demetrios Papageorgis, "Effectiveness of Forewarning in Developing Resistance to Persuasion," *Public Opinion Quarterly* 26 (1962), 24–34; Demetrios Papageorgis and William J. McGuire, "The Generality of Immunity to Persuasion Produced by Pre-Counterarguments," *Journal of Abnormal and Social Psychology* 62 (1961), 475–481.

[40]Richard E. Petty and John T. Cacioppo, "Forewarning, Cognitive Responding, and Resistance to Persuasion," *Journal of Personality and Social Psychology* 35 (1977), 645–655. This study was updated and confirmed by the same authors in "Effects of Forewarning of Persuasive

Intent and Involvement on Cognitive Responses and Persuasion," *Personality and Social Psychology Bulletin* 5 (1979), 173–176.

[41]Bobby J. Calder, Chester A. Insko, and Ben Yandell, "The Relation of Cognitive and Memorial Processes to Persuasion in a Simulated Jury Trial," *Journal of Applied Social Psychology* 4 (1974), 62–93; Arthur A. Lumsdaine and Irving L. Janis, "Resistance to 'Counterpropaganda' Produced by One-Sided and Two-Sided 'Propaganda' Presentations," *Public Opinion Quarterly* 17 (1953), 311–318.

[42]Litigation Sciences, "Affective and Cognitive Jurors," *Trial* 18 (1982), 95.

[43]Richard M. Markus, "A Theory of Trial Advocacy," *Tulane Law Review* 56 (1981), 119.

[44]Rikki J. Kleiman, "A Checklist for Opening Statements," *Trial Diplomacy Journal* (Summer 1985), 35.

[45]Thomas A. Mauet, *Fundamentals of Trial Techniques* (Boston: Little, Brown, 1980), 51.

[46]John C. Elam, "Persuasion in the Opening Statement: The Defendant's Approach," in Grace W. Holmes, ed., *Persuasion: The Key to Damages* (Ann Arbor, Mich.: The Institute of Continuing Legal Education, 1978), 97.

[47]Raymond W. Buchanan, "Opening Statements and Closing Arguments: A Response from the Communication Perspective," in Ronald J. Matlon and Richard J. Crawford, eds., *Communication Strategies in the Practice of Lawyering* (Annandale, Va.: Speech Communication Association, 1983), 454.

[48]W. Lance Bennett, "Storytelling in Criminal Trials: A Model of Social Judgment," *Quarterly Journal of Speech* 64 (1968), 1–22; W. Lance Bennett and Martha S. Feldman, *Reconstructing Reality in the Courtroom* (New Brunswick, N.J.: Rutgers University Press, 1981), chap. 3.

[49]Jeans, op. cit., 202.

[50]Michael G. Parkinson, "Verbal Behavior and Courtroom Success," *Communication Education* 30 (1981), 22–31.

[51]Lucy V. Katz, *Winning Words: A Guide to Persuasive Writing for Lawyers* (New York: Harcourt Brace Jovanovich, 1986), 8.

[52]Quoted in Nicholas M. Cripe, "Fundamentals of Persuasive Oral Argument," *Forum* 20 (1985), 351.

[53]Thomas L. Long, "Opening Statement in Product Cases," *Trial* (November 1985), 55.

[54]Alfred S. Julien, "Rules on Opening Statements," *American Bar Association Journal* (October 1985), 64.

[55]"Proximate What? Only Ph.D. Knew," *American Bar Association Journal* 64 (1978), 660.

[56]Don Peters, "Participatory and Persuasion: Strategies and Research Needs in Opening Statements and Closing Arguments," in Ronald J. Matlon and Richard J. Crawford, eds., *Communication Strategies in the Practice of Lawyering* (Annandale, Va.: Speech Communication Association, 1983), 403–404.

[57]Craig Spangenberg, "Basic Values and the Techniques of Persuasion," *Litigation* (Summer 1977), 16.

[58]Dennis S. Gouran, "Principles Affecting the Choice of Persuasive Strategies in Opening and Closing Arguments," in K. Phillip Taylor, ed., *Trial Advocacy: Strategic Considerations in Persuasion* (Orlando, Fla.: Institute for Study of the Trial, 1980), 22.

[59]Tom Riley, "The Opening Statement: Winning at the Outset," *American Journal of Trial Advocacy* 3 (1979), 233–234.

[60]Carl I. Hovland, Irving L. Janis, and Harold H. Kelley, *Communication and Persuasion* (New Haven: Yale University Press, 1953), 290.

[61]Philip G. Zimbardo and Floyd L. Ruch, *Psychology and Life* (Glenview, Ill.: Scott, Foresman, 1975), 232–273.

[62]Douglas Ehninger et al., *Principles and Types of Speech Communication* (Glenview, Ill.: Scott, Foresman, 1986), 43–47.

[63]Shelly Chaiken and Alice H. Eagly, "Communication Modality as a Determinant of Message Persuasiveness and Message Comprehension," *Journal of Personality and Social Psychology* 34 (1976), 605–614.

[64]Decof, op. cit., 1–37.

[65]V. Hale Starr, "From the Communication Profession: Communication Strategies and Research Needs on Opening Statements and Closing Arguments," in Ronald J. Matlon and

Richard J. Crawford, eds., *Communication Strategies in the Practice of Lawyering* (Annandale, Va.: Speech Communication Association, 1983), 440.

[66]Robert J. Jossen, "Opening Statements: Win It in the Opening," *The Docket* (Spring 1986), 13.

[67]Edward T. Hall, *The Hidden Dimension* (New York: Doubleday, 1969), chap. 10.

[68]Ehninger et al., op. cit., 277.

[69]Eckhard A. Hess, "Attitude and Pupil Size," *Scientific American* (April 1965), 46–54.

[70]Kenneth Friedman, "Learning the Arabs' Silent Language: Edward J. Hall Interviewed," *Psychology Today* (August 1979), 46–47.

[71]Adapted from Lawrence J. Smith and Loretta A. Malandro, *Courtroom Communication Strategies* (New York: Kluwer, 1985), 57–64.

[72]Morton Cooper, "The Impressive Voice in the Courtroom," *Trial* (July 1979), 53.

[73]Crawford, op. cit., 11.

[74]Stern, op. cit., 323.

[75]Judges, unlike juries, occasionally interrupt an opening and ask attorneys for clarification. There are times, in fact, when the opening becomes a running colloquy between the judge and attorney in bench trials. Martin W. Littleton, "Opening to the Court or Jury," in Harry Bodin, ed., *Civil Litigation and Trial Techniques* (New York: Practicing Law Institute), 310.

[76]John C. Elam, "Persuasion in the Opening Statement: The Defendant's Approach," in Grace C. Holmes, ed., *Persuasion: The Key to Damages* (Ann Arbor, Mich.: The Institute of Continuing Legal Education, 1969), 97.

[77]William A. Trine, "Motivating Jurors Through Opening Statements," *Trial* (December 1982), 83.

[78]Donald E. Vinson and Philip K. Anthony, "Stating Your Case, Making Your Case," *Barrister* (Winter 1983), 16.

[79]Carl I. Hovland, "Summary and Implications," in Carl I. Hovland et al., eds., *The Order of Presentation in Persuasion* (New Haven: Yale University Press, 1957), 139.

[80]F. H. Lund, "The Psychology of Belief: The Law of Primacy in Persuasion," *Journal of Abnormal and Social Psychology* 20 (1925), 183–191.

[81]Carl I. Hovland, E. H. Campbell, and T. Brock, "The Effects of 'Commitment' on Opinion Change Following Communication," in Carl I. Hovland et al., eds., *The Order of Presentation in Persuasion* (New Haven: Yale University Press, 1957), 23–32.

[82]Solomon E. Asch, "Forming Impressions of Personality," *Journal of Abnormal and Social Psychology* 41 (1946), 258–290.

[83]A. S. Luchins, "Primacy-Recency in Impression Formation," in Carl I. Hovland et al., eds., *The Order of Presentation in Persuasion* (New Haven: Yale University Press, 1957), 33–61.

[84]Vernon A. Stone, "A Primacy Effect in Decision-Making by Jurors," *Journal of Communication* 19 (1969), 239–247.

[85]Richard T. Marshall, "The Telling Opening Statement," *Practical Lawyer* 19 (1973), 32.

[86]Norman H. Anderson, "Primacy Effects in Personality Impression Formation Using a Generalized Order Effect Paradigm," *Journal of Personality and Social Psychology* 2 (1965), 1–9.

[87]Interference is contradictory information. There is basically nothing to contradict the plaintiff's or prosecutor's opening statement. However, the defense's opening is full of inconsistent information, which people tend to discount or give lower weight or truth probability. It is easier to discount later information than it is to change the impression created by the initial material. Norman H. Anderson and Ann Jacobsen, "Effect of Stimulus Inconsistency and Discounting Instructions in Personality Impression Formation," *Journal of Personality and Social Psychology* 2 (1965), 531–539.

[88]Martin F. Kaplan, "Context Effects in Impression Formation: The Weighted Averaging Versus the Meaning-Change Formulation," *Journal of Personality and Social Psychology* 19 (1971), 92–99; Robert S. Wyer, Jr., and Stanley F. Watson, "Context Effects in Impression Formation," *Journal of Personality and Social Psychology* 12 (1969), 22–33.

[89]For an elaboration of these three variables, see Robert E. Lana, "Controversy of the Topic and the Order of Presentation in Persuasive Communications," *Psychological Reports* (1963), 163–170; Robert E. Lana, "Familiarity and the Order of Presentation of Persuasive

Communication," *Journal of Abnormal and Social Psychology* 62 (1961), 573–577; Robert E. Lana, "Interest, Media, and Order Effects in Persuasive Communications," *Journal of Psychology* 56 (1963), 9–13.

[90]William C. Costopoulos, "Persuasion in the Courtroom," *Duquesne Law Review* 10 (1972), 394.

[91]Harvey Cromwell, "The Relative Effect on Audience Attitude of the First Versus the Second Argumentative Speech of a Series," *Speech Monographs* 17 (1950), 105–122.

[92]Robert G. Lawson, "The Law of Primacy in the Criminal Courtroom," *Journal of Social Psychology* 77 (1969), 121–131.

[93]Robert G. Lawson, "Order of Presentation as a Factor in Jury Persuasion," *Kentucky Law Journal* 56 (1967–1968), 523–555.

8
CHAPTER
EVIDENCE

FUNCTION AND NATURE OF EVIDENCE

EVIDENCE RELEVANCY AND ADMISSIBILITY

NONTESTIMONIAL EVIDENCE
Depositions / Documentary Proof / Demonstrative Material

The evidentiary process at trial works in the following way. After opening statements, the prosecution or the plaintiff opens by presenting its witnesses and other evidence. These witnesses are subject to direct examination by the prosecutor or plaintiff. Whenever attorneys examine their own witnesses, that is, witnesses for their side, the examination is direct. Then the witnesses face cross-examination by the theoretically unfriendly defense lawyer. Cross-examination questions and answers are designed either to secure admissions that will help the cross-examiner's case or to discredit the witness's story.

After direct examination and cross-examination, periods of redirect and recross follow. The prosecutor or plaintiff may conduct a redirect examination to deal with matters raised during defense questioning. In turn, the defense may deal with redirect during a recross examination. When prosecutor's or plaintiff's attorneys have finished the presentation of all their witnesses (called the case-in-chief), the defense then presents its case by offering evidence. The procedure for presenting the defense's evidence is the same as it was for the prosecutor or plaintiff. This chapter and the one that follows analyze the role evidence plays in the drama of a courtroom trial.

FUNCTION AND NATURE OF EVIDENCE

In order to reach decisions in court, judges and juries must be finders of fact. Evidence, then, is anything offered in court to guide the judge or jury in deciding the relative truth or falsity of a fact at issue. Evidence originates from sources other than the lawyers and is offered in support of the lawyers' claims or issues. The presentation of evidence, mainly through a question and answer format, constitutes the bulk of any trial. So, it is important that "facts are communicated effectively [in order to give the] . . . decision-makers . . . the information necessary to make informed judgments."[1]

Does evidence really persuade jurors? Studies of the effects of evidence, done outside courtroom settings, show that there are significant attitudinal differences favoring the persuasive effects of speeches containing good evidence over speeches without evidence.[2] This is particularly true when "the source is initially perceived to be moderate-to-low credible, when the message is well delivered, and when the audience has little or no prior familiarity with the evidence included or similar evidence."[3] This is not to say that other factors in the courtroom situation might not also be important, but research does point to the significance of having evidence serve as the raw material of proof in legal settings.

What does evidence do when it persuades? Research shows that evidence is "both a topic-related variable (when it has an effect, it affects attitude toward topic) and a source-related variable (it affects attitude toward source . . .)."[4] The persuasive function of evidence in general settings has been explained as follows:

Evidence enhances the learning process in listeners, thereby strengthening what they already know and feel. Evidence enables them to perceive things in a new way. . . . It gives friendly audiences support for their own beliefs, whereas discrepant evidence gives unfriendly audiences a chance to weigh their opposing evidence against the persuader's evidence. It provides neutral audiences with information that might lead to the conclusion, "I never realized this was so important; you've caused me to think about it in a new way." Evidence can give a sense of "logic" to persuasion and enhances the chance of an audience making a logical choice, for its use appeals to the rational nature of people.[5]

If evidence works this way generally, imagine how potent it must be in trial settings, where juries are constantly reminded to base their decisions on the evidence alone.

To better comprehend how evidence is used in jury or judge decision making, we must understand that there are two somewhat different viewpoints on the nature of evidence. One viewpoint is that evidence is used to *recreate* or *reconstruct* events in the minds of a judge and jury. For example, suppose two people were present when a contract was signed between them three years ago. Now the contract is in dispute, and a trial ensues that focuses on the interpretation of that written agreement. As evidence, the contract is read, both individuals testify regarding their understanding of the meaning of the agreement, and subsequent documents arising out of the agreement (e.g., budgets, memoranda) are presented and explained. This information is supposed to show to the jury what was on the minds of the contract parties when the document was signed. In other words, the evidence allows us to discover the truth of an event that took place three years ago.

Another viewpoint is that the presentation of evidence is a *creative* or *constructive* process, that is, that legal evidence constructs the conception of an event that best serves the needs of justice today. Events do not just happen as a matter of truth or fact. Events are subject to interpretation by the parties involved, and they all may have different interpretations of what took place. There may be a dispute over the paths two cars took in a personal injury accident case. There may be disagreement over road conditions involving the same accident. And so it goes. Juries and judges do not recreate truly what happened at that accident; they only interpret and then create a situation in order to best meet the needs of justice.

Regardless of your viewpoint regarding the nature of evidence in court (and I must admit that I endorse the latter approach), evidence becomes "fact." Often, conflicting evidence must be resolved. For instance, several interpretations of the facts would have been possible if Jack Ruby had gone to trial for murdering Lee Harvey Oswald. The television cameras pointed toward the "fact" that Ruby

was the killer. Yet, evidence accumulated by Melvin Belli, Ruby's defense counsel, indicated that (a) Ruby was having tea with an elderly lady about fifty miles from the scene of the shooting; (b) Ruby was at the scene, but was quickly handed the gun by a young college student who actually fired the shot; (c) the anti-Semitic police were really responsible for killing Oswald and they were out to get Ruby, a Jew; or (d) Ruby shot in self-defense because Oswald was about to attack him. As you can see, evidence often conflicts, and it is up to judge or jury to determine which evidence best constructs reality. These various recollections of past events constitute the evidence out of which facts are constructed.

EVIDENCE RELEVANCY AND ADMISSIBILITY

All of the information gathered to construct reality in court cannot necessarily be presented to a jury. Certain rules of evidence are applied to the information to make certain that it is both relevant and admissible.[6] Let us look at some of these rules in a nutshell.

Evidence is relevant when it has something to do with what is to be proven in court; that is, relevant evidence must have probative value. When something is too remote to be worthy of consideration, then the evidence is immaterial, or not relevant. For example, it is irrelevant in a larceny trial to try to prove that a defendant had poor grades in high school, unless those grades have some sort of probative value in relation to the issues at hand. If information about grades has no demonstrable bearing on the taking of property with criminal intent (larceny), it is deemed irrelevant and cannot be presented to the court. To hear about the character of someone when character is not an issue is irrelevant.

Legally irrelevant evidence might be inflammatory, confusing, or time wasting, and this is why it is kept out of the trial. After all, facts should not be used as a ruse to prejudice a jury or to draw their attention away from the real issues of a case. Nor should facts confuse the issues or cause undue delay, as through the needless presentation of cumulative evidence.[7] Logical and legal rules of relevance, then, are the very spirit of rationality in the courtroom.[8]

Rules of evidence admissibility further govern what can and cannot be heard in court. For instance, the source of the evidence must be *competent*. Here are some examples. Expert witnesses cannot be considered competent to testify until a foundation has been laid that demonstrates their expertise. Children can be declared incompetent, a decision based not on their age, but on their memory, their level of intelligence, and their ability to separate truth from falsehood.[9] A privileged communication, such as that between attorney and client, physician and patient, or member of the clergy and parishioner, can be declared incompetent by a judge after a lawyer objects to the presentation of such information. A mentally ill person without the ability to understand the proceedings, observe, remember, or narrate is generally thought to be an incompetent witness. Illegally obtained information, such as an unauthorized wiretap, an inappropriate search and seizure, or a coerced confession, is incompetent under the exclusionary rule. Except as provided by statute, every person is thought to be competent as a witness and can testify in court unless incompetence is proven. "Any objections to the competency of the witness to give evidence must be made before the witness commences his testimony, provided that the disqualification is known to counsel at that time."[10]

Next, *hearsay* evidence is usually inadmissible. The hearsay rule is baffling, complex, and difficult to apply. Hearsay is a report that is at least secondhand information on what someone did or said.[11] There is an old party game in which someone whispers a story into another person's ear and then the story is passed down the line so that everyone can hear how distorted it gets by the time the whole group hears it from the last person. This game may liven a party, but such stories cannot be told in court. Witnesses are not to testify in court about what they have heard, but only about what they know to be true. It is unlawful to say, "A told me that Z occurred."

The reason for the hearsay rule is that such information is typically not subject to cross-examination. The only way to cross-examine the evidence is to question the original source of the statement. The Sixth Amendment says that an accused person has the right to confront an opposing witness, but this right is lost when hearsay is presented. As with so many rules, however, there are exceptions to disallowing hearsay from being heard in court. Hearsay information can be heard when the original source of the information is unavailable (e.g., the person is dead or too ill to testify). Hearsay information can also be heard in court if it can be verified by some primary or original source. These two exceptions are frequently granted, although the jury is advised that they are hearing hearsay information.

Finally, *circumstantial* evidence may be inadmissible. Circumstantial evidence is inferential or indirect evidence. The defendant's fingerprints from a burglarized house, bloodstains from the door handle of a murder suspect's car, and the sudden wealth of a store clerk suspected of theft are all illustrations of circumstantial evidence. If a local sheriff peers through a window and observes people playing poker and wagering money, he has directly observed gambling. However, if that sheriff legally breaks into that room, but sees only playing cards, money, and burning cigarettes in the ashtrays, he may infer that someone has been gambling there recently, but the evidence is indirect or circumstantial. Direct or eyewitness evidence is almost invariably admissible so long as it is relevant. However, circumstantial evidence is admissible from a witness only after a foundation has been laid to satisfy a judge that the witness can form reasonable opinions, that is, opinions that are rationally based on clear perceptions. In cases in which such circumstantial evidence is allowed, the jury is once again instructed that they are hearing evidence that is inferential in nature.

Naturally, lots of circumstantial evidence is presented by witnesses. For instance, dimensions can be inferential ("I think the car was approximately fifteen feet away from the curb"). Property values can be inferential ("The stolen goods amount to roughly two thousand dollars"). Identification of handwriting can be inferential ("That certainly looks like my boss's signature"). Testimony about the physical condition of another can be inferential ("Since he was staggering and had bloodshot eyes, I assumed he had been drinking"). Lots of evidence in court is circumstantial, and it usually requires the laying of a foundation in order for the personal opinion to be admissible.

Rules of evidence, then, are designed to keep the jury from hearing certain evidence, on the grounds that such information is irrelevant or legally inadmissible. These rules "represent the most careful attempt to control the process of communication to be found outside the laboratory."[12] The underlying premise of evidence rules is to be fair and objective to both sides. What can the jury safely hear and see? Judges have a good deal of discretion in what can and cannot be presented. In nonjury cases, the tendency is to de-emphasize the rules; in jury cases, the rules tend to be more closely followed. Attorneys must know how the rules of evidence will be applied because these rules "affect persuasion in a dramatic way, for they are the rules that determine whether evidence on which to base a persuasive argument can be produced."[13]

NONTESTIMONIAL EVIDENCE

Once evidence is determined to be relevant and admissible, it can then be presented in court in one of two forms—*nontestimonial* or *testimonial*. Nontestimonial evidence comes in the form of depositions, documentary proof, and real or demonstrative material that the jury can see. Testimonial evidence comes out of the mouths of witnesses. Testimonial evidence will be discussed in Chapter 9.

Depositions

Depositions are used as evidence when witnesses are unavailable for trial. A deposition may be used in place of a witness who is unavailable because of "death or illness, as well as any witness who cannot be found or is beyond the jurisdiction's subpoena power."[14] Depositions from an adversary's witnesses may also be used during cross-examination, with the possibility of weakening an opposition's case. If a deposition is used for the latter purpose, counsel says, "Your Honor, at this time I wish to read to the jury certain portions of Mr. Davis's deposition, taken on March 5, 1986, in the office of his attorney." Then those parts of the deposition are read which will weaken a witness's testimony (e.g., by showing a possible contradiction between what was said earlier and what is said on the stand). Depositions were discussed as a method of discovery in Chapter 3.

From a communication standpoint, two matters must be considered before an attorney uses a deposition at trial. First, if depositions are read aloud rather than presented to the jury in writing, they should not be read aloud by a single attorney. This can prove to be a deadly dull one-person form of human communication. The oral soliloquy should be replaced by surrogate witnesses who are called to the stand to play the roles of the persons who were the deponents. They read the script with the attorney, going through the questions and answers verbatim. Because people are influenced as much by how a person says something as by what the person says, surrogates should be chosen for the rhetorical and dramatic impact they might have on the jury. They should also be roughly the same age and sex as the original deponents.

Second, the judge in chambers should be advised which parts of a deposition are going to be read by counsel if the entire document is not to be read aloud. Opposing counsel can always object or designate other parts that they want to read.[15] "To avoid interruptions from objections in the presentation counsel should seek an *in limine* ruling on all objections to the deposition testimony to be offered."[16] Interruptions can reduce the dramatic impact of the deposition presentation. A further discussion of depositions used during cross-examination will be covered in Chapter 9.

Documentary Proof

Documents include such papers and records as tax returns, deeds, birth certificates, death certificates, letters, business records, leases, wills, and personal checks. Before any document is admissible as evidence, it must be authenticated for the court. "Authentication is a legal process of proof that is designed to establish the genuineness of the writing."[17] There is a well-defined procedure for the authentication of documentary proof in all courts. Generally, counsel who wants to present documentary evidence first has it marked for identification; that is, he or she asks the clerk of the court to place a mark on the material so that it can be used for future reference. The document is then shown to opposing counsel for inspection. Barring objection, the document is examined and authenticated by a witness on the stand who is familiar with the material. For instance, a witness authen-

ticating a contract might say that he or she saw Mr. X place his signature on that document, now recognizes and identifies Mr. X's signature, and claims that the contract is in the same condition now as when it was executed. This is called the *past-recollection-recorded* technique of introducing documents. Documents may also be introduced by an *official records* method, in which certificates from official document custodians take the place of live authenticators.

Once authenticated, the document is again marked by the court reporter, and counsel moves for the admission of it into evidence. The document is neither seen by the jury nor thought of as evidence until it is marked as such by the court clerk and approved by the judge. Frequently, adverse counsel will object to having a certain document admitted as evidence and will ask the court to rule on its admissibility. If it is admitted as evidence, the jury can have access to the written material during their deliberations.

From a communication standpoint, several considerations must be made. One matter to consider is that the documentary evidence must not overkill. Frequently there is too much detail in a particular document for an attorney to want it admitted as evidence. The major information easily gets lost. In those cases, it may be best to have a witness read to the jury only the important part of the document, rather than to have the jury view the entire piece. Naturally, the material should be read with appropriate voice inflection, pausing, and emphasis.

Another consideration is that the document may have both favorable and unfavorable information in it. A tax return may show charitable contributions to some group the jury might oppose. In a case such as this, it is strategically wise not to present the information from the tax return as documentary proof, but rather through witness testimony that refers only to the favorable information.

Some final considerations:[18] (1) since the most effective documents are those that relate to the judge's instructions, these essential documents should be distinguished from unimportant ones; (2) good documents should be exploited by having counsel read them aloud, by handing individual copies to each juror, or by blowing them up to billboard size by using an overhead projector and showing them again during closing argument; (3) in cases in which numerous documents are to be presented, an attempt should be made to get the less important ones introduced as a group in a few seconds with little fanfare rather than to drag out a trial with dull testimony about lifeless bits of paper.[19] Too many documents ineptly presented "can figuratively drive the jury to embrace the opposition's side. A case can be destroyed by the unnecessary use of reams of complicated documents that will both bore and confuse the jury."[20]

Demonstrative Material

Demonstrative materials, or visual exhibits, are physical illustrations of facts presented.[21] Demonstrative material has been used in the courtroom for years, especially by personal injury lawyers. It provides a silent visual stimulus for a jury, which is often more damning than any oral stimulus. One writer notes that we learn 85 percent from sight, 10 percent from hearing, and 5 percent from touch, taste, and smell.[22] So there is some merit to the saying "One picture is worth a thousand words," and attorneys should get in the habit of becoming courtroom Rembrandts. Several types of interesting and potentially exciting demonstrative exhibits are available to counsel.

Courtroom demonstrations are one possibility. For instance, a personal injury plaintiff's attorney may ask the client to step down, stand before the jury box, and show the jury scars on his legs. This in-court demonstration or performance can be objected to by adverse counsel as histrionics or theatrics. In a number of jurisdictions, injured plaintiffs cannot be personally exhibited to the jury.[23] Nevertheless, when such demonstrations are allowed, they have persuasive potential.

Real or physical objects may come to the jury as a form of demonstrative material. Real evidence is the thing itself. Scientific evidence, such as fingerprints, footprints, blood samples, bloodstains, and pieces of hair or cloth, may be introduced at trial. In a murder case, prosecutors might want to qualify as evidence the weapon that caused a death. Should real objects not be available, counsel might consider using closely similar items. For example, a bomb identical to one that exploded and caused death, or an electrical switch like one that caused a personal injury, may be presented to a jury if the objects are sufficiently similar in nature.[24]

The jury view is another kind of demonstrative material. The jury view is essentially presence at the scene, "observing places or objects material to the litigation but which cannot feasibly be brought into, or reproduced, in the courtroom."[25] The courts disagree over whether or not a jury view is really evidence,[26] but it certainly is demonstrative. Viewing the scene in which an incident took place allows jurors to get a sharp perspective on what happened there.

Chalkboard drawings by witnesses can be used, although they "lead to difficulty in making a record, preserving the exhibit for review, and even preserving the exhibit during the trial."[27] Quick erasures and accidental smudges are common. Therefore, blackboard information is the least preferred form of demonstrative material. If the chalkboard sketch is to be preserved, it can be photographed for the record.

Photographs and slides are also forms of demonstrative material. They have been used in court for more than a hundred years, as indicated by the 1875 trial photo of the scene of a Pelham, Massachusetts, accident, in which a plaintiff's horse and buggy had driven over the side of an unguarded embankment.[28] Photographs and slides may be of such things as holes in a road, damage to two vehicles, a patient in traction, or a stairwell involved in a slip-and-fall accident. In many ways, photographs are superior to slides, because they can more easily enter the jury room afterward. Photographs are admissible as long as they can be authenticated, that is, shown to be substantially identical with the actual condition in controversy. For instance, photographs taken after the actual time an event occurred must not contain scene changes that misrepresent the relevant condition. Additionally, the color in a photograph or slide must be fair and impartial, although this condition is difficult to achieve. One study found that plaintiffs received greater monetary damages when the jury viewed color slides of an injury than when they did not.[29] In another study, color photographs yielded greater monetary awards to the severely injured plaintiff than did black-and-white photographic evidence.[30] If a judge rules that a color photo of a nude victim in a pool of blood is too gruesome, inflammatory, and prejudicial, counsel should be ready to have a black-and-white photo of the same scene available. On the other hand, it can be argued that "if photographs are being used to depict damage to an automobile, black-and-white photographs could be misleading in that they may tend to minimize the true extent of the damage by reducing contrast and colors."[31] Professional forensic photographers are available to give advice to counsel; names of photographers may be obtained from the Evidence Photographers International Council in Maplewood, New Jersey.[32]

Videotapes and motion pictures are used more and more at trial to portray "a day in the life" of a seriously injured accident victim. This material can be quite graphic for juries. Videotape and film can additionally be used to show an expert conducting an experiment, such as a ballistics test or an automobile brake test—a much more cautious approach than having such experiments actually conducted in court. Tape or film can also be used to demonstrate a traffic signal sequence, the operation of heavy machinery, or any other action that may be important to the case, even though such material is potentially deceptive and objectionable because of inaccuracies from lens settings, film interruptions, elimination of unfavorable frames, and so forth.

X rays and computer techniques constitute other forms of demonstrative material. To complement a physician's oral testimony describing a fractured femur, an X ray can be a vivid portrayal of the injury. Computer-generated reconstructions can show the movements of many objects in a three-dimensional world and can be used to show what happened in a midair collision. The computer is programmed with aircraft velocities, headings, rates of descent or climb, and so forth. Jurors view the reconstructed animation of the accident on a television monitor hooked up to the computer.[33]

Three-dimensional models can be effective visual aids. They may or may not be dismantled. They may or may not have moving parts attached to them in order to show critical movements. Models are especially useful in representing a large object, showing spatial relationships or topographical features, or demonstrating a complex mechanical matter to a jury, such as the aerodynamic nature of an airplane wing during a howling snow and ice storm. Probably the most commonly used models in court are reproductions of the human skeleton and its organs.

Diagrams, in the form of charts, graphs, or maps, have potential as well. A poster-size chart or graph equipped with transparent acetate overlays allows several witnesses to illustrate their testimony with grease pencils. Charts of computations help in the presentation of numerous statistical data and are especially good when calculating how the amount of damages is determined. Bar, line, or pie graphs can show relationships within sets of figures. Charts can also be used to visually summarize case facts into a coherent whole. Maps may be admitted so that the jury may better understand something like the floor plan of a robbed bank, rather than having to fill in details from their own banking experiences. If a magnetic board map is used, it is convenient to show how people moved about in the bank during a robbery. Charts, maps, and graphs are ideally designed to show, in the simplest terms, complicated facts to the court. This means, then, that the diagram should be self-explanatory and that labels and other words should be kept to a minimum.[34] Finally, colors on diagrams must be carefully selected. For instance, if an accident involves automobiles, the drawing should contain the true colors of the vehicles.

Several aspects of the presentation of demonstrative material will be addressed next. Visual material should be concealed until it is needed. "Where greater dramatic impact is desirable, such evidence may be located prominently in the courtroom but covered to conceal its identity, heightening the jury's curiosity and fascination until it is finally to be unveiled."[35] Timing may be critical, too. Good advice to follow is that explanatory, run-of-the-mill visuals should be presented by witnesses early in the trial whereas emotionally evocative evidence should come near the conclusion. If an emotional effect is desired, it should come close to the time when a jury will render its verdict.[36]

Witnesses should be thoroughly prepared to use visual aids at trial. After all, the witnesses have to be able to put exhibits into words. Dry runs with the witnesses using the material are useful. Also, if a witness is to draw something in court, counsel must be certain that the witness has the ability to draw accurately and clearly, or else that person may lose credibility in the minds of the jury. There is always some risk in having a witness create a visual aid in court.

Once a visual aid is unveiled by a witness, pointers should be used so that the judge and jury can see what is happening. Demonstrative exhibits should either be large enough or blown up enough for the entire jury to see, or multiple copies should be made so that each juror can have his or her own copy. If the exhibit is enlarged, transportation, storage, and use factors must be considered. When referring to demonstrative material at trial, a lawyer and a witness should choose words to accompany the presentation that will have meaning to an appellate court if they peruse the trial transcript. For instance, "right here" is not as clear for the record as "at the point on plaintiff's exhibit G where I will place a red X on the map." Finally, visuals should be used not only by witnesses, but again by lawyers during closing arguments in order to ensure the full persuasive value of the material.

In general, demonstrative material should be used only if it directly aids in conveying information. It should educate and simplify. Demonstrative material should not be used if it is merely spectacular and has little relevance to what juries must resolve. Sometimes, the temptation exists to use an elaborate demonstration to illustrate a minor point, but this may only serve to "convince the jury that counsel is more interested in conducting a three-ring circus than in helping them reach the correct solution to a difficult problem."[37]

Because the courts have recognized the persuasive effect that exhibits have on juries, they require a rigorous foundation to qualify demonstrative material for use at trial.[38] Qualifying demonstrative exhibits for admissibility depends on their relevance, authenticity, the hearsay rule, and the best-evidence rule. To have relevance, the exhibit must help the jury better understand the case without creating undue confusion or prejudice. To have authenticity, the exhibit must be a fair and accurate representation of, shall we say, a highway intersection. Authenticity is affirmed by a testifying witness. The hearsay rule says that an exhibit cannot contain hearsay, that is, that the witness producing the demonstrative evidence must be available for questioning to test the reliability of the exhibit. The best-evidence rule calls for the strongest or most authentic evidence available. The rule applies to documents, films, videotapes, recordings, and X rays. It is a competence rule designed to prevent fraud, and it says that the content must be proven by the medium itself or else the content must be adequately explained to the court. In all cases, it is less difficult to qualify visual material as an exhibit for illustrative purposes than it is as evidence. When visual material is only an exhibit, it cannot be taken into the jury room during deliberations.

Research based on the principles of Gestalt psychology shows that visual material increases attention, adds clarity to a message, and improves perception, comprehension, and retention.[39] Furthermore, visual aids that supplement, not supplant, oral messages positively affect both the speaker's credibility and the audience's attitude change.[40] In general, "factfinders give greater weight to visualizations than verbalizations."[41] Studies that have examined how much verbal testimony a jury will recall after hearing it have shown "that as little as twenty percent is retained for a period of twenty-four hours. The same studies have shown that better than fifty percent of what a juror sees is retained for that period of time, and some go as high as seventy percent."[42] It is obvious that if there is a way to use nontestimonial evidence, a lawyer should seize the opportunity to do so.

Whatever medium an attorney wishes to use as nontestimonial evidence—depositions, documentary proof, or demonstrative material—its basic purpose is to teach, to allow greater comprehension and memory, and to allow a greater understanding by the court and jury. In addition, nontestimonial evidence has a persuasive effect insofar as it enhances the credibility of both the speaker and the speaker's ideas. The value of using nontestimonial evidence in court cannot be underestimated.

Notes

[1]"Civil Procedure—Directing a Verdict in Favor of the Party With the Burden of Proof," Casenotes, *Wake Forest Law Review* 16 (1980), 607–620.

[2]Robert S. Cathcart, "An Experimental Study of the Relative Effectiveness of Four Methods of Presenting Evidence," *Speech Monographs* 22 (1955), 227–233; Thomas B. Harte, "The Effects of Evidence in Persuasive Communication," *Central States Speech Journal* 27 (1976), 42–46; James C. McCroskey, "The Effects of Evidence in Persuasive Communication," *Western Speech* 31 (1967), 189–199; James C. McCroskey, "A Summary of Experimental Research on the Effects of Evidence in Persuasive Communication," *Quarterly Journal of Speech* 55 (1969), 169–176; James C. McCroskey, "The Effects of Evidence as an Inhibitor of Counter-Persuasion," *Speech Monographs* 37 (1970), 188–194.

[3]McCroskey, "Summary of Research," 175.

[4]Charles Larson and Robert Sanders, "Faith, Mystery, and Data: An Analysis of 'Scientific' Studies of Persuasion," *Quarterly Journal of Speech* 61 (1975), 187.

[5]Victoria O'Donnell and June Kable, *Persuasion: An Interactive-Dependency Approach* (New York: Random House, 1982), 139–140.

[6]These rules vary somewhat from jurisdiction to jurisdiction and undergo continuous revision.

[7]Ronald L. Carlson, Edward J. Imwinkelried, and Edward J. Kionka, *Materials for the Study of Evidence* (Charlottesville, Va.: Michie, 1983), 237–242.

[8]Lee Loevinger, "Facts, Evidence, and Legal Proof," *Western Reserve Law Review* 9 (1958), 164.

[9]If a child's competence is in doubt, the trial judge conducts a private examination of the child. Only when the judge is satisfied that the child understands and will probably testify truthfully will the child be allowed to take the stand.

[10]Bernard Manning, *The Criminal Trial* (South Berlin, Mass.: Research Publishing, 1975), 77.

[11]James W. McElhaney, *Trial Notebook* (Chicago: American Bar Association, 1981), 63.

[12]Edward W. Cleary, "Evidence as a Problem in Communication," *Vanderbilt Law Review* 5 (1952), 282.

[13]Charles W. Joiner, "Rules of Evidence: Do They Help or Hinder Persuasion?" in Grace W. Holmes, ed., *Persuasion: The Key to Damages* (Ann Arbor, Mich.: The Institute of Continuing Legal Education, 1969), 186.

[14]Thomas A. Mauet, *Fundamentals of Trial Techniques* (Boston: Little, Brown, 1980), 171.

[15]James Jeans, *Trial Advocacy* (St. Paul, Minn.: West Publishing, 1975), 226.

[16]Jay S. Blumenkopf, "Deposition Strategy and Tactics," *American Journal of Trial Advocacy* 5 (1981), 250.

[17]Julian R. Hanley and Wayne W. Schmidt, *Legal Aspects of Criminal Evidence* (Berkeley, Calif.: McCutchan, 1977), 246.

[18]Janeen Kerper, "Documents: Keeping Judge and Jury Awake," *Litigation* (Spring 1981), 18–20.

[19]Rule 1006, Federal Rules of Evidence, states, "The contents of voluminous writings, recordings, or photographs which cannot be conveniently examined in court may be presented in the form of a chart, summary, or calculation. The originals, or duplicates, shall be made available for examination or copying, or, both, by other parties at a reasonable time and place. The judge may order that they be produced in court."

[20]Robert McFigg, Ralph C. McCullough II, and James L. Underwood, *Civil Trial Manual* (Los Angeles: Joint Committee on Legal Education of the American Law Institute and the American Bar Association, 1974), 285.

[21]Thomas A. Heffernan, "Effective Use of Demonstrative Evidence: 'Seeing is Believing,'" *American Journal of Trial Advocacy* 5 (1982), 427.

[22]Thomas F. Parker, "Applied Psychology in Trial Practice," *Defense Law Journal* 7 (1960), 33.

[23]Melvin M. Belli, Sr., *Modern Trials,* vol. 4 (St. Paul, Minn.: West Publishing, 1982), 433.

[24]Francis Xavier Busch, *Trial Procedure Materials* (Indianapolis: Bobbs-Merrill, 1961), 190.

[25]Douglas M. Moore, Jr., "Basic Practice Guide for Demonstrative, Experimental and Scientific Evidence," *Insurance Counsel Journal* 50 (1983), 279.

[26]Compare *Snyder v. Massachusetts,* 291 U.S. 97, 54 S.Ct. 330, 78 L.Ed. 674 (1934) and *Beatty v. Depue,* 103 N.W.2d 187 (S.D. 1960).

[27]J. Eric Smithburn and James H. Seckinger, "Visual Evidence," *Litigation* (Winter 1983), 34.

[28]*Blair v. Inhabitants of Pelham,* 118 Mass. 420 (1875).

[29]Edward Oliver and William Griffit, "Emotional Arousal and 'Objective' Judgment," *Bulletin of the Psychonomic Society* 8 (1976), 399–400.

[30]Denise H. Whalen and Fletcher A. Blanchard, "Effects of Photographic Evidence on Mock Juror Judgment," *Journal of Applied Social Psychology* 12 (1982), 30–41.

[31]Mark A. Dombroff, "Utilizing Photographs as Demonstrative Evidence," *Trial* (December 1982), 73.

[32]Larry Shavelson, "Photography as Demonstrative Evidence," *Trial* (February 1984), 42–45.

[33]Mark A. Dombroff, "Demonstrative Evidence: Computer Reconstruction Techniques," *Trial* (July 1982), 52–54.

[34]Jonathan R. Crane, "Graphic Testimony and Presentations," *Trial Diplomacy Journal* (Winter 1982–83), 23.

[35]Bruce T. Wallace, "Demonstrative Evidence: Some Practical Pointers," *Trial* (October 1976), 52.

[36]George Vetter, *Successful Civil Litigation* (Englewood Cliffs, N.J.: Prentice-Hall, 1977), 241.

[37]Ralph C. McCullough II and James L. Underwood, "How to Prepare and Use Demonstrative Evidence in a Civil Trial," *Practical Lawyer* (March 1, 1982), 20.

[38]Smithburn and Seckinger, op. cit., 33.

[39]Rudolph Arnheim, *Visual Thinking* (Berkeley: University of California Press, 1969); John M. Kennedy, *A Psychology of Picture Perception* (San Francisco: Jossey-Bass, 1974); Leonard Zusne, *Visual Perception of Form* (New York: Academic Press, 1976).

[40]William J. Seiler, "The Effect of Visual Materials on Attitudes, Credibility, and Retention," *Speech Monographs* 38 (1971), 331–334.

[41]Richard M. Markus, "A Theory of Trial Advocacy," *Tulane Law Review* 56 (1981), 114–115.

[42]Joseph Kelner and Francis E. McGovern, *Successful Litigation Techniques: Student Edition* (New York: Matthew Bender, 1981), p. 12-2.

9

CHAPTER

EXAMINATION OF WITNESSES

TESTIMONIAL EVIDENCE: DIRECT EXAMINATION
Preparation of Witnesses / Communication Strategies
for the Attorney in Direct Examination

TESTIMONIAL EVIDENCE: CROSS-EXAMINATION
Nature and Scope / Waiving Cross-Examination /
Planning and Preparation / Adverse Witnesses /
Impeachment / Communication Strategies for the
Attorney in Cross-Examination

EXPERT WITNESSES

REDIRECT, RECROSS, AND OBJECTIONS

Clear and cogent facts never walk into a courtroom or fly in through the courthouse windows. They must be dragged into a trial through testimonial evidence. These facts constitute the script for the play that is about to unfold. They must be presented carefully and logically so that the case (the drama) is in an understandable and persuasive form for the judge and jury. The witnesses constitute the main cast of characters in the play. Attorneys serve as their directors. It is not enough for just the attorney to understand each witness's place in the overall scheme of proof; counsel must ensure that these witnesses communicate accurately and convincingly in court.

TESTIMONIAL EVIDENCE: DIRECT EXAMINATION

After trial counsel have outlined the plot for a case, they should determine which witnesses are needed to develop the drama. In what could be called the tryout phase, some lawyers assemble all the potential witnesses for a particular case in one place at one time. Basic case theme orientation and general advice about testifying are covered at this session. "Such a conference often results in the development of circumstances not previously learned by counsel, and, . . . it gives the witnesses confidence from the knowledge that others will also testify."[1] There are those lawyers who believe that the team conference makes for a more united front and less discrepancy in the overall narrative testimony.

There are also those counsel who think that the group session is dangerous. Opposing counsel at trial can accuse the other side of having established a "school for witnesses," in which each of them was instructed as to the subject of their testimony.[2] Some witnesses may be tempted to tailor their testimony to those of the other witnesses and then, on cross-examination, be forced into discrepancies. Or the group might start arguing with each other, thereby reducing confidence in the witnesses when a meeting of minds cannot be reached. Therefore, witness conferences prior to trial appear to have merit to some, but disadvantages for others.

Preparation of Witnesses

One important factor that permeates a trial is an atmosphere of tension. A trial is a dramatic undertaking. The litigants rely heavily on the outcome, running the risk of losing money, property, status, or freedom. The stakes are high. The issues are usually close and could be decided either way by a judge or jury. Furthermore, trials are inherently unpredictable. No matter how well witnesses have been prepared by attorneys, they may unknowingly blurt out answers that destroy their testimony or the entire case. Important witnesses may fail to show up. A major witness might turn out to be highly incoherent. Unpredictability abounds. Even the most experienced trial lawyer is under extreme pressure during the course of a trial. There is no way that the atmosphere of tension can be completely avoided.

However, careful pretrial preparation of witnesses minimizes the effect of courtroom tension on them. Louis Nizer once advised his colleagues as follows:

I hope you are not the kind of a lawyer who puts a witness on the stand relying upon the preparation which your assistant or associate has made and who has handed you a note as to what this witness will testify to. I hope you are not the kind of a lawyer who puts the witness on the stand after you have yourself perfunctorily examined him to determine the nature of his testimony.

If you are that kind of a lawyer, may I suggest that you are overlooking some of the elementary facts of life.

Put yourself in the position of the witness. He has never faced an audience before in his life.

Suddenly he is placed on a platform, and to his right sits a . . . justice with a black robe, which in itself is sufficient to put him in awe and in terror. To his left there are twelve jurors looking at him very skeptically and critically, and who examine every motion which he makes, as well as every word which he utters. In front of him are a sea of faces, and by this time he sees, out of the corner of his eyes, already dimmed, the leering faces of the defendant and his witnesses looking up at him. In front of those hostile faces he sees opposing counsel sitting anxiously on the edge of the seat. He imagines by this time that the cross-examiner is slowly sharpening a knife, waiting to spring at him and cut him to pieces.

And while all these confusing surrounding circumstances are pressing in upon him, and his blood is pounding in his head, you stand there presenting questions to him. It is surprising that he can even answer the first questions put to him by the court attendant: "What is your name and where do you live?" and if you expect him, in the light of these circumstances, to be descriptive, to be articulate, to be finely sensitive to a point that you wish him to develop—well, you are simply expecting too much from human nature. There is no use going to the restaurant during recess hour and complaining about your fool witness; how he made incredible answers against his own interest and in violation of the truth. The fault is yours and mine. If we put him on the stand without greater preparation and take that risk the fault is not his.[3]

Witness preparation is nothing new in litigation circles. In the 19th century, New York attorney William J. Fallon is said to have rehearsed witnesses in the carriage sheds near the White Plains courthouse. This practice caused James Fenimore Cooper to coin the phrase "horse-shedding the witness."[4] Although the term has a conspiratorial ring to it, witness preparation is not meant to be witness indoctrination. Instead, it refers to the enhancement of witness credibility in order to reach the ideal for each person who will take the stand.

What is the ideal witness? It is someone with high credibility, or what Aristotle called *ethos*. "Aristotle perceived ethos as a power-ful proof supplied by the source himself and through judgments made of his character, sagacity, and goodwill."[5] Years later, social psychologists replaced the term *ethos* with *source credibility*. Their research indicated that the reactions to a message are significantly affected by cues as to the communicator's expertness (authoritativeness, competence, experience, and training) and trustworthiness (friendliness, gentleness, fairness, hospitality, and ethicality). In other words, presentations tend to be judged more favorably when made by communicators with these characteristics than by those without them.[6] The authors of a book on persuasion note this link between ethos and attitude formation when they write,

If we assume that a persuasive interchange begins with a definite ethos of the persuader in the mind of the persuadee, then the utterances and actions of the persuader will be measured against this initial ethos. Actions and utterances will be constantly judged as consistent or inconsistent with expectations, and the credibility at the beginning of the interaction will be reinforced or changed as the message continues.[7]

Therefore, to enhance witness ethos, expertise and trustworthiness must be identified and highlighted during witness preparation.

Sometimes, strong witness credibility develops with relatively little advice from counsel; at other times, extensive witness coaching is necessary. The amount of time preparing a witness "will be directly related to the importance of the witness in the case, together with the amount of 'cleaning up' necessary to smooth over any undesirable characteristics he may have."[8] Insufficiently coached witnesses have little vitality, freshness, clarity, or spontaneity, and, therefore, they are easily disbelieved. On the other hand, overcoached witnesses focus awkwardly on memorizing exact words, not on an exact reporting of the events. They appear mechanical and untruthful on the stand and are disbelieved as well.

To make the best impression, witnesses should be "dignified without being painfully stiff, serious without being devoid of humor, flexible in their attitude, but positive in their statements."[9] So direct examination without coaching is a big gamble, but too much pretrial drilling is troublesome too.

What, then, constitutes effective pretrial witness preparation for direct examination? To begin, the lawyer should prepare an outline of the matters to be covered in direct examination. There is no better way to organize one's thoughts than to construct them on paper. The witness to be examined should be made aware of that outline. The witness should be handed, not a written copy of the exact questions that will be asked, but only a list of the topics to be covered. Once the list is presented to the witness, the lawyer should discuss the key points of the testimony with that person.

Generally, this discussion alone will constitute inadequate pretrial witness preparation. Also needed are practice sessions with each witness, preferably using videotaping and feedback.[10] These sessions should be cooperative ventures; that is, the lawyer should solicit witness input by asking, "Is there anything I've overlooked? Is there anything you think is particularly important?"[11] The practice sessions are designed to give witnesses a feel for the questioning experience. Giving them this familiarity can boost their confidence and, in turn, their credibility in court.[12] One recent experiment compared briefed, or coached, prosecution eyewitness testimony to the testimony of eyewitnesses who had received no preparation. Mock jurors viewing both types of testimony on videotape perceived higher witness confidence for briefed witnesses than for nonbriefed witnesses, and as a result, the percentage of guilty verdicts increased from 30.5 percent to 50.5 percent.[13]

The number of practice sessions needed depends on the perceived persuasiveness of the witness. In the case of a vital witness or a witness with obvious problems in communicating, counsel may find it necessary to go through this procedure many times before trial. Several factors related to jury appeal should be carefully monitored as these sessions progress: listening skills, perception and memory ability, attitude and emotional state, nervousness, appearance, physical and vocal delivery, and language.

Listening skills should be monitored because most people are poor listeners. Are questions understood before they are answered by the witness? Does the person correctly ask to have unclear questions repeated or reframed? Are answers blurted out before questions are ended? Is the witness only guessing what the questions might be? "Persons, who are to be witnesses, should be, as part of the preparation, taught and admonished to listen to the entire question and to answer only what is asked by such question. It may become necessary to hold sessions with certain witnesses, whereby this can be accomplished, and insure that the answers will be responsive."[14] In addition, witnesses should be instructed to become silent at once if the judge interrupts or if the other attorney poses an objection during questioning.

Each witness's *perception and memory ability* ought to be evaluated as well. Although we would like to believe that witnesses observe and report events accurately, we know that perception and memory are really quite capricious and "influenced by needs, attitudes, a situational context, and a host of other variables."[15] "Psychologists have shown that people tend to forget 10 percent of what they are exposed to within 24 hours and 90 percent within a week."[16] It is unlikely, then, that witnesses can recall in significant detail something they experienced months earlier.

Fallibility of human perception and memory is due to both internal (physiological and psychological) states and external (environmental) factors.[17] *Physiological internal factors* affecting memory and perception include such obvious matters as age and health; older, ill folks tend to be less than reliable. One of the *psychological internal factors* causing inaccuracies in testimony is the situational expectations people have (e.g., hunters who mistake other hunters for deer and then shoot them).[18] Sometimes witnesses expect to see certain things, and they later report on them as though they had seen them. Another psychological factor is personality. Punitive or authoritarian types observing a simulated kidnapping, for instance, tend to recall details more accurately than nonpunitive persons.[19] "One explanation for this is that punitive people are more expectant of malice from others and are therefore more alert to threatening situations."[20] A final psychological factor is emotional stress. To a point, emotionally important events arouse perceptual acuteness and enhance memory, but if the emotional arousal is extreme, details begin to blur.[21]

External factors affect memory and perception too. Elements in the environment, such as movement, distance, lighting, and noise, affect witness accuracy. For instance, action events, such as assassinations, ensure greater witness accuracy than do background events, such as crowd noise.[22] Even pretrial publicity, such as newspaper reports, can serve as an external factor to fill in certain gaps in information for potential witnesses.[23]

Since the turn of the century, considerable research on memory and perception has focused on the ability of eyewitnesses to recount events or identify things correctly.[24] "The influence of improper suggestion upon identifying witnesses probably accounts for more miscarriages of justice than any other single factor—perhaps it is responsible for more such errors than all other factors combined."[25] Yet juries often give eyewitness testimony a weight far out of proportion to other trial testimony,[26] regardless of the confidence shown through the communication of the eyewitness.[27] So it is incumbent upon trial attorneys to locate the best possible eyewitnesses. The ideal eyewitness is a person who

"(a) perceived all that transpired during the event, (b) accurately encoded these perceptions, (c) exhaustively stored the encoded perceptions in memory, and (d) fully and accurately retrieved the encodings from memory in the form of late report(s)."[28] Unfortunately, eyewitness performance in each of these four areas has been far from ideal. Let us examine the findings from some of the landmark studies.

We cannot possibly know everything that goes on around us.[29] Even in what we do sense, distortions regarding distance, time, size, speed, and weight are common.[30] Encoding information studies—studies of the acquisition and initial storage of information concerning an event—demonstrate that eyewitness testimony becomes more unreliable as the number of exposures to stimuli becomes smaller,[31] as the time of the event observed is shortened,[32] as the event observed becomes increasingly complex,[33] and as stress caused by the event increases to the point where arousal impairs viewing performance.[34] In one experiment, students were asked to describe a fight in one of their classrooms. The fight had been staged by confederates. Students most upset by the incident gave highly inaccurate testimony.[35]

Retention studies show that storage of information is quite difficult for the human brain inasmuch as "changes in the memorial representation can take place during the interval between the original encoding and the subsequent eyewitness report."[36] Extended intervals of time are associated with forgetting.[37] In experiments regarding lineups, face identification after a few days has a 30 percent error rate,[38] and white people more accurately recognize other white faces than black or oriental faces.[39] Memories become fragile when inconsistent information is observed,[40] postevent information is received,[41] or guessing is used to complete information gaps.[42]

Finally, retrieval-of-information studies indicate that verbal reporting can be biased or distorted by the type of question asked.[43] In sum, eyewitness testimony is quite prone to error.[44] Attorneys need to watch for such errors and, in eyewitness preparation, search for questions whose answers will satisfy the court of the fidelity of the witnesses' observational and reporting capabilities.

The witness's *attitude and emotional state* should be monitored too. The witness should be in the right frame of mind for trial. "The ideal witness is one who gives the appearance that he is simply testifying to his best memory of the facts and that he is not overeager for 'his side' to win. Such a witness is a rare jewel."[45] Following is a list of some of the attitudinal and emotional characteristics of specific kinds of problem witnesses who need coaching, with some suggested measures to help reduce the problems.[46] In each case, a witness trait is such that it might interfere with the effectiveness of that person's testimony. Of course, major and permanent improvements cannot be performed by attorneys. However, proper coaching can seek to neutralize some of the problems that might induce the jury or judge to reject a witness's testimony.

The Long-Winded Witness

Every question requires a speech for an answer. Being impulsive and talkative is risky because the witness is supplying additional information, which can be effectively cross-examined. In addition, the overly talkative person is not particularly persuasive.

Solution: The attorney should go over the lengthy and repetitive answers in practice. Point out those sections of the answer which are unresponsive and voluble. Restrain the witness.

The Short-Winded Witness

One who imitates a sphinx on the witness stand, giving one-word answers and forcing the examiner to drag out the answers. Forces the lawyers to use leading questions to prod the witness, and this looks bad to a jury.

Solution: Indicate the importance of giving sufficiently detailed answers. Do so in coaching as well as on the witness stand if necessary.

The Opinionated Exaggerator

One who thinks that a strongly partisan argument is successful direct examination. Wants to "win" the case. Uses adjectives, metaphors, and hyperbole. May even tell falsehoods and begin to believe in them. Jury will be turned off by this kind of person. What is desired are the essentials of a story without exaggeration, imagination, and opinion.

Solution: Identify the opinions and exaggerations in practice sessions and subtly urge their omission. Convince the witness of the undesirability of testifying to anything other than the salient facts, without offending the witness's vanity.

The Antagonistic, Hostile Witness

A lawsuit is a personal affront, and the other side is perceived as the enemy. The subsequent display of anger, hatred, and contempt certainly is not persuasive to a jury. On the stand the witness becomes stubborn, vindictive, malicious, and argumentative.

Solution: This witness may be avoided altogether, but if used, the witness must be made to understand that fury is the sign of a weak case and will be distasteful to the judge and the jury. This witness should be advised against exhibiting emotional outbursts on the stand.

The Dull Witness

Ho hum.

Solution: There is little that can be done to "clean up" this witness before trial. The lawyer should try to teach some language and imagery techniques, coach in delivery skills, and probably try to keep the direct examination as short as possible. Of course, if the person is dull because he or she is not very bright, keep the examination from becoming too complex. Spend ample time going over the facts of the case again and again with this witness before the trial. Perhaps avoid redirect, since this will only highlight the dullness.

The Ham

This is a frustrated actor, usually without much acting talent. The person tries to mimic some "exciting" witness he or she has seen in television or movie dramas. The jury will perceive this kind of person as a phony.

Solution: Coach the witness to "cool it," and if necessary, show how ridiculous his or her caricature mannerisms are. Try to get the person to use language that is standard and plain.

The Forgetful Witness

The person who lapses into an "I don't remember" state is devastating under direct examination. Such answers leave bad impressions on juries.

Solution: The lawyer should attempt to freshen the witness's memory. Leading questions may be asked if a sufficient foundation has been laid to show that the witness could not recall if asked nonleading questions. Attention in the leading questions may be directed to a prior question, conversation, event, or circumstance. The witness may be shown a deposition. An attorney should "attempt to get the witness to relive rather than recall. 'You testified that it was cold when you went outside. I want you to try to relive that moment in your mind; try to feel the cold, see what you saw then. Place yourself at the scene. What

happened immediately after you went outside?'"[47]

The Very Important Person

A condescending person who really does not want to spend time on this matter. This self-centered person's busy schedule outside of court is readily apparent. The jury will not like this kind of person.

Solution: Patience and tact on the part of the lawyer are necessary. Try to have the inflated ego of this witness temporarily veiled by discussing the matter with the witness before trial. If necessary, frame questions in the trial so that they call for simple yes or no answers.

The Thinker

This person has long pauses between questions and answers. This delay is perceived by the jury as time for fabricating a reply. Extreme slowness is not convincing and lacks spontaneity.

Solution: Go over all the questions and answers with the witness in advance. Have the person think over the content of the answers and not search for exact wording.

The Disorganized Thinker

This person has difficulty putting thoughts into words. Juries will quickly tune out; they do not like tangents and rambling.

Solution: Review all answers in coaching sessions, and have the person recognize the central part of each answer.

The Qualifier

A very cautious witness who gives qualified replies, this person will say, "I think it was this way . . ." or "I believe it was . . ." This is often a witness who also speaks slowly— in a hesitant, deliberate, and often timid fashion. This approach to testimony creates an impression of evasiveness.

Solution: Point out that trials do not deal in speculation. Educate the witness before trial to increase his or her probative value as a witness.

Everyone's Friend

This is a witness who scrupulously tries to avoid offending or hurting anyone. He or she wants to keep everyone happy. A witness like this is prone to contradicting his or her direct examination testimony under cross-examination. The person can be recognized in the interview process because she or he is always giving answers the lawyer wants to hear.

Solution: Avoid using this witness.

The Vacillator

From moment to moment, one gets a different story regarding distance, speed, time, and so on from this witness. This careless account of the facts will never persuade a jury.

Solution: Do not use this witness unless he or she can be strengthened in recalling and telling the facts of the case.

The Child as Witness

There may be a tendency to use vivid imaginations and stretch the truth. Children are highly suggestible, and their memories can be easily manipulated.

Solution: "Children can be excellent witnesses . . . if parents do not impose their own views on their children's statements and if lawyers did not ask them leading questions on the stand."[48]

Nervousness is quite common among witnesses. Many witnesses are unfamiliar with the trial environment, and it scares them. Yet, if they give "wrong" answers because of ap-

prehensiveness, a case could be lost. However, in one study, researchers found that jurors' attributions of confidence accounted for nearly 50 percent of the variance between jurors' decisions to believe witnesses.[49] In order to build witness self-confidence during pre-trial preparation, an attorney should at some point in witness preparation accompany the potentially nervous witness either to sit in a courtroom and watch a trial, preferably the same courtroom in which the case will be tried, or to have practice sessions in an empty courtroom.[50]

How can counsel put a witness at ease during an actual trial? There are several ways. Opening questions to the uncomfortable witness should be easy ones—questions that place no serious mental strain on the respondent. If a witness continues to appear nervous after a short time on the stand, counsel might ask that person why he or she feels uneasy. This question can cut the tension, and the witness can be encouraged to sit back and try to relax. A comment can be made for the jury, such as, "Now, everyone gets nervous testifying in court, especially if it is the first time. We all understand what you're going through. So take your time and try to relax as much as possible." Attorneys must neither display displeasure at witness nervousness nor rush the witnesses through their direct examination.

Appearance is yet another area for monitoring. It makes sense for lawyers to advise witnesses how to appear at trial, because outer attractiveness or appearance plays a role in personal encounters. For example, during the 1960s, long hair took on a major significance in structuring interpersonal responses. Even today, men with long hair are seen as less credible and serious and more immature than are men with shorter hair.[51]

There is an abundance of research to show that physically attractive people initially are more influential than physically unattractive people,[52] even in the courtroom environment,[53] although this difference wears off after a period of time.[54] Initially, we tend to think of older men (over thirty) with beards as dignified, intelligent, independent, extroverted, sophisticated, mature, and masculine, but this is not so for younger men. Young males have more initial credibility (i.e., an honest, nonradical, and open image) without beards.[55]

Clothes communicate too. Your male instructors who wear suits and ties send nonverbal messages different from those of instructors who wear jeans and sneakers. What a witness wears in court is important as well. Dark colors are more professional than light colors. Red conveys excitement or defiance; pale blue conveys tenderness or unhappiness; dark blue conveys power and security; orange conveys distress or contariness; brown conveys protectiveness or melancholy; black conveys defensiveness, unhappiness, hostility, or power; green conveys calm and serenity; purple conveys dignity; yellow conveys joy.[56] If any fabric has a design in it, small patterns are superior to large patterns.[57] Males with eyeglasses are seen as more intelligent and industrious than are their nonspectacled counterparts. Females in eyeglasses are seen as religious, conventional, and unimaginative.[58]

It is imperative, then, that trial lawyers contemplate their witnesses' hairstyles, clothing, and use of artifacts. Witnesses should not appear as something they are not. It is unlikely that a metal forger would appear in court in a three-piece Brooks Brothers suit. But it is equally senseless to have that person look distasteful, offensive, or unattractive at trial. Some attorneys go to witnesses' homes and tactfully help them pick out their clothes for trial. Dress should be on the conservative side; there should be no loud ties or socks and no flashy jewelry such as long, dangling earrings. Conservative dress makes the witness appear more reasonable to the jury.[59]

Grooming should be in conformity with local practice. Hair should be neatly arranged and neither unusual nor extreme. Fingernails should be clean. The witness should be instructed not to chew gum. And, at all times, a client or witness should appear to be attentive and interested in the course of the trial. Appearance is important because witnesses really are exhibits. Their visual images communicate quite a bit to the jury. That is why criminal defendants are no longer allowed to be brought to court in black-and-white striped suits and shackles. To do so makes them appear guilty.

Coaching witnesses in the areas of *physical and vocal delivery* is important because "judgments of the demeanor of witnesses are central to the trial process."[60] Jurors rely heavily on these nonverbal cues in evaluating the credibility of witnesses.[61] Research demonstrates that if witnesses are to appear strong and confident, they should use forceful and rhythmic gestures, considerable eye contact, a relatively high vocal volume and fast speaking rate, a relaxed posture, facial activity, affirmative head nods, and voice intonations.[62]

Witnesses should stand upright when taking the oath and say "I do" in a clear voice. They should be told not to slouch in the witness stand because such posture communicates disrespect or indifference. They should sit up alertly but should not appear tense or belligerent. Leaning slightly toward the judge or the jury projects a message that the witness can be trusted and communicates "a feeling of closeness and rapport."[63] Witnesses should be encouraged to use effective gestures; open hands with palms up communicate sincerity and confidence; clenched hands or palms down communicate anger and tension. The arms should remain unfolded. Witnesses should avoid looking at their shoes, at the floor, or around the courtroom while testifying. When eye contact is avoided, the jury may think the witness is trying to hide something. However, witnesses should not stare persistently at the jury during the entire trial, since a fixed gaze implies suspicion. Eye contact should be maintained with the attorney who is doing the questioning, unless that attorney instructs the witness to look at the jury or somewhere else. An occasional, natural, small, and friendly smile is helpful.

There is a widespread tendency for listeners to attribute specific personality characteristics to speakers on the basis of their voices,[64] although those perceptions may be far from accurate. Research demonstrates that we identify sexuality by how masculine or feminine a person's voice is; age, size, and health by how strong or weak a person's voice is; and dominance versus submissiveness by how loud or soft a person's voice is.[65] A breathy female voice communicates youth, femininity, and petiteness.[66] A nasal voice comes generally from an unpleasant, complaining, and undesirable personality.[67] A tense-sounding male voice indicates someone who is unyielding, cantankerous, high-strung, or emotional.[68] The loud, fast voice is associated with being resourceful and self-sufficient; the loud, slow voice is associated with being aggressive and secure; the soft, fast voice reflects enthusiasm and happiness; and the soft, slow voice is correlated with stress and withdrawal.[69] A booming, resonant voice depicts a person who is authoritarian, energetic, healthy, lively, and gregarious.[70] People with monotones are boring, cold, and sluggish.[71] Persons with foreign accents have lower credibility than persons without foreign accents.[72] Vocal characteristics such as coughs, yawns, moans, or crying have an effect on the messages they accompany.[73] Vocalized pauses between words and sentences ("um" and "ah") lower a person's credibility.[74] Lots of silent time due to extensive pauses communicates uncertainty.[75] People who speak too fast seem over-prepared, insincere, and trite.[76] Witness coaching should take these perceptions into consideration. Witnesses should talk to jurors in a normal, relaxed manner, as though they were talking to friends or neighbors. Witnesses should be further coached so as to be heard by the judge and jury. There is a tendency for fearful and tense witnesses to lower their voices to the point that they are nearly inaudible. Volume problems are further compounded by the fact that many courtrooms are acoustically bad and have no microphones. Witnesses should neither be hesitant in their delivery nor speak too rapidly.

Finally, witnesses should be advised how to leave the stand at the conclusion of their testimony. They should not leave the stand with extreme expressions reflecting either dejection or relief; these expressions can damage the jury's confidence in their testimony. Nor should they leave the stand in triumph; this expression can convince the jury that the witness believes he or she has put something over on them.

Finally, appropriate *language* should be developed in witness preparation, because it can influence a trial verdict. The right choice of words should be encouraged. Speech shortcomings, such as saying "you know" or "OK," should be corrected if they are extreme and distracting. Grammar needs close attention too. Parkinson found that defendants who spoke in more grammatically complete sentences were acquitted more often than other defendants.[77]

A phrase like "let me be honest with you" carries the implication that "the rest of the testimony might not be honest, or that honesty is a matter of casual choice for the witness."[78] Phrases need attention. Suppose a witness uses the descriptive phrase "The car went like a red streak past me" instead of saying "The car was going fast," or "It feels like a hot poker being driven into my ribs" rather than "It's a pain in my side." An alert attorney should reward the witness for using the first sentence in both cases. Why? Because the analogies are more descriptive and pay greater homage to the power of words than do the plain statements. The plaintiff's attorney in particular wants the jury to have a vivid picture of very rapid motion or pain and suffering, and the more colorful testimony does a better job in that regard.

Vivid information is much more potent than nonvivid information from the witness. In one study, the degree of detail or the concreteness of information on critical points was related to the credibility of the story in the mind of the jurors.[79] In another study, mock jurors read testimony from a hypothetical trial about drunken driving. Testimony was either pallid for the prosecution and detailed for the defense or vice versa. Those exposed to vivid prosecution testimony were more likely to render guilty verdicts than were those who consumed pallid evidence.[80] Vivid descriptions that appeal to the senses affect juror attitudes, and pallid information is more likely to be ignored. Descriptions are deemed pallid when too many hedge words (e.g., "I guess," "I might have," "possibly," "kind of," "it seems") are used. Such words create an impression of uncertainty and indecisiveness.[81]

Other research regarding witness language shows that successful defendants are polite and deferential (e.g., they say "please," "thank you," "yes, sir") and rely on third-person rather than first-person pronouns, whereas successful plaintiffs are verbose (they use adverbs and adjectives extensively and give a large quantity of specific information).[82] One group of researchers presented testimony to subjects that was either powerful or powerless and found that witness attractiveness and credibility were affected. Powerless speech includes hesitations ("well," "um," "ah," "you know," "er"), answering questions with questions, and hedging. Greater acceptance of the witness's testimony was found as powerless speech was decreased, regardless of the sex of the witness.[83] Meanwhile, intensifiers ("very," "surely," "certainly"), a form of powerful speech, were found to signify speaker commitment, add force to a message, and increase the influence of certain witnesses.[84]

Lawyers must educate witnesses that certain words have power and impact. Some-

times, powerful language is appropriate, as in the case of expert testimony; other times, powerless language is appropriate, as in the case of a victim's testifying. However, whatever the situation, lawyers should never choose a vocabulary for their witnesses. Witnesses should use words with which they are familiar. Lawyers should let the witnesses unwittingly discover their own descriptive words, and when good descriptions are chosen, they should congratulate their witnesses for those "right" words.

As lawyers measure the jury appeal of each of their witnesses during the practice sessions they should ask themselves, "Which potential witnesses should be kept and which ones should be discarded?" If two witnesses will be saying essentially the same thing, but only one of them has persuasive potential, the possible loser might be forgotten.

To summarize, "witness preparation is a mandatory obligation which the advocate owes to the client"[85] in any litigation. A group of researchers discovered the importance of preparing witnesses before trial when they had role-playing jurors randomly assigned to hear testimony presented by a strong witness or a weak witness. To control for possible contaminating factors (physical appearance, sex, etc.), the same professional actor portrayed both witnesses. The researchers concluded,

In the strong witness condition, the actor responded to the attorney's questions in a confident, assertive way, displaying few distracting nonverbal and paralinguistic behaviors. By contrast, his responses in the weak witness condition were halting, unsure, and accompanied by a number of nervous bodily and vocal behaviors. After hearing the testimony, all role-playing jurors completed an instrument designed to measure their retention of the information presented by the witness, their perceptions of the witness's credibility, and their verdicts in the case.

Although verdict was not significantly affected by witness strength, both retention of information and ratings of credibility were. In two separate studies, jurors who heard the strong witness retained significantly more of the testimonial information and rated the witness as significantly more credible. Thus, holding both message content and the fixed attributes of the witness constant, presentational skill exerted a strong impact on juror response.[86]

Although witness preparation is crucial, it does not mean telling witnesses what their testimony should be. It is, in fact, unethical to graft something onto "the truth." Rather, witness preparation means suggesting or indicating to witnesses what is desired of them regarding "demeanor, actions, reactions, and responsiveness"[87] when they take the stand. "The prime purpose of the witness is to tell what he or she knows about the circumstances under trial, but also to impress the trier of the facts that he knows and tells it honestly, forthrightly, and completely."[88] Should opposing counsel in cross-examination ask a witness if he or she has been coached for trial, the witness should be able to say with confidence, "Yes, I discussed my testimony in some detail with lawyer X, and she told me to tell the truth as persuasively as I could!"

The bottom line on witness preparation is to assure and reassure witnesses that they will do all right when they testify. Although this section of Chapter 9 offers many areas for criticism, counsel must avoid giving too much negative feedback to the witnesses. Positive criticism is important too; witnesses should be reinforced for what they do right. "Remember criticism is meant to be *creative,* to fix something."[89] Witnesses "fix it" best if lawyers show faith in them.

Communication Strategies for the Attorney in Direct Examination

Several strategic questions for direct examination should be posed by every trial lawyer. First, *how many witnesses should be used?*

One author says to "make it simple, make it fast, and then quit."[90] Another confirms that by saying, "Get in, score, and get out."[91] In other words, brevity yields clarity. As the number of witnesses an attorney calls to testify increases, so do opportunities for troublesome opposition cross-examination. There is no need to gild the lily, with many witnesses boring the jury by making the same point over and over again.

Second, *in what order should witnesses be presented?* What is discussed here is an ideal. Last-minute problems require flexibility and adaptation by trial lawyers. Nevertheless, if they can be followed, the principles of primacy and recency apply to the order of proof. Primacy has to do with initial impression; juries tend to believe more deeply what they hear first. They begin with a relatively blank slate, and the first thing written on that slate will be the most impressive. In a simulated rape trial, it was found that the greatest number of guilty verdicts occur when the strongest "guilty" witnesses come first in the order of presentation.[92] So an attorney should have a strong and important witness testify first in direct examination, with weaker, dull, or incidental witnesses in the middle.[93]

At the same time, and to the extent that it is possible, the testimony ought to unfold in approximately the same order as the story or occurrence told in the opening statement. Thus, in a personal injury case, the issue of liability might be presented by witnesses to the accident before other witnesses (e.g., practicing physicians) testify about injury and damages. Also, corroboration witnesses should be called immediately after the witness they are corroborating in order for the jury to more easily fit the supporting material to the original testimony. What we have said so far is that primacy should be considered first in witness selection, followed by a chronological or logical development of the story.

When we reach the end of the witness list, recency must reign. The lid on a case should be slammed tightly shut with a strong and important witness at the end of direct examination.[94] The last witness should be impressive and memorable; after all, what the last witness says "is freshest in the minds of the jurors during their formal deliberations."[95] For instance, defense attorneys should probably call upon the defendant as their last witness. The jury will be waiting to hear from that person anyway. In addition, defendants can sit through a trial and be in a position to explain prior and possibly inconsistent testimony from others. Recency dictates that an important witness should be saved for the end of the case-in-chief.

Third, *how should the direct examination begin?* Most witnesses are probably in a strange and scary environment. To put them at ease, direct examination should begin with nonthreatening, preliminary matters. Initially, some personal characteristics of the witness should be presented to the jury. They include the witness's name, age, occupation, place of residence, marital status, education, and so forth. Questions such as these can put a witness at ease. Each of these questions should be posed individually. It is unwise to coldly say, "For the record, please give us your name, age, present address, and place of employment." By the time the witness gets to employment, he or she may have forgotten the balance of the question, and this can cause unnecessary nervousness. It is better to begin by warmly saying, "In order for the jury to get to know you better, please tell us your name." As questions like these are answered, personal features with which the jury can easily identify should be highlighted.[96]

In cases in which a witness is going to describe an event or occurrence, an attempt should be made to build up initial witness credibility with the jury. This means that some time should be spent having witnesses note the exact position they were in with regard to the event they are describing. What must be demonstrated is "where the witness was at the time of the occurrence; what line of vision he had; what, if any, obstructions or distrac-

tions were present; and what the degree of visibility was at that time."[97] How much of this introductory questioning is needed depends on the nature of the witness. For instance, a parent fighting for child custody or a pedestrian viewing a hit-and-run accident will want to have his or her personal characteristics or viewing position explored at some length.

Once the preliminary groundwork has been established, the witness's knowledge of the essential facts can be explored. This next step in direct should be preceded by a punch line; that is, the jurors should hear the focus of a story right away. Counsel questioning a plaintiff whose automobile was hit by a truck might say, "Mr. Samuels, did something happen to you on the night of October 10, 1985?" The plaintiff can answer, "It sure did. That was the night I was rammed into by a truck." Now the jury knows what Samuels' testimony will cover, and they should be interested in hearing the rest of what he has to say.

Fourth, *what form of question should be posed to witnesses in direct examination?* In direct examination, the witness is the star. As a result, open-ended questions are best. Early research noted that witness errors increased when closed-ended, specific questions were asked instead of allowing the witness to provide narrative testimony.[98] Later research confirms that when lawyers fail to allow witnesses to narrate during direct examination, the authoritativeness and believability of the testimony decreases in the minds of the jury,[99] and the credibility of the lawyer is substantially damaged.[100] So, in direct examination, an attorney should maintain a low profile and let the witness tell the story. "The more complete and detailed the description, the more convincing the testimony will be."[101]

Leading questions are generally disallowed in direct examination.[102] A leading question is one that suggests the answer. "Was it raining that night?" is leading and objectionable. The question will not be allowed because it clues the witness to the desired answer. "What was the weather like that night?" is not leading. There are only a few rare circumstances in which counsel on direct examination may be allowed to lead a witness. Leading is allowed in order to maintain an orderly structure for the questioning and to develop important detail.[103] For example, leading is permissible to expedite preliminary matters, such as the witness's background. Leading questions can be used where a witness has tremendous verbal difficulty answering simple questions, such as is sometimes the case with someone who cannot speak the language well. Leading may also be employed when a witness is hostile to counsel. Suppose, for example, that a witness on direct examination called by the prosecution is a close friend of the defendant and is antagonistic and sarcastic to the questioning attorney. The prosecutor may have to seek permission of the court to treat the witness as a hostile witness and examine him with leading questions. Finally, leading questions are properly permitted in direct examination when witnesses surprise attorneys by their answers. Unexpected testimony is subject to leading in order to refresh the witness's memory regarding prior information that runs contrary to the surprising and new information. Here is a sample series of leading questions to refresh a witness's recollection, which would probably be appropriate for direct examination:

Q: Are you able to remember the names of any other persons who were present at the meeting to which you referred?

A: No, I can't. I'm certain that there were some others there, but I just can't seem to come up with their names now.

Q: You have exhausted your recollection of those who were present?

A: Yes, I am afraid so. I just have a mental block.

Q: Would it ring any bells if I suggested to you that Mr. Carlos Rodriguez also attended that meeting?

A: You're right! I remember now. Rodriguez was there, too.

Generally, however, leading questions in direct examination are disallowed.

Witness interrogation need not be entirely in question form (e.g., "What is your name?" "Where do you live?" "Where do you work?" "Where were you on the morning of August 23?"). By the time important testimony comes, the question form has become monotonous and lost its impact. To break the repetitious pattern of asking questions, an attorney can use this form: "State your name and address." "Tell the jury where you work." When the more substantive questioning begins, counsel then can shift to the question form (e.g., "What happened in the bank after you first laid eyes on the defendant?").

Vague questions should at all times be avoided in direct examination. They are an unproductive question form that will "bring forth a lot of . . . objections from your opponent . . . [and] cause you a great deal of consternation and embarrassment."[104] If a lawyer says to a witness, "Tell us something about the incident," the witness can go off in all directions, thereby undermining his or her credibility. Instead, "Tell us what happened when you first entered the bank" allows a witness to better understand the time frame surrounding the question. Vague questions are damaging to an attorney in direct examination inasmuch as they are a roadblock to clarity.

A question form that can effectively be used in direct examination is one that places emphasis on certain parts of a witness's testimony that are significant to counsel's case. Although lawyers are not allowed to repeat questions, they can repeat key phrases and words in subsequent questions. One such method is called the loop-back question, a question that includes the prior answer. For example: "What happened next?" "I opened the window." "And after you opened the window, what did you do?" Backtracking, or looping back, is a recommended way of emphasizing favorable and important witness information for jury memory enhancement.[105]

Another linguistic technique using repetition is to create word pictures with key words. For instance, suppose that an attorney wants to emphasize that a traffic light was red. This is a critical piece of information and not a minute detail. To make the red signal have a lasting impression, counsel might pose questions such as those that follow: "Where were you, Mr. Smith, when the light became yellow?" "Did you observe any traffic then?" "Where were you when it turned to red?" "Did you observe any traffic then?" "Approximately how long was the signal red before Mr. Jones entered the intersection?" "Mr. Smith, could you visually describe for the jury the traffic control device that was red?" And so forth. Questions such as these, which focus on the red traffic control light, call attention to the importance of the red light by creating a slow-motion word picture of something that happened in a very short span of time and by repeating the word "red" several times.

The form of the question should be kept relatively plain and simple. "About how many times have you crossed that intersection as a pedestrian?" is superior to "Why don't you tell us about the number of occurrences in which you exited from the sidewalk to get from one side of the intersection to the other side of the intersection that we have identified for the court?" Less wordy questions are clearer questions. Here are some examples of convoluted, confusing, and complex questions, which, unfortunately, are the badge of many lawyers. Each question is followed by a translated improvement.

Note that in each of the translations only one fact is sought. Questions should always be broken down to just one fact.

The use of negatively constructed questions creates ambiguity and confusion too.[106] "Jurors take longer to process negative sentences and have more difficulty in remembering them."[107] "Didn't you hear Sally Foerster leave the house?" is an unclear question. Does a yes answer mean that she left the house or that she did not leave the house? "Even if the jury understands the witness'

Unclear Question	Translation
For how long a period of time have you been so employed?	How long have you worked at Kessler Tool and Die?
Would you indicate for the court, please, what distance the plaintiff's motor vehicle was from your motor vehicle when you first observed it?	How far away was the other car when you first saw it?
For what period of time did you maintain surveillance over the defendant, the subject in question?	How long did you watch Mr. Turner?
Did not a time come when you had occasion to observe the defendant departing from his residence?	Did you ever see Mr. Turner leave his home?

meaning from inflection or expression, those factors do not appear in the written record."[108] For example, the negatively constructed question "So, there is no light in the stairwell, is there?" is much improved by the positive phrasing "Was there a light in the stairwell?" Suppose a witness answers the negatively constructed question in the affirmative. Does that mean there was no light? Or does it mean there was a light? It is unclear. Multiple negatives are even worse. How would you answer these questions? "Do you not agree that color confusion is not uncommon?" "You never did see the train, is that not correct?" Questions phrased affirmatively yield significantly better comprehension than their negatively phrased counterparts. But a combination of a positive question and a negative one should be avoided too. A question such as "You never heard Sally Foerster leave the house, is that right?" is unclear. Either an affirmative or a negative response will be ambiguous.

Pretentious verbiage creates added confusion. Here is a list of gobbledygook words that tend to be overused:

aware that	is it correct that
client	observe
consecutive with	occasion
contact with	previous to
direct your attention to	subsequent to
incident	vehicle
in lieu of	what, if anything
in relation to	with respect to

Often these words can be deleted entirely—and should be, because the jury has to make too great an effort to listen to them. Psycholinguistic research has shown that jurors do not easily understand such language.[109] Attorneys should from time to time review their own trial transcripts with a critical eye to look for awkward words and phrases that get in the way of clear speech. Stilted language, like

"subsequent to" or "in lieu of" can be replaced with plainer language, such as "after" or "instead of." Similarly, if a witness's answer makes little sense because of a lack of simplicity, a narrowly phrased question of clarification or explanation is helpful (e.g., "Excuse me, Ms. Farnsworthy, I didn't quite follow what you were saying. Exactly where were you standing when you saw the shooting incident?"). Naturally, this practice requires that attorneys listen carefully to their witnesses' answers.

Language choice in the phrasing of questions is an extremely important matter. University of Washington psychologist Elizabeth Loftus conducted a series of experiments to determine the effect word choice has on witness answers. After viewing a film showing an automobile accident, 50 students were asked an implicative question with a definite article ("Did you see *the* broken headlight?"); a disjunctive question was asked to 50 more students, with an indefinite article ("Did you see *a* broken headlight?"). More than twice as many subjects answered in the affirmative when the definite article was used, whether or not the broken headlight was in the film. This effect probably occurred because the definite article implies that there was a broken headlight whereas the indefinite article does not.[110] Another group of students was asked to estimate the speed of one vehicle. Those who were asked, "How fast was the yellow car going when it *smashed* into the other car?" averaged 40.8 miles per hour; those who were asked, "How fast was the yellow car going when it *hit* the other car?" averaged 34 miles per hour.[111] Suggestive words in the attorney's questions influence a witness's mental image and, in turn, the response given.

Fifth, *in what order should an attorney's questions be asked in direct examination?* The order should be chronological if an occurrence is to be described. Stories recited in time sequence are easier to "perceive and abstract"[112] than information communicated in some random fashion. One author provides us with the following example of the order of a plaintiff's testimony in an automobile collision case:[113]

a. His background
b. Description of collision location
c. What occurred just before the collision
d. How the collision actually occurred
e. What happened immediately after the collision
f. Emergency room and initial treatment
g. Continued medical treatment
h. Present physical limitations and handicaps
i. Financial losses to date

If a witness is not testifying about an occurrence, or is only called to make one or a few points, a logical or topical order should be used. Here, questions are framed around the points an attorney wants to make with the particular witness. For instance, expert witnesses might present their main conclusions first and then go through their reasoning later. In this way, the jury hears the most important information while they are still attentive. Or consider the case of a physician who is charged with medical malpractice for failing to identify the decedent plaintiff's cardiac arrest in the hospital emergency room. After the patient came in, the doctor was called away to treat victims of an airplane crash and left a nurse to take tests and monitor the heart patient. Chronology implies chaos and confusion. However, asking a doctor to first list the normal procedures for possible heart attack patients (testing and monitoring) and then note whether these procedures were followed in this particular case will make the defendant's testimony appear more reasonable than if the chronology of disorganization is emphasized. This order of questions focuses on the issues the attorney wishes to stress.

The finish to each direct examination must be carefully planned too. A witness's testimony "must be brought . . . to a ringing affirmation of that which went before, a well defined conclusion, a bang and not a whimper."[114] Climax is important. Consider these examples:

Defense Attorney: Michael, did you rob that bank?
Defendant: No, sir, I did not!
Defense Attorney: Your Honor, I have no other questions.

or

Prosecuting Attorney: How well can you identify the burglar?
Witness: I am certain that I will never forget that face as long as I live!

Final questions such as these put appropriate exclamation points at the end of a lawyer's direct examination.

Sixth, *should unpleasant or negative information be raised in direct examination?* Yes, it should be raised if opposing counsel is aware of the fact and the unpleasant information is of some significance. For example, the plaintiff in a medical malpractice case claims damage to her leg. Yet she plays golf daily and walks the entire course. How can this potential weakness in the plaintiff's case be explained? In direct examination, counsel should have her explain that she plays golf even though she constantly experiences considerable pain. The explanation and the attitude conveyed when this information is revealed "should be matter-of-fact so as to suggest it has no adverse bearing on the value of the witness' testimony."[115] Negative information should be buried somewhere in the middle of the direct examination because "when jurors hear favorable evidence first, it strengthens the approach tendency to the point where unfavorable evidence can be accepted without causing a loss of the initial approach response. However, if unfavorable evidence is presented first, the avoidance tendency is established and it might be difficult to overcome."[116]

Disclosure of weaknesses will make a witness a "human being to the jury and will protect the witness from attack on cross-examination."[117] Raising damaging information on direct examination has the effect of inoculating the jury against its eventual exposure by the opposition. Generally, subjects who hear two-sided arguments or refutational defenses are less persuaded by counterargument than are those who initially hear a one-sided argument.[118] Inoculation by two-sided arguments works in courtroom persuasion in much the same way as measles vaccinations immunize children against measles.[119]

Seventh, *what nonverbal behaviors should an attorney elicit prior to and during direct examination?* Prior to direct examination, lawyers should attempt to secure the table nearest to the jury to allow personable and attractive clients to be as visible as possible. The lawyer should use rewarding nonverbal behavior with the client as well. She or he should not lean away from the client, avoid eye contact with the client, or stack books and other objects between the lawyer and the client. Such nonverbal cues communicate distance between the two parties. Rather, counsel should act as though the client is a special friend. Smiling and good eye contact demonstrate a psychological closeness for the jury.[120]

During direct examination, physical and vocal cues from the lawyer should help make a witness's testimony memorable. If a lawyer is permitted to stand almost anywhere in the courtroom during direct examination,[121] he or she should be positioned to avoid obstructing the jury's view of the witness in any way. Standing in the way prevents the witness from seeing all the jurors. In turn, "the jurors are unable to see, or perhaps even hear, the tes-timony. Similarly rapport . . . will be lost as jurors lose the ability to relate one-on-one with the witness."[122] Counsel should be positioned a long distance from the witness, on the other side of the jury, leaving an expanded personal territory for the witness. This arrangement can cause the witness to look at the jury and to project his or her voice. It is best, then, to stand in a baseline position beside and at the far end of the jury box, as the X in the diagram illustrates:

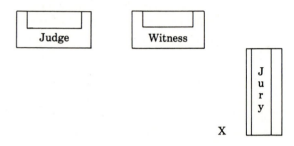

Questioning a witness while remaining seated is unwise; the table is a real barrier to effective communication. However, some attorneys begin their direct examination while seated, and when they hit the meaty part of the witness's testimony, they rise from their chairs and move to point X in order to dramatize what is about to occur. It is from and to point X that an advocate must depart and return from time to time, such movement "calculated to supplement and increase the impact and effectiveness of communication and rapport."[123] Consider the following illustration:

In a murder case, when asking of the eyewitness, "And what did he do with the knife?," the impact of the answer can be highlighted by forcing the jury to consider the weight of the question. Moving toward the witness along an imaginary line, between the end of the jury-box and the middle of the witness stand, while asking the all important question will psychologically intensify the witness' response. Asking the question from a stationary position, and then moving toward the witness before the witness' answer, will accomplish the same result. First, the change, in and of itself, will serve to put the jury on notice. Second, as the distance between the examiner and the witness decreases, the impact of the answer increases. Asking the question while moving toward the witness and timing the move to end at the witness stand as the question is finished creates an aura of anticipation in counterpoint to the questions asked earlier from the rear of the jury-box.[124]

Eye contact with a witness is essential; attorneys should not read questions from a yellow pad in a routine manner with little apparent interest in what the witness is saying. Notes should be unobtrusive. If they are held in the hands of the attorney, "they will give the impression of a rehearsed story."[125] Eye contact with the witness during the answer helps an advocate pay closer attention to the witness. At no time should a lawyer use the eyes or any other part of the body to show skepticism for the case. Every so often you see attorneys displaying nonverbal displeasure at an answer given by one of their own witnesses. Even though irritation might be inwardly felt by counsel, it must not be shown to a jury. The jury easily senses skepticism or impatience and watches for such signs. Lawyers must remain nonverbally confident, calm, and patient in the courtroom, even when witnesses utter surprising and unfavorable messages.

Attorneys should think about their vocal cues as well. Since direct examination is usually the time for the presentation of friendly witnesses, a conversational and friendly tone of voice should be used. The voice should be firm, clear, and loud enough to be heard by all. "The habit of some lawyers of prefacing each question with an "ah" or "uh," and then haltingly evolving the next inquiry, works greatly to their disadvantage"[126] in terms of holding the jury's interest. The attorney should not sound bored. The pace should

move along rather quickly so as to avoid tedium, but not so fast as to lose the jury with regard to what is being said. At important points in a witness's testimony, counsel should either slow down or speed up the pace to emphasize and dramatize what is being said. Witnesses, after all, will usually adapt to the pacing the questioner uses. Pure silence is also effective. After a very important answer, "a pause linked to a gesture, such as putting down . . . your notes, taking off your glasses, taking a breath, or taking a step toward the witness, makes the jury stop and consider what has just happened."[127]

This concludes the discussion of direct examination. "If the direct examination is properly and skillfully conducted, the impression thus made by an honest witness is more lasting than any argument of counsel. The vivid story of a single witness told in a winning way will leave a first impression upon a juror's mind that no eloquence can efface."[128] With these words in mind, let us next turn our attention to certain principles of cross-examination.

TESTIMONIAL EVIDENCE: CROSS-EXAMINATION

Lawyers are entitled to cross-examine witnesses once the witnesses have completed direct testimony. Unchanged over time, cross-examination is "the surest trial procedure yet devised for correcting error, eliciting suppressed facts, and confounding the perjurer."[129] The respected author Henry Wigmore called cross-examination "the greatest legal machine ever invented for the discovery of truth."[130]

Cross-examination is often perceived as a highly dramatic moment of confrontation in a trial. Indeed, it is to a trial what a fight is to a hockey game. The jury waits for a hammer-and-tongs type of excitement to happen, perhaps because they are conditioned by what they see on television or in the cinema, where cross-examination is presented in its most savage form. Even though the jury expects sparks to fly, it is wrong for a lawyer to put greater stock in cross-examination than in any other part of the case. To do so affords too much importance to the opponent's cause. Instead of adopting a defensive posture, attorneys should focus primarily on selling the merits of their own cases through direct examination. This is not to de-emphasize the importance of cross-examination in any way; it certainly is an important part of the trial process. However, cross-examination is not *the* most important part by any means.

Nature and Scope

There are two possible purposes for cross-examination. A cross-examining attorney should know which of these he or she is trying to attain. One purpose is to clarify the direct testimony or to elicit additional information that was not revealed in direct examination but is helpful to the questioner's case. "The fact that a witness is being cross-examined does not mean that the cross-examiner is dragging something out of the witness against his will. It may well be that . . . the cross-examination is merely instrumental in bringing out the unalloyed facts."[131]

The second purpose of cross-examination is to test witnesses in order to weaken or demolish their direct testimony. Weakening is accomplished by attacking a witness's knowledge, accuracy, perception, memory, truthfulness, or overall credibility. (Obviously, this objective should be seen as an alternative to the first purpose of cross-examination. Only in rare cases would both objectives be sought with a single witness.) If the second and more aggressive objective of cross-examination is sought to its fullest extent, a witness may reach the point of being discredited and seen as unreliable. This result is known as impeachment, and it will be explored more fully later in the chapter.

There are three prevailing rules in the United States regarding what can be covered in cross-examination. The "English Rule," or wide-open rule, allows a witness to be examined fully on all matters relevant to the case. The narrower "American Rule" limits cross-examination, except for impeachment purposes, to those facts and circumstances covered in direct examination.[132] If the narrow rule applies and a cross-examiner wants to range farther afield, he or she must call that witness as part of his or her own case. This practice will be discussed later under the section entitled "adverse witnesses." The compromise view, called the "Michigan Rule," is a half-open door. Under that rule, the cross-examiner "may question about any fact on which the opponent has the ultimate burden of proof, but may not question about part of his or her own affirmative case unless the witness mentions that fact on direct."[133] There is always a considerable amount of discretion by the judge with regard to the scope of any cross-examination.

Waiving Cross-Examination

There are times when cross-examination should be waived because it is too much of a gamble. There are several possible risks. Although it is possible to confront witnesses with inconsistencies, fluent witnesses may be able to successfully squirm out of internal contradictions in what they say. In an attempt to prove bad character of a witness, sympathy by the jury for that witness and the case he or she supports can be provoked. In an attempt to bring out matters about which an adversary failed to inquire, in the belief that these matters will be favorable to one's own client, one might uncover more evidence favorable to the adverse party who called the witness. Even to insist upon clearer answers from a witness can possibly lead to an unexpected and unfavorable disclosure. Sometimes it is best to leave alone an unclear answer or a rambling story from direct examination. Finally, cross-examination is pointless if a witness has not harmed the case "unless counsel feels that he has a reasonably good chance to extract information from the witness that is favorable to his side."[134] To cross-examine minor witnesses who have been used to establish some independent fact, and who have not hurt the case, serves no useful purpose.

Cross-examination has the potential to backfire. Sometimes it works and sometimes it does not. When it does not work, an attorney may end up looking foolish in the eyes of the jury. At the same time, he or she actually strengthens the effect that the adverse witness had on the jury. If the witness is an intelligent, articulate individual and seems to be telling the truth, the best cross-examination may be none at all. The key to whether or not to cross-examine is careful planning, combined with experience and instinct. Lawyers must know exactly what they are looking for in cross-examination; fishing expeditions are almost always unwise. Noted attorney Leon Jaworski provides us with this cautionary anecdote:

I once faced an elderly witness, a pathetic figure. He obviously was falsifying. His direct testimony convinced me that he was senile, and I felt certain that most of the jury had reached the same conclusion. On the close of his direct testimony, I did what I think each of you would have done, I remained silent. The judge, looking at me, said, "Let's proceed with the cross-examination." I paused a few seconds. Measuring my words carefully, I replied, "I do not believe I need to ask this witness any questions." I was later told by several jurors that they appreciated this gesture.[135]

There is one other matter to be considered regarding a cross-examination waiver. Juries and clients probably expect some cross-examination of witnesses. The expectation and desire of juries to hear cross-examination must be factored into any decision regarding waiver. Pleasing the client must be considered too. "Clients often feel that a failure to cross-examine is a sign of a lack of interest in the case. If counsel explains his strategy to the client, such a critical attitude may be forestalled. . . . [After all,] a favorable result in the case as a whole is more important than the pyrrhic victory of one witness."[136]

There is a lot of gambling to be done in making the decision whether or not to cross-examine. The best bottom-line rule to follow is never to cross-examine more than is absolutely necessary. A noted lecturer on trial advocacy put it this way: "Don't cross-examine unless you can say to yourself, from the heart and not from the ego, 'I know I have to.' Cross-examine not to be a great performer, but to be a good lawyer."[137]

Planning and Preparation

Three concerns should affect lawyers' preparation for cross-examination. First, *there should always be clear ends and means for each examination.* Earlier, two purposes for cross-examination were identified. Once a lawyer knows which purpose he or she is trying to fulfill for a given witness, that lawyer must concentrate on the methodology to be employed to accomplish that objective.

Suppose counsel's purpose is to discredit a witness's testimony. Then the cross-examiner should determine in advance what are the potential weaknesses in the witness's story. Are there limitations to the witness's knowledge, recollection, perception, action by words or conduct, state of mind, or operation of mind? "What, if anything, do you know about . . ." gets at a witness's lack of knowledge. "What do you remember about . . ." get at a witness's inability to recollect. "What did you hear when . . ." gets at a flaw in perception. "What, if anything, did you say when . . ." gets at a witness's inaction. "What were your feelings with respect to . . ." opens up the possibility of a shaky emotional state.

"What is your opinion about . . . " can focus on faulty conclusion drawing. Each of these questioning procedures serves as a specific technique for discrediting a witness in cross-examination.

One technique that generally should *not* be used in a cross-examination in which a witness's testimony is to be discredited is to have a witness simply repeat testimony from direct examination. Sometimes attorneys do this hoping for a contradiction or some other faux pas. Questions such as those that follow are a waste of time: "You say you saw the accident? You saw the plaintiff driving down Main Street? You saw the defendant driving down the wrong side of Main Street?" These questions waste time because a prepared witness will simply buttress the original direct examination about how the accident occurred.

Of course, exceptions always exist. One of the great anecdotes of the trial bar concerns New York trial attorney Max Steuer.[138] Earlier in this century, many Jews migrated from Eastern Europe to New York City. Several of their children worked in garment industry sweatshops. One of the shops, the Triangle Shirt Waist Company, was an eight-story factory building employing nearly six hundred young women. The building had fire escapes, where the young women would go to smoke their cigarettes. The owners, upset at this practice, one day nailed the fire doors shut. Shortly thereafter, a fire ensued, and four hundred employees were burned to death. The owners were indicted for manslaughter, and Max Steuer became their lawyer. One prosecution witness was a small survivor named Sophie Shapiro. She dramatically told the story of the day of the fire. She was on the fourth floor and was talking to another employee, who had been having a cigarette in a stairwell. The young woman told Sophie she had smelled smoke. Sophie told her it might have been her own cigarette, so they went back to work. Five minutes later, the smell of smoke was stronger. They looked in the stairwell and saw fire. They tried to pry the fire escape doors

open, but failed. Soon the fire entered the room. Panic followed. Sophie stepped into a broom closet and fainted. The next thing she remembered was being in the arms of a fireman.

How would you cross-examine Sophie Shapiro? Steuer stood up and violated the advice just offered. He said, "Sophie, tell it again." She did. He then said a second time and even a third time, "Sophie, tell it again." Each time, she told the story using exactly the same words. But the fourth time the story was told, she substituted a "that" for a "which." When she finished, Steuer said, "Sophie, didn't you make a mistake? Didn't you say 'that' instead of 'which' when you were telling about the burning flesh?" She responded, "Oh, yes, I made a mistake. I'm sorry." Steuer asked nothing else. This story is a rare phenomenon. He had a clear, definite, and most unusual objective. The defendants were acquitted because Steuer had turned the prosecution witnesses into tape-recorded parrots. Generally, however, this technique will backfire on an attorney. After all, very few practitioners at the bar are of the caliber of a Max Steuer. Generally, testimony from direct examination should not be repeated in any detailed fashion.

The best procedure to use for deciding what ends and means to employ in cross-examination is to outline and index opposing counsel's witness depositions in detail. "Sometimes the outline should merely indicate the subject discussed on each page of the transcript. Sometimes the outline should contain brief excerpts of language from the transcript. The guiding principle is counsel's ability to pick up the outline at trial and quickly find testimony he needs to cross-examine the witness."[139] Rarely will actual questions be prepared from the outline before the trial, because flexibility and spontaneity are needed too.

Second, *cross-examination questions should be structured carefully*. Generally, the cross-examination should ignore peripheral material and be brief. While there may be hundreds of possible areas for cross-examining each witness, only a few of them should make the final cut. Juries have a limited capacity to retain information they hear. "The jury receives facts aurally, and it receives them only once. Attempting too much on cross-examination will invariably create two problems: the impact of your strongest points will be diluted, and the less significant points will be forgotten entirely by the time the jury deliberates on its verdict."[140] One author maintains that if he were cross-examining a mother who testified in support of an alibi defense for her son, he would ask one and only one cross-examination question: "You are his mother, aren't you?!?"[141]

There is a tendency for some lawyers to begin cross-examination where direct examination left off. That is usually the wrong place to start questioning, because the opposing lawyer has probably ended direct by making a strong point. Where, then, should cross-examination begin? It should start at a place where (1) the witness has less confidence and (2) the cross-examining attorney can immediately have the jury focus on his or her specific objective. "It is the theory of the case, then, that provides the starting point for organizing cross-examination. . . . An example is in order. The defendant is charged with murder and pleads self-defense. An assistant medical examiner testifies for the state that the victim died as the result of a gunshot wound. A careful cross-examiner might ask a few questions designed to show that the medical examiner has no way of knowing whether the man was shot in self-defense or whether he was an innocent victim."[142] The point to be made by the cross-examination is the place where cross-questioning should begin.

The sequence of questions is important too. For instance, the extremely important question should not be posed until a foundation has been laid to ask it. This means that cross-examination questioning should move inductively; evidence should be assembled to support a conclusion the examining attorney wishes to make before stating that conclusion. Subsidiary questions should precede key questions. If a doctor testifies in direct that someone died from aponeurosis (a rupture of connective tissue at the base of the brain) and refers to damage at the base of the "skull," the cross-examination might begin with the subsidiary question "Doctor, is the brain inside the skull?" The groundwork can thus be laid to get to an important question concerning the physician's competence.

The body of the cross-examination might follow Bergman's "Safety Model" approach.[143] Bergman claims that the safer the cross-examination, the more likely an attorney is to accomplish his or her purpose. "The model is hopefully a more useful way of phrasing the familiar Golden Rule of Cross-Examination, 'Do not ask a question that you do not know the answer to.' This advice, while sound in and of itself, is no easier to follow than the advice that one should 'neither a borrower nor a lender be.'"[144] The model asks cross-examiners to rank proposed questions in terms of their safety, with high-safety questions, such as those based on prior witness statements, a much better bet than fishing-expedition, low-safety inquiries.

Cross-examination should end on a high note. A brilliant cross-examination period must not be anticlimactic. To proceed beyond the point of climax distracts the attention of the jury from the main thrust of the examination. Suppose a lawyer has reached a point where the jury has trouble believing a witness's story because the witness has just said something implausible or self-incriminating. This is the high note, and cross-examination should cease. A perfectly awful last question would be "Then why should we believe what you said?" That question allows witnesses to argue in defense of their challenged testimony. That cross-examination has been destroyed by one too many questions. A masterly cross-examination of a defendant does not end with him whimpering before the jury, "I confess." That only happens in motion picture and television scripts. Rather, an outstanding cross-examination ends on a high note when it merely sets up the point for closing argument. Only in closing argument should the drama of cross-examination be used to make the point that the witness's testimony should be disbelieved.

Younger gives us the marvelous example of a defense lawyer cross-examining an eyewitness:

Q: Where were the defendant and the victim when the fight broke out?
A: In the middle of the field.
Q: Where were you?
A: On the edge of the field.
Q: What were you doing?
A: Bird watching.
Q: Where were the birds?
A: In the trees.
Q: Where were the trees?
A: On the edge of the field.
Q: Were you looking at the birds?
A: Yes.
Q: So your back was to the people fighting?
A: Yes.

Now what do you do? You stop and sit down. And what will you argue in summation? He could not have seen it. His back was to them. You have challenged perception. Instead, you ask the one question too many:

Q: Well, if your back was to them, how can you say that the defendant bit off the victim's nose?
A: Well, I saw him spit it out.

That is the kind of answer you will get every time you ask the one question too many.[145]

Third, *lawyers should coach their own witnesses for cross-examination as part of the practice sessions for direct examination.* Prepare witnesses for cross-examination by discussing with them a few general guidelines:

1. Witnesses should be courteous in their demeanor to the questioning lawyer. They should not needlessly argue with counsel. At the same time, they should not be afraid of forcefully defending their testimony when the occasion requires it.

2. Witnesses must try to be directly responsive to the attorney's question. Avoid beating around the bush.

3. If they can, witnesses should try to avoid answering too many questions with yes or no answers. Some answers need brief explanations.

4. Witnesses should make their answers to questions as short as possible. This guide is suggested because when witnesses make long, rambling, narrative answers, they may confuse themselves or give more information than is needed.

5. Witnesses should not volunteer any information that is not sought in the cross-examination question.

6. Witnesses should not guess at answers if they do not know them. Witnesses are entitled to answer, "I do not know."

7. Witnesses should listen for the "facts" built into the cross-examiner's leading questions. Are they accurate or not?

8. Witnesses should not answer questions they do not fully understand. They should ask that such questions be repeated.

9. Witnesses should not let themselves be rushed into giving answers. At the same time, they must not be too hesitant or halting.

10. Witnesses should not look to their own counsel for answers.

11. Witnesses should break the steady rhythm of the cross-examiner. For instance, after an especially long and complex question, the witness can ask, "Would you please repeat the question?"

12. Witnesses should always tell the truth.

If possible, it is also wise to discuss with each witness the opposing counsel's style, delivery, idiosyncrasies, and likely areas for cross-questioning. For some, it may be wise to have dry-run cross-examination sessions, with an associate asking the questions. During the mock cross-examination, the witness should be confronted with all the challenging questions that can be anticipated at trial.[146] The questions should not be asked in a disbelieving way, which might reduce the confidence of the witness. Witnesses should know that grueling mock sessions have been designed to allow them to face cross-examination without fear.

In sum, careful planning and preparation takes into account (1) the objectives of and available methodologies for cross-examination, (2) an understanding of human behavior in the courtroom, (3) the structure of each cross-examination period, and (4) witness preparation. Careful planning and preparation are far more likely to bring solid results than an anticipated moment of inspiration.

Adverse Witnesses

An adverse witness is one that is hostile to the attorney who calls that witness to testify. Witnesses of this kind are used if opposing counsel does not produce them at trial or if, when produced, they fail to discuss in direct examination something the cross-examiner desires to have discussed. The primary purpose of presenting proof through an adverse party is not to destroy the credibility of the witness. Rather, it is to obtain information vital to the questioning counsel's case. Questioning should be limited only to that information which the adverse witness can provide. For instance, proof of ownership of a weapon that is within sole control of the hostile witness might be solicited when this witness testifies. Of course, it is foolish to call an adverse witness to the stand unless counsel is rather certain that such information can be realized.

Defendants are sometimes called as adverse witnesses by the plaintiff. If the defendant is called, it is strategically wise to have that person testify before the plaintiff or victim is called. As one author notes, "If you suspect that the defendant is willing to adapt his story to suit the occasion, your calling him to the stand as the first witness deprives him of the advantage of knowing before he is called upon to give his testimony what contentions he will have to meet; it affords you the opportunity of cross-examining him before he knows your theory of the case and what you are hoping to get him to admit."[147] The disadvantage of this strategy is that it gives the defendant the opportunity to make the initial impression. If this impression is favorable, the strategy backfires. But if a very strong and highly believable witness is put on the stand immediately after the defendant, the damaging parts of the defendant's statement can be destroyed before they have had a chance to set like concrete in the minds of the jury.[148]

The adverse witness procedure begins when a lawyer requests permission for a voir dire of a hostile witness. Once the lawyer has proven to the court that the witness is indeed adverse, questioning commences. The lawyer's technique for adverse witness examination should be somewhere between the approach for a friendly witness and ordinary cross-examination. "It is obvious that if the witness were to be asked a vital question, point-blank, his answer would likely be unfavorable, but that by a delicate approach, . . . an admission may be obtained which may logically or necessarily lead to a concession upon the principal issue."[149]

An example of successful examination of an adverse witness occurred in the government's World War II fraud trials of aluminum foundries that had made castings for airplane motors. Packard Motor Car Company, the prime contractor, issued specifications for the castings. However, the foundries were charged with ignoring some of the welding specifications. One of the government's adverse witnesses was the chief metallurgist from Packard. To best understand the testimony that follows, it is important to know that *peening* refers to a process for repairing defective castings.

Q: Paragraph 7 of the Specifications contains this language: "Castings shall not be repaired, plugged, nor welded without written permission." Do you recall now whether it was in your mind at that time to prohibit peening by that language?

A: It was not.

Q: Your thought was that peening, being a regularly accepted foundry practice, would be permitted notwithstanding that language? (Note this question broadens the previous testimony by suggesting that the specifications were not intended to exclude accepted foundry practices.)

A: Yes, sir.

Q: And you expected the defendant to disregard the language that castings should not be repaired without your consent insofar as repairing by peening was concerned?

A: Yes, sir.

Q: You knew at the time these specifications were framed that peening was a well-established foundry practice in the manufacture of aluminum castings?

A: I knew that we peened in our own factory eight or ten years before, yes.

Q: And you know you had found it necessary to peen in order to produce castings in quantity?

A: Yes, sir.

Q: And you expected the aluminum manufacturers to read this specification in the light of established foundry practices so far as peening was concerned?

A: Yes, sir.[150]

Note how vital the final question is. Note too that this was testimony that could come only from a Packard official as an adverse witness.

Impeachment

Impeachment is the process of discrediting a witness's testimony. Here is an example:

Q: Mr. Ford, you testified on direct examination that the first time you saw the defendant was on the evening of the alleged murder. Is that correct?

A: Yes, that's what I said.

Q: Mr. Ford, do you recall giving police officer Miller a written statement on the morning following the murder?

A: Yes, I do.

Q: I show you what purports to be a copy of that statement, dated April 18, 1986, bearing your signature. Is this your written statement?

A: Yes, it is.

Q: Would you refer to the first paragraph of that statement and read it aloud please?

A: "I first saw the defendant on the morning before the killing. He came to my house and asked if my wife was home."

Q: Then your statement is different from your testimony under oath, is it not?

A: Yes, it is. I guess I just forgot.

Counsel may then point out in closing argument that the witness has been impeached and may not be worthy of being believed. It has been shown empirically that once testimony has been impeached, juries will, at the very least, ignore the testimony and base their verdicts on the remaining evidence.[151] Impeachment is indeed a powerful and dramatic force.

When should impeachment be undertaken? The first impulse of many lawyers is to impeach all of the other side's witnesses, but such an attempt is unwise. If impeachment is pursued, it ought to have a sound basis. Unsuccessful attempts are worse than mere failures. An impeachment attempt that fails causes opposing counsel's witnesses to look stronger then when they began. The witness has withstood an impeachment attempt, and juries tend to sympathize with people who have had false charges filed against them. So impeachment should be approached cautiously. It should be undertaken only when there is a reasonably good chance of success.

What techniques of impeachment will yield the best results? It is best to start impeachment fairly early in a cross-examination because a witness is usually more nervous and less poised at that time. This timing catches the witness off guard and susceptible to impeachment. Discrediting questions should not come out at the very beginning of the cross-examination. Instead, cross-examiners should conceal their objective initially but then move quickly into a series of questions aimed at the impeachment purpose. This advice does not mean that an advocate should try to develop rapport with a witness at the beginning of cross-examination. "The jury has a nose for phony friendliness."[152] Rather, some courtesy and humanity should be displayed toward an opponent; anger and hostility are not the best behaviors to use at the start of a cross-examination effort.

Question form plays a role in the success of an impeachment attempt. Questions should be specific and sequential in order to keep constant pressure on the witness. Consider this example:

Q: The traffic light was red when you arrived at the intersection, wasn't it?

A: I don't believe so. I think it was green when I arrived at the intersection.

Q: Mr. Phelps, do you recall testifying this morning on direct examination that the light was red?

A: I'm not sure. I don't remember.

Q: Well, let me refresh your memory. Didn't you say this morning [reading from transcript], "As I approached the intersection, I had a clear view of the traffic light"?

A: Yes.

Q: Do you recall testifying, "I looked at the light carefully and noticed the color of the signal"?

A: Yes.

Q: So you clearly saw the traffic light, right?

A: Yes, I did.

Q: Do you have any doubts that you saw it clearly?

A: No.

Q: Do you recall further testifying this

morning, "The light was red when I arrived at the intersection"?

Mr. Phelps has been led into eating his own words as the agony of impeachment was prolonged by a series of leading questions. It was not done through a single question followed by a confession. Nor is impeachment the result of a free-wheeling inquiry. Effective impeachment comes from "a series of questions designed to elicit a series of responses each one more damning in its implication. The purpose is to take the jurors by the hand and lead them into a deeper and deeper conviction of the impropriety of the witnesses' action.[153]

Impeachment should stop just short of the climax. Impeaching lawyers sometimes are so successful that they believe they have to make the final kill while questioning. They want to reduce the witness to a blubbery shambles and consummate the case then. This should not be done! Consummation comes in the closing argument. Cross-examination only supplies the facts from which that final argument is later made. Something should be left hanging at the end of the impeachment process.

What are some areas in which impeachment is possible? First, there might be *internal contradictions.* A poll of Oregon jurors showed that watching a witness squirm when being impeached with a prior inconsistent statement was, to them, the most impressive part of a trial.[154] If there is an internal contradiction in someone's testimony, the cross-examiner should first lay the foundation regarding the circumstances of what was said in a prior instance, be it direct examination, written deposition, oral statement, pleadings, or omissions.[155] The exact language of that prior statement should be quoted. Then counsel should go over the testimony in court to show the contradiction. If necessary, the court reporter can read the testimony in court from the trial transcript or an attorney can read it from a deposition. If a contradiction is shown, the attorney points out to the jury in closing argument that this witness is unworthy of belief and that his or her testimony should be discounted.

Note the following example and running commentary provided by Morrill:

Q: You testified in court today that when you first saw Mr. White's automobile, it was traveling about 40 mph.
A: That's correct.
Q: Now, Mr. Smith, do you recall giving your deposition about six months ago?
A: Yes.
Q: That depostion was taken in your lawyer's office, was it not?
A: Yes.
Q: I was there at that time and asked you some questions, did I not?
A: Yes.
Q: And your lawyer was present the entire time I was asking you those questions?
A: Yes.
Q: There was a court stenographer present at that time, just as there is one here in court today?
A: Yes.
Q: And that court stenographer was taking down all of the questions I asked of you and all of the answers that you gave?
A: Yes.
Q: Before you testified, were you sworn to tell the truth?
A: Yes.
Q: Before I proceeded to ask you any questions, I asked you to listen carefully to my questions and told you I would be happy to repeat any questions you did not understand; is that correct?
A: That is correct.
Q: Do you remember this question being asked of you and this answer being given by you?
   "Q: Can you estimate the speed of Mr. White's automobile when you first saw it?"
   "A: Yes. It was traveling about 25 mph."
   Do you recall that question being asked of you and that answer being given by you while you were under oath?
A: Yes.

At this point, the witness has been impeached. There are several possible questions to ask next in following up the impeachment in order to highlight the inconsistencies. Some of the more commonly used are as follows:

Q: Were you lying then or are you lying now?
Q: At the time you gave your deposition, less time had gone by and you undoubtedly remembered the facts more clearly at that time; is that not so?
Q: Mr. Smith, would you like to change your testimony at this time?

I feel it is usually preferable to say nothing at all. If the point has been properly made by the cross-examiner, it is not necessary to give the witness a slap in the face. I do not feel such a slap adds any emphasis to the point already made, and it is always possible that the jurors may sympathize with the witness and dislike the examiner for what they may feel is an unnecessary affront.[156]

Furthermore, if Mr. Smith is asked to explain the contradiction in his testimony, he "has a chance of coming up with a plausible explanation of the conflict in his two versions."[157]

A second area for impeachment comes when a witness has a *poor reputation for truthfulness*. It is always possible that witnesses will deliberately lie on the stand. Should this be suspected, counsel must determine what precipitated the fraudulent testimony. Is the witness a congenital liar, who is morally incapable of distinguishing truths from falsehoods? Or is the witness so prejudiced for one litigant or against another in the case as to ignore his or her oath to tell the truth? To answer the first question, some courts allow evidence about a person's reputation for telling the truth to enter the trial.[158] Such evidence "is designed to show that the conscience of the witness would not be disturbed if he falsified."[159] Persons familiar with the witness's background behavior regarding truth and veracity in the community (called "collateral" witnesses) are called to the stand to testify as part of the impeachment process.

To answer the second question, a relationship between the witness and a party in the case must be proven. This relationship must be of a kind that would cause the witness to significantly color his or her testimony. The loving mother of a defendant is more likely to falsify information than is a distant cousin of that defendant. Proving the connection between personal relationships and lying is tricky business indeed and should be approached cautiously by counsel. Outstanding evidence is needed to make the attack successful. If the witness is only wounded by insinuation, the cross-examiner may "be cursed as a bullying pettifogger."[160]

Third, the witness may have *deficient perception, memory, or recall ability*. Faulty perception may be due to an emotional or physical impairment of some sort. One type of emotional impairment is stress. When we are calm, our perceptory ability is more likely to be accurate than when we are under duress. Under stress, the brain does not allow us to be precise.[161] For example, air force flight crews in trouble lose their attention for details such as time and color.[162] Physically, eyewitnesses may have the impairment of bad hearing. They could still testify with some accuracy about what they saw at a scene, because the failing hearing would impeach only one part of their testimony.

"Perception lasts for about one quarter of a second. After that, we rely on short-term memory, which has a reduced capacity for holding information."[163] This psychological phenomenon has important implications for impeachment. An eyewitness's account would be valuable if he or she were questioned a quarter of a second after observing an incident. But such is not the case. So impeachment is a time to focus on the numerous problems associated with short-term memory storage. We lose information in transferring from perception to memory. We hold only four to six unrelated items at a time in our short-term memory.[164] We lose infor-

mation along the way, and most of it is lost forever. In fact, if information in the short-term memory is not continually reviewed and studied, it is not etched into our long-term memory. We must carefully classify and file information in order for it to be stored for the long term. Even then, some of the information may be lost. If you observe an elderly lady with white hair and wrinkled skin who is wearing a flowered dress and straw hat and speaks with a foreign accent, all those data might be filed as "old lady." And that will be the only information you can later recall. Only a fraction of what we perceive do we remember.

Furthermore, we assimilate the information we receive to conform with our stereotypes and expectations.[165] Stereotyping skews both perception and recall insofar as we assign to others actions in which they had no part. In one study, subjects viewed a subway scene in which a black man and a white man were facing each other. The white man was holding a razor. But when later asked to recall who was holding a razor, only a few more than half the subjects said it was the white man.[166] Expectations, or mind sets, also skew perceptions and recall. What we think we see is often what we expect to see. Coins seem larger to poor children than to their rich peers because money has greater value to the poor.[167] Aces of spades colored red are ignored and not counted by card players, who expect spades to be black.[168] Expectations cause us to report what we think we observe rather than what we really observe, thereby laying the groundwork for impeachment.

These, then, are some of the areas for impeachment. Some witnesses are more primed for impeachment than others, and analysis of each witness is important for counsel. As the great Roman advocate and educator Quintilian said nearly two thousand years ago, "In the examination of a witness, the first essential is to know his type." The flippant or smart-aleck witness is generally disliked by juries, and impeachment by getting that person to overextend is appreciated by the audience. The witness who recited a carefully prepared story is easily confused and subsequently impeached if the cross-examiner changes the order of the story and the logic behind the witness's conclusions. The evasive witness can be impeached by asking, "Don't you want to really answer the question?" Juries appreciate rough treatment in these instances. On the other hand, it is much more difficult to impeach a timid and frail witness. That is why analysis and adaptation of each witness is important for the cross-examiner who embarks on an impeachment mission.

Communication Strategies for the Attorney in Cross-Examination

Throughout the questioning of witnesses, lawyers must be cognizant of their communication techniques and the effect they are having on the judge or jury. What follows are eight guidelines trial lawyers should heed when cross-examining witnesses.

Keep the jury's attention. Belief is closely tied to attention and interest. The examiner should be the person holding the audience's interest during cross-questioning, and opposing counsel should not be center stage, distracting from the examination by doing such things as rattling papers, whispering, squeaking a chair, tapping a pencil, or deliberately and hurriedly looking for a piece of paper in a briefcase. When blatant distractions such as these occur, examining counsel should approach the judge and ask to have the opposing attorney reprimanded. During cross-examination, examining counsel should do everything possible to get the jury to pay attention to what the examiner and the witness are saying.

Throughout cross-examination, the tone and mood of the questioning should vary to reduce boredom. A good blend of the casual, soft-spoken method, which lulls the witness into a sense of security, and the dramatic, vigorous, rapid-fire method is highly recommended. Vocal modulation should suit the subject under discussion, but there should be frequent modulation to ensure a dynamic delivery. Dynamism in questioning is associated with being tough-minded, task oriented, assertive, and self-assured,[169] precisely the traits a cross-examiner wants to exhibit. Well-known cross-examiner Melvin Belli comments, "The experienced examiner, like a baseball pitcher, relies upon a change of pace to suit the varying conditions in the game. . . . The gentler approach is better calculated to elicit the concessions which the examiner desires. The . . . vehement style . . . ordinarily makes the hostile witness more hostile."[170]

There should be no inordinately long pauses between questions. Trials seem lengthy to jurors anyway, and their attention span is often exceeded when questioning does not move along at a fairly quick clip. "The skillful cross-examiner keeps an examination confined to a definite line of inquiry and conducts it in a snappy, vigorous manner."[171] In addition to holding the attention of the jury, quick questioning gives witnesses less time to consider the effects of their replies, and they are kept off balance when facing constant pressure from the questioner. "A witness answering rapidly is more likely to contradict himself than one who answers after having been given plenty of time to deliberate."[172] A brisk examining pace does not mean that an attorney should rush the examination along to the point of losing a jury, but it does mean that the questioning should not be strung out unnecessarily to the point of beating a dead horse.

Finally, the jury has just finished hearing testimony that was presented chronologically. To bore the jury by following chronology again is a mistake. "Cross-examination should always be organized by themes."[173] The cross-examiner wants to focus on the issues raised in the testimony. Direct examination laid the foundation for those issues. The jurors should have their attention drawn to those issues in order to provide focus and excitement in the trial.

Avoid copious notes. It is disconcerting to a jury to see a lawyer rely on a morass of notes during cross-examination. Extensive lists of precise questions prepared in advance cause an attorney not to listen, not to follow up on answers, and to spend too much time on trivialities. The jury thinks that the lawyer is ill prepared for the examination of witnesses when he or she becomes wedded to a yellow pad. Some notes, such as brief outlines of the battle plan, are permissible; extensive notes are unwarranted.

During opposing witnesses' direct examination, copious notes need not be written. It is far more crucial to study each witness and to make notes only on those portions of the testimony which help to underscore or alter the previously planned cross-examination. However, when questioning those witnesses in cross-examination, there is one dimension of note taking that can be quite effective. Witnesses and jurors constantly scrutinize the nonverbal behavior of the questioning attorney. When a lawyer occasionally pauses to write something down during cross-examination, it appears as though important information or a significant concession has been made by the person testifying, and this act can unnerve the witness.

Do not badger the witness. Savage sarcasm, loudness, gestures of disgust, and other discourtesies designed to pulverize a witness are generally to be avoided because juries will become alienated by this tactic. "It must be kept in mind that the witness is entitled to courteous treatment. A jury is ordinarily quick to sense and resent a discourtesy."[174] Juries are more likely to sympathize with those who are bullied and browbeaten than with those who do the bullying and browbeating. Even when a witness is obviously biased or lying, lawyers must resist the temptation to lose their tempers. An advocate should not allow the cross-examination to become a fencing match, no matter how adverse the witness is. "Juries are apt to regard an advocate who has lost his temper as one who is covering a weak case with bluster."[175]

Insist that the witness's answers be clear. Witnesses who are cross-examined often frame evasions to questions. When this occurs, the cross-examiner should try to pin the witness down to a clear answer. Consider the following illustration:

Q: Have you talked with anyone about your testimony in this case?
A: I don't know what you mean. I talked to you. [*Evasive.*]
Q: Have you talked with anyone other than me?
A: This friend of mine. [*Evasive.*]
Q: What friend?
A: Carl Jones.
Q: How many times did you talk with Mr. Jones?
A: Two times. Maybe three. I don't know.
Q: Let's start with the first time you talked with Mr. Jones about the case. Will you recall that time and please be exact?

Notice how the evasive witness is pressed. But how far should an attorney go to get a clear answer? It depends on the importance of the information solicited. Even if a witness is obviously evasive after some pressing on an important matter, the pressing can be stopped because the evasiveness will be apparent to the jury and will reflect unfavorably on the reliability of that witness's testimony. If a witness continues to give evasive answers, a lawyer can request the court to instruct the witness to clearly answer the question.[176] The instruction from the judge usually works.

Avoid cross-interruptions with a witness. Duke University studies on language and law concluded that cross-interruptions and simultaneous talk with a witness during cross-examination cause a perceived loss of lawyer control and reduced attorney credibility.[177]

Cross-interruptions occur when lawyers break into witness answers. Simultaneous talk is overlapping dialogue between lawyer and witness. Since a lawyer's control over a witness is perceived to diminish when the lawyer and a witness talk at the same time or interrupt each other, it is strongly advised that lawyers do what they can to avoid these instances. If a witness attempts to explain an answer on cross-examination, counsel should not interrupt, but should follow up with a loop-back question incorporating part or all of the explanation to emphasize something favorable to the examiner's position. Loop-back questions, rather than interruptions and simultaneous speech, allow the lawyer to regain control of the witness.

Avoid open-ended questions, and use leading questions. Open-ended questions give witnesses a chance to explain their answers. Long, narrative answers allow witnesses to slip in unfavorable and damaging information. When answers are limited to a yes, no, or short reply by closed-ended or leading questions, counsel can accomplish a lot of control over a witness in the cross-examination period. Leading questions offer two advantages: "First, if the witness is anxious to give the right answer, and is friendly toward the questioner (or at least neutral) the witness is likely to accept the answer implied by the question. Second, leading questions may stimulate a memory of a fact or event which is consistent with other beliefs the witness holds about the event in question."[178] The net result is that there is a greater chance of diminished witness credibility with leading questions than with nonleading questions.[179]

The following is one author's example, with commentary, of a successful use of leading questions:

Assume the following facts in representing a defendant: Two automobiles collided at an intersection where one street is regulated by a stop sign, while the other street is a through street; the defendant, who had the stop sign, struck the side of the plaintiff's car while it was traveling through the intersection. To paraphrase the testimony, the defendant states that he brought his car to a stop, looked both ways, decided he had time to proceed through the intersection and started up, striking the side of the plaintiff's automobile, which, he says must have been coming at a fast rate of speed; the plaintiff testifies he was traveling at a reasonable speed and did not notice the defendant until he was struck in the side. Assume, further, that the plaintiff is an articulate person with an above-average ability to persuade a jury. The proper way to cross-examine this plaintiff is to give him no opportunity to explain or give narrative answers. Questions calling for explanations might be as follows:

Q: Now, if the visibility was good and nothing interfered with your vision, why was it that you didn't see Mr. White's car until it hit you?

A: It just never occurred to me that a car coming from Green Street with the stop sign would drive right into my side. I was going along at a reasonable speed in a wide, open intersection, and there just isn't a reason in the world why Mr. White should not have waited for me until I passed through the intersection.

Q: But, if you were paying attention, how is it that you didn't see Mr. White's car until the accident?

A: The only explanation must be that I didn't expect a car and never really noticed it until he suddenly drove into my side.

Now compare the following examination:

Q: You have driven down Main Street in the past?

A: Yes.

Q: As a matter of fact, you have driven down Main Street quite a number of times in the past; isn't that correct?

A: Yes.

Q: You were, therefore, quite familiar with the intersection of Main Street and Green Street?

A: Yes.

Q: Then I'm sure you were aware that the street you were on was a through street?

A: Yes.

Q: And you knew that Green Street had a stop sign?

A: Yes.

Q: You had driven on Green Street in the past?

A: Yes.

Q: This accident occurred at about 11:00 in the morning?

A: Yes.

Q: This was a clear, bright day; wasn't it?

A: Yes.

Q: There wasn't anything to obscure visibility at that time?

A: No.

Q: And as you drove on Main Street that day, there was nothing to prevent you from seeing cars traveling in either direction on Green Street?

A: Correct.

Q: That is, you could see cars moving from your left to your right or from your right to your left; isn't that true?

A: Yes.

Q: I believe you testified that you approached Green Street at about 45 mph?

A: Yes.

Q: The posted speed is 50 mph?

A: Yes.

Q: Then you weren't speeding at the time?

A: No.

Q: You were paying attention to your driving?

A: Yes.

Q: There wasn't anything to distract you from your driving?

A: No.

Q: You can see a considerable distance on Green Street both to the left and right as it approaches Main Street; is that correct?

A: That is true.

Q: When you were some distance from the intersection, there was nothing to interfere with your vision in seeing Mr. White's car, was there?

A: No.

Q: And as you continued to approach Green Street, was there anything to interfere with your vision in seeing Mr. White's car?

A: No.

Q: And as you began to enter the intersection of Green Street, was there anything to interfere with your vision in seeing Mr. White's car?

A: No.

Q: And as you entered the intersection, I take it there was still nothing to interfere with your vision in seeing Mr. White's car?

A: Yes.

Q: And after you were driving in the intersection, I take it there still was nothing to interfere with your vision in seeing the other car?

A: That is correct.

Q: And then there was an accident?

A: Yes.

Q: And I believe you testified that you did not see Mr. White's car until the accident?

A: Yes.

Q: You wouldn't know whether Mr. White stopped at the stop sign, would you?

A: No.

Q: Or how long he waited at the stop sign before proceeding?

A: No.

Q: And the reason you wouldn't know whether he stopped is that you never even took the simple precaution of looking out for other cars as you drove into that intersection.

The lawyer is now provided with material for his summation: "How can the plaintiff contend he was exercising ordinary care before and at the time of the occurrence? There was nothing to interfere with his vision. It was a bright, clear day. All he had to do was look—just look. John's white car did not drop out of the sky. If only the plaintiff had taken the one, simple precaution of looking, none of us would be here today.

"Under the law, and it is this jury's sworn duty to follow the law, the plaintiff cannot collect ten cents unless he proves that before and at the time of the accident he was exercising ordinary care for his own safety . . ."[180]

As this cross-examination shows, it is the attorney who makes the assertions and statements of fact. It is not the witness. The witness responded with yes-or-no answers. Although counsel cannot demand yes-or-no replies, a tactic resented by the jury and judge, he or she can request the court to direct an evasive witness to answer yes or no. At times, the witness may respond by saying,

"I don't know." This is not a bad reply, because research shows that the more times a lawyer gets a witness to say "I don't know," the more unreliable that witness will appear.[181]

Use suggestive language. Suggestion is generated in the minds of listeners during communication. Lawyers who attempt to channel those suggestions through their own words are simply capitalizing on a present and unavoidable force.[182] Cross-examination is a time when lawyers can assert their views of a case in their own words.[183]

One way to suggest what ought to be important to the judge and jury is to highlight vital answers and key phrases. Repetition enhances memory. Hence, key words in vital answers should be used in subsequent questions. If a "concealed rotten railing" is important to the case and such words are used in a witness's testimony, "that concealed rotten railing" should be the words used in many questions to follow. However, repeating all or some part of *every* answer, regardless of its importance, minimizes the effectiveness of an examination. That is not what is suggested here. Also, the rhythm created by repetition can be an influential factor. Consider a police officer who is cross-examined about a collision.[184] The plaintiff's attorney has gotten the officer to state that a bus rear-ended the car of the injured plaintiff. A defense theory is that the officer has no way of remembering what happened years ago. Now, consider the rhythm of these questions: "Now, you've indicated that skid marks *appeared* to come from both the car and the bus?" "What tires on the car did the skid marks *appear* to come from?" "What tires on the bus did the skid marks *appear* to come from?" "Does your report show what tires they *appeared* to come from?" The same key word, tied to the defense attorney's theme, is cleverly built into each cross-examination question for the persuasive effect repetition affords.

Suggestion can also be accomplished through the use of tag questions. In one experiment, subjects watched one of two versions of a film. One version contained a bicycle; the other did not. Afterward, subjects received one of two questions: "Did you see the bicycle?" and "You did see a bicycle, didn't you?" The latter question has a tag on it. Tag questions produced many more "yes" answers, irrespective of whether a bicycle was actually present.[185] The tag itself creates a negatively constructed question. As noted in the section on direct examination, negatively constructed questions are confusing to respondents. This may be why there were more "yes" answers to such questions in the experiment. Although attorneys do not want to confuse their own witnesses and should avoid tag questions in direct examination, tags are excellent forms of suggestion for leading questions in cross-examination.

Another suggestive technique is to assert facts indirectly in the questions posed. For example, if a rape victim is questioned about her prior sexual history, juries will infer that the premise underlying these questions is valid and that the victim may have encouraged the rape. One study found that when rape victim history questions are asked, defendants receive lighter sentences than when such questions are not asked.[186] Another study noted that more guilty verdicts were issued the more jurors constructed in their minds an increasingly violent crime, and that such a construction of reality was linked to the specificity of violent words in the prosecutor's leading questions. A nonspecific question was "How much of the incident did you see?" A specific question was "How much of the fight did you see?"[187] Also, when the question "Is Curtis a friend of yours?" is asked, the implication is that Curtis is on good terms with the witness. When the question "Is Curtis an enemy of yours?" is asked, the implication is that Curtis is an enemy. If counsel wants to show in cross-examination that the witness has a vendetta against his or her "enemy," Curtis, the latter question is suggestive of this "fact."

One study of the suggestive implications of language offered questions to its subjects regarding whether a certain person was an extrovert or an introvert. Words used in the question included "talkative" and "life of the party," or "not outgoing" and "feel left out." The results show that the assumptions contained in the questions were treated as conjectural evidence by the observers making their judgments about people.[188] Even the description of faces is subject to suggestive questioning. Eyewitnesses who are given false information, such as the mention of a mustache when indeed none existed, incorporate the false information into their subsequent verbal descriptions.[189] Phrasing questions that lead the listener to expect something neither explicitly stated nor necessarily implied in the question "provides a very potent means to create a picture or model of the events described in the minds of jurors—a model which may go far beyond the actual words spoken. In other words, more is inferred than need be stated."[190]

Use nonverbal communication techniques when cross-examining. Because of its ease of use, nonverbal communication is a major source of meaning[191] in the cross-examination exchange. Three dimensions of nonverbal communication will be discussed: kinesics, paralanguage, and proxemics.

Kinesics is the study of gestures and body movement. It includes movement of the hands, head, limbs, and other parts of the body, as well as posture, facial expressions, and eye movements. Some of the obvious research findings in the area of kinesics are that recurring gestures and movements tend to communicate messages following certain patterns. For example, shaky hands communicate nervousness. Clasped hands communicate tension. Tapping or snapping fingers communicate impatience. Hitting a table with a fist communicates anger. Crossed legs and turned-away shoulders communicate dislike. Open arms communicate trust and honesty. The lowered head communicates a feeling of inferiority or insecurity.[192] On the other hand, a sudden change from baseline kinesic behavior communicates something too. A sudden nervous gesture or movement in the chair, a glance toward the other lawyer, or a rapid change in vocal cues reveals what may be a sensitive area for questioning. Kinesic changes signaling witness deception include an awkward smile, a rigid body, blushing, perspiring, difficulty in breathing, shaking, playing with fingernails or facial hair, and sudden shifting of body, leg, and foot movements.[193] Knowing and identifying these kinesic characteristics can help a lawyer who is trying to detect deceit, although it should be stressed that these behaviors may not stem solely from deception. The cues are only signs that, if intensified through additional questioning, may become signs of dishonesty.[194]

One finding particularly interesting for cross-examination purposes is that hypokinetic persons (those who move and talk slowly) have problems communicating with hyperkinetics (those who move and talk rapidly). Dialogue between them becomes exasperating because they communicate at different rates.[195] Imagine a lawyer using this information when trying to exasperate a witness in court.

Finally, facial and eye expressions are rich in communication potential for the cross-examining attorney. Questioning lawyers should attract and hold the eyes of their responding witnesses. A lot can be learned from standing near witnesses and studying their eye expressions. Visual feedback signals that a communication channel is open.[196] How many times, when an instructor posed a question in class, have you looked away or put your head down to avoid eye contact and hoped that in turn you were closing the communication channel so that you would not have to answer that question? By the same token, avoidance of eye contact or increased blinking is an indication that a witness does not want to communicate with the examining lawyer and desires to have that particular interaction cut off.[197] In addition, pupils enlarge, or dilate, when witnesses have positive feelings toward something, and they contract or constrict when those witnesses have negative feelings, including difficulty with what they are saying.[198]

Lawyers need to be aware of their own eye contact cues as well. For instance, if an examiner gets a devastating answer to a question, he or she should remain poker-faced as if nothing has happened. This facial control minimizes the effect of the damaging answer. Or, if an examiner receives a wonderful reply to a question, he or she should emphasize that reply by turning to the jury and looking at them so they can think about the information they just heard. Furthermore, tight nonverbal control over witnesses, by means of a fixed gaze, can be used by an attorney in cross-examination in order to create a certain degree of tension. Gazing is used to dominate and influence.[199] On the other hand, too much of a fixed stare on witnesses can make them feel uncomfortable, and this is not a good idea if the attorney's main purpose is to elicit information.

Paralanguage is the study of the human voice. To some extent, lying or deception can be perceived by listening to a witness's voice.[200] Individuals shifting toward deception tend to talk less, more slowly, and with greater disfluencies.[201] They have longer delays in responding as they search for good answers, and their responses become shorter.[202] In addition, their pitch becomes higher.[203]

Proxemics is the study of the use and perception of social and personal space. We all have privacy needs. We need to maintain some degree of distance from others. Some space is seen by us to be completely ours and inviolate. The term *territoriality* is given to our tendency to claim and defend certain spaces as our very own. We all have certain territories we call our own—perhaps an entire bedroom or perhaps one chair in a given classroom. When those territories are invaded, human behavior is affected. When we feel crowded in our own territory, we become less cooperative, less friendly, and more hostile. Positive communication channels close. Anxieties grow.[204]

In addition to territory, we all have our own personal space, a distance between people at which they can both feel comfortable. This is not a fixed place like territory, but an invisible bubble of space that travels with us. The bubble expands and contracts according to the situation; it is large in a hostile environment but shrinks in a friendly setting.[205] Strangers in an elevator stand farther apart than do loved ones. To increase anxiety in someone else, personal space can be invaded. So, with regard to territoriality and personal space, "the violation of distance norms or expectations has perhaps its greatest impact in negatively affecting interpersonal relationships."[206]

Think of what a good working knowledge of proxemics does for a lawyer during cross-examination. The lawyer should physically dominate the courtroom. If local rules allow, counsel should stand during cross-examination. Standing attracts the jury to what the lawyer is saying. The X marks on the diagram that follows indicate where an attorney should stand and then move during cross-examination if the attorney wants to invade a witness's territory and personal space, thereby creating discomfort and anxiety.

Notice in the diagram how counsel approaches and dominates the witness's terri-

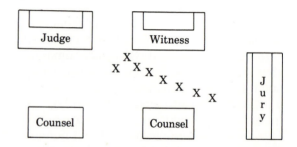

tory with his or her presence. Nonverbal domination is important during cross-examination.[207] To come on strong and dominate a witness, an attorney should move closer to the stand if such a move will not receive disapproval from a jury. To the extent moving in on the witness is allowed, it has the advantage of diminishing the witness's importance or status, controlling the witness's answers, and allowing the jury to focus on the lawyer's leading questions.

Equally important as nonverbal awareness and evaluation in the courtroom is the related phenomenon of listening, a skill needed for cross-examination and for direct examination as well. Bad listening is identified in several ways. Pretending to listen by acknowledging the message while hearing only the sound of a witness's voice is not listening. Sporadic comprehension of what a witness says is not listening. Giving up trying to understand a complex message is not listening. Listening to argue, not to understand, is not listening. However, being aware of these bad listening habits and then concentrating, remaining objective, trying to understand, and posing questions about what is not understood are recommended skills for effective listening. Good listening does not just happen; lawyers questioning witnesses must work hard at developing this dimension of the communication process.[208]

EXPERT WITNESSES

As noted in Chapter 4, the outcome of a great deal of litigation is determined by the opinions of expert witnesses. Because of the importance of experts, many lawyers have them testify last so that they can be used to summarize prior witness testimony and offer their own well-founded opinions. Experts may be used in one of three ways. First, they may be used as fact witnesses. For example, a victim's doctor can be called to testify about the party's injury. Second, they may be used to teach the jury certain scientific principles to help them evaluate the facts of a case. For instance, a speech scientist can testify about the validity of voiceprint information. Third, they may be used to express an opinion about the facts of the case at hand. For example, a ballistics expert might offer a judgment about a certain gun's being the one used in a shooting incident.[209]

Attorneys want their experts to have high credibility with the jury. Credibility consists of competence, trustworthiness, and dynamism. Competence refers to the witness's training, experience, and professional expertise and is established as "attorneys attempt to convince the judge and jury to formulate a positive evaluation of the . . . witness by having the witness recite a litany of educational and experiential credentials during the voir dire."[210] Voir dire in this context is a period of examination by an attorney to establish the expert's qualifications. Voir dire occurs before the expert presents any substantive opinions. Trustworthiness refers to the sincerity, honesty, and objectivity of the witness. References to the taking of an oath, allegiance to a code of professional ethics, lack of partisanship, and a disclaimer of personal gain or motive may be used to establish trustworthiness. Speakers are also considered trustworthy and objective when they use authority-based assertions, that is, references to treatises and other kinds of evidence from outside sources.[211] Also, the expert must appear sincere.[212] Dynamism refers to the witness's presentation. As noted in Chapter 3, the personality and demeanor of the expert are on trial. During the expert's presentation, he or she must come across as aggressive, emphatic, forceful, bold, active, energetic, and efficient—not meek and hesitant.[213] In addition, the expert must be a model teacher, "prepared as consummate actor and communicator, pursuing every educational strategem and device that an excellent instructor would adopt,"[214] especially communicating in words the jury would understand and believe. Finally, experts should "dress at or near the top of the 'power dress continuum.'"[215] This means a dark blue or dark gray suit, a white shirt, executive shoes, and a conservative tie for males and a skirted suit, a plain white blouse, heels, and conservative makeup for women. Short hair is needed for both sexes.

Once a trial judge is convinced that the person testifying is qualified in a given field, then the expert may be questioned about the case. An examination of the expert's observations and methodology should be organized in the same way as an assault on Mt. Everest: first, climb the mountain; second, plant a flag; third, climb down. In climbing up, experts should detail all the preparation, study, experimentation, rejection of alternative conclusions, and analysis that they have undertaken to formulate their conclusions or opinions. The flag at the pinnacle is the experts' statements of opinion. In climbing down, experts may explain the bases or reasons that support their conclusions.[216] Taken in this order, the testimony should be easy for a jury to follow.

"For a trial, the structure of an adversary's case often depends heavily upon . . . cross-examination directed toward [the] expert. . . . Unlike other witnesses, this witness will testify on ultimate conclusions which may be controlling if accepted."[217] However, even though cross-examination of an expert is so vital, the risks of cross-examining an expert are acute. Experts are partisan. Many have experienced the rigor of forensic combat. "At times they develop a remarkable ability to answer all around a question without directly answering it."[218] They frequently have the upper hand over a lawyer in the area of specialization in which they are testifying. Therefore, experts are often able to maintain their equilibrium and build on their original testimony under cross-examination. When there is a competent expert and an incompetent lawyer, the cross-examination can be disas-

trous for the lawyer. Hence, expert witnesses should not be cross-examined unless the questioner can answer four questions:

1. Has the testimony on direct examination hurt my case?

2. If it has, can I impeach that testimony in cross-examination?

3. Can I obtain testimony helpful to my case?

4. Do the probable benefits of cross-examination outweigh the possible dangers of cross-examinination by a big enough margin to justify the risks?[219]

In order to cross-examine expert witnesses successfully, lawyers must be well prepared. This is especially true if the goal of the cross-examination is impeachment. If impeachment is counsel's goal, he or she should strike for the jugular at the beginning of cross-examination, while the witness is apprehensive and the jury is attentive. Impeachment of an expert can be accomplished in one of three ways.

First, experts may be ill qualified, even if the court has deemed them experts in a given trial. Qualifications can be undermined, either through cross-examination of the experts on the stand or by independent evidence from other sources. It is perfectly appropriate to probe an alleged expert's faulty educational background, lack of experience, or personal bias. However, only a very thorough investigation by the questioning attorney before trial prevents this approach from failing. A high degree of success virtually must be assured before counsel embarks on this goal for cross-examining an expert.

Probing the expert's educational background and experience as a line of attack often gets into the distinction between qualifying generally as an expert and giving opinions in the specific case. A person may be qualified as a mechanical engineer but lack the expertise to testify about skid marks and tire tread. Attacking the qualifications of an expert under voir dire or cross-examination can possibly block the presentation of that individual's opinion. Here is an example of an expert who, under cross-examination, is shown to have significant limitations as an expert:

Q: Doctor, you testified that you are a neurosurgeon?
A: Yes.
Q: Are you also a psychiatrist?
A: No.
Q: Are you an X-ray specialist, a radiologist?
A: No.
Q: Are you a specialist in orthopedic surgery?
A: We do some of the same kinds of work.
Q: Are you a specialist in that field?
A: No.
Q: There has been testimony in this case about brain waves or electroencephalograms. Are you a specialist in interpreting those tests?
A: I review many of them.
Q: But doctor, aren't there physicians who do that type of work almost exclusively?
A: Yes.
Q: Often they practice in hospitals, don't they?
A: Yes.
Q: And when your patients have brain wave tests done at such hospitals, you generally rely on those specialists for interpretation of such brain wave tests, don't you?
A: Yes.[220]

Personal bias might be proven as well. Bias represents the experts' attitudinal set, and it can be shown by causing the experts to acknowledge that they have testified on many occasions for the same side or for the same position. It might be shown that they accumulate a substantial portion of their total income in this way, or that their personal prejudice has made them particularly attractive to parties taking the other side in that type of litigation.

The previous paragraph implies that some lawyers try to impeach by pointing to the remuneration received by experts for their appearances in court. Indeed, such is the case. The thinking behind this approach is that the jury will believe that the money will influence the experts' opinions and that partisanship is inevitable. To the contrary, all experts are paid for their testimony, and this attempt to impeach generally falls on deaf ears. "Even if the jury knows the witness is paid, this knowledge will not make them distrust the expert as long as there is no attempt to conceal" that fact.[221]

Second, the expert may be impeached because of inconsistent opinions. If writings, speeches, and prior depositions or court testimony of an expert are combed, counsel might discover earlier opinions that were quite different from the testimony just heard on the witness stand. "If the witness has testified with some frequency previously, his testimony has probably been transcribed as part of a record for appeal which is available for inspection at the courthouse. For counsel who have a substantial volume of litigation involving expert witnesses, it may be wise to prepare an index of expert testimony contained in appellate records filed at the courthouse. . . . Nothing is quite as devastating to a witness and his testimony as being confronted by a completely ordinary statement made by him in another circumstance or context."[222] Consider this hypothetical example:

Q: Doctor Pryor, I believe you said that in your opinion this boy did not have phonoronia, is that correct?
A: That is correct.
Q: And you drew that conclusion for three reasons: one, he had a normal heartbeat; second, he had a normal neurological examination; and third, he was not rendered unconscious. Is that correct?
A: Yes.
Q: All right. Now, doctor, would you agree with this statement:
"I don't think that unconsciousness

could be used as an index at all in connection with phonoronia because we have penetrating wounds of the polomax in which very frequently consciousness is not lost. I don't think that unconsciousness has any diagnostic significance in regard to the possibility of phonoronia.''

A: Absolutely not.

Q: Doctor, I am reading to you, if it will assist you, a special address you gave to the American Medical Association on February 20, 1980. Now would you like to read your own speech?

Self-contradiction undermines an expert's credibility. To accomplish this method of impeachment, counsel simply asks the witness whether he or she did in fact testify earlier to a certain fact, which the jury can see is inconsistent with his or her present conclusion. In this way, the jurors note the conflict, and the expert has no concurrent opportunity to attempt an explanation.

A variation on the prior-inconsistency approach is to use the adverse expert to develop portions of the cross-examiner's own case. For example, an artfully prepared line of questioning may cause a medical expert to agree that the nature of injuries is consistent with one's own position regarding liability. Here is an illustration:

Q: Doctor, did you see any evidence that John Franklin's condition was caused by his being hit in the head by a baseball?

A: Did you say hit in the head by a baseball?

Q: Yes.

A: No, I saw no evidence of that.

Q: Can we rule that out?

A: Yes, I would have seen other signs if there had been damage from being hit in the head by a baseball.

Q: Did the plaintiff's lawyer tell you that a witness of mine will consider that a real possibility?

A: No, this is the first I've heard of it.

Adverse experts will typically not know where they are being led until after they have helped the questioner.

Another variation on the prior-inconsistency approach is to accomplish reversals by the expert on opinions expressed in direct. Quite often, expert conclusions are based on certain assumed facts. "To emphasize that these . . . facts are the necessary predicate for the conclusions expressed by the witness, it may be helpful in appropriate cases to list those assumed facts for the jury on a blackboard or chart, particularly when they are disputed facts. The witness is then . . . asked whether his answer would change if each of the facts individually was modified or contradicted.''[223] For example:

Q: If the motor control test of his left hand had been positive, would that have been significant?

A: It would be relevant.

Q: And if spasms in the palm of the left hand had also been present, would that cause you to modify your opinion?

A: I didn't find any spasm.

Q: I understand, but if a competent orthopedist had found that spasm and a positive motor control test, at the same time as your examination, would that cause you to modify your conclusion that he had fully recovered when you saw him?

A: Well, if you can assume those things, I suppose so.

A final variation on the use of inconsistencies is to show a conflict between the witness's conclusions and the jury's own common sense and experience. Consider the following:

Q: Let me ask you this: Assume Ms. Crandell has a traumatic neurosis. If she gets every single penny she asks for, will she get well the next day, the next week, or the next month?

A: I think she will feel very much better as soon as she gets appropriate payment for the pain she has suffered.

Q: How about headaches and dizziness? Will they disappear the same day she gets the check? Put the money in her pocket and that's it?

A: She may have headaches from different causes.

Q: But this condition is going to go away on the day payment is made, is that right?

A: That is my medical opinion, yes.

Q: It won't even taken a week, it will be just that day, that first day?

A: That's right.

Notice that the physician is pushed into taking a ludicrous position. The doctor has demonstrated a clear lack of objectivity, and most juries are willing to disregard testimony that counters common sense and personal experience. "If the expert's testimony sounds implausible or inconsistent with human experience, . . . it is necessary to 'close the door' after the answer and to avoid explanation by the witness. Rigid control is required to accomplish this."[224]

Ultimately, counsel may pose a hypothetical question, which asks an expert to assume certain facts as a foundation for inferences to be drawn from those facts. The theory is "that the jury must be put in the position to accept or reject the inference, depending on whether they accept or reject the specific facts upon which it rests."[225] The scope of a hypothetical question is in the hands of the presiding judge. Some attorneys maintain that a well-propounded hypothetical can be quite persuasive, although there are those who claim that it is a confusing interruption of the normal presentation of evidence. One author goes so far as to say that the hypothetical "is, perhaps, the most abominable form of evidence that was ever allowed to choke the mind of a juror or throttle his intelligence."[226] From a communication viewpoint, I tend to agree with that position and find the hypothetical not very advisable. In fact, the hypothetical is being used less and less in court.

Essentially what an attorney asking a hypothetical does is to pose a rather long question to an expert witness. The question contains specific hypothetical facts, which are a synopsis of previously sworn testimony. The examining attorney then asks the expert to reach a conclusion about those facts. For instance, an attorney may describe an accident in which a woman fell while stepping off a city bus and ask the expert to assume the facts in the incident to be true. Then, counsel may say, "Based on those facts, could such a fall result in amnesia?" The expert renders an opinion and states the reasons for that opinion. If a hypothetical is used, it should be prepared in writing early, with copies of the question given to the expert, the judge, and opposing counsel.

Third, an expert may be impeached when there are contrary views from other experts in the field. Textbooks and treatises from other sources can be quoted. When they are, contrary books and articles from respected authors should be piled high on counsel's table. When books or articles from experts other than the person on the witness stand are the subject of inquiry, the opposing author's name, full qualifications, and viewpoint are read aloud to the jury so that they can hear the opposing opinions one after the other. If the witness denies that the source is authoritative, all is not lost, especially if the witness refuses to acknowledge a second and a third and a fourth of these authoritative publications by authors with impressive credentials. Ultimately, the jury must conclude either that the witness is ignorant in his or her own professional field or that he or she is adamant, stubborn, and untruthful.

One technique for making headway in cross-examination is to get the expert to agree continually to leading questions. "Why" questions should be avoided at all costs. Note the following:

Q: Is safety an important consideration in good design?
A: Of course it is.
Q: And the greater the danger involved, the more important it is that a good design should include efforts for safety?
A: I suppose so.
Q: And certainly where a large piece of machinery on an assembly line could cause its operator to lose his eyesight if it malfunctions, that is a very serious danger, isn't it?
A: Yes.
Q: Is it good practice to test a machine design after the machine is constructed?
A: Yes.
Q: Can this be done by operating the machine?
A: Certainly.
Q: And should such tests be conducted several times to see how the machine will function?
A: Yes.

Throughout a cross-examination of this kind, a relatively tight rein must be held on the witness so that he or she is not free to make lengthy and possibly diverting explanations that are beyond the control of the examining counsel. If a witness is diverted, he or she should be brought back to a certain point, and the questioner should insist upon a responsive answer. Cross-examining an expert witness can be a tricky business. If the proper question form and order are working, the cross-examination should proceed on course. However, "the art of advocacy . . . dictates

that one should abandon any line of questioning if the witness' response is upbeat."[227]

REDIRECT, RECROSS, AND OBJECTIONS

After a party has been cross-examined, the lawyer who called the witness to the stand may question that witness again. This examination is called redirect. Its purpose is (a) to clarify matters that became confused during cross-examination or (b) to straighten out or rehabilitate a witness whose testimony has been placed in doubt by effective cross-examination. In either case, lawyers hope that the redirect will reestablish witness credibility. Redirect cannot simply repeat what was said in direct; it can only go over either what could have been said or direct on any new matter introduced in cross-examination.[228] Redirect can occur immediately after cross-examination, or a witness can be subject to recall later in a trial for further questioning.

Redirect should be kept short and emphatic. For example, suppose that under cross-examination, the witness admits that he was involved in a serious traffic accident in 1983. On redirect, the attorney can explain away this accident as follows:

Q: Did the police investigate the traffic accident you had in 1983?
A: Yes, they did.
Q: And what did they conclude?
A: They assured me that the accident was entirely the fault of the other driver.

Rehabilitation has now been completed. When redirect questions are asked, they should be phrased in a calm, friendly manner so as not to convey to the witness that he fell apart under cross-examination.

If nothing particularly damaging occurs in

cross-examination, redirect might not be attempted. After all, redirecting shows some dissatisfaction with a particular witness under cross-examination. "By asking redirect questions, counsel is in effect conceding to the tribunal that the cross-examiner has developed something requiring clarification. . . . Declining redirect can imply to the tribunal that the cross-examiner's score is zero. This is similar to declining cross-examination in the first place to imply that the impact of the direct on relevant issues may have been nil."[229] The prudent advocate must weigh the option of redirect carefully. Sometimes the original direct testimony should stand as is. After all, there is no requirement that a witness be called for redirect examination. Anyway, "the implication of issues raised on cross-examination can sometimes be dealt with in closing argument, in lieu of redirect."[230]

Recross is conducted by the cross-examining attorney after redirect has been completed. The guidelines parallel those for redirect. Recross may be done either to ask something an attorney forgot to ask in cross-examination or to go over something brought out in redirect. The opportunity to recross rests with the court.

Throughout the examination of witnesses, objections are always possible. The primary reason for objection is to exclude improper evidence. Improper-evidence objections are designed to protect the record and prevent inadmissible and inappropriate answers from reaching the jury.[231] An example follows:

Q: What did Mr. Smith tell you about the conversation between Jones and Taylor?
Interruption: Objection, Your Honor. Hearsay.

Objections may also be used to prevent the opposition from using an improper manner of questioning.[232] Improper-manner-of-

questioning objections are pointed toward question form. Improper questions may be leading, misleading, repetitive, compound, and so forth. This objection is to the question itself, not the answer. For instance:

Q: Did you arrive at the bank at eight A.M. and immediately open the safe?
Interruption: Objection, Your Honor. Compound and leading question.

After an objection is raised, the judge serves as an umpire on the contention and the reasons underlying it. Judges will either overrule or sustain objections. Lawyers are bound by the trial judge's ruling, unless they are given permission to argue it. Judges will rarely exclude evidence to which counsel has not raised an objection. A judge may, however, interrupt testimony and call counsel to the bench to coach him or her to begin raising objections to something consistently done in error by the other side.

It is important for an attorney not to go overboard by becoming an automatic jack-in-the-box, presenting nonmeritorious objections. Making too many objections makes counsel appear obstructive. It looks to the jury as though the objecting counsel is trying to have certain facts concealed from them, and this situation becomes even worse when the objections are frequently overruled.[233] Objections should never be frivolous, made just for effect. Sometimes they are used to make speeches, and that is not their purpose. Sometimes they are used to interrupt the pace and flow of a damaging cross-examination, and this tactic is often exposed for what it is—unjustified obstructionism. Embarrassing warnings from the bench look bad for an objecting attorney.

Objections from attorneys should always be specific. They should not follow the boilerplate approach: "I object. Incompetent, irrelevant, and immaterial." "Many objections are made because of the reflex action of trial counsel in reacting to a legally improper question. Others arise from counsel's impulse to display his knowledge of the rules of evidence. In either event, the wiser course would generally be to restrain yourself and let the situation pass uneventfully."[234] If an objection is to be raised, the specific reason should be known to the objector, to the opposing attorney, and to the judge. If the testimony causes no harm, counsel might refrain from objecting, even if the question is objectionable.

Objections should be made without argument. "The making of an objection coupled with a lengthy argument in support of it is certain to brand the attorney as inexperienced. More than that, it is not proper trial conduct, and a good trial court will not permit it."[235] If an argument is necessary, permission from the court should be requested. Judges who grant such permission usually will hear argument in support of and in opposition to the objection outside the presence of the jury.

On occasion, when a situation becomes outrageous, a lawyer can object with righteous indignation. Generally, however, "the appropriate tone will be one of patience and courtesy perhaps even prefaced with 'Pardon me, your Honor, I must object to that question because I am afraid it calls for a hearsay response.'"[236] Jurors should not be offended by the manner of making objections; politeness is very important.

When making objections, an advocate should be timely. Objections should be made as soon as the basis for them becomes apparent. If an inappropriate question is asked, the witness answers it, and the answer is followed by a late objection, the judge may disallow the objection because it was late. If an objectionable question is asked and it is not possible to raise an objection until part of the witness's answer has been given, the objection should still be made, with an accompanying

motion from counsel to strike the answer from the record. If the objection is sustained, the judge will instruct the jury to disregard both the objectionable question and the answer.

For maximum effectiveness, attorneys should stand when making objections. Objections should be addressed to the judge and not to opposing counsel.[237] Judges appreciate the courtesy. Also, standing "will divert the attention of the witness to [the lawyer presenting the objection]."[238]

An appropriate response to objections endears a lawyer to a jury. Inappropriate responses are (a) to assume the other lawyer is always correct and move on to the next question, (b) not to wait for a ruling by the judge, and (c) to automatically argue against every objection the other side raises. The appropriate reaction is to think carefully how best to respond to each and every objection and then to follow through accordingly. Then, after objections have been raised and ruled on, questioning lawyers must carefully note where they left off so that they can easily pick up at the point at which they were interrupted. Should a lawyer get an unfavorable ruling on an objection, he or she must be careful not to bicker with the judge about the ruling or display disappointment or bitterness. Emotions must be held in check.

Used sensibly, objections can become a strategic part of a trial. They not only help in removing irrelevant and inadmissible information from the trial, but also become part of the official court record, serving as the basis for an appeal should a judge rule unfairly. To be effective, a trial lawyer must know when to object, what to object to, and how to object.

Since the presentation of evidence constitutes the bulk of a trial, its sheer volume indicates its importance. Communication scholarship shows that defective evidence retards positive source credibility and attitude change, particularly for a communicator with moderate initial credibility, whereas the inclusion of solid evidence facilitates persuasion.[239] The persuasive potential of evidence is enormous in affecting the outcome of trials.

Notes

[1]Robert McFigg, Ralph C. McCullough II, and James L. Underwood, *Civil Trial Manual* (Los Angeles: Joint Committee on Legal Education of the American Law Institute and the American Bar Association, 1974), 401.

[2]Hubert Hickam and Thomas M. Scanlon, *Preparation for Trial* (Philadelphia: Joint Committee on Continuing Legal Education of the American Law Institute and the American Bar Association, 1963), 283.

[3]Louis Nizer, "The Art of the Jury Trial," *Cornell Law Quarterly* 32 (1946), 65–66.

[4]Gene Fowler, *The Great Mouthpiece: A Life Story of William J. Fallon* (New York: Blue Ribbon Books, 1931), 93.

[5]Kenneth E. Andersen, *Persuasion: Theory and Practice* (Boston: Allyn and Bacon, 1978), 235.

[6]Carl I. Hovland, Irving L. Janis, and Harold H. Kelley, *Communication and Persuasion* (New Haven: Yale University Press, 1953), 35.

[7]Winston L. Brembeck and William S. Howell, *Persuasion: A Means of Social Influence* (Englewood Cliffs, N.J.: Prentice-Hall, 1976), 184.

[8]Alan E. Morrill, "Direct Examination," *Insurance Law Journal* 543 (1968), 309–310.

[9]Lewis Lake, *How to Win Lawsuits Before Juries* (New York: Prentice-Hall, 1954), 48.

[10]John A. Call, "Psychology in Litigation," *Trial* (March 1985), 48–58.

[11]Leonard Packel, "How to Prepare and Conduct a Direct Examination of a Witness," *Practical Lawyer* (January 15, 1982), 70.

[12]Gary L. Wells, R. C. L. Lindsay, and Tamara J. Ferguson, "Accuracy, Confidence, and Juror Perceptions in Eyewitness Identification," *Journal of Applied Psychology* 64 (1979), 440–448.

[13]Elizabeth F. Loftus, "Eyewitnesses: Essential but Unreliable," *Psychology Today* (February 1984), 24.

[14]Herbert A. Kuvin, *Trial Handbook* (Englewood Cliffs, N.J.: Prentice-Hall, 1965), 140.

[15]Gerald R. Miller and F. Joseph Boster, "Three Images of the Trial: Their Implications for Psychological Research," in Bruce Dennis Sales, ed., *Psychology in the Legal Process* (New York: Spectrum, 1977), 24.

[16]Harold B. Hayes, "Applying Persuasion Techniques to Trial Proceedings," *South Carolina Law Review* 24 (1972), 383.

[17]Amiram Elwork, Bruce Dennis Sales, and David Suggs, "The Trial: A Research Review," in Bruce Dennis Sales, ed., *Perspectives in Law and Psychology: The Trial Process* (New York: Plenum, 1981), 41.

[18]Robert F. Sommer, "The New Look on the Witness Stand," *Canadian Psychologist* 8 (1959), 94–100.

[19]James Marshall, *Law and Psychology in Conflict* (Indianapolis: Bobbs-Merrill 1966), 89–100.

[20]Elwork, Sales, and Suggs, op. cit., 42.

[21]Robert Buckhout, "Eyewitness Testimony," *Scientific American* (December 1974), 23–31.

[22]Marshall, op. cit.

[23]C. Bird, "The Influence of the Press Upon the Accuracy of Report," *Journal of Abnormal and Social Psychology* 22 (1927), 123–129; D. S. Greer, "Anything but the Truth? The Reliability of Testimony in Criminal Trials," *British Journal of Criminology* 11 (1971), 131–154.

[24]J. McKeen Cattell, "Measurements of the Academy of Recollection," *Science* 2 (1895), 761–765; Hugo Munsterberg, *On the Witness Stand: Essays on Psychology and Crime* (New York: Clark, Boardman, 1908); John B. Watson, "Psychology As the Behaviorist Views It," *Psychological Review* 20 (1913), 158–177. A splendid review of eyewitness research is found in L. Craig Parker, *Legal Psychology* (Springfield, Ill.: Charles C. Thomas, 1980), chap. 2.

[25]Patrick M. Wall, *Eye-Witness Identification in Criminal Cases* (Springfield, Ill.: Charles C. Thomas, 1965), 26.

[26]Elizabeth F. Loftus, *Eyewitness Testimony* (Cambridge: Harvard University Press, 1979), 8–19.

[27]Gary L. Wells and Edward F. Wright, "Practical Issues in Eyewitness Research," in Martin F.

Kaplan, ed., *The Impact of Social Psychology on Procedural Justice* (Springfield, Ill.: Charles C. Thomas, 1986), 117.

[28]Steven Penrod, Elizabeth Loftus, and John Winkler, "The Reliability of Eyewitness Testimony: A Psychological Perspective," in Norbert L. Kerr and Robert M. Bray, eds., *The Psychology of the Courtroom* (New York: Academic Press, 1982), 121.

[29]Donald A. Norman, *Memory and Attention: An Introduction to Human Information Processing* (New York: Wiley, 1976).

[30]Dillard S. Gardner, "The Perception and Memory of Witnesses," *Cornell Law Quarterly* 18 (1933), 391–409; W. F. Grether and C. A. Baker, "Visual Presentation of Information," in Harold P. Van Cott and Robert G. Kincaide, eds., *Human Engineering Guide to Equipment Design* (Washington, D.C.: Government Printing Office, 1972).

[31]Gardner, op. cit.

[32]Thomas M. Graefe and Michael J. Watkins, "Picture Rehearsal: An Effect of Selectivity Attending to Pictures No Longer in View," *Journal of Experimental Psychology: Human Learning and Memory* 6 (1980), 156–162; Douglas L. Hintzman, "Repetition and Memory," in Gordon H. Bower, ed., *The Psychology of Learning and Motivation* (New York: Academic Press, 1976), 47–91.

[33]Alvin G. Goldstein and June C. Chance, "Visual Recognition Memory for Complex Configurations," *Perception and Psychophysics* 9 (1971), 237–241; George Mandler, "Recognizing: The Judgment of Previous Occurrence," *Psychological Review* 87 (1980), 252–271.

[34]Brian R. Clifford and Jane Scott, "Individual and Situational Factors in Eyewitness Testimony," *Journal of Applied Psychology* 63 (1978), 352–359.

[35]Robert M. Hutchins and Donald Slesinger, "Some Observations on the Law of Evidence," *Columbia Law Review* 28 (1928), 432–440.

[36]Penrod, Loftus, and Winkler, op. cit., 134.

[37]David Egan, Mark Pittner, and Alvin G. Goldstein, "Eyewitness Identification: Photographs v. Live Models," *Law and Human Behavior* 1 (1977), 199–206; Jack P. Lipton, "On the Psychology of Eyewitness Testimony," *Journal of Applied Psychology* 62 (1977), 90–93; Jean M. Mandler and Gary H. Ritchey, "Long Term Memory for Pictures," *Journal of Experimental Psychology: Human Learning and Memory* 3 (1977), 386–396; James Marshall, "The Evidence: Do We See and Hear What It Is? Or Do Our Senses Lie?" *Psychology Today* (February 1969), 48–52; Roger N. Shepard, "Recognition Memory for Words, Sentences, and Pictures," *Journal of Verbal Learning and Verbal Behavior* 6 (1967), 156–163.

[38]Alvin G. Goldstein, "The Fallibility of the Eyewitness: Psychological Evidence," in Bruce Dennis Sales, ed., *Psychology in the Legal Process* (New York: Spectrum, 1977), 223–248; J. W. Sheperd and H. D. Ellis, "The Effect of Attractiveness on Recognition Memory for Faces," *American Journal of Psychology* 86 (1973), 627–634; John W. Shepard, Jan B. Deregowski, and Haydn D. Ellis, "A Cross-Cultural Study of Recognition Memory for Faces," *International Journal of Psychology* 9 (1974), 205–211.

[39]Elaine S. Elliott, Elizabeth J. Wills, and Alvin G. Goldstein, "The Effects of Discrimination Training on the Recognition of White and Oriental Faces," *Bulletin of the Psychonomic Society* 2 (1973), 71–73; Roy S. Malpass and Jerome Kravitz, "Recognition for Faces of Own and Other Race," *Journal of Personality and Social Psychology* 13 (1969), 330–335.

[40]Elizabeth F. Loftus, David G. Miller, and Helen J. Burns, "Semantic Integration of Verbal Information into a Visual Memory," *Journal of Experimental Psychology: Human Learning and Memory* 4 (1978), 19–31.

[41]Baruch Fischoff, "Perceived Informativeness of Facts," *Journal of Experimental Psychology: Human Perception and Performance* 3 (1977), 349–358.

[42]Reid Hastie, Robert Landsman, and Elizabeth F. Loftus, "Eyewitness Testimony: The Dangers of Guessing," *Jurimetrics Journal* 19 (1978), 1–8.

[43]Lipton, op. cit.; Kent H. Marquis, James Marshall, and Stuart Oskamp, "Testimony Validity as a Function of Question Form, Atmosphere and Item Difficulty," *Journal of Applied Social Psychology* 2 (1972), 167–186; Mark Snyder and Seymour W. Uranowitz, "Reconstructing the Past:

Some Cognitive Consequences of Person Perception," *Journal of Personality and Social Psychology* 36 (1978), 941–950.

[44]Buckhout, op. cit.; Elizabeth F. Loftus, "Reconstructing Memory: The Incredible Eyewitness," *Psychology Today* (December 1974), 117–119; Wall, op. cit.; Gary L. Wells, "Applied Eyewitness Testimony Research: System Variables and Estimator Variables," *Journal of Personality and Social Psychology* 36 (1978), 1546–1557; A. Daniel Yarmey, *The Psychology of Eyewitness Testimony* (New York: Free Press, 1979).

[45]Howard H. Spellman, *Direct Examination of Witnesses* (Englewood Cliffs, N.J.: Prentice-Hall, 1968), 66.

[46]The list is freely adapted from Morrill, op. cit., 310–316.

[47]Kenney F. Hegland, *Trial and Practice Skills in a Nutshell* (St. Paul, Minn.: West Publishing, 1978), 138.

[48]Gail S. Goodman and Joseph A. Michelli, "Would You Believe a Child Witness?" *Psychology Today* (November 1981), 83.

[49]Wells, Lindsay, and Ferguson, op. cit.

[50]One source says that having an apprehensive witness observe a trial can be dangerous and should therefore be cautiously approached. "Exposure to trials in which witnesses receive unusually severe treatment may transform apprehension into paralyzing fright. Therefore, before suggesting that a witness view a particular trial, the attorney should thoroughly investigate the nature of the proceedings." McFigg, McCullough, and Underwood, op. cit., 239.

[51]Lawrence B. Rosenfeld and Jean M. Civikly, *With Words Unspoken: The Nonverbal Experience* (New York: Holt, Rinehart and Winston, 1976), 62.

[52]Victor M. Catano, "Impact on Simulated Jurors of Testimony as a Function of Non-Evidential Characteristics of Witness and Defendant," *Psychological Reports* 46 (1980), 343–348.

[53]Carolyn Lown, "Legal Approaches to Juror Stereotyping by Physical Characteristics," *Law and Human Behavior* 1 (1979), 87–100; V. Hale Starr and Mark McCormick, *Jury Selection* (Boston: Little, Brown, 1985), 339–343.

[54]Judee K. Burgoon and Thomas Saine, *The Unspoken Dialogue: An Introduction to Nonverbal Communication* (Boston: Houghton Mifflin, 1978), 145–148.

[55]Daniel G. Freedman, "The Survival Value of the Beard," *Psychology Today* (October 1969), 36–39; Robert J. Pellegrini, "Impressions of a Male Personality as a Function of Beardedness," *Psychology* (February 1973), 29–33; Rosenfeld and Civikly, op. cit., 66–67.

[56]David C. Murray and Herdis L. Deabler, "Colors and Mood-Tones," *Journal of Applied Psychology* 38 (1954), 432–435; L. B. Wexner, "The Degrees to Which Colors (Hues) Are Associated With Mood-Tones," *Journal of Applied Psychology* 38 (1954), 432–435.

[57]Norma H. Compton, "Personal Attributes of Color and Design Preferences in Clothing Fabrics," *Journal of Psychology* 54 (1962), 191–195.

[58]Michael Argyle and Robert McHenry, "Do Spectacles Really Affect Judgments of Intelligence?" *British Journal of Social and Clinical Psychology* 10 (1971), 27–29; Paul N. Hamid, "Style of Dress as a Perceptual Cue in Impression Formation," *Perceptual and Motor Skills* 26 (1968), 904–906; G. R. Thornton, "The Effect of Wearing Glasses Upon Judgments of Persons Seen Briefly," *Journal of Applied Psychology* 28 (1944), 203–207.

[59]For a detailed discussion of witness appearance, see Lawrence J. Smith and Loretta A. Malandro, *Courtroom Communication Strategies* (New York: Kluwer, 1985), 29–64.

[60]Gerald R. Miller and Judee K. Burgoon, "Factors Affecting Assessments of Witness Credibility," in Norbert L. Kerr and Robert J. Bray, eds., *The Psychology of the Courtroom* (New York: Academic Press, 1982), 169.

[61]Michael Argyle, Florisse Alkema, and Robin Gilmour, "The Communication of Friendly and Hostile Attitudes by Verbal and Non-Verbal Signals," *European Journal of Social Psychology* 1 (1971), 385–402; John E. Hocking, Gerald R. Miller, and Norman E. Fontes, "Videotape in the Courtroom: Witness Deception," *Trial* (April 1978), 52–55; Albert Mehrabian and Morton Wiener, "Decoding of Inconsistent

Communications," *Journal of Personality and Social Psychology* 6 (1967), 108–114.

[62]Cathy Maslow, Kathryn Yoselson, and Harvey London, "Persuasiveness of Confidence Expressed via Language and Body Language," *British Journal of Social and Clinical Psychology* 10 (1971), 234–240; Albert Mehrabian and Martin Williams, "Nonverbal Concomitants of Perceived and Intended Persuasiveness," *Journal of Personality and Social Psychology* 13 (1969), 37–58; B. Timney and Harvey London, "Body Language Concomitants of Persuasiveness and Persuasibility in Dyadic Interaction," *International Journal of Group Tensions* 3 (1973), 48–67.

[63]Henry B. Rothblatt, "The Defendant—Should He Testify?" *Trial Diplomacy Journal* (Fall 1979), 24.

[64]Edith B. Mallory and Virginia R. Miller, "A Possible Basis for the Association of Voice Characteristics and Personality Traits," *Speech Monographs* 25 (1958), 255.

[65]Gary Patrick Nerbonne, "The Identification of Speaker Characteristics on the Basis of Aural Cues," Ph.D. diss. (East Lansing: Michigan State University, 1968).

[66]David W. Addington, "The Relationship of Selected Vocal Characteristics to Personality Perception," *Speech Monographs* 35 (1968), 492–505.

[67]David W. Addington, "The Effect of Vocal Variations on Ratings of Source Credibility," *Speech Monographs* 38 (1971), 492–505.

[68]Addington, "The Relationship of Vocal Characteristics."

[69]Norman N. Markel et al., "Personality Traits Associated With Voice Types," *Journal of Psycholinguistic Research* 1 (1972), 249–255.

[70]Burgoon and Saine, op. cit., 83; Ernest Kramer, "The Judgment of Personal Characteristics and Emotions From Nonverbal Properties of Speech," *Psychology Bulletin* 60 (1963), 408–420.

[71]Addington, "The Relationship of Vocal Characteristics."

[72]Bradford Arthur, Dorothee Farrar, and George Bradford, "Evaluation Reactions of College Students to Dialect Differences in the English of Mexican-Americans," *Language and Speech* 17 (1974), 255–270; Joyce F. Buck, "The Effects of

Negro and White Dialectical Variations Upon Attitudes of College Students," *Speech Monographs* 35 (1968), 181–186; Anthony Mulac, Theodore D. Hanley, and Diane Y. Prigge, "Effects of Phonological Speech Foreignness Upon Three Dimensions of Attitude of Selected American Listeners," *Quarterly Journal of Speech* 60 (1974), 411–420.

[73]George L. Trager, "Paralanguage: A First Approximation," *Studies in Linguistics* 13, nos. 1 and 2 (1958), 1–12.

[74]Gerald R. Miller and Murray A. Hewgill, "The Effect of Variations in Nonfluency on Audience Ratings of Source Credibility," *Quarterly Journal of Speech* 50 (1964), 36–41; Kenneth K. Sereno and Gary J. Hawkins, "The Effects of Variations in Speaking Nonfluency Upon Audience Ratings of Attitude Toward the Speech Topic and Speaker's Credibility," *Speech Monographs* 34 (1967), 58–64.

[75]Donald S. Boomer, "Hesitation and Grammatical Encoding," *Language and Speech* 8 (1965), 148–158.

[76]Frieda Goldman-Eisler, "Sequential Temporal Patterns and Cognitive Processes in Speech," *Language and Speech* 10 (1956), 122–132.

[77]Michael Parkinson, "Language Behavior and Courtroom Success," Paper presented at the International Conference on Language and Social Psychology (University of Bristol, England, July 1979).

[78]James W. McElhaney, "Trial Notebook: The Horse Shed," *Litigation* (Summer 1981), 44.

[79]Martin F. Kaplan and Gwen D. Kemmerick, "Juror Judgment as Information Integration: Combining Evidential and Nonevidential Information," *Journal of Personality and Social Psychology* 30 (1974), 493–499.

[80]Robert M. Reyes, William C. Thompson, and Gordon H. Bower, "Judgmental Biases Resulting From Different Availabilities of Arguments," *Journal of Personality and Social Psychology* 39 (1980), 2–12.

[81]John M. Conley, William M. O'Barr, and E. Allan Lind, "The Power of Language: Presentational Style in the Courtroom," *Duke Law Journal* 6 (1978), 1375–1399.

[82]Brenda Danet, "Language in the Legal Process,"

Law and Society Review 14 (1980), 445–464; Michael G. Parkinson, Deborah Gersler, and Mary Hinchcliff Pelias, "The Effects of Verbal Skills on Trial Success," *Journal of the American Forensic Association* 20 (1983), 17, 22.

[83]Bonnie Erickson et al., "Speech Style and Impression Formation in a Court Setting: The Effects of 'Powerful' and 'Powerless' Speech," *Journal of Experimental Social Psychology* 14 (1978), 266–279.

[84]John Waite Bowers, "Some Correlates of Language Intensity," *Quarterly Journal of Speech* 50 (1964), 415–420; James J. Bradac and Anthony Mulac, "A Molecular View of Powerful and Powerless Speech Styles," *Communication Monographs* 51 (1984), 307–319; John W. Wright and Lawrence A. Hosman, "Language Style and Sex Bias in the Courtroom," *Southern Speech Communication Journal* 48 (1983), 137–152.

[85]Roberto Aron and Jonathan L. Rosner, *How to Prepare Witnesses for Trial* (Colorado Springs: Shepard's/McGraw-Hill, 1985), 11.

[86]Gerald R. Miller et al., "The Effects of Videotape Testimony in Jury Trials," *Brigham Young University Law Review* 1 (1975), 331–373; Gerald R. Miller et al., "Jurors' Responses to Videotaped Trial Materials: Some Further Evidence," *Michigan State Bar Journal* 54 (1975), 278–282.

[87]Kuvin, op. cit., 143.

[88]Ibid.

[89]Sonya Hamlin, *What Makes Juries Listen* (New York: Harcourt Brace Jovanovich, 1985), 195.

[90]Thomas A. Mauet, *Fundamentals of Trial Techniques* (Boston: Little, Brown, 1980) 18.

[91]James Jeans, *Trial Advocacy* (St. Paul, Minn.: West Publishing, 1975), 220.

[92]Donald C. Pennington, "Witnesses and Their Testimony: Effects of Ordering on Juror Verdicts," *Journal of Applied Social Psychology* 12 (1982), 318–333.

[93]"Jurors tend to remember the evidence which is presented first and that which is presented last. They tend to forget the evidence which is presented in the middle of the trial." Thomas F. Parker, "Applied Psychology in Trial Practice," *Defense Law Journal* 7 (1960), 35.

[94]Morrill, op. cit., 341.

[95]Robert E. Keeton, *Trial Tactics and Methods* (Boston: Little, Brown, 1973), 23.

[96]Underscoring does not mean repeating the witness's answer. "Repetition of the answers of your witness will only annoy the court, cause objections by the prosecutor, and make it appear to the jury as if his testimony is unsatisfactory. If any important portion is slurred over by the witness, restate the question in a different form so that the important portion is repeated without its being obvious." Henry B. Rothblatt, *Successful Techniques in the Trial of Criminal Cases* (Englewood Cliffs, N.J.: Prentice-Hall, 1961), 85.

[97]Joseph Kelner and Francis E. McGovern, *Successful Litigation Techniques: Student Edition* (New York: Matthew Bender, 1981) pp. 13-4, 13-5.

[98]Helen Mary Cady, "On the Psychology of Testimony," *American Journal of Psychology* 35 (1924), 110–112; William Stern, "The Psychology of Testimony," *Journal of Abnormal and Social Psychology* 34 (1939), 3–20; Guy Montrose Whipple, "The Observer as Reporter," *Psychological Bulletin* 6 (1909), 153–170; Paul L. Whitley and John A. McGeoch, "The Effect of One Form of Report Upon Another," *American Journal of Psychology* 38 (1927), 280–284.

[99]Randall K. Stutman, "Testimony Control and Witness Narration During Courtroom Examination: An Empirical Elaboration of Bennett's Storytelling Theory," Paper presented at the Western Speech Communication Association Convention (Tucson, Ariz., February 1986).

[100]William M. O'Barr and John M. Conley, "Language in the Courtroom: Vehicle or Obstacle?" *Barrister* (Summer 1976), 1–9.

[101]Elizabeth F. Loftus, Jane Goodman, and Chris Nagatkin, "Examining Witnesses: Good Advice and Bad," in Ronald J. Matlon and Richard J. Crawford, eds., *Communication Strategies in the Practice of Lawyering* (Annandale, Va.: Speech Communication Association, 1983), 299.

[102]Federal Rule of Criminal Procedure 611(c) states, "Leading questions should not be used on direct examination except as may be necessary to develop his testimony."

[103]Mark P. Denbeaux and D. Michael Risinger, "Questioning Questions: Objections to Form in

the Interrogation of Witnesses," *Arkansas Law Review* 33 (1979), 439–489.

[104]Hegland, op. cit., 26.

[105]Robert G. Crowder, *Principles of Learning and Memory* (Hillsdale, N.J.: Erlbaum, 1976).

[106]Sandra E. File and Alison Jew, "Syntax and the Recall of Instructions in a Realistic Situation," *British Journal of Psychology* 64 (1973), 65–70; John F. Grady, "From the Bench," *Litigation* (Fall 1979), 62–63; Jacques Mehler, "Some Effects of Grammatical Transformations on the Recall of English Sentences," *Journal of Verbal Learning and Verbal Behavior* 2 (1963), 346–351; Stella Vosniadou, "Drawing Inferences From Semantically Positive and Negative Implicative Predicates," *Journal of Psycholinguistic Research* 11 (1982), 77–93.

[107]Leroy J. Tornquist, "A Response to Legal Strategies, Communication Strategies and Research Needs in Direct and Cross-Examination," in Ronald J. Matlon and Richard J. Crawford, eds., *Communication Strategies in the Practice of Lawyering* (Annandale, Va.: Speech Communication Association, 1983), 354.

[108]Jeffrey L. Kestler, *Questioning Techniques and Tactics* (Colorado Springs: Shepard's/McGraw-Hill, 1982), 74.

[109]Robert P. Charrow and Veda Charrow, "Making Legal Language Understandable: A Psycholinguistic Study of Jury Instructions," *Columbia Law Review* 79 (1979), 1306.

[110]Loftus, "Reconstructing Memory"

[111]Elizabeth F. Loftus and John C. Palmer, "Reconstruction of Automobile Destruction: An Example of the Interaction Between Language and Memory," *Journal of Verbal Learning and Verbal Behavior* 13 (1974), 585–589.

[112]Richard M. Markus, "A Theory of Trial Advocacy," *Tulane Law Review* 56 (1981), 104.

[113]Mauet, op. cit., 88.

[114]Jeans, op. cit., 220.

[115]Loftus, Goodman, and Nagatkin, op. cit., 302.

[116]Michael F. Colley, "Friendly Persuasion: Gaining Attention, Comprehension, and Acceptance in Court," *Trial* (August 1981), 45.

[117]Mark J. Kadish and Rhonda A. Brofman, "Direct Examination Techniques for the Criminal Defense Attorney," *Trial Diplomacy Journal* (Winter 1980), 41.

[118]Arthur A. Lumsdaine and Irving L. Janis, "Resistance to 'Counterpropaganda' Produced by One-Sided and Two-Sided 'Propaganda' Presentations," *Public Opinion Quarterly* 17 (1953), 311–318.

[119]William J. McGuire, "Inducing Resistance to Persuasion: Some Contemporary Approaches," in Leonard Berkowitz, ed., *Advances in Experimental Social Psychology* (New York: Academic Press, 1964), 192–231.

[120]Smith and Malandro, op. cit., 72–73.

[121]"Some local court rules limit the ambulations of counsel by requiring that he position himself at the counsel table or a podium." Jeans, op. cit., 215.

[122]Jeff Wolfe, "A Strategy for the Effective Use of the Courtroom During Direct Examination," *American Journal of Trial Advocacy* 8 (1984–85), 207.

[123]Ibid., 213.

[124]Ibid.

[125]Sydney C. Schweitzer, *Cyclopedia of Trial Practice* (Rochester, N.Y.: Lawyers Cooperative, 1970), 513.

[126]Francis Xavier Busch, *Trial Procedure Materials* (Indianapolis: Bobbs-Merrill, 1961), 191.

[127]Hamlin, op. cit., 211.

[128]Francis L. Wellman, *Day in Court* (New York: Macmillan, 1931), 142.

[129]Busch, op. cit., 212.

[130]John Henry Wigmore, *A Treatise on the System of Evidence in Trials at Common Law* (Boston: Little, Brown, 1904), 1697.

[131]Morrill, op. cit., 421.

[132]Part of Federal Rule of Evidence 611(b) reads, "Cross-examination should be limited to the subject matter of the direct examination and matters affecting the credibility of the witness. The court may, in the exercise of discretion, permit inquiry into additional matters as if on direct examination."

[133]Ronald L. Carlson, Edward J. Imwinkelreid, and Edward J. Kionka, *Materials for the Study of Evidence* (Charlottesville, Va.: Michie, 1983), 73.

[134]Jacob W. Ehrlich, *The Lost Art of Cross-Examination* (New York: Putnam, 1970), 18, 25.

[135]Leon Jaworski, "Cross-Examination of Witnesses," *Arkansas Law Review* 19 (1965), 44.

[136]McFigg, McCullough, and Underwood, op. cit., 418.

[137]John A. Burgess, "Principles and Techniques of Cross-Examination," *Trial Diplomacy Journal* (Winter 1979), 20.

[138]Irving Younger, *The Art of Cross-Examination* (Chicago: American Bar Association Section on Litigation, Monograph Series, no. 1, 1976), 25–28.

[139]M. Melvin Shralow, "Cross and Re-Direct Examination," *Trial Diplomacy Journal* (Summer 1981), 38.

[140]Mauet, op. cit., 241.

[141]Younger, op. cit., 22.

[142]James W. McElhaney, "The Story Line in Cross-Examination," *Litigation* (Fall 1982), 46.

[143]Paul Bergman, *Trial Advocacy in a Nutshell* (St. Paul, Minn.: West Publishing, 1979), 184–229.

[144]Ibid., 185.

[145]Younger, op. cit., 30–31.

[146]John Nicholas Iannuzzi, *Cross-Examination: The Mosaic Art* (Englewood Cliffs, N.J.: Prentice-Hall, 1982), 102.

[147]Keeton, op. cit., 21.

[148]Jacob D. Fuchsberg, "How I Decide in What Order to Present Witnesses," in Grace W. Holmes, ed., *Excellence in Advocacy* (Ann Arbor, Mich.: Institute of Continuing Legal Education, 1971), 33.

[149]Harry Bodin, *Civil Litigation and Trial Techniques* (New York: Practicing Law Institute, 1976), 559–560.

[150]Ibid., 560–561.

[151]Nina Hatvany and Fritz Strack, "The Impact of a Discredited Key Witness," *Journal of Applied Social Psychology* 10 (1980), 490–509.

[152]Hamlin, op. cit., 244.

[153]Elizabeth Loftus, "Leading Questions and the Eyewitness Report," *Cognitive Psychology* 7 (1975), 560–572.

[154]James W. McElhaney, *Trial Notebook* (Chicago: American Bar Association, 1981), 56.

[155]"Confrontation is essential. To introduce any prior inconsistent statement, . . . the witness must first be confronted with particularity concerning the prior statement. In other words, the witness must have his attention directed to the time, place and circumstances under which the prior inconsistent statement was made and asked if he made it. . . . If the inconsistent statement is in writing, the witness must be shown the instrument and given an opportunity to read it. These confrontation requirements are known as the rule in *Queen Caroline's Case,* 2 Brod.&Bing 284, 313, 129 Eng.Rep. 976 (1820), adopted uncritically by American courts. . . . Except for a few jurisdictions, the rule in Queen Caroline's Case continues to be law in most state courts." Ibid., 112–113.

[156]Alan E. Morrill, *Trial Diplomacy* (Chicago: Court Practice Institute, 1972), 64.

[157]Walter Barthold, *Attorney's Guide to Effective Discovery Techniques* (Englewood Cliffs, N.J.: Prentice-Hall, 1975), 151.

[158]Federal Rule of Evidence 609 states, "For the purpose of attacking the credibility of a witness, evidence that he has been convicted of a crime shall be admitted if elicited from him or established by public record during cross-examination but only if the crime (1) was punishable by death or imprisonment in excess of one year under the law under which he was convicted, and the court determines that the probative value of admitting this evidence outweighs its prejudicial effect to the defendant, or (2) involved dishonesty or false statement, regardless of the punishment." Federal Rule of Evidence 608 states, "The credibility of a witness may be attacked or supported by evidence in the form of opinion of reputation, but subject to these limitations: (1) the evidence may refer only to character for truthfulness or untruthfulness, and (2) evidence of truthful character is admissible only after the character of the witness for truthfulness has been attacked by opinion or reputation evidence or otherwise."

[159]Mason Ladd, "Some Observations on Credibility: Impeachment of Witnesses," *Cornell Law Quarterly* 52 (1966–67), 241.

[160]Jeans, op. cit., 314.

[161]Murray Aborn, "The Influence of Experimentally Induced Failure on the Retention of Material Acquired Through Set and Incidental Learning," *Journal of Experimental Psychology* 45 (1953), 225–231; Harry P. Bahrick, Paul M. Fitts, and Robert E. Rankin, "Effect of Incentives Upon Reactions to Peripheral Stimuli," *Journal of Experimental Psychology* 44 (1952), 400–406; Edward E. Johnson, "The Role of Motivational Strength in Latent Learning," *Journal of Comparative and Physiological Psychology* 45 (1952), 526–530; Hugh Kohn, "Effects of Variations of Intensity of Experimentally Induced Stress Situations Upon Certain Aspects of Perception and Performance," *Journal of Genetic Psychology* 85 (1954), 289–304; Robert E. Silverman and Bernard Blitz, "Learning and Two Kinds of Anxiety," *Journal of Abnormal and Social Psychology* 52 (1956), 302–303.

[162]Buckhout, op. cit.

[163]Thomas Sannito, "How to Discredit Eyewitness Testimony," *Trial Diplomacy Journal* (Winter 1981), 6.

[164]Ibid.

[165]Frederic C. Bartlett, *Remembering* (Cambridge: Cambridge University Press, 1932).

[166]Gordon W. Allport, "Change and Decay in the Visual Memory Image," *British Journal of Psychology* 21 (1930), 133–148.

[167]Jerome S. Bruner and Cecile C. Goodman, "Value and Need as Organizing Factors in Perception," *Journal of Abnormal and Social Psychology* 42 (1947), 33–44.

[168]Jerome S. Bruner and Leo Postman, "Emotional Selectivity in Perception and Reaction," *Journal of Personality* 231 (1974), 23–31.

[169]W. Barnett Pearce and Forrest Conklin, "Nonverbal Vocalic Communication and the Perception of a Speaker," *Speech Monographs* 38 (1971), 235–241.

[170]Belli, op. cit., 710.

[171]Albert S. Osborn, *The Problem of Proof* (New York: Matthew Bender, 1926), 397.

[172]Belli, op. cit., 712.

[173]Daniel H. Skerritt, "Cross-Examination: Torching the Calendar," *Litigation* (Winter 1986), 24.

[174]Francis Xavier Busch, *Law and Tactics in Jury Trials* (Indianapolis: Bobbs-Merrill, 1949), 533.

[175]Richard Harris, *Hints on Advocacy* (St. Louis: William H. Stevenson, 1943), 60.

[176]"Judges generally will not give an instruction to the witness unless the evasion by the witness is clear cut, and the refusal of the judge to give an instruction . . . may be interpreted by the jury as an indication that the judge thinks the witness is answering properly and not in the least evasively." Keeton, op. cit., 145.

[177]Conley, O'Barr, and Lind, op. cit.

[178]K. Phillip Taylor, Raymond W. Buchanan, and David U. Strawn, *Communication Strategies for Trial Attorneys* (Glenview, Ill.: Scott, Foresman, 1984), 87.

[179]Wells, Lindsay, and Ferguson, op. cit.

[180]Morrill, *Trial Diplomacy*, 61–62.

[181]Robert Dunstan, "Context for Coercion: Analyzing Properties of Courtroom 'Questions,'" *British Journal of Law and Social Psychology* 7 (1980), 61–77.

[182]Robert T. Oliver, "Speech Techniques in Cross-Examination," *Rocky Mountain Law Review* 22 (1950), 256.

[183]Brenda Danet et al., "An Ethnography of Questioning in the Courtroom," in Roger W. Shuy and Anna Shnukal, eds., *Language Use and the Uses of Language* (Washington, D.C.: Georgetown University Press, 1980), 222–234.

[184]Tony L. Axam and Robert Altman, "The Picture Theory of Trial Advocacy," *Litigation* (Winter 1986), 10.

[185]Elizabeth F. Loftus, "Language and Memories in the Judicial System," in Roger W. Shuy and Anna Shnukal, eds., *Language Use and the Uses of Language* (Washington, D.C.: Georgetown University Press, 1980), 257–268.

[186]Hubert S. Feild, "Rape Trials and Jurors' Decisions: A Psycholegal Analysis of the Effects of Victim, Defendant and Case Characteristics," *Law and Human Behavior* 3 (1979), 261–284.

[187]Danuta Kasprzyk, Daniel E. Montano, and Elizabeth F. Loftus, "Effect of Leading Questions on Juror's Verdicts," *Jurimetrics Journal* 16 (1975), 48–51.

[188]William B. Swann, Jr., and Daniel Wegner,

"Where Leading Questions Can Lead: The Power of Conjecture in Social Interaction," Unpublished manuscript (Austin: University of Texas, 1980).

[189]Elizabeth F. Loftus and Edith Greene, "Warning: Even Memory for Faces May Be Contagious," *Law and Human Behavior* 4 (1980), 323–334.

[190]Jane Goodman and Elizabeth F. Loftus, "Social Science Looks at Witness Examination," *Trial* (April 1984), 55.

[191]Ray L. Birdwhistell, *Kinesics and Context* (Philadelphia: University of Pennsylvania Press, 1970); Albert Mehrabian, *Nonverbal Communication* (Chicago: Aldine-Atherton, 1972).

[192]Rosenfeld and Civikly, op. cit., 113–117.

[193]F. K. Berrien and G. H. Huntington, "An Exploratory Study of Pupillary Responses During Deception," *Journal of Experimental Psychology* 32 (1943), 443–449; R. J. Cutrow et al., "The Objective Use of Multiple Physiological Indices in the Detection of Deception," *Psychophysiology* 9 (1972), 578–588; Paul Ekman and Wallace V. Friesan, "Detecting Deception from the Body or Face," *Journal of Personality and Social Psychology* 29 (1974), 288–298; Paul Ekman and Wallace V. Friesan, "Hand Movements and Deception," *Journal of Communication* 22 (1972), 353–374; Paul Ekman and Wallace V. Friesan, "Nonverbal Leakage and Clues to Deception," *Psychiatry* 32 (1969), 88–106; Paul Ekman and Wallace V. Friesan, *Unmasking the Face* (Englewood Cliffs, N.J.: Prentice-Hall, 1975); Robert S. Feldman, Linda Devin-Sheehan, and Vernon L. Allen, "Nonverbal Cues as Indicators of Verbal Dissembling," *American Educational Research Journal* 15 (1978), 217–231; Ira Heilveil, "Deception and Pupil Size," *Journal of Clinical Psychology* 32 (1976), 675–676; Mark L. Knapp, Roderick P. Hart, and Harry S. Dennis, "An Exploration of Deception as a Communication Construct," *Human Communication Research* 1 (1974), 15–29; Charles C. McClintock and Raymond G. Hunt, "Nonverbal Indicators of Affect and Deception in an Interview Setting," *Journal of Applied Social Psychology* 5 (1975), 54–67; Bert Pryor and Charner Leone, "Behavioral Stereotypes of Deception Communication," *Trial* (June 1981), 14–19, 70.

[194]Louis Nizer, "Witness Examination," *Trial Diplomacy Journal* (Fall 1980), 23.

[195]Abne M. Eisenberg and Ralph R. Smith, *Nonverbal Communication* (Indianapolis: Bobbs-Merrill, 1971), 100–101.

[196]Phoebe C. Ellsworth and Linda M. Ludwig, "Visual Behavior in Social Interaction," *Journal of Communication* 22 (1972), 380.

[197]Adam Kendon and Mark Cook, "The Consistency of Gaze Patterns in Social Interaction," *British Journal of Psychology* 60 (1969), 481–494; Albert Mehrabian, "Inference of Attitude From Posture, Orientation and Distance of a Communicator," *Journal of Consulting and Clinical Psychology* 32 (1968), 296–308.

[198]Eckhard H. Hess, "Attitudes and Pupil Size," *Scientific American* (April 1965), 46–54; Eckhard H. Hess and James M. Polt, "Pupil Size in Relation to Mental Activity During Simple Problem-Solving," *Science* 143 (1964), 1190–1192.

[199]Mark L. Knapp, *Essential of Nonverbal Communication* (New York: Holt, Rinehart and Winston, 1980), 198.

[200]John E. Hocking et al., "Detecting Deception From Verbal, Visual, and Paralinguistic Cues," *Human Communication Research* 6 (1979), 33–46; John E. Hocking and Dale G. Leathers, "Nonverbal Indicators of Deception: A New Theoretical Perspective," *Communication Monographs* 47 (1980), 119–131; Norman R. F. Maier and James A. Thurber, "Accuracy of Judgments of Deception When an Interview Is Watched, Heard, or Read," *Personnel Psychology* 21 (1968), 23–30.

[201]Albert Mehrabian, "Nonverbal Betrayal of Feeling," *Journal of Experimental Research in Personality* 5 (1971), 64–73.

[202]Glen D. Baskett and Roy O. Freedle, "Aspects of Language Pragmatics and the Social Perception of Lying," *Journal of Psycholinguistic Research* 3 (1974), 117–131; James J. Bradac, John Waite Bowers, and John A. Courtright, "Three Language Variables in Communication Research: Intensity, Immediacy, and Diversity," *Human Communication Research* 5 (1979), 257–269; R. J. Cutrow et al., op. cit.; Ekman and Friesan, "Detecting Deception"; Ekman and Friesan, "Hand Movements"; Paul Ekman, Wallace V.

Friesan, and Klaus R. Scherer, "Body Movement and Voice Pitch in Deceptive Interaction," *Semiotica* 16 (1976), 23–27; Feldman, Devin-Sheehan, and Allen, op. cit.; Knapp, Hart, and Dennis, op. cit.; Robert E. Kraut, "Verbal and Nonverbal Cues in the Perception of Lying," *Journal of Personality and Social Psychology* 36 (1978), 380–391; Joseph D. Matarazzo et al., "Interview Speech Behavior Under Conditions of Endogenously-Present and Exogenously-Induced Motivational States," *Journal of Clinical Psychology* 26 (1970), 141–148; J. A. Meerloo, "Camouflage Versus Communication: In the Beginning Was the Lie," *Communication* 3 (1978), 45; Mehrabian, "Nonverbal Betrayal of Feeling"; Michael T. Motley, "Acoustic Correlates of Lies," *Western Speech* 38 (1974), 81–87; Miron Zuckerman et al., "Facial and Vocal Cues of Deception and Honesty," *Journal of Experimental Social Psychology* 15 (1979), 378–396.

[203] Ekman, Friesan, and Scherer, op. cit.

[204] James C. Baxter and Bettye F. Deanovich, "Anxiety Arousing Effects of Inappropriate Crowding," *Journal of Consulting and Clinical Psychology* 35 (1970), 174–178; Nancy Jo Felipe and Robert Sommer, "Invasions of Personal Space," *Social Problems* 14 (1966), 204–214; Jeffrey David Fisher and Donn Byrne, "Too Close for Comfort: Sex Differences in Response to Invasions of Personal Space," *Journal of Personality and Social Psychology* 32 (1975), 15–21; Mardi J. Horowitz, Donald F. Duff, and Lois O. Stratton, "Body Buffer Zones," *Archives of General Psychiatry* 11 (1964), 651–656; Miles L. Patterson, Sherry Mullens, and Jeanne Romano, "Compensatory Reactions to Spatial Intrusion," *Sociometry* 34 (1971), 114–121; Robert Sommer, *Personal Space: The Behavioral Basis of Design* (Englewood Cliffs, N.J.: Prentice-Hall, 1969).

[205] Michael Argyle and Janet Dean, "Eye Contact, Distance and Affiliation," *Sociometry* 28 (1965), 289–304.

[206] Dale G. Leathers, *Nonverbal Communication Systems* (Boston: Allyn and Bacon, 1976), 65.

[207] Nancy M. Henley, *Body Politics—Power, Sex, and Nonverbal Communication* (Englewood Cliffs, N.J.: Prentice-Hall, 1977).

[208] William A. Haskins, "The Art of Listening," *Litigation* (Summer 1984), 46–48.

[209] Edward J. Imwinkelreid, *Evidentiary Foundations* (Indianapolis: Michie/Bobbs-Merrill, 1980), 136.

[210] Steven C. Bank and Norman G. Poythress, Jr., "The Elements of Persuasion in Expert Testimony," *Journal of Psychiatry and Law* (Summer 1982), 176.

[211] Mortimer H. Nickerson, "The Expert Technical Witness on Trial," *American Bar Association Journal* 50 (1965), 732–733; Jack L. Whitehead, Jr., "Effects of Authority-Based Assertion on Attitude and Credibility," *Speech Monographs* 38 (1971), 311–315.

[212] Richard Eisenger and Judson Mills, "Perceptions of the Sincerity and Competence of a Communicator as a Function of the Extremity of His Position," *Journal of Experimental Social Psychology* 4 (1968), 224.

[213] Erwin P. Bettinghaus, *Persuasive Communication* (New York: Holt, Rinehart and Winston, 1973), 106.

[214] Aron and Rosner, op. cit., 283.

[215] James Rasicot, *Jury Selection, Body Language, and the Visual Trial* (Minneapolis: AB Publications, 1983), 83.

[216] Peter I. Ostroff, "Experts: A Few Fundamentals," *Litigation* (Winter 1982), 64.

[217] Richard M. Markus, in Jeans, op. cit., p. 327.

[218] William Henry Gallagher, "Technique of Cross-Examination," in Bodin, op. cit., 573.

[219] George Vetter, *Successful Civil Litigation* (Englewood Cliffs, N.J.: Prentice-Hall, 1977), 213.

[220] Markus in Jeans, op. cit., pp. 329–330.

[221] Ruth McGaffey, "The Expert Witness and Source Credibility—The Communication Perspective," *American Journal of Trial Advocacy* 2 (1978), 62.

[222] Markus, in Jeans, op. cit., pp. 336–337.

[223] Ibid., pp. 333–334.

[224] David B. Baum, "Taking On the Opposing Expert," *Trial* (April 1984), 78.

[225] Vetter, op. cit., 206.

[226] Francis L. Wellman, *The Act of Cross-Examination* (New York: Collier, 1962), 119.

[227] John M. Dawson, "Cross-Examination of the Expert Witness," *Employee Relations Law Journal* 8 (1982), 306.

[228] Carlson, Imwinkelreid, and Kionka, op. cit., 76.

[229]Richard A. Givens, *Advocacy: The Art of Pleading a Cause* (Colorado Springs: Shepard's/McGraw-Hill, 1980), 157.

[230]Ibid.

[231]Tornquist, op. cit., 364.

[232]Keeton, op. cit., 166.

[233]William M. O'Barr, *Linguistic Evidence: Language, Power, and Strategy in the Courtroom* (New York: Academic Press, 1982), 121.

[234]Wilfred R. Lorry, *A Civil Action: The Trial* (Philadelphia: Joint Committee on Continuing Legal Education of the American Law Institute and the American Bar Association, 1959), 91.

[235]Al J. Cone and Verne Lawyer, *The Art of Persuasion in Litigation* (Des Moines: Dean-Hicks, 1966), 285.

[236]Jeans, op. cit., 353–354.

[237]Mark A. Dombroff, *Key Trial Control Tactics* (Englewood Cliffs, N.J.: Executive Reports Corporation, 1984), 339.

[238]Hegland, op. cit., 126.

[239]Joseph A. Luchok and James C. McCroskey, "The Effect of Quality of Evidence on Attitude Change and Source Credibility," *Southern Speech Communication Journal* 43 (1978), 371–383.

10
CHAPTER

CLOSING ARGUMENTS

After all the evidence has been presented, attorneys deliver closing arguments to the court. In this chapter, we will consider the following aspects of the closing argument: its purpose, preparation, content, structure, emotional appeal, delivery, and the additional dimension of recency.

THE PURPOSE OF THE CLOSING ARGUMENT

Closing arguments separate the meaningful from the trivial and pull together everything that went on during a trial. Since the court "recognizes that the evidentiary part of a trial may appear disjointed, confusing, and even contradictory, . . . attorneys are given the opportunity to bring it all back together into a logical relationship, weaving the testimony, documents, and other evidence into the cohesive story presented originally in opening statements."[1] Closing arguments are designed to persuade the jury to adopt a certain version of the case facts; they are argumentative speeches designed to focus on and clarify certain issues, which will guide the jury in their deliberations by giving them arguments they can use as they face each other in the jury room. While it is true that a lawyer is involved in persuasion throughout a jury trial, the most apparent persuasive part of the process is the closing argument. A lawyer's rhetorical purpose in making a closing argument is to affect attitude formation.

For instance, in the celebrated 1984 John DeLorean case, the prosecutor wanted to have the jury emphasize the issue of conspiracy to sell and distribute cocaine; the defense lawyers wanted to have the jury ponder the matter of government entrapment. Apparently, the defense lawyers did the superior job of guiding the jury to the issues to consider. As is the case in so many trials, closing argument was the high point of advocacy in the DeLorean case.

Some people call the closing argument a *summation*. Indeed, the term *summation* will be used here as well. However, should the term *closing argument* conjure up advocacy and persuasion and *summation* imply wrapping up or reviewing, a wrong image would be evoked. What happens during this part of any trial is more than a summarizing of the evidence. "Argument does not suggest a mere summary. Argument brings to mind persuasion addressed to the thorniest problems a case can present."[2] Trials should end with good attempts at argument, no matter what the attempt is called.

Little information is available concerning the quantifiable importance of the final argument. Some trial practitioners believe that "final argument is the most important single feature of any lawsuit";[3] others think that "lawsuits are won during the trial, not at the conclusion of it."[4] However, almost all lawyers agree that lawsuits can be lost by "fumbling, stumbling, incoherent, exaggerated, vindictive closing arguments."[5] Indeed, in one of the earliest studies investigating jurors' reactions to summation, it was found that the closing argument was an "important" stage of the trial that influenced the jurors' opinions.[6]

On occasion, and usually in bench trials rather than jury trials, lawyers waive closing arguments. Sometimes the trial judge dispenses with final arguments, since the trial briefs are considered adequate to present the parties' positions.[7] However, in jury trials, waiving is generally not a good idea, and judges have no right to dispense with them. After all, jurors expect to hear a dramatic, clarifying summation at the close of most trials. Waiving may be misconstrued as a sign of weakness.

Summations may vary in other ways between judge and jury trials. Before a jury, counsel is precluded from urging his or her own interpretation of the law, whereas an attorney may have differing views from the judge on matters of law in a bench trial.[8] Occasionally, judges in a bench trial interrupt counsel during closing argument to pose questions and engage in debate. When questioning occurs, an attorney should "ordinarily address himself on the question or comment even if it involves an interruption of the train of thought."[9] Also, attorneys can use more technical language and be less repetitious with a judge alone than they can with a jury.[10] Be it before judge or before jury, however, the purpose of closing argument remains the same—to clarify and to persuade.

PREPARING THE CLOSING ARGUMENT

Closing arguments are sometimes given immediately after the last witness has testified, or after a short or overnight recess. Since lawyers usually do not know how much preparation time they will have for giving the closing argument, careful planning must occur throughout the course of a trial. After all, "very few lawyers can make an effective impromptu argument."[11] "The best final argument is one that has been carefully planned and prepared."[12]

Preparation for the closing argument is an ongoing process throughout litigation. Before and during trials, lawyers should jot down items that might be included in the summation. These items can be kept on removable pages in a trial notebook. When items are kept one to a sheet, the material can easily be indexed for ready reference throughout the trial and then reshuffled at the conclusion of the case to form an outline of the matters to be covered in summation. Collating this material is a good task for a new assoicate or a legal intern.

At or near the end of a trial, a lawyer should sort through the items and assemble them into a cogent outline. The speech must not be written out verbatim. Like an architect designing a home, who has a clear picture of the building before he or she proceeds with the

details, an attorney must know the major ideas to be covered and the images to be formed. The outline should be organized to summarize the case theory in a logical and dramatic way that, of course, is consistent with what was said in the opening statement and with the witnesses' testimony. "Without a well-designed plan for summation, counsel will frequently fail to recognize not only the various logical points on which the summation could be terminated, but also the most effective point at which it should be terminated."[13]

As attorneys prepare their closing remarks, they need to engage in audience analysis, that is, think about how to adapt to the particular judge or jury in the case. "Often, statements made during the [voir dire] examination may provide a valuable clue to points that should be emphasized on summation."[14] Jury decisions are not made on intelligence and case facts alone, but also on emotions, feelings, and prejudices. For instance, when a plaintiff's attorney is trying to convince a jury in a personal injury case that the plaintiff has had damage to his mental health, counsel must recognize that the problem is an invisible one to the jury. Therefore, in closing, the attorney must deal directly with a juror's disinclination to accept subjective symptoms of suffering. How can the lawyer arouse in the jury a sense of identification with the plaintiff? The attorney must figure out how to use exciting language to make the mental anguish as vivid as possible. More will be said about such rhetorical techniques later in the chapter. The lawyer must also play upon lawyer-client-juror value similarities that are relevant to the influence attempt.[15] More will be said about value similarities later as well.

Rehearsal of the final argument is advised. Practicing aloud can give counsel some notion of how the summation will sound. If possible, a tape recorder or a listener to give feedback to the practiced argument is helpful. "A review of the presentation . . . will usually lead to a change in delivery. Even experienced trial attorneys discover they must make adjustments."[16] So preparation of the final argument involves several considerations—general planning, notetaking, outlining, audience analysis, and rehearsal.

THE CONTENT OF THE CLOSING ARGUMENT

Wide latitude is given to counsel in making their summations, although attorneys are not free to say anything they wish during closing arguments. Some argument is improper, and an infraction can cause a case to be appealed. What follows is a discussion of some of the more common boundaries.

Asserting a new fact or point in closing that was not adduced during the presentation of evidence is a violation. For example, a prosecutor would risk an objection if he or she said, "The defense has made a big point of the absence of bloodstains on the stabbing victim's car seat. Perhaps I should have brought in the bloodstained cushion." The existence of the bloodstained cushion was not put in evidence. Similar improper tactics deal with evidence distortion—misquoting, quoting out of context, or omitting unfavorable information.

Blatantly appealing for sympathy and making inflammatory appeals to prejudice and passion also constitute unethical content. A prejudicial slur by a defense counsel might be something like this: "Here we have an avowed atheist seeking to prevent praying in the school that our God-fearing, taxpaying neighbors are paying for." Arguments are improper that appeal to racial or religious prejudice, nationalism or sectionalism, or prejudice regarding the wealth or poverty of the parties.[17] Although displaying emotion in the closing argument is permitted, appealing to prejudice is not.

Still another infraction is the golden-rule approach, which asks the jury to imagine themselves in a client's position, thereby inviting the jurors to disregard their oaths and become nonobjective viewers of the evidence.[18] Plaintiff's attorney cannot say, "Place yourself in the position of this young couple, who lost their home, their belongings, and their cat and dog." An attorney can, however, properly remind a jury of the oath and promises made during voir dire concerning their lack of bias and their fair consideration solely of the issues and evidence.

One final example of improper conduct in summation is to make discourteous or insinuating remarks about opposing counsel or that counsel's client. One winning appeal was based on a comment by plaintiff's attorney when the defendant was a large business. Plaintiff's counsel referred in closing to "the distinguished, highly learned gentleman who represented this rich corporation." The appeals court found the remark prejudicial.[19]

Therefore, lawyers are forbidden to make improper argument in their summations. Sometimes these remarks are grounds for a decision reversal, particularly if the improper conduct was noted through an objection by opposing counsel at the time of the alleged infraction.[20] Although what has been said here makes it seem as though an attorney needs to exercise extreme caution in the closing argument, Justice Brown said, "If every remark made by counsel outside of the testimony were grounds for a reversal, comparatively few verdicts would stand, since in the ardor of advocacy, and in the excitement of a trial, even the most experienced counsel are occasionally carried away by this temptation."[21]

What content ought to appear in the closing argument? Generally, items for summation are plucked from critical testimony and set into a crown either of guilt or liability on the one hand or of a presumption of innocence or freedom from liability on the other. Five essential matters are covered in most summations: a statement of issues, a statement of the amount of proof required, a statement of evidence, some discussion of adverse evidence, and a statement of how the law applies to the facts.

First, all cases should boil down to a few determinate issues, which form the game plan for the case. Smith explains:

An issue is a key or pivotal question of fact or philosophy raised by the contentions of the party. For example, in a simple intersectional case, the key issue would be which party had the green light. If the plaintiff had witnesses establishing the issue, then he should stress this issue. The defendant may then defend his case on collateral issues . . . or side issues on which the defense can win.[22]

An issue (e.g., the green light) is not a theme (e.g., safety and the value of human life). Themes are central motivating ideas that pervade the entire case and closing argument; issues are major points to be supported by evidence. Highlighting the issues in the closing argument means that a lawyer refers to the pleadings that started the case. One method in a civil case is to show that the plaintiff made good or failed to make good the original complaint, or that the defense made good or failed to make good the original answer. In many personal injury cases, the only two issues for the plaintiff are liability and injury leading to damages. A review of final arguments from several civil cases found lines of ten more specific issues from the plaintiff: (1) The plaintiff is an innocent victim of circumstance; (2) the plaintiff has acted admirably in adverse circumstances; (3) the defendant's missing witness confirms defense culpability; (4) the incident giving rise to plaintiff's losses was preventable; (5) the defendant will not take responsibility for any loss, unlike other good people; (6) the defendant's selfish motives led to plaintiff's losses; (7) money is appropriate compensation and only form of compensation available; (8) the jurors are the sole judges of the amount to be assessed; (9)

the plaintiff no longer leads a normal life and must be compensated for this loss; (10) justice, not sympathy, must guide the jury's decision.[23] The exigency of the trial situation limits counsel almost completely to common lines of argument.[24]

While the lawyer for the plaintiff tries to fix the jury's attention on the main issues, the defense is more likely to scatter it over several collateral points, especially when its case on the main issues is not strong. In defending against a damage claim when the plaintiff clearly has the advantage on the liability issue, counsel might employ the "How about this, and how about that?" tactic that academic debaters have experienced: "If the injury was as serious as claimed, why did the plaintiff decline first aid on the spot? And why hasn't he missed a softball game since the accident?" This strategy is intended to minimize the amount of the jury's award.

Second, after highlighting the issues, a lawyer in closing argument weighs the burden of proof. The proof that is needed to establish or refute conviction or right of recovery needs an attorney's explanation and interpretation. For instance, in a civil case, plaintiff's lawyers explaining "preponderance of the evidence" may want to draw the scales of justice on a blackboard—or use their arms as the scales—and point out that a slight tilting in their favor—"no matter *how* slight—is sufficient to carry the burden of proof."[25] From the plaintiff's point of view, jurors must understand that "beyond a reasonable doubt" does not apply. By way of analogy, in a baseball game, a team can win by a 3–2 margin; the score does not have to be 3–0.

The defense will remind the jury that the plaintiff or prosecutor has a serious burden of proof. In a criminal case, the defense lawyer should refer to as many reasonable doubts as possible and not to a single reasonable doubt. To do this, counsel must probe the testimony for foggy memories, inconsistencies, or lack of evidence.[26] The prosecutor or plaintiff will attempt to offset this by recounting, point by point, how he or she met that responsibility.

Third, key evidence must be reviewed in the summation speech. Reviewing all of one's own witnesses' testimony in great detail is a waste of time; only the essential facts need to be analyzed. What does the evidence mean? How does it relate to the issues? Are the sources of evidence credible? Why is the evidence supporting the advocate's version of the facts probably true? Is there a numerical preponderance of the facts supported by the evidence for the advocate's side? As the questions are answered, counsel should not say,"I believe the evidence shows that . . . " This language sounds hopeful and apologetic. Phrasing like "The evidence convincingly establishes that . . . " is more positive and persuasive. Each corpus of facts should be categorized and analyzed under each of the pertinent case issues.[27] An issue-by-issue summary is sometimes referred to as *marshaling the evidence*.

Fourth, although the thrust of a summation should be the positive aspect of one's own case, some attention should be given to disarming the opposition with discussion of the lack of credibility and the insufficiency of adversary evidence. In one respect, little time should be spent pointing out deficiencies in the entire case of the opposition; to do so turns the trial into a picayune debating match. On the other hand, important two-sided argumentation—presenting and then refuting a counterargument—is persuasive, particularly when the audience is familiar with the issues on both sides of a controversy, as they are in a trial.[28] Two-sided arguments build lawyer credibility because they communicate candor, fairness,[29] intelligence, and an ability to argue both sides.[30]

Fifth, an attorney may want to comment on how the facts relate to legal principles. This does not mean to argue the law, but to show how the law, which the judge will present to the jury, applies to the issues and facts at hand. For example, what requirements have to be met to prove assault? Have these requirements been met? The prosecutor will want to show that all the legal requirements have been met; the defense lawyer will focus on those elements he or she contends have not been met. In addition, an advocate will want to secure a copy of the instructions the judge will later give to the jury to "be able to incorporate [them] . . . and the law into the argument,"[31] using the same language the judge will use. This strategy weaves a thread between the case evidence and the standard the judge will ask the jury to use in reaching their decision.

Two additional items of advice concerning the content of closing arguments should be followed by trial lawyers. First, case weaknesses should be admitted. Jurors appreciate and respect candor and honesty.[32] Of course, the insignificance of these weaknesses should also be noted, and the unfavorable information should be quickly mitigated.[33] At no time should an advocate apologize for these weaknesses or for anything else he or she thinks may have offended the jury during the course of the trial. It is better to act confident throughout the summation.

Second, explicit logic should be used. Logical argument is discussed at some length in the section on issue analysis in Chapter 3. "The difference between explicit and implicit arguments is really one of degree, not of kind."[34] An implicit conclusion to an argument is "Can you really trust the testimony of Mary Smith?" An explicit conclusion to an argument is "We cannot place any faith in the testimony of Mary Smith." The art of developing explicit conclusions is essential for a closing argument to be logically persuasive. And when explicit conclusions are stated, the advocates should explain how they got from evidence to the conclusions. For example, a lawyer might say, "Witness A said that fact Z exists. From that, we can infer that fact X also exists." The basis of such an inference is common experience. Or, "The testimony of John Doe was thus. I am trying to establish this. Now, how does that testimony relate to the issue?" Answering this question exposes the inference-making process of counsel. Such reasoning helps make cases clear and convincing to juries and judges.[35]

It is not enough for the lawyer to merely lay out the information and hope the jury will arrive at a logical decision. Wishful thinking is not enough. Rather, he or she must realize that since other factors come into play, it is up to the attorney to analyze the available information for the jury. It is up to the attorney to delineate the steps that go into the analysis so that the jury will be able to answer in their own minds the question "why?" Why did they arrive at a particular verdict?[36]

THE STRUCTURE OF THE CLOSING ARGUMENT

Because structure and order achieve balance and reduce confusion and frustration,[37] summations must be well organized to make it easier for both the speaker and the listeners to remember the message. The impact of a closing argument is significantly related to its structure. Let us then consider what goes into the overall structure of the closing argument: the introduction ("tell them what you are going to tell them"), the body ("tell them"), and the conclusion ("tell them what you told them").

An appropriate mood needs to be created in the introduction to the summation. In only a few sentences, not too profuse or flowery, an attorney might begin by saying, "Good afternoon. We have now reached the point in the trial where closing arguments will be presented. This is the time when the lawyers will tell you what their cases are all about." An informative statement of this nature can be followed by a brief word of thanks to the jury for their attentiveness and patience. Generally, what a lawyer is doing is expressing sincerity to the jury; after all, sincerity is comfortable

and flattering. Ingratiation theory indicates that, unless the attempt is too obvious, showing appreciation yields a jury more receptive to what is in the summation than if the lawyer immediately stands up and begins arguing.[38]

The introduction is also the place where counsel briefly previews the theme for the final speech. What is this case all about? This is not the time to go into detail; counsel should simply tell the jury the basic theme. For instance: "Calvin Bond will never to able to use his right arm for the rest of his life. His prospects of ever leading a normal life were ruined when an armed man entered Calvin's clothing store and shot him in the arm after taking all of the money out of the cash register." It is extremely important that, when this concise introduction is finished, counsel have the attention of the jury focused on important parts of the message to follow.

The heart of the closing is found in the body of the speech. The body is organized around the major issues, which were discussed in the previous section on content. The issue or issues an attorney stands on, whether legal, factual, or philosophical, must be made clear. If a lawyer stands on a legal issue, the question might be "Why don't you ponder all the aspects of loitering as they are outlined in the relevant statute?" If a stand is taken on a factual issue, the question would be something like "Did it happen, or didn't it?" If the stance is philosphical, the lawyer should say, "The basic issue here is whether we will let a slumlord get away with renting firetraps to poor people." As noted earlier, the body of the summation is to be organized around the issues themselves.

The body of the summation begins with a simple road-map summary of the issues. One author provides us with the following example:

The judge will instruct you that you should return a verdict for Jane Porter if you believe four things: first, that the defendant either drove at an excessive speed or was intoxicated; second, that her conduct was negligent; third, that Jane Porter sustained injuries as a result of such negligence; and fourth, that the driver Jones was operating the Ajax Company truck within the scope of his employment by Ajax. These are issues you must decide.[39]

Little time needs to be spent developing the uncontested issues (e.g., Jones was driving the truck as part of his job). However, detailed evidence summaries should accompany the discussion of the contested issues (e.g., the defendant was under the influence of alcohol). The main goal of providing detail is to resolve the contested issues. The detail might show that counsel's own witnesses had consistent facts, demonstrated common sense, and were credible. Counsel might further show that he or she had the greater quantity of evidence. In outline form, a contested-issues argument looks like this:

Statement of issue
Summary of relevant evidence
Discussion
Statement of next issue
Summary of evidence relevant to that issue
Discussion, etc.[40]

Some thought needs to be given to the number of different issues raised. Research suggests that there is an upper limit to the number of issues or arguments a person can present and still have persuasive effect. One group of researchers exposed subjects to anywhere from one to sixteen criminal case arguments.[41] The subjects were then asked to rate their strength of belief in the defendant's guilt. Ratings of guilt increased steadily as the number of prosecutorial issues increased, up to about ten arguments. Thereafter, the effect of adding more arguments was negligible. The most persuasive effect took place when seven to ten arguments were used.

Additional thought needs to be given to the order in which the issues are presented.

Should lawyers begin with weaker arguments and build to the strongest one, or should they start with the strongest argument for their side and then cover the rest in descending order? After studying research in communication and social psychology, one author concludes that "arguing 'climax–anticlimax,' which is going from strong to weak, . . . is . . . the most persuasive pattern of argument."[42] Counsel's own strongest argument should be stated first; a lawyer who waits to put the strongest issue last may be facing a skeptical jury, who has been asked to accept weaker positions in the case first.

The conclusion, or peroration, should bring the closing argument to a resounding climax. This is where most of the emotional appeal should appear.[43] More will be said about emotion later. The closing part of each summation should be concise and forceful. This is the time for oratory and eloquence.[43] Although the following example may go overboard for most attorneys, the dramatic ending of defense attorney Sir Edward Marshall in the *Greenwood* murder case eloquently emphasizes the dreadful finality of a jury's verdict:

Your verdict is final, necessarily final. Science can do a great deal; these men with their mirrors, multipliers, and milligrams can tell you to the ten-thousandth or millionth part of a grain the constituents of the human body. Science has enabled us to talk from here to thousands of miles away without any intervening wire or visible means of communication. Science has enabled us to kill thousands by obnoxious gases, and can enable us to blow ourselves to pieces with one little explosive. But science cannot do one thing: that is to find the vital spark which converts inert clay into a human being. Once the life is gone out of a man, be it as a result of a jury's verdict of murder, or be it by any other cause, life is at an end, and no power of science can replace it. I ask you to remember the scene in "Othello," where the jealous Moor made up his mind to kill Desdemona; Othello enters Desdemona's chamber, makes up his mind to kill her relentlessly, for he believes her to be unchaste, and seeing her lying there he thinks of the effect of killing her as compared with putting out her light, and says: "Put out the light," and then he puts out the light. . . . Are you by your verdict going to put out that light? Gentlemen of the Jury, I demand at your hands the life and liberty of Harold Greenwood.

Notice that the final words of this closing argument appropriately end with a specific request for action.

The last few words said to a jury should be strong ones. Melvin Belli says that the last few lines could even be memorized.[44] In show business, entertainers try for strong finishes with what they call "tag lines." Attorneys should do likewise. The "put out the light" reference, combined with a reminder of the awesome power a jury has on its shoulders, constituted an effective tag line for Sir Edward Marshall.

How long should a closing argument last? In the days of Daniel Webster or Clarence Darrow, when the trial served as a form of public entertainment, summations often consumed two or three days.[45] Today, closings generally go from a few minutes to many hours. "A one-hour summation, or possibly two hours, is about as long as it should go."[46] Unfortunately, very little research exists on how long the suitable closing argument should be. Anyway, speed is not of the essence; eloquence is. The complexity of the case and the speaking ability of the attorney ought to be factors in determining the length of the closing argument. And when the climax of the speech is reached, the time for an attorney to quit is at hand.

With increasing frequency, the courts are allocating time for closing arguments. Equal time, such as 20 minutes apiece, is given to both sides. A bailiff keeps the time and informs the lawyers when they have but a few minutes remaining. If the jury is unaware that there are time limits, the lawyers should not tell the jury what the limits are, because the

jurors will watch the clock too closely. Pacing is important when lawyers face time limits during their closing arguments. Counsel should leave their watches where they can unobtrusively see them so the time can be observed. Practicing and timing the speech beforehand is advised as well.

EMOTIONAL APPEAL IN THE CLOSING ARGUMENT

Emotion is "that type of affective state characterized by considerable intensity and where the organism is experiencing more widespread visceral and somatic changes than is true of the more mild feelings we may have over some person, object, or event; it is both a physiological and psychological response to a stimulus."[47] Appealing to the emotions in argument is often denounced. Perhaps emotionalism should be denounced if it goes to an extreme. However, if undue emotional appeals are avoided, some emotionalism in summations is strategically wise. Why? Because lawyers are really selling points of view; they are urging belief in the stories they tell. "Dry appeals purely to the intellect with no emotional content are not very persuasive."[48] Therefore, some emotional appeal should be found in the summation.

Emotionalism in the closing argument can take one of several forms. One form is the *dramatic presentation*. Only lawyers capable of using a dramatic voice and manner should try this approach; incapable lawyers appear phony. Dramatic presentations involve speaking from a whisper to a shout or parading around the courtroom and playing center stage. More will be said later in the chapter about delivery of the summation.

Emotions can also be aroused through an exciting use of *visual aids*. "The lawyer who ignores the use of visual aids in persuasion ignores the whole framework in psychology."[49] One author suggests that a defense lawyer can dramatize the idea of contributory negligence by tearing a sheet of paper into a large piece and a tiny one, holding them up for contrast, and saying, "If my client was negligent . . . (showing them the large piece of paper), and the plaintiff was negligent . . . (showing the small piece), then under the law it is the sworn duty of this jury to find my client not guilty. It is not a matter of weighing which one was the most (more) negligent. Before he can collect ten cents, the plaintiff must prove that he, himself, was not even guilty of that much negligence (again showing the small piece of paper)."[50]

All kinds of visual aids are permitted in the closing argument, and they can be used to help communicate the case theme and issues to the jury. For example, "it is often helpful to list the elements of the cause of action on a chart or blackboard, and cross out or erase the uncontested ones."[51] Charts can also be used to show damage computations, chronology of events, lists of witnesses, and so on. Diagrams of accident scenes can recreate the movement and relative positions of the parties. The presentation of real evidence such as the murder weapon in a homicide is an effective persuasive technique. "Tangible, visual evidence involves the eye and is powerfully persuasive"[52] when used in the closing argument.

Another form of emotionalism is the *emotional appeal* itself. Sir Edward Marshall has given us an example of an emotional appeal to fear and sympathy. Emotional appeals should be aimed directly at the value systems and attitudes of the jurors. By value systems, I mean such familiar ingredients as love of family, justice, Puritan morality, freedom, success, work, practicality, rationality, quantity (bigness, speed, etc.), safety, comfort, generosity, patriotism, conformity, and so forth. Attitudes that are related to these values are complex mixtures of affective, cognitive, and behavioral elements. These three elements involve how one feels, and what one knows or believes, and predispositions to act.

In appealing emotionally to attitudes and values, an advocate tries to anchor the case to them—to show consonance or compatibility between them and the decision that is being urged. Anchoring technique is based on consistency theory.[53] Attitudes and values flowing from the case are shown to be consistent with, or anchored to, the jurors' basic belief systems. The authors of one book offer the following advice regarding anchoring technique:

The point to remember is that if you can anchor your case to one of these widely accepted foundations you will make it difficult for your opponent to sway the jury because their belief about your case cannot be altered without changing the other beliefs to which it is anchored. Since changing two or more interlocking beliefs is more difficult than changing an isolated belief, successful anchoring creates resistance to the persuasive attempts of your opponent. Obviously, the more firmly your case is anchored in the deeply held values and beliefs of the jurors, the more resistant they will be to counter-persuasion.[54]

Emotion resides in the attitudes and values of the jurors; when these attitudes and values are tapped, moving people to action is likely to occur. Here is an illustration, an appeal to the value of life: "I am proud that our country places a high value on life because you judge a civilization by what it thinks of human life. I believe that it is a mark of our civilization that we hold to the principle that life is our most precious and expensive commodity. Our forefathers thought so when they said that each man is entitled to life, liberty, and the pursuit of happiness." As long as the rhetoric is not condescending, this value appeal should help to shape belief in one or more issues in the closing argument.

Other ways to approach this value are through the rhetorical question or by capitalizing on voir dire commitments. A rhetorical question is one whose answer is so obvious it does not demand an answer. "Rhetorical questions will work only if the attorney is absolutely sure of how the jury will respond to the question. The theory behind the use of the rhetorical question is that the juror who answers that question in his own mind then becomes an advocate for that point of view in the jury room. That answer becomes his own."[55] So the rhetorical question could be asked, "Doesn't justice demand that we place a high value on life, liberty, and the pursuit of happiness?" Likewise, I noted in Chapter 5 that individuals need to be consistent with prior commitments. So, if a lawyer asked the jury in voir dire to make a commitment to value life, the closing argument could proceed with a reminder and a discussion of that commitment as it applies to decision making in the case at hand.[56]

Some writers on persuasion explain that language that holds attention is the key to the whole process of using emotional appeals successfully. After reviewing years of research in the Duke University Law and Language project, John M. Conley concludes, "The manner in which a person speaks may be as important as what he says in shaping the conclusions of his audiences."[57] Numerous other studies clearly link speaker credibility, audience interest, and language choice.[58] The idea is to control listeners' perceptions to keep attention on the speaker's message by using language that is vivid. Vivid language causes humans to think and deal in mental pictures. The opposite of vivid language, abstractness, is not likely to elicit mental pictures similar to those desired by the advocate. Words like *book, relative, insect,* and *family planning* are general; words like *paperback novel, father, killer bee,* and *contraceptive* are more concrete and vivid. Since vivid words evoke sensory images, word choice has much to do with persuasion. Notice what a difference it makes to call someone a "troublemaker" instead of a "social critic" or to say "a wound

that is oozing pus" rather than "a lesion that is suppurating." Lawyers in closing arguments have many occasions to choose vivid words for pain, suffering, anguish, worry, fear, grief, embarrassment, shame, and the like.

The words chosen for closing argument should have punch to them. Short adjectives, nouns, and verbs can evoke visual images. Words like *happy, healthy, crash, smash-up, mangled,* and *ruined* evoke images more effectively than words like *satisfactory, negligent, incident,* and *direct result.* Why? Because they appeal to the senses. "Sensory language is to the communicator as the rainbow of colors is to the painter."[59] The lawyer who says, "He heard a piercing screech, followed by a loud crash," is appealing to our auditory sense. The lawyer who says, "he saw a green Volvo run the red light and hit the brown Toyota broadside," is appealing to our visual sense. The lawyer who says, "She felt scared to death and helpless when she realized she was trapped in her car," is appealing to our kinesthetic or internal feelings sense. Attorneys who frame their speeches in sensory language will appeal to the sensory channels of the jury. Notice, in the following portion of a closing argument about the accidental blinding of a man with five children, how visual imagery is used in the first paragraph, kinesthetic imagery in the second paragraph, auditory imagery in the third paragraph, and visual imagery again in the fourth paragraph. A full sensory experience is created.

When we came to this court today, on this *beautiful springtime morning,* the *profusion of flowers* was *radiant* and *breathtaking.* Each *bloom* seemed to be vying with its neighbor, and altogether they almost outdid themselves. What a *sight* to gladden our hearts and soothe our spirits; Longellow spoke of the *flowers* thus: *"Stars* of the earth, these *golden flowers; emblems* of the *bright and better land."* But the *flowers* and their message of inspiration were for you and me not for John Demmons. He could not, and did not, *see a flower* as he came to court today. He will never *see a flower* again. . . .

In *happier times,* when John Demmons came home from work, his youngest children met him at the gate of his *humble* rented cottage, and he would *hold them close,* then *throw them into the air* and *catch them* as they came down, *holding them close* so that he *felt their little heartbeats—flesh of his flesh, blood of his blood, and bone of his bone!* For all fathers this *feeling* is about as *great a boon* as God can grant unto you. But now John cannot have the *ecstasy* and *happiness* he formerly knew. He might not be able to *catch the child,* so he *dare not throw it into the air.* How much is the *loss* of the *privilege worth?* It seems almost *profane* and *vulgar* to *equate* that *father-child relationship* with mere dollars. . . .

Go with me now inside the little rented cottage at mealtime. Seven people sit around a table: the father, the mother, and five little children. Before the meal begins each one clasps the hand of another and form a family-circle. John *tells* one of them to *say grace,* to *'Ask the blessing.'* And he carefully *listens* to the child as he *prays:*

God is great, God is good
God we *thank* Thee for this food.

John used to *peep to see* if all of the children had *closed their eyes*—a father's privilege. He cannot *peep* now; he cannot *see* them. The meal is eaten, but somehow things have changed, and it will never be as it once was.[60]

"One of the most powerful tools used in summation"[61] for making language vivid is the analogy. It is said that nothing moves jurors more convincingly than "an apt comparison to something they know from their own experience is true."[62] For instance, the lawyer for the plaintiff injured in a nuclear power plant accident might compare the facility to a boiling tea kettle, or counsel might make reference to the chameleon, which changes color when it gets scared, as a comparison to the other side when they change their story. Analogies are vivid and persuasive because they "first provoke and then reward the listeners' intellectual pride."[63] Knowing what they do about boiling tea kettles or chameleons, the jurors reach conclusions before the speaker does. Analogies are also effective because they are a form of storytelling if they are filled with detail and repeatedly referred to in summation "in order to squeeze out the final ounce of persuasive impact from each example."[64] So, as long as the analogy does not violate the golden-rule prohibition by requesting that the jury put themselves in the shoes of one of the parties, it is "perhaps the most powerful form of argument we know."[65]

Similar to the analogy is the metaphor, another linguistic tool to achieve vividness. A metaphor is a referent evoking an intense reaction from the audience by taking a term out of its habitual association and placing it in, while comparing it to, another more emotional association. For example, "abortion is legalizing *murder*" is a death metaphor, and "allowing this water polluter to go free means the *rape* of our environment" is a sex metaphor. After experimentally comparing discourse with and without metaphors, one researcher concluded that a metaphor nearly always communicates a stronger attitude than does a conventional expression.[66]

Finally, with reference to effective use of language, three familiar qualities of style should be mentioned: *clarity, intensity,* and *appropriateness.* Clarity, or clearness or perspicuity, is generally desirable, but "Clearness to whom?" is the question. In closing arguments, clearness to judge and jury is the test. Clarity and simplicity are interrelated, and simplicity comes from the use of everyday language. Phrases like "Isn't that hard to swallow?" or "The bottom dropped out of his case" incorporate slang and clichés, but if not overused, they provide clarity. Terse sentences are usually clearer than longer, complex ones. Moderate redundancy aids clarity because it reminds and reinforces.[67] Finally, whereas prosecuting and plaintiffs' attorneys should remain consistently clear, there is some evidence that somewhat abstract speech with less clarity works to the advantage of a defense attorney.[68]

Intensity refers to the degree to which the stance of the language deviates from neutrality.[69] Generally, speakers appear more dynamic and credible when intense language is used.[70] For instance, the word "must" is more intense than the word "hope." "I'm firm, but he's pigheaded" is another example of an intense expression. Successful prosecutors are verbally assertive (intense); while unsuccessful prosecutors are more tentative and polite. Meanwhile, in criminal cases, successful defense attorneys use few adverbs and affective words, whereas unsuccessful defense attorneys used demonstrative language.[71]

Some words of caution need to be given regarding intensity. If a listener perceives too many intensifying adjectives (e.g., "very clear," "surely appreciate," and definitely help"), the result is not convincing because the communication is lengthened, the persuasive punch noted in our earlier discussion regarding vividness is removed,[72] and a boomerang effect is created, which leads to attitude change in the opposite direction from that desired.[73] Also, one study showed that male communicators can be more effective than female communicators when using highly intense language, perhaps because we expect females to use less intense language than males.[74] "When a female communicator does use highly intense language, there may be a violation of expectations for an audience member which could lead to the rejection of the source and her message."[75] Right or wrong, stereotypes do play a role in persuasive communication.

Appropriateness of language or fitness of expression is a subjective judgment, but clearly such matters as foul or abusive language are normally considered inappropriate. A statement like "The case is quite simple" is inappropriate for jurors who may see it as complex. A statement like "This is the most important decision you will ever make" puts too much of a burden on the panel. Equally inappropriate are worthless phrases. One writer cites the following ones:

"We are here today . . . "
"It must be remembered that . . . "
"It must be noted that . . . "
"I would submit that . . . "
"I would contend that . . . "
"If I should misstate the evidence, follow your own recollection and not mine."[76]

Also, referring to "my client" sounds too impersonal and as though the lawyer is ready to have the cashbox ringing.[77] Finally, some words and grammar are more appropriate for one side of a case than they are for the other side. In the highly publicized war-of-the-words 1975 trial in which Boston obstetrician-gynecologist Kenneth Edelin was convicted of manslaughter in connection with a late abortion, the term used to characterize the object of the abortion was appropriately "baby" or "child" for the prosecution and "fetus" or "product of conception" for the defense.[78] In civil suits, the plaintiff's attorney should use "collision"; the defense attorney should say "accident." The plaintiff should use subjective language about people and physical referents; defense counsel should appear objective. The plaintiff should avoid the passive voice; the defendant's lawyer should avoid the present tense.[79]

Taken together, vividness, clarity, intensity, and appropriateness all add to a powerful attorney style. Research findings support the claim that such style is directly related to jury judgments of lawyer competence in the courtroom.[80] Thus, it behooves each and every attorney to be aware of the importance of the linguistic dimension of closing argument.

Emotionalism, in the form of dramatic presentations, visual aids, appeals to the emotions, and language that is vivid, clear, intense, and appropriate, is advised for the summation when it is used in moderation. Since the jury is already informed about the case, and since the judge will ask them to look at the evidence, the effect of emotionalism may be expected to be less than in other persuasive settings.[81] Nevertheless, some emotionalism should be used by advocates during closing argument.

DELIVERING THE CLOSING ARGUMENT CONVINCINGLY

After an extensive summary of research on how we speak, one author draws this conclusion: "Many, and sometimes most, of the critical meanings generated in human encounters are elicited by touch, glance, vocal nuance, gesture, or facial expression without the aid of words."[82] We get meaning from nonverbal cues, and this means that misunderstanding can come from a listener's insensitivity to those cues or a speaker's failure to use nonverbal cues congruent with verbal ones. Thus, if a lawyer's words express sympathy in the summation, while the voice and face suggest indifference, the jury is likely to believe the latter. Let us then examine some of the vocal and physical delivery techniques attorneys can use to make their final presentations effective.

Regarding *vocal delivery*, "oration will not do the job. The . . . attitude should be friendly, conversational and direct."[83] The jury should be talked with, not at. After all, research shows that a calm and measured style of vocal delivery will make the attorney more highly credible than will a strident and intense voice.[84]

The summation should be neither too loud nor too soft. Neither should it be too fast nor too slow. Too much speed implies slipperiness and shallowness;[85] yet slow talkers are dull and not persuasive.[86] Slowness is usually a more serious problem in summations than is speed. Vocal variety should replace monot-

ony in order to keep the jury interested in the message. The voice can be raised or lowered when an important point is reached, as long as the pitch does not get too high. Extremely high-pitched voices are less credible than those with deeper pitches.[87]

Pauses should be used to create suspense and drama; they are particularly useful before and after making main points. Pausing is the equivalent of punctuation in writing and is inappropriate in the middle of an idea or after every few words. The summation should be neither memorized nor read verbatim. Canned speeches sound insincere and unimpressive. Lastly, the nonfluency "uh," a vocalized pause between sentences and thoughts, causes significantly lower listener ratings on speaker credibility, dynamism, and competence.[88]

Physical delivery involves a consideration of one's eyes, gestures, movement, and use of space. The most important thing to understand about physical delivery is not how to communicate with it, but how to keep from sending the wrong message. Direct eye contact should be established with the jurors as the summation is being delivered. Eye contact should not be with the floor or at some spot above the jurors' heads. Effective eye contact enhances sincerity and honesty; it also allows for feedback. In order to ensure maximum eye contact, minimal notes should be used. Reading aloud should be limited to quoting directly from the record.

Gestures should be natural, yet not so frequent as to appear like a perpetual windmill. With regard to movement, a lawyer should not be locked physically to one spot unless the court requires the practice of remaining behind a lectern. Even then, lawyers must not anchor themselves to the lectern. If movement is allowed, counsel should move (not pace) in order to gain attention.

Space is most important. Large and loud attorneys may want to be as much as 20 feet away from the jury when speaking; attorneys smaller in stature with a gentler style may want to be as close as 12 feet away. One study indicates that distances between the speaker and listener of more than 12 feet are the most effective for one-way persuasion.[89] An attorney should stand directly in front of the jury box to get them to pay close attention. At the same time, attorneys do not want to intimidate the jury by their sheer physical domination. "Hollering, speaking loudly, pounding on the jury rail, and getting into the face of the jury . . . may look good on television, but such behavior does not win lawsuits."[90]

How does an attorney develop effective vocal and physical delivery? The answer is *not* to think of what one is doing during performance; "an awareness . . . destroys naturalness and spontaneity; . . . [it] results in self-consciousness."[91] The road to improvement in delivery is found instead in being prepared, feeling comfortable, practicing aloud, and performing often.

RECENCY AND THE CLOSING ARGUMENT

One part of the trial context is the speaker order, which is not the same everywhere. In many jurisdictions, the defense delivers the first closing argument and the plaintiff or prosecutor speaks last. In other jurisdictions, the plaintiff or prosecutor speaks first, the defense speaks next, and the plaintiff or prosecutor replies in rebuttal. In both situations, the plaintiff or prosecutor gets the last word in closing arguments. As you may remember, the plaintiff and prosecutor also got the first chance to speak in opening statements.

Is there an advantage in speaking last? Research on what is called the recency effect indicates an advantage insofar as the last word is often the most memorable and influential word. One study found that when 160 undergraduates read jury trial excerpts, a significant recency effect appeared regarding both their

opinion of the case and their retention of information. When the prosecution spoke last, his words were more impressive and better retained; when the defense attorney spoke last, his words were better remembered and more persuasive.[92] The recency effect even increases in strength if there is some delay between the two closing arguments.[93] Subsequent research has consistently confirmed the recency phenomenon.[94] Perhaps there is a distinct advantage given to prosecutors and plaintiffs in the trial format by giving them the last speech and leaving their arguments uppermost in the jurors' minds.

In an earlier chapter, we noted that the psychological principle of primacy assists the party with the burden of proof. That principle is that what is said first and accepted is difficult to turn around. The primacy advantage rests with the prosecutor or plaintiff. Now the same attorney profits from the psychological principle of recency. Some thought-provoking questions are raised about the trial format. "How does the . . . order which combines both primacy and recency effects balance the burden of proof? Or does it offer a balancing effect at all? Is it an unfair advantage for either the plaintiff or prosecutor?"[95] These are difficult questions to answer, and so far there is only speculation. Some defense attorneys argue that the burden of proof has actually shifted to the defense. Research on this matter is sorely needed.

The defense antidote for overcoming the effects of primacy and recency is to present the problem directly to the jury. Here is an illustration pertaining to a tripartite argument procedure:

Ladies and gentlemen, throughout the trial Mr. Plaintiff Lawyer has talked to you first, and I have talked to you second. He talked to you in voir dire *first,* and I talked second; he talked to you in opening statement *first,* and I talked second; he presented evidence to you *first,* and I presented evidence to you second; and he talked to you now *first,* and I am talking to you once again, second.

Psychologists tell us that people are more influenced by what comes first in a two-part presentation simply because it comes first and for no other reason. They call this the *primacy* effect. . . . [Now,] I ask you, I implore you— remember that primacy effect and please wait and listen to all of the argument, including Mr. Defendant's, before you make up your mind about this case.

. . . In additon to that primacy effect, . . . there is also another such effect called the "recency effect." Psychologists tell us that all persons tend to have a better recall of material presented to them last, . . . since it is more recent or more fresh in their minds. In this case the prosecutor not only talks with you first in argument, but he also talks with you last in argument. So please, after I am finished, remember that he has the last word. Try not to remember that last word more vividly than what is now offered to you because of some mind-affecting psychological process.[96]

Summation or closing argument is an art form and "the nearest thing to free speech the trial will afford."[97] It is a crucial part of any trial, although the closing most often rests on the strength of what preceded it. Nevertheless, a trial attorney must be a skilled communicator as he or she approaches this final presentation to the jury. The summation should be planned well in advance in terms of content, organization, emotional appeals, and delivery. Appendix F offers a model closing argument, which appears to have been carefully planned.

Although this chapter has presented the viewpoint that closing arguments should be a time for outstanding advocacy, a word of caution is warranted. Argumentative overkill in one's zeal to persuade "is seen as presumptuous and overbearing. It can turn jurors off so completely that they become passive, unresponsive, and, ultimately, advocates against counsel."[98] All of the rhetorical techniques discussed here can be overdone. However, if they are used tactfully, the summation can be properly executed to be simple, logical, sincere, and persuasive, and it will be an effective conclusion to any lawyer's case.

Notes

[1]Raymond W. Buchanan, "Opening Statements and Closing Arguments: A Response From the Communication Perspective," in Ronald J. Matlon and Richard J. Crawford, eds., *Communication Strategies in the Practice of Lawyering* (Annandale, Va.: Speech Communication Association, 1983), 453.

[2]James W. McElhaney, "Solving Problems With Final Argument," *Litigation* (Winter 1983), 43.

[3]Murry Sams, Jr., "Closing Argument: New Answers to Some Old Problems," in Grace W. Holmes, ed., *Excellence in Advocacy* (Ann Arbor, Mich.: Institute of Continuing Legal Education, 1971), 86.

[4]James H. Seckinger and Kenneth S. Broun, *Problems and Cases in Trial Advocacy* (St. Paul, Minn.: National Institute for Legal Advocacy, 1979), 186.

[5]Ibid.

[6]H. P. Weld and E. R. Danzig, "A Study of the Way in Which a Verdict is Reached by a Jury," *American Journal of Psychology* 53 (1940), 531.

[7]Leslie H. Vogel, "Final Argument," in Harry Bodin, ed., *Civil Litigation and Trial Techniques* (New York: Practicing Law Institute, 1976), 646.

[8]Ibid.

[9]Prentice H. Marshall, "Persuading Judges in Bench Trials," *Litigation* (Summer 1977), 12.

[10]Myron L. Gordon, "Nonjury Summations," in *Am Jur Trials* (San Francisco: Bancroft-Whitney, 1967), vol. 6, 776–777.

[11]Joseph Kelner and Francis E. McGovern, *Successful Litigation Techniques* (New York: Matthew Bender, 1981), p. 17–3.

[12]Frank J. McGarr, "Prosecution Summations," in *Am Jur Trials* (San Francisco: Bancroft-Whitney, 1967), vol. 6, 878.

[13]Harry A. Gair, "Summations for the Plaintiff," in *Am Jur Trials* (San Francisco: Bancroft-Whitney, 1967), vol. 6, 651.

[14]Robert McFigg, Ralph C. McCullough II, and James L. Underwood, *Civil Trial Manual* (Los Angeles: Joint Committee on Legal Education of the American Law Institute and the American Bar Association, 1974), 446.

[15]Ellen Berscheid, "Opinion Change and Communicator-Communicatee Similarity and Dissimilarity," *Journal of Personality and Social Psychology* 4 (1966), 670–680.

[16]John J. Cleary, "The Final Argument in a Criminal Case," *Practical Lawyer* (September 1, 1981), 45.

[17]Francis Xavier Busch, *Trial Procedure Materials* (Indianapolis: Bobbs-Merrill, 1961), 526–527.

[18]Herbert A. Kuvin, *Trial Handbook* (Englewood Cliffs, N.J.: Prentice-Hall, 1965), 283.

[19]Edward J. Thompson, "Lawyers' Courtroom Conduct and Manners," *Case and Comment* (September–October 1967), 22.

[20]J. Alexander Tanford, *The Trial Process: Law, Tactics and Ethics* (Charlottesville, Va.: Michie, 1983), 142.

[21]*Dunlop v. United States,* 165 U.S. 486, S.Ct. 375, 41 L.Ed. 789 (1897).

[22]Lawrence J. Smith, *Art of Advocacy: Summation* (New York: Matthew Bender, 1981), 1–17.

[23]Sharon L. Occhipinti, "Lines of Argument: A Generic Component of Summations," Paper presented at the Speech Communication Association convention (Chicago, 1984).

[24]For a further discussion of the rhetorical situation, see Lloyd F. Bitzer, "The Rhetorical Situation," *Philosophy and Rhetoric* 1 (1968), 1–14.

[25]J. D. Lee, "Final Strokes: Painting the Whole Picture at Summation," *Trial* (July 1983), 66.

[26]David Cohen, "Responsible Doubt in Summation," *Trial Diplomacy Journal* (Spring 1981), 32.

[27]D. Jeffrey Hirschberg and Godfrey Issac, *Advanced Criminal Trial Tactics* (New York: Practicing Law Institute, 1978), 204–205; McFigg, McCullough, and Underwood, op. cit., 453.

[28]Michael F. Colley, "Friendly Persuasion: Gaining Attention, Comprehension and Acceptance in Court," *Trial* (August 1981), 46; Russell A. Jones and Jack W. Brehm, "Persuasiveness of One- and Two-Sided Communications as a Function of Awareness There Are Two Sides," *Journal of Experimental Social Psychology* 6 (1971), 47–56; Robert G. Lawson, "Relative Effectiveness of One-Sided and Two-Sided Communications in Courtroom Persuasion," *Journal of General Psychology* 82 (1970), 3–16.

[29]Steven H. Goldberg, *The First Trial: Where Do I Sit? What Do I Say?* (St. Paul, Minn.: West Publishing, 1982), 204–205.

[30]Paul Bergman, *Trial Advocacy* (St. Paul, Minn.: West Publishing, 1979), 321.

[31]Mark A. Dombroff, "The Last Word," *Trial* (March 1986), 60.

[32]Thomas A. Mauet, *Fundamentals of Trial Techniques* (Boston: Little, Brown, 1980), 301.

[33]John P. Miller, "Opening and Closing Statements From the Viewpoint of the Plaintiff's Attorney," *Practical Lawyer* (October 1964), 92.

[34]Bergman, op. cit., 312.

[35]Charles I. Hovland and Wallace Mandell, "An Experimental Comparison of Conclusion-Drawing by the Communicator and by the Audience," *Journal of Abnormal and Social Psychology* 47 (1952), 581–588; Donald L. Thistlewaite, Henry DeHaan, and Joseph Kamenetsky, "The Effects of 'Directive' and 'Nondirective' Communication Procedures on Attitudes," *Journal of Abnormal and Social Psychology* 51 (1955), 107–113.

[36]Donald E. Vinson and Philip K. Anthony, "The Closing Argument: Applications of Attribution Theory," *Trial Diplomacy Journal* (Spring 1984), 34.

[37]John J. Makay and Thomas C. Sawyer, *Speech Communication Now: An Introduction to Rhetorical Influences* (Columbus, Ohio: Merrill, 1973), 142.

[38]Norman E. Fontes and Robert W. Bundes, "Persuasion During the Trial Process," in Michael E. Roloff and Gerald R. Miller, eds., *Persuasion: New Directions in Theory and Research* (Beverly Hills, Calif.: Sage, 1980), 249–266.

[39]Tanford, op. cit., 156.

[40]Bergman, op. cit., 252.

[41]Bobby J. Calder, Chester A. Insko, and Ben Yandell, "The Relation of Cognitive and Memorial

Process to Persuasion in a Simulated Jury Trial," *Journal of Applied Social Psychology* 4 (1974), 62–93.

[42]Smith, op. cit., p. 1–34.

[43]Phillips R. Biddle, "An Experimental Study of Ethos and Appeal for Overt Behavior in Persuasion," Ph.D. diss. (Urbana: University of Illinois, 1966); Hovland and Mandell, op. cit.; Howard Leventhal and Robert P. Singer, "Affect Arousal and Positioning of Recommendations in Persuasive Communications," *Journal of Personality and Social Psychology* 4 (1966), 137–146.

[44]Melvin M. Belli, "Techniques of Final Argument," *Trial Diplomacy Journal* (Winter 1979), 39.

[45]Scott Baldwin, "Jury Argument," *Trial* (April 1984), 59.

[46]Stanley E. Preiser, "The Criminal Case: Tips on Summation," *Trial* (October 1979), 53.

[47]Winston L. Brembeck and William S. Howell, *Persuasion: A Means of Social Influence* (Englewood Cliffs, N.J.: Prentice-Hall, 1976), 106.

[48]Craig Spangenberg, "Basic Values and the Techniques of Persuasion," *Litigation* (Des Moines: Dean-Hicks, 1966), 335.

[49]Al J. Cone and Verne Lawyer, *The Act of Persuasion in Litigation* (Des Moines: Dean-Hicks, 1966), 335.

[50]Alan E. Morrill, *Trial Diplomacy* (Chicago: Court Practice Institute, 1979), 95.

[51]Tanford, op. cit., 156.

[52]Don Peters, "Participatory Persuasion: Strategies and Research Needs in Opening Statements and Closing Arguments," in Ronald J. Matlon and Richard J. Crawford, eds., *Communication Strategies in the Practice of Lawyering* (Annandale, Va.: Speech Communication Association, 1983), 409.

[53]William J. McGuire, "Cognitive Consistency and Attitude Change," *Journal of Abnormal and Social Psychology* 60 (1960), 345–353.

[54]K. Phillip Taylor, Raymond W. Buchanan, and David U. Strawn, *Communication Strategies for Trial Attorneys* (Glenview, Ill.: Scott, Foresman, 1984), 83.

[55]Lawrence J. Smith and Loretta A. Malandro, *Courtroom Communication Strategies* (New York: Kluwer, 1985), 764–765.

[56]Robert E. Cartwright, "Winning Psychological Principles in Summation," *Trial Lawyer's Quarterly* 16 (1984), 9–10.

[57]John M. Conley, "Language in the Courtroom," *Trial* (September 1979), 35.

[58]Eldon E. Baker, "The Immediate Effects of Perceived Speaker Disorganization on Speaker Credibility and Audience Attitude Change in Persuasive Speaking," *Western Speech* 29 (1965), 148–161; Howard Giles and Peter F. Powesland, *Speech Style and Social Evaluation* (New York: Academic Press, 1975); L. S. Harms, "Social Judgments of Status Cues in Language," Ph.D. diss. (Columbus: Ohio State University, 1959); Gerald R. Miller and Murry A. Hewgill, "The Effects of Variations in Nonfluency on Audience Ratings of Source Credibility," *Quarterly Journal of Speech* 50 (1964), 36–44; Anthony Mulac, "Assessment and Application of the Revised Speech Dialect Attitudinal Scale," *Communication Monographs* 43 (1976), 238–245; Paul I. Rosenthal, "Specificity, Verifiability, and Message Credibility," *Quarterly Journal of Speech* 57 (1971), 393–401; Kenneth K. Sereno and Gary J. Hawkins, "The Effects of Variations in Speaker's Nonfluency Upon Audience Ratings and Attitudes Toward the Speech Topic and the Speaker's Credibility," *Speech Monographs* 34 (1967), 58–64.

[59]Stephanie L. Swanson and David Wenner, "Sensory Language in the Courtroom," *Trial Diplomacy Journal* (Winter 1981–82), 14.

[60]Judge Randall Evans, Jr., *Opening and Closing Arguments: The Law in Georgia* (Norcross, Ga.: Harrison, 1978), 42–48.

[61]Smith and Malandro, op. cit., 759.

[62]Spangenberg, op. cit., 13, 16.

[63]Peters, op. cit., 404.

[64]Richard J. Crawford, "Closing Argument: High Noon at the Penthouse Corral," *Trial Diplomacy Journal* (Winter 1982–83), 15.

[65]James W. McElhaney, "Analogy in Final Argument," *Litigation* (Winter 1980), 37.

[66]John Waite Bowers, "Some Correlates of

Language Intensity," *Quarterly Journal of Speech* 50 (1964), 415–420.

[67]John T. Cacioppo and Richard E. Petty, "Effects of Extent of Thought on the Pleasantness Rating of P.O.X. Triads: Evidence for Three Judgmental Tendencies in Evaluating Social Situations," *Journal of Personality and Social Psychology* 40 (1981), 1000–1009; Warner Wilson and Howard Miller, "Repetition, Order of Presentation, and Timing of Arguments and Measures as Determinants of Opinion Change," *Journal of Personality and Social Psychology* 9 (1968), 184–188.

[68]Michael G. Parkinson, "Verbal Behavior and Courtroom Success," *Communication Education* 30 (1981), 31.

[69]John Waite Bowers, "Language Intensity, Social Introversion, and Attitude Change," *Speech Monographs* 30 (1981), 345.

[70]William J. McEwen and Bradley S. Greenberg, "The Effects of Message Intensity on Receiver Evaluations of Source, Message and Topic," *Journal of Communication* 20 (1970), 340–350.

[71]Parkinson, op. cit., 29.

[72]Marilyn R. Abbey and William M. O'Barr, "Law and Language: The Duke University Studies," *Trial Diplomacy Journal* (Winter 1981), 26.

[73]Bowers, "Language Intensity and Attitude Change," op. cit.

[74]Michael Burgoon, Stephen B. Jones, and Diane Stewart, "Toward a Message-Centered Theory of Persuasion: Three Empirical Investigations of Language Intensity," *Human Communication Research* 1 (1975), 240–256.

[75]Erwin P. Bettinghaus, *Persuasive Communication* (New York: Holt, Rinehart and Winston, 1980), 127.

[76]James W. McElhaney, "The Stock Phrases," *Litigation* (Summer 1982), 44.

[77]Ibid.

[78]Brenda Danet, "'Baby' or 'Fetus'?: Language and the Construction of Reality in a Manslaughter Trial," *Semiotica* 32 (1980), 187–219.

[79]Michael G. Parkinson, "Two Studies of the Relationship Between Presentation Style and Verdict," Unpublished paper, 1982.

[80]James J. Bradac, Michael R. Hempill, and Charles H. Tardy, "Language Style on Trial: Effects of 'Powerful' and 'Powerless' Speech Upon Judgments of Victims and Villains," *Western Journal of Speech Communication* 45 (1981), 327–341; Bonnie Erickson et al., "Speech Style and Impression Formation in a Court Setting: The Effects of 'Powerful' and 'Powerless' Speech," *Journal of Experimental Social Psychology* 14 (1978), 226–279; E. Allan Lind and William M. O'Barr, "The Social Significance of Speech in the Courtroom," in Howard Giles and Robert St. Clair, eds., *Language and Social Psychology* (Baltimore: University Park Press, 1979), 66–87.

[81]Paul C. Lewan and Ezra Stotland, "The Effects of Prior Information on Susceptibility to an Emotional Appeal," *Journal of Abnormal and Social Psychology* 62 (1961), 450–453.

[82]Dean Barnlund, *Interpersonal Communication* (Boston: Houghton Mifflin, 1968), 535–536.

[83]Henry B. Rothblatt, *Successful Techniques in the Trial of Criminal Cases* (Englewood Cliffs, N.J.: Prentice-Hall, 1961), 95.

[84]W. Barnett Pearce and Bernard J. Brommel, "Vocalic Communication in Persuasion," *Quarterly Journal of Speech* 58 (1972), 296–306; W. Barnett Pearce and Forrest Conklin, "Nonverbal Vocalic Communication and Perception of a Speaker," *Speech Monographs* 38 (1971), 235–241.

[85]James MacLachlan, "What People Really Think of Fast Talkers," *Psychology Today* (November 1979), 112–117.

[86]Norman Miller et al., "Speed of Speech and Persuasion," *Journal of Personality and Social Psychology* 34 (1976), 615–625.

[87]David W. Addington, "The Effects of Vocal Variations on Rating of Source Credibility," *Speech Monographs* 38 (1971), 242–247.

[88]Miller and Hewgill, op. cit.

[89]Stuart Albert and James M. Dabbs, Jr., "Physical Distance and Persuasion," *Journal of Personality and Social Psychology* 15 (1970), 265–270.

[90]Lee, op. cit., 70.

[91]John Stefano, "Body Language and Persuasion," *Litigation* (Summer 1977), 32.

[92]Stanley Zdep and Warren Wilson, "Recency Effects in Opinion Formation," *Psychological Reports* 23 (1968), 195–200.

[93]Chester A. Insko, "Primacy Versus Recency as a Function of the Timing of Arguments and Measures," *Journal of Abnormal and Social Psychology* 69 (1964), 381–391; Chester A. Insko, E. Allan Lind, and Stephen LaTour, "Persuasion, Recall and Thoughts," *Representative Research in Social Psychology* 7 (1976), 66–78; Norman Miller and Donald T. Cambell, "Recency and Primacy in Persuasion as a Function of the Timing of Speech and Measurements," *Journal of Abnormal and Social Psychology* 59 (1959), 1–9.

[94]Laurens Walker, John Thibault, and Virginia Andreoli, "Order of Presentation at Trial," *Yale Law Journal* 82 (1972), 216–226; William Wallace and Warner Wilson, "Reliable Recency Effects," *Psychological Reports* 25 (1969), 311–317.

[95]V. Hale Starr, "From the Communication Profession: Communication Strategies and Research Needs in Opening Statements and Closing Arguments," in Ronald J. Matlon and Richard J. Crawford, eds., *Communication Strategies in the Practice of Lawyering* (Annandale, Va.: Speech Communication Association, 1983), 437.

[96]David L. Herbert and Roger K. Barrett, *Attorney's Master Guide to Courtroom Psychology* (Englewood Cliffs, N.J.: Executive Reports Corporation, 1980), 1108–1109.

[97]Jacob Fuchsberg, "Preface," In Smith, op. cit., vii.

[98]Sonya Hamlin, *What Makes Juries Listen* (New York: Harcourt Brace Jovanovich, 1985), 311.

11
CHAPTER

TRIAL JUDGE COMMUNICATION

JUDGE–ATTORNEY COMMUNICATION

JUDGE INSTRUCTIONS TO THE JURY

PATTERNED INSTRUCTIONS

There are over thirty thousand judges in the American legal system; approximately half of them are elected and half are appointed. All federal judges are appointed. To most citizens, the judge is the embodiment of justice, and the position itself is considered to be of high status. To underscore the status of judges, they sit in positions higher than anyone else in court and wear robes. Judges are addressed by such honorific titles as "Your Honor," "the Court," and "the Bench."[1] Often, when lawyers are appointed to judicial positions, it is considered to be the apex of their careers. This chapter will look at some dimensions of a trial judge's communication patterns.

JUDGE–ATTORNEY COMMUNICATION

Justice Cardozo was quoted as saying that "there is no guarantee of justice except the personality of the judge." It is the judge's style and tone that give each courtroom a distinct character and flavor. The dynamic interplay between the style and tone of each lawyer and those of each judge affects the outcome of a trial. So it is imperative that lawyers analyze the attitudes and personalities of judges as audiences.

When lawyers become judges, their prior attitudes are seldom left behind. Attitudes vary among judges with respect to types of crimes, sex of litigants, kinds of evidence, sentencing, life-styles, extenuating circumstances, conduct of bail, and so forth. Judges differ in the treatment of traffic, drug, and liquor law violators; some hesitate to ruin the career of a physician, for example, but they do not mind punishing a blue-collar laborer. Judges have attitudes toward attorneys, too. One judge might suggest to a female lawyer that she not wear her large, floppy hat in court or she will risk being jailed for contempt of court. Another judge might threaten a male lawyer who appears in court without a necktie.

Research on judges' attitudes has revealed that Democratic judges are more liberal than Republican judges[2] and that liberal judges are prodefendant in criminal cases, progovernment in business regulation cases, proplaintiff in motor vehicle accident cases, and proemployee in employee injury cases.[3] Unfortunately, not enough research has been done on judicial attitudes to tell us much more than this. "Attempts to correlate backgrounds to behavior have simply been too crude to produce meaningful results. . . . The connection between judicial attitudes and voting behavior remains uncertain."[4] About the best an attorney can do is speculate about judges' attitudes using common sense, consulting publications written by a particular judge, examining published judicial profiles (e.g., *Almanac of the Federal Judiciary*), and directly observing a given judge's style in the courtroom.

In addition to evaluating a judge's attitudes, an examination of personality is important. Such an examination has been undertaken.[5] The examiners observed judges in a city court and came up with six personality types: the intellectual scholar, the routine hack, the political adventurer-careerist, the judicial pensioner, the hatchet man, and the tyrant-showboat-benevolent despot. The first two types are workhorses, although the former of the two is more legally knowledgeable. The third type has little interest in judicial administration, but is interested in a higher office. The fourth type is winding down a professional career and, for all practical purposes, has retired. The fifth type is usually a former prosecutor who is authoritarian and wants swift justice. The sixth type is a sadistic exhibitionist—deeply hostile, frustrated, ambitious, and either severe or soft depending on his or her mood.

Recognizing that a wide range of both attitudes and personality types exists among judges, lawyers must learn how to adapt and communicate effectively across courtrooms. In their adaptation, lawyers must avoid confrontation and emphasize cooperative behavior "since cooperation maximizes case productivity."[6] This is not to say that the judge must dictate the rhetorical situation, only that the lawyer must be aware of his or her relationship with the bench at all times. Attorney understanding and patience fosters rapport. "It is not suggested that lawyers curry favor. It is only suggested that lawyers remember their duty to their clients and not diminish the credibility or persuasiveness of their cases by taking side trips down antagony lane with judges."[7]

Above and beyond knowing and adapting to the attitudes and personalities of judges, respect for the court is an absolute and constant must for attorneys. Lawyers who are flippant and arrogant lose judicial respect. Lawyers who are inattentive or poorly prepared demonstrate a lack of respect. Disrespectful conduct toward the court can and probably should influence judicial behavior against a thoughtless attorney. In sum, attorneys must be aware of the way they interact with judges in and out of court at all times.

JUDGE INSTRUCTIONS TO THE JURY

One of the major circumscribed responsibilities of the judge is to keep the jury informed of what is happening throughout a trial so that the jury can render a fair and informed decision. Although there are many times when a judge talks to or educates a jury, five specific instances are most crucial.[8]

First, a judge talks to the venire (potential jury panel) when they first arrive at the courthouse for jury duty. Sometimes this is a live talk; sometimes it is videotaped. This preliminary talk is a relatively short message, covering such topics as the history and significance of trial by jury, the length of jury service, the hours of work and where to report, the physical arrangement of the courthouse, and standards of jury conduct.[9]

After members of the venire have been randomly chosen to go to a courtroom to be considered for a particular case, a judge addresses the potential jurors for a second time. She or he swears them in to answer questions truthfully during the voir dire that is to follow. She or he then explains the charge or suit in the particular case, introduces the attorneys and their clients, explains the process of voir dire, and frequently begins the voir dire questioning with such stock matters as asking the jurors to give their names, ages, and occupations and the names and occupations of spouses.

After the jurors for a given trial have been chosen and sworn in, the judge then offers a third major communication to the panel. Most of this commentary focuses on juror conduct during the course of the trial (e.g., being on time, not talking during the trial or to the litigants or witnesses outside of court).

The fourth speech a judge gives to a jury is a set of substantive instructions prior to the jury's deliberation. On rare occasions, this set of instructions is given before closing arguments, but the usual pattern is to have them presented immediately after the lawyers' summation speeches. Suggestions for what is to be said in these instructions can be filed by the attorneys with a judge early in any trial. The pretrial conference is an excellent time to discuss the points on which instructions will be required.[10] Early submission of proposed instructions allows counsel and the judge to examine them without the pressure of the trial at hand.[11] Some judges prefer such counsel assistance on instructions; other judges prepare their own. In any case, attorneys should prepare and tender instructions, either to persuade the judge to use the lawyer's language when charging the jury or to preserve for appeal a question arising from the court's refusal to give the proffered instruction. Much of the remainder of this chapter will be devoted to these instructions, since they are such a vital part of judge communication.

The fifth time a judge addresses a jury is just before they are discharged from their trial assignment. The judge thanks the jury for their work and informs them that they may discuss the case freely but cannot be compelled to do so if they choose not to.

In the fourth communication that judges have with juries, several things take place. First, the issues of the case are clarified. Issues are central points or contentions on which questions of guilt or liability should focus. For instance, the injured plaintiff claims that the defendant failed to keep his automobile under proper control. Meanwhile, the defendant argues that the plaintiff was not injured to the extent claimed. Issues are points of controversy. Most of the issues in a case ought to have been known by the judge since the time of the pretrial conference with the lawyers. The judge cannot comment on the merit of the evidence regarding these issues but can only tell the jury that they cannot arrive at a decision unless and until certain issues have been considered and resolved.

Second, certain aspects of the weight of evidence are discussed by the judge. For instance, the judge must tell the jury that the burden of proof rests with the plaintiff or prosecutor. The jury must be reminded that the presumption rests with the defense. Judges also instruct juries regarding circumstantial, conditional, or withdrawn evidence. For example, if a prosecutor relies exclusively or heavily on circumstantial evidence, the judge must tell the jury that they can convict only if all reasonable hypotheses except the defendant's guilt have been ruled out. Juries are furthermore instructed about conditionally admitted evidence, that is, evidence that was admitted only under the condition that some disputed prior fact was true. For instance, before a jury can decide that there was a conspiracy between two parties, the jury must first decide the disputed fact that the two defendants actually met and conversed. One final instance of a judge's instructing the jury about evidence is to point out evidence that was withdrawn. Juries should not consider improperly admitted and later withdrawn evidence. Ordinarily, when judges discuss evidence with juries, they cannot comment on or review specific case evidence;[12] judges can talk only about the theory of evidence for the jurors.[13] The jurors are the exclusive triers of the facts.

Third, points of applicable law must be conveyed by the judge to the jury. After finding the facts of a case, juries must apply those facts to the relevant law. Judges tell juries what the statutory law is but cannot interpret the law for the jury. This is a very delicate distinction. The law must be explained clearly, but if a judge goes outside his or her explanation mission and into the area of interpretation, he or she is beginning to make statutory law, and this constitutes grounds for an appeal. As a result, many judges fulfill this third objective simply by reading the applicable law to the jury and nothing else.

In a few instances, juries are asked to recommend punishment in a criminal trial or damages in a civil trial. When this is the case, a fourth objective in judge instructions is to tell the jury what punishments may be imposed if guilt is found or what damages may be awarded if liability is found.

Two other instructions are occasionally used in our courts. One is the directed verdict; the other is the Allen charge. In a directed verdict, judges ask juries to find no liability or acquit only in cases in which the evidence from the plaintiff or state has been so extraordinarily weak that no verdict other than not liable or not guilty could ever stand. In other words, the directed verdict asks the jury to dismiss a civil or criminal case.[14]

The Allen charge, sometimes referred to as "the dynamite charge," is used when a jury has been deliberating for an exceptionally long period of time. The jury informs the court that they are hopelessly deadlocked. Then the court issues a special instruction that asks dissenters to strongly reconsider their positions, even though each juror is reminded that he or she should make an independent judgment. If the language of the Allen charge is coercive, a mistrial could be declared.[15] Therefore, Allen charges are very rarely used, and in some states, they are outlawed.

PATTERNED INSTRUCTIONS

Next we will examine the communication dimensions of the judge's charge to the jury prior to deliberations. Patterned instructions, sometimes called standardized or uniform instructions, have been developed through the years to alleviate the numerous appellate court reversals based on faulty judge communication to the jury. For instance, in Illinois from 1930 to 1955, 38 percent of the reversals were caused in whole or in part by erroneous instructions.[16] Prior to the development of patterned instructions in Alabama, one-third of the appeals taken in that state were due to an alleged error in instructions.[17] In Montana, the percentage was the same;[18] in Missouri, it was 42 percent.[19]

The use of patterned instructions began in California in the 1930s, when Los Angeles Superior Court Judge William J. Palmer began keeping a file of the instructions he read to his juries.[20] He worked very carefully on the language of his instructions to avoid case reversals. Based on Palmer's files, sets of instructions on evidence, the law, and other matters were published in each state, and by the federal government in 1938. They became known as *Basic Approved Jury Instructions* (BAJI). Today, they appear as loose-leaf sheets, which can be pulled and reorganized at will by American judges. Some judges must read them verbatim; they may not deviate from the language of the patterned instruction. Other judges are not required to read instructions verbatim, but many do so anyway.

Still other judges simply use BAJI as a guideline for drafting their own set of instructions in language suitable to a specific case and jury.

Several advantages exist in using patterned instructions exclusively. They save court time because the law has been thoroughly researched and annotated in advance.[21] Think of all the time judges would have to take if they had to research all the pertinent case law before instructing each jury in each case. The accuracy of the instructions is enhanced. Given the fact that BAJI are carefully drafted by judges and lawyers, technical precision is fostered. In most states, the result has been a significant decrease in the case reversal rate for error in instructions.[22] Finally, because patterned instructions supposedly have been prepared with jury comprehensibility in mind, BAJI should improve the jurors' understanding of what judges are telling them. If the preparation of instructions is left in the hands of the judge, the possibility of garbled verbiage and verbal garbage exists. If clear BAJI are used, lay understanding of the instructions is enhanced.

Unfortunately, regarding this last advantage, researchers have found that the drafters of the BAJI in each state have not always achieved clarity.[23] Many of the patterned instructions read like Supreme Court opinions. This is because "the most reliable way to assure that instructions will be acceptable to the appellate courts is to use language that follows closely that used in previous appellate decisions."[24] "Trial judges must possess unusual talents of communication; talents not widely shared by members of the legal profession. . . . A run-of-the-mill trial judge will phrase his instruction to the jury in impenetrably technical terms, . . . hardly more influential on the jury's deliberation than it would have been if delivered in classical Greek."[25] The instructions are wordy, they contain numerous legalistic terms, and the language is stilted. The result is that jurors are not fully understanding the patterned instructions currently administered in many jury trials.[26] In one experiment, 34 volunteer jurors in Nevada were read patterned instructions for an attempted murder. Only one juror could tell the difference between the highest and lowest charges.[27] In 405 trials in the state of Washington, jurors were consistently confused about the criminal terms "intent" and "reasonable doubt."[28] In another study, jurors could not understand 45 percent of the important elements of a patterned instruction.[29] A United States district judge in Northern California found, after reading patterned criminal instructions to more than one hundred jurors, that nearly one-half thought they should disregard circumstantial evidence and did not understand what the prosecutor's burden of proof meant.[30]

This brings us, then, to the disadvantages of reading the BAJI verbatim to a jury. Reading word for word reduces juror comprehension. Since so many of the instructions were not written for oral presentation, they are very hard to follow when read aloud. The jury does not have a written copy of the instructions before them when the judge is reading aloud. Many judges read poorly anyway. Frequently, jurors sit absolutely bewildered during the reading of instructions. To compound the problem of verbatim reading, patterned instructions are usually read aloud to a jury only once. It is doubtful that jurors can comprehend a one-time oral reading. In one simple experiment, college students heard a 14-minute lecture on birds by a skilled public speaker. A recall test was given to each student. The highest score was 57 percent, even though college students are probably more attuned to receiving information from lectures than are the average jurors.[31]

Since jurors' attitudes toward the law are influenced by their understanding of what a judge tells them about the law,[32] what improvements can be made to help judges communicate more effectively? First, when patterned instructions are used, they should be allowed in writing in the jury room deliberations. Even in those states where this action is permitted, some judges deny this privilege to the jury because they believe "the practice is disruptive and tends to prolong the deliberations of the jury."[33] In the notorious Harrisburg Seven trial in Pennsylvania, the jury deliberated longer than any other federal jury in history. During the entire 7-day deliberation, the jury was confused over the judge's charges to them. There had been 64 witnesses in a 56-day trial. There were 7 defendants, each faced with 10 charges. Thus, thousands of decision combinations were possible. The jury repeatedly requested a copy of the instructions that the judge had presented to them orally over a two-hour period of time. Each time, the jury's request was denied. The result was a deadlocked jury admittedly confused over the judge's instructions.

Would the results have been different had the patterned instructions been allowed in the deliberation room? Possibly so. Researchers have found that there is generally more comprehension following the reading of a text than after listening to a lecture.[34] One researcher concludes, "Quantitative analysis of the juries' performance revealed that the juries that had been provided with written copies of instructions for each juror were more efficient and exhibited higher quality deliberations. Jurors with written instructions made fewer explicit comments about confusion, spent less time inappropriately applying the law, wasted less time trying to ascertain the meaning of instructions, and concentrated more on relevant facts and proper application of the law."[35] The ideal situation, then, is to have the judge read the jury instructions once and then give them a written version of the instructions for clarification. After all, "hobgoblin fears that this practice might somehow taint the jury's deliberations have not materialized."[36]

A second improvement that can be made in the use of patterned instructions is in their arrangement prior to presentation. Instead of pulling out a set of loose-leaf instructions and reading them in random order to a jury, a judge should carefully consider the organizational pattern that will make those instructions most meaningful to the jury. After all, "organization accounts for much of why and what people remember."[37] A logical outline should be used to help the jury see the relationship among the various sets of instructions. A logical structure is one in which each idea is causally or temporally connected to succeeding ideas. Such a structure furthers comprehension.[38] Furthermore, transitions between sets of instructions serve as summaries of previous points and signposts preparing a jury for the next main thought.

One organizational innovation in judge instructions, which shows "a potential over traditional instructions for juror comprehension,"[39] is the algorithmic, step-by-step process instruction, a proven technique for increasing goal clarity and efficiency in problem-solving groups.[40] The process instruction not only explains the law, but also gives a jury a sense of the direction they should follow in reaching their decision. The process instruction does so by asking the jury to answer a series of questions on the component issues of the case, each question building on the other questions. Should any question be either answered in favor of the defense or unresolvable, the prosecutor has lost the case. In research using those instructions, less time was required by a jury to reach a verdict, and the jury was better able to orient itself toward the crucial issues in a case.[41] So process instructions have merit in improving both juror comprehension of the law and the quality of the content of deliberation.[42]

A third set of recommendations focuses on the way judges should read patterned instructions to juries. One presentational technique they should use is verbal redundancy;[43] that is, they should repeat key words and phrases in order to increase juror retention of certain information. What is not repeated is likely to

be forgotten. If everything is repeated, nothing is gained. But if the essentials are repeated, the jury can focus on what is most important.[44]

Another presentational technique judges should use when reading patterned instructions aloud is vocal variety. However, the manner of delivering instructions commonly in existence has been described by one judge thus:

One of the most widespread abuses is the manner in which many judges deliver their instructions. First, there is the experienced judge who has given the same instructions for so many years that he forgets that he is giving them for the benefit of those who have never heard them, and reads so rapidly and in such a flat and unmodulated voice that it is difficult for anyone to understand him. The opposite of this is the judge who looks in amazement at the printed words before him and stumbles over them as if it were his first experience with legal phraseology. Probably the least helpful is the judge who mumbles or speaks in such low tones that he cannot be heard, even by the most attentive juror. One of the above types of delivery usually occurs after counsel has pointed out the sanctity of the law and has repeatedly stressed that only by a complete understanding of the instructions by His Honor can the jury render a verdict based upon justice. Then the twelve unfortunate people in the jury box, who have listened to days of testimony and oratorical display by counsel, are suddenly confused and dismayed to hear a delivery of one of the above types.[45]

After viewing numerous videotapes of trial judges, the authors of one paper concluded that "most of the judges tended to give every point, even every sentence equal vocal weight."[46] Reading aloud in a dull, listless monotone makes attentiveness difficult if not impossible. One trial judge was even reversed after jurors complained that he could not be heard, read too fast, and read in a manner that did not foster comprehension.[47] Reading aloud without a monotone assists audience attentiveness. Vocal variety can also be achieved through the effective use of pauses. Pauses should not be made arbitrarily, at the end of a certain number of words or at the end of a typewritten line, but rather after thought units. The best way for judges to develop vocal variety is to practice reading the BAJI aloud ahead of time and to solicit criticism concerning their performances.

A fourth improvement in pattern instructions is to have them written for lay juror utility. Several techniques are possible to make the instructions more comprehensible. The active voice should be substituted for the passive voice.[48] Sentences should be short and grammatically simple.[49] Excessive words should be deleted (e.g., use "if" to replace "in the event that"). Affirmative sentences should replace negative forms unless the negation expresses an exception to a rule.[50] For instance, instead of saying "A manufacturer is not relieved of any responsibility to inspect an article before delivery," it is better to say "A manufacturer is required to inspect all articles before delivery." Omitted pronouns (e.g., "that," "which," "who") should be inserted (e.g., "that" in "if you are convinced that it is erroneous").[51] Ordinary words should replace polysyllabic language.[52] Words such as "whereas" and "aforesaid" should be omitted from the instructions. Technical terms and legalistic words that might not be understood by lay persons must be avoided. Concrete words should replace abstractions inasmuch as the concrete words increase retention and comprehension.[53] These simple, concrete words should be of a high-frequency variety, that is, words that are most frequently used in widely read magazines or newspapers. Several psycholinguistic researchers have shown that high-frequency words are more easily recognized, recalled, and comprehended than are low-frequency words.[54] Research shows that when jury instructions are rewritten in simpler, easier-to-understand language, the level of juror understanding can rise by as

much as 30 percent.[55] As noted before, jury instruction drafting committees usually are composed of judges, lawyers, and law professors, whose emphasis is on legal accuracy in the instructions. "While these individuals communicate very well with each other in the special language of the law, few are well enough versed in semantics to communicate legal concepts to jurors in a short time with a high rate of success."[56] This problem is one that needs to be remedied in future drafting endeavors.[57] Consider, for example, the following two instructions; the first was used in federal courts a few years ago, and the second is a revised version of the same instruction composed by linguists affiliated with the Federal Judicial Center:[58]

Impeachment by Proof of Conviction of a Crime–Defendant

A defendant's prior conviction is admitted into evidence solely for your consideration in evaluating the credibility of the defendant as a witness. It is not evidence of the defendant's guilt of the offense with which he is charged. You must not draw any inference of guilt against the defendant from his prior conviction. You may consider it only in connection with your evaluation of the credence to be given his present testimony in court.

Defendant's Testimony: Impeachment by Prior Conviction

You have been told that the defendant, (name), was found guilty in 19xx of [e.g., bank robbery]. This conviction has been brought to your attention only because you may wish to consider it when you decide, as with any witness, how much you will believe of his testimony in this trial. The fact that the defendant was found guilty of another crime does not mean that he committed this crime, and you must not use his guilt for the crime of _____ as proof of the crime charged in this case. You may find him guilty of this crime only if the government has proved beyond a reasonable doubt that he committed it.

Instructions should also be as brief as possible. At present, instructions can be very long, negatively influencing comprehension.[59] Editing is essential because the listening span for any audience is very short, and there are limits to the amount of information the mind can absorb.[60] One study demonstrated what a chore listening can be for jurors, even with a relatively simple and short case. The judge read 20 minutes of instructions to experienced jurors. They were read orally in the morning, when people were mentally alert. A test was immediately given to each juror, and they accurately comprehended approximately half of the information. The jurors' lowest scores were in the area of understanding the law (e.g., the meaning of contributory negligence). As the instructions got longer, juror comprehension decreased.[61]

Florida is one state where the comprehensibility of the BAJI has been a serious concern. Prior to the use of patterned instructions in Florida, an estimated 40 percent of the jurors could not figure out what the judge's instructions meant. Initially, patterned instructions were not much better. But in the 1970s, research by communicologists on the BAJI in Florida led to improvement of the language in them and of the way they were being presented to juries. In 1978, researchers surveyed a group of 116 Florida venirepersons. They asked about instructions the jurors had received in breaking-and-entering cases. The same judge was used for all the presentations, and his remarks were videotaped. A 40-item comprehension test was administered. On their final day of jury service, each juror took the examination. The patterned instructions that were used had been edited by communication experts to ensure maximum clarity. Meanwhile, another group of jurors heard instructions that were not carefully edited, and they took the same test. The results were clear: comprehension was better among those jurors who heard the edited, well-presented patterned instructions than among

those who did not. Only 27 percent of the instructions were misunderstood by the group who heard the model patterned instructions.[62]

That research indicates that if patterned instructions are well written and effectively presented by judges, they can be relatively well comprehended by jurors. Perhaps that comprehension level can be further increased by allowing those written instructions to go into the jury room during deliberations. However, if the BAJI are not written well, not read aloud well, and not seen by the jury, trial judge communication with jury is far from what it should and could be.

Notes

[1]Jerome Frank said, "Unfrock the judge, have him dress like ordinary men, become in appearance like his fellows, and he may well be more inclined to talk and write more comprehensibly. Plain dress may encourage plain speaking." *Courts on Trial: Myth and Reality in American Justice* (Princeton: Princeton University Press, 1949), 259.

[2]Sheldon Goldman, "Voting Behavior on the United States Court of Appeals Revisited," *American Political Science Review* 69 (1975), 491–506.

[3]Stuart S. Nagel, *The Legal Process from a Behavioral Perspective* (Homewood, Ill.: Dorsey, 1969), 199–236.

[4]Anthony Champagne and Stuart Nagel, "The Psychology of Judging," in Norbert L. Kerr and Robert M. Bray, eds., *The Psychology of the Courtroom* (New York: Academic Press, 1982), 167–268.

[5]Alexander B. Smith and Abraham S. Blumberg, "The Problem of Objectivity in Judicial Decision-Making," *Social Forces* 46 (1967), 96–105.

[6]Champagne and Nagel, op. cit., 269.

[7]Terry W. Mackey, "The Trial Lawyer and The Trial Judge—Or 'The Unholy Alliance,'" *Trial* (May 1982), 75.

[8]Jack Pope, "The Judge-Jury Relationship," *Southwestern Law Journal* 18 (1964), 46–49.

[9]Many courts have adopted a juror's handbook, which briefly explains these matters. This booklet either replaces or supplants the preliminary judge instructions.

[10]Don Musser, "Instructing the Jury—Pattern Instructions," in *Am Jur Trials* (San Francisco: Bancroft-Whitney, 1964), vol. 6, 953.

[11]"Early delivery of jury instructions to the court lets the trial judge know what legal path the lawyer has embarked upon. The key instructions should be prepared, and one or two alternatives should likewise be a ready weapon in the litigator's instruction arsenal. If the lawyer comes to court with only one expression of a key instruction and that instruction, for whatever reason is rejected by the court, counsel is left bereft of any opportunity to have the jury instructed on a relevant issue. By submitting an alternative or two, a more expansive discussion of the legal proposition under consideration may ensue, and the court may be persuaded to give one of the three or four additionally preferred instructions on the given key issue." James Kruger, "Jury Selection and Jury Instructions," *Trial* (August 1981), 24–25.

[12]In those jurisdictions which do not adhere to common law procedures, such as the federal courts, the judge may explain and comment on the facts presented.

[13]"Comments: The Jury Instruction Process—Apathy or Aggressive Reform," *Marquette Law Review* 49 (1965), 140, 141.

[14]Robert L. McBride, *The Art of Instructing the Jury: 1978 Supplement* (Cincinnati: Anderson, 1978), 17–18.

[15]"The Allen Charge Dilemma," *American Criminal Law Review* 10 (1972), 637–670.

[16]Gerald C. Snyder, "Pattern Jury Instructions—A Boon to the Bench and Bar," *Missouri Bar Journal* 20 (1964), 53.

[17]Ingram Beasley, "Pattern Charges," *Alabama Lawyer* 27 (1966), 181–192.

[18]W. W. Lessley, "Montana Jury Instruction Guides," *Montana Law Review* 27 (1966), 125–129.

[19]Robert S. McKenzie, "Pattern Jury Instructions," *Insurance Counsel Journal* 36 (1969), 215–221.

[20]Susan A. Henderson "Pattern Jury Instructions: Answers to Some Common Questions," *Judicature* 52 (1969), 339.

[21]Philip H. Corboy, "Illinois System of Instructing Jurors in Civil Cases," *DePaul Law Review* 8 (1959), 141–164.

[22]Philip H. Corboy, "Pattern Jury Instructions—Their Function and Effectiveness," *Insurance Counsel Journal* 32 (1965), 57–65; Robert G. Nieland, "Assessing the Impact of Pattern Jury Instructions," *Judicature* 62 (1978), 185–194.

[23]Amiram Elwork, James J. Alfini, and Bruce D. Sales, "Toward Understandable Jury Instructions," *Judicature* 65 (1982), 432–443; Robert F. Forston, "Judge's Instructions: A Quantitative Analysis of Jurors' Listening Comprehension," *Today's Speech* 18 (1970), 34–38; Joseph J. O'Mara, "Standard Jury Charges—Findings of Pilot Project," *Pennsylvania Bar Association Quarterly* (January 1972), 166–175; David U. Strawn and Raymond W. Buchanan, "Jury Confusion: A Threat to Justice," *Judicature* 59 (1976), 478–483.

[24]E. Allan Lind, "The Psychology of Courtroom Procedure," in Norbert L. Kerr and Robert M. Bray, eds., *The Psychology of the Courtroom* (New York: Academic Press, 1982), 27.

[25]McBride, op. cit., 92.

[26]Raymond W. Buchanan et al., "Legal Communication: An Investigation of Pattern Instructions," *Communication Quarterly* (Fall 1978), 31–35.

[27]"Study Urges Plain Language for Jury Instructions," *New York Times,* June 7, 1981, p. 25.

[28]Lawrence J. Severance, Edith Greene, and Elizabeth F. Loftus, "Toward Criminal Jury Instructions The Jurors Can Understand," *Journal of Criminal Law and Criminology* 75 (1984), 198–233; Lawrence J. Severance and Elizabeth F. Loftus, "Improving Criminal Justice: Making Jury Instructions Understandable for American Jurors," *International Review of Applied Psychology* 33 (1984), 97–119.

[29]Robert P. Charrow and Veda R. Charrow, "Making Legal Language Understandable: A Psycholinguistic Study of Jury Instructions," *Columbia Law Review* 79 (1979), 1306–1374.

[30]William F. Schwarzer, "Jury Instructions: We Can Do Better," *Litigation* (Winter 1982), 5.

[31]"Comments: Jury Instruction Process," 143.

[32]K. Phillip Taylor et al., "An Affective-Cognitive Consistency Explanation for Comprehension of Standard Jury Instructions," *Communication Monographs* 47 (1980), 68–76.

[33]Thomas J. Cunningham, "Should Instructions Go Into the Jury Room?" *California State Bar Journal* 33 (1958), 280.

[34]K. C. Beighley, "An Experimental Study of the Effect of Four Speech Variables on Listener Comprehension," *Speech Monographs* 19 (1952), 249–258; S. M. Corey, "Learning From Lectures and Learning From Reading," *Journal of Educational Psychology* 25 (1934), 459–470; H. B. Siegel, "McLuhan, Mass Media, and Education," *Journal of Experimental Education* 41 (1973), 68–70.

[35]Robert F. Forston, "Sense and Non-Sense: Jury Trial Communication," *Brigham Young University Law Review* (1975), 601.

[36]Bernard S. Meyer and Maurice Rosenberg, "Questions Juries Ask: Untapped Springs of Insight," *Judicature* 55 (1971), 107.

[37]Bruce Dennis Sales, Amiram Elwork, and James J. Alfini, "Improving Comprehension for Jury Instructions," in Bruce Dennis Sales, ed., *Perspectives in Law and Psychology: The Criminal Justice System* (New York: Plenum, 1977), 58.

[38]James G. Greeno and David L. Noreen, "Time to Read Semantically Related Sentences," *Memory and Cognition* 2 (1974), 117–120; Ralph Y. Sasson, "Semantic Organizations and Memory for Sentences," *American Journal of Psychology* 84 (1971), 253–267; Herbert W. Seliger, "The Discourse Organizer Concept as a Framework for Continued Discourse Practice in the Language Classroom," *International Review of Applied Linguistics* 9 (1971), 195–207.

[39]David U. Strawn and G. Thomas Munsterman, "Helping Juries Handle Complex Cases," *Judicature* 65 (1982), 445.

[40]Marvin E. Shaw, *Group Dynamics: The Psychology of Small Group Behavior* (New York: McGraw-Hill, 1976), 312–324.

[41]K. Phillip Taylor et al., "How Do Jurors Reach a Verdict?" *Journal of Communication* 31 (1981), 37–42.

[42]Jon F. Schamber, "The Influence of Process Jury Instructions and Pattern Jury Instructions on the Content of Jury Deliberation and Comprehension of the Law in a Simulated Jury Trial," Unpublished paper, 1982; Francine F. Vahlenkamp and William J. Jordan, "Linguistic Barriers to Communication in Jury Charges: Special Issues Versus General Instructions," Unpublished paper, 1982.

[43]Grant Fairbanks, Newman Guttman, and Murray S. Miron, "Auditory Comprehension in Relation to Listening Rate and Selective Verbal Redundancy," *Journal of Speech and Hearing Disorders* 22 (1957), 23.

[44]Amiram Elwork, Bruce D. Sales, and James J. Alfini, "Juridic Decisions: In Ignorance of the Law or in Light of It?" *Law and Human Behavior* 1 (1977), 163–190.

[45]Thomas J. Cunningham, "Instructing Juries," *California State Bar Journal* 32 (1957), 127, 133.

[46]Paul Page and Gordon Zimmerman, "Effective Communication in Jury Instructions," *Judges Journal* 14 (1975), 13.

[47]*Kinser v. Kruse,* 283 N.E.2d 120 (1972).

[48]Severance and Loftus, op. cit., 108.

[49]Kenneth I. Forster and Leonie A. Ryder, "Perceiving the Structure and Meaning of Sentences," *Journal of Verbal Learning and Verbal Behavior* 10 (1971), 163–170; V. M. Holmes, "Order of Main and Subordinate Clauses in Sentence Perception," *Journal of Verbal Learning and Verbal Behavior* 12 (1973), 285–293; William F. Schwarzer, "Communicating With Jurors: Problems and Remedies," *California Law Review* 49 (1981), 731–769; Alexander J. Wearing, "The Recall of Sentences of Varying Length," *Australian Journal of Psychology* 25 (1973), 155–161.

[50]Elizabeth R. Cornish and P. C. Watson, "The Recall of Affirmative and Negative Sentences in an Incidental Learning Task," *Quarterly Journal of Experimental Psychology* 22 (1970), 109–114; Philip B. Gough, "Grammatical Transformations and Speed of Understanding," *Journal of Verbal Learning and Verbal Behavior* 4 (1965), 107–111; Sheila Jones, "The Effect of a Negative Qualifier in an Instruction," *Journal of Verbal Learning and Verbal Behavior* 5 (1966), 497–501; Dan I. Slobin, "Grammatical Transformations and Sentence Comprehension in Childhood and Adulthood,"

Journal of Verbal Learning and Verbal Behavior 5 (1966), 219–227; P. C. Watson, "Response to Affirmative and Negative Binary Statements," *British Journal of Psychology* 52 (1961), 133–142.

[51] Francine F. Vahlenkamp and William J. Jordan, "A Comparative Analysis of Linguistic Complexity in Two Forms of Jury Charges," *Journal of Applied Communication Research* 12 (1984), 1–16.

[52] Ordinary word choice does not mean that the "language of the street" should be used, because "the law is not the 'language of the street'; but certainly instructions can be simplified and made much clearer and more understandable to a lay jury than many that are now used." Kenneth M. Wormwood, "Instructing the Jury," *Defense Law Journal* 15 (1966), 10.

[53] Richard H. Bloomer, "Concepts of Meaning and the Reading and Spelling Difficulty of Words," *Journal of Educational Research* 54 (1961), 178–182; William F. Dukes and Jarvis Vastian, "Recall of Abstract and Concrete Words Equated for Meaningfulness," *Journal of Verbal Learning and Verbal Behavior* 5 (1966), 455–458; Aloysia M. Gorman, "Recognition Memory for Nouns as a Function of Abstractness and Frequency," *Journal of Experimental Psychology* 61 (1961), 23–29; Allan Paivo, *Imagery and Verbal Processes* (New York: Holt, Rinehart and Winston, 1971); Wilma A. Winnick and Kenneth Kressel, "Tachistoscopic Recognition Threshholds, Paired-Associate Learning, and Free Recall as a Function of Abstractness-Concreteness and Word Frequency," *Journal of Experimental Psychology* 70 (1965), 163–168.

[54] Ian Begg and Edward J. Rowe, "Continuous Judgments of Word Frequency and Familiarity," *Journal of Experimental Psychology* 95 (1972), 48–54; Kate Loewenthal, "Semantic Features and Communicability of Words of Different Form-Classes," *Psychonomic Science* 17 (1969), 79–80; Clyde E. Noble, "The Familiarity-Frequency Relationship," *Journal of Experimental Psychology* 47 (1954), 13–16; Leo Postman, "Effects of Word Frequency on Acquisition and Retention Under Conditions of Free-Recall Learning," *Quarterly Journal of Experimental Psychology* 22 (1970), 185–195; Roger C. Smith and Theodore R. Dixon, "Frequency and the Judged Familiarity of Meaningful Words," *Journal of Experimental Psychology* 88 (1971), 279–281.

[55] Amiram Elwork, Deborah A. Hansen, and Bruce Sales, "The Problem with Jury Instructions," in Martin F. Kaplan, ed., *The Impact of Social Psychology on Procedural Justice* (Springfield, Ill.: Charles C. Thomas, 1986), 220; "Study Urges Plain Language," op. cit.

[56] Robert G. Nieland, *Pattern Jury Instructions: A Critical Look at a Modern Movement to Improve the Jury System* (Chicago: American Judicature Society, 1979), 23.

[57] Dorean Koenig, "Jury Instructions for Jurors: Proposals for the Simplification of Michigan Instructions on Murder," *Wayne Law Review* 21 (1974), 1–30.

[58] E. Allan Lind, "Substantive Contributions to Federal Court Policy and Procedures," in Martin F. Kaplan, ed., *The Impact of Social Psychology on Procedural Justice* (Springfield, Ill.: Charles C. Thomas, 1986), 44.

[59] O'Mara, op. cit.

[60] George A. Miller, "The Magical Number Seven, Plus or Minus Two: Some Limits on Our Capacity for Processing Information," *Psychological Review* 63 (1956), 81–97.

[61] Forston, "Judge's Instructions," op. cit.

[62] Buchanan et al., op. cit.

JURY
DECISION MAKING

COMMUNICATION DIRECTED AT JURORS PRIOR TO DELIBERATION
Communication Outside the Courtroom /
Communication Inside the Courtroom / Note Taking
During the Trial / Lawyer Influence on the Jury /
Witness Influence on the Jury / Evidence Influence on
the Jury / Judge Influence on the Jury

THE CONTENT AND PROCESS OF JURY DELIBERATIONS
What Jurors Discuss / Forepersons and Leaders /
Communication Networking and Hung Juries /
Applicable Decision Rules / Jury Size / Rendering the
Verdict

How do jurors tell right from wrong, guilt from innocence? In Burma, litigants light candles of equal size; the winner is the party whose candle lasts the longest. In Borneo, opponents pour lime juice on two shellfish; the decision depends on which fish squirms first. But here in the United States, litigation decisions often are made by juries.

There is a considerable mystique about the way juries reach decisions. No one can eavesdrop on what they are doing—not the attorneys, not the judge, not the bailiff, not even a person interested in conducting scholarly research on juries. Nor are members of a jury required to justify their verdicts or explain how their process of deliberation unfolded. Yet, jury decisions must be accurate. Juries are expected to prevent conviction of the innocent in a consistent, rational, and unbiased manner all the time.

Because jury decision making is such a mystery, it has been the subject of a burgeoning amount of research in recent years. Small group research has been conducted either by using mock juries or by interviewing real jurors after a trial is over. Such research examines the jury as a social group that is goal directed and task oriented. "Its goal is to reach a verdict, but there are very few guidelines as to how to go about the task."[1] This chapter will, for the most part, be a review of research on jury task. After considering communication directed at jurors prior to deliberation, an attempt will be made to piece together a coherent picture of the deliberation process.

COMMUNICATION DIRECTED AT JURORS PRIOR TO DELIBERATION

Jurors engage in almost no communication with others about a trial while it is under way. They cannot talk among themselves. They cannot talk with outsiders. They cannot communicate with the witnesses or lawyers in a case. Often, they cannot even remind themselves of something pertinent by taking notes in court. Restrictions on jury communication prior to deliberation are common.

Communication Outside the Courtroom

During a trial, jurors eat in public restaurants, walk along the courthouse halls, and live at home. Very rarely is a jury sequestered, or locked up and kept away from others, while a trial is in progress. Therefore, jurors are in contact with nonjurors throughout the course of a trial. However, jurors are instructed not to discuss cases they are hearing with anyone other than their fellow jurors.[2] Even then, discussion among jurors cannot take place until the jury officially begins its deliberations.

Should a lawyer or witness be seen or heard conversing with a member of the jury, a mistrial can be declared. Such conduct, should it be witnessed by others, should be reported at once to the presiding judge. The judge can then either declare a mistrial at that point or allow the trial to continue, but an appeal on the alleged prejudicial misconduct can later be filed. In one case, the Harry Barfield Company sued for refund of federal income taxes in a United States district court.[3] While leaving the building during a noon recess, the president of the company happened to enter an elevator with three of the jurors in the case. A conversation ensued, in which one of the jurors and the company president exchanged a brief thought about family relationships, but made no mention of the case. This conversation was brought to the court's attention following the recess. The judge said there was not enough harm to declare a mistrial. The trial proceeded, and the jury ruled in the company's favor. The case later went to appeal, and under questioning, the involved juror said that his decision was not affected by the conversation in the elevator. However, the appellate court reversed the lower court's decision, on the grounds that conduct that gives even the appearance of prejudice must be scrupulously avoided. The president's action was deemed unfair.

Why is predeliberation communication among jury members so controlled? The reason is to avoid having the jurors influenced by anything other than what is officially said in court. To communicate in an unauthorized fashion is an act carefully monitored in our jury system. Generally, however, the rule is not as rigidly enforced as it was in the Barfield case. Usually, communication is judged to be prejudicial only if it might clearly influence a juror's decision.[4]

Communication Inside the Courtroom

Juror communication inside the courtroom is limited too. In nonlegal fact-finding settings, messages commonly travel in more than one direction. For example, in a congressional hearing, messages travel in several different directions as the parties involved communicate with each other. Such multidirectional communication, in which immediate feedback is offered, enhances message accuracy and understanding among the communicators. However, in the courtroom setting, communication is a one-way street. Jurors cannot verbally respond to stimuli from attorneys or witnesses, the result being that "as messages become longer and more complex under one-way communication, the communication is received less accurately and with more frustration and hostility."[5] If jurors fail to comprehend what is going on, they certainly might find it difficult to come up with a maximally rational judgment.[6]

Some suggest the jurors should be allowed to ask questions during a trial. There is a historical basis for such a practice. After the Normans conquered England in the eleventh century, citizens were summoned by the king to resolve disputes. These citizens went out and gathered the facts of a case and later asked questions of the litigants at trial. Unfortu-nately, there were heavy penalties against those individuals who rendered a verdict that was improper from the royal point of view. So the practice of juror questioning disappeared along with the rest of the Norman procedure. As trial procedures were established in America, jurors were asked to remain silent,[7] although the reason for this practice is obscure. Judges are permitted to ask for clarification, but jurors are to remain passive participants during a trial.

Juror intervention through question asking would have its benefits. The feedback would allow a more accurate reception of the evidence. Even simple juror feedback, such as "I don't understand what you just said," or "Please speak more slowly," could enhance juror comprehension. Furthermore, allowing the jurors to ask questions or make remarks like those just mentioned might make jury duty more interesting.

Naturally, there are problems with juror questioning. A juror could say something that might prejudice the proceedings. Not knowing the rules of evidence, a juror might say something improper, inflammatory, or irrelevant. In addition, trials could be delayed for an inordinate amount of time if jurors got too actively involved.

If juror intervention were permitted, there would have to be a period of orientation of jurors; that is, jurors would have to get instructions regarding their duties and limitations in asking questions, These instructions could be in writing or could be presented orally by the judge, or both. Juror comments and questions could be presented in one of three ways. First, a direct oral exchange with the lawyer or witness could occur. This kind of exchange provides maximum communication and is not very time-consuming, but the likelihood for improper communication is high. Second, the juror could exchange words privately with the judge, and the judge could then repeat those words in permissible form. This procedure increases the time involved in incorporating jury intervention into the trial, but reduces the likelihood of prejudical communication. Third, the juror could write out the question or comment, present the written message to the judge, and the judge could do what he or she wished with the information. Spontaneity would be lost, but this practice is the best way to ensure against prejudice.[8] In all cases, the most appropriate moment to ask a question would be when the examination of a witness was completed. "This procedure causes minimal disruption to trial procedure and allows counsel freedom to elicit testimony without interference."[9] Unfortunately, lawyers and judges generally seem opposed to juror intervention during a trial. There are only isolated instances of any of these three practices taking place in our jury system.[10]

Note Taking During the Trial

Another aspect of predeliberation communication by jurors is note taking during a trial. States are split over this practice.[11] Attorneys and judges can take notes freely during a trial. Sometimes jurors are allowed to do so, but other times, they are forbidden to take notes. Note taking operates at the discretion of the trial judge.

The objections to juror note taking are numerous.[12] Some argue that the more literate would have an advantage in taking notes.[13] Furthermore, the information in their notes would take on added and perhaps disproportionate importance in the deliberations. Worse yet, if their written information was imperfect, inaccurate, or incomplete, the jury decision could be based mostly on an erroneous set of notes. Another objection is that better notes would be taken at the beginning of a trial than at the end. If so, there would be a more complete written record of the case of the prosecutor or plaintiff than there would be for the defense. Finally, the physical process of scribbling notes might be distracting

both to the note taker and to other jurors. Unfortunately, no one knows for sure if any of these objections are valid; they have not been thoroughly tested.

The major argument for note taking is that notes can compensate for faulty memories, particularly during lengthy, complex trials.[14] Jurors in Illinois who were permitted to take notes rated the quality of their deliberations higher than those who were not allowed to take notes. The note takers there also found cases less difficult to decide than those jurors who could not take notes.[15] All the jurors in this Illinois experiment who were allowed to take notes did so, and the quality of notes per juror ranged from one to thirty pages.[16]

Jurors seem to want to take notes. A survey of approximately five hundred New Mexico jurors in criminal trials, who were not allowed to take notes, shows that a majority of them wish they had had the opportunity.[17] There is indeed an irony in forbidding jurors to take notes, because the person more familiar with the courtroom setting, the judge, can take notes, but the jurors cannot. From a communication viewpoint, it seems as though optional note taking can serve as a worthwhile memory aid for jurors. As long as (1) all jurors have an equal opportunity to take notes, (2) none of the jurors are coerced to do so, (3) the jurors are promised that their notes will remain confidential, (4) jurors are reminded that the notes of their colleagues are fallible, and (5) the notes are destroyed at the end of a trial,[18] then the discretion to take notes should be left with the jury and not with the court.[19] "The value to be derived from allowing jurors to take notes outweighs the dangers from the practice."[20]

The next item in this chapter is a consideration of those aspects of the trial itself that influence jury decision making. What is the influence of the lawyer? The witnesss? The evidence? The judge? Also, what happens when a jury is faced with making multiple decisions? Of course, no aspect works independently; all factors intertwine regarding jury verdicts, a point to remember as we proceed to look at each aspect individually.

Lawyer Influence on the Jury

Social science research has shown that the credibility of a lawyer is a variable in jury decision making. Anecdotal data gathered by one researcher show that juries respond to personal traits, habits, and appearance of lawyers. Even attorney facial expressions and courtesy were found to influence juror attitudes.[21] From his investigation of 23 cases, that author concludes, "Liking or disliking a lawyer solely because of his personality and performance at the trial was a material factor affecting juror voting behavior in at least nine of the civil and three of the criminal cases studied."[22]

In another study, researchers interviewed real jurors and found that few would hire the attorneys they voted against and that most would prefer to be represented by the counsel for the side for which they had voted.[23] Characteristics given to the attorneys they voted for were "very bright, fair, good, sharp, very convincing, a good actor, and a person who aroused sympathy for his side." Characteristics of counsel who were voted against were "boring, not convincing, dishonest, too well dressed, cruel, harsh, insincere, and lacking in eloquence."[24]

In another study, real jurors who were interviewed after a variety of criminal trials found the victorious attorneys very attractive, confident, good-natured, verbal, expert, intelligent, intellectual, and honest. Meanwhile, the impression of the losing attorney was expressed in comments like the following: "It would be difficult to meet and talk with him." "He just wouldn't fit into my circle of friends." "I don't like the way he looks." "He would be a poor problem solver."[25] These comments support the claim that juries carefully evaluate lawyers in court as part of the decision-making process.

It was discovered a long time ago that attorney credibility was important to juries.[26] For years, it has been a point of fascination for lawyers to find out just how important they really are. A recent study provides some insight into that matter. The investigators discovered that in many matches, counsel were so evenly balanced that their credibility was of little importance. However, "in 25 percent of the cases in which defense counsel is superior he will have some share in moving the jury toward disagreement."[27] Presumably, this would be true for prosecutor's and plaintiff's attorneys as well.

On the other hand, another investigator studied 16 jury deliberations, and after conducting a computer-assisted content analysis, discovered that only 0.8 percent of jury deliberation time is devoted to a discussion of the attorneys in a trial.[28] So we really do not know how important attorney credibility is in jury verdicts, but it is a variable that must be considered. Sometimes the lawyer is an insignificant factor in jury decision making; other times, he or she is a major factor, probably when there is an imbalance in the ethos of the attorneys for both sides.

Before we leave the subject of counsel credibility and jury decision making, we ought to take note of the research on attorney gender as a factor in rape trials. In one study, 80 female and 80 male jurors gave signficantly more not-guilty verdicts when the defense attorney was female (71 percent acquittal rate) than when he was male (49 percent acquittal rate).[29] Perhaps this result is due to the fact that a female lawyer is especially persuasive in a rape trial because it seems not in her best interest as a woman to defend an actual rapist.

To the extent that an attorney can make a difference in jury verdicts, what important lawyer qualities best predict the outcome of a trial? In a sweeping survey of jurors in criminal trials, it was found that proficiency in lawyering skill and likability were the strongest predictors of outcome, while attorney dress was the least significant factor.[30] It is not what a lawyer wears, but what he says, that influences jurors the most.

Witness Influence on the Jury

As you might imagine, if the credibility of counsel is at stake, so too is the credibility of witnesses. In fact, one study found witness credibility more widely discussed by jurors than lawyer credibility.[31] Dimensions of witness credibility for jurors have been studied from a variety of nonevidential variables. Although these variables overlap, they include witness attractiveness, character, race, socioeconomic status, and emotional state. Language was already discussed at length in Chapter 8. These variables are viewed as nonevidential because "they have no direct legal relevance to the guilt or innocence of the defendant."[32] Evidence as a variable will be considered later in this chapter.

One study examined witness attractiveness.[33] An example of an attractive defendant is a 33-year-old female secretary, white, five feet three inches tall, weighing 103 pounds. She wears appealing clothes that show off her figure. In fact, she has been a clothes model for a national magazine. She is friendly and a good worker. An unattractive defendant is a 33-year-old female janitor, an introvert, white, five feet three inches tall, weighing 180 pounds. Her appearance is poor; her teeth are rotting, and a number of them have fallen out; she wears tattered clothes and smells as though she has not showered recently. She is a twice-divorced person. That study concluded that unattractive defendants get heavier sentences from juries (even though their subjects did not interact with each other) than attractive defendants, and that defendant attractiveness was a more important variable than victim attractiveness.[34] In fact, "no witness holds greater persuasive potential than the defendant in a criminal case."[35]

In another study on attractiveness, in which 102 jurors interacted, group discussion was shown to lessen the importance of defendant attractiveness. The researchers found that jurors actually overcompensated for their biases against an unattractive defendant. In their study, the unattractive defendant received a less severe sentence (5.48 years) than did the attractive defendant (8.40 years).[36] The findings of the earlier research could not be replicated. In a similar study, investigators also found increased leniency toward unattractive defendants as a result of group discussion.[37]

On balance, however, attractiveness serves as a potentially important variable in witness credibility. In the literature, attractiveness relates to any or all of the following: personality traits, social desirability of behavior, physical appearance, and attitude similarity to jurors. For the most part, likability attracts.[38] Testimony of likable witnesses has much greater influence (believability) than that given by unlikable witnesses.[39] Several studies show that when the jury feels positively toward the defendant, the defendant's chances of going free substantially increase. Or, conversely, when the jurors dislike a victim, they tend to be more lenient toward a defendant.[40]

It has been empirically discovered that subjects exposed to an attractive plaintiff and an unattractive defendant in an automobile negligence trial more often found in favor of the plaintiff and awarded more money in damages than did subjects that viewed an unattractive plaintiff and an attractive defendant.[41] Other studies confirm this finding.[42] Another series of experiments on attractiveness used criminal rape cases. Again, the findings show attractiveness to be an important variable. One investigator learned that jurors gave greater credence to an alibi when it was offered by an attractive defendant than when it was presented by an unattractive defendant.[43] Other researchers found that jurors gave assailants of attractive women harsher sentences than assailants of unattractive women.[44] The authors of another study on rape found a significant correlation between the attractiveness of a defendant and the verdict. They write, "When jurors were aesthetically impressed, they were more prone to acquit, and the more their eyes were offended, the greater was their tendency to convict. Also, the more they agreed 'the defendant was likable,' the more . . . certain they were that he was innocent."[45]

Numerous additonal studies involving rape and other kinds of criminal cases confirm that attractive defendants are evaluated with less certainty of guilt and less severe recommended punishment.[46] With few exceptions, all investigations conducted to date reveal that attractiveness is "an advantageous social commodity."[47] Those few studies, noted earlier, which appear to have difficult results may be explained either by their using cases in which attractiveness was unrelated to the particular suit or charge[48] or by their using cases in which the attractiveness of witnesses on the two sides was relatively equal.

Another witness variable is something called character or honesty. One study found a direct correlation between a juror's attitude toward a plaintiff and that plaintiff's character.[49] As the evaluation of the plaintiff's honesty improved, the amount of the award granted to that party increased. A prior record is one dimension of honesty, and research shows that prior records increase the likelihood of subsequent convictions over the likelihood of conviction for a first-time accused person.[50] In addition, in another study, simulated jurors believed that a defendant's character and past history should be a factor influencing their decisions.[51]

Race influences verdicts and sentencing recommendations as well. According to a summary of sentencing patterns for black and white inmates in Texas prisons for murder, rape, or burglary, blacks receive longer sentences, regardless of the race of the victim.[52] The same has been found true for juveniles.[53] Black males are more likely to be found guilty than white males.[54] Black defendants receive longer sentences than white defendants.[55] In rape cases, both black and white jurors judge a dissimilar-race defendant more harshly than a similar-race defendant.[56] Black offenders are treated more harshly than white ones in rape cases, unless the victim is a black woman.[57] In another study, respondents were supplied with a list of ten crimes and ten possible male offenders, five of whom were white and five of whom were black. Each offender was to be paired with the crime he had committed. Crime-specific racial stereotypes emerged: blacks are associated with violent crimes, such as mugging, and whites are associated with white-collar crimes, such as embezzlement.[58] Signs clearly point toward juries' being influenced by the race of the defendant. What unfortunately appears to be happening is that jurors are assigning characteristics and propensities to individual racial group members based on the stereotypes they possess about the characteristics and propensities of that racial group generally.[59]

Another possible dimension of witness credibility is the socioeconomic status of the individual. Socioeconomic status is measured by a person's income or education. Following a case of burglary, a low-income defendant was found guilty by only 52 percent of the jurors, all factors except income being equal.[60] However, this difference here and in other studies was not statistically significant.[61]

Some studies have found that low-status individuals are in a more unfavorable position than high-status individuals in those rare cases where juries recommend sentencing.[62] In one study, social status was manipulated to test its effect on both verdict and sentencing judgments. Following deliberations over a murder trial, jurors were found to give a defendant with more education and a higher income (a medical intern) no greater or lesser a verdict of guilt than a defendant with little education and low income (a maintenance employee). However, jurors gave a longer sentence when defendant status was high than when it was low, perhaps because a medical intern is judged more responsible for his action because of his special training in life processes.[63] In sum, the results of the research on socioeconomic status is mixed, indicating that defendant income and education do not seem to be important variables in jury decision making.

Finally, how do the perceived emotional states of defendants affect their credibility? One study shows that sad and distressed defendants are perceived as punishing themselves; they get favorable evaluations. Happy-go-lucky defendants are perceived as not offering restitution, and they are evaluated poorly. Angry defendants get even more negative reactions from the jury.[64] Other studies show that remorseful defendants receive shorter sentences than unremorseful ones.[65] In fact, degree of repentance by the defendant has the power to minimize the attractiveness factor discussed earlier.[66]

Witness anxiety is another dimension of emotional state. Behaviors such as nervous fidgeting, poor eye contact, and speech errors are predicted to stereotype defendants as anxious, deceptive, and guilty.[67] Indeed, the prediction is accurate; the more a defendant exhibits these communication behaviors, the more the jurors perceive a high-anxiety emotional state. Lower perceived anxiety conditions produce the lowest percentage of guilty verdicts.[68]

Evidence Influence on the Jury

In the ideal world of litigation, facts should determine jury verdicts. Happily, research confirms the ideal. The authors of one article write, "The strongest determinant of a jury's deliberation and verdict is the material evidence presented. . . . This fact is so self-evident that no researchers, to our knowledge, have tried to dispute it."[69] In one study, the amount of evidence was more than three times as powerful as juror attitudes, and the strength of the evidence was more than seven times as powerful, as jurors were deliberating toward a verdict.[70]

Although verdicts are based on the amount of strength of the evidence, evidence "is not a completely objective factor introduced into the courtroom; each juror will interpret . . . the evidence in some degree of concordance with his or her attitudes."[71] In other words, the amount and strength of the evidence is relative. Attitudes toward issues, attractiveness of witnesses, race of the defendant, and so forth enter the decision-making process. As equally strong amounts of evidence appear at trial, other "factors begin to have determinative effects on deliberations and verdicts."[72] Nevertheless, evidence has a far greater effect on jury judgments than do the extralegal factors.[73] In fact, the importance of nonlegal factors in jury decision making can "be reduced by increasing the factual material available on the case."[74]

But what kinds of factual material should be generated? Therein lies the rub. What the research has not told us is what kinds of facts incline a jury to its decision. Will an insignificant or immaterial fact appear superior to such extralegal information as the speaking ability of the attorney? We do not know. All we know is that facts are the primary basis for jury decisions and that only when facts are missing will the jury increase its focus on nonevidentiary matters.

Three categories of research on evidence have been conducted to date. These categories survey the ability of the jury (1) to accurately recall the facts, (2) to accurately perceive credible testimony, and (3) to dismiss inadmissible evidence.

The first category of research covers recollection of the facts that a jury hears. How accurate is the juror's recall of the evidence? One study found that, during deliberations, almost every relevant fact of a case is recalled and is deemed significant by one or more of the jurors.[75] In other words, collective recall works well. Another study used a true-false test on jurors and determined that jurors can collectively help each other in recalling facts accurately, even though their accuracy level diminishes as trials get longer (84 percent accuracy mark for a two-hour trial and a 72 percent accuracy mark for a two-day trial).[76]

The second research category pertains to a jury's ability to perceive evidence validly. In one study, jurors found it extremely difficult to assess the veracity of witness testimony; truthfulness and deceitfulness were almost impossible for laypersons to determine.[77] In another study, jurors were unduly receptive to eyewitness identification evidence; they virtually believed every eyewitness was telling the absolute truth.[78] In yet a third study, simulated jurors were much more likely to vote for conviction if there was an eyewitness corroboration of the crime than when there was no eyewitness testimony.[79] This same finding occurs even when the eyewitness is discredited in cross-examination.[80] Naive jurors seem to rely on common sense in evaluating eyewitness testimony, even though common sense may not accurately reflect a true state of affairs. In a study of three cases, 83.7 percent of the jurors overestimated the accuracy of eyewitness identification.[81] So jurors do not assess the validity of evidence with much accuracy, especially in terms of recognizing eyewitness deception. Perhaps the only way to make jurors more sophisticated is to teach them how to estimate the accuracy of testimony more carefully.[82]

The third category covers reactions to inadmissible testimony. As noted in earlier chapters, jurors are frequently instructed by judges to ignore inadmissible testimony. But can they? A survey of 500 New Mexico jurors showed that 75 percent of them wanted to consider in their decision evidence that was ruled inadmissible on legal grounds.[83] Another study showed that inadmissible evidence influences judgments when the rest of the evidence is weak and unconvincing.[84] In still another study, subjects read trial transcripts. Later, the subjects were told to dismiss some of the information. They clearly did not do so.[85] In civil cases, the knowledge that

a defendant has insurance is associated with giving the plaintiff higher awards, even though judges in such cases direct juries to ignore this information.[86]

Inadmissible testimony is considered by jurors only when it comes from certain sources; it is not considered from a police officer but is considered from an eyewitness.[87] Also, not only do jurors ignore the instruction to disregard inadmissible testimony, but they give greater weight to evidence that is objected to and ruled inadmissible than to any evidence that is admitted into the trial.[88] Furthermore, the stronger the admonition to disregard the evidence, the more the jurors ignore the admonition.[89] Inadmissible testimony, once heard, is virtually written into the record with indelible ink. Judicial instructions to disregard inadmissible evidence are inconsequential. The solution to this phenomenon may rest in using videotaped witness testimony so that inadmissible material can be expunged and the jury will never hear it.[90]

Judge Influence on the Jury

Judges have an opportunity to play an important role in jury decision making. In fact, juries often look to judges for cues on which decision to make.[91] However, cues that judges give to jurors frequently confuse them,[92] particularly during the judge's closing instructions to a jury. Numerous instances of juror misunderstanding exist, particularly of legal terminology (e.g., contributory negligence, reasonable doubt).[93] Other studies confirm that such confusion is common and that jurors misunderstand 30–40 percent of the judge's instructions.[94] One researcher discovered that jurors even construct their own laws at times, regardless of the judge's instructions.[95] Since lay jurors do not have the necessary background in the law, as lawyers and judges do, judges wind up not influencing juries directly as much as they could.

One way judges indirectly influence juries

is by giving them various verdict alternatives. Research shows that with only two alternatives (e.g., guilty or not guilty on the charge of first-degree murder), juries tend to be more lenient than if they are presented additional options.[96] Given two alternative choices, one defendant was found not guilty by 54 percent of the jurors. However, given three alternative choices (manslaughter included) the same defendant was found not guilty by only 8 percent of the jurors.[97] In another study involving an automobile accident case, a choice between first-degree murder and not guilty resulted in 76 percent voting not guilty. However, when the jury had the option to vote for first-degree murder, second-degree murder, or not guilty, only 43 percent voted not guilty.[98] Therefore, the more choices there are for a jury to make, the greater the chances are that a defendant will be found guilty of something.[99]

Communication directed at jurors prior to deliberation comes from lawyers, witnesses, and judges. All of this communication influences jury verdicts, although what is presented as evidence seems to have the greatest influence on decisions. Although all these sources of information are important inputs into the jury's thinking, signs point toward trial content (what witnesses, lawyers, and judges say) as significantly more important than such nonlegal matters as the physical appearance or vocal patterns of any of the parties in litigation.[100] In other words, juries consider the issues, the evidence, and the law paramount when making their decisions.

THE CONTENT AND PROCESS OF JURY DELIBERATIONS

Much of the jury deliberation research got its impetus from general studies on how groups develop consensus or agreement.[101] Outside the legal setting, it was found, a snowballing effect by a majority in a small group makes dissent increasingly difficult. In fact, a point is

reached at which dissent by the minority seriously rankles the majority, so most groups move toward a defined majority rather than toward a defined minority.[102] (Those of you familiar with the motion picture *Twelve Angry Men* may be disappointed to learn that the behavior of the characters was highly atypical.)

The landmark jury study was published by Kalven and Zeisel in 1966. This study, often referred to as the University of Chicago Jury Project, got its start with a $400,000 grant from the Ford Foundation. The grant was issued in 1956, and advanced several years thereafter, to further behavioral science research in law. Harry Kalven was a lawyer-academician; Hans Zeisel was a statistician; another partner, Fred Strodtbeck, was a small-groups analyst. Their interdisciplinary research resulted in one of the most important jury studies ever undertaken. They analyzed approximately 3,600 criminal trials, asking if judges and juries make basically the same decision. Data came from a questionnaire filled out by judges. So, to the extent that judges' inferences about jury reasoning are valid, the work is a major contribution to the literature on juries. This research team was pleased to discover that juries understand the cases they hear and almost always concur with decisions given by judges (85 percent of the time). When they disagree, juries are slightly more lenient than judges. Kalven and Zeisel concluded that the group process minimizes error, and this conclusion gave them great faith in jury decision making.[103]

The University of Chicago project actually had a rather shaky start. In their pilot program in the mid-1950s, Kalven and Strodtbeck bugged a jury room during a real jury's deliberations, with the cooperation of a Kansas court. Tape recorders and microphones recorded deliberations without the jurors' knowledge. This took place at the time that Senator Joseph McCarthy was a member of the Judiciary Committee. After investigating this research, the Senate committee claimed an invasion of privacy had occurred and that possible Communist subversion was afoot.[104] So bugging juries became expressly prohibited by law.[105]

Alternative research strategies for studying real deliberating jurors had to be developed. One approach is the field study. Field research involves postdeliberation interviews with jurors. Although such research has value, the findings are often considered "soft" data because the researchers must do a lot of guessing about the numerous decision-making variables. Fieldwork does not allow for systematic control of any of the variables. Furthermore, jurors often forget or distort their recollection of what really took place in the deliberations.

Another strategy has been research conducted with experimental mock juries, in which the researcher can construct trial elements so that they differ only in the variable or variables being studied. One of the most serious possible methodological weaknesses in experimental designs is that the subjects are college students acting as role-playing jurors.[106] The weakness of using college students in these studies is that they might be dissimilar from typical juries, thereby resulting in different findings.[107] According to one writer, "researchers should stop deluding themselves with the wishful thought that exclusive reliance on the species, *akademia moros,* will yield empirical generalizations which meet the predictive tests of the [judicial] marketplace."[108]

Other weaknesses in experimental design are that data are sometimes gathered from individual jurors, who do not get a chance to deliberate with other subjects. Such studies do not analyze the jury as a unit; thus, they make deliberation relatively unimportant in decision making. It is reasonable to assume jurors persuade other jurors. Furthermore, sometimes subjects get only brief, written case summaries, rather than watching videotapes of a reenacted trial or seeing live pre-

sentations in which actors play the roles of judges, attorneys, and witnesses. As a result, some dimensions of message transmission, such as nonverbal cues, are omitted, and this could make a difference in decisions. Also, partial trial information can affect the verdict because not enough information is supplied to the subjects being tested.[109]

A final objection to the use of simulated jurors is that they may not have the motivation of real jurors. Although they are asked to role-play, they may be "inadequate to the task of understanding real juries."[110] However, many researchers who have used mock juries note anecdotally that their subjects get deeply and seriously involved in deliberations.[111] In one study, it was discovered empirically that student juries deliberate about the same length of time, apply the same criteria for determining reasonable doubt as do real juries, and deliver verdicts nearly identical to those of real juries hearing the same cases, especially when they are led to believe that they are deciding real cases.[112]

In spite of the possible limitations of simulated jury research, most of our knowledge about juries today is based on mock jury studies. That research is organized here around the subjects of what information jurors receive (already discussed in the first section of this chapter), what information they discuss (the content of jury deliberations), and how groups network with each other and are structured (selection of leaders, applicable decision rules, and jury size). Each will be considered in turn.

What Jurors Discuss

Ultimately, jurors reach consensus on a decision. "But unlike most problem-solving groups they need not worry about implementing their decisions; they need only report their finding to the court; and the institution will take over its implementation."[113] Juries frequently begin the process of deliberating by orienting themselves to such procedures as foreperson selection and to evidence, issues, themes, and counterthemes.[114] At first, this is a general and softly focused exploration. After the first vote is taken, however, the focus becomes much sharper, "with advocates of competing views confronting each other rather directly on the points of disagreement."[115] The first vote is a turning point in the intensity of the deliberations. The first vote, unless decisive, identifies factions. That vote forces people into committing themselves and defending their positions to others. An early first vote can obviate altogether a general and friendly discussion of evidence and issues.[116]

There have been a variety of findings regarding what actually transpires during jury deliberations. One researcher recorded and analyzed the content of deliberations of ten criminal juries. She found that one-half of their discussion was devoted to personal experiences and opinions, 25 percent of their communication concerned procedural matters, 15 percent focused on witness testimony, and 8 percent of their discussion was over judge instructions.[117] Meanwhile, mock jurors discussing a murder trial in Massachusetts spent 53 percent of the time discussing testimony and 25 percent of the time referring to judge's instructions.[118] Most of what mock jurors say in deliberations is relevant to their decisions, and most of the discussion is "of 'high quality' in the eyes of attorneys, law students, and social scientist observers."[119]

Another investigator discovered that, in mean percentages, jury discussion time in civil cases is spent as follows: determination of liability—57.1 percent, judge instructions—9.5 percent, witness credibility—8.5 percent, procedures, such as how and when to vote—5.6 percent, lack of evidence in the trial—2.5 percent, damages—1.5 percent, and the attorneys—0.8 percent, with the rest of the time devoted to miscellany.[120] In another study, 65 jurors who had completed their service in ten California felony trials said that they attached much more importance to

witness testimony in arriving at verdicts than they did to what the lawyers or judges said. In addition, the importance of the defendant's appearance was negligible.[121] So most jury discussion and decision-making time is apparently spent getting down to the business of determining and evaluating the facts of the case, with a considerable amount of additional time spent discussing applicable law. Very little time is spent in social and immaterial interaction.

Let us examine more closely some studies on a few of the content areas juries discuss. Research in which jurors deliberated over a videotaped reenactment of a bank fraud case showed that they inevitably reached points of factual disagreement. When this happened, they began to speculate. For example, the male defendant allegedly received more cash from a female bank teller than he was entitled to. Although there was no such evidence, the jury speculated that the defendant and the bank teller were having an affair.[122] In essence, juries make up facts in order to construct complete stories. In another content area, Kalven discovered that the lawyer's estimated contingency fee, usually one-third of the plaintiff's award, is taken into account by juries even though it is not supposed to be a factor.[123] Jurors wanting to give high awards keep the figure high by referring to the attorney's fee in their arguments with individuals who favor low damages. The argument frequently works. What juries do not do in arriving at damages is to poll each juror to give a figure and then take a mean average of the figures each juror wants to award, although "a simple arithmetic average is a good predictor of the award finally agreed upon" through negotiation.[124] Generally, damage award determinations are the result of a greater willingness to negotiate and compromise than are guilty–not guilty verdict discussions, which tend to be more pointed and direct.[125]

What jurors discuss is closely related to structure—how the group is formed and what rules the group must follow. Four aspects of process and structure will next be examined: the selection of forepersons and leaders, the effect of communication networking on in-decisions in juries, the decision rule variable, and the relationship between jury size and decision making.

Forepersons and Leaders

There is a myth about forepersons that says that they are like lions among sheep. Re-search denies this myth. Forepersons are not necessarily opinion leaders. First of all, not much thought goes into foreperson selection. Seldom are there nominations or democratic elections. The job of foreperson is often given to the individual who speaks first,[126] who vol-unteers for the position,[127] or who is sitting at the head of the table.[128] Less than a minute is used to make the appointment.[129] Within each jury, there is a central work group made up of active and influential participants, and there are peripheral observers who are non-influential and rather inactive. The foreperson could be from either group; no pattern has emerged that indicates that forepersons are jury leaders.

What are the demographic characteristics of the foreperson? The odds are that the as-signment will go to a man[130] (seven times out of ten) who is white (95 percent of the time), whose average age is 47, who has had about two-and-a-half years of college, and who is earning about $35,000 a year. When the foreperson is a woman, her average age is 33, she has had about two years of college, and her family income is about $30,000 a year.[131] Both male and female forepersons are usually white-collar professionals.[132] They are ver-bally fluent and have affable and confident demeanors.[133] A disproportionately large per-centage of them have served as jurors previ-ously, and they have an even better chance of being selected if they were forepersons previously.[134]

Who, then, are the jury opinion leaders, the speakers, and the persuaders? What kinds of people make up the central work group? One researcher found that in 82 percent of the twelve-person juries studied, only three of the jurors account for one-half of the ver-bal acts. At times, as many as 25 percent of the jurors do not speak at all during the delib-erations.[135] The working core accounts for as many as 70 percent of the verbal statements exchanged during deliberation.[136] The per-suaders in the central work group are usually male, white, well educated, and holding high occupational status.[137] They speak frequently about facts, issues, fact-issue relationships, and comments of other jurors, whereas the less persuasive jurors are quieter, find deci-sion making difficult, and feel ill at ease with any verdict.[138] Leaders are generally fastidi-ous, intelligent, buoyant, self-confident, dom-inant, decisive and sensitive.[139] Therefore, be-cause forepersons exhibit some of these traits, they may be a part of the jury leader-ship. However, when this happens, much of the forepersons' communication is of a housekeeping nature and procedural. Ac-cording to one study, forepersons participate a great deal at first by reading the judge's in-structions and getting the group started, but as the deliberations proceed, they participate no more than what approximates the group norm.[140] In other words, a foreperson tends to adopt a moderator or organizational role rather than serving as an advocate who will strongly influence verdicts.[141] When a fore-person has low status (e.g., is a laborer or a housewife with few organizational skills), the chances are greater for a hung jury than in a group that is led by a professional with lead-ership ability.[142]

Communication Networking and Hung Juries

A coherent picture of the jury deliberation process in a criminal case is given in Figure 12.1.[143] The first time a jury votes is noted in step 2 of the diagram. This vote is an initial check to determine if the needed number of

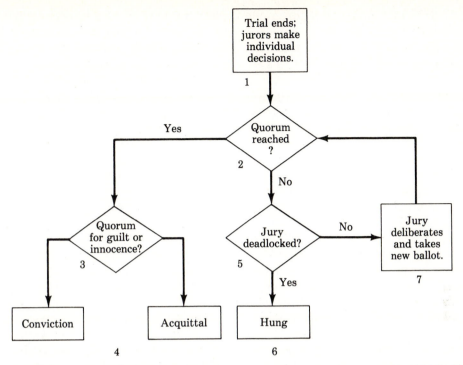

FIGURE 12.1   A FLOWCHART DIAGRAMMING THE SEQUENCE OF DECISIONS MADE DURING DELIBERATION

votes has been reached for either side. If not, the divergent viewpoints of the group are, as noted earlier, brought out into the open. If the required number of votes (a quorum) is obtained, as seen in steps 3 and 4, a decision has been reached, and the deliberations may end. However, if a quorum (verdict) is not reached, the jury must proceed. Very rarely will a jury be so pessimistic when the first vote does not result in decision that they will simply give up (step 5). Rather, they will discuss with each other for a while before taking a new ballot (step 7). The discussion phase continues through steps 2, 5, and 7 until the jury renders a verdict or admits it is hung (step 6).

A hung jury is one that has deliberated for a proper period of time but cannot agree on a decision. As a result, a mistrial is declared, and the hung jury is discharged by the court. An estimated 5.5 percent of all criminal trials result in hung juries.[144] This means that there

are thousands of deadlocked jury trials annually. A high proportion of these cases deal with crimes against property or persons or with sex and drug offenses.[145] In 63 percent of these cases, a minority of the jurors want acquittal; in 27 percent of these cases, the minority want conviction.[146] In other words, most hung juries lean toward guilty verdicts.

When a criminal jury is hopelessly deadlocked, 40 percent of the cases are dismissed and never come back to trial; the defendant is set free. In 34 percent of the cases, there are negotiated guilty pleas. The rest of the cases—26 percent—are tried again, at a conviction-to-acquittal ratio greater than 2:1. Significantly fewer than one percent of those cases that are retried result in hung juries again.[147]

We can begin to understand why juries reach points of indecision by laying out the sequential phases of task-oriented small group discussion. The phases of communication in such a group include orientation, open conflict, conflict resolution, and reconciliation.[148] During orientation, the group's task is defined, and initial ideas and preferences are revealed. During open conflict, differences of opinion are shared. During conflict resolution, a decision acceptable to all begins to surface and is discussed. During reconciliation, consensus is reached, and an attempt is made to heal the wounds of conflict. In this last stage, the group aims for solidarity and a commitment to the final decision as the right one. "The channeling of communication in the deliberating jury seems to follow such a sequence."[149]

The *orientation* phase of deliberation finds jurors communicating in ways that are neither antagonistic nor combative. The emphasis is on getting along with each other. There is tension among the members, associated mostly with the uncertainty of the task and with the awesome responsibility of being in the jury room and having to reach a decision. Lots of questions are asked of each other. Most of the communication is ambiguous and innocuous. There is some joking. Some procedures are discussed. A foreperson is selected. In general, the group is beginning to get accustomed to each other.[150]

Soon the jurors are eager to learn what the others are thinking. As they do, messages become sharpened, issues become better focused, and at some point, a first vote is taken. Some juries take an early vote; others wait a while. The verdict-driven jury begins with an early public ballot, followed by discussions of the evidence and frequent balloting. This jury is hurried and not interested in the complete story; their evaluation of the evidence becomes disjointed and fragmented. Their style of deliberation is adversarial. The evidence-driven jury ballots late and then only to validate that a quorum has been reached. Evidence is reviewed without reference to a verdict. The evidence-driven jury is trying to construct a credible story. They take more

time to reach decisions than a verdict-driven jury. The jurors appear more open-minded to persuasion than in verdict-driven juries. Jurors who follow the evidence approach are generally more satisfied with the group's performance than those who use a verdict approach.[151]

During the *open-conflict* phase in either the verdict-driven or the evidence-driven jury, disagreements surface. The shift from orientation to open conflict is gradual and subtle. However, as positions are taken, coalitions begin to form. Peripheral jurors continue to function as though they were in the orientation phase; they make socially facilitating comments to keep the group happy, or they remain quiet. Meanwhile, central work group members debate the issues and evidence.[152] There is considerable pressure for conformity to the majority opinion.[153] In fact, about 90 percent of the majority opinions after a first vote are the same as the final decisive vote.[154] Sometimes disagreement gets so heated, juries reach a point of irreconcilable difference. But deadlocks usually occur when a substantial minority faction exists from the outset, "even though a minority of one might hang the jury at the end of deliberation."[155] Or if a broad range of verdict preferences are shared on the first ballot, the jury may deadlock.[156] However, if a significant number of jurors (say, two-thirds) favor a verdict after the first vote, then in all likelihood the jury will return to the courtroom with a verdict.[157] One computer model simulation of jury deliberations showed that 3 out of 12 jurors form a relatively weak coalition, but 4 or 5 people on a 12-person jury can be much more influential and may hang the panel.[158]

The *conflict-resolution* phase gets us past the debate over facts and issues and into a consideration of the emerging decision. Once again, the discussion gets ambiguous, not to facilitate social cohesion, as in the orientation phase, but rather to allow a mediating of opposition forces. Putting forth an ambiguous new proposition is a signal of willingness to abandon an old position that could hang the jury. Nonverbal behavior of the minority, in the form of doodling, cleaning of nails, and so forth, also signals that they want the disagreement to finally end.[159]

Finally, the *reconciliation* phase cements the jury's consensus on a decision. This may not be a pleasant time for what was the minority. So the majority will try to create a spirit of togetherness. Names and addresses may be exchanged; jokes may be told again, particularly about the deliberations; the minority may say they are glad closure could be accomplished.[160]

A key element regarding jury indecision is the size and makeup of the minority faction[161] and whether or not the jury is verdict-driven or evidence-driven.[162] Juries voting too early or too often tend to deadlock more than juries trying to carefully piece together a story. To the extent that the minority in a combative, verdict-driven jury is large, vocal, and adamant, the conflict resolution phase of jury deliberations probably will not be completed. The minority faction in that environment will remain firm in its position "even when reasonable argumentation appeared to have undermined all of the bases for initial verdict preference."[163]

During voir dire, attorneys must consider the possibility of a minority faction and how members of a panel will mix and interact. "It is not enough to select the right evaluators of your case; you must know how to put them together."[164] The best minority juror for the lawyer who has argued the majority position is one who will acquiesce to social pressure. Even though there are no demographic or personality characteristics to differentiate holdouts from other jurors, it is usually the bright, vocal person who has a low perception of the seriousness and thoroughness of jury deliberations who will polarize the group and who will not likely conform to the majority.[165] If this kind of person can be detected

during voir dire, he or she should be struck if conformity is the lawyer's goal. However, the reverse is true in cases where defense counsel can benefit from a deadlocked panel. Group dynamics are crucial as they relate to the problem of hung juries.[166]

Hung juries are psychologically costly. Members of a hung jury panel think they have failed because they could reach no clear and unequivocal decision. Hung juries are economically wasteful, too. As the data cited earlier indicate, most of the hung juries are leaning in the direction of a guilty verdict, and most of the retried cases result in a guilty verdict. Therefore, what might be done to avoid hung juries has been a topic of concern in legal circles for many years. For instance, judges might admonish juries to communicate with an open mind and not to vote too soon. Other remedies that have been proposed and sometimes implemented are discussed in the next two subsections of this chapter: lowering the number of votes required for a decision and reducing jury size.

Applicable Decision Rules

The origin of the unanimous-decision (e.g., 12–0) rule for juries is unknown, but it has been with us in English common law since the latter half of the fourteenth century.[167] The first time that something other than a unanimous-decision rule was used in America was in Oregon in 1934, when the legislature permitted a 10–2 decision to find a defendant guilty.[168] Since then, many states have eliminated the unanimous-decision rule in certain cases. Why? Because studies have shown that unanimous-rule juries are hung more frequently than nonunanimous-rule juries.[169] Kalven and Zeisel found that in jurisdictions where unanimous verdicts were required, 5.6 percent of the juries deadlocked, compared with only 3.1 percent in jurisdictions that had nonunanimous-decision rules.[170] In Multnomah County (Oregon), the number of hung criminal juries where 10–2 decisions are required is only 2.5 percent.[171]

The United States Supreme Court in separate 5–4 decisions has upheld the principle of nonunanimity by allowing 10–2 and 9–3 guilty verdicts.[172] The Court said that unanimity is not constitutionally required in rendering a guilty verdict and that decision-rule changes do not influence jury behavior.[173] They also said that since most cases are settled by plea bargaining or are clear-cut, few defendants would be affected by the use of the nonunanimous-decision rule.[174]

During the debate preceding and following the two Court decisions, four arguments surfaced in the defense of nonunanimity over unanimity. First, nonunanimous decisions are more reasonable because there is always the chance that one stubborn juror will impede justice just for the sake of being obstinate. That person will remain blind and deaf to rational argument and valid evidence.[175] However, opponents to nonunanimity point to research that shows that the obstinate juror thesis is bogus. Those jurors who remain on a panel are generally reasonable people and will doubt their positions if others insist they are mistaken. If minority positions develop, they do so because of juror confusion, not sheer stubbornness.[176]

Second, nonunanimous decisions are preferred because there is always the chance that one juror can be corrupted.[177] In 1966, the British Parliament authorized jury verdicts of 10–2 after several notorious instances of jury tampering.[178] However, opponents to nonunanimity note that there are virtually no cases of unscrupulous jurors serving in the United States and that, therefore, this argument for nonunanimity has little foundation.[179]

Third, nonunanimity is superior to unanimity because the latter is an unreasonable expectation. It is difficult to get 12 people in any setting to agree on anything controversial. Why should we expect otherwise in the courtroom?[180] But those who defend unanimity respond by arguing that no other setting has anything like a burden of proof requirement and that part of the definition of this burden is to influence not some, but all, of the members of a jury.[181]

Fourth, nonunanimity is superior to unanimity because of the economic burden of asking juries to reach unanimous decisions and then finding them hung. It is true that having to retry a case is time-consuming and costly. Millions of dollars are spent each year on retried cases. Does a nonunanimous decision rule reduce the number of deadlocked juries? That question has already been answered affirmatively. In separate studies, researchers concluded that the reason there are fewer hung juries with a nonunanimous decision rule is that compromise comes quicker and disagreement is lessened by the minority, who see less of an opportunity to sway the rest of the group to their side.[182] A unanimity requirement creates longer jury deliberations, more total comments from everyone, greater disagreement and exchange of opinions, suggestions, and information—particularly when the minority position is for a not-guilty verdict—and more polling during deliberations.[183] In spite of the fact that there is a difference in deliberation time, the minority viewpoint is just as robustly expressed regardless of whether a unanimous or nonunanimous decision is required.[184] In addition, most empirical studies show that nonunanimous juries lean no more toward either the prosecution or the defense than juries speaking with a single voice.[185] Indeed, only one study found that mock jurors watching a videotaped murder trial had three times as many convictions under a nonunanimous-decision rule as under a unanimous-decision rule.[186] In civil cases, one study found no significant differences in negligence decisions or in damage awards between 12–0 and 10–2 juries.[187]

The strongest argument against nonunanimity is that the burden-of-proof standard is weakened. The validity of this argument depends on your perspective on burden of proof. In civil litigation, the plaintiff and defendant are almost in a parity relationship.[188] The plaintiff must prove his or her case only by a preponderance of the evidence. Since the amount of proof for the plaintiff is far from absolute, why must jury agreement be unanimous? However, in criminal law, definitions of reasonable doubt do not specify whether the doubt must be measured by an individual standard or a group standard. If an individual standard is used, nonunanimous decisions are satisfactory. If a group standard is used, nonunanimous decisions are unsatisfactory, because the 11–1 or 10–2 decision shows some group doubt. Some argue that the criminal-case reasonable-doubt standard is weakened by the nonunanimous-decision rule.[189] Surveyed jurors say they feel more comfortable with the correctness of group decisions than they do with individual decisions; the aggregate certainty of guilt is easier for them to justify than having their individual decisions highly emphasized.[190]

Other than a possible burden-of-proof problem, there is no compelling evidence against the nonunanimous-decision rule. Differences in the product or outcome of jury deliberations are nil. Therefore, since non-unanimity lessens the number of hung juries, state courts have made the nonunanimous-decision rule more and more common, particularly in civil and nonfelony criminal cases.[191]

Jury Size

Closely related to the matter of decision rule is jury size. All the states have the option to reduce jury sizes to levels specifically approved by the Supreme Court. The traditional jury size has been twelve members. Speculation about where the number twelve originated ranges from the twelve Apostles to the 12 tribes of Israel to the number of months on the calendar to the number of grades in our school system to the number of signs in the zodiac.[192] The number twelve does indeed have a mystical quality to it. Whatever speculations one wishes to believe, the number twelve for jury size is apparently nothing more than historical accident; there is no firm empirical ground that justifies the figure.

In 1970, and again in 1973, the Supreme Court said that the Sixth Amendment insured a trial by jury but that it did not guarantee that the panel be composed of twelve persons. The Court said that a six-person jury does not adversely affect group processes and is satisfactory in all but capital crime cases.[193] They based this claim on a collection of studies that have been seriously challenged by many legal scholars and social scientists as mere ornament, as haphazard, as irrelevant, or as uncontrolled.[194] One author summarized the complaint as follows:

The Court used actual empirical studies which it seriously distorted in its portrayal of them, and used intuitive mathematics that were at odds with explicit and well-established statistical principles. . . . On the basis of non-studies and misread studies, the Supreme Court decided *Williams*. On the basis of the flawed studies conducted after *Williams,* the same conclusion was reinforced in *Colgrove*.[195]

In 1978, the Court looked at a five-person panel in a criminal case and set a bottom line when it ruled that the number of jurors could not fall below six. To do so would threaten Sixth and Fourteenth Amendment guarantees.[196] With this decision, the Court noted the need for more and better data before making any further decisions about jury size. Speaking for the Court, Justice Blackmun said more information was needed linking jury size to effective group deliberation, accuracy of verdict, the representation of minority jurors, and protection for the defendant. In the latter area, the Court was particularly concerned about how a defendant might be disadvantaged by smaller juries, especially because there would be fewer hung juries.

The major argument convincing the Supreme Court to reduce the size of a jury from twelve to six seems to have been the promotion of greater efficiency at a reduced price.[197] Because there is less time to impanel smaller juries and there are fewer people to pay, a smaller jury was seen to be economically advantageous. Indeed, studies in Minnesota, New York City, and Worcester, Massachusetts, confirm that case backlog is reduced and millions of dollars are saved when courts go from twelve- to six-person juries.[198] Furthermore, since the "empirical studies" show no apparent difference between verdicts rendered by twelve-person juries and those rendered by six-person juries, why not opt for efficiency?

The Court heard some arguments against reducing jury size. The claim of greater efficiency was challenged by data, notably from Washington, D.C., to show that there were no significant savings in time or money with smaller juries.[199] There was also the claim that a cross-section of the community is more difficult to obtain with a six-person jury than it is with a twelve-person jury, resulting in different decisions.[200]

Since the early 1970s, considerable data have been gathered on jury size. We have learned that an exceptionally aggressive member of a jury has a better chance of imposing his or her opinion on a small group than on a large group.[201] This situation is a possible drawback to a small jury insofar as an active and aggressive communicator could impose his or her will on the others easily. In a larger group, a more sizable opposition can unite to overcome the persistence of a dominant leader. However, research has also demonstrated that fewer people dominate talk in large groups than in small groups.[202] Indeed, there is a positive correlation between total group participation and smaller group

size,[203] with the minority viewpoint heard more often and in greater depth in the smaller group.[204] Because satisfaction corresponds with a member's level of participation in a group, juror satisfaction is more easily facilitated in smaller groups.[205]

We still do not know if there are fewer hung juries when the size of the group is reduced from twelve to six. One author saw no significant differences in the frequency of deadlocked juries according to jury size.[206] However, most other studies have found fewer hung juries when six-person rather than twelve-person panels are used.[207] In fact, Zeisel discovered that the percentage of hung juries could be reduced to 2.4 percent from more than 5 percent by cutting jury size in half.[208]

On the question of whether twelve-person juries are more representative of a cross-section of a community than six-person juries, one investigator found that they are. For instance, in one black community studied, there was an 80 percent chance that a black would serve on a twelve-person jury and only a 41 percent chance that a black would serve on a six-person jury. In one highly conservative community, there was a 75 percent chance that an extreme conservative would sit on a twelve-person jury but only a 40 percent chance that an extreme conservative would sit on a six-person jury.[209] Another researcher reached the same conclusion when she learned that there were blacks on 59 percent of the six-member juries and on 78 percent of the twelve-member juries she studied. Also, women constitute 30 percent of all six-member juries but 57 percent of all twelve-member juries. A greater variety of ages and occupations was also found on twelve-person juries.[210] Just as in public opinion polling, the larger the sample, the more representative it is.

Finally, do decisions differ depending on jury size? In civil suits, all studies except one found no statistically significant differences favoring the plaintiff when juries of six and twelve were compared.[211] That one study found that juries are biased against the plaintiff in decisions and awards.[212] Criminal litigation verdicts also do not differ between six-person and twelve-person juries given the same case material,[213] although twelve-person juries are somewhat more consistent in reaching the same decision on the same case than are multiple six-person juries when they are given identical information.[214]

To summarize, there is no clear pattern in the research to show the most desirable jury size. Neither twelve nor six has captured the honors for superior characteristics and performance. Most of the jury-size research has been drenched with criticism, and only a few studies remain unscathed. Nevertheless, investigations show that large juries spend more time deliberating, are less influenced by aggressive leaders, attain better community representation, and produce more consistent verdicts. Small juries allow more talk from all the group members, have higher group ratings of satisfaction with decision making, increase efficiency in the courts by reaching decisions quickly and costing less, reach approximately the same verdicts in civil and criminal cases as large juries do, and tend to be deadlocked less than larger panels.

For some, the interrelated issues of reduction in jury size to six and the removal of the unanimous-decision rule constitute a significant erosion of our judicial system.[215] To set aside those fears somewhat, the Supreme Court in 1979 required unanimous verdicts in criminal trials when the jury was composed of only six persons.[216] Meanwhile, to make use of the merits of various jury sizes and the non-unanimous decision rule combined, one author has imaginatively proposed that a jury of twelve be impaneled. After the trial, this group would divide itself into twin juries of six members each. Both juries would deliberate, and each panel would have to reach at least a 4–2 decision to find for the prosecutor or

plaintiff.[217] Since jury size and decision rule seem to be no more than a matter of personal preference, what do you think of Saks' suggestion?

Rendering the Verdict

After the jury has reached its decision, the panel returns to court to render its verdict. This is often the dramatic high point in litigation. The verdict is read by the foreperson in open court. In a criminal case, the jury finds the accused "guilty" or "not guilty" of the charges. In a civil case, the jury finds for the plaintiff and awards a certain sum of money, or finds for the defendant. The jury does not have to explain its verdict; it merely states a conclusion. If requested to do so by the attorneys, the judge can poll each member of the jury individually to confirm that conclusion.

This chapter has essentially been an encyclopedia of research on jury decision making. Even though much more research is bound to be done, we know enough now to be able to conclude that studies of jury behavior suggest that jurors take their work very seriously. They strive to reach fair decisions. They carefully review the testimony and issues. After studying 2000 jurors, Simon concluded that "they were concerned that the verdict they reached was consistent with the spirit of the law and with the facts of the case."[218] The group judgment system used in American trials, although imperfect, still is a highly satisfactory mechanism. It is also the final act of communication in the legal process.

Notes

[1]Beth Bonora, Rosalyn Linder, Richard Christie, and Jay Schulman, "Jury Selection," in Beth Bonora and Elissa Kraus, eds., *Jurywork: Systematic Techniques* (Berkeley, California: National Jury project, 1979), 206.

[2]Without an explicit explanation from the judge of the reasons for not talking, jurors disobey the rules from time to time. Elizabeth F. Loftus and Douglas Leber, "Do Jurors Talk?" *Trial* (January 1986), 59–60.

[3]John Edd Stepp, Jr., "Communications Between Parties and Jurors May Be Irrebuttably Prejudicial as a Matter of Law," *Houston Law Review* 4 (1966), 583–588. (See *United States v. Harry Barfield Co.* 359 F. 2d 120 [5th Cir. 1966]).

[4]Thomas J. Bice, "Jury Misconduct in Iowa," *Drake Law Review* 20 (1971), 643.

[5]Robert F. Forston, "Sense and Non-Sense: Jury Trial Communication," *Brigham Young University Law Review* (1975), 629.

[6]Lisa M. Harms, "The Questioning of Witnesses by Jurors," *American University Law Review* 27 (1977), 132.

[7]Jurors are permitted to ask questions in British courts today.

[8]Harms, op. cit., 151–154.

[9]Ibid., 156.

[10]Bertram Edises, "One-Way Communication: Achilles' Heel of the Jury System," *Judges' Journal* 13 (1974), 78; Forston, op. cit., 631.

[11]*Facts of the Jury System: A Survey* (Denver: National Center for State Courts, 1976), 28.

[12]For a detailed list of objections, see Tommy L. Holland, "Trials: Jurors' Notes Approved in Oklahoma," *Tulsa Law Journal* 7 (1971), 56–65.

[13]"The answer to that objection is that the present system gives advantage to the person who purports to have the better memory, or who has the more domineering personality—under no system would all jurors have equal influence." Forston, op. cit., 632.

[14]Arthur L. Newell, "May a Juror Take Notes in Illinois?" *Chicago-Kent Law Review* 46 (1969), 255; Dragan D. Petroff, "The Practice of Jury Note Taking—Misconduct, Right, or Privilege?" *Oklahoma Law Review* 18 (1965), 140.

[15]Victor E. Flango, "Would Jurors Do a Better Job if They Could Take Notes?" *Judicature* 63 (1980), 440–441.

[16]Ibid., 442.

[17]Thomas L. Grisham and Stephen F. Lawless, "Jurors Judge Justice: A Survey of Criminal Jurors," *New Mexico Law Review* 3 (1973), 355.

[18]Elvin J. Brown, "Note Taking by Jurors," *Judges' Journal* 10 (1971), 27–28.

[19]Numerous times during the 1950s, the federal courts have ruled uniformly that the matter of note taking by jurors rests in the sound discretion of the trial court. Edwin L. Scherlis, "Note Taking by Jurors," *Temple Law Quarterly* 37 (1963–1964), 334.

[20]Donald S. Buzard, "Jury Note-Taking in Criminal Trials," unpublished paper (1951).

[21]Dale W. Broeder, "The Impact of the Lawyers: An Informal Appraisal," *Valparaiso Law Review* 17 (1966), 40–76.

[22]Ibid., 42.

[23]Harold M. Hoffman and Joseph Brodley, "Jurors on Trial," *Missouri Law Review* 17 (1952), 243.

[24]Ibid.

[25]Margaret L. McLaughlin, et al., "Juror Perceptions of Participants in Criminal Proceedings," *Journal of Applied Communications Research* 7 (1979), 92–102.

[26]H. P. Weld and E. R. Danzig, "A Study of the Way in Which a Verdict is Reached by a Jury," *American Journal of Psychology* 53 (1940), 536.

[27]Harry Kalven, Jr., and Hans Zeisel, *The American Jury* (Boston: Little, Brown, 1966), 372.

[28]Forston, op. cit., 606–612.

[29]Nora K. Villemur and Janet Shibley Hyde, "Effects of Sex of Defense Attorney, Sex of Juror, and Age and Attractiveness of the Victim on Mock Juror Decision Making in a Rape Case," *Sex Roles* 9 (1983), 879–889.

[30]Thomas Sannito and Edward Burke Arnolds, "Jury Study Results: The Factors at Work," *Trial Diplomacy Journal* (Spring 1982), 9.

[31]Forston, op. cit., 606–612.

[32]Francis C. Dane and Lawrence S. Wrightsman, "Effects of Defendants' and Victims' Characteristics on Jurors' Verdicts," in Norbert L. Kerr and Robert M. Bray, eds., *The Psychology of the Courtroom* (New York: Academic Press, 1982), 84.

[33]David Landy and Elliot Aronson, "The Influence of the Character of the Criminal and His Victim on the Decision of Simulated Jurors," *Journal of Experimental Social Psychology* 5 (1969), 141–152.

[34]This is not to say victim attractiveness or unattractiveness is unimportant. In one

experiment, the respectability of the victim made a difference. One rape victim was either married or a virgin; another was divorced. All other information being equal, the defendant was given a longer sentence when the victim he raped was either married or a virgin. Cathaleene Jones and Elliot Aronson, "Attribution of Fault to a Rape Victim as a Function of Respectability of the Victim," *Journal of Personality and Social Psychology* 26 (1973), 415–419.

[35]K. Phillip Taylor, Raymond W. Buchanan, and David U. Strawn, *Communication Strategies for Trial Attorneys* (Glenview, Ill.: Scott, Foresman, 1984), 103.

[36]Ronald M. Friend and Michael Vinson, "Leaning Over Backwards: Jurors Response to Defendants' Attractiveness," *Journal of Communication* 24 (1974), 124–129.

[37]Richard R. Izzett and Walter Leginski, "Group Discussion and the Influence of Defendant Characteristics in a Simulated Jury Setting," *Journal of Social Psychology* 93 (1974), 271–279.

[38]James H. Davis, Robert M. Bray, and Robert W. Holt, "The Empirical Study of Decision Processes in Juries," in J. L. Tapp and F. J. Levine, eds., *Law, Justice, and the Individual in Society: Psychological and Legal Issues* (New York: Holt, Rinehart and Winston, 1977), 330.

[39]Luis T. Garcia and William Griffitt, "Impact of Testimonial Evidence as a Function of Witness Characteristics," *Bulletin of the Psychonomic Society* 11 (1978), 37–40.

[40]William Griffitt and Thomas Jackson, "Simulated Jury Decisions: The Influence of Jury-Defendant Attitude Similarity–Dissimilarity," *Social Behavior and Personality* 1 (1973), 1–7; Izzett and Leginski, op. cit.; Herman E. Mitchell and Donn Byrne, "The Defendant's Dilemma: Effect of Jurors' Attitudes and Authoritarianism," *Journal of Personality and Social Psychology* 25 (1973), 123–129; Sannito and Arnolds, op. cit., 9.

[41]Richard A. Kulka and Joan B. Kessler, "Is Justice Really Blind? The Influence of Litigant Physical Attractiveness on Juridical Judgment," *Journal of Applied Social Psychology* 8 (1978), 366–381.

[42]Cookie Stephan and Judy C. Tully, "The Influence of Physical Attractiveness of a Plaintiff on the Decisions of Simulated Jurors," *Journal of Social Psychology* 101 (1977), 149–150; Elaine

Walster, "Assignment of Responsibility for an Accident," *Journal of Personality and Social Psychology* 3 (1966), 73–79.

[43]Marsha B. Jacobson, "Effects of Victim's and Defendant's Physical Attractiveness on Subjects' Judgments in a Rape Case," *Sex Roles* 7 (1981), 247–255.

[44]Hubert S. Feild and Leigh B. Bienen, *Jurors and Rape: A Study in Psychology and Law* (Lexington, Mass.: Lexington Books, 1980), 142.

[45]Sannito and Arnolds, op. cit., 9. "Jury Study Results."

[46]Karen K. Dion, "Physical Attractiveness and Evaluation of Children's Transgressions," *Journal of Personality and Social Psychology* 24 (1972), 207–213; Michael G. Efran, "The Effects of Physical Appearance on the Judgment of Guilt, Interpersonal Attraction, and the Severity of Recommended Punishment in a Simulated Jury Task," *Journal of Research in Personality* 8 (1974), 45–54; Martin F. Kaplan and Gwen D. Kemmerick, "Juror Judgment as Information Integration: Combining Evidential and Nonevidential Information," *Journal of Personality and Social Psychology* 30 (1974), 493–499; Kalven and Zeisel, op. cit., 193–218; Gloria Leventhal and Ronald Krate, "Physical Attractiveness and Severity of Sentencing," *Psychological Reports* 40 (1977), 315–318; Robert M. McFatter, "Sentencing Strategies and Justice: Effects of Punishment Philosophy on Sentencing Decisions," *Journal of Personality and Social Psychology* 36 (1978), 1490–1500; Charlan Nemeth and Ruth H. Sosis, "A Simulated Jury Study: Characteristics of the Defendant and the Jurors," *Journal of Social Psychology* 90 (1973), 221–229; David E. Reynolds and Mark S. Sanders, "Effect of Defendant Attractiveness, Age, and Injury on Severity of Sentence Given by Simulated Jurors," *Journal of Social Psychology* 96 (1975), 149–150; Harold Sigall and David Landy, "Effects of the Defendant's Character and Suffering on Juridic Judgment," *Journal of Social Psychology* 88 (1972), 149–150; Harold Sigall and Nancy Ostrove, "Beautiful but Dangerous: Effects of Offender Attractiveness and Nature of the Crime on Juridic Judgment," *Journal of Personality and Social Psychology* 31 (1975), 410–414.

[47]Gerald R. Miller, "The Unwanted Juror?" in Michael E. Roloff and Charles R. Berger, eds.,

Social Cognition and Communication (Beverly Hills, Calif.: Sage, 1982), 239.

[48]Sigall and Ostrove, op. cit.

[49]Dale E. Broeder, "The Pro and Con of Interjecting Plaintiff Insurance Companies in Jury Trial Cases: An Isolated Jury Project Case Study," *Natural Resources Journal* 6 (1966), 269–287.

[50]David E. Hatton, John R. Snortum, and Stuart Oskamp, "The Effects of Biasing Information and Dogmatism upon Witness Testimony," *Psychonomic Science* 23 (1971), 425–427; Landy and Aronson, op. cit.; Nemeth and Sosis, op. cit.

[51]Efran, op. cit.

[52]Henry Allen Bullock, "Significance of the Racial Factor in the Length of Prison Sentences," *Journal of Criminal Law, Criminology, and Police Science* 52 (1961), 411–417.

[53]Terence P. Thornberry, "Race, Socioeconomic Status, and Sentencing in the Juvenile Justice System," *Journal of Criminal Law and Criminology* 64 (1973), 90–98.

[54]Richard P. McGlynn, James C. Megas, and Daniel H. Benson, "Sex and Race as Factors Affecting the Attribution of Insanity in a Murder Trial," *Journal of Psychology* 93 (1976), 93–99.

[55]Michael J. Hindelang, "Equality Under the Law," *Journal of Criminal Law, Criminology, and Police Science* 60 (1969), 306–313.

[56]Denis Chimaeze E. Ugwuegbu, "Racial and Evidential Factors in Jury Attribution of Legal Responsibility," *Journal of Experimental Social Psychology* 15 (1979), 133–146.

[57]Feild and Bienen, op. cit., 141.

[58]Michael J. Sunnafrank and Norman E. Fontes, "The Effects of Ethnic Affiliation on Juror Responses: General and Crime-Specific Ethnic Stereotypes." Paper presented at the Western Speech Communicaiton Association Convention (Los Angeles, 1979); Michael J. Sunnafrank and Norman E. Fontes, "General and Crime Related Racial Stereotypes and Influence on Juridic Decisions," *Cornell Journal of Social Relations* 17 (1983), 1–15.

[59]Elaine S. Brand, Rene A. Ruiz, and Amado M. Padilla, "Ethnic Identification and Preference: A Review," *Psychological Bulletin* 81 (1974), 860–890; John C. Brigham, "Ethnic Stereotypes," *Psychological Bulletin* 76 (1971), 15–38; Harold

Sigall and Richard Page, "Current Stereotypes: A Little Fading, A Little Faking," *Journal of Personality and Social Psychology* 18 (1971), 247–255; Marylee Taylor, "Race, Sex, and Expression of Self-Fulfilling Prophecies in a Laboratory Teaching Situation," *Journal of Personality and Social Psychology* 37 (1979), 897–912.

[60]Robert I. Gordon and Paul D. Jacobs, "Forensic Psychology: Perception of Guilt and Income," *Perceptual and Motor Skills* 28 (1969), 143–146.

[61]Freda Adler, "Socioeconomic Factors Influencing Jury Verdicts," *New York University Review of Law and Social Change* 3 (1973), 1–10; Theodore G. Chiricas and Gordon P. Waldo, "Socioeconomic Status and Criminal Sentencing: An Empirical Assessment of a Conflict Proposition," *American Sociological Review* 40 (1975), 753–772; James M. Gleason and Victor A. Harris, "Group Discussion and Defendant's Socioeconomic Status as Determinants of Judgments by Simulated Jurors," *Journal of Applied Social Psychology* 6 (1976), 186–191; John Hagan, "Extra-Legal Attributes and Criminal Sentencing: An Assessment of a Sociological Viewpoint," *Law and Society Review* 8 (1974), 357–383.

[62]Landy and Aronson, op. cit.; John P. Reed, "Jury Deliberations, Voting, and Verdict Trends," *Southwest Social Science Quarterly* 45 (1965), 361–370.

[63]Robert M. Bray et al., "The Effects of Defendant Status on the Decisions of Student and Community Juries," *Social Psychology* 41 (1978), 256–260.

[64]Jeffrey C. Savitsky and Marguerite E. Sim, "Trading Emotions: Equity Theory of Reward and Punishment," *Journal of Communication* 24 (1974), 140–146.

[65]W. Austin and M. K. Utne, "The Differential Impact of an Offender's Suffering on Simulated Jurors' Convictions and Sentencing Behavior," Unpublished paper (Charlottesville: University of Virginia, 1976); Michael G. Rumsey, "Effects of Defendant Background and Remorse on Sentencing Judgments," *Journal of Applied Social Psychology* 6 (1976), 64–68.

[66]Ellen K. Solender and Elizabeth Solender, "Minimizing the Effect of the Unattractive Client on the Jury: A Study of the Interaction of Physical

Appearance with Assertions and Self-Experience References," *Human Rights* 5 (1976), 201–214.

[67]Mark L. Knapp, Roderick P. Hart, and Harry S. Dennis, "An Exploration of Deception as a Communication Construct," *Human Communication Research* 1 (1974), 15–29.

[68]Bert Pryor and Raymond W. Buchanan, "The Effects of a Defendant's Demeanor on Juror Perception of Credibility and Guilt," *Journal of Communication* 34 (1984), 92–99.

[69]Amiram Elwork, Bruce Dennis Sales, and David Suggs, "The Trial: A Research Review," in Bruce Dennis Sales, ed., *Perspectives in Law and Psychology: The Trial Process* (New York: Plenum, 1981), 23.

[70]Michael J. Saks, Carol M. Werner, and Thomas M. Ostrom, "The Presumption of Innocence and the American Juror," *Journal of Contemporary Law* 2 (1975), 46–54.

[71]John R. Hepburn, "The Objective Reality of Evidence and the Utility of Systematic Jury Selection," *Law and Human Behavior* 4 (1980), 96.

[72]Elwork, Sales, and Suggs, op. cit., 23.

[73]Kaplan and Kemmerick, op. cit.

[74]Roy F. Baumeister and John M. Darley, "Reducing the Biasing Effect of Perpetrator Attractiveness in Jury Simulation," *Personality and Social Psychology Bulletin* 8 (1982), 286–292.

[75]H. P. Weld and Merrill Roff, "A Study of the Formation of Opinion Based Upon Legal Evidence," *American Journal of Psychology* 51 (1938), 609–628.

[76]Hoffman and Brodley, op. cit., 248–249.

[77]Gerald R. Miller et al., " . . . and Nothing but the Truth," in Bruce Dennis Sales, ed., *Perspectives in Law and Psychology: The Trial Process* (New York: Plenum, 1981), 145–179.

[78]Patrick M. Wall, *Eyewitness Identification in Criminal Cases* (Springfield, Ill.: Charles C. Thomas, 1965).

[79]Elizabeth F. Loftus, "Eyewitness Testimony: Does the Malleable Human Memory Interfere With Legal Justice?" *Social Action and the Law Newsletter* 2 (1975), 5.

[80]Elizabeth F. Loftus, *Eyewitness Testimony* (Cambridge: Harvard University Press, 1979);

Nathan R. Sobel, *Eyewitness Identification: Legal and Practical Problems* (New York: Clark Boardman, 1972); Wall, op. cit.

[81]John C. Brigham and Robert K. Bothwell, "The Ability of Prospective Jurors to Estimate the Accuracy of Eyewitness Identifications," *Law and Human Behavior* 7 (1983), 19–30.

[82]Kenneth A. Deffenbacher and Elizabeth F. Loftus, "Do Jurors Share a Common Understanding Concerning Eyewitness Behavior?" *Law and Human Behavior* 6 (1982), 15.

[83]Grisham and Lawless, op. cit., 356.

[84]Stanley Sue, Ronald E. Smith, and Cathy Caldwell, "Effects of Inadmissible Evidence on the Decisions of Simulated Jurors," *Journal of Applied Social Psychology* 3 (1973), 345–353.

[85]Sharon Wolf and David A. Montgomery, "Effects of Inadmissible Evidence and Level of Judicial Admonishment to Disregard on the Judgments of Mock Jurors," *Journal of Applied Social Psychology* 7 (1977), 205–219.

[86]When the defendant disclosed he or she had no liability insurance, the average award was $33,000; when the defendant disclosed he or she had liability insurance, the average award was $37,000; and when the jury was instructed to disregard the fact that the defendant had liability insurance, the average award increased to $46,000. Dale W. Broeder, "Plaintiffs' Family Status as Affecting Juror Behavior: Some Tentative Insights," *Journal of Public Law* 14 (1965), 131–141.

[87]John C. Reinard, "Effects of Inadmissible Evidence From Law Enforcement Officers on Jury Decisions." Paper presented at the Western Speech Communication Association Convention (San Jose, Calif., 1981).

[88]John C. Reinard, "Inadmissible Testimony in the Courtroom: An Experimental Study of Sources and Types on Verdicts, Sentence Recommendations, and Credibility," Paper presented at the Speech Communication Association Convention (Chicago, 1986); John C. Reinard and Rodney A. Reynolds, "The Effects of Inadmissible Testimony Objections and Rulings on Jury Decisions," *Journal of the American Forensic Association* 15 (1978), 91–109.

[89]Vincent F. Follert, "Reactance in the Jury Room:

Decision by Men and Not by Laws." Paper presented at the Central States Speech Association Convention (Milwaukee, Wis., 1982).

[90]Gerald R. Miller and Robert W. Bundens, "Juries and Communication," in Brenda Dervin and Melvin J. Voight, eds., *Progress in Communication Sciences,* vol. 3 (Norwood, N.J.: Ablex, 1982), 144–146.

[91]Joseph J. O'Mara, "The Courts, Standard Jury Charges—Findings of a Pilot Project," *Pennsylvania Bar Journal* 120 (1972), 166–175.

[92]Joan B. Kessler, "An Empirical Study of Six- and Twelve-Member Jury Decision-Making Processes," *University of Michigan Journal of Law Reform* 6 (1973), 712–734.

[93]Amiram Elwork, Bruce Dennis Sales, and James J. Alfini, "Juridic Decisions: In Ignorance of the Law or in Light of It?" *Law and Human Behavior* 1 (1977), 163–189; Forston, op. cit., 610–612; Robert F. Forston, "Judge's Instructions: A Quantitative Analysis of Jurors' Listening Comprehension," *Today's Speech* 18 (November 1970), 34–38; Bert Pryor et al., "An Affective-Cognitive Consistency Explanation for Comprehension of Standard Jury Instructions," *Communication Monographs* 47 (1980), 68–76.

[94]Taylor, Buchanan, and Strawn, op. cit., 100.

[95]Dale W. Broeder, "The University of Chicago Jury Project," *Nebraska Law Review* 38 (1959), 744–760.

[96]Edith Greene and Elizabeth F. Loftus, "When Crimes Are Joined at Trial," *Law and Human Behavior* 9 (1985), 193–207; Norbert L. Kerr, "Severity of Prescribed Penalty and Mock Jurors' Verdicts," *Journal of Personality and Social Psychology* 36 (1978), 1431–1442.

[97]Neil Vidmar, "Effects of Decision Alternatives on the Verdicts and Social Perceptions of Simulated Jurors," *Journal of Personality and Social Psychology* 22 (1972), 211–218.

[98]Kalman J. Kaplan and Roger I. Simon, "Latitude and Severity of Sentencing Options, Race of the Victim, and Decisions of Simulated Jurors: Some Issues Arising From the 'Algiers Motel' Trial," *Law and Society Review* 7 (1972), 87–98.

[99]Kathleen Carrese Gerbasi, Miron Zuckerman, and Harry T. Reis, "Justice Needs a New Blindfold: A Review of Mock Jury Research," *Psychological Bulletin* 34 (1977), 337.

[100]Ronald J. Matlon et al., "Factors Affecting Jury Decision-Making." Paper presented at the Speech Communication Association Convention (Chicago, 1985).

[101]Dorwin Cartwright and Alvin Zander, eds., *Group Dynamics: Research and Theory* (New York: Harper & Row, 1960), 165, 167, 286.

[102]Muzafer Sherif, *The Psychology of Social Norms* (New York: Harper, 1936), 138.

[103]Kalven and Zeisel, op. cit.

[104]United States Congress, Senate, Internal Security Subcommittee of the Committee on the Judiciary, *Hearings, Recording of Jury Deliberations,* 84th Cong., 2d sess., 1955; see also *New York Times,* October 6, 7, 8, 13, and 14, 1955.

[105]18 U.S.C. § 1508.

[106]Gerald R. Miller et al., "Methodological Issues in Legal Communication Research: What Can Trial Simulations Tell Us?" *Communication Monographs* 50 (1983), 35.

[107]Robert M. Bray and Norbert L. Kerr, "Methodological Considerations in the Study of the Psychology of the Courtroom," in Norbert L. Kerr and Robert M. Bray, eds., *The Psychology of the Courtroom* (New York: Academic Press, 1982), 287–323.

[108]Gerald R. Miller, "On Rediscovering the Apple: Some Issues in Evaluating the Social Significance of Communication Research," *Central States Speech Journal* 30 (1979), 22.

[109]Joan B. Kessler, "The Social Psychology of Jury Deliberations," in Rita James Simon, ed., *The Jury System in America: A Critical Overview* (Beverly Hills, Calif.: Sage, 1975), 71–72.

[110]Ronald C. Dillehay and Michael T. Nietzel, "Constructing a Science of Jury Behavior," in Ladd Wheeler and Phillip Shaver, eds., *Review of Personality and Social Psychology* (Beverly Hills, Calif.: Sage, 1980), vol. 1, 250.

[111]Bray and Kerr, op. cit., 209; Kessler, op. cit.; Rita James Simon, *The Jury and the Defense of Insanity* (Boston: Little, Brown, 1967), 38; Fred L. Strodtbeck, "Social Process, the Law, and Jury Functioning," in William M. Evan, ed., *Law and Sociology: Exploratory Essays* (New York: Free Press of Glencoe, 1962), 144–164.

[112]Norbert L. Kerr, David R. Nerenz, and David

Herrick, "Role Playing and the Study of Jury Behavior," *Sociological Methods and Research* 7 (1979), 337–355.

[113]Michael J. Saks and Reid Hastie, *Social Psychology in Court* (New York: Van Nostrand Reinhold, 1978), 93.

[114]Reid Hastie, Steven D. Penrod, and Nancy Pennington, *Inside the Jury* (Cambridge: Harvard University Press, 1983), 24.

[115]Saks and Hastie, op. cit., 93.

[116]Charles H. Hawkins, "Interaction Rates of Jurors Aligned in Factions," *American Sociological Review* 27 (1962), 689–691.

[117]Rita M. James, "Status and Competence of Jurors," *American Journal of Sociology* 69 (1959), 563–570.

[118]Hastie, Penrod, and Pennington, op. cit., 83–98.

[119]Reid Hastie, Steven D. Penrod, and Nancy Pennington, "What Goes On In a Jury Deliberation," *American Bar Association Journal* 69 (1983), 1848–1849.

[120]Forston, "Sense and Non-Sense," 609–612.

[121]Diane L. Bridgeman and David Marlowe, "Jury Decision Making: An Empirical Study on Actual Felony Trials," *Journal of Applied Psychology* 64 (1979), 91–98.

[122]Gerald R. Miller and Norman E. Fontes, *Real Versus Reel: What's the Verdict? The Effects of Videotaped Court Materials on Juror Response* (Final Report, NSF-RANN Grant APR75–15815, 1978).

[123]Harry Kalven, Jr., "The Jury, the Law, and the Personal Injury Damage Award," *Ohio State Law Journal* 19 (1958), 158–178.

[124]Saks and Hastie, op. cit., 94.

[125]Charles H. Hawkins, "Interaction and Coalition Realignments in Consensus-Seeking Groups: A Study of Experimental Jury Deliberation," Ph.D. diss. (Chicago: University of Chicago, 1960).

[126]Fred L. Strodtbeck, Rita M. James, and Charles Hawkins, "Social Status in Jury Deliberations," *American Sociological Review* 22 (1957), 713–719.

[127]Edward Burke Arnolds and Thomas Sannito, "Jury Study Results Part II: Making Use of the Findings," *Trial Diplomacy Journal* (Summer 1982), 15; Bridgeman and Marlowe, op. cit.; Strodtbeck, James, and Hawkins, op. cit.

[128]Hawkins, "Interaction and Coalition Realignments"; Fred L. Strodtbeck and L. Harmon Hook, "The Social Dimensions of a Twelve-Man Jury Table," *Sociometry* 24 (1961), 397–415.

[129]Rita J. Simon, *The Jury: Its Role in American Society* (Lexington, Mass.: Lexington Books, 1980), 42.

[130]In Kentucky, 89 percent of the forepersons are male, whereas males compose only 56 percent of the jurors who serve on trials. Ronald C. Dillehay and Michael T. Nietzel, "Juror Experience and Jury Verdicts," *Law and Human Behavior* 9 (1985), 179–191. See also Bray et al., op. cit.; Carol J. Mills and Wayne E. Bohannon, "Juror Characteristics: To What Extent Are They Related to Jury Verdicts?" *Judicature* 64 (1980), 22–31; Strodtbeck, James, and Hawkins, op.cit.

[131]Sannito and Arnolds, op. cit., 8.

[132]Hawkins, "Interaction and Coalition Realignments"; Sannito and Arnolds, op. cit.; Simon, *The Jury: Its Role in American Society,* op. cit.; Strodtbeck, James, and Hawkins, op. cit.

[133]Sannito and Arnolds, op. cit., 8.

[134]Dillehay and Nietzel, "Juror Experience and Verdicts," op. cit.; Kerr, "Effects of Prior Juror Experience on Juror Behavior, op. cit.; Norbert L. Kerr, Douglas L. Harmon, and James K. Graves, "Independence of Multiple Verdicts by Jurors and Juries," *Journal of Applied Social Psychology* 12 (1982), 12–29.

[135]Hawkins, "Interaction Rates of Jurors Aligned in Factions," op. cit., 689–690.

[136]Murray Levine, Michael P. Farrell, and Peter Perrotta, "The Impact of Rules of Jury Deliberation on Group Developmental Processes," in Bruce Dennis Sales, ed., *The Trial Process* (New York: Plenum, 1981), 263–304.

[137]John A. Call, "Psychology in Litigation," *Trial* (March 1985), 50; Hastie, Penrod, and Pennington, *Inside the Jury,* op. cit., p. 145.

[138]Hastie, Penrod, and Pennington, *Inside the Jury,* 146.

[139]Ralph M. Stogdill, "Personal Factors Associated With Leadership: A Survey of the Literature," *Journal of Personality and Social Psychology* 25 (1948), 35–71.

[140]Hawkins, "Interaction and Coalition Realignments," 26–27.

[141]Bridgeman and Marlowe, op. cit., 97; Hastie, Penrod, and Pennington, *Inside the Jury*, 145; Saks and Hastie, op. cit., 92.

[142]Fred L. Strodtbeck and Richard M. Lipinski, "Becoming First Among Equals: Moral Considerations in Jury Foremen Selection," Unpublished manuscript (1983).

[143]Steven Penrod and Reid Hastie, "A Computer Simulation of Jury Decision Making," *Psychological Review* 87 (1980), 133–159.

[144]Kalven and Zeisel, op. cit., 56–57; Penrod and Hastie, "Computer Simulation," op. cit.

[145]Leo J. Flynn, "Does Justice Fail When the Jury Is Deadlocked?" *Judicature* 61 (1977), 131.

[146]Ibid.

[147]Ibid., 133.

[148]Robert F. Bales and Fred Strodtbeck, "Phases in Group Problem-Solving," *Journal of Abnormal and Social Psychology* 46 (1975), 485–495; Warren G. Bennis and Herbert A. Shepard, "A Theory of Group Development," *Human Relations* 9 (1956), 415–437; B. Aubrey Fisher, "Decision-Emergence: Phases in Group Decision-Making," *Speech Monographs* 37 (1970), 53–66; Thomas Scheidel and Laura Crowell, "Idea Development in Small Discussion Groups," *Quarterly Journal of Speech* 50 (1964), 140–145.

[149]Garold Stasser, Norbert L. Kerr, and Robert M. Bray, "The Social Psychology of Jury Deliberations: Structure, Process and Product," in Norbert L. Kerr and Robert M. Bray, eds., *The Psychology of the Courtroom* (New York: Academic Press, 1982), 228.

[150]Philip K. Anthony and Edward M. Bodaken, "Jury Communication: Phases in the Deliberation Process," *Trial Diplomacy Journal* (Fall 1982), 23–24.

[151]Hastie, Penrod, and Pennington, *Inside the Jury*, 163–165.

[152]Anthony and Bodaken, op. cit., 24–25.

[153]Saks and Hastie, op. cit., 96–97.

[154]Kalven and Zeisel, op. cit., 488.

[155]Hastie, Penrod, and Pennington, "What Goes On," 1848.

[156]Hastie, Penrod, and Pennington, *Inside the Jury*, 166.

[157]Steven Penrod and Reid Hastie, "Models of Jury Decision Making," *Psychological Bulletin* 86 (1979), 462–492.

[158]Penrod and Hastie, "A Computer Simulation," op. cit.

[159]Anthony and Bodaken, op. cit., 25.

[160]Ibid.

[161]James H. Davis, "Group Decision and Social Interaction: A Theory of Social Decision Schemes, *Psychological Review* 80 (1973), 97–125; Hawkins, "Interaction Rates," op. cit.; Hastie, Penrod and Pennington, *Inside the Jury*, chap. 6.

[162]Hastie, Penrod, and Pennington, *Inside the Jury*, 166–167.

[163]Hastie, Penrod, and Pennington, *Inside the Jury*, 166.

[164]Thomas Sannito, *A Psychologist's Voir Dire* (Dubuque, Iowa: Forensic Psychologists, 1979), 20.

[165]Hastie, Penrod, and Pennington, *Inside the Jury*, 149.

[166]Several mathematical models have evolved to account for communication networking processes in juries. These models can predict verdicts with considerable accuracy. The predictions are based on the model's understanding of group decision-making processes. See W. Lance Bennett, "Storytelling in Criminal Trials: A Model of Social Judgment," *Quarterly Journal of Speech* 64 (1978), 1–22; Alan E. Gelfand and Herbert Solomon, "Analyzing the Decision-Making Process of the American Jury," *Journal of the American Statistical Association* 70 (1975), 305–309; Alan E. Gelfand and Herbert Solomon, "Modeling Jury Verdicts in the American Legal System," *Journal of the American Statistical Association* 69 (1974), 32–37; Alan E. Gelfand and Herbert Solomon, "A Study of Poisson's Models for Jury Verdict in Criminal and Civil Trials," *Journal of the American Statistical Association* 68 (1973), 241–278; Martin F. Kaplan, "A Model of Information Integration in Jury Deliberation," *Academic Psychology Bulletin* 5 (1983), 91–96; Alvin K. Klevorick and Michael Rothschild, *A Model of the Jury Decision Process* (New Haven: Cowles Foundation for Research in Economics at Yale University, 1983); Alvin K. Klevorick, Michael Rothschild, and Christopher Winship, *Information Processing and Jury Decision*

Making (New Haven: Cowles Foundation for Research in Economics at Yale University, 1982); Stuart S. Nagel and Marian G. Neef, *Decision Theory and the Legal Process* (Lexington, Mass.: Lexington Books, 1979); Nancy Pennington and Reid Hastie, "Juror Decision-Making Models: The Generalization Gap," *Psychological Bulletin* 89 (1981), 246–287; Penrod and Hastie, "Models of Jury Decision Making," op. cit.; Steven Penrod, "Mathemetical and Computer Models of Jury Decision Making," in H. H. Blumberg et al., eds., *Small Groups and Social Interaction* (New York: John Wiley, 1983), vol. 2, 47–56; Penrod and Hastie, "A Computer Simulation," op. cit.; Sarah Tanford and Steven Penrod, "Computer Modeling of Influence in the Jury: The Role of the Consistent Juror," *Social Psychology Quarterly* 46 (1983), 200–212.

[167]Sir Patrick Devlin, *Trial by Jury* (London: Stevens and Sons, 1956), 48.

[168]Laird C. Kirkpatrick, "Should Jury Verdicts Be Unanimous in Criminal Cases?" *Oregon Law Review* 47 (1968), 418.

[169]Robert D. Foss, "Structural Effects in Simulated Jury Decision Making," *Journal of Personality and Social Psychology* 40 (1981), 1055–1062; Norbert L. Kerr et al., "Guilt Beyond a Reasonable Doubt: Effects of Concept Definition and Assigned Decision Rule on the Judgments of Mock Jurors," *Journal of Personality and Social Psychology* 34 (1976), 282–294; Alice M. Padawer-Singer, Andrew N. Singer, and Rickie L. J. Singer, "An Experimental Study of Twelve vs. Six Member Juries Under Unanimous vs. Nonunanimous Decisions," in Bruce Dennis Sales, ed., *Psychology in the Legal Process* (Jamaica, N.Y.: Spectrum, 1977), 77–86; Saks and Hastie, op. cit., 84.

[170]Kalven and Zeisel, op. cit., 461.

[171]Van Dyke, op. cit., 209.

[172]*Apodaca v. Oregon,* 406 U.S. 404 (1972); *Johnson v. Louisiana,* 406 U.S. 356 (1972).

[173]Charlan Nemeth, "Rules Governing Jury Deliberations: A Consideration of Recent Changes," in Gordon Bermant, Charlan Nemeth, and Neil Vidmar, eds., *Psychology and the Law* (Lexington, Mass.: Lexington Books, 1976), 178, 181.

[174]"Constitutional Law—Jury Unanimity No Longer Required in State Criminal Trials," *North Carolina Law Review* 51 (1972), 134–145.

[175]William Haralson, "Unanimous Jury Verdicts in Criminal Cases," *Mississippi Law Journal* 21 (1950), 185–202; Kirkpatrick, op. cit., 419–420.

[176]S. E. Asch, "Effects of Group Pressure Upon the Modification and Distortion of Judgments," in G. E. Swanson, Theodore M. Newcombe, and Eugene L. Hartley, eds., *Readings in Social Psychology* (New York: Holt, 1952), 2–10; Kalven and Zeisel, op. cit., 462–463.

[177]Charles Kellogg Burdick, "Criminal Justice in America: Possibilities of Improvement by Statutory Changes and Constitutional Amendments Affecting Procedure," *American Bar Association Journal* 11 (1925), 510–515; Keith Mossman, "Justice and Numbers," *Trial* (November–December 1974), 25.

[178]Alec Samuels, "Criminal Justice Act," *Modern Law Review* 31 (1968), 24.

[179]Robert M. Brady, "The Jury: Is It Viable?" *Suffolk University Law Review* 6 (1971–72), 912; Van Dyke, op. cit., 210.

[180]Ruth B. Ginsburg, "Special Findings and Jury Unanimity in the Federal Courts," *Columbia Law Review* 65 (1965), 268.

[181]Kirkpatrick, op. cit., 421–422.

[182]Robert Buckhout et al., "Jury Verdicts: Comparison of Six Versus Twelve Person Juries and Unanimous Versus Majority Decision Rule in a Murder Trial," *Bulletin of the Psychonomic Society* 10 (1977), 175–178; Foss, op. cit.

[183]Hastie, Penrod, and Pennington, "What Goes On," 1850; Nemeth, op. cit., 178.

[184]Michael J. Saks, *Jury Verdicts: The Role of Group Size and Social Decision Rule* (Lexington, Mass.: D. C. Heath, 1977), 92–94.

[185]Robert M. Bray, "Decision Rules, Attitude Similarity, and Jury Decision-Making," Ph.D. diss. (Urbana: University of Illinois, 1974); James H. Davis et al., "The Decision Process of 6- and 12-Person Mock Juries Assigned Unanimous and Two-Thirds Majority Rules," *Journal of Personality and Social Psychology* 32 (1975), 1–14; Bernard Grofman, "The Slippery Slope: Jury Size and Jury Verdict Requirements—Legal and Social Science Applications," *Law and Policy Quarterly* 2 (1980),

293; Valerie P. Hans, "The Effects of the Unanimity Requirements on Group Decision Processes in Simulated Juries," Ph.D. diss. (Toronto: University of Toronto, 1978); Hastie, Penrod, and Pennington, "What Goes On," 1850; Kerr et al., "Guilt Beyond a Reasonable Doubt," op. cit.; Nemeth, op. cit., 171; Pawader-Singer, Singer, and Singer, op. cit.; Saks, op. cit., 98–99.

[186] Buckhout et al., op. cit.

[187] Broeder, "The University of Chicago Jury Project," op. cit.

[188] W. James Kronzer and John N. O'Quinn, "Let's Return to Majority Rule in Civil Jury Cases," in Glenn R. Winters, ed., Selected Readings: The Jury (Chicago: American Judicature Society, 1971), 77.

[189] Anthony A. Morano, "Retreat From Unanimity and Reasonable Doubt in Criminal Cases," University of Toledo Law Review 1969 (1969), 337–347; "In the Wake of Apodaca v. Oregon: A Case for Retaining Unanimous Jury Verdicts," Notes, Valparaiso University Law Review 7 (1973), 249–264.

[190] Charlan Nemeth, "Interaction Between Jurors as a Function of Majority v. Unanimity Decision Rules," Journal of Applied Social Psychology 7 (1977), 38–56; Saks, op. cit., 95.

[191] In 1981, 29 states permitted less-than-unanimous votes in certain civil cases. Five states allowed nonunanimous decisions in some criminal cases.

[192] J. Gordon Forester, Jr., "Return the 12-Man Jury," Litigation (Summer 1984), 4; Edward Thompson, "Six Will Do," Trial (November–December 1974), 14.

[193] Williams v. Florida, 399 U.S. 78, 90 S.Ct. 1893 (1970); Colgrove v. Battin, 413 U.S. 149, 93 S.Ct. 2448 (1973).

[194] Gordon Bermant and Rob Coppock, "Outcomes of Six- and Twelve-Member Jury Trials: An Analysis of 128 Civil Cases in the State of Washington," Washington Law Review 48 (1973), 593–596; Philip M. Cronin, "Six-Member Juries in District Courts," Boston Bar Journal (April 1958), 27–29; Shari S. Diamond, "A Jury Experiment Reanalyzed," University of Michigan Journal of Law Reform 7 (1974), 520–532; Grofman, "Recent Supreme Court Cases," op. cit.; Richard O. Lempert, "Undiscovering

'Nondiscernible Differences': Empirical Research and the Jury Size Cases," Michigan Law Review 73 (1975), 643–708; Lawrence R. Mills, "Six-Member and Twelve-Member Juries: An Empirical Study of Trial Results," University of Michigan Journal of Law Reform 6 (1973), 671–711; L. Craig Parker, Jr., Legal Psychology (Springfield, Ill.: Charles C. Thomas, 1980), 130–142; R. H. Phillips, "A Jury of Six in All Cases," Connecticut Bar Journal 30 (1956), 354; Albert M. Rosenblatt and Julia C. Rosenblatt, "Six-Member Juries in Criminal Cases: Legal and Psychological Considerations," St. John's Law Review 47 (1973), 615–633; Michael J. Saks, "Ignorance of Science Is No Excuse," Trial (November–December 1974), 18–20; Saks and Hastie, op. cit., 76–83; "Six-Member Juries Tried in Massachusetts District Court," Journal of the American Judicature Society 42 (1958), 136; Peter W. Sperlich, " . . . And Then There Were Six: The Decline of the American Jury" Judicature 63 (1980), 262–279; Edward A. Tamm, "The Five-Man Civil Jury: A Proposed Constitutional Amendment," in Glenn R. Winters, ed., Selected Readings: The Jury (Chicago: American Judicature Society, 1971), 30–39; David A. Vollrath and James H. Davis, "Jury Size and Decision Rule," in Simon, The Jury: Its Role, 73–106; David F. Walbert, "The Effect of Jury Size on the Probability of Conviction: An Evaluation of Williams v. Florida," Case Western Reserve Law Review 22 (1971), 529–554; Lloyd L. Wiehl, "The Six-Man Jury," Gonzaga Law Review 4 (1968), 35–44; Hans Zeisel, "Twelve Is Just," Trial 10 (November–December 1974), 13–15; Hans Zeisel and Shari Seidman Diamond, "'Convincing Empirical Evidence' on the Six-Member Jury," University of Chicago Law Review 41 (1974), 281–295.

[195] Saks, Jury Verdicts, op. cit., 37–38.

[196] Ballew v. Georgia, 435 U.S. 223, 89 S.Ct. 1029 (1978).

[197] David M. Powell, "Reducing the Size of Juries," Journal of Law Reform 5 (197), 87–108; Edward Thompson, "What Is the Magic of Twelve?" Judges' Journal (October 1971), 88.

[198] Edward J. Devitt, "Six-Member Civil Juries Gain Backing," American Bar Association Journal 57 (1971), 1111–1113.

[199] William R. Pabst, Jr., "Statistical Studies of the

Costs of Six-Man Versus Twelve-Man Juries," *William and Mary Law Review* 14 (1972), 372; William R. Pabst, Jr., "What Do Six-Member Juries Really Save?" *Judicature* (June–July 1973), 6.

[200]Irving R. Kaufman, "Harbingers of Jury Reform," *American Bar Association Journal* 58 (1972), 696.

[201]Hare, op. cit.; John R. Snortum, Jeff S. Klein, and Wynn A. Sherman, "The Import of an Aggressive Juror in Six- and Twelve-Member Juries," *Criminal Justice and Behavior* 3 (1976), 255–262.

[202]Robert F. Bales, *Interaction Process Analysis: A Method for the Study of Small Groups* (Reading, Mass.: Addison-Wesley, 1950); Robert F. Bales and Edgar F. Borgatta, "Size of Group as a Factor in the Interaction Profile," in A. Paul Hare, Edgar F. Borgatta, and Robert F. Bales, eds., *Small Groups: Studies in Social Interaction* (New York: Knopf, 1955); Philip E. Slater, "Contrasting Correlates of Group Size," *Sociometry* 21 (1958), 129–139.

[203]Saks, *Jury Verdicts,* 78–80; Strodtbeck, James, and Hawkins, op. cit.

[204]Kessler, "An Empirical Study," op. cit.

[205]Saks, *Jury Verdicts,* 81; Strodtbeck, James, and Hawkins, op. cit.; Edwin J. Thomas and Clinton J. Fink, "Effects of Group Size," *Psychological Bulletin* 60 (1963), 371–384.

[206]Saks, *Jury Verdicts,* 89–90.

[207]Norbert L. Kerr and Robert J. MacCoun, "The Effects of Jury Size and Polling Method on the Process and Product of Jury Deliberation," *Journal of Personality and Social Psychology* 48 (1985), 349–363; Padawer-Singer, Singer, and Singer, op.

cit.; Michael J. Saks and Thomas M. Ostrom, "Jury Size and Consensus Requirements: The Laws of Probability v. The Laws of the Land," *Journal of Contemporary Law* 1 (1975), 163–173; Angelo C. Valenti and Leslie L. Downing, "Differential Effects of Jury Size on Verdicts Following Deliberation as a Function of the Apparent Guilt of a Defendant," *Journal of Personality and Social Psychology* 32 (1975), 655–663.

[208]Hans Zeisel, " . . . And then There Were None: The Diminution of the Federal Jury," *University of Chicago Law Review* 38 (1971), 710–724.

[209]Saks, *Jury Verdicts,* 90–91.

[210]Padawer-Singer, Singer, and Singer, op. cit.

[211]Bermant and Coppock, op. cit.; Kessler, "An Empirical Study, op. cit.; Mills, op. cit.

[212]Beiser and Varrin, "Six-Member Juries in the Federal Courts," *Judicature* 58 (1975), 424–433.

[213]Davis et al., "Decision Processes of Mock Juries," op. cit.; Alice M. Padawer-Singer and Allan H. Barton, "Experimental Study of Decision-Making in the Twelve- Versus Six-Man Jury Under Unanimous Versus Non-Unanimous Decisions," Unpublished paper (New York: Columbia University Bureau of Applied Social Research, 1975).

[214]Saks, *Jury Verdicts,* 86–87.

[215]Justice Marshall in *Williams v. Florida,* op. cit.

[216]*Burch v. Louisiana,* 99 S.Ct. 1623 (1979).

[217]Saks, *Jury Verdicts,* 107–108; Saks and Hastie, op. cit., 87–88.

[218]Simon, *The Jury: Its Role,* 52.

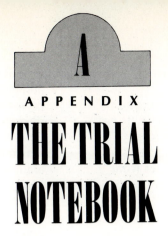

THE TRIAL NOTEBOOK

A trial notebook might include the following sections. Obviously, certain of these categories would be inappropriate in particular cases.

1. **Things to Do.**   A reminder of matters that require immediate attention.
2. **Checklist or Agenda.**   A list of the steps to be followed in preparing the case. As each step is taken, it is checked off. As other steps occur, they are added to the agenda. This becomes a blueprint for preparation for trial.
3. **Statement of Facts.**   Contains basic information, such as date, location, time, type of occurrence, diagram of the occurrence. They should be outlined in sufficient detail to explain the situation and answer anticipated inquiries. They may be in chronological order, in order of importance, or in the order in which witnesses will be presented at trial.
4. **Pleadings.**   The outlines of allegations by both sides. Place in columns. A summary of all issues.

5. **Jury Selection.**   Should contain key questions to be asked during voir dire. Should also identify the authority for asking certain questions. A chart with information about each juror should be provided.
6. **The Law.**   Notes on propositions of law and how they control the facts in the case. Note citations supporting each proposition. This is a handy reference in support of theories for such matters as admissions of proof.
7. **Witnesses.**   A sheet listing all possible witnesses, plus a separate sheet for each witness who will appear at trial. Background information and the nature of their testimony are needed. Outline key questions that should be asked. Opposite key questions should be citations referring to the law of the case.
8. **Opening Statement Notes.**   Outline of what should be covered in opening remarks. Also include what opposing counsel says in opening remarks.
9. **Direct Examination Sheets.**   A record of everything you must elicit from your

witnesses in the order in which you will elicit it.

10. **Cross-Examination Sheets.** Notes on each witness from the other side. These notes should focus on what cross-examination questions should be asked.

11. **Depositions and Interrogatories from Discovery.** Notes and outlines of the discovery depositions and interrogatories that have been taken and can be used.

12. **Motions.** Notes made about all motions filed before and during the trial. Responses to those motions and orders should be included.

13. **Exhibits.** A list of exhibits, numbered and described (e.g., bills, receipts, correspondence, maps, photographs, diagrams).

14. **Final Argument Notes.** Blank sheets on which to jot down ideas about closing argument during preparation and trial.

15. **Instructions.** Notes regarding anticipated requested instructions, or requests to charge the jury, that will be presented to the court.

16. **Index and Cross-Indexes.** The nature of the case will determine how complex these should be. In huge cases nowadays, computer experts program this material.

APPENDIX

CHECKLIST FOR PREPARING A WITNESS FOR A DISCOVERY DEPOSITION

I. Importance of the Deposition
II. The Proceedings
   A. Location of the deposition
   B. Persons Present
      1. You
      2. Attorneys for each party
      3. Court reporter
   C. Sequence of events
      1. Administration of oath
      2. Questions by opposing counsel
      3. Objections
      4. Possible cross-examination
      5. Termination
   D. Events after the deposition
      1. Interval for transcribing the testimony
      2. Reading, correction, signing, and filing of the transcript
      3. Possible later use of the deposition
III. Suggestions for Testifying
   A. Tell the truth
   B. When answering, do as follows:
      1. Listen carefully
      2. Study the questions carefully and think through answers
      3. Give no more and no less than asked; be concise
      4. Do not volunteer information
      5. Insist on finishing your answer
      6. Don't exaggerate
      7. Admit ignorance when necessary
      8. Ask for explanation of questions you don't understand
      9. Use words, not nods or gestures
   C. Scrutinize documents shown during the deposition carefully
   D. Avoid the following:
      1. Nervousness and fear
      2. Anger
      3. Sarcasm
      4. Arguing
      5. Speculation
      6. Interrupting
   E. If necessary, consult with counsel before answering
   F. If necessary, talk "off the record"
IV. Miscellany
   A. Wear what you would to court; present your best appearance
   B. Speak slowly and enunciate clearly
   C. Maintain a pleasant demeanor

SAMPLE INTERROGATORIES TO A DEFENDANT

1. What are the names and addresses of all persons with knowledge of the accident that gave rise to this cause of action?
2. Were any photographs taken at the scene of the accident or at any time subsequent to the accident?
3. What is the name and address of the registered owner of the automobile being driven by you at the time of the accident?
4. Does any person other than the registered owner have a claim to the legal ownership of the automobile driven by you at the time of the accident?
5. If you are not the owner of the vehicle in question, was the automobile being driven by you with the knowledge and permission of the owner?

SPECIMEN OF VOIR DIRE QUESTIONS

The following series is a complete voir dire examination of one prospective juror by a judge, a defense attorney, and a prosecuting attorney in a murder trial. The examination is a hypothetical one. In the case, the defendant has pleaded not guilty to the charge of murdering a police officer. Notice the use of objections and a challenge for cause.

The Clerk: Thomas M. Blair, do you solemnly swear that you will truly answer the questions asked you, touching upon your qualifications to act as a trial juror in the case now pending before this court?

Mr. Blair: Yes.

Judge: Mr. Blair, do you live in Middlevale?

Blair: Yes.

Judge: Before you came into court today for jury service, had you heard anything concerning this case?

Blair: If I did, I don't recall.

Judge: At this time do you have an open mind with regard to the question of the defendant's guilt or innocence?

Blair: Yes, I do, but I don't know if I would be allowed to serve on the jury. I have a cousin who is a policeman.

Judge: Where does he work?

Blair: In Centertown.

Judge: Is he in any way connected with this case?

Blair: No.

Judge: All right. Do you know anyone in the district attorney's office of this county?

Blair: No.

Judge: Do you know the defense counsel who is seated here?

Blair: No, sir.

Judge: Do you have any quarrel in your own mind with the fundamental proposition, which applies to all criminal cases, that the defendants on trial are presumed to be innocent and are entitled to be found not guilty, unless the jurors find from the evidence that their guilt has been established beyond a reasonable doubt? Do you have any quarrel with that in your own mind?

Blair: No.

Judge: If you are selected as a juror in this case, will you give to the defendant on trial here the full benefit of that presumption and require that degree of proof before you vote guilty?

Blair: Yes.

Judge: Do you entertain any conscientious opinion concerning the death penalty that would cause you to be unable to find a defendant guilty of murder in the first degree even if the evidence should justify such a finding?

Blair: If evidence existed that would cause me to find a person guilty, I would. But I'm somewhat opposed to capital punishment.

Judge: Would your opposition to capital punishment deter you from returning a verdict of murder in the first degree?

Blair: No.

Judge: Then we get past that point and you, as a juror, now have to determine the penalty. Could you impose the death penalty?

Blair: I think so.

Judge: Do you know of any reason why you could not act as a fair and impartial juror in this case if selected?

Blair: No.

Judge: Thank you. Mr. Defense Attorney, do you have additional questions?

Defense: Thank you, Your Honor. Mr. Blair, what is your wife's occupation?

Blair: My wife is a bookkeeper.

Defense: By whom is she employed?

Blair: She's at the nearby army base. She's a civil servant there.

Defense: How long has she been employed by the federal government?

Blair: Six or seven years.

Defense: Has she ever been involved in law enforcement work?

Blair: No.

Defense: Is she a member of any organization, or are you a member of any organization, that is dedicated to the betterment of the law or the more effective enforcement of the law?

Blair: No.

Defense: Are you or is she a member of any law enforcement or auxiliary law enforcement organization?

Blair: No.

Defense: Now, you did mention, Mr. Blair, that you have a cousin who is a patrolman. Is that correct?

Blair: Yes.

Defense: Have you had occasion to take any particular interest in his work? What he does? What his duties are?

Blair: No.

Defense: Does he visit your home frequently or do you visit his home?

Blair: On occasion.

Defense: And on the occasion of these visits, have you gotten involved in any conversations concerning any of his specific cases or arrests or any gun battles he might have been involved in, anything like that?

Blair: Nothing extensive, no.

Defense: Now, I cannot recall, but did you state to the Court that you do recall something about this case that we are discussing here today?

Blair: No, but there is a point I would like to mention. My mind is kind of ill at ease about something that I said earlier, and that's the death penalty. I would have difficulty on that. I would have difficulty requesting anything stronger than life imprisonment.

Defense: Mr. Blair, as long as that has come up, let me ask you this question. You have already heard the Court ask Mr. Franklin if he could follow the law as the Court gives it to him and if he could apply the law to the facts in rendering a verdict. Do you recall that?

Blair: Yes.

Defense: Mr. Franklin said he could. Now, if you are selected as a trial juror in this case, you will be sworn as a juror to discharge your duties. And one of those duties is to follow the law as the Court gives it to you. So the question really is, if the Court advised you that if you found certain facts to be true, you must return a verdict of first-degree murder, could you follow that law, even though you might have some problem as far as the death penalty is concerned?

Blair: I could return a verdict of first-degree murder if the evidence showed that.

Defense: All right. Now, the next step, then, Mr. Blair. You're still under oath as a juror, and if the jury has found that the verdict should be first-degree murder, then we reach the penalty phase. If, under the instructions from the Court and under all the evidence, you felt that the case called for a death penalty, could you vote that even though you might oppose it?

Blair: I honestly don't know. I would find it difficult. I don't know.

Defense: I take it that you are uncertain but that you would have to assess the whole situation at that time and then decide, is that correct?

Blair: I guess so. I would find it difficult.

Defense: Now, Mr. Blair, turning to the fact that you have a cousin who is a member of a police department; because you have become somewhat interested in his work, which is of course natural, do you feel that the interest would make it more difficult for you to weigh the evidence and apply the law as the Court gives it to you and to guarantee to the defendants their presumption of innocence, because it's this kind of case?

Blair: No, I don't believe so.

Defense: In other words, the fact that a police officer was involved here would not make you tend to place some greater burden upon the defendants here than otherwise might be the case, is that correct?

Blair: I don't think so. No.

Defense: I take it, then, that the mere fact that the defendants have been charged with a crime in this case does not lead you to believe that it's likely that they're guilty of the crime.

Blair: No.

Defense: That's up to the evidence and up to the law as the Court gives it to you, is that correct?

Blair: Yes.

Defense: I have no further questions to ask Mr. Blair at this time, Your Honor.

Judge: Mr. Prosecutor, you may proceed.

Prosecutor: Now, Mr. Blair, you indicated that you have some difficulty with imposing the death sentence.

Blair: That's right.

Prosecutor: Now, concerning that, have you belonged to any organizations that have advocated the abolition of the death penalty?

Blair: No. It's just a personal feeling.

Prosecutor: It would be a rather difficult decision to make, would it not?

Blair: Yes, it would.

Prosecutor: Almost any decision a juror would have to make concerning life or death would be an important, difficult decision, would it not?

Blair: Yes.

Prosecutor: Now, you indicated that you think you would have some difficulty.

Blair: That's right.

Prosecutor: Does that, in your mind, make you feel that because of that you would have difficulty bringing in a first-degree murder verdict?

Blair: No.

Prosecutor: Do you think you can totally divorce the question of penalty from the question of guilt?

Blair: I think so. If the evidence shows that a person is guilty, I think they should be punished. However, as far as the death penalty goes, if I were to try and impose it on somebody, I would feel a bit like a murderer myself, quite frankly. If I were responsible for sending somebody to the gas chamber and they died, I would feel like a murderer.

Prosecutor: If you would feel that way, then do you think you could give the People a fair trial on that question?

Blair: On guilt or innocence, yes; but I sincerely hope they would get life imprisonment.

Prosecutor: You would hope that?

Blair: Yes.

Prosecutor: But what happens, Mr. Blair, when you are in the jury room and eleven of the other jurors feel this is a proper case for the imposition of the death penalty? There is no question in their minds, after hearing the background and history of the defendant, that this is a proper case for the death penalty. There are 11 jurors voting for death, and there's you, who has told me that you think it would be difficult. I want to know, for the benefit of the people of our state, whether it would be impossible.

Blair: I'd find it hard to live with.

Prosecutor: I realize that. It's a difficult decision. It's an unpleasant decision. You would find it hard to live with. The question is, Could you do it? You would have to come down into the open courtroom, Mr. Blair, and face that individual sitting over there, and tell him that for the murder of a policeman, he is to die.

Defense: I object, Your Honor. That's not necessarily true. It depends on what he hears.

Judge: The objection is sustained with the question in that form.

Prosecutor: Let me rephrase it. If the jury brings in a first-degree murder verdict, the question to you, Mr. Blair, is, Do you feel that you could come down into the courtroom and state your opinion in open court that the penalty for first-degree murder is death? Could you do that?

Blair: I don't think so.

Prosecutor: And is it fair to say, Mr. Blair, that, in your present state of mind, you just feel that life imprisonment should be the punishment, and you just couldn't bring in the death penalty?

Blair: I would find it most unpleasant. I think capital punishment should be abolished.

Prosecutor: Can you conceive of a case where, even though it would be most unpleasant to you, you could come into this courtroom and state your verdict in open court that this defendant should die, even though it would be unpleasant?

Defense: Your Honor, I object to that. I don't think that's the question at all, what Mr. Blair could or could not state in open court. That is asking him to speculate. The question is what he could vote for in this case.

Judge: What is meant by this question is that when the jury does reach a verdict and comes into court, each side has the right to poll the jury, that is, to ask each juror if the verdict rendered is the verdict that you voted for. And the question is, Could you conceive of any facts in the case that would cause you to vote for the death penalty and then come into court and, being asked if that was your verdict, answer yes? Could you do that?

Blair: I don't think so.

Prosecutor: May I, Your Honor.

Judge: Yes.

Prosecutor: Mr. Blair, I am just trying to get you to understand that whether you think it's difficult or you don't think so, the question should be yes or no. If you don't think so, that leaves a possibility that perhaps you could. But if you're sure in your mind right now that you could not bring in the death sentence, will you please tell us?

Blair: I couldn't.

Prosecutor: Mr. Blair, are your opinions concerning the death penalty such that you would automatically refuse to impose it without regard to the evidence that might be developed during the trial of the case?

Blair: Yes.

Prosecutor: Thank you, Mr. Blair. Your Honor, we would challenge for cause.

Judge: The Court will allow the challenge. Mr. Blair will be excused. Thank you for attending, Mr. Blair. Will you please step down and take the slip that the bailiff will hand you, and return it to the jury commissioner's office for further instructions.

MODEL
OPENING STATEMENT

The following material, reprinted with the permission of the Court Practice Institute, is taken from Frederic G. Levin, "Strategy for Opening Statement: A Case Study," Trial Diplomacy Journal 4 (Fall 1981), 13–21, 55–64. Mr. Levin is a member of the Pensacola, Florida, law firm of Levin, Warfield, Middlebrooks, Mabie and Magie. His practice is limited to plaintiffs' personal injury law. He is a member of the Inner Circle of Advocates and is a Board Certified Civil Advocate of the National Board of Trial Advocacy. Mr. Levin has written numerous articles on trial tactics and insurance law and has lectured extensively on the same subjects.

On November 9, 1977, a Louisville & Nashville Railroad Company train derailed in Pensacola, Florida. Two tank cars carrying anhydrous ammonia ruptured, and the toxic gas leaked onto the nearby property of Dr. Jon Thorshov. As a result of inhaling the gas, Dr. and Mrs. Thorshov died and their two children were permanently injured.

The subsequent wrongful death action, *Thorshov v. Louisville & Nashville Railroad Company*, went to trial in February of 1980. On February 27, 1980, the jury returned verdicts totalling more than $18 million ($10 million of which was for punitive damages) for the deaths of Jon and Lloyda Thorshov. According to Frederic G. Levin, counsel for the plaintiffs, "The case was, for all practical purposes, over after the opening statements."

The plaintiffs' opening statement painted a picture of the defendants wearing black hats, and that was the image the defense labored under for the rest of the trial. To understand how this was accomplished, it is necessary to begin with a brief background of the case.

Pensacola has several major industrial plants which employ thousands, and which are dependent on rail transportation. The Louisville & Nashville (L&N) has served the Pensacola area since the mid-1800's. Starting in 1976, the L&N began having derailments in Escambia County, of which Pensacola is the county seat. The derailments became newsworthy when one caused a major rupture of an anyhdrous ammonia tank car in the north Escambia County area and several people were hospitalized as a result. Between the time of that accident and the deaths of Dr. and Mrs. Thorshov, the news media reported an average of one derailment every month. In one accident, thousands of residents had to be evacuated; another derailment caused an explosion of propane gas and a fire that lasted two days.

In numerous meetings between the City of Pensacola and L&N officials, the L&N maintained that there was no cause for alarm, that the tracks were in excellent condition.

In the summer of 1977, Doctor Jon Thorshov, age 38, his wife Lloyda, age 28, and their two children (Daisy, age three, and Gamgee, age one) moved to Pensacola. Dr. Thorshov entered into practice as a pathologist, at a salary of $55,000 per year. He was to become a partner after one year, and would have made about $100,000 after taxes in 1979 if he had lived. The Thorshov family was exemplary—the children had been left with a babysitter only once in their lives.

Within a week following the derailment and Dr. Thorshov's death, both the maternal grandparents (Hutchens) and the paternal grandparents (Thorshov), who were the personal representatives for the estate, hired the Pensacola law firm of Levin, Warfield, Middlebrooks, Mabie & Magie, P.A. to file suit against the L&N. The personal injury claims for the two children were severed from the two wrongful death claims.

Plaintiff's attorneys included Fred Levin, D. L. Middlebrooks and Dan Scarritt. Levin was chosen to handle the opening statement.

Levin realized that *Thorshov* was the "ultimate dream case" in many respects: substantial damages, clear liability and deep-pocketed defendants. "But, even the ultimate dream case has disadvantages," Levin heeded. Surprisingly, as the plaintiffs' team developed their theory, they found as many disadvantages in the case as advantages. "The purpose of an effective opening statement," according to Levin, "is to cover the disadvantages in the best light and at the same time present the advantages."

Many of the disadvantages Levin listed were similar to the problems faced in almost any civil case from the plaintiff's viewpoint. For example:

☐ Pensacola is a railroad town, and the community is extremely conservative. The jurors would not be naturally inclined to award large damages for a handsome, wealthy doctor and his beautiful wife.

☐ The facts of the accident were complex and technical.

☐ The jurors would not be sequestered, and the case was to be the most publicized civil case in Pensacola's history. TV cameras would be allowed in the courtroom, and all three networks would carry the trial.

☐ The defense team was led by Bert Lane, who had an impressive record of defense victories and was well liked by jurors because of his "good old boy," folksy way.

☐ Plaintiffs did not know prior to trial whether they would be permitted to discuss the facts of specific derailments which had occurred before November of 1977.

☐ "The Louisville & Nashville Railroad Company had several hundred employees living in the Pensacola area," Levin explained. "Many of these employees were 'old timers' who made excellent defense witnesses, since they would relate well to a local jury." On the other hand, plaintiffs' witnesses were well-educated, bright and quick.

☐ Seven years prior to the accident, the L&N Railroad had been taken over by the Seaboard Coastline Railroad. Several bright, young, educated executives came over from Seaboard Coastline (SCL) to run the L&N. These new L&N executives also made excellent witnesses.

☐ Railroad regulations require a railroad to accept every car sent over its line. The tank cars carrying anhydrous ammonia on November 9, 1977, were not owned by L&N, and did not have head shields (extra heavy pieces of metal placed at both ends of the tank cars), even though the federal government had passed a regulation requiring that all tank cars have head shields by January 1, 1980. Although head shields would not have prevented the derailment, they would have prevented the puncture of the two tank cars carrying anhydrous ammonia. It was evident that L&N would argue the commonsense position that had it not been for government regulations requiring the L&N to accept these tank cars on its line, the Thorshovs would not have died as a result of the derailment. The owner of the tank cars had not been sued in this case. Although this argument had no real basis in law, it was going to be appealing to the jury.

One of the greatest advantages the plaintiffs had was that "we knew more about the case than defense counsel," Levin told us. "The railroad was unwilling to hire any independent experts to explain how the accident occurred. The railroad relied on its own employees. Defense counsel's opinion as to how the accident actually occurred was limited to the opinion of L&N's own employees. We had hired independent experts, and therefore had a better view of what had actually occurred in the accident. By the time of trial, defense counsel sincerely believed that the railroad had done nothing wrong. This situation created an atmosphere in which we could destroy the defense with an effective opening statement."

Timing was crucial to Levin's opening statement. The defense would be hearing for the first time the plaintiffs' theory of how the accident happened, and Levin did not want to give them a chance to prepare their response. Levin's opening statement ended at 3:30 in the afternoon, and the defense was forced to proceed after only a ten minute break.

The following transcript, slightly edited for publication, is accompanied by Levin's comments in italics.

Mr. Levin: May it please the Court, counsel, Mr. and Mrs. Hutchens, Mr. and Mrs.

Thorshov, and you, ladies and gentlemen of this jury. What we lawyers are getting ready to do now is to make our opening statements. And it is here that we tell you what we expect the evidence in the case is going to be, and what we expect the judge is going to tell you the law is at the end of the case. But the opening statement itself is not evidence, and it is not law; it is lawyer talk.

The evidence is going to come to you from the witness stand, and the law is going to come to you from His Honor, the judge.

How many times has the plaintiffs' lawyer sat down after opening statement and heard the defense counsel say, "What you have just heard is lawyer talk"? The above remarks stole a little of the defendant's thunder. The plaintiffs' attorney should try to diffuse everything that he thinks the defense attorney wants to say in the defendant's opening statement. If counsel for the defendant is a likeable individual, an attempt should be made to cover every possible situation that plaintiffs' counsel believes the defendant will attempt to cover in defendant's opening. This will prevent defense counsel from using his likeable personality at the start of the case. Of course, the converse is likewise true: If defense counsel has an obnoxious personality, give him the opportunity to show it to the jury.

I would like to congratulate you. You eight people have been selected from what I believe is the largest panel of jurors ever called for a civil case. And the reason you were selected was because both sides of this case believe that you will be fair and unbiased, in other words, that you will judge this case solely on the evidence and the law.

Let the jury know just how important the case is. The purpose was to insinuate that the court believes that this must be a very large case or the court would not have called that many potential jurors.

I would like to reiterate what the judge has already told you and what he will tell you every evening. And that is if you are watching television or reading a newspaper or listening to a radio, if there is anything that comes on or that you see about this case, about railroads in general, about the L&N, please stop, turn it off, get away from it. If somebody wants to talk to you, whether it is your husband or your wife, parents, children, friends, neighbors, co-workers, tell them you cannot, just cannot talk about this case, because if the judge believes that maybe you will be influenced, he does have the power to sequester the jury. That means he has the power to lock the jury up, and nobody wants that. You don't, the judge doesn't, nor do the lawyers. So if anybody tries to talk to you or if you see anything, please just totally get away from it. Now, this case is going to last, in our opinion, somewhere between three weeks and a month. And it is going to be difficult not to hear things, so again, I urge you to please try to stay away from it.

We recognized that the jury selected in this case was an excellent plaintiff's jury. The case would last several weeks and the possibility existed that there could be another derailment during the trial. Such an event would be well publicized and could cause a mistrial. In fact, there was a derailment that occurred the day before closing arguments. In addition, we were deeply concerned that the jurors would be influenced by friends, neighbors, family, etc. A general rule to follow is that when asking for tremendous sums of money, outside influence will normally work to the disadvantage of the plaintiff.

On the defense side of this case for the L&N Railroad is, in my opinion, three of the finest defense railroad lawyers in the country. Mr. Bert Lane is the finest defense lawyer I have ever been up against, and he has been asked to come back out of retirement to try this case. His son Gary is an excellent trial lawyer, and Ms. Dawn Welch, in my opinion, is probably the brightest associate I have seen. But I am not telling you that to gain sympathy for us, because I feel like we are adequate to the task, we are certainly well prepared, and we believe that we are on the right side of the case. And no matter how good you are, you can't change the facts.

The purpose of the above was to stress the importance of the case and the fact that it was going to be a large case. Complimenting opposing counsel can be a very dangerous tactic if it is insincere. If opposing counsel is not competent, do not compliment him. The worst defeat I ever suffered in a courtroom was when I complimented defense counsel and defense counsel had totally wrecked the defendant's case. In that situation, the jury felt that I was making fun of counsel for the defendant, and the jury sympathized with him.

Now, on November 9, 1977, there was a derailment. Now, as a result of this derailment a young doctor and his lovely wife were killed and two children were very seriously injured. This case involves just the death action, the two cases, one for the death of Jon Thorshov and one for the death of Lloyda Thorshov. The injuries to the children are not being tried at this time. Their condition, though, is going to become important to you in deciding this case.

And you will understand what I mean when I say "condition" by the time I get through with the opening statement.

Again, I was attempting to steal some of the defendant's thunder. Defense counsel will certainly point out that there are other cases which involve the injuries to the two children. Also, this was an attempt to get the jury ready to understand that the condition of the children will be an issue in the case, whether or not their condition was caused by this accident.

Now, all of you, all of us have seen criminal cases on television and in the movies, and in those cases you see the criminal defense lawyers and they are exciting and there are all kind of surprises going on, and there is hidden evidence and tactics and delays. Well, that doesn't go on in a civil case. And it's unfortunate, but it's not going to be—we are friends, the lawyers are friends and there are not going to be any fistfights in the courtroom. I saw a movie just recently where the prosecution jumped up and beat the defense lawyer while the judge was trying to call order. That is not going to happen. There is not going to be any cursing in this courtroom. In other words, it is going to be a good, well-tried civil case for damages.

And, I know what must be going through your mind, "Oh, my God, we're going to be here a month listening to this dull civil case." But, if there ever was a civil case, if there ever was a case for damages that was made for television or made for the movies, it is going to be this one because it is going to run the gamut of emotions. When you think of love, and you are going to hear from the witness stand of the love that Jon had for Lloyda and that they had for their children, and it is a true love story. It is the thing that a movie would be made out of. Sympathy, you've got a young doctor and his attractive wife and two beautiful children, well-mannered children, and the doctor and his wife die a horrible death and the children are very seriously injured. And the evidence is going to tear at your heart when you hear the story—well, the psychiatrist will tell you about little Daisy Thorshov, six years old, who sleepwalks at night looking for her mommie and daddy, because she thinks that they were taken from her because she was a bad girl and they will come back if she is a good girl.

The trial is going to last several weeks and there will be a great deal of technical testi-mony. The purpose of the above was to tell the jury that the case will be interesting. If you tell someone that the movie they are getting ready to see is a good movie, it is more likely that they will enjoy the movie than if you had told them that it is a horrible movie.

I think as the evidence comes in you are gong to possibly feel disgust toward the railroad. This case—it's not just a simple little accident, it wasn't going too fast or not coming to a complete stop at a stop sign or maybe having a couple of drinks and driving off a road. No, I think you will find in this case that this was the worst stretch of track in the whole L&N system for serious derailments.

In a deposition of one of the defendant's employees, he mentions (out of context) the fact the Escambia County has been the worst area in the total L&N system for serious derailments. This comment was made in a very lengthy answer to a question propounded by plaintiffs' attorney. There were thousands of pages of depositions, and it was hoped that lead counsel for the defendant had no knowledge that the statement had been made. The reader will note that the comment is repeated several times in the opening statement. In the opening statement for the defendant, counsel made the mistake of saying, "The evidence will be that this section of track was one of the best sections of track on the total L&N Railroad system."

Now, I think you will find in this case that they just didn't care.

You're going to find the case interesting, and being normal people you are going to have normal emotions. But, a month from now when you go into that jury room, you have to leave your emotions behind because a jury room is no place for emotions. You have got to judge this case on the cold hard facts, the cold hard evidence, and the cold hard law. What I am saying to you is that we don't want any sympathy verdict. Now, again, I think what must be going through your minds, "Here Fred Levin is, he represents the family and he is telling us that they don't want a sympathy verdict. He must be pulling our leg." No, I am sincere when I tell you we don't want a sympathy verdict.

If the railroad was not at fault in this case, you took an oath, and I would hope that you would back up your oath and walk in that jury room and find zero damages for these children. But if the evidence justifies a verdict in the tens of millions of dollars, I hope that you will again abide by your oath and have the backbone to say, "I don't care, I'm going to put it down, because the evidence justifies it."

Now, we don't want a sympathy verdict because as the evidence comes in you will start to see that there are two different philosophies, two different theories. One is the emotional approach. We ought to find enough money to take care of these children to cover their needs for the rest of their lives. But that is not the law, that is a sympathy verdict. That is charity and we don't want charity. And the law says we're not entitled to get that. The other side of the coin is that you should award damages for the fair value of what has been taken, and there is a big difference between what these children need and the fair value of what has been taken from them.

Plaintiff should always tell the jury that he does not want a sympathy verdict. This is simply stealing defendant's thunder. The most important purpose of the above was to begin to explain to the jury the difference between "taking care of the children" and following the law and awarding "the fair value of what has been taken from the children." The natural tendency of a jury in a death case is to take care of those left behind. Sometimes, this can work to the advantage of the plaintiff. However, in this case, what was taken was substantially more than what the children needed.

For example, we believe that the evidence in this case will show that Jon Thorshov, the doctor, had he not been killed on November 9, 1977, and had he lived out his normal life expectancy, which would have been about 33 or 34 years from the date of the accident—approximately 31 years from now—that during that period of time, considering inflation, he would have made over $20,000,000. This will come to you from professors of economics. Well, children don't need that kind of money, and we know they don't need that kind of money. The law says, and you have taken an oath to follow the law, that you should award what you believe has been taken, which is the fair value of what has been taken from them.

The evidence in this case will show that Jon and Lloyda Thorshov were two of the finest parents that you could ever imagine. Those children, the two children were left with a babysitter one time in their life. They were left without at least one parent with them one time in their life. They were devoted to their children. Now, children don't need, they really don't need parents that are that devoted or that wonderful, but that is what has been taken from these children, and that is what you will be asked to replace. Now, at the end of this case we're going to ask you for approximately $12,000,000 for the compensatory damages, that is, the damages for what has been taken. And I am here to tell you that two children don't need $12,000,000, but if you find that that is the value of what has been taken, then you have taken an oath to award that kind of money. So, when I tell you that we don't want a sympathy verdict, we don't want charity, I am sincere. I want you, we ask you to follow the law.

Do you mention a dollar amount in the opening statement when you're going to talk about extremely large sums of money? In this case, we thought so. This case was going to re-

ceive tremendous publicity. It would have been impossible for the jurors to totally avoid the publicity. We felt that the media should refer to the case as a multimillion dollar case, and in order to do this, the figures needed to be mentioned in opening statement. In fact, every mention of the case included the adjective "multimillion dollar."

It was easy to discuss the amount we were requesting of $12,000,000 when reference could be made to the fact that the deceased would have earned over $20,000,000 during his lifetime. However, this is a dangerous tactic in some cases. For example, assume the case involved the death of a child. In such a case, it would probably be a mistake to mention that plaintiffs were demanding $3,000,000. That evening, when the juror gets home and mentions $3,000,000 to his or her spouse, neighbors, etc., someone is going to start talking about insurance rates, profiteering over the loss of a loved one, etc. As a general rule, mention substantial figures in opening statement only when it can be logically justified with actual economic losses.

Now, the judge is going to tell you that we have the burden of proof in this case, that is, the Thorshov family must prove their case to you by the greater weight of the evidence, and that means exactly what it says, greater weight, 51 percent of the evidence. I like to look at it as the scales of justice. On one side of the scales is our evidence, on the other side is theirs. Which weighs the most in your mind? If you would think about football, if there is a football score 21 to 20, the team that got 21 points wins. We don't have to wipe them out, we don't have to beat them 21 to nothing. In other words, it is simply the greater weight, 51 percent of the evidence. And we don't have to prove anything beyond a reasonable doubt because that is the test for a criminal case, and no matter what you do a month from now nobody is going to go to jail. It is not a criminal case, it is a civil case for damages.

Always tell the jury that no one is going to go to jail and that no one is going to lose their job because of the case and the verdict. Note that I forgot to mention that no one was going to lose his job. This proved to be a mistake. The case was against the L&N Railroad and the engineer. The engineer was a resident of Florida and was made a party to prevent the removal to Federal Court. When the jury returned a verdict in this case, it found against the railroad but found no negligence on the part of the engineer. As will be seen, a substantial part of the negligence attributed to the railroad was in the actual operation of the train by the engineer. The jury's finding for the engineer on the negligence count could have been critical had the case gone to an appellate court. Therefore, where appropriate, always tell the jury that the defendant is not going to lose his job, and that no one is going to go to jail.

Now, what is the evidence going to show? I think you are going to have to back up many, many years where the evidence starts in Minneapolis, Minnesota. Mr. and Mrs. Roy Thorshov. Mr. Thorshov was a very successful and *is* a very successful engineer and architect. They are Norwegian and his father before him was an architect-engineer, and it was expected that their son, that the Thorshov's son was going to be an architect-engineer. He was born on February 27, 1939. His name was Jon, J-o-n. At the start he was going to be an architect-engineer like his father, but by the time he got into the second or third grade he decided he was going to be a doctor. He was an outdoor-type boy, a loving boy, his family was very proud of him. He was extremely bright. You will see some poems that he wrote, and to be perfectly honest with you, half of the words in there I had to go look up in a dictionary. I mean, he was just an extremely bright young man. He graduated from the University of Minnesota High School, and then he went to the University of Minnesota College and graduated there, and then to the University of Minnesota Medical School where he graduated in 1964. He then joined the Air Force and he went into the Air Force and he continued his training, and he became licensed as a pathologist, a medical doctor with the United States Air Force.

(I am beginning the narrative which paints the plaintiffs with white hats.)

About ten years after Jon was born, in a little town called Rangely, Colorado, in the ranch area, Lloyd and Phillis Hutchens had a little girl. They came from a middle-class background, were not wealthy people, and they had this daughter, and her name was Lloyda, and it's L-l-o-y-d-a, and she was born on October 5, 1949. Now, she graduated from high school and did not go to college. She joined the Air Force and became an x-ray technician. And while they were both in the Air Force, the doctor in the doctor's office, and Lloyda in the x-ray office as a technician, they met each other and started dating and they fell in love. But as usual, what occurred was the doctor, or the officer, leaves town and she was left there at the Air Force base. Jon was shipped off to Germany, and he was in Germany about three weeks and got leave and decided that he loved her, came back to the states and got Lloyda, and said, "Marry me." She did and they took off and went to a judge's office and got married.

Pensacola is a military town. One of the jurors in this case was a very attractive, single lady in her late 20's. The typical situation in a military community is for the young officer to date the local beauties. Normally, the officer has a good time and then ships out, leaving the

young lady behind. The purpose of the above was to show that Dr. Thorshov was not the typical officer, and we hoped that this might have some effect upon the young, attractive female juror.

As soon as she got out of the Air Force she came to live with him in Germany, and about a little over a year after they got married their first child, Daisy, was born. And she was born November 12, 1973. And then about three years later on May 23, 1976, they had their first and only son Gamgee, which is G-a-m-g-e-e. Jon was then a lieutenant colonel in the Air Force. And then in 1977 an old friend of his, a very good friend of his, Dr. Michael O'Brien, called him, and Dr. O'Brien told him of an excellent opportunity here in Pensacola at the Medical Center Clinic. And Jon and Lloyda Thorshov came to Pensacola with the family, looked it over, and decided to accept the position. Within one year he would have been a partner in the Medical Center Clinic. He was that good. He joined the Medical Center as an associate on August 1, 1977. This was after he left the Air Force. He remained in the Air Force reserve.

Jon, Lloyda and the two children loved Pensacola. They bought a beautiful home out on Scenic Highway out overlooking Gull Point. It is up on a cliff and it overlooks Escambia Bay, and down below the cliff runs the railroad, and they loved the trains. Jon used to come home early so that they could take the children down to the cliff and look at the train come by. They did everything together; they went shopping together; they went to the movies together; everywhere they went the whole family went together. Jon built pens, he was an outdoor type, for rabbits and chickens for the children there at the home. The family was happy, they were making friends, and everybody who met them were impressed. They were impressed because they were the perfect family.

All but Gamgee were in excellent health. Jon and Lloyda and Daisy were in excellent health. Gamgee had been having some kidney problems with one kidney, and they were hopeful that with medication, possibly surgery, this would be corrected.

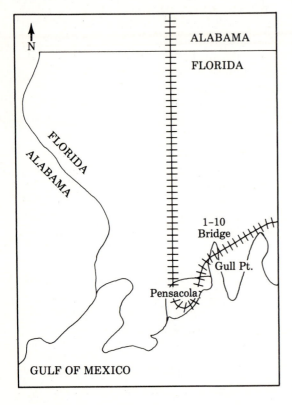

On Wednesday, November 9, 1977, Jon was off work, and as usual, he came home and the whole family went early Christmas shopping. The family automobile was a new pickup truck, it wasn't a Mercedes, it wasn't a Cadillac, but a new pickup truck for him and the family. And they went out shopping, and they came home about 5:00. Lloyda began preparing hamburgers for Jon and Daisy and Gamgee, and about 6:05 they heard the train coming north heading up toward the Escambia Bay trestle, coming toward Gull Point. The hamburgers were in the oven, there was vegetables on the stove and she was preparing the hamburger buns. Daisy was eating an apple, and on the radio was WMEZ. Anyhow, they were listening to WMEZ, easy listening music, and at that moment I cannot imagine that they felt that they were ever safer in their lives than they were at that particular moment, nor could they have felt that they could be any happier than they were at that particular moment.

The above was an attempt to bring the jury into the story that was being told. Note that several unimportant details are mentioned in the same manner that one would do in a normal conversation. Of course, the reference to the pickup truck, not being a Cadillac or a Mercedes, was made for the purpose of trying to show that this was not the typical wealthy doctor.

Now, we're going to have to back up again to pick up the evidence, except this time we have got to go way back, way before any of us were even born. Many, many years ago the L&N, or whatever it was called then, decided to run their tracks into Pensacola from Alabama. The railroad tracks, and I am not too good of an artist, but I am going to try as best I can, came out of Alabama, came south through Century and Molino and Barth and on into the, what they call the Goulding yards now, which is a little north, this is north up here (indicating), up Fairfield and came down into downtown Pensacola and then—well, they built the passenger station, which I will mark right here (indicating), it turned east. As the tracks continued it crosses Ninth Avenue, then the 14th Avenue crossing, then the 17th Avenue crossing, then that little trestle that goes over the Bayou on down the beach and then it swings back north, and it starts heading north up until it gets to Gull Point, and then it makes a sharp turn left and heads on up.

As I was giving the above directions, I was drawing a map on the board in order to make it more understandable for the jury. The significant parts of the above remarks were the references to Molino, Barth, and the 17th Avenue crossing. There had been a major derailment in the Barth area some time prior to the accident which injured a number of people. This particular derailment could not be referred to at trial. There had been another major derailment subsequent to the Gull Point derailment in Molino, which likewise could not be mentioned at trial. Also, there had been a major derailment at the 17th Avenue crossing which required the evacuation of thousands of people. Without mentioning the derailments, it was hoped that the jury would recall them by simply mentioning the area and writing the names of those areas on the board.

Now, it is underneath the Interstate to the Escambia Bay trestle which crosses over the Escambia Bay. And if the directions I had given you are correct, the railroad goes south then east then north until it gets to Gull Point and makes a sharp turn to the left and goes up.

Now, when we talk to the railroad people about direction, any time that train leaves Alabama and starts into Florida, no matter what direction it is going, it's heading south. So, when they are on the stand and they say, "Well the train, we were heading south, railroad south at the time," they were actually going north. Now, we will try to keep it straight and we will try to get them to remember that it is geographic north, heading north, even though it's railroad south. A lot of us who drive a lot realize that, for example, I guess the Pensacola Bay Bridge is actually north and south, but it's called 98 East and 98 West. Anyhow, when the train was going up around Gull Point, it was going geographic north, but the railroad people say it was going railroad south. It continues railroad south until it gets to

Chattahoochee, Florida, at a place called River Junction, which is the Chattahoochee River. And at that point the railroad tracks belong to the Seaboard Coastline Railroad, it's turned over to them.

The above was simply to give the background and to explain some railroad terminology. The opening statement is the place to explain any terminology problems.

For years passenger and freight trains came through Pensacola, and as a kid we used to wave at the engineer and he would blow his horn and at the station when the crew would get off, the passenger station, I remember, you used to look at them the way today in an airport you look at the airline crew, the captain and the co-captain, and the stewardess getting off, there was just this air about them. But times change and in the 1960's it became necessary to stop passenger service through here and we only had freight. And the L&N always made good money, it was always a good railroad. The tracks were well maintained. The old time railroad people wore their railroad caps with pride, and they wore those striped baseball type hats with the big red L&N.

The above was mentioned for the benefit of any jurors who felt close to the railroads. We knew that none of the jurors had any present connections with railroads or railroad employees. However, it was recognized that some of the jurors, especially the older ones, had to have had some connection with railroads or railroad employees in the past. This was simply an attempt to contrast the wonderful old railroad with what was now becoming a corporate giant that was only concerned with making money.

Now, while all of this was going on in Pensacola, over in Jacksonville, Florida, there were some other things occurring. There was a railroad called Seaboard Airline Railroad, and they had a bunch of bright young good college educated executives, and they got together with a railroad called the Atlantic Coastline Railroad and merged forming the Seaboard Coastline Railroad. And the Seaboard Coastline Railroad Company, or holding company, or whatever it is, started buying up other companies. And they called themselves the family company or the family line, and when we speak of the SCL, that is who we are talking about. And during this case you will hear us refer to the Seaboard Coastline Railroad or the SCL, and they started looking over toward the L&N because the L&N was very profitable, very well maintained, and its employees were very happy.

And in the 1960's they started buying up stock in the L&N and by December 31, 1971, they had 98.2 percent of the stock. And by early 1972 they had bought 100 percent, they had total control of the L&N Railroad.

1972 was a critical date, as would be shown by the testimony. In an economic analysis of the L&N, maintenance expenses took a tremendous drop in 1972 and continued on through 1977. As a practical matter, the Seaboard Coastline Railroad had control of the L&N since 1967. The purpose of the above was to stress the year 1972 as the year of the takeover. This was a very significant part of the theme of the case. We recognized that defense counsel did not understand the significance of the year 1972. Note that this was being woven into the general narrative about the background of the railroad. By the time defense counsel realized the significance of the takeover in 1972, it had been mentioned so many times in evidence that it was too late to do anything about it.

And then the Seaboard Coastline Railroad started sending the bright young executives over to Louisville to help run the L&N. And

they set down some new policies, and those policies were, "We need to save on maintenance. For every dollar you can save on maintaining our tracks, it moves over into profit."

Of course, the old time L&N people said, "What about our safety rules? They require that we spend a lot of money on maintenance." And they started talking about this, especially in this day and time when trains were getting heavier, the chemical cars were getting larger.

Mr. Lane: Your Honor, we object to this line of discussion. What the L&N spent on maintenance has absolutely nothing to do with this case except on that line of track that went around Gull Point; but what it spent in Louisville or Oregon or Chicago, or Atlanta, has absolutely nothing to do with this case.

The Court: Objection overruled.

Mr. Levin: And they began spending less and less money. And they, of course, like the old L&N people said, "What about our safety rules, and the old safety rules require that we spend money on maintenance because especially nowadays when the tracks were under heavy trains, heavy cars, chemicals, things like that." And most of these rules, these safety rules, are by the L&N and by the AAR—the AAR is the American Association of Railroads—and this organization consists of all the railroads in the country.

There were many rules and rulebooks developed by the L&N and the American Association of Railroads. The above is an attempt to distinguish between the old time L&N employees and the new young executive that came over from the Seaboard Coastline. As one can see, the theme of the case is starting to develop. We begin to see the picture of the money-grabbing corporate giant coming in and taking over this wonderful old railroad back in 1972. The attempt is to make the old time L&N employee an example of what is good about railroads. Note the technique of using an alleged conversation in the above. If the lawyer feels comfortable using this technique, it can be very effective.

Almost all of these rules concern preventing derailments. Now, a derailment is when a train leaves the track and most derailments occur in a curve. And most derailments are caused by a thing called lateral forces. As you drive a car around a curve there is a force trying to throw you off the curve. Now, when I was in school they called it centrifugal force, but what we are talking about today and we will be talking about for the next month is a thing called lateral forces. Things that will try to derail the train, and that is what most of these rules were for.

The above is simply definitions. Never assume that a jury understands everything that you understand. The word "derailment" could probably not be defined by 50 percent of the population.

At this point in the opening statement, we had a blackboard in front of the jury. On the board were twelve numbered items. Number one was "heavy train." Number two was "wide gauge." Number three was "bad ties," and so on for twelve specific items. This was a visual display of what we contended were the twelve things that contributed to causing the derailment. In fact, there are over fifty different things that could contribute to a derailment. We decided that the twelve situations would be stressed in opening statement as if there were only twelve possible things that could cause a derailment. We thought that since the L&N employees had convinced defense counsel that nothing was wrong, defense counsel would probably be totally unaware of how many different possibilities existed that could cause derailments.

And these rules concern 12 things, the rules that we will be talking about. There are 12 things that can cause a derailment. There are 12 things that can create what we call these lateral forces. And the first one up there is the heavy train, and there are rules against trains that are too heavy. AAR and the L&N have rules. As a locomotive comes into a curve it starts turning. Well, as the locomotive is turning it is not moving as fast forward as the train behind it, and obviously the more weight you have behind it, the more chance that locomotive has of getting pushed off of the outside rails. And the L&N and the AAR both have rules against that.

The gauge between tracks, it is 56½-inch gauge between the two rails. This is an exact thing and it has been the same for years and years and years. Now, the L&N has a rule, and that is if that gauge gets to 57 inches we've got to correct it, and the reason we've got to correct it is if that train is able to shake back and forth it starts to create more lateral forces. It is the same situation as pushing a car back and forth to get it to move. And the L&N had rules about that.

Bad ties, which is the third thing up there. The L&N has rules, and it has a rule about bad ties. A tie is the timber, the pieces of wood upon which the rail is fastened. And the L&N has a rule that if that tie is bad and rotten we've got to take it out. That is the old time L&N safety rules, and it is still in existence today, and it says we've got to put in new timbers. And then you will hear about the FRA, the Federal Railroad Administration, the Federal Government who governs these railroads. Now, they say they've got minimum, minimum rules. They say, "L&N, you can have a rotten tie and you don't have to do a thing in the world about it, but if you have three totally rotten ties together, you've got to replace one of them." In other words, they can abide by the federal rules by having two rotten ties, one good tie, two rotten, one good, two rotten, one good for the whole line. And so those are the rules in regard to ties.

Now, spikes. The L&N has rules about their spikes. Now, the spikes, you've got a rail, and under the rail is a thing called a tieplate that holds the rail. And these tieplates have these big heavy metal spikes that are driven into the tieplate, into the timber that holds the rails and tries to maintain the gauge. Well, L&N has rules and those rules are, don't let those spikes get too loose. Don't let it be where a train can ride along and the spikes just jump out. And they also have rules that on certain curves, if it's a real sharp curve, you've got to put a certain number of spikes in there to make sure you can hold that rail down.

And then the L&N and the AAR have two rules about train makeup, and that is five and six. The L&N and the AAR say that on a heavy freight train, which we will be involved with in this case, don't ever put light cars up next to the locomotive. Don't put a light car up next to the locomotive with the heavy train behind it because it will again create excessive lateral forces, and the computers tell them this. And then the L&N and the AAR have very strong rules about this long car-short car hookup. They say— and their rules are definite—on a very heavy freight train such as this, don't put a long car-short car hookup next to a locomotive because as they apply the brakes it has a tendency to pop off the track.

As you drive a car around a highway, a major highway, you notice it's banked. Well, railroads have the same thing. When they go around a curve they have a thing called super elevation, and that means the outside rail is higher than the inside rail. They call that super elevation. And the L&N has rules, and they've always had rules that if they design a curve for a super elevation of three and a half inches they must maintain it because the computer says that exact super elevation is necessary for the speed to go around that curve.

And then they have this thing called super elevation runoff. Now, the L&N has a very specific rule that you cannot allow that super elevation in the curve, the high outside rail, to run off into the tangent track. Now, tangent track is straight track. In other words, if you had tracks leading up to the curve this is called tangent, straight track. The L&N rules say under no set of circumstances can you let that run off into the tangent. And the reason for that is, as you can tell, if you're riding along on a straight track and it lifts you up and you shift the weight down and you're on this rail as you start around the curve, you've thrown your weight from here to there, the same as rocking a car creating lateral forces and creating a situation that could cause you to overturn a rail.

I continued to explain each of the twelve numbered items on the board. At this point, I drew freehand a picture of a rail to show the head of the rail and the web of the rail.

Now, the next thing is the 132-pound rail. This is the head of the rail and this is the web, and up until 1947 the standard rail in this country was called 131-pound rail. Now, what that meant was that for every one yard of rail it weighed 131 pounds, and over the 1920's and 1930's and 1940's they started realizing in the late 1930's that these rails were breaking, the head was breaking away from the web and they started having troubles. And so the American Railway Engineering Association, and you will hear them talk about the AREA, that is their own engineering association, said back in the 1940's, "We have got to do something to stop this." So, they added some weight, one pound per yard at the head and web to increase the strength of it. And it did a good job and it became known as 132-pound rail, and they never again, never again made 131-pound rail since 1947 in this country. But there is a lot of it still in use, and on those tracks where they have 131-pound rail it requires an eye inspection, they walk along with a mirror and they inspect the rail to make sure cracks are not forming.

And then in the late, I guess, the late 1960's, these trains started becoming heavier and these four-axle locomotives, you will hear a lot about four-axle and six-axle locomotives. An axle has two wheels, so if you were looking at the side of a locomotive going past you, a four-axle locomotive would have four wheels facing you. Well, then because the trains were getting bigger and they needed to have bigger locomotives they made a six-axle locomotive, and that is a tremendous thing, it weighs almost 400,000 pounds, and it has six wheels on each side. But, when they started using these six-axle locomotives they began to realize that these six-axle locomotives were causing the outside rails to overturn in some curves, not the four-axle, but the six-axle. And so the industry, the railroad industry, suggested slow the speeds down. If 35 miles an hour was a safe speed around a curve for a four-axle, then we ought to reduce the speed for the six-axle.

Now, there are only two rules about the operation of a train, and that is number 11 and 12.

Speed. Obviously the faster you go around a curve the more lateral forces you're going to create. And the L&N has some very, very specific rules in regard to speeding. They will tell you if they catch an engineer going one mile over the speed limit, some of them say we fire him, others say we discipline him strongly. And there is a reason for that, a strong reason for that, because whereas 55 miles per hour on the interstate highway is the maximum legal speed, it is not the maximum safe speed. You could drive 70 miles an hour, we could five years ago, and it was a safe speed to drive. But on a railroad track they determine what the maximum safe speed is and the engineers are told to drive at that speed, don't go over it. Don't go over it because

the computer says it can cause problems. In other words, you're driving at the fastest maximum speed, you've got speed limits and that is what you follow.

And, of course, braking in a curve. That is just good common sense, and all engineers realize that. You don't throw on your brakes in a curve. Now, all of these rules are rules that were created by the old time L&N employees, and even recently the old time L&N employees that remained there kept making these safety rules.

Some of the L&N rulebooks were written in 1974. This is counter to the theme of the case that the new SCL–L&N employees, after taking over in 1972, were interested only in making money. We had to prevent defense counsel from pointing out that many of the rulebooks were written after the takeover. As will be seen later, we point out a reason for the rulebooks to have been written as late as 1974. This will be discussed under the new bonus plan.

And these rules are sent down to all L&N employees. But then the SCL executives who had come into the L&N went around to the L&N executives that were making these rules, and they would tell the L&N people it cost money to rearrange a train and take the light cars off of the front and put them in the back. It takes money to take a long car-short car out of a train and put it in the back. It costs money to slow a train down, it costs money to maintain gauge, ties, timbers. It costs money if we don't put enough weight, the more weight we put on a train the more money we make. And we can get more speed if we run off that super elevation onto the tangent track. Of course, the L&N people who had been there for years asked, "What about the safety rules that we have?" Well, the new SCL–L&N executives said, and you will hear it time and time again from that witness stand, "That is not a rule, that is a guideline." So they came in and told them to disregard these safety rules, these are

crossing and you see an L&N train go by, you start to see cars from the B & O, the Chessie System, the Union Pacific, the Southern Pacific—well, at midnight, every night, whoever has those cars on their system, they pay per diem, they pay rent on those cars.

Now, this doesn't mean the locomotives, there is a different price for that. And the per diem on an average train is $10,000 a day. Now, the L&N people began to realize—on train number 407, we can pick up those cars in New Orleans after midnight, take them all the way through Pensacola, through Santa Rosa County and get them to River Junction and Chattahoochee before midnight and, you know, you can save $10,000. And on number 407 they started doing that. Now, recognize that the L&N does turn the train over to the Seaboard Coastline at Chattahoochee, but the Seaboard Coastline, even though they own the L&N, is a separate company, and the L&N profits would start to look better. And the crew on train number 407 realized very well what per diem was.

The per diem was not going to be a surprise to counsel for the defendant. In some situations, it might have been well to have saved this point for summation. However, it was consistent with the strategy of the case to put everything possible in opening statement. At this point in the opening, the total background had been presented to the jury. Everything had been brought up to the point of the day of the accident. The theme of the case had now become evident to everyone in the courtroom. The board with the twelve violations was still in front of the jury and remained there as I began to tell the jury about the accident.

And now for the first time, no matter what you've read or what you've heard, we believe you are going to hear what actually occurred.

On Wednesday, November 9, 1977, the train was scheduled to leave Goulding yard at 4:00 o'clock. As it started to pull out they had brake problems and it had to be delayed an hour and a half. And train number 407 actually left Goulding yard at 5:31, and started heading down through Pensacola.

On the locomotive in the front, the engineer was Walter Brewer; the reserve engineer was Jerry Phillips; the brakeman was Wayne Johnson; and on the caboose at the rear of that train was Warren Kelly, the conductor, and Charles Martin, the flagman.

Now, Mr. Brewer well understood this train was an hour and a half late already. He well understood per diem—I mean to tell you he well understood per diem—since the L&N about five months before then said, "We aren't going to run those four axles anymore, we're going to run those six axles," and that was on May 29, 1977, about five months before this accident. And Mr. Brewer knew what to do because he had been speeding regularly on train number 407. And the railroad knew it and they didn't say a word about it.

Plaintiffs' counsel had evidence that 80 percent of the time that train number 407 ran during the five months preceding the accident, it must have been speeding at some point during the run. Also, there was evidence that Mr. Brewer must have been speeding 80% of the time he ran train number 407. These records were obtained from the L&N and analyzed by plaintiffs' computer. The inference could easily be drawn that the L&N had the same knowledge that the plaintiff had.

So 407 left Goulding with three locomotives, three six-axle locomotives, the train was a mile and a half long and there were nine thousand trailing tons not including the weight of the locomotive.

Now, there was a 10-mile-per-hour speed limit through Pensacola, and as far as Mr.

Brewer was concerned that continued until the caboose crossed 17th Avenue. As far as the railroad it was when the caboose crossed Blount Street, and then it went to 15. But as far as Mr. Brewer knew and what Mr. Brewer testified to, that he was to run that train at 10 miles an hour until the caboose crossed the 17th Avenue trestle. And Mr. Brewer knew the city police, like the city of Pensacola, was looking out for him, and he knew if he went by the Blount Street crossing and the 14th Avenue crossing and the Ninth and the 17th Avenue crossing there could be a police car there, and they've got radar guns, so Mr. Brewer knew to keep that train down to 10 miles an hour.

But he also knew when he got beyond the 17th crossing there weren't any more crossings between there and Santa Rosa County. The only crossing was a little dirt road crossing at Gull Point, and there wasn't going to be any police car on that dirt road just waiting for a train when they didn't know what time it would be there.

After 17th Avenue, after the caboose crossed 17th Avenue, the rules allow the train to get up to 40 miles an hour until it gets to the Gull Point curve, when it had to get down to 35 miles an hour. Now, as I said, as the train left and got to the point where the caboose crosses 17th Avenue he was doing all right, he was perfectly within the speed limit.

The L&N knew that his train violated the AAR weight limit not just by a few pounds, because that train on just the Gull Point curve that we are concerned with was 50 percent too heavy, 50 percent too much weight for the minimum AAR safety rules. They say 6,000 trailing tons for that curve, and they had 9,000.

The wide gauge, number two up there, the L&N knew that the gauge was too wide, and they had known about it for about a year. The reason they had known it, there is a thing called a geometry car, and that

geometry car runs—it's got computers on it and everything, and it has to run under the law twice a year around these tracks. And when this occurred in June of 1977 it showed the gauge was too wide. And they did it back before then in February of 1977 and it showed the gauge was too wide. Well, what did the L&N do? Nothing. Because it was going to cost money to straighten out that gauge.

Bad ties. The L&N knew from 17th Avenue to the Escambia Bay trestle the tie conditions were so bad they violated even those minimum FRA rules, three bad ties in a row. But it is going to cost money to go in there and lift that track and pull and put new timbers in there.

The L&N knew that on the front of the train they had not one, but four light cars on the front of this extra heavy freight train, in violation of the AAR rules and their own rules. But it would have cost money to have taken those cars out and put them behind.

The L&N knew that the first two of those light cars, the first car connected to the three locomotives, and the second car was a long car-short car combination in direct violation of the AAR rules, but again, it would cost money to straighten that out. You know, just to change it around would cost fuel and it takes time, effort and money.

On the super elevation in the Gull Point curve they designed it for three-and-a-half inches, the outside rail. The L&N knew that when that geometry car ran across there five months before that the three-and-a-half inch super elevation had dropped to two inches. They knew that it was in violation and they should have corrected it. But, it cost money to come in and lift up the track and get it straightened out.

They knew when they put that rail in Gull Point in 1975 that they wanted to go a little faster. They knew they let that super elevation run off into the straight track in direct violation of their own rules in order to allow more speed. But it costs money to slow a train down, and they didn't have to slow it down if you give the train that super elevation runoff.

And the L&N knew that the 132-pound welded rail track included one section, at least one section that was made in 1943 of 131-pound welded rail. And you see that was saving them a few dollars by using old 1943 track. That was the track over in that pile, and every once in a while you can slip it in and save a few dollars.

And the L&N knew the only times they had been having any trouble were with these six-axle locomotives, but they didn't slow the speed limit down for them. They just let them run because they had to have them in order to pull that much weight at a good speed.

And we believe you will find from the evidence that on November 9, 1977, everything that they could possibly do wrong in regard to lateral forces and maintenance, they did wrong and they knew it, for the particular stretch of track that we are talking about. In fact, we believe that the evidence will show you that for the stretch of track between 17th Avenue and Escambia Bay trestle, the one they were so proud of, that there were at least forty FRA violations. These are the minimum standards. If a railroad has forty in its whole system in one year, that would be a lot. We will show forty in this stretch of track that they were so proud of.

I say to you that there will be direct evidence of all ten of the first ten things. Now, I know it sounds unbelievable, because I am not giving you evidence, it is strictly lawyer talk, but listen to the evidence.

So, on November 9, 1977, Brewer has got all these things in front of him that he is facing as he comes across 17th Avenue, and he hears from the conductor as the caboose crosses the 17th Avenue crossing. It is about 6:00 o'clock, and the conductor calls to him, "Brewer, you know, we have crossed 17th, now you can go ahead and do what we have to do." And Brewer knows what he has got to do because he has got to beat that per diem, and he goes full throttle. And he gets up to 10, to 15, to 20, to 25, 30, 35, 40. And it's about 6:02, 6:03, and at this time the Thorshov family are in their home. They are cooking, listening to the radio, the children are playing, the food is on, and it's 6:06. There is a crash out in front of the Thorshov's home. Now, what happened between 6:03 and 6:06, there is some dispute because you see, we weren't on that train, and we don't have anybody on that train willing to testify. So, first I am going to tell you what they say, and then I'm going to tell you what we are going to try to infer from the evidence that we will put on.

The crew says, "We're going 40 miles an hour, we're paying good attention, we're getting into the Gull Point curve and we know there is a 35-mile-speed limit and Brewer slows that thing down to 35." They say, "Brewer blows the whistle for the Gull Point crossing," and they say, "We're in that lead locomotive, all three of us, and we're watching out, everybody is looking as they start into the Gull Point curve." The crew tells you that they were going—all three of them say they were going 35 miles an hour as they came into the curve.

Now, as they go around the curve we do know that the second locomotive overturned the outside rail, and that the third locomotive and 15 or 20 cars thereafter traveled on the overturned rail. As the locomotive overturned the right side rail and continued on around, it kept overturning the rail in front of it. And the right wheels of the second locomotive on back for every one of those cars, the flange, the little thing that sticks down—I am not an artist for sure—anyhow, it is a little thing that sticks down from the wheel. The flange had overturned the track and it was riding in the web. All the right wheels were riding in the overturned web of that track.

The left wheels were over in the dirt. They had already come into the inside of the track and they were just chewing up the dirt and the ties and the timbers. And the crew said, "We were just riding along minding our own business, and the mere fact that we had thrown thousands and thousands of tons behind us, digging up this dirt and everything, we didn't even notice it until our locomotive got beyond the crossing. Eleven or twelve hundred feet we had been riding along derailed, and at that time that doggone 131-pound rail, the head broke off of it and the cars started going every which a way. And at that time the cars broke loose from the coupling, the emergency brakes went on and then, of course, we came to a stop. And that is how the accident happened."

We had the testimony of the engineer about a simulated run that the engineer made shortly after the accident. If the testimony was to be believed as to his speed from the time he started until the caboose crossed 17th Avenue, then the train had to be going approximately 70 miles per hour at the Gull Point curve in order for the derailment to have occurred at 6:06 p.m. However, counsel recognized that it was impossible for that particular train to be going in excess of 50 miles an hour from the computer studies. Also, there were two witnesses that claimed to have heard the screeching of brakes for 15 to 30 seconds prior to the sound of the derailment. The L&N trial team had no knowledge of the two ear-witnesses. How do you handle strong testimony on behalf of the plaintiff when you recognize that it is likely going to be proved to be impossible? How do you handle the surprise of the testimony about braking when the L&N could put on evidence that the screeching actually occurred from the right wheels running in the web of the rail (after the derailment)? In other words, the screeching could have been occurring after the outside rail overturned, and lasted for approximately 15 seconds before the cars began to derail. The following is how we handled these problems.

Now, it's not critical to our case what they did on that train, but I think you will find from the evidence that what they did is that when Brewer and the crew in the locomotive got up to 40 miles an hour, he knew he had to make the per diem. It was about 6:02, 6:03, and he let it go up to 45, maybe 50, maybe 55, maybe 60, we don't know, but we know he wasn't paying attention. And at 6:05 we believe the evidence to be that he was going—that he could have been going over 60 miles an hour, that he was well exceeding the speed limit, and that he was going into the Gull Point curve and it was raining. It was drizzling, and maybe he didn't have his wipers on, I don't know what happened, but all of a sudden he realizes as he is about to blow the whistle for the Gull Point crossing, he realized the speed he was traveling, and it was excessive. He knew it, and he knew he couldn't make it and he put on his brakes. Now, again, there is no direct evidence of any of this, but we think that from the evidence there is a good possibility of what I just told you. The first 10 things, there is going to be direct evidence of, but the other two things, we weren't there, so we don't know, but we think the evidence will indicate it. We do know the outside rail did overturn, we do know the second locomotive, the third locomotive, all of these cars behind it were riding along with right hand wheels in the web. And we do know that the left hand wheels were digging up that dirt out there. There wasn't anything in the world they could do at that time because the train was already in emergency.

We believe that there is a good possibility that that 131-pound rail, the only rail that broke in a lengthwise direction, the rail that caused the pile up, we believe it is a good possibility that it was already cracked. Now, I say it is a good possibility, because we have a witness that said when he saw the rail it was rusted. But the L&N took that rail and they sent it up to the AAR laboratory, sent it up to their own labs, and said, "Check and see if this is a new crack in that rail or was it an old one that we should have discovered before." And the AAR came back with this opinion to the L&N that it was a new crack.

So, we said, "Let us see it. Let our experts look at it."

And they said, "We threw away those rails." Knowing that millions of dollars were involved, the AAR just threw the rail away, and they said, "We no longer have this rail." But we do know that the rail did break, and when the rail broke the cars started piling up; wheels started throwing every which a way, and some of the wheels hit two ammonia cars.

Although it was insignificant in the case, it was important to point out that the rail had been thrown away, contrary to established procedures for any laboratory. This point became extremely important in summation. During the trial of the case, several things were uncovered for the first time that indicated there had been some toying with evidence subsequent to the derailment by the L&N.

Now, the L&N knew that they were forced to carry these ammonia cars because you've got to carry them. You just can't say, "I'll take this car, I won't take that car." But they knew that these cars didn't have head shields on them. The L&N had to carry them, and they did it for a profit. But they knew they should have slowed the train down because they had cars without head shields. Head shields are extra pieces of metal up on the front.

Again, the above is simply stealing the defendant's thunder. They would say that they were required to accept every car sent over its line because of federal regulations. I was putting this situation in its best light by saying that the L&N should have reduced their speed when they realized that the tank cars did not have head shields.

Jon Thorshov and his family are in the home at this point. The two cars of ammonia are pouring ammonia up over this cliff onto the Thorshov home. They had come home about 5:00, as I have said, in the pickup truck, and Scenic Highway is about this height (indicating) and the home was about on this level, and the cliff, anyhow, the driveway goes downhill to his home. He had pulled the pickup truck facing the water, facing the railroad cars. Jon grabs the little girl and Lloyda grabs the young child. And obviously they made up their minds that we're going to run through this and we're going to get in the truck and we'll back it up to Scenic Highway and try to get out. And at this time the ammonia is spreading.

They ran out of the house, they get into the truck, he gets it started, he gets it into reverse, and about the time he starts to move it it stops because there is no oxygen. He grabs Daisy, he goes out of the driver's side, he gets about 10 yards and he falls. Lloyda, at the same time, the wife, grabs the little boy, Gamgee, she goes out the passenger side and gets about 15 yards and falls.

Now, before any of this occurs, when the ammonia is spreading out over everywhere, the train has stopped. Now the train stopped just oh, four or five hundred feet beyond the crossing, and the crew gets off and they start walking back to see what's happened. "God knows, everything's done, let's see what we did." And they are walking back and they are looking and they see this cloud of ammonia spreading out over the Thorshov's home. And they knew—I think they testified that they knew there were lights on in the house, that the people were there, and the thought goes through their mind, "Boy, if we had those air packs, if the L&N had paid for those air packs we could go on in there and save those people, because well—no," they said, "no, we'd better go back to the engine."

Well, they start back to the engine and over to their right, to the east of the tracks is Gull Point and there are lots of homes down there and this whole track is blocked, cars are overturned, and everything else. And if that wind changes these people are in trouble. Oh, I am sure the thought must have gone through their mind, "Let's go knock on these people's doors and warn them," or "Let's go run back to the train and blow the whistle and just keep blowing the whistle until they realize what is going on." But, no, they decided not to do that, even though the first L&N safety rule says help people that are in danger. But that was a rule, and the rules were guidelines, and those guidelines didn't apply in Pensacola. So they ran back to the train and they did the smart thing, they unhooked the first locomotive, all three of them jumped in there and they got the hell out of there. No whistles, no calling, no knocking, no nothing. Well, fortunately the fire department didn't feel that way, because they were immediately notified and the fire department crew started in. And they grabbed their air packs, and they are some— you'll probably hear from them tomorrow, and they are some real heroes.

The firemen's oxygen was running out and they went up under train cars, everywhere else, trying to save the people that were trapped in Gull Point. Anyhow, they put on air packs, they go into the Thorshov home and they can't find anybody. And as they were going out they find Daisy, they grab her and get her to an ambulance. The accident happened at 6:06 and at 6:30 Daisy is on an ambulance. They get her on the ambulance and they take her to the hospital.

Well, they know that nobody has left the little girl there alone and they note that there must be other people there, and they go back in again and they find Gamgee, they bring him out. They find Lloyda and Jon and they bring them out and they are put on an ambulance five minutes later.

Jon dies on the way to the hospital and Lloyda and the two children are put into the hospital. Daisy has gotten about 25 minutes of ammonia and she probably has—there is the possiblity that she has some lung damage, probably not—

Mr. Lane: If Your Honor please, we object to the discussion of these injuries. That is involved in the big case yet to be tried.

Mr. Levin: Your Honor, I really appreciate the reference to the big case for some injuries while we know that the wrongful death cases are the real substantial cases, but in this case, the condition of these children, whether or not they are going to be dependent to age 22 or for life, is critical.

Mr. Lane: We object, Your Honor. That is exactly why he got the cases severed, because he didn't—

The Court: Objection overruled.

Mr. Levin: Daisy got out in 25 minutes and she has very little, if any, lung damage. Gamgee was in there 30 minutes and the doctors will testify that he probably has severe lung damage. He could be a pulmonary cripple.

Jon got out in about 30 minutes, the father, he died on the way to the hospital.

Lloyda got out in 30 minutes, and she lived for 75 days on a respirator and then died.

Daisy had to have a corneal transplant, and you will see some cosmetic difficulties with her eyes when you see her. We are going to bring her in and—

Mr. Lane: Your Honor, we renew our objections. It is just not involved in this case.

Mr. Levin: Your Honor, if the Court please,

in the standard jury instructions, under wrongful death, under loss of services and support it is for as long as these children will be dependent—would have been dependent on their parents. Their physical condition is an issue, not whether it is related to the accident or not, but their condition is relevant in this case.

The Court: Objection overruled.

Mr. Levin: Daisy had a corneal transplant and there is the possibility that she will go blind in both eyes.

There is a small possibility of lung damage, and she obviously has psychiatric problems as indicated by the sleepwalking.

Gamgee went ahead and lost the one kidney, probably not related to the accident. But it is important that he only has one kidney, and as the Court overruled Mr. Lane when he continued to object, this will be important to you at the end of the case. Gamgee has definite permanent lung damage and he may be a pulmonary cripple. He also has the same possibility of going blind that Daisy does.

Now, we filed suit and we basically alleged all of the things that I just told you, and the L&N answered in a magnanimous fashion and said, "we deny everything; and L&N can do no wrong." They even denied that they were in any way at fault.

When advantage can be taken of the pleadings, take it. The above is simply a method of rubbing in the fact that defendant denied responsibility.

Now, we also joined Mr. Brewer in this case. We believe Mr. Brewer is at fault, or we would not have filed suit against Mr. Brewer. But, as far as going and collecting the kind of money that we are talking about from Mr. Brewer, there isn't any chance. We are going after the L&N. And the reason Mr. Brewer remains in this case is because we don't want to be in federal court. We want to try this case here in state court.

The above was an attempt to explain to the jury why the engineer was a party to the case. As explained earlier, the jury found that Mr. Brewer was not negligent because the jury did not want Mr. Brewer to lose his job. This information was obtained from a juror subsequent to trial. We should have explained to the jury that Mr. Brewer was a member of the union and had no chance at all of losing his job.

Now, the L&N says that neither it nor any of its employees did anything wrong. It just happened. "We don't know what happened. It just happened. The train just went off the track. Why do you blame us?" That is what the L&N says.

And they sent in one of the bright SCL–L&N executives who is now a big vice president over there for us to take his deposition. He had come in and taken over the L&N maintenance in 1972, and he was in charge in '75 when they laid this track and in '77 when they had the derailment. He did such a good job in handling everything after the derailment they made him the vice president. So they sent him to us and they said, "If you want to know what is wrong with our tracks, ask him."

So, we asked Mr. Parker, who is now their vice president up there in Louisville, who came over from the SCL in Jacksonville. We asked, "Mr. Parker, tell us what is wrong with that track?"

And he said, "You know, I took my own time and came down to Pensacola after that little derailment down there and nobody else wanted to do it. I walked the track from 17th Avenue all the way around—and, of course, in the Gull Point area it was messed up, so I couldn't tell about that, and I walked all the way around to the Escambia Bay trestle." And he said, he told us under oath, that "that track was in perfect condition. There wasn't anything wrong with that track."

Mr. Parker was the L&N's key witness. The above was simply painting him with the black hat. Throughout the opening statement all of the new SCL–L&N executives had been painted with black hats. The attempt was now being made to make Mr. Parker the perfect example of the new SCL–L&N executive.

Shortly after the derailment, the L&N had crews working on the track where the derailment happened. They also had crews heading back toward 17th putting those new timbers in, putting those spikes in, making sure it was in good condition. By the time the city got around in December to come and look at all of this track they thought it was beautiful. So Mr. Parker stated, under oath, "The tracks were perfect." The one thing that he doesn't know to this very moment, and I am sure that all of the L&N people will tell him about it because it is going to be here when he takes the stand, we took pictures and he didn't know that.

Between the time of the derailment, after he had looked at it, and before repairs, we went out and took pictures, and he didn't know about it. We were right in front of the L&N crews. They were coming along getting that track straightened out, and we were about a mile in front of them just going right along taking pictures. Not me, personally, but we had people out there, and he didn't know about it until now. But he will know about it tonight for sure.

And so we are going to have pictures, and when they put Mr. Parker on the stand, or if we've got to, we'll put him on the stand, and we'll show him the pictures and we'll ask him to tell you how this was such a perfect track. That is their vice president.

Obviously, anybody who believes what I have told you would be sickened. They would be disgusted. And I am here to tell you, when it comes from the witness stand it is going to be worse.

Now, we have the burden of proof. Yes, we've got to prove one of these 12 things by 51 percent of the evidence.

And as I told you, the L&N denies everything. And we had to go out, because this is highly technical stuff when you start talking about lateral forces and super elevations and all of these things like that, we had to go out and find some people who knew something about it. And we have got some former executives, Ed Mann, the executive vice president from Penn Central Railroad, and the vice president from Conrail, and the vice president from Amtrak. These are former railroad people. You know it is rough to get a railroad man to testify against another railroad, but they are coming in and they are going to lay it on you. They are going to let you and the people of Pensacola know how bad it was.

The above is an attempt to paint the plaintiffs' witnesses with white hats. I was saying that the plaintiff's witnesses must be honest and good men in order to be willing to testify against their own industry.

And during this case you will also hear from some employees who actually worked tracks for the railroad, excuse me, former employees. They couldn't be working for them now, believe me. Former employees of other railroads will come in and tell you the same thing.

At this part of the opening statement, it became necessary to get into the most difficult part of the case, the law of damages. The jury had pads and pencils. The jury was eventually going to be given a special verdict form. All of the testimony as to special damages such as loss of support and services were going to be calculated by economists.

At the end of this case you are going to be given a special verdict form, and the first question probably is going to ask, "Was the L&N negligent?"

Negligence is the failure to do what is

right. Any one of those 12 things. And if the railroad or any of its employees were negligent in any of those ways, then you will be required to fill out the damages.

At this point, the board facing the jury was replaced with a sample special verdict form.

And there will be a space for damages to the property, the damage that was done to the Thorshov property. And you will hear testimony as to what damage was done. And then there will be a place on that form that will ask what were Lloyda's medical and funeral expenses, and they were something over $45,000. That is going to be a pretty simple figure to put in, it will be introduced into evidence. And then a space for Jon Thorshov's funeral expense, which was a little over $2,000; and then there will be a place for his accumulations. If Jon Thorshov had lived out his normal life expectancy, how much would he have saved and invested, and how much would have been left for these children? Now, this starts to get a little bit more difficult, and this and most of the other damage questions are going to be more difficult than the $45,000. That is the reason you have been given pads and pencils, because there are going to be so many figures to keep track of.

In determining damages, you are going to first have to decide from the evidence, what does the future hold for Daisy and Gamgee Thorshov. In other words, how much longer would they have been dependent if their parents had not been killed and only the children had been involved in the accident.

We do know that healthy children of doctors normally go through four years of college. So we do know that one alternative, that if you believe the children will regain their health, you will determine that they would have been dependent to age 22. That's age 22 for both Daisy and Gamgee. But, of course, the children aren't healthy,

and what we believe you will probably find from the evidence is that Daisy, even though she is not healthy would have gone off to college, will go to college, will get out, and she would no longer be dependent. If her parents had lived she would no longer have been dependent on them, and she would have gone off and married and had her own life.

But we believe you will find that Gamgee, because of the possibility of the serious condition that occurred to him, that he may be dependent for the rest of his life, and then of course, the figures vary greatly. They change greatly when you support somebody to age 22 or you support somebody for life.

You will be asked at the end of this case to put in the figures for loss of support for Gamgee, loss of services, net accumulations, loss of Jon Thorshov's parental guidance, his companionship for Gamgee, and for Gamgee's mental pain and suffering. And then you will be asked to do the same thing for Daisy, for each of these elements. They will be combined into one figure, for Daisy for the loss of her father. And then it's going to be necessary to do this for the mother.

Now, three of these things, support, services, and net accumulations, are subject to economic testimony, and we are going to bring in an economist to testify to it because he can give exact figures to you.

Companionship, guidance, mental pain and suffering, no. These are things you're going to have to rely on your common sense and experience. Nobody is going to take the stand and say that the value of the loss of Jon Thorshov's companionship for Gamgee or Daisy was worth two million dollars or six hundred thousand or so much. These are things that we are not going to be able to present evidence about, and that is left to your common sense and experience.

But, on support, services and net accumulations, we intend to bring in some of America's most outstanding professors of economics and they will put figures on the board. They will take Jon Thorshov's salary for the year 1979, what it would have been in '79, and then they know what pathologists have made in the past. They do know what is happening with different economic things, and then they project these figures, the same way they project social security figures, and they know how much money today is going to be worth in the future.

So, they take the salary, and they increase it each year. Then they determine his savings because they know how much the average man in that income category saves. So let's say the doctor after paying income tax would have made $100,000. They know that a man with two children, which is the situation he would be in if he had lived, would have saved a blank percentage, and I think it's 25 percent. So, they put that off to the side for 1980, and then the next year how much would he have made, and then they keep increasing it with inflation until the year he would have died.

This money would then be a tremendous sum of money, 31 years from now. So, then they say, "Well, we are going to replace that money today." How much money will it take today, in dollars invested at a tax free rate of interest, that 31 years from now will replace exactly what they believe Jon Thorshov would have left for these children had he lived, and that is what they will be talking to you about.

And as to support, they do it the exact same way. They will come in and they will take his income after taxes, and then they will remove the amount that he is going to save. They will then take how much he would have spent on himself, and then they will divide the difference between the two children until each child is no longer dependent. And this is the reason it is important for you to determine whether those children would have been supported beyond age 22, because there is a

tremendous difference between supporting Gamgee to 22 and supporting him for the life of his father.

They then take the gross figures for the loss of support and they bring it down to its present value. That is how much money invested today at a tax free rate of interest will produce the exact amount, in their opinion, of lost support that Daisy and Gamgee would have had.

For the services of the father they do the exact same thing, and for the services of the mother they do the same thing. In other words, a mother who was with these children full time. They are going to have to find somebody to clean and cook and somebody to stay with them. And they go through these figures and they tell you what these things are going to be, and then they bring them back down. The economists will determine how much invested today, when you return your verdict, will it take to pay these amounts for these children as long as they would have been dependent.

Now, I am going to suggest to you that when the professors of economics come in and testify that you take two pages of your pad, one of them for each professor, and put down 22 and 22. Because we'll give you a list of figures for each of these things assuming each child being dependent to age 22. And then on the next page he will then give you figures for Daisy to 22; Gamgee for life.

And at the end of the case you will add those figures of loss of the support, services, and net accumulations, and add those figures to the parental guidance and to the companionship, and the mental pain and suffering. It's not going to be all that dull. I am going to have them talk to you about what causes inflation and what prices are going to be like, and it will astound you, 20, 30, 40, 50 years from now. And they will go into the fact that there aren't going to be things called pennies, nickels, quarters, probably, and they will go into astounding things, what wages are going to be some 40 or 50 years from now, and what homes are going to cost and what cars are going to cost and how this all comes into play.

The above part of the opening was extremely dull and very difficult to understand. I used the blackboard in explaining some of the complications. Most often, the blackboard was being used to write down certain key words with the hope that the jury would copy those words onto their pads. Also, it was an attempt to get the jurors excited about the testimony of the economists.

Now, the L&N Railroad has listed three economic witnesses, and if they disagree with what the professors of economics testify to, if they disagree as to what prices are going to be in the future, then I say to the L&N Railroad, don't rely on your lawyer talk in your closing argument here, put your economists on the witness stand. They have got three economists listed. If any one of them is willing to say that Professor Goffman is wrong or President Sliger is wrong, then let him come on. Don't let Mr. Lane come on at the end of this case and say everybody knows plaintiffs' economists are wrong, let L&N come on with their evidence, let them come in and say there is not going to be any inflation.

The above remarks were extremely important in the eventual outcome of the case. (The L&N had listed three economists as potential witnesses. We doubted that the railroad intended to call them as witnesses, and we believed they had simply listed them in order to require us to prepare for their expected testimony.) We wanted to be able to say in closing argument, "The L&N economists must have agreed with plaintiffs' economists, because L&N did not put these witnesses on the stand."

Finally, we believe the Judge—and this is the end—will allow you to answer one more question at the end of the case: Did the L&N Railroad, through its employees, act in a wanton manner or in a manner that was with reckless indifference to the rights of others? Now, this is different from simple negligence. I have been telling you about simple negligence, and that is any one of these 12 things for simple negligence. But, if their conduct was so bad, so horrible, and you find they did so many bad things that you determine that they were reckless, they were indifferent, they didn't care, and if you find that, then the Judge will give you an opportunity at the end of this case to do what the government couldn't do to them, and that is, control. You have that power. And the Judge will tell you, and these will be his words, "Look at how much the L&N Railroad is worth and come up with an amount of money in punitive damages that would keep them from ever doing this again."

And I believe you will find from the evidence that the L&N Railroad knew how bad this was, and they knew this stretch of track was the worst in their system; they knew derailments were happening, and they knew ammonia was escaping. Now, they didn't want Jon Thorshov and Lloyda Thorshov to die—but they knew somebody was going to, somebody was going to get seriously injured out there. But the L&N said, "We are willing to take that gamble," and I think that is what you will find, and I think you will find that Jon and Lloyda Thorshov lost that gamble.

Thank you.

AUTHOR'S NOTE: Although this is an excellent opening statement, there is room for some improvement. Readers of the book are encouraged to consult Chapter 7, utilizing the information found there to edit Mr. Levin's opening remarks.

MODEL CLOSING ARGUMENTS

The following material is reprinted with permission from Joseph Kelner and Francis E. McGovern, Successful Litigation Techniques (New York: Matthew Bender, 1981), 17/15–17/28.

PLAINTIFF'S CLOSING ARGUMENT

Compliment the Jury

Ladies and Gentlemen of the Jury, as the trial is fast drawing to a close, I would be remiss in my duty if I did not commend the twelve (12) of you for your rapt attention to the testimony in the case. The very fact that you were selected by both sides in this case demonstrates the high regard and esteem in which each of you are held in the community in which you live. On behalf of the Plaintiff, Rita Smith, and her husband, Stanley Smith, I want you to know that we will be happy with whatever verdict you render in this case. We know that your verdict will be based upon the law and the evidence in the case and will be fair and just to all concerned.

Facts

The evidence has clearly proven that Rita Smith was a student at the Alexander City State Junior College on the date of her injury. She was riding from Alexander City south on Alabama State Highway #63 from Alexander City to Tallahassee. Phyllis Jones was driving the automobile and there was a total of five (5) young ladies in the automobile. Rita Smith was riding in the left rear seat of the automobile and had no control whatsoever over the operation of the motor vehicle being driven by Phyllis. The Defendant, in utter disregard for the safety of Rita Smith and her friends, pulled out into the highway directly in front of the automobile in which Rita was riding without warning. It was raining, and the road was wet. As soon as Phyllis saw the automobile suddenly and unexpectedly pull out in front of her, she hit her brakes, her car skidded, and the left side of the automobile in which Rita Smith was riding crashed into the right side and rear of the automobile operated by the Defendant. Rita Smith was permanently injured.

Burden of Proof

The burden of proof, Ladies and Gentlemen of the Jury, is on the Plaintiffs, Rita and Stanley Smith, to prove that the wreck and Rita's personal injuries and Stanley's consequent injuries were the result of the negligence of the Defendant. The burden that is on Rita and Stanley is not to be confused with the burden on the prosecution in a criminal case, which is to satisfy you beyond a reasonable doubt. The confusing thing is that the word "reasonable or reasonably" appears in both definitions. On occasions in the past, I have discovered on talking with jurors after the return of a verdict that some mistakenly favor the defense although they felt that the Plaintiff was probably right, where they were not satisfied beyond a reasonable doubt that the Defendant was guilty of negligence. They erroneously believed that they had to be moved to a conclusion beyond a reasonable doubt that the Plaintiff was entitled to recover. This is mistaken and these jurors were honestly misled and mistaken. They were victims of a system and the Plaintiff was a victim of a system, in which the same jurors who sit at a civil trial like this can serve as jurors in criminal cases. There, a man's liberties are at stake and the burden of proof is beyond a reasonable doubt and to a moral certainty. The same jurors' only exposure to the law is through television programs focused on criminal trials where the burden is, of course, to satisfy the jury beyond a reasonable doubt. The easiest way to illustrate Rita Smith's burden of proof in this case, which is a civil case, is to say that Rita merely needs to have 51 percent of the evidence. In making this determination it does not matter how many witnesses each side has. If you consider the effect of both sides' testimony and the Plaintiff has 51 percent of the effective testimony, then she is entitled to win. It is the same type of reasoning process that is used in everyday decisions in life, business decisions. A man chooses between a Ford and a Chevrolet. He cannot gather evidence sufficient to move him to be satisfied beyond a reasonable doubt. He merely exercises his reason and judgment, examines the evidence of the good points of both, and makes a decision when he is rea-sonably satisfied which one is best. If he waited until he was satisfied beyond a reasonable doubt, he would never buy a car—he would end up walking. The same is true of any business decision of the hundreds a person makes each month. That is all you will be required to do in this case. The decision you have to make in a civil case is in the nature of a business decision. It is different from the special problem that exists when a man is on trial for his life in a criminal case. The philosophy of criminal law is that it is better to free 99 guilty people than to convict one innocent one. This is not the point here. Certainly, it is not better to free 99 people guilty of careless driving than to send away empty-handed 99 innocent victims of their carelessness. If a guilty defendant in a criminal case is acquitted, there is no real loser; but we cannot acquit a guilty defendant in a civil case without injustice to the innocent victim of his carelessness. Therefore, the law in a civil case imposes on the Plaintiff an entirely different burden of proof. That is why it is enough if you simply are reasonably satisfied that the Plaintiff's case is just. The tool that you jurors work with in making a decision in this case is "preponderance of the evidence." If you can imagine the blind scales of justice and you put the Plaintiff's evidence on one side of the scales and the Defendant's evidence on the other, if the scales are tipped ever so slightly in favor of the Plaintiff, then the Plaintiff has met his burden by the preponderance of the evidence. In everyday life when you decide to take one job over another, you make that decision by the preponderance of the evidence. You make investments and decide whether to marry one girl over another by the use of the tool called the preponderance of the evidence. It is called the rule of scales.

Duty

The Court will charge you at the end of the case that the Defendant owes a duty not to negligently injure Rita Smith or anyone else on the public highways of this State. The evidence in this case clearly shows that the wreck occurred on a public highway in this state and that the Defendant breached his legal duty to Rita Smith by his careless driving.

Causation of Injury

In this particular case, I feel that it is beyond question that Rita's injuries were definitely the result of the carelessness and the negligence and the fault of the Defendant. We are in this Court because of Rita's injuries. What caused those injuries? The careless, heedless, and negligent driving of the Defendant.

Contributory Negligence

The judge will charge you at the conclusion of this case that contributory negligence is not a defense in this case. In my judgment there is absolutely no evidence of contributory negligence on the part of Phyllis, who was driving the automobile in which Rita Smith was riding at the time of the wreck. However, even if Phyllis was in some way contributorily negligent, the Defendant's negligence has been well established and Phyllis' contributory negligence cannot be imputed to Rita. Rita is entitled to recovery against the Defendant irrespective of whether or not Phyllis was guilty of any negligence.

Plaintiff's Injuries

This wreck occurred on October 29, 1973. The doctor's testimony clearly shows the following:

Patient complains of pain in the neck and back and upper dorsal spine area; neck muscle tenderness. Her neck. Pain medication and muscle relaxers prescribed. November 2—continued severe neck pain; rib belt was applied. December 2—continued severe neck pain occipital headaches; soft neck brace prescribed. December 9—severe pain in neck and severe headaches. Ultrasound treatment applied again. Continued on medication. January 7—Ultrasound treatment. January 25—still wearing neck brace; still taking pain medication; residual headaches. February 6—still under Dr. Russell's treatment. March 15—Dr. Sheehan, an orthopedic surgeon, confirmed a fractured left rib; daily headaches; headaches began at the top of the head and involved the forehead and eyes; pain in right trapezius muscle between shoulder blades of upper back; moderate muscle spasm of right cervical spine; tenderness of spinous processes of C4, C5, and C6 posteriorly; acute cervical strain. Treatment: cervical collar, hydrocollator heat and packs and liniment, darvotran capsules for pain in muscles. April 5—Continuation of pain in upper back and right upper trapezius muscle; difficulty driving. Treatment: heat twice a day, muscle relaxants for head pain and muscle spasms in upper trapezius muscles. April 21—Diagnosis: Chronic cervical strain. 5 to 10 percent permanent disability to the cervical spine.

Actual Medical Expenses

Rita's actual out-of-pocket medical expenses total $213.70. Additionally, she was required to miss approximately 10 days out of class as a result of the injury. Her ability to attend to her household duties and to see and care for her children had been hindered for a long period of time.

Permanent Partial Disability

Ladies and Gentlemen of the Jury, it is awfully important for you to distinguish between an anatomical or medical disability and a functional or actual disability, the point being that a 10 percent loss of efficiency can represent 100 percent disability to obtain employment and to compete. For example, a watch with a 10 percent disability would lose 24 hours a day. A $100 watch that loses 24 hours a day is not worth $90. It is not worth 90 cents if it cannot be fixed. Yet, this is the exact amount that the Defendant has taken from the Plaintiff if he has inflicted a 10 percent disability.

The critical difference that 10 percent can make can be measured in athletic contests. No one in history ever ran a mile in less than 4 minutes until a few years ago. But if anyone could reduce the time by 10 percent, he could run a mile in 3 minutes 36 seconds, a figure that needs no elaboration. There are a hundred golfers on the professional circuit who can shoot the average course in 72 any day, but a 65 is the score of a champion at his best. Take a basketball player 6 feet tall and add 10 percent and you have a star of 6 feet 6 inches.

We are not merely juggling figures: these are practical objective computations of physical differences that 5 to 10 percent can make in performance, function and ability to compete. The injured Plaintiff must be employed and employable. She must compete to get a job and hold it. A loss of 5 to 10 percent can handicap an accident victim for the rest of her life to a serious and important extent. Doctors who examine applicants for employment and men who hire them often turn a 5 to 10 percent permanent physical handicap into a 100 percent disability to land a job.

One flat tire on an automobile, if you cannot fix it, renders the car 100 percent useless as a means of transportation; and while a human body is a machine of marvelous efficiency, it has the practical difficulty that you cannot write to the factory and get a replacement part. A 5 to 10 percent permanent disability means one that can never be repaired.

When the company doctor finds an applicant 10 percent disabled, the employer does not hire him at 90 percent of the time. The employer simply does not hire him at all, and he remains 100 percent out of a job; and in this day when the unemployment rolls are increasing daily, the average employer is not going to hire a 10 percent disabled worker and expose himself to liability if the worker injuries himself or somebody else and run the risk that the 10 percent disabled worker cannot produce at 100 percent efficiency all the time.

Before the Defendant caused the wreck and Rita's injury, Rita was in excellent health. The shock of this injury has now slowed her gait by at least 10 percent. Now, if Rita were competing in the 100-yard dash, she would be on the 90-yard line when the others crossed the finish line.

Rita must compete to get a job in the future and hold it. Rita is now more vulnerable to injury. Her recovery will now be more difficult. She has now suffered an impairment of her general health. Rita's whole family has been injured. Rita was rightfully in the road. The Defendant wrongfully pulled out into the road and caused the wreck. Rita was a passenger. She had no control over either automobile. The law gave her the right to be where she was and the Defendant has now permanently injured her.

Pain and Suffering

The medical testimony shows that Rita was in pain from October 19, 1973, through the last treatment by the orthopedic surgeon on April 21, 1974. She had daily headaches, neck pain, and pain between her shoulder blades. Her final diagnosis was chronic cervical strain. You heard her testimony. She still has the severe occipital-type headaches described by the doctor and she still has neck muscle tenderness. Ladies and Gentlemen, a headache does not just affect your head. If you have a headache, your whole body hurts. A splinter in your finger is not restricted just to your finger. A grain of sand in your eye affects your whole body. If you didn't sleep well last night because of pain, then you don't feel well today all over. The pain and lack of sleep affects the whole man or the whole woman. The jury must object to pain and show disapproval of the infliction of pain by awarding a money judgment in these type of cases.

Very few people who have been the victims of intense and prolonged pain ever received a jury verdict that even approaches adequate compensation for what they have suffered. Pain is not only unpleasant to endure; it is unpleasant to think about. The only chance for a Plaintiff to gain a fair trial on the issue of pain and suffering is to persuade the jury to steel themselves to the disagreeable task of looking at the shocking reality of pain and what pain does to a man or woman. It is human nature to turn our minds from the impact of other people's troubles just as we must turn our minds from the thought of our eventual deaths. If we did not have the mental block, we would all be the victims of such anxiety and concern that we could not stand it. We would become insane. I, as a trial lawyer, and you, as a trial jury, have the duty to overcome the abhorrence and look at pain and see it for what it is. It is like opening a window into hell.

Pain is the blood brother of death. They are partners and allies as the chief enemies of man. Consider, however, that although a man in great pain may ask for death to give him peace, no man has ever asked for pain. Pain is a cruel monster—choosing as its victims the helpless and the sick who are least able to bear it. It loves to prey on children. It attends every human birth and it torments the last minutes of the dying. If you are religious, you believe that an omnipotent God thought nothing worse as a supreme punishment in hell than to make it a place of pain. If you are not religious, then you believe that the accumulated imagination of man could imagine nothing worse.

Look at the law's attitude toward pain, wherever it arises, outside of an action for damages. The law forbids cruel and unusual punishments. The law says to the State, you can inflict capital punishment; you can take a man's life, but you must do it without pain; you can kill him, but you may not hurt him.

What about the men who invented anesthesia? The men of medicine who taught us how to get rid of pain for an hour during an operation are immortal. They are heroes of science because they taught us to push back pain for an hour.

The finger of pain leaves its trace on the human face, in the look in a man's eyes and the very way he carries himself. Long continued pain enervates and saps the life and strength of a man and his organs.

Pain is the opposite of pleasure. The antithesis of comfort. A man thinks nothing of spending as much money as he can for an evening of pleasure or a day of comfort, but it is hard for him to see how heartless it is to deny some miserable wretch a few dollars a day compensation for suffering pain the rest of his life.

When the time comes for the Defendant to pay for the misery he has inflicted, he asks that you take an attitude of tolerance toward pain as if it were not really worth much money. He is asking that your mind tolerate pain which is something your body will never do. An hour of pain is a sample of hell. It is this sickening horror, this tool of torturers, this scourge of mankind that you are asked to belittle so as to deny a woman a dollar a day as compensation. I do not see how a man can ask you to make friends with the idea of pain or to tolerate it or belittle it any more than he would ask you to accept and fraternize with a murderous enemy of your country or to say of a malignancy in your body: it is nothing but a cancer. I had a friend whose little child had an ailment that caused constant and daily pain. Fortunately, there was a medicine that could relieve this pain but that medicine cost $5 for a day's supply. Can you imagine her parents sitting with her one morning almost feeling her pain themselves and saying to her: As $5 a day is excessive even for severe pain, we will withhold the medicine today and put the $5 in some practical investment such as a common stock in a railroad or in an insurance company. No parent would take that position while the child suffered 10 minutes, and any parent who did so would be unworthy to have the child's custody.

The courtroom is the only place in all human experience where anybody contends that pain is of less account than money. However, we administer justice in a courtroom by the same standards and the same values that rule the outside world of men and affairs. The Defendant who says that a few dollars a day is too much to award for pain because it comes to a large amount in a lifetime, stands utterly alone and without precedent or support in human experience. If the Plaintiff cannot ask a jury to be ruled by sympathy, the Defendant has no right to ask you to be ruled by cruelty.

There are 168 hours in a week. Rita Smith will sleep 56 of those hours and she will work or go to school at least 40 hours a week. This will leave 72 hours for living. You know, the 40 hours that some people work makes them a slave. The 56 hours they sleep, they may as well be dead. The 72 hours that is left is what a man or a woman works for. When we permanently disable a person and inflict permanent pain on her, we have impaired her joy of living. We live for more than just survival.

Verdict

Rita Smith is 21 years old. She is not a veteran and she is not entitled to any monthly disability payment from the Veterans' Administration. She has 44 years to live before she reaches the age of 65 years. If you awarded her $1 a day for her 10 percent permanent disability and the pain that she suffers, you would award her $16,060. You may feel that she is entitled to more than that. The amount of your verdict is up to you. I know you want

your verdict to reflect credit upon you. I know that it will. The law plainly provides for reasonable compensation. The Judge will tell you that there is no measuring stick for pain. Pain cannot be bought in the marketplace. However, we do know that relief from pain can be bought. I urge you to consider this in reaching your verdict. Thank You.

DEFENDANT'S CLOSING ARGUMENT

Ladies and Gentlemen of the jury, my client, Mr. Jones, and I join Mr. Hornsby in thanking you for the close attention that you have given to the attorneys and witnesses. I am sure that by now you appreciate very deeply the heavy responsibility that rests upon your shoulders in deciding this case. We all have functions to perform in the trial of a case. It is the duty of the attorneys to question the witnesses and to object to any question which they feel calls for inadmissible testimony and, finally, at this stage of this case to review with the jury the testimony that has been given and see if we can assist you in applying that testimony to the legal issues involved in the case. That is exactly what I will attempt to do. It, of course, is the duty of the witnesses to tell you what they know about the occurrence; it is the duty of the judge to rule upon all objections that might be made during the course of the trial. After the attorneys finish their closing remarks the judge will explain to you the law that you will need to understand in order to decide the case. Your function, however, is by far the most important. It is your responsibility to determine just what the truth is and then apply that truth as you find it to be to the legal principles that will be explained to you by the judge.

There are two parts to this case. The first part presents the question "Is there any liability on the part of Mr. Jones? Unless you find that Mr. Jones is liable to the plaintiff, then you will not come to consider the second part. But if you find that he is liable, then you will come to consider what injuries and damages the plaintiff actually sustained as a result of the accident.

I noticed with interest how casually Mr. Hornsby touched upon the liability issue. Basically this is what he said: Rita Smith was not driving the automobile in which she was riding and had no control over it and that Mr. Jones, in utter disregard for the safety of Rita Smith and her friends, pulled out without warning into the highway directly in front of the automobile in which Mrs. Smith was riding. Well, ladies and gentlemen, I do not believe you are going to decide this case on the basis that Mr. Jones acted in disregard of the safety of anyone. You heard him when he testified; you had the opportunity to look him in the eye right now. If he has given you the impression that he did act in utter disregard of the safety of himself and other people on the highway and that he did pull out into the highway with reckless indifference to the consequences of his doing so, you should bring in a verdict in favor of the plaintiff.

Before making that determination, however, I respectfully ask that you consider all of the testimony in the case and just see what it was. Mr. Jones was on his way to work; he was not out carousing around looking for an accident to happen. He is a family man; he did not want to get hurt himself; and he did not want to hurt anyone else. He had the right to use the highway on the morning of this accident to get to work, and I agree wholeheartedly with what Mr. Hornsby said concerning the duty that he was under on that occasion. Certainly, he was under the duty to exercise reasonable care to see that he did not hurt himself nor anyone else. What is reasonable care? It is that degree of care which a reasonable person would have exercised on the occasion and under the conditions that existed on the morning of the accident. What were those conditions? It was raining and visibility was poor. What did he do? He pulled up to the stop sign, stopped, looked in both directions, and he saw an autombile that was several hundred feet from the intersection. He assumed, as he had the right to do, that it was traveling at a lawful rate of speed and that he had ample time to get across before it reached the intersection. Does that indicate a reckless disregard for the consequences of what he was doing or does it indicate the degree of care which a reasonable person would have exercised? Ladies and gentlemen of the jury, all of you travel on busy highways, and you know that when you stop at an intersection you cannot just sit there all day; when it appears to be safe to cross, you cross and that is what he did. The unfortunate part of this situation was that the vehicle in which this young plaintiff was riding was traveling so fast that the driver utterly lost control when she attempted to slow down. All of the testimony shows that the car she was in went into a skid and was completely out of control when the collision occurred. Has the plaintiff proved to you that Mr. Jones was to blame for this accident, or has the evidence satisfied you that it resulted solely from the excessive speed of the automobilie in which the plaintiff was riding? I am not talking about contributory negligence now because the court will tell you that the contributory negligence of the driver of the automobile in which the plaintiff was riding would not bar the plaintiff from recovery, but I ask that you listen further to his Honor's charge to you, and I think he will tell you that if the negligence of that young lady in driving that car was the sole proximate cause of the collision, Mr. Jones would not be liable. From the argument which the plaintiff's attorney has made, I think you can deduce that he must realize that the testimony is awfully weak in proving that Mr. Jones was to blame for this accident. He has likened the burden of proof in this case to a person who goes down to buy an automobile and has difficulty in deciding whether he wants a Chevrolet or a Ford. Well, I do not know what that argument means because we are not dealing with the purchase of automobiles here; we are dealing with a claim that a citizen of this town who was on his way to work to earn a living for his family was guilty of reckless driving and operated his automobile in a reckless manner and in disregard of the rights of other people on the highway. That, ladies and gentlemen, is what we are dealing with; and I say to you that when you are sitting here as disinterested jurors, judging the conduct of one of your fellow men, you should take far more proof before convicting him and holding him liable in damages than you would to make a decision as to whether or not you want to buy a Chevrolet or Ford automobile. We are dealing with a serious matter in this case, and I tell you now that the judge will not charge you that the burden resting on the plaintiff has anything to do with a decision as to whether you buy a Ford or a Chevrolet car. He will, I think, tell you that before the plaintiff would be entitled to a verdict at your hands you must be reasonably satisfied by the preponderance of the testimony that Mr. Jones was gulity of negligence. Ladies and gentlemen, when you have considered all the evidence and when you have considered it in an honest and sincere manner, I believe that you will, by your verdict, say to Mr. Jones, "Mr. Jones, we do not believe you are guilty of negligence, and we do not believe you were to blame for this accident."

The plaintiff's attorney also has talked about proximate cause. Ladies and gentlemen, his Honor will in a few minutes explain to you what proximate cause is, but I expect that he will define it as being that cause which, unbroken by any independent cause, produces the injury. Well, ladies and gentlement, when you hear the judge use that term, independent cause, I ask that you consider whether or not the skidding of the automobile that the plaintiff was riding in and the loss of control by the driver of that car was an independent cause. I say it was, and if you

agree and if you find that Mr. Jones was guilty of negligence but his negligence was not the proximate cause of the injury, then the plaintiff still would not be entitled to recover. I respectfully submit, ladies and gentlemen, that when you have considered all of the evidence in this case, you will not find that Mr. Jones was guilty of negligence and certainly he was not guilty of the type of conduct which Mr. Hornsby has charged him with of being careless, heedless and negligent in the driving of his automobile. We expect your verdict will be in favor of the defendant and we respectfully ask that you find Mr. Jones not liable.

As I stated in the beginning, however, there are always two parts to a lawsuit. I sincerely believe that you will not come to the second part, but I never know whether the jury is agreeing with what I say or not. It could be that you are looking me in the eye and saying, "I don't agree with what you have said about liability. I think Mr. Jones was careless, heedless and negligent and that he should pay for the injuries which the plaintiff received." Therefore, in justice to my client, I am compelled to discuss the injuries received by the plaintiff. By making this argument, however, I hope that you will not think that my position about no liability has changed in the least, because it has not.

Mr. Hornsby has talked about pain and he said, "Pain is the blood brother of death." He has used the old stock argument about a watch that loses a certain percentage of its effectiveness, of a mile runner, and last of all, the usual argument about one flat tire on an automobile. But, ladies and gentlemen of the jury, as reasonable people, I ask you what does that type of argument have to do with a strained neck? Let's be objective about the testimony in this case. I realize that the doctor stated that in his opinon the plaintiff probably has 5 to 10 percent permanent disability to the neck. What did he base this opinion on, however? I ask that you recall just as much of his testimony as you possibly can, and I am going to review it a little bit, and I am going to do it as honestly and as fairly as I can. The plaintiff repeatedly complained to him of pain in her neck. The plaintiff repeatedly complained to him of headaches. The plaintiff repeatedly complained to him of pain in her shoulder and upper back. That is what she told the doctor. Now look at the testimony of the doctor to see what he found. I think an accurate appraisal of his actual findings was that he found nothing. The x rays showed nothing. On one occasion his notes showed that there was a "moderate muscle spasm of the right cervical spine." He also told you what a muscle spasm is, and that it is nothing in the world except a tightening of the muscle. You will have with you when you go back to the jury room the office records of the doctor. I ask that you look through them carefully and see if you can find in them anything which the doctor actually found himself. Every notation is about complaints made to him by the plaintiff. In giving appropriate weight to the complaints that she made to the doctor, I ask that you, ladies and gentlemen, bear in mind that prior to the time she made those complaints she had filed, and it was then pending, a lawsuit in which her attorney had alleged in the complaint the exact and same complaints. Based upon these complaints made by the plaintiff both to the doctor and to you, her attorney is asking that you give her $16,060. Well, what are her actual damages? She had a doctor bill of $213.70, and, at the most, she was off work for ten days. I hope, ladies and gentlemen, that you have done the same thing that I have during the course of this trial and that is to observe this plaintiff as she has walked up and down the halls of this courthouse. If you have, I be-

lieve you have noted that when she is not in the courtroom she exhibits no signs of any stiffness in her neck as she has while sitting here in your presence. We again come back to the burden of proof which rests on the plaintiff. That burden is to prove to your reasonable satisfaction by the preponderance of the evidence that this plaintiff has in fact received the injury which she claims to have received. If she has not done that, then she is not entitled to payment for some alleged injury which she has not proved that she in fact sustained.

Ladies and Gentlemen, my time is up, and I am about to sit down. I will not have an opportunity to talk with you again. The plaintiff's attorney will be permitted to talk with you once more. That is by reason of the fact that he does have the burden of proof. I have attempted to answer what he said in his opening argument and to anticipate some of the things that he might say in this final argument but I ask that you do this for me if you will. In the event he makes some statement which I have not previously answered and which I have not anticipated, that you say to yourself: "What would the defendant's attorney have said in response to that statement if he had been permitted to respond to it?"

Again, I want to thank you for your services here, and I know that the verdict that you return will reflect your honest and sincere determination of the issues in the case.

AUTHOR'S NOTE: Although these are fine examples of closing arguments, readers are encouraged to consult Chapter 10 for the purpose of editing these summations and making them even more powerful models of effective courtroom communication.

INDEX